Tip of the Spear

VF-154 F-14A on *Constellation*, May 1985. (author)

TIP OF THE SPEAR

U.S. Navy Carrier Units and Operations 1974-2000

Rick Morgan

Schiffer Military History
Atglen, PA

Book Design by Ian Robertson.

Library of Congress Control Number: 2006931697

Printed in China.
ISBN: 978-0-7643-2585-4

Published by Schiffer Publishing Ltd.
4880 Lower Valley Road
Atglen, PA 19310
Phone: (610) 593-1777
FAX: (610) 593-2002
E-mail: Info@schifferbooks.com.
Visit our web site at: www.schifferbooks.com
Please write for a free catalog.
This book may be purchased from the publisher.
Please include $3.95 postage.
Try your bookstore first.

In Europe, Schiffer books are distributed by:
Bushwood Books
6 Marksbury Avenue
Kew Gardens
Surrey TW9 4JF, England
Phone: 44 (0) 20 8392-8585
FAX: 44 (0) 20 8392-9876
E-mail: Info@bushwoodbooks.co.uk.
Visit our website at: www.bushwoodbooks.co.uk
Free postage in the UK. Europe: air mail at cost.
Try your bookstore first.

Contents

Dedication

To paraphrase the columnist George F Will, few people in the United States realize that at any moment of the day or night there are aviators braving the elements and risking their lives while flying off and back onto aircraft carriers somewhere in the world. The very fact that there are these individuals who leave their families for months at a time, while putting their own lives at risk, allow the rest of us to chase the American dream.

Therefore, this book is dedicated to the Men, Friends, Warriors, shipmates, and drinking buddies I've known through the years who have died while in the service of their country:

The drama of Naval Aviation: VF-74 F-4S AA104 (157309) blasts down a ridgeline at Fallon. Flying doesn't get much better than this. 10 May 1982. (Robert Lawson)

1st LT Steve Scott	13 Feb 80	VT-25	TA-4J	Yuma AZ
LT Dave Hankins	14 Feb 80	VT-25	TA-4J	Port O'Conner TX
LTJG Dave Huckaba	14 Feb 80	VT-25	TA-4J	Port O'Conner TX
LTJG Tom Cook	16 Dec 80	VF-171	F-4J	Fentress, VA
1st LT Chris Taylor	2 Jan 81	VMAT(AW)-202	A-6E	North Carolina
LT Jim Mallory	29 Oct 81	VAQ-138	EA-6B	Virginia Beach VA
LT Frank Kertscher	4 Aug 82	VQ-1	EA-3B	Indian Ocean
LTJG David Pies	4 Aug 82	VQ-1	EA-3B	Indian Ocean
LT Dave DeBartolomeo	10 Jul 84	VAQ-135	EA-6B	CV-66
LT Joe Durmon	13 Jan 86	VF-213	F-14A	CVN-65
LT Jim Guzy	9 Jun 86	NATC	SH-60B	Atlantic Ocean
LCDR Don Holderby	5 Dec 88	VAQ-139	EA-6B	W-291
LT Scott Threlkeld	5 Dec 88	VAQ-139	EA-6B	W-291
LT John Wilcox	5 Dec 88	VAQ-139	EA-6B	W-291
LT B.A. Jacobs	5 Dec 88	VAQ-139	EA-6B	W-291
LT John "Zeke" Zibel	24 Jul 89	VAQ-129	EA-6B	North Island CA
LCDR Steve Garcia	8 Aug 89	VA-128	A-6E	Whidbey Island WA
LCDR Barry Cooke	2 Feb 91	VA-36	A-6E	Persian Gulf
LT "BJ" Dwyer	5 Feb 91	CVW-8	F/A-18A	Persian Gulf
LCDR Dan Dewispelaere	15 Oct 91	VA-155	A-6E	VR-1350, WA
LT Chuck Gurley	3 Nov 92	VAQ-129	EA-6B	El Centro CA
CDR Seadog Fodor	Nov 89	CO,VAQ-139	Leukemia	Oak Harbor WA

The flight deck of an aircraft carrier has been rightly described as among the most dangerous places on earth. The hazards are many and unforgiving, and working on the roof for long hours in extremes of weather is both fatiguing and disorienting, yet it is also undeniably exciting and compelling to watch. There's no other place quite like it. Here a yellowshirt directs an unseen aircraft taxiing up the bow, while a VS-41 S-3B is moved aft to *Lincoln's* cat 2 during FRS CQ on a gray day off San Diego on 15 Oct '92. (author)

An anonymous Naval Aviator from VA-122 taxis his A-7E *Corsair II* during FRS CQ on *Ranger* in September 1987. He represents those that volunteer and succeed in mastering the complex, exacting, and dangerous task of flying aircraft off and back on aircraft carriers day and night in almost all weather conditions. (author)

Preface and Acknowledgments

The term "The Tip of the Spear" refers to a truly select group of warriors. It signifies those at the "Pointy End" of the U.S. forces—those who are the first to respond when the Commander in Chief decides its time to unleash the U.S. military.

The term has been used to describe a lot of military specialties, but only a few organizations within the Department of Defense really approach its true meaning. Marine amphibious units, as well as the Army's special forces, such as the Rangers and Green Berets, certainly fit within this category. Naval aviation—and the carrier based forces, in particular—also occupy a truly unique place under this definition.

Time after time, when an international crisis flares, the President and his advisors ask the question "*Where are the Carriers?*" Tailhook aviation has always proven to be ready on arrival, and among the nation's true warrior elite.

During the 1980s, when Muammar Qaddafi woke up every morning and took his daily brief, he undoubtedly asked the same exact question: "*Where are the Carriers?*" Libya's Maximum Leader had to concern himself with the ships off his coast, and not soldiers in Texas or bombers in Louisiana. While the other services certainly have their own unique and important capabilities, the Navy's deployed carriers influence the world in a profound and tangible fashion on a daily basis.

Call it what you will—either gunboat diplomacy, or shade it as a modern version of Alfred Thayer Mahan's theories—between 1974 and 2001 carrier airpower was the National Command Authority's initial military response to many global events, and it truly was at "The Tip of the Spear."

This book is my attempt to record the accomplishments of those that go to sea in these magnificent ships, and fly aircraft off and then back aboard them.

This work was started about a decade ago as a compilation of historical notes I have kept for years. It really goes back to 1971, when my family stopped at NAS Alameda during a trip to California. I already had a fascination with military aviation (my Dad was actually in Thailand flying USAF F-4Es at the time), and I was amazed with the color and *panache* that Naval Aviation had. Please forgive the pun, but I've been hooked ever since and, from 1974, made it my life. During my four years at the University of Missouri I discovered "Naval Aviation News" and started reading, and absorbing things like squadron histories, when I probably should've been more concerned with calculus or physics. I had my priorities though—I still have no plans to write a book on those subjects, something I assure you the Western World is a safer place for.

My goal here is to provide a single-source basic reference on U.S. carrier aviation and its units for the last quarter of the 20th Century. The period covered herein, 1 January 1974 to 31 December 2000, was picked because it represents the time frame between Vietnam and the start of the new millennium. This period includes years of violent peace and, as we now know, was punctuated by events that would lead to the "Global War on Terror," which officially started after the attacks of 11 September 2001. This is not an in-depth analysis of world events, but I hope this book becomes the one someone picks up when he wants to know what, say, VA-66 or VAW-114 was doing in 1977, what air wing was assigned to *Constellation* in 1985, or to get details on what carrier aviation's role was over Lebanon in 1983.

Because there is so much more to tailhook aviation than just the carrier-based units, I've included not only the squadrons that deploy in carriers—the familiar VF, VA, and VFA units—but also deal with the land-based outfits that directly supported carrier operations, including the RAGs, CompRons, and FEWSG.

If I have one regret about this book, it is in the total number of photographs and illustrations I could cram in it. I had, literally, thousands of color slides to choose from, and am truly sorry that I could not put more in this work. I've tried to present a selection of pictures running from the routine to the unusual for this work, and I hope the reader will approve of what he sees.

In a similar vein, I had to make a difficult decision not to include squadron insignia in this book, largely because the inclusion of 200+ color logos would have probably put the price of this work into low earth orbit.

There are a lot of people who need to be recognized in helping me prepare this book. On the top of the list are three other men who have spent years observing and recording Naval carrier operations: Rick Burgess, Mike Weeks, and Tom Kaminski. Their help and willingness to share their knowledge with me has certainly made my job easier. Dave "Heyjoe" Parsons provided additional help and insight into the fighter community. My older brother Mark helped go through many chapters to proofread and offer comments, as well as the occasional raspberry. His help is greatly appreciated.

The staff of the Tailhook Association's magazine "The Hook"—Steve Millikin, Doug Siegfried, and Jan Jacobs—also deserves a lot of credit. They always made me feel welcome on my rare visits to San Diego, and opened up their library to me. "The Hook," which really started as a true magazine in 1977 is, without question, one of the two top periodicals on carrier aviation available, and is highly recommended to anyone interested in the business and its history.

A similar nod needs to go the Naval Aviation History Office at the Washington Navy Yards. Roy Grossnick and Mark Evans maintain the official records, and write tremendous history when they are given the time and budget to do so. Their help has been absolutely critical to this study.

Another invaluable source is the service's publication "Naval Aviation News," which has provided an immense value through the years as a source of information. In spite of occasional attempts by some to kill it, or turn the magazine into a trendy "feel good" Oprahesque service pulp, "NavAv News" has remained the standard, enduring reference on the subject since it was made public after World War II. The magazine's annual operations reviews, in particular, mark this as a rare, and highly valuable, source of historical information.

Thanks needs to go to several enthusiasts who helped, and two in particular who deserve special mention for their pioneering work in this niche field of Naval Aviation History. Lindsay Peacock and Duane Kasulka have been publishing on this subject since the late 1960s in a variety of obscure enthusiast publications, monographs, and small books. Their efforts and dedication to keep track of squadrons and ships in a period before computers and the internet are nothing short of amazing. Both of these men's work has made it easier for the rest of us, and they have my undying admiration.

There are others, of course, who have published superior material in this area: Peter Mersky's considerable body of work merits praise, and Rene' Francillon also deserves credit for his endeavors, particularly his important book *Tonkin Gulf Yacht Club*, which set the standards for this kind of historic-reference effort. Patrick Martin's book *Hook Code* also needs to be noted as a great source of information, and a ready reference while trying to sort things out for this book. His work should be on the shelf of anyone interested in keeping track of Navy and Marine squadrons since 1960. Writer Tony Holmes provided information that helped clarify *Tomcat* operations and combat usage of the *Phoenix* missile.

Finally, I wish to make a particular point to thank the photographers whose pictures I use in this work. Bob Lawson and Michael Grove literally went through cases of Kodachrome to bring you many of the pictures you see in this book. Bob, who is also a superb writer, has never really received the credit he deserves for his groundbreaking work in the area of airborne photography. His material featured in "The Hook" remains some of the best Navy aerial photography ever conducted, and set the standard for many commercial aviation photographers that have followed. (Bob practically invented "ACM photography," in particular.) Michael made a habit of shooting almost every Air Wing that visited Fallon for many years—his collection (along with his fellow photographer Doug Olsen's) ranks as one of the best depicting Naval Aviation through the years. Other photographers helped as well: Brian Rogers, a retired Air Force Colonel, and Pete Clayton, a former Blackshoe Naval officer also contributed, as did retired Pennsylvania Police Officer David Brown. John Pouch, an old friend from New Mexico, and another retired Air Force officer, also graciously allowed me to print his material. I have also been able to tap into the Navy's Public Affairs digital collection and use a number of their images. Thanks again guys, for letting me use your wonderful photos. I hope I've done them justice.

And, finally, a very special thank you to my wife of 25 years—Julie, who has put up with me for these many years and tolerated my passion in this area.

Above all, at the age of 50 I still can't believe I had the opportunity to be part of the team that is Naval Aviation. I look back at what I participated in—carrier ops, combat, and even an ejection from an EA-6B—with a mostly wistful gaze. The camaraderie and sense of accomplishment remain indelibly embossed in my memory. Simply stated, I will never have a better job in my life.

Final note: In case it isn't obvious, this book is about Naval Aviation, so in the interest of inter-service relations I have chosen to include the occasional pithy comment about the Navy's sister organizations. All kidding aside (and believe it or not!), I have a great deal of admiration, and even affection for the other parts of the DOD, so If my comments manage to offend anyone, then please catch me at the bar some time, and I promise to engage you in a frank and professional discussion about the matter.

Rick Morgan
St. Louis, 2006
FLY NAVY! GO TIGERS!

Introduction

Historical Context to Air Wings

The organization of Naval Aviation is in a constant state of change. Understanding the previous ten-year period, which included Vietnam, is therefore critical to comprehend what the service went through during the following period.

As of 1964 Naval Aviation featured two distinct types of carrier organizations: Attack Carrier Air Wings (CVW), which were assigned to attack carriers (CVA/CVAN); and Anti-Submarine Air Groups (CVSG), which flew off of ASW carriers (CVS). There were 15 CVWs and nine CVSGs at that time.

Ten years later there were 14 CVWs in the Navy, which was down only slightly from the Vietnam war apogee of sixteen. The service would disestablish two of these wings (19 and 21) by 1977, only to add a pair (13 and 10) for a short period in the 1980s during the Reagan-Lehman build up years. By *Desert Storm* the number had stabilized at twelve, and then was reduced again back to ten by 2000. The Reserves did not have cohesive carrier air wings until their massive reorganization of 1970, after which there were two. One of these would be cut following Desert Storm. Table 1 reflects the Carrier Air Wings that existed from the start of the Vietnam war through 2000.

VF-84 used the tails of their F-4 *Phantoms* to good effect, producing one of the enduring images in Naval Aviation history. F-4B AE202 is shown at Holloman AFB, NM, on 20 May 1974. The following month the unit would start getting F-4Ns, and soon return to the *Franklin Roosevelt* for another Med deployment. (author)

Wing	Code	Fleet	
CVW-1	AB	Lant	
CVW-2	NE	Pac	
CVW-3	AC	Lant	
CVW-5	NF	Pac	
CVW-6	AE	Lant	disestablished 1992
CVW-7	AG	Lant	
CVW-8	AJ	Lant	
CVW-9	NG	Pac	
CVW-10	AK	Lant	disestablished 1969
CVW-10	NM	Pac	established 1987, disestablished 1988
CVW-11	NH	Pac	
CVW-13	AK	Lant	established 1984, disestablished 1991
CVW-14	NK	Pac	
CVW-15	NL	Pac	disestablished 1995
CVW-16	AH	Pac	disestablished 1972
CVW-17	AA	Lant	established 1966
CVW-19	NM	Pac	disestablished 1977
CVW-21	NP	Pac	disestablished 1975
CVWR-20	AF	Reserves	established 1970
CVWR-30	ND	Reserves	established 1970, disestablished 1994

Note: CVW-16 was established in 1960 as an Atlantic Fleet asset and moved to the Pacific Fleet in 1963, yet it retained the AirLant "AH" code throughout.

Table 1: Air Wing Quick Reference 1964-2000

Since the late 1950s air wings had roughly standardized with five primary mission squadrons (VF and VA, the latter being sub-divided into light and medium attack categories) and detachments, or squadrons that covered heavy attack (VAH), photo-recon (RVAH or VFP), electronic warfare (VAW, later VAQ), and airborne early warning (VAW) mission areas. Table 2 reflects the changes in the numbers of squadrons in each of the carrier communities between 1964 and 2000.

Note how the ASW community was completely subsumed by the Carrier Air Wings after Vietnam as the "CV Concept" was adopted fleet wide, and the CVSGs were disestablished.

	1964	1968	1974	1991	2000	Mission aircraft
CVW	15	16	14	12	10	
VF	30	30	26	22	12	F-3, F-4, F-8, F-14
VFA	0	0	0	22	24	F/A-18
VA(L)	29	33	30	2	0	A-4, A-7
VA(M)	14	13	12	15	0	A-1, A-6
(R)VAH	11	10	9	0	0	A-3, RA-5C
VAW	2	10	12	13	10	E-1, E-2
VFP	2	1	1	0	0	RF-8
VAQ	2	2	8	13	10	EA-1, EKA-3B, EA-6B
CVSG	9	8	0	0	0	
VS	18	16	10	10	10	S-2, S-3
VSF	0	2	0	0	0	A-4
HS	9	8	10	13	10	H-3, H-60

Table 2: Fleet Squadron Strength 1964-2000

Note: Table does not include readiness squadrons (RAGs).

VF: **Fighter squadrons.** The Navy assigned two VFs to most CVWs through 1993, when they started disestablishing units with an immediate goal of having only one F-14 unit per Wing. The last F-3 *Demon* unit (VF-161) transitioned to *Phantoms* in Sept. 1964. F-8s survived in VFs until 1976, while *Phantoms* lasted another decade.

VA: Attack squadrons: Informally subdivided into Light (L) and Medium (M), with most wings having a single VA(M) and two VA(L) units assigned (see chap 3 for exceptions and other details). Transition of the light attack forces to strike-fighters (VFA) started in 1983. They were completely replaced by *Hornets* in 1991, and the last regular Navy VA(L) squadrons disestablished. The final deployment for the Douglas A-1 in the attack role was in 1968, with VA-25. The *Intruder*, and the medium attack community, was closed out in 1997.

The desire to be identified with a winning team is strong, and over the years a number of Navy squadrons adopted the insignia and traditions of elite units that had been lost in time. The *Sundowners* are one example—taking the persona of a distinguished WWII era organization in 1956. The distinctive sharkmouth on this *Tomcat* defines it as a VF-111 F-14A, as it prepares to taxi at Miramar on 30 Jan 1981. (Bob Lawson)

VFA: The "Strike-Fighter" title was coined for the new F/A-18 units that began to appear in 1983. The type quickly replaced light attack (A-7) and would, eventually, supersede the remaining VF outfits as well.

(R)VAH: Heavy attack units typically operated with eight to ten A-3Bs on "big decks," or as 3 or 4 aircraft dets on smaller ships. The last VAH was disestablished, or redesignated as a VAQ, by the end of 1971. RA-5C *Vigilantes* started going to sea in 1966 in RVAH units, and continued in fleet service for another 13 years.

VAW: Airborne Early Warning: As of 1964 two units (VAW-11, -12) sent E-1B dets to carriers. In 1967 their detachments were re-formed into separate squadrons, as E-2s quickly replaced the *Willy Fudds* on most carriers. E-1 dets continued to be used on "small decks" through 1977.

VAQ: **Tactical Electronic Warfare Squadrons:** Prior to 1968, two specific VAW units (13 and 33) supplied EA-1F dets to carriers for the EW role. In 1968 the VAQ community was formed, and EKA-3Bs quickly took over the job. EA-6Bs arrived from 1972 as four aircraft squadrons replaced detachments.

VFP: Light Photographic Squadrons: Two outfits (VFP-62 and -63) provided RF-8 detachments to those ships that did not have RA-5C squadrons assigned. VFP-62 was disestablished in 1968, leaving VFP-63 to soldier on until it too stood down, in 1982.

VS: **Anti-Submarine Squadrons**: CVSGs normally deployed with two VS and one HS unit, along with VAW and, as available, VSF dets. VS squadrons were equipped with S-2 *Trackers* through 1976, when they were completely replaced by S-3 *Vikings*, which had been introduced in 1974. From that point the Navy quickly lowered the number of VS units to match the air wings that had them.

VSF: Anti-Submarine Fighter Squadrons: Two VSFs (1 and 3) were established at Alameda by 1967 to provide A-4 dets to ASW carriers as basic fighter protection. Both units would actually make deployments as light attack units in CVWs due to a shortage of VA squadrons during the Vietnam War. They would both be disestablished in 1970.

HS: Helicopter Anti-Submarine: All were equipped with SH-3As in 1964, and successively received SH-3D and SH-3H aircraft before the SH-60F arrived following *Desert Storm*. CVWs used HC detachments with HH-2B/C *Seasprites* and, later, SH-3G *Sea Kings* until the HS units were assigned following Vietnam.

On Squadron Histories

Note: A version of this section was originally published in the Winter 2005 edition of "The Hook."

Although this book deals with the quarter-century period after Vietnam, it is certainly appropriate to discuss the broader subject of Navy squadron lineages.

It has been said that tracking the lineage of Naval Aviation squadrons is about as easy to follow as a French art film. It is often that confounding. The Navy's habit of frequently redesignating squadrons has led to decades of confusion among aviation historians. This is compared to the Marines, where a number is only used once (for instance, VMA-214, the fabled *Black Sheep*, have always been number "214" no matter what the prefix, and will undoubtedly always stay that way).

The World War II Navy squadrons that survived to 1946 went through a massive reorganization that was so complex and confusing that the service was forced to carry out yet another complete fleet redesignation again only two years later. The 1948 plan was both well thought out and somewhat elegant, in that the squadrons in an Air Group were initially numbered lineally using the Group's number as a guide (CVG-4 having squadrons numbered 41 through 45, CVG-11 units 111 to 115, etc.).

This simple system lasted only up to the start of the Korean War, when operational realities forced the service to move squadrons around, and it didn't take long before the sequential 1948 system was hopelessly scrambled. During the same period the Navy also formed eight "Air Task Groups" (ATGs), which were ad hoc organizations that acted as "temporary" Air Groups with "spare" squadrons. ATGs existed only between 1950 and '59, but they certainly helped jumble unit organization and identity.

Through this volatile period the Navy (and AirPac in particular) had a policy of changing squadron designations when they moved between Air Groups in an effort to keep all units within a CVG sequentially numbered. Unfortunately, the timing of these changes never seemed to follow a plan, as it could vary from the time of transfer to several years afterward. (The *Fighting Red Cocks* of VA-63, for example, were assigned to CVG-2 for nine years before they finally became VA-22.)

The absurdity of this paper drill was probably best exemplified on 9 March 1959, when VF-24 and VF-211 swapped designations on the same day while switching air groups. Since one was called the *Checkertails* and the other the *Fighting Checkmates*, confusion was guaranteed for years. In 1964 these two units were joined in CVW-21, which has effectively sealed their co-mingled histories.

Similarly, there were two California based outfits designated VF(AW)-3. One, based at Moffett Field, was the former VC-3, a night fighter unit that became, in effect, the first fleet replacement squadron for high-performance jets. It was disestablished on 2 May 1958, and replaced the very same day by another unit with the same designation at North Island. The *Blue Nemesis* was actually a unique squadron that flew colorful F4D-1 *Skyrays* under NORAD operational control until 1963. The two, historically distinct squadrons, have been confused ever since.

This bureaucratic tomfoolery finally ended in the fall of 1964 when three Miramar based fighter squadrons were moved between air wings. VF-24 went from CVW-2 to 21, VF-213 moved to CVW-11, and the VF-111 *Sundowners* moved over to CVW-2. All three were directed to change their designations with the moves, with AirPac directing VF-111 to become VF-26, VF-213 to VF-116, and VF-24 to change to VF-214. One, or more, of them complained,[1] and the order was rescinded, but not before several aircraft were repainted. On 1 September 1964 CNO ordered an end to this policy, and from then on units were allowed to keep their designations after moving between air wings. Since then the actual changing of squadron numbers during redesignation has been limited to only a few, special cases (such as VA-67 becoming VA-15) that have been a lot easier to track.

On terminology

Terminology used by the service tends to be confusing, and even though there is a specific written instruction covering the issue, many units and people do not follow it when writing about the subject. This includes many within the service itself, which has led to no small amount of chaos—particularly with amateur historians and aviation enthusiasts that, not surprisingly, usually assume that the "official source" has to be correct.

Up to 1998 the Navy used **OPNAVINST 5030.4D** to set squadron historical guidelines. As of 1974 the following terms were used to describe squadron histories:

Established / Disestablished: A squadron's history and lineage officially begins on the date it is established and, up to 1998, when it was disestablished. By instruction, aviation units had finite lives—when disestablished they went away forever, and could not be brought back. For example, while there have been three squadrons designated VF-93, they were all separate units with distinct lineages, histories, and honors. The reason for this practice is reportedly derived from ship tradition, in that while there have been multiple vessels named *Enterprise*, CVAN-65 could not claim to have been at the Battle of Midway, like the proceeding *Enterprise* (CV-6) was.

With this policy in mind, new units established (*never* "re-established") with a previously used designation were, officially, completely separate and distinct units, a fact that many outfits ignored, or did not understand. Officially, new units *could not* (at least officially) claim the history or honors of squadrons that had gone before them.

Official policy not withstanding, "the fleet" frequently clamors to bring back old and historic outfits when it comes time to form a new squadron. This was particularly true during the "growth years" while John Lehman was SecNav. In order to allow new units to re-use popular old insignias the Navy *did* allow them to "adopt" the logos and "traditions" of older organizations, but not their history. For example, the first two VAQ squadrons established for "joint" duty in the 1990s (VAQ-133 and -137) both returned the designations, names, and insignias of disestablished units to Whidbey Island—at VAQWing's specific request. In spite of this, officially, they are all new units, and not "re-established" organizations.

Redesignation: Is the term used when a squadron is directed to change its title, such as VA-147 becoming VFA-147. As this does not interrupt a squadron's history or lineage, the unit retains a defined line of history. Example: The *Tophatters* of VF-14 can trace an uninterrupted line back to 1919, through no less than 14 redesignations, and are therefore able to claim a continuous history back to the Woodrow Wilson Administration. On the other hand, a squadron that was established in, say, October 1972, is not allowed to claim the history or honors of a unit prior to that date, even if it had the same designation, or wears the same colors and insignia of a previous unit. The current VF-2, for instance, cannot legitimately claim to be the same as, or even related to, the VF-2 that was on the *Langley* (CV1), or any of the three other VF-2s that have existed through the years.

Two other words frequently misused are **Commissioned and Decommissioned**, which are, officially, used *only* for ships and commissioned officers, never squadrons, wings, or other modern aviation entities. Nonetheless, these terms are often used in official correspondence, even if incorrectly. Compounding the confusion is that many good sources of information, including "Naval Aviation News" and "The Hook," used these words for many years without realizing they were incorrect. It was not until the mid- to late 1980s that correct terminology became "common knowledge" among those who paid attention to such things.

In 1998 the Navy issued **OPNAVINST 5030.4E**, which dramatically changed the way the service tracked squadron lineages and honors. The Navy now uses what is basically the same system used by the Marines and Air Force. Squadrons are still established, but are now **deactivated** instead of disestablished. Now, when a squadron is deactivated, its lineage and honors are maintained, and they may return at a later date with full honors.

When a squadron returns to life, it is now **reactivated**. Officially, however, it must use the last designation it was assigned prior to deactivation. A squadron cannot be reactivated and designated on the same day; therefore, at least one day must elapse between reactivation and redesignation. For example, if VP-65 is deactivated, and the Navy later reactivates it as a fleet logistics (VR) squadron, it must be reactivated as VP-65, and a day must elapse before it is redesignated VR-65.

Once a letter/number combination has been assigned to a squadron, that combination can never be assigned to another squadron. For example, VFA-15's lineage includes VA-67 and VA-15. None of those designations can be used by any other existing, or newly established squadron(s).

Frustratingly (and perhaps predictably), the change in policy has again been largely ignored within the service subsequent to "4E's" release, or with 5030.4F, which has subsequently replaced it. Most official documents still direct units to "decommission" or "disestablish"—both of which are incorrect and/or obsolete terms. As of 2005 official directives from the office of the Chief of Naval Operations (CNO) are still using the terms "disestablish" when shutting down squadrons. It would appear that some things never change.

Examples: When the A-7B squadron VA-155 was disestablished at Lemoore in 1977, it was the historical end of the line for the *Silver Foxes*, who had been able to trace a legacy back to World War II. Ten years later another VA-155 was established, this time with A-6Es at Whidbey Island. Even though it took the same nickname, it was a distinct unit from the prior VA-155.

The *Sundowners* of VF-111 used the famous insignia and nickname of the WWII unit of the same name, yet they were not officially related. The original VF-111, which held the lineage of the historical VF-11 *Sundowners* of WWII, was disestablished with FJ-3 *Furys* in 1958. On the same day, the F11F-1 *Tiger*-equipped VA-156 was redesignated VF-111, and it adopted the name and logo of the previous outfit. Officially, they are two distinct squadrons, although easily confused. Several other famous squadrons, including the *Red Rippers* of VF-11, fall in this same category as, although the famous Gordon's Gin Boar's Head logo dates from the bi-plane Navy, the current unit that claims the title only goes back to 1950, and has used that insignia and nickname since 1959.

In a more extreme example of creative historical bookeeping, the VT designation was used for Torpedo squadrons until 1947, when the

VB and VT communities were joined as Attack (VA) squadrons. Nonetheless, at least one current-day Training (VT) squadron has claimed to be related to a World War II Torpron of the same designation, even though today's Training Squadrons (VT) date only from 1960.

On Nicknames and Insignias

Nicknames can be changed by a Commanding Officer at the wave of a hand. There is no official approval required to change names—witness E-2 units that went through up to three names in only a few years. In some cases a unit's officially bequeathed radio callsign becomes interchangeable with its nickname, particularly when the ready room or CO do not really care for their title: VA-196 (*Main Battery/Milestones*) and VA-93 (*Blue Blazers/Ravens*) came under this category. (But then again, some squadrons don't want anyone calling them by their officially bequeathed callsigns—VA-65 "Cupcake" and VAQ-33 "Honeymoon" come to mind) There are other cases where long established nicknames and identities are changed on the call of a new CO because he doesn't like the one he has inherited—VF-33's 1987 makeover from *Tarsiers* to *Starfighters* being an excellent example, as is VA/VFA-27, which has been known as the *Royal Maces*, *Chargers*, and then *Royal Maces* again.

Insignias, on the other hand, *do* require official approval, through the Naval History Office. There are set standards (OPNAV Instruction 5030.4) and rules for insignia. Not surprisingly, these rules are not always followed as well—and in some instances, squadron COs directed new insignia without going through the official procedure. These changes can be as simple as a change of color to an existing logo (In November 2000 VAQ-139 officially changed the blue in their insignia from a light "Carolina" shade to one much deeper when a new CO didn't like what was being used), to a complete change (VFA-97 dumping their unique Vietnam era logo for a generic and decidedly unimaginative "diving bird & F-18."). At least two squadrons (VS-32 and VF-211) went "retro" in the 1990s, and officially adopted logos that looked much more like WWII insignias. Some units have changed insignias without going though the formal approval process specified in 5030.4, and have gone years, only to realize that the Navy still shows a long forgotten "retired" logo to still be the only officially recognized one.

The instruction covering squadron insignias specifically forbids use of recognizable aircraft on a logo, because a timeless design does not need to be changed when they convert to a new type of aircraft (think VF-14 *Tophatters* or VF-31 "Felix"). Nonetheless, a number of units felt the need to add their specific aircraft, either in planform or head-on, to their logos, and used these designs as their patch. These include VF-33, VFA-131, and VFA-106. Although not quite legal by instruction, all were approved by CNO as official insignia.

In some cases units have their old, established patches retired to "remember" other, disestablished units. VAW-120 took VAW-110's old "diving chicken," and VA-42's forty-year old *Green Pawn* was replaced by VA-176's much younger and less distinguished *Thunderbolt*. Both are good examples, but probably the best known of these cases of "patch envy" involves the classic *Jolly Roger*.

Case Study: The Jolly Roger

Few insignia in Naval Aviation are as familiar as the "Jolly Roger," the legendary skull and crossbones pirate motif. Three distinct squadrons have used the same insignia and nickname through seven decades and several wars. They are all historically separate squadrons.

VF-17 was established during World War II, and was destined to be the first Navy unit to take Vought's F4U-1 *Corsair* into combat. "Fighting Seventeen" was taken out of Air Group-17 (AG-17) and off *Bunker Hill* (CV17) for a variety of reasons, and ended up as a land based outfit in the Solomon Islands. Known then as "Blackburn's Irregulars" (Lt. Cdr. Tommy Blackburn being their initial C.O.), they went on to a distinguished combat record, with the black pirate flag becoming their legendary insignia. The unit returned to the United States in March 1944, and was completely reorganized with Grumman *Hellcats* before returning to combat in *Hornet* under Lt.Cdr. "Marsh" Beebe.[2] VF-17 actually had more kills (161) with *Hellcats* than it did with *Corsairs* (152), and ended WWII as the Navy's leading Fighter Squadron.

Fighting-17 survived the war, and was redesignated VF-5B ("Fighting Five-Baker") on 15 Nov 1946, and subsequently VF-61 on 28 July 1948. After flying *Bearcats*, *Panthers*, *Cougars*, and *Demons*, they were disestablished on 14 Apr 1959, thus ending the lineage of the first "Jolly Roger" squadron.

The *Sluggers* of VF-103 adopted the name, insignia, and traditions of the *Jolly Rogers* in 1995. Suitably marked F-14B AA100 heads for the duty runway at Oceana in October 1997. The "Mutha" inscription on the tail refers to an annual fighter award given by the F-14 RAG, in its role as the senior ("mother") *Tomcat* unit. (David Brown)

The powerful "Jolly Roger" logo, and everything it implies, led another unit to drop a previous insignia and nickname in favor of VF-61's retired pirate flag in 1959.

VA-86 was established on 1 July 1955 and, in one of those odd admin drills the service periodically goes through, was redesignated the same day as VF-84. The

Vagabonds flew FJ-3 *Furies* for several years when, in 1959, the final Commanding Officer of Fighting-61 was assigned to finish out his CO tour.

The new Skipper apparently did not care for the existing nickname or logo, and proposed a squadron makeover with his old unit's identity. The ready room voted in the affirmative, and the *Vagabonds* became the *Jolly Rogers* of VF-84. The squadron flew F8U *Crusaders* before re-equipping with F-4B *Phantoms IIs*. It is with this classic McDonnell product that the unit became truly famous, as it used the F-4's broad tail surface as a canvas for its pirate flag, and subsequently painted them entirely black, with their white crossed bones and leering skull. Their appearance early in the Vietnam War is believed by some to have been the reason the communists started using the term "Yankee Air Pirate" to describe American flyers.

These markings stayed on through conversion to F-14s, where even the Soviet media noticed them, the paper *Pravda* at one time showing a picture of their *Tomcats* to prove to the proletariat that the U.S. Navy was indeed a pirate organization, comparing their insignia to the Nazi SS, among other organizations.

In 1979-80 the squadron was picked to "star" in the movie "The Final Countdown." The unit subsequently saw combat in *Desert Storm*, and carried out ten deployments in the F-14 before it was disestablished in the post-*Desert Storm* drawdown on 1 Oct 1995.

Once again, the allure of the *Jolly Roger* logo induced another squadron to give up its own identity. On 29 Sept 1995 the *Sluggers* of VF-103 officially changed their names to the *Jolly Rogers*, whereupon they adopted the logo and traditions of VF-84.[3] Fighting-103 itself dates from 1 May 1952, and has flown *Cougars*, *Crusaders*, and *Phantoms*, and seen combat in Vietnam and *Desert Storm*. The unit now holds the encased bones of Ens Jack Ernie, the VF-17 pilot who was shot down and killed in 1945. The result is that the "Skull and Bones" was retained on Navy combat aircraft, and VF-103 is now known by a new generation as "the one and only" *Jolly Roger* outfit.

Fortunately for historians, the Naval Aviation History Office has reference material available on its web site that covers the current instruction, as well as the recognized and official lineages of most active squadrons. The Office has also published two tremendous books covering the VA/VFA and VP communities and their squadrons, both of which can be downloaded for free from the web. These works are the definitive sources on the subject of squadron lineage in these communities. It can only be hoped that the history office is given the time and resources to complete the series for all of the other squadrons in the service's remarkable history.

Book Organization

Each of the chapters on carriers, Air Wings, and squadrons is arranged in roughly the same fashion.

Carriers: Are organized by hull number, which also places them largely in chronological order of construction. Each carrier is shown with its major deployment dates, and what Air Wing accompanied them. Readers will have to go to the relevant CVW page in order to find out what squadrons were assigned to the wing. Deployment locations are provided in shorthand, once again to save space. A key is provided to help the reader sort it out.

As far as dates are concerned, trying to keep track of actual deployment dates can drive the researcher to drink—and I mean heavy drink. I have tried to use the dates published by the Naval Historical Center, or in annual "Naval Aviation News" reviews wherever possible in this book, but be advised, these can and will be off by several days, as squadrons move prior to the actual ship's "away from the pier" day. In a similar vein, I've tried to use reasonable sources (once again, usually "NavAv News") for establishment or disestablishment dates. Many times bases, wings, or squadrons will have a formal ceremony prior to, or even well after, the prescribed calendar day that the office of CNO says is their "official" date. This is usually done for convenience (particularly if the prescribed day is actually on a weekend) or, as has happened in some cases, in order to have a decent ceremony before the bulk of the unit is transferred elsewhere. I have tried to note ceremonial, along with official dates, wherever I was aware of them.

Wings: CVWs are listed numerically, with each major deployment being tabulated, along with the squadrons assigned by what side number ("modex") they occupied. This chapter is the real meat of the book as far as I'm concerned.

Squadrons: Unit chapters are arranged by community—fighter, attack, early-warning, and so forth. This is how the service breaks up its squadrons, so it seemed like the right way to do it here. VFA units are combined with the VA squadrons in chapter 5, since that is where most of them came from. Squadron listings include unit lineage (as recognized by the Naval History Office, which is—no matter what some writers would have you believe—the final word on the subject), and a list of deployments undertaken during the 1974 to 2000 timeframe. "Nice to know information" is included on most squadrons, although space does not allow much more than a limited amount for most organizations. In order to save paper, information on specific underway dates for CVW-5 units while forward deployed are listed only in chapter 2 (Air Wings).

Deployment Shorthand Used Througout this Book:

Carrier deployments are normally planned to last around six months, although shorter cruises to the Northern Atlantic or Central and Northern Pacific are not uncommon. The following terms are used throughout this book:

Carib: Caribbean: Usually under 2nd Fleet, only mentioned when it involved significant operations, such as off Grenada and Haiti. Most Atlantic Fleet carriers routinely worked off Puerto Rico as part of their work ups as well.

Fwd Deployed: Unit is assigned to CVW-5 on the Japan based carrier, either *Midway*, *Independence*, or *Kitty Hawk,* depending on the time frame. Subject to frequent at sea periods to WestPac, IO, and PG areas. In order to save space, actual underway dates are covered only in the ship and air wing chapters.
Horn: Carriers from the *Midway* class and later have been built too wide to use the Panama Canal, so when they move between coasts "the short way" they have to go around South America via Cape Horn. This route is typically used for ships either proceeding to, or returning from, major overhauls or nuclear refueling.
IO: Indian Ocean: A ship operating between the Strait of Malacca and the Horn of Africa. Typically under 7th Fleet command. The Arabian Sea switched to 5th Fleet command when it was established on 1 July 1995.
MED: Mediterranean. A ship proceeds through the Straits of Gibraltar, and operates within the Mediterranean Sea under the control of 6th Fleet.
NorLant, NL: North Atlantic: Usually indicates support of NATO operations off Iceland, England, or Norway. Frequently included flight operations from inside Norwegian fjords in order to baffle Soviet targeting efforts and scare ships' navigators. Usually under 2nd Fleet command.
NorPac: Northern Pacific: Under 7th or 3rd Fleet command, usually included operations off Alaska and/or the Kuril region of Japan or the Soviet Union.
PG: Persian Gulf. Also called the Arabian Gulf. Indicates a ship went through the Strait of Hormuz to operate inside the Gulf. Either under 7th or 5th Fleet command, depending on time frame.
RS: Red Sea: Typically a ship that transits the Suez Canal going to or from the Indian Ocean. Some battle groups go no further, specifically *Saratoga* and *John F. Kennedy* during *Desert Shield/Desert Storm*. Ships that transit from the Med to the IO/PG region are assumed to have transited the Suez and Red Sea unless otherwise noted.
Shakedown: Following new construction or a major refit (like SLEP), carriers make short at sea periods in a non-combat ready condition in order to test systems. See sidebar in chapter 2.
SoLant, SL: Southern Atlantic: A ship working in the southern hemisphere, frequently to or from the Indian Ocean via the Cape of Good Hope, off South Africa.
SoPac, SP: Southern Pacific: Under 3rd Fleet, significant operations off Central and South America without going around the Horn.
World: An "Around the World" deployment, which entails moving between the U.S. coasts "the long way." Can be either east to west or vice versa. See notes for details.
WP: Western Pacific, or WestPac. A ship under the command of 7th Fleet operating west of Hawaii, in or around the Philippines, Japan, and/or Australia.

The Naval services' enlisted personnel make the flight deck work. A V2 division Safety Observer, identified as AB2 Matthew Angus, observes operations on *TR* during *Allied Force* on 29 Jun 1999, while the props of a VRC-40 C-2 spin only feet away. (U.S. Navy; PH2 Jonathan Byrd)

1

Deployments and Major Actions

When a crisis erupts in the world, the first question asked in Washington is "WHERE ARE THE CARRIERS?"

The U.S. Navy exists to project power in support of the foreign policy of the American government. The service's preferred weapon is the aircraft carrier, and its embarked Carrier Air Wing. Since the end of World War II the U.S. Navy has continuously deployed carrier battle groups overseas so that they would be in position in the event their power was required. They provide real presence in a troubled world.

As of 1974, the service was winding down from almost ten years of continuous combat in South East Asia. Most of its carriers were in serious need of maintenance, and the service was looking at the transition of whole communities to the F-14A, A-6E, E-2C, EA-6B, and S-3A. While the Army and Air Force were generally able to return to garrison at the end of the war, the Navy and Marine Corps still deployed men on ships to exotic locales overseas for six months, or more, at a time.

Work-Ups

Six months underway on a large gray ship with 5000 of your closest friends was (and is) considered a real test of sailors and their families. What was often unnoticed was that there's a lot more to these major

The Grumman F-14 *Tomcat* series achieved iconic status both inside and outside the Navy. This picture, taken 26 Jan 2000, shows a *Black Knight* F-14A (NF113, 162611) below the overcast, and heading for the break at Kadena AFB, Okinawa. It displays where the F-14 series came from—the AIM-54 *Phoenix* on the port wing pylon, representing the fleet air defense mission it was originally designed for, and where the type went, as it carries a LANTIRN targeting pod on the starboard side, which denotes the bombing role it assumed late in life. (U.S. Navy, PH1 Chris Desmond)

deployments than the actual cruise. The formal work-up cycle proceeding deployment would run for months prior to the actual departure, and only add to the time away from home. Many individuals (particularly wives) find the work-up period to be harder to deal with than the formal deployment due to their frequency, short durations, and "hard on the family" nature.

Work-ups themselves are usually arranged in a "walk before you run" sequence of at sea periods, during which the ship and air wing melds together as a team.

Early in the work-up cycle the wing would carry out a Weapons Training Exercise (WepTraEx, later called Advanced Tactical Phase—ATP—or, as always, just the "Fallon det") at Fallon, Nevada, where the CVW joined its squadrons together for the first time to conduct unified warfighter training over a two or three week period. Prior to this individual squadrons would have been conducting crew and unit level training and, if lucky, would have participated in a *Red Flag*, *Maple Flag*, or similar combat exercise.

Normal work-ups usually start with an at sea period called "Refresher Training," or RefTra. During RefTra flying frequently seems secondary to shipboard events, such as General Quarters (GQ), Engineering, and Damage Control drills, as well as other Blackshoe training.

The air wing would also work to re-qualify its pilots in carrier landings. Pilot landing requirements are spelled out in detail in the Navy's Landing Signal Officer (LSO) NATOPS manual. Things like duration between landings, both day and night, as well as pilot experience, are all taken into account to keep Naval Aviators both proficient and safe behind the boat.

Subsequent at sea periods would include various other training evolutions that went by a variety of names and acronyms, most of which are irrelevant here. Most featured increased operational tempos and more complex exercises.

East coast ships would typically work off the Virginia Capes (Vacapes) or Jacksonville (Jax Op Area), or might go as far as the Puerto Rican Operating Area (PROA). Caribbean operations were almost always conducted as part of work-ups, and typically involved the warning areas located off Puerto Rico, with the "island paradise" of Vieques being used as a bombing range. Although *Theodore Roosevelt* pulled into Trinidad-Tobago in 1990, port calls at Caribbean locations other than the Virgin Islands were rare. In some cases, pre-deployment training would include local operations that led to port calls into places like Boston, Fort Lauderdale, or New York. The *Kennedy*, in particular, with its politically revered name, was frequently used as a "show boat" for trips to the two big Northeast ports.

Almost all Pacific Fleet work-ups were conducted in the vast W-291 ("Whiskey-291") warning areas off San Diego. Pacific Fleet ships might also move away from California to take part in an exercise off Hawaii (a "Pineapple Cruise") or Alaska. Special port calls to annual "Fleet Week" celebrations at locations like Seattle or even San Francisco were not uncommon.

A successful work-up period would usually end with some sort of Operational Readiness Exercise or Inspection (ORE/ORI), where the ship/air wing team went through a formal "graduation exercise" to prove they were ready for deployment.

Once work-ups were complete, the ship and its air wing would leave its homeport and deploy for six, or more, months in faraway locations. The carrier was the centerpiece of a Carrier Battle Group (CVBG), made up of the "bird farm," as well as a host of consorts, including cruisers, destroyers, and frigates, which provided additional anti-air and anti-submarine protection.

It needs to be noted that the dates given throughout this book are the actual dates the ship pulls out of and returns to its homeport. Travel dates for squadrons could vary by several days either way. A Pacific fleet unit deploying on an Atlantic carrier might move two to three days before the ship gets underway, and the enlisted troops would not actually return to their homes and families until a day or two afterwards, depending on the availability of airlift.

Most ships and air wings also participated in numerous exercises while on deployment. This was particularly true during the "quiet" period between the end of Vietnam and *Desert Storm*, when it seemed

An Air Wing's trip to Fallon, Nevada, is an absolutely critical part of its turnaround cycle prior to cruise, as it's the first time the wing gathers all of its squadrons together for unified training. Here a division of A-7Es from VA-195 run across the irrigated fields near Fallon on their way to the bomb ranges on 20 July 1976. (Ens. Mark L. Morgan, USN)

like every public affairs story heralded squadrons' participation in heavily scripted events like "Display Determination" and "Northern Wedding." While these events do have some value in terms of operational training, to many aircrew they also frequently seemed to be more trouble than they were worth. These exercises are too numerous to list, and would add little, if any, value by being included in this work.

Atlantic Fleet Deployments

The Mediterranean, which had been almost out of mind during the Vietnam War, resumed its importance in the mid-70s, as the service concerned itself once again with the Soviet Navy. For several years a lack of operating money led to many ships spending 50%, or more, of their time in port at anchor. This changed from the early 80s, as operations off Libya and Lebanon led to a series of crises that required ships to stay at sea.

During the 1970s and '80s the Med was full of exotic places to stop, and port calls could include Palma, Marseille, Monaco, Naples, Athens, Rhodes, Antalya, Alexandria, Benidorm, and Haifa. Up through the early 1980s it was not unusual to have squadron officers' wives follow ships from port call to port call, and men frequently complained about not having enough time at sea to save money for the next visit. This problem generally vanished through the 1980s and '90s, as things heated up, operational ("steaming") money increased, and carriers started spending more time underway.

During the early '80s, the area off of Lebanon was initially given the title "Bagel Station," as battle groups started to patrol off the troubled country. This was declared to be offensive to certain ethnic groups, and it soon became generally known as "Beno Station" (as in "Be No Fun, Be No Liberty," etc). It was from this locale that the 1983 strikes into Lebanon were conducted.

The area off Libya was famed for the "Line of Death," which was the "do not cross" line drawn across the Gulf of Sidra by the regime of Muammar al-Qaddafi. The U.S. government, which recognized only a twelve mile national limit off Libya, declared that the rest of the Gulf was International Waters, and routinely sailed ships into the area under what were called "Freedom of Navigation Operations," or FonOps. It was these events that directly led to the confrontations between the two countries during the mid-1980s.

A few Atlantic Fleet ships supported 7th Fleet operations in the Indian Ocean during the '70s and '80s. Initially this was done by rounding the southern tip of Africa due to the reticence of the Egyptian Government to letting U.S. warships (particularly nuclear powered) through the Suez Canal. In 1986 *Enterprise* was permitted to transit from the Red Sea through the Canal to enter the Med on a one-time basis. By 1990 Egypt allowed use of the Canal by carriers in both directions, and this has become the routine ever since, particularly as Atlantic Fleet battle groups continued to support Central Command requirements in the Persian Gulf.

Northern Atlantic (NORLANT) cruises could be made as a short four to six week "warm-up" period conducted several months prior to the six-month Mediterranean deployment, or as an adjunct to a Med cruise. They usually involved exercises with NATO in the North Sea or Atlantic, and could include flight operations from within Norwegian fjords in an attempt to confuse potential Soviet targeting systems, while also scaring the ship's navigator and Officer of the Deck (OOD: the man actually conning the vessel). Portsmouth, England, was the most common port call for a NorLant, although other locations were also occasionally visited.

Pacific Fleet Deployments

Carriers deploying to the Western Pacific (WestPac, or WP) utilized Cubi Point, the Republic of the Philippines, as the primary support base. Here the Navy had a large facility that allowed pierside berthing (a rarity for a carrier anywhere outside of the U.S.), repair facilities, a fully equipped Naval Air Station, and the exotic pleasures of Olongopo City for recreation. Most, if not all, WestPac carriers would call on Cubi at some point in their deployments. Typical Pacific fleet liberty port calls would include Hong Kong, Pusan, Korea, Singapore, Pataya Beach, Thailand, and Japan. Most ships would also pull into Pearl Harbor going both to and from WestPac, as well.

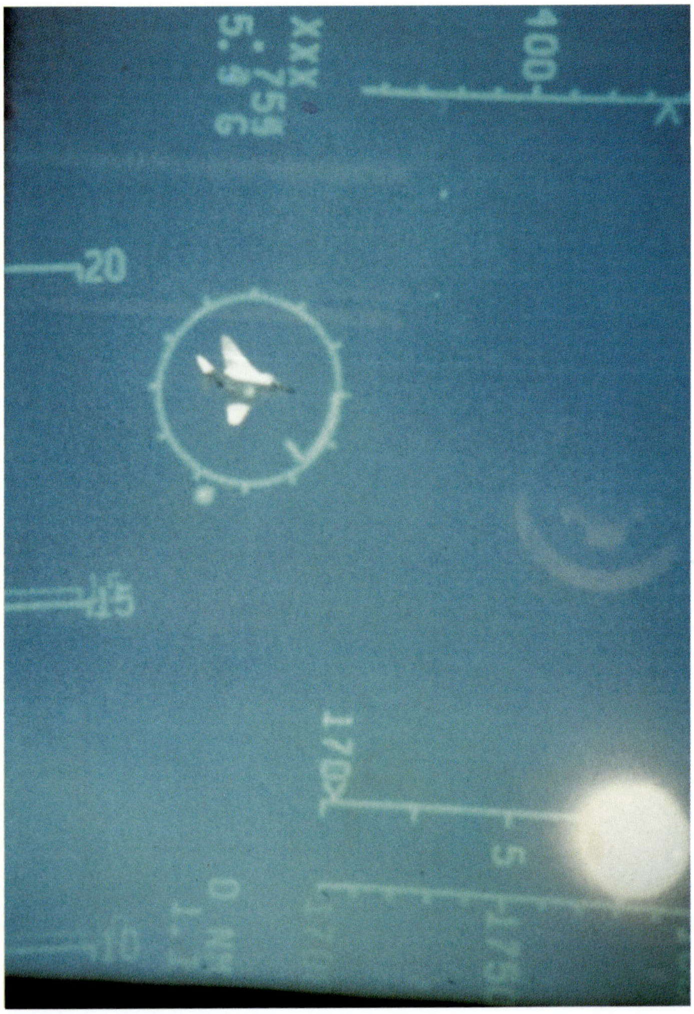

Hello Sailor! Training continues even while on cruise, and sometimes you provide it for your sister services. In this case a VF-31 F-4J suffers from a severe case of pipper burns in a shot taken through the HUD of a pursuing USAF F-15A in 1980. The *Phantom* is flying off *Saratoga* during the ship's Med cruise. The *Eagle* is from the Soesterberg, Netherlands, based 32nd TFS flying out of Decimomanu, Sardinia. The Air Force fighter is in a 90 degree right hand bank/18 degrees nose up, doing 0.75mach while pulling over 5 Gs, and is undoubtedly enjoying himself thoroughly. (USAF, via Lt Col R.H. Morgan)

Trips to the Northern Pacific (NorPacs), never really common, would see ops in the Aleutians, or even into the Bering Sea, off the Soviet Union. These trips were usually notable for the notable reaction from Soviet aviation, as well as what was frequently starkly miserable weather. Ships were known to occasionally pull into Anchorage, Alaska, for liberty on these visits as well.

Events in Iran from 1979 led to ships routinely working in the Indian Ocean, with the British owned archipelago of Diego Garcia providing support. Keeping battle groups of multiple ships and thousands of sailors at sea in the IO was a Herculean task. Diego Garcia (also called "Day-Gar," or "Dodge") was almost two thousand miles away from the Arabian Gulf, yet the U.S. Navy made the process look deceptively easy. Certainly no other navy in the world could have maintained so large a force so far from home as well as the U.S. Navy did.

Pacific Fleet Battle Groups usually entered the IO via the Strait of Malacca, and frequently ended their stay with a port call at Fremantle (Perth), Australia. Other IO port calls included Mombassa, Kenya, Hobart Tasmania, Sydney, Australia, and even Karachi, Pakistan, in a few rare cases.

In 1974 *Constellation* became the first modern carrier to enter the Persian (Arabian) Gulf, as a show of support for the Shah of Iran. Tensions with Iran's new government from late 1979 led to ships working well into the Gulf of Oman (the "GOO"), but short of the narrow Strait of Hormuz entrance to the Gulf. This is the body of water from which *Enterprise* launched its 1986 *Praying Mantis* strikes.

The carrier operating area in the Gulf of Oman soon received the title "Camel Station" from the sailors in the region. Higher authority again decided that this name was probably offensive to some unspecified ethnic group, so it soon was rechristened "Gonzo Station" (although some now referred to it as "Camelot Station"). The actual origin of this title is unknown, and although it may well have come from the cynical work of author Hunter S. Thompson, before long it was assumed to mean the cute, shaggy, blue Muppets character. It was probably this connotation that led the US-3As to get the unofficial nickname "Miss Piggy," as they tirelessly plied their trade between Diego Garcia and the carriers off Oman.

Up through *Desert Shield* the Navy (initially as Commander, Middle Eastern Force, ComMidEastFor under 7th Fleet, but later this operation became 5th Fleet, as it took over as a separate organization in 1995) refused to put carriers into the Persian Gulf due to the fear of trapping capital ships inside the narrow Strait of Hormuz, and resulting "fish in a barrel" vulnerability concerns.

This all changed during *Desert Shield*, when it became apparent that the carriers needed to get closer to Iraq if they were going to be a relevant force. Once the decision was made to go into the Gulf, the Navy sent in over 100 vessels, including four carriers and two battleships, and they worked these waters with great success during *Desert Storm*.

Carrier Battle Groups routinely operated within the Gulf for the remainder of the decade, as the Navy supported Operation *Southern Watch*. Ships in the Gulf would normally call on Dubai and Bahrain for liberty.

Naval Carrier Combat Operations 1 Jan 1974 to 31 Dec 2000

"No wonder Americans do well at war, as war is chaos, and Americans practice chaos on a daily basis." - Familiar, if slightly exaggerated foreign view on how the U.S. conducts war

The following work lists those actions where carrier based units have been involved in combat. Behind every engagement are an incredible array of other squadrons whose contributions allowed the combatant units to function; however, space does not allow the listing of the numerous support units that backed up the combatants, nor little more than top-level descriptions. Deeper analysis for many of these events may be found through the bibliography.

***EAGLE PULL*: 12 April, 1975:**

Carrying CH-53 *Sea Stallions* of Marine Squadron HMH-463 in lieu of a CVW, *Hancock* provided support and cover for the evacuation of American personnel from Phnom Penh, Cambodia. Actual threat was limited to small arms fire in Cambodia. Another Marine H-53 unit, HMH-462, carried out similar duties from *Okinawa* (LPH-3).

***FREQUENT WIND*: 29 April, 1975:**

Four carriers (*Enterprise*, *Hancock*, *Coral Sea*, and *Midway*) cover and support the withdrawal of American Citizens from Saigon, South Vietnam, prior to its capture by North Vietnamese forces in their final push to forcibly re-unify the two countries. *Enterprise* (with CVW-14) and *Coral Sea* (CVW-15) provided top cover and support, while *Hancock* and *Midway* off-loaded their air wings, and were used as helicopter platforms. This operation featured the first use of the F-14A *Tomcat* in combat conditions, as *Enterprise* and CVW-14 provided CAP over Saigon during the evacuation.

Hancock retained Marine CH-53 unit HMH-463 after having covered the evacuation of Cambodia earlier in the month. During the final evacuation of Saigon every ship off South Vietnam seemed to have helicopters trying to land on it, with the carriers obviously leading the list of preferred candidates. Rotary-wing aircraft that participated ran the gamut from South Vietnamese aircraft that had no experience at ship landings, to the superb Air Force rescue units and their *Jolly Green Giants*, as well as Air America *Hueys*. Up to 100 Vietnamese H-1s and H-47s alone made the trip out to CTF-76, with the aircraft using any deck available to land on.

The chaotic event led to a number of colorful incidents. In one reported case an Air Force HH-53 landed on an unprepared Navy amphibious assault ship (LPD) after mistaking it for the much larger carrier *Midway*, which was several miles away. The amphib, which still had its HF whip antennas surrounding the landing area in the "up" position, took the *Jolly Green Giant* anyway, even if the pilot's basic ship recognition was a wee bit off.

One *Knox*-class Frigate (FF) had two Vietnamese UH-1 *Hueys* land on its tiny helo-deck in spite of repeated attempts to wave-off the desperate aircraft. A South Vietnamese Air Force O-1 *Birddog* managed to land on *Midway* with a pilot and his large family onboard. (Although this was widely reported as the "first ever" time this type of aircraft had ever landed on a carrier, there were several cases of Marine observation aircraft doing the same through the 1950s.) Many of the helos were pushed overboard during the evolution, although several thousand Vietnamese were saved from the depredations of the new Communist government by this incredible evolution.

Midway subsequently pulled into Thailand and craned aboard about 95 former VNAF aircraft (including Northrop F-5s and Cessna A-37s), and took them to Guam, in spite of strenuous complaints, threats, and demands from the new "unified" Vietnamese government, who claimed the airframes belonged to them. Following the event *Enterprise* returned to Hawaii carrying CH-53A/Ds of HMH-463, along with CVW-14, which created a somewhat unusual deckload for the carrier.

MAYAGUEZ INCIDENT 12-14 May, 1975:

Coral Sea, with CVW-15, along with Air Force units flying out of Thailand, supported Marines as they attempted to rescue 39 crewmembers from the U.S.-flagged merchant vessel SS *Mayaguez*, which had been seized on the open seas by units of the Khmer Rouge armed forces. Operations included strikes on Koh Tang Island, where the crewmen were thought to be held, and on Naval targets in Cambodia proper. Fifteen Marines, Airmen, and Navy Corpsmen were killed in action on the ground, with several Air Force CH/HH-53s and an OV-10 being shot down by unusually fierce ground fire from the island. Three Marines were inadvertently left behind during the final helo withdrawal, and were executed by the Cambodians. No Navy aircraft were lost.

EAGLE CLAW: 24-25April 1980:

The seizure of the U.S. embassy in Tehran, Iran, on 4 Nov 1979 by "students" (one of which was reported to be a future President of Iran) led to the capture of 66 American citizens. Although several plans for their forced release were apparently evaluated, the actual operation, named *Eagle Claw*, involved a very complex evolution that included all four services.

Eight RH-53Ds from HM-16 were shipped surreptitiously to the Indian Ocean, leaving CONUS around Sept 1979. The aircraft were reportedly off-loaded at Diego Garcia, and later flown aboard *Nimitz*, from which the RH-53Ds took off for the mission with Marine crews

A carrier pilot's reputation can be made—or broken—by the way he looks coming back aboard the boat. We're in a VAQ-139 *Prowler* on 26 July 1985 while in the IO, and coming aboard *Constellation*. Lt Billy "Prep" Martin has us on final, and the ball is half a cell high, but he'll get us aboard in fine fashion. Note the CVW-14 aircraft spotted right up to the foul line, as well as the LSOs visible on their platform. (author)

Egypt's Suez Canal was closed from the Six Day War of 1967 through 1975, when it was finally reopened for traffic. *America* was the first U.S. aircraft carrier to subsequently use the channel, in May 1981, and *Enterprise* became the first nuke to be allowed through it, in 1986. Since then the Suez has proven indispensable for moving ships between the Med and IO. Here *Eisenhower* (CVN-69) "does the ditch," northbound on 27 Feb 1992, with CVW-7 on deck. The broad expanse of desert beyond the ship is the Sinai Peninsula. (U.S. Navy, CWO2 A.A. Alleyne)

The establishment of a continuous carrier presence in the Indian Ocean and Gulf of Oman in the 1980s quickly led to a requirement for a utility transport aircraft to help support these ops. The C-2 was too slow and short ranged, and new construction was out of the question, so the Navy converted six S-3 Vikings to US-3As to haul passengers and mail between Diego Garcia and the carriers. Known throughout the fleet as "Miss Piggy," the US-3s provided valuable service for over 15 years before being retired. Here RG713 (158668) is about to plug a VA-196 KA-6D before starting the roughly 1800 mile trek to "Dodge." Two VFA-25 *Hornets* wait their turn alongside. (author)

on 24 April. Two of the helicopters returned to the *Nimitz*, and six made the refueling point inside Iran, named "Desert One," where they met a force of MC/EC-130s that had arrived from Oman with Army Special Forces and fuel.

When another RH-53D went down at the landing site the decision was made to abort the mission due to a lack of helos. While refueling in preparation for the return trip a helicopter that was repositioning itself was engulfed in a dust cloud ("brownout"), and hit a USAF EC-130 that was being used for ground refueling. The resulting explosion and fire killed eight American servicemen.

The remaining personnel were placed in the surviving C-130s, which returned to Oman. The five other RH-53Ds were abandoned at the site for the Iranians to find. The hostages would have to wait until 20 January 1981 before being released after diplomatic negotiations.

Along with *Nimitz*/CVW-8, *Coral Sea*/CVW-14 was on station to provide tactical air support for the exfiltration of the raiders and hostages on 25 April. Both air wings painted recognition markings on their aircraft for the event, consisting of large, colored stripes on the starboard wings. All of the squadrons involved painted these markings out prior to returning to CONUS, with the exception of VA-86 who, since the orange/black stripes were their squadron colors, left them on for the fly-in at Cecil Field.

***GULF OF SIDRA*: 19 Aug, 1981:**

For some time Libya's maximum leader Muammar al-Qaddafi had maintained that the Gulf of Sidra in the Mediterranean south of the 32°-30' line (which soon gained the inspired title "Line of Death") was Libyan waters, and therefore off limits to U.S. naval forces. The U.S. Government held the gulf was international waters, and conducted what it called "Freedom of Navigation Operations" (FONOPS) in the area with both surface and air units of the 6th Fleet. Frequent visits by Libyan Air Force aircraft were met by Navy aircraft from several carriers, and were escorted back towards land. Provocative actions by both sides were occasionally reported, but things did not go "hot" until the morning of 19 August 1981. *Nimitz* (with CVW-8) and *Forrestal* (CVW-17) were manning CAP stations in the Gulf with *Tomcats* and *Phantoms*, respectively. A section of VF-41 F-14As were vectored onto northbound Libyan aircraft, which turned out to be an element of SU-22 "Fitters," Soviet-built ground attack aircraft that were only minimally capable as fighters. One of two Sukhoi pilots, who apparently had no idea how far in over his head he was, shot an AA-2 "Atoll" missile at the F-14s, and the fight was on. The *Tomcats* returned fire, splashing both "Fitters" with AIM-9 *Sidewinder* missiles. Leading the flight was VF-41's Commanding Officer, Cdr. Hank Kleeman. The U.S. Navy held a press conference afterwards with the four aircrew involved, while Libya conducted a SAREX. The event seemed to catch Libya by surprise and, at least initially, they appeared to pull back from further direct confrontation with U.S. forces.

***URGENT FURY* 25-31 Oct 1983:**

When President Reagan decided to overthrow a budding Marxist Government on the island of Grenada, carrier *Independence*, with CVW-6 embarked, was chosen to provide close air support for the effort. Although USAF units, including F-15Cs and A-10s, were prepared for involvement, the island's relative isolation meant that this would be a largely Navy/Marine tactical air war.

"Indy" left Norfolk 18 October for a scheduled Med cruise, where it was due to relieve *Eisenhower*. Instead, the ship turned south and proceeded to the Caribbean. CVW-6 flew about 700 sorties over seven days of operations in support of Marine and Army units on the ground.

The *Valions* of Atkron-15 were involved in action in both Grenada and Lebanon during their 1983-84 cruise in *Independence*. They lost one A-7E during the 4 Dec strikes, and had another aircraft damaged. AE306 (160879) is shown at Fallon in June 1984, and its heavily weathered TPS finish shows the signs of aggressive anti-corrosion work by the squadron's maintenance troops. (Michael Grove)

Threats were limited to small to medium AAA, which shot down several Army and Marine helicopters, although no Navy jets were hit. Attack Squadrons 15, 87, and 176 provided the majority of the support, while VF-14 and -32 established CAP stations against possible Cuban involvement. VAW-122 conducted vital command and control for the entire joint operation, and VS-28 kept an eye on area shipping. After establishing that the Grenadans were not using radar fire control for their weapons VAQ-131 was largely out of the fight, although they were also used to escort curious media aircraft out of the area. In a wee bit of misidentification, one TV crew, in a *King Air*, would describe a *Lancer Prowler* as a "heavily armed Navy fighter jet."

***LEBANON* 4 Dec, 1983:**

The disintegration of Lebanon as a country through foreign-aided civil war led the U.S. to station 6th Fleet carriers off the coast as a show of force, and to monitor Syrian troop movements. On several occasions Syrian and Muslim troops fired on Navy aircraft, particularly F-14 TARPS reconnaissance flights. On the morning of 4 December, Commander in Chief Europe (CINCEUR) directed limited strikes on specific military targets in Lebanon, with hard early morning target times. Carriers *Kennedy* and *Independence* (fresh from Grenada) had prepared for weeks for such strikes, but were given virtually no warning prior to the arrival of the actual execute order early on the morning of the 4th.

With minimal time to prepare their strikes in order to meet the specified target times, crews were rushed and aircraft launched with incomplete bomb loads. Concern about possible Syrian radar-directed SAMs led to the strikes proceeding inland at low altitudes, which put them in the heart of infra-red guided missile envelopes. The result was that two aircraft were destroyed by IR guided SAMs. *Kennedy* lost a VA-85 A-6E, with the pilot, Lt. Mark Lange, being killed, and the B/N, Lt. Bobby Goodman, falling into Syrian hands, and remaining a functional POW for four weeks. CVW-7's CAG, Cdr. Ed "Hunyak" Andrews, was in a VA-15 A-7E when hit while pulling off target. He was able to nurse his crippled *Corsair* just off the coast before ejecting, and was subsequently rescued. Another *Valion* A-7E in the same division was hit by a probable SA-7, but was able to recover safely on *Independence* with damage to his tail cone area.

Little is believed to have been accomplished in terms of military damage by the Navy aircraft. Post-action analysis emphasized the confusion and rushed nature of the event, and many believed that delays in passing the execution order from Washington, when combined with hard time-on-target requirements (which were rumored to coincide with delivery in Damascus of a "stern letter from the State Department"), led to the fiasco. (There was another story told fleet wide, perhaps apocryphal, that Israeli military officials, when asked their opinion of the attack replied something to the effect of "with the tactics you used we can't believe you lost *only **two*** aircraft!")

There were also complaints that the targets selected by higher authority for the strike were not appropriate for the action taken and the time directed, as early morning placed the sun in the face of the attackers and to the advantage of the defenders, while making some preferred electro-optical weapons, including *Walleye*, impossible to use.

The strike was a major embarrassment within the Navy, and led to some level of finger pointing in the service. In a positive sense, it did reinforce an ongoing drive towards more realistic training, through what became "Strike U" at Fallon, and a serious reevaluation in Navy command and control. Later successes in combat are frequently attributed to the lessons learned in this operation, particularly the trend away from low altitude "Alpha Strike" attacks in the teeth of enemy defenses, as well as continued development of precision weapons, instead of large amounts of iron ("dumb") bombs.

***Achille Lauro:* 7 Oct 1985**

An Italian cruise ship, the *Achille Lauro*, was highjacked by a small group of heavily armed Palestinian Terrorists. While onboard the terrorists murdered a U.S. citizen, Leon Klinghoffer. They subsequently docked the ship in Egypt, where they were given asylum. When attempts by the U.S. government to carry out a formal extradition of the individuals failed, *Saratoga* and CVW-17 were ordered to intercept the aircraft carrying them from Egypt to Tunisia. VF-74 and VF-103 *Tomcats* made the intercept, under the control of a VAW-125 *Hawkeye*. Contrary to many reports, no EA-6B *Prowlers* were involved. The Egyptian airliner, a Boeing 737-200, was forced down at Sigonella, Sicily, where Italian authorities interceded, and took the surprised terrorists into custody.

***PRAIRIE FIRE:* 24-25 March, 1986:**

American forces, once again conducting Freedom of Navigation Operations (FONOPS) in the Gulf of Sidra, came to blows with Qaddafi's military. A large force under 6th Fleet built around carriers *Saratoga* (carrying CVW-17), *America* (CVW-1), and *Coral Sea* (CVW-13) was conducting operations in the disputed waters when long-range SA-5 SAMs were fired at Navy aircraft. HARM anti-radiation missiles from F/A-18s and A-7Es were fired back while under the electric cover of EA-6Bs, with some damage being recorded. During the night and following morning several Libyan Navy patrol boats were engaged by both aircraft and surface units, with at least one "Nanuchka II" Corvette (hit by VA-55 and VA-85) and one "La Combattante" PTG (*Waheed*, through VA-34 delivered *Harpoons* and VA-85 dropped *Rockeyes*) being destroyed by A-6Es. An additional "Nanuchka" was heavily damaged by VA-85 *Intruders* as well. Claims by surface ships that they engaged and destroyed additional Libyan Naval units with *Harpoon* could not be corroborated. The Libyan air force chose to sit this one out, much to the disgust of Navy fighter crews. No Naval aircraft were damaged during the fracas. This incident featured the first combat use of the F/A-18 *Hornet*, HARM, and *Harpoon* missiles.

***EL DORADO CANYON* 14-15 Apr, 1986:**

Following *Prairie Fire*, an American soldier was killed and 50 wounded by a terrorist bomb at a nightspot in Berlin. Qaddafi was blamed, and President Reagan authorized limited strikes against terrorist and military targets in Libya in response. The two remaining 6th Fleet carriers, *Coral Sea* (with CVW-13) and *America* (CVW-1), launched strikes into Benghazi, while Air Force F-111Fs from the 48th TFW flew circuitous routing from Lakenheath, UK, to hit Tripoli in

The *Black Ravens* had a wild 1985-86 New Years Eve, as they were recalled from revelry to travel to the Med and join CVW-13 underway off Libya. 72 hours later they had aircraft on *Coral Sea* and were ready for combat. The trip ended with participation in Operations *Prairie Fire* and *El Dorado Canyon*. AK607 (161350) sits at Whidbey in August 1986 before the unit moved on to CVW-11. (author)

an impressive piece of airmanship. *Intruders* from both ships went over the beach, with VA-34 hitting targets located in Benghazi, while VA-55 struck Benina Airfield. Carrier aircraft (VAQ-135 and VMAQ-2 EA-6Bs, VA-46 and -72 A-7Es, and F/A-18s from VFA-131, 132, VMFA-323, and -314) provided defense suppression, along with USAF EF-111A *Ravens* from the 42nd ECS. Battle Group *Hawkeyes* (from VAW-127 and 123) carried out vital command and control duties, as well. The result was that only one F-111 (70-2389) was lost with its crew to very heavy enemy defenses. Actual bombing results were mixed, although dramatic F-111 bombing video had the desired impact on media worldwide.

PRAYING MANTIS 18 April 1988:

Although the U.S. hostages had been released by the Iranians in 1980, tensions in the Persian Gulf had continued to build, particularly as Iran fought a bloody war with its neighbor, Iraq. Iranian forces had begun to imperil the flow of oil leaving the Persian Gulf, and the U.S. Navy was called upon to escort tankers, amid increasing rhetoric and threats of violence from the Ayatollah Khomeini. On 14 April the U.S. Frigate *Samuel B. Roberts* (FFG-58) struck an Iranian laid mine in the Gulf and almost sank. Four days later aircraft from *Enterprise*, which operated from the Gulf of Oman, carried out strikes against Iranian naval targets and oil platforms in conjunction with surface units and Marine helicopters located inside the Persian Gulf. Local command was under Commander Joint Task Force Middle East (COMJTFME) embarked in *Coronado* (AGF-11) The 1350 ton Saam-class frigate *Sabalan*, in particular, was considered a "high interest" target, as it had reportedly attacked several merchant ships in the proceeding months, with the Commanding Officer being known to taunt his victims over bridge-to-bridge radio.

Making things more problematic was the presence of a severe haze across most of the Gulf, with visibility reported as being of less than a mile in places. Ship identification, in particular, was made very difficult by the weather phenomenon, which would complicate the locating and targeting of the Iranian Navy ships and Revolutionary Guard speedboats that were expected to respond to the U.S. attacks.

Action began at 0900 when ships from Surface Action Groups (SAGs) Bravo (*Merrill*, DD-976; *Lynde McCormick*, DDG-8; *Trenton*, LPD-14; with elements of HMLA-167 embarked) and Charlie (*Wainwright*, CG-28; *Bagley*, FF-1069; and *Simpson*, FFG-56) began to shell two Iranian oil platforms that had been used as bases for mine-laying and small boat attacks on merchant shipping. Assaults on the platforms by Marines and SEALS followed, with two of the bigger structures being put out of action. CVW-11 provided top-cover in the event the Iranian Air Force tried to intervene, and as Surface CAP against Iranian ships or boats.

At about 1300 the Iranian Navy finally made an appearance, as the missile-patrol boat *Joshan* approached SAG Charlie. After being warned the PGM shot a *Harpoon* missile at the Americans, which missed, and they responded with overwhelming fire, quickly sinking the 800 ton vessel. Later in the day *Wainwright* engaged an Iranian F-4 with Standard SAMs. The *Phantom* II was damaged, and managed to land at its base.

Attacks by Boghammer speedboats on merchant shipping were met by CVW-11 aircraft which destroyed or damaged several with *Rockeye*. Other aircraft scoured the Gulf, while looking at contacts that proved to be either merchant ships or neutral warships, which included units from the UAE, and even the Soviet Union.

While this was going on an A-6E from *Enterprise* located a possible warship in the Strait of Hormuz. Poor visibility required the crew to make a low pass, during which they drew fire and identified it as a Vosper/Saam-class frigate, which could have been any one of four the Iranians possessed.

The *Intruder* returned fire, and additional CVW-11 aircraft (at least one A-6E and six *Corsairs*) joined the event by unloading *Harpoons*, *Skippers*, dumb bombs, and a *Walleye* on the hapless ship, which was soon identified as the *Sahand*. DDG *Joseph Strauss* also pumped a *Harpoon* into the vessel for good measure, and the target was soon a blazing wreck. The stubborn ship finally sank several hours later.

Not long afterward, another Iranian Frigate was located and more aircraft attacked. This one turned out to be the "high interest" *Sabalan*, which promptly collected several laser guided and dumb bombs from A-6s and A-7s. It was at this point that the battle was ceased after a call from Washington, D.C., and the battered warship, now dead in the water, was allowed to be towed back into port.

E-2Cs from VAW-117 were given credit for providing excellent command and control during the event, while VAQ-135 *Prowlers* carried out jamming support, as well. One Marine AH-1T (161018) and its crew of two from HMLA-167, flying from *Trenton*, were lost during the action, although the exact cause was apparently never determined, although it was described as "combat related."

Praying Mantis was certainly a success within its stated goals, that being to spank the Iranians, and show them that the U.S. would not stand by while it threatened shipping inside the Persian Gulf. That being said, it also led to a tremendous amount of self-congratulation within the service, as well as inflated statements trying to enhance the event's historical importance, particularly when one senior officer involved grandly described it as the most significant U.S. Naval engagement since Korea.

In the end, the largest Navy in the world had conducted a successful one-day action against a second-level opponent. More than a few observers felt that portraying it as a "great victory" ranking up with the battle of Midway as being somewhat overdramatic. Any other result would have been considered unthinkable.

Gulf of Sidra 4 Jan 1989:

In a repeat of the 1981 shootdown, two Libyan aircraft, this time MiG-23 "Floggers," were judged to be a threat to a pair of VF-32 F-14As off *Kennedy*. One was destroyed by AIM-9 *Sidewinder*, the other with an AIM-7 *Sparrow*, out of a total of four missiles fired (three *Sparrows*, one *Sidewinder*).

DESERT SHIELD 2 Aug 1990-16 Jan 1991:

The surprise Iraqi invasion of Kuwait on 2 August, 1990 led to the deployment of several carriers to cover the build up of coalition forces on the Arabian Peninsula. *Independence* was already present in the Gulf of Oman, while the *Eisenhower* transited the Suez Canal to arrive in the Red Sea on 8 August. Pressure to get the eastern carriers closer to potential targets (and thereby reduce tanker requirements) led to the movement of *Independence* into the Persian Gulf. Although NavCent was highly concerned with the restricted waters (and much higher potential vulnerability) presented by the PG, all subsequent combat operations from the east side would be flown from these waters.

Although not involved directly in combat, these two ships contributed a great deal in providing cover for the initial units that deployed to the region, as well as by establishing initial operating procedures for the units that would conduct

the eventual liberation of Kuwait. Both vessels remained on station until relieved by *Midway* and *Saratoga*. These ships were joined by *Ranger* and *Kennedy* prior to the 17 Jan start of *Desert Storm*.

DESERT STORM 17 Jan to 28 Feb 1991:

In the greatest focused use of naval airpower since *Linebacker II* in Vietnam, six carriers carried out combat operations against Iraq over a six week period that led to the liberation of Kuwait. From the night of 17 January, Task Force 155/Battle Group Yankee (*Kennedy*/CVW-3 and *Saratoga*/CVW-17) launched strikes from the Red Sea, while Task Force 154/Battle Group Zulu (*Ranger*/CVW-2 and *Midway*/CVW-5) attacked from the Persian Gulf. Newly arrived *America*/CVW-1 began operations from the Red Sea on the 18th, while *Theodore Roosevelt*/CVW-8 started flights in the Persian Gulf on 20 January, after making a high-speed transit around the Arabian Peninsula from the Suez Canal.

First night strikes involved four air wings sending aircraft deep into Iraq against the teeth of the enemy air defense system. Combat

Bound for glory. This *Sunliner* F/A-18C was one of two of the squadron's *Hornets* that was used to shoot down MiG-21s on the first morning of *Desert Storm*. AA410 (163502) would be the mount of Lt. Nick Mongillo for the kill. It's shown here at Fallon in Oct '89. (Michael Grove)

Desert Storm could not have been carried off without the incredible amount of aerial tanking available for tactical aircraft. The KC-135s, KC-10s, and their crews never quite got the credit they deserved for their role in the war, particularly from their own service. Here a VF-41 F-14A from *Theodore Roosevelt* gets its fill over the Persian Gulf. It will soon depart for a TARPS escort mission with the VF-84 photo bird sitting off the right side. A VF-102 *Tomcat*, flying North Gulf CAP off *America*, observes from the port side. The tanker in this case is a Pennsylvania ANG KC-135E (59-1457), and the date is 25 Feb '91. (author)

operations were continuous until 28 Feb, with the exceptions of *Midway*, which suspended flights for one week mid-war to repair worn flight-deck non-skid, and *America*, which shifted from the Red Sea to the Persian Gulf by 15 Feb. Her arrival in the PG raised the strength of TF154 to four carriers in time to support the imminent invasion of Kuwait by coalition ground forces.

With long distances to travel to their targets, the Red Sea air wings typically launched two to three major strikes a day, while Persian Gulf aircraft, being sometimes within 100 miles of their targets, generally conducted cyclic ops throughout the war. The result was that TF155 aircrew typically flew fewer total sorties from the Red Sea, but had more flight hours, while TF154 crews flew more missions but less total hours.

Initial Navy flights, particularly from the Red Sea, were highly dependent upon coalition (largely USAF and RAF) tankers. Persian Gulf launched missions became less reliant on tanking as they closed on Iraqi targets later in the war. Red Sea carriers were virtually invulnerable to attack, while PG ships faced a constant threat from mines. Potential attacks by "Silkworm" and *Exocet* missiles, although taken seriously, never materialized on the carriers themselves.

In spite of some pre-war analysis predicting heavy attrition, the Navy lost only a single aircraft on night one, a *Saratoga*-based F/A-18C. Four other USN aircraft would be shot down over the following six week war: three A-6Es and an F-14. Three of the combat losses (60%) would be from one air wing, CVW-17. Four additional aircraft (an A-7E, A-6E, and two F/A-18As) were lost to operational reasons during the same period. (see appendix A for more details) Only *Midway*/CVW-5 lost no aircraft during the war; *Kennedy*/CVW-3 and *America*/CVW-1 suffered operational mishaps, but did not lose any due to enemy action.

Only three air-to-air kills were made by Navy aircraft during *Desert Storm*. *Saratoga*-based *Hornets* from VFA-81 shot down a pair of MiG-21s on 17 Jan. On 6 Feb a VF-1 F-14A from *Ranger* destroyed a solo Mi-8 or -17 helicopter, for which the crew became the most highly decorated CVW-2 aviators of the war.

Desert Storm would prove to be the largest carrier combat operation conducted by the Navy in roughly twenty years. While the war showed that old war horses like *Ranger*, *America*, and *Midway* still had plenty of fight left in them, it also proved to be something of a last hurrah for battle groups of oil burning aircraft carriers, with only one nuke (*Roosevelt*) participating.

SOUTHERN WATCH 27 Aug 1992 to 17 Mar 2003:

Operation *Southern Watch* (OSW) was fallout from the end of *Desert Storm*, where Allied air forces (U.S., RAF, and French) continued to patrol southern Iraq airspace to enforce compliance with post-war non-fly directives. OSW was conducted under the auspices of Central Command (CentCom) for over eleven years, using carriers operating in the Persian Gulf, as well as rotational Air Force units flying out of Saudi Arabia and the Gulf States.

Although the official date was from Aug 1992 (following an announcement by President G.H.W. Bush on the 26th), the operation, in effect, began with the end of hostilities in Feb 1991. Air Force flights typically flew out of Prince Sultan Air Base (PSAB), located near Al Kharj ("Al's Garage"), Saudi Arabia, and the Navy usually kept at least one carrier in the Persian Gulf to fly these missions as well. From March 1998 expeditionary EA-6B squadrons joined the Air Force at PSAB, replacing their EF-111A *Ravens*.

Although all flights north of the Iraqi border were considered "combat," most did not involve release of ordnance. On occasion flights did drop bombs for reasons of self protection, or as "response options" following provocative Iraqi actions. On two occasions (27 Dec 1992 and 17 Jan 1993) USAF F-16s engaged and shot down Iraqi fighter aircraft that penetrated "no fly" areas. Between 16 and 20 Dec

1998 the United States conducted a three-day combat operation dubbed ***Desert Fox***, which involved strikes from the carriers *Enterprise* (with CVW-3) and *Carl Vinson* (CVW-11). *Enterprise* launched 281 sorties during the event, while *Vinson* arrived in time to participate in one night of operations.

On 5 January 1999 VF-213 F-14Ds engaged Iraqi MiG-25s at long range with a pair of AIM-54 *Phoenix* AAMs, without result. This appears to have been the first combat use of the *Phoenix* in U.S. Navy history. A similar event occurred on 9 Sep 1999, when a VF-2 F-14D shot at a fleeing Iraqi MiG-23. Although neither action ended in a kill, both of these engagements were reportedly made at the extreme edge of the missile's envelope against receding targets, and had a low probability of a kill. It needs to be said that Iran claimed in excess of 100 kills with the weapon during its previous war with Iraq, and although there is a significant lack of hard evidence to confirm the real level of success, there seems to be no doubt that the Iranian Air Force scored the only kills with the legendary *Phoenix*.

It's probably safe to assume that every carrier that entered the Persian Gulf between 1992 and 2003 logged combat time as a part of OSW, although in most cases it involved armed patrol of Iraqi airspace, and returning to the carrier with their un-dropped ordnance. It became a routine part of cruise and, by 2000, OSW had become, in effect, a method of reducing what remained of the Iraqi Integrated Air Defense System (IADS), with specific radars, operations centers, and missile sites being targeted for destruction. This unofficial campaign would pay off dividends when the final invasion of Iraq occurred in March 2003, during *Iraqi Freedom*.

RESTORE HOPE: 9 Dec 1992 to 4 May 1993

U.S. operations in the Horn of Africa region were a result of internal strife in the region, and centered on the nation of Somalia, which had fallen into a civil war controlled by various tribal leaders and local warlords. In August 1992 President Bush announced that the country would support United Nations attempts to bring famine assistance and stability to Somalia under the name Operation ***Provide Relief***. Initial attempts were met by more violence and extreme graft on the part of the Somali warlords.

In December 1992 the U.S. increased direct military involvement in the country in order to bring order, as well as protect UN efforts to feed the country's starving population. This event was named ***Restore Hope***, which was done under UN Security Resolution 794, which authorized the U.S. "...to use all necessary means to establish a secure environment for humanitarian relief operations in Somalia as soon as possible." Marines and other U.S. troops went ashore and

While some pre-war analysis predicted heavy attrition during what would become *Desert Storm*, there were relatively few actual combat losses during the war. There were also a small number of operational mishaps, including this VA-72 A-7E, which suffered a nose gear failure during a cat shot on 26 Jan '91. The pilot was able to get the aircraft airborne, and brought it back for a barricade arrestment on *Kennedy*. In spite of the heroics, the *Corsair* (158830, AC403) was subsequently stripped and pushed overboard. (U.S. Navy)

achieved a small measure of control until the UN officially took over under Operation ***Continue Hope*** in May 1993.

UN-run operations continued against rising violence, even with direct U.S. military support. Attempts to restrict local warlords led to the disastrous raid by Army troops on 3/4 October that became the "Black Hawk Down" engagement, where two Army helos were destroyed and 18 soldiers killed. U.S. forces would subsequently be withdrawn by March 1994.

Carrier aviation participation in Somalia was limited largely to a support role during the early parts of the operation. *Ranger* was the first to arrive, and it was relieved by *Kitty Hawk* in Dec 1992. Flight operations usually involved low fly-bys for "shock" value, and E-2s being used to control air traffic over the country. TARPS-equipped *Tomcats* were heavily used for photo-recon, and in a more novel role, S-3s were used to drop propaganda leaflets via their sonobouy tubes.

***NORTHERN WATCH:* 31 Dec 1996 to 17 Mar 2003:**

The Air Force's portion of *Desert Storm* that flew out of Turkey went by the name Joint Task Force *Proven Force*. It was succeeded post war by a joint operation designated *Provide Comfort*, which rendered support and coverage to the Kurdish people in the northern part of Iraq.

In time this operation was renamed *Northern Watch*, which became the European Command (EUCOM) counterpart to *Southern Watch*, and involved routine patrol operations over northern Iraq that occasionally led to "response option" strikes in the face of Iraqi provocation. Operations were centered out of Incirlik, Turkey, and usually flown by U.S. Air Force or Allied units seconded to the 7440th Wing and (from 15 Sep '97) the 39th AEW. Although both *Theodore Roosevelt* and *Forrestal* flew missions into northern Iraq from the Med in 1991 during *Provide Comfort*, carrier-based aircraft were not normally used to cover *Northern Watch*. From December 1997 expeditionary EA-6B units were deployed to Incirlik to provide EW support for Air Force participants. ONW continued up to 17 March 2003 and the start of *Iraqi Freedom*.

***DENY FLIGHT* 12 April 1993 to 20 Dec 1995**
***DELIBERATE FORCE* 29 Aug to 14 Sep 1995**

The unraveling of Yugoslavia in the late 1980s and early 1990s led to increasing factionalism, as the nation divided into multiple countries. Reports of genocide by Serbians against Muslim population in what was now called Bosnia-Herzegovina led to an outraged world press, and calls for both political and military action against the Serbs.

Military and relief efforts in the Balkans region would run through most of the 1990s, and take multiple names along the way. What followed was a long and very complex series of operations that would involve threats and posturing by the United Nations, as well as—in the end—the first combat operations ever undertaken by the North Atlantic Treaty Organization (NATO).

NATO, using forces assigned to Allied Air Forces Southern Europe (AFSOUTH), initiated ***Deny Flight*** to ensure compliance with UN Security Council Resolution 816, which banned flights by the Serbian military in the airspace of Bosnia-Herzegovina. The operation would be flown by U.S. forces, as well as many other NATO allies, from bases in Italy and cooperative Balkan states. A number of carriers conducted operations in the Balkans as part of *Deliberate Force*. In Aug/Sep 1993 the Navy also placed a reinforced EA-6B squadron into Aviano to support NATO flights. This effort was headed by VAQ-141 (strengthened with additional *Prowlers* from VAQ-130 and -209), which moved off the *Theodore Roosevelt* as needed to cover coalition operations. Other carriers involved included the French Navy's *Clemenceau* and the United Kingdom's HMS *Ark Royal*.

Deny Flight was frequently an exercise in frustration for aircrew (being called, among other things "Operation Please Don't Fly" by some members of CVW-8), as they dealt with NATO restrictions and the realities of coalition "war." Nonetheless, on occasion, things did get busy, as on 28 Feb '94, when USAF F-16Cs from the 86th Fighter Wing shot down what was believed to be four Yugoslavian *Super Galeb* light-attack aircraft (accounts differ—the targets are also described as *Galebs* in some accounts, although the two types are substantially different) that were conducting strike operations on Bosnians.

On 2 June 1995 an Air Force F-16C (89-2032) from the 31st FW hanging out without EW support was shot down by an SA-6. The pilot, Capt Scott "Zulu" O'Grady, was rescued six days later by Marine helicopters and a large covering force, which included the Navy EA-6Bs operating out of Aviano.

Carried out within *Deny Flight*, **Deliberate Force** involved a month of strikes on Bosnian Serb targets in response to continued aggression against civilians. The United Nations had issued multiple mandates to protect the largely Muslim Serbs from Christian Bosnian Serb forces. When these "orders" were ignored NATO organized a month-long air campaign in response. Part of this response was *Dead Eye*, which was intended to destroy Serbian air defense sites. Operations were conducted under NATO's AFSOUTH with French, German, Italian, Dutch, Spanish, Turkish, British, and U.S. forces. Over 3500 sorties were flown, with the loss of a single French Mirage 2000N on 30 August to an IR missile. Its crew was taken prisoner and eventually returned. U.S. Navy participation included ten EA-6B *Prowlers* flying from Aviano, and the carriers *Theodore Roosevelt* (CVW-8) and *America* (CVW-1). This action marked the first heavy use of the F-14 *Tomcat* in an air-to-ground combat role. *Deliberate Force* helped bring the warring parties to the peace table for the December 1995 signing of the Dayton Accords, which would lead to another series of NATO operations to maintain the unstable peace between the two sides.

***UPHOLD DEMOCRACY* 12 Sep to 22 Oct 1994**

In the fall of 1994 the Clinton administration watched the impending collapse of its favored regime in Haiti with concern. The Army was ordered to deploy elements of the 10th Mountain Division, as well as Special Forces to prop up the Haitian government, and two aircraft carriers were directed to embark Army helicopters to support the operation.

Eisenhower interrupted her normal work-up cycle to take portions of the 10th Mountain to the island, along with all or part of three Navy helo squadrons for support. The ship was used to move a good deal of the division's helicopters and wheeled vehicles, the latter of which were taken to the beach by Army and Navy helos.

Amazingly, at least one Army publication subsequently printed an article congratulating the service for "inventing" the ship-to-shore movement tactics and techniques that the Navy and Marines had been using for years for this same purpose. It also claimed that the Navy had to be "taught" how to sling loads from hovering helicopters—something that VERTREP units and ships had been doing at sea for decades. The Army's take on the event notwithstanding, *Eisenhower* returned home to Norfolk after ten days and, less than a month later, re-loaded CVW-3, and headed for the Med for its normal six-month cruise. What had been a major evolution for the Army had proven little more than a slight interlude in the warship's normal routine.

America loaded elements of the 160th Special Operations Aviation Regiment (160th SOAR), and was used over seven weeks to provide support during the event with these highly professional Army warriors.

Placing Army helicopter units on carriers led to a significant number of issues which included, but were not limited to, HERO (electromagnetic/ordnance safety) concerns, berthing, and flight deck safety. Other areas of concern included learning to work with Army helos, most of which did not have folding rotor blades, EMI hardening, or protection against a saltwater environment. Nonetheless, the Navy-Army team made things work in a fine fashion. "Air wing" configuration is provided below, since it does not fit into the normal Carrier Air Wing organization found in chapter 3.

The use of *America* as a Spec Ops platform would be repeated by *Kitty Hawk* during Operation *Enduring Freedom* off Afghanistan in 2002, in a highly successful joint operation conducted by both services.

Eisenhower		**13 to 23 Sept 1994**		**Haiti**
HS-7	SH-3H	AG610	SAR	
HCS-4	HH-60H	NW	detachment	Combat SAR
HC-2	CH-53E	HU	detachment	VERTREP, Heavy lifting

Elements, 10th Mountain Division, U.S. Army
CH-47, UH-60, OH-58, AH-64 (1850 troops, 51 helicopters)

America **12 Sept to 22 Oct 1994** **Haiti**
Elements, 160th Special Operations Aviation Regiment, U.S. Army ("The Night Stalkers")
MH-47, MH-60, MH/AH-6 (64 helicopters)

The September 1994 "invasion" of Haiti in Operation *Uphold Democracy* involved the very unusual use of conventional aircraft carriers as helicopter platforms for the U.S. Army. *Eisenhower* carried 51 helos and over 1800 troops from the 10th Mountain Division to the island for the op. This picture was shot on 14 Sept as the vessel departs Norfolk, with numerous soldiers pictured among the ship's sailors. Army UH-60As, OH-58s, and at least one AH-64 are seen on the "Ike's" flight deck—where they emphasize their lack of rotor fold—as well as a single *Dusty Dog* SH-3H from HS-7, who provided traditional planeguard coverage for the trip. (U.S. Navy, PH2 Steve Eufield).

***ALLIED FORCE/NOBLE ANVIL* 24 Mar 1999 to 10 Jun 1999**
Continued unrest in the Balkans led to major combat operations against the former Yugoslavia in support of ethnic Muslims in Kosovo in 1999. Serbian troops were deemed to be conducting operations within Kosovo in violation of UN Security Council Resolution 1199 of 23 Sep 1998.

Allied Force would be the name used for the entire operation, while *Noble Anvil* was the U.S. portion of the bigger effort.

NATO, with Allied Air Forces Southern Europe (AFSOUTH), initiated air operations against the former Yugoslavia on 24 March 1999 to stop what were declared to be "ethnic cleansing" operations being undertaken in Kosovo.

U.S. Naval involvement centered once again on the *Theodore Roosevelt*/CVW-8 team. By now *TR* had more actual time in combat than the rest of her *Nimitz* class sisters combined. The Navy also supported an ad hoc "Electronic Attack Wing Aviano" of EA-6Bs from VAQ-140, -138, and -209 to cover coalition operations between February and July 1999. The Marines had a separate large *Prowler* unit present as well, made up of personnel and airframes from VMAQ-1, -2, and -4 for the same purpose. At the height of operations there were 29 EA-6Bs located at Aviano.

On 27 Mar an Air Force F-117A (82-0806) from the 49th FW was shot down by Yugoslavian SAM forces, and an F-16C (80-0550, 555th FS, 31st FW) was destroyed on 2 May, again by a surface-to-air missile. The Air Force would later officially admit in a publicly released 2002 paper by its Historical Research Agency that both had been shot down by SA-3s. In 2005 the Serbs would claim that both were shot down by the same missile battery. Five Serbian MiG-29s were downed by USAF F-15Cs, an F-16C, and a sole Dutch F-16. *Allied Force* resulted in the withdrawal of Serbian forces from Kosovo, and the tenuous establishment of a largely unstable peace to the region.

Red Flag and the Navy

Following the end of the Vietnam War, the Air Force started looking for ways to better prepare its pilots for combat. The Tactical Air Command (TAC), under General Bobby Dixon (known TAC-wide as "The Tidewater Alligator"), developed a periodic exercise at Nellis AFB, Nevada, where entire units would fly in and conduct training on a somewhat realistic basis over the vast range areas located north of the base. The exercise was christened *Red Flag*, and it has since become the blueprint for large-scale unit training throughout the military aviation world. The stated goal of the exercise was to provide aircrew an equivalent to ten "combat" missions in a more benign training environment before they saw the real thing.

The Air Force spent millions of dollars developing threat simulators, missile launchers, and providing aggressor aircraft for use at the Nellis ranges. Large, well equipped buildings and training facilities were constructed on base for visiting units, as well. Briefings were standardized and professionally delivered. Post-flight debriefs were done en masse, with a video playback available of the entire battle.

What started out in the late '70s as a moderately scaled affair turned into a massive endeavor, where over 100 aircraft could launch on a single event. By the mid-1980s Nellis AFB would host up to six *Red Flags* annually, with one usually featuring an electronic warfare-heavy environment and labeled *Green Flag*.

Red Flag gave the Air Force the chance to bring units together for training that was not available on a scale anywhere else. USAF flyers frequently remarked that this was the only place they could get together with other types of aircraft, compare tactics, and work as a team, something Navy crews did routinely at Fallon and on the boat. Fighters, bombers, tankers, AWACS, and trash haulers all participated. Until the 1990s this two-week trip to Nevada might be the major deployment for many Air Force units through their entire year.

Navy and Marine squadrons came as well, as did allied units from places like England, Canada, Chile, France, and Singapore. Not surprisingly, inter-service rivalries also appeared, and Navy crews had to learn how to do business "the Air Force way." Things like the Navy's slightly relaxed flight suit standards were frequently brought up, as did the notorious "red line entry" at Air Force ramps, where you had to enter or exit a flight line *only* at specific points. Cross the red line painted on the ramp anywhere else, and you could quickly find yourself sprawled on the concrete with a rifle pointed at your head. (Typical Navy response, while picking gravel out of your face: "Red line? What red line?") All kidding aside, *Red Flag* was the beginning of a true joint flight training environment, and it paid off in spades down the road during operations like *Desert Storm*.

For most Navy crews *Red Flag* was considered a "Good Deal," and not to be turned down. While it might have been the biggest annual training event for some USAF units, to Navy squadrons two weeks in Las Vegas made *Red Flag* a nice interlude before leaving CONUS for six months on a boat.

Red Flag spawned a whole host of other exercises in the Air Force under similar colored names, some of which emphasized command and control, logistics, and other "warfare" areas. The Canadians developed *Maple Flag*, a highly regarded exercise on a slightly smaller scale out of Cold Lake, Alberta.

Red Flag was (and is) a monumental training event that helped prepare the U.S. forces for world events of the 1980s and '90s. Between 1984 and 1990 the author participated in four *Red Flags* and their *Green Flag* cousins. Most of the training was still directed with the Soviets in mind, even if the stark western U.S. desert wasn't where most of us thought we might have to fight.

Nonetheless, in October 1989 the author flew in a *Red Flag* that included English *Jaguars* and *Tornadoes*, Italian *Tornadoes*, USAF RF-4Cs out of Bergstrom, Eglin-based F-15Cs, and Seymour-Johnson F-15Es, as well as B-52s, EF-111s, and E-3As. Little did we know that, only about a year later, many of these same men and machines would be in combat over terrain very similar to Nevada.

The Navy started participating in exercises with the Air Force at Nellis AFB, Nevada, in a big way during the late mid- to late 1970s, and continued through to 2000. These operations included the well know *Red Flag* series, as well as a number of lesser known ops, such as *Gunsmoke*, a periodic weapons competition. Here a section of VFA-97 *Warhawk* F/A-18As depart Nellis during *Gunsmoke* '95. (David Brown)

2

Carriers

"Give me a fast ship, for I intend to go into Harm's Way"
- John Paul Jones, paraphrased

1974 was a turning point for the carrier Navy. The Vietnam War was over, and the service had a fleet of tired ships to deal with. Fourteen carriers were in the fleet, along with four stored in "mothballs" for possible later use. In addition, there was a single training carrier (AVT), the *Lexington*, based in Pensacola, and *Intrepid*, the last of the ASW carriers (CVS), which had only a few months left in service. All but one of the ships were oil burners, *Enterprise* being the only nuclear powered carrier in service. Two of the active fleet carriers were "27 Charlie" *Essex* class approaching the ends of their lives, three were of the *Midway* class, and the remaining eight were so called "Supercarriers" of the *Forrestal* and latter classes.

Big changes were on the way, though, as *Nimitz*, the Navy's second CVAN, was rapidly approaching completion. The *Nimitz*s would prove to be the largest single class of carriers built since the *Essex*

Ranger makes a hard turn while working in the W-291 area off San Diego on 27 July 1990. CVW-2—one of the so-called "All-Grumman Air Wings"—is arrayed on deck. (Robert Lawson)

types, and would dominate the fleet by the end of the millennium. For ship's company, the vessels were a great step forward from earlier ships, as their air conditioning usually worked, and water hours, where crew's fresh water was rationed, generally became a thing of the past. The *Nimitz*, and her eight subsequent sister ships are, arguably, the most important class of warships built by any Navy since World War II.

Starting in 1972, the Navy began to redesignate "Attack" carriers (CVA/CVAN) to multi-purpose carriers (CV/CVN), as they mixed the former attack and anti-submarine roles into the CVWs.

Saratoga was the first redesignated, with others following. All remaining carriers were redesignated on 30 June 1975.

The Navy had increased its deploying carrier force from 14 to 15 prior to *Desert Storm*, but economic realities caught up with it in the '90s, as *Midway*, *America*, and all of the *Forrestals* were retired, with only three new *Nimitzs* coming on line (*Washington*, *Stennis*, and *Truman*). In the fall of 1995, the service declared that the *Kennedy* would be a reserve training vessel, and not be used for normal cruises, which actually dropped the number of deployable decks to 11. This proved impractical, and she was brought back up to regular manning levels, and returned to the Mediterranean in the spring of 1997.

As of December 2000, the carrier Navy had twelve CV/CVNs in service: three oil burners and nine nukes. All of the "27Cs," *Forrestals*, and *Midways* were gone: either scrapped ("turned into razor blades," as commonly stated), stored, or converted into museums.

	Total	*Essex* 27C/125	*Midway*	*Forrestal*	*K.Hawk/JFK*	*Enterprise*	*Nimitz*
1974	**14**	2	3	4	4	1	0
1985	**14**	0	2	4	4	1	3
2000	**12**	0	0	0	3	1	8

Table 3: Active Fleet Carriers

Class	Displacement	Length	Beam	Crew	Catapults	Elevators
Essex	27,100 tons	894 ft	93 ft	3500	2	3
Midway	62,000 tons	979 ft	113 ft	4700	2/3	3
Forrestal	79,000 tons	1046 ft	129 ft	5400	4	4
Kitty Hawk	80,800 tons	1060 ft	129 ft	5500	4	4
Enterprise	85,600 tons	1100 ft	133 ft	5600	4	4
Nimitz	96,000 tons	1100 ft	134 ft	5600	4	4

Table 4: Carrier Dimensions

Source of data is the U.S. Navy, although numbers can vary considerably depending on ship's configuration and date of information. Crew numbers include embarked air wing. Just about every member of the *Nimitz* class seems to have claimed the "World's Largest Warship" title at one time or another, depending on things like minute measurements of the deck, the phase of the moon, and the way the crew's laundry was hanging. For most intents and purposes, they're all about the same.

Listings: Deployment dates show day the ship left its homeport until it returned. Actual deployment dates for the air wings and/or individual squadrons frequently vary. Dates listed are as recorded by the Naval Aviation History office. Actual ceremonial dates are listed if known to be different.

Shorthand for cruise locations: Lant: Atlantic; WP: Western Pacific; NP: Northern Pacific; IO: Indian Ocean; Carib: Caribbean; RS: Red Sea; Med: Mediterranean; World: "around the world"; and CA: Central America. More details can be found in the introduction.

Intrepid (CVS-11)

Class: 27C/125 *Essex*
Homeport: Norfolk, VA
Comm. CV-11 16 Aug 1943, decom. 22 Mar 1947, r/d CVA-11 1 Oct 52, comm. 18 Jun 54, r/d CVS-11 31 Mar 62, decom. 15 Mar 74.
The fourth ship to bear the name *Intrepid*, the "Evil I" was in service Jan 1974 with no air wing assigned. The ship, a distinguished veteran of World War II, Vietnam, and the Cold War, had returned from her last deployment as an ASW carrier in 1973. She would be used for fleet and training command carrier qualifications until decommissioned and stricken in March 1974, and placed in storage at Philadelphia Naval Shipyard. *Intrepid* is preserved as a museum at New York, NY, which opened in August 1982.

Hornet (CVS-12)

Class: 27A/125 *Essex*
Comm. CV-12 29 Nov 43, decom. 22 Mar 47, r/d CVA-12 1 Oct 52, comm. 1 Oct 53, r/d CVS-12 27 Jun 58, decom 26 Jun 70.
The second carrier to carry the name *Hornet* after CV-8, which was sunk in the Battle of Santa Cruz in Oct. 1942. The ship was in storage at Bremerton, WA, as of Jan 1974. Stricken for scrap on 25 July 1989, the ship was retained until 26 May 1998, when it was donated and moved to the former NAS Alameda, CA, where it became a museum.

Lexington (CVT-16, AVT-16)

Class: 27C/125 *Essex*
Homeport: Pensacola
Comm. CV-16 17 Mar 43, decom 23 Apr 47, comm. CVA-16 1 Sep 55, r/d CVS-16 1 Oct 62, r/d CVT-16 1 Jan 69, r/d AVT-16 1 Jul 78, decom 8 Nov 91.
Lexington was the second carrier to carry the name of the opening battle of the Revolutionary War, and was named after the loss of CV-2 at Coral Sea in 1942. In service as a dedicated training carrier as of Jan '74, the Lex went by the nickname "Blue Ghost." The ship was

27C & SLEP

The twenty-four *Essex* (CV-9) class carriers easily rank among the most important group of warship he U.S. Navy has ever operated. Although some sources break them into two groups—the original *Essex* and later "long-hull" *Ticonderogas*—most fleet sailors recognized them as a single class. They saw combat in three major wars (WWII, Korea, and Vietnam), and served in five different decades. Most were decommissioned following World War II, and would return to service during and after the Korean War naval buildup. Built with straight-decks, the class needed to be heavily modified in order to operate jet aircraft in a safe fashion. Three major modernization programs were subsequently conducted on a selected number of vessels through the 1950s, and would define the survivors of this class forever.

The first of these efforts was called **SCB-27A**, which involved the addition of newer H-8 hydraulic catapults, and removal of the five-inch gun turrets from alongside the heavily redesigned island. Ten vessels received the "Twenty Seven Alpha" mod. *Oriskany*, which had not been finished during WWII, was completed as the first 27A vessel, and was commissioned in 1950 as the blueprint for nine subsequent ships.

SCB-27C ("Twenty Seven Charlie") was conducted in 1954 and 1955, and involved equipping seven ships with new steam catapults, as well as the extensive island modifications. The first three of this program (*Intrepid*, *Hancock*, and *Ticonderoga*) all initially deployed as straight-decked 27Cs.

The third major program was called **SCB-125**, which added angled decks and hurricane (enclosed) bows to fourteen of the 27A/27C ships from 1955 to 1959. Three ships received the 27C/125 modifications at the same time, which has led to confusion ever since as to what the mods really entailed, and they have been collectively called "27 Charlies" ever since. *Oriskany* was the only 27A to be subsequently rebuilt with steam catapults and the other 27C details, making seven of that modified class overall. One 27A (*Lake Champlain*) did not receive the angled deck, and was decommissioned as a straight deck.

The last 27A to cruise with an attack carrier air group was *Essex*, who deployed to the Med with CVG-10 in 1959-60. From then on the less capable "27 Alphas" were used as anti-submarine carriers (CVSs), and operated with ASW groups and A-4 *Skyhawks* through the early '70s. The last 27As were decommissioned in 1973.

As the most capable members of their class, the ships improved with the 27C/125 mods became the final *Essex* class to operate. With smaller decks and more Spartan living quarters than their "Supercarrier" replacements, the 27Cs became legendary in the fleet as they operated the fleet's last A-4s and F-8s. *Intrepid*, *Oriskany*, *Hancock*, *Bon Homme Richard*, *Shangri-La*, and *Ticonderoga* all achieved distinguished combat records in Vietnam. *Lexington* became the training carrier, and operated out of Pensacola until 1991.

As of 2005 four *Essex* 27A/27Cs (*Yorktown*, *Lexington*, *Hornet*, and *Intrepid*) survive as museums, at Charleston, SC, Corpus Christi, TX, Alameda, CA, and New York, NY, respectively.

SLEP

Four conventionally powered carriers went through a Service Life Extension Program (SLEP) at Philadelphia, PA. The program involved two *Forrestals* and two *Kitty Hawks* from 1980 through 1993. SLEP was a massive overhaul that included new or improved arresting gear, catapults, crew living arrangements, electronics equipment, and weapons systems. A typical SLEP took three years to complete, and was said to add 15 years to the life of the ship, although only *Kitty Hawk* would last that long.

The "mothball fleet" at Bremerton, Washington, had four *Essex* class carriers present when this picture was taken on 23 Oct '83. They include two "27 Charlies" (*Oriskany* and *Bon Homme Richard*) and a pair of "27 Alphas" (*Bennington* and *Hornet*). Stored for possible later use, only one would eventually survive (the *Hornet*), as a museum at Alameda. The four flattops are in company with a number of destroyers, submarines, and landing ships. The pier on the far left has two missile cruisers (*Chicago* and *Oklahoma City*) and the battleship *Missouri* tied to it, as well as a sole LSD. (author)

not configured to support intermediate level maintenance (AIMD), underway refueling, or ordnance handling, and was therefore unable to function as a deploying carrier. "Lady Lex's" normal operating area was the Gulf of Mexico, from Key West to Texas, in support of Training Command, and some FRS CQ requirements. The *Lexington* could handle most non-afterburning aircraft, including S-2, C-1, T-2, T-28, TA-4, A-6, and A-7. Due to ship size and safety concerns RA-5, A-3, F-4, and F-14 FRS squadrons normally qualified on available fleet decks.

The ship was re-designated as an auxiliary training carrier (AVT-16) on 1 July 1978. The "Lex" helped introduce over a generation of Naval Aviators in the fine art of carrier landings, a vocation that was certainly fraught with danger, as on 29 Oct 1989, when a student pilot was killed when his VT-19 T-2C (158876) crashed into the ship's island while carrying out initial carrier qualification training.

Lexington was decommissioned on 8 November 1991 as the last of the famed "27 Charlies" to operate. She was stricken on 30 Nov, and subsequently donated to the city of Corpus Christi, TX, for use as a museum.

***Hancock* (CVA-19, CV-19)**
Class: 27C/125 *Essex*
Homeport: Alameda
Comm. CV-19 15 Apr 44, decom 9 May 47, comm. CVA-19 1 Mar 54, r/d CV-19 30 Jun 75, decom 30 Jan 76.

8 May 1973-8 Jan 1974	WP/IO	CVW-21, (HMH-463)
18 Mar to 20 Oct 1975	WP	CVW-21

The fourth U.S. Navy ship to be named after the first signatory of the Declaration of Independence. A distinguished veteran of both WWII and Vietnam, the *Hancock* was returning from the Western Pacific as of January 1974. The ship was redesignated CV-19 30 June 1975, even though she never embarked ASW aircraft.

Hancock's final deployment was a somewhat unusual one as, although CVW-21 was assigned, they were off-loaded at Cubi Point to make room for Marine CH-53 squadron HMH-463 for contingency operations off South East Asia (SEA). From 12 April the ship was involved in Operation *Eagle Pull*, the evacuation of Cambodia. On 29 April the ship was used in *Frequent Wind*, the evacuation of Saigon. When these operations were completed CVW-21 was re-embarked, and the ship continued its normal deployment. The 1975 cruise marked the last forward deployment of Navy A-4s. *Hancock* was decommissioned 30 Jan 1976, stricken the following day, and sold for scrap.

***Bennington* (CVS-20)**
Class: 27A/125 *Essex*
Comm. CV-20 6 Aug 44, decom 8 Nov 46, comm. 30 Nov 51, r/d CVA-20 1 Oct 52, r/d CVS-20 30 Jun 59, decom. 15 Jan 70.
Bennington, named for a Revolutionary War battle in Vermont where Colonial militia wiped out a "Hessian" unit, was one of the less familiar of her class. She served in World War II, and was an early (1959) convert to the ASW carrier configuration. *Bennington* was in reserve at NS Bremerton, WA, as of Jan 1974, having been decommissioned in January 1970. She was stricken on 20 Sep 1989, and sold for scrap on 1 December 1994.

***Bon Homme Richard* (CVA-31)**
Class: 27C/125 *Essex*
Comm. CV-31, 26 Nov 44, decom. 9 Jan 47, comm. CVA-31 1 Nov 55, decom. 2 Jul 71.
In reserve, NS Bremerton, WA, as of Jan 1974. The "Bonnie Dick" (or "BHR") bore the name of Revolutionary War naval hero John Paul Jones' ship, which defeated the Royal Navy's frigate *Serapis* off England in September 1779. *Bon Homme Richard* was the last Attack Carrier (CVA) in the Navy inventory, as it was never redesignated CV. She was stricken on 20 Sep 1989, and sold for scrap on 4 Feb '92.

The *Lexington* was the last of the fabled "27 Charlies" to operate. The ship had belonged to Training Command since 1962, and was generally kept in the Gulf of Mexico to carrier qualify student pilots, as well as some RAG squadrons. She's shown here circa 1980 coming into port. A-7Es from VA-174 and VA-86 are on the bow, while three HH-46As from HC-16 are spotted aft. (U.S.Navy)

***Oriskany* (CVA-34, CV-34)**
Class: 27C/125 *Essex*
Homeport: Alameda
Comm. CV-34 25 Sep 50, r/d CVA-34 1 Oct 52, r/d CV-34 30 Jun 75, decom 30 Sep 76.

18 Oct 73-5 Jun 74	WP/IO	CVW-19
16 Sep 75-3 Mar 76	WP	CVW-19

In commission and on deployment as of January 1974. *Oriskany* was named for a Revolutionary War battle in New York during the Saratoga campaign. The ship's 1975-76 WestPac would be the last for U.S. Navy F-8 *Crusaders* in the VF role. *Oriskany* was a valiant ship that saw combat in Korea (one trip) and Vietnam (seven deployments), and was used in the filming of the 1954-55 movies "Bridges of Toko-Ri" and "Men of the Fighting Lady." Redesignated CV-34 30 June 1975, even though the "O-Boat" never carried ASW assets. The last *Essex* class carrier to forward deploy, *Oriskany* was decommissioned 30 Sept 1976, and sat in reserve at NS Bremerton, WA, until sold for scrap on 9 Sept 1995. The hull then bounced around the West and Gulf Coasts, as various groups tried to agree on how to dispose of it. These included attempts to make it a museum, and even a proposal to tow it to Japan for development into a tourist attraction. When these plans fell through the vessel ended up tied to a pier in Beaumont, TX. Finally, in 2003, it was announced that she would be sunk off Pensacola, Florida, as an artificial reef. It would not be until 2006 that the right agency gave its final approval for this action.

***Shangri-La* (CVA-38)**
Class: 27C/125 Essex
Comm. CV-38 15 Sep 44, decom. 7 Nov 47, comm. CVA-38 1 Feb 55, r/d CVS-38 30 Jun 69, d. 30 Jul 71.
Shangri-La was the mythical Himalayan location in the James Hilton novel "Paradise Lost," and the launching point, as reported by President Roosevelt, of the World War II Doolittle raid on Japan. The new *Essex*-class hull CV-38 was subsequently given the name. The ship had been decommissioned on 30 July 1971, and was in reserve (Philadelphia Naval Shipyard) as of January 1974. She was stricken from the register 15 July 1982, and sold for scrap in August 1988.

***Midway* (CVA-41,CV-41)**
Class: *Midway*
Homeport: NS Yokosuka, JA
Comm. 10 Sep 45 as CVB-41, r/d CVA-41 1 Oct 1952, r/d CV-41 30 Jun 75. decom. 11 Apr 1992.
Midway was the first of three "Battle" carriers built at the end of WWII, and the second named for the pivotal Naval engagement of that conflict. These large carriers were the first U.S. warships that were too wide for the Panama Canal. None of the trio saw combat during the Korean War, being used instead in the Atlantic and Med, watching the Soviets in the early years of the Cold War. The class ship was the second carrier named *Midway*, the first being CVE-63, which was renamed *St. Lo* in October 1944 to make *Midway* available for CVB-41. It would be lost in action at Leyte Gulf only a few weeks later, on 25 Oct, leading many Naval observers to note that it's considered bad luck to rename a ship once its christened.

After an early (1965) deployment to Vietnam *Midway* went through a major overhaul, which produced a large flight deck for her displacement that featured only three arresting gear wires and two catapults. The five-year hiatus also meant that the ship made fewer Vietnam deployments (three) than most of her Pacific Fleet counterparts, although her fighter aircraft did shoot down the first and last MiGs of the war for the Navy. She would be transferred to a "forward deployed" status in Japan from October 1973, where she remained until returning to CONUS for decommissioning in 1992. During this 18 year period *Midway* made frequent deployments to all parts of the Western Pacific and Indian Ocean. The co-locating of a carrier and its complete air wing led to an exceptionally close knit team throughout its tenure in Japan, as well as a flight deck crew that was the envy of every other carrier in the Pacific Fleet.

Midway was involved in Operation *Frequent Wind*, the evacuation of Saigon, during April 1975. The ship was used by a large number of South Vietnamese and Air America helicopters evacuating the doomed country. Most were pushed into the sea to make room for following aircraft. One VNAF O-1 *Bird Dog* also landed on the ship, with its pilot and his family. In May 1975 the ship was used to transport over 95 ex-South Vietnamese A-37s and F-5s to Guam, the aircraft having been craned aboard in Thailand.

Between 1973 and 1991 the *Midway*, with CVW-5, was the Navy's only permanently forward deployed carrier, being based in Yokosuka, Japan. The ship/air wing team earned an enviable record while overseas. She's shown here underway in the Western Pacific on 18 Aug 1984 with only a small portion of the wing present. (Robert Lawson)

In 1987 the ship went into a Japanese shipyard and had side "blisters" installed to help stabilize the vessel, which had only grown in weight over the years. Instead the "cure" only made things worse in certain sea conditions, and the ship was known to roll uncomfortably at times. On 8 October '88 she survived a 24+ degree roll during a storm, which some engineers apparently thought was past her limit. The frightening event became something of a legend in the ship's long history.

In 1991 *Midway* was the flagship of TF154 for Operation *Desert Storm* while operating in the Persian Gulf. *Midway* was replaced by *Independence* in the autumn of 1991 as the forward deployed carrier, and the ship was decommissioned at San Diego on 11 Apr 1992, and moved to Bremerton, WA, for storage. Stricken from the Navy list on 17 March 1996, she returned to San Diego in 2004 to become a very successful museum.

Deployments:

29 Jan to 6 Mar 1974	WP	CVW-5	
18 Oct to 20 Dec 1974	WP	CVW-5	
13 Jan to 18 Feb 1975	WP	CVW-5	
31 Mar to 29 May 1975	WP	CVW-5	*Frequent Wind*
4 Oct to 19 Dec 1975	WP/IO	CVW-5	
13 Mar to 26 Apr 1976	WP	CVW-5	
19 May to 22 Jun 1976	WP	CVW-5	
9 Jul to 4 Aug 1976	WP	CVW-5	
1 Nov to 17 Dec 1976	WP	CVW-5	
11 Jan to 1 Mar 1977	WP	CVW-5	
19 Apr to 5 May 1977	WP	CVW-5	
27 Sep to 21 Dec 1977	WP/IO	CVW-5	
11 Apr to 23 May 1978	WP	CVW-5	
9 Nov 1978 to 23 Dec 1978	WP	CVW-5	
11 Jan to 20 Feb 1979	WP	CVW-5	
7 Apr to 18 Jun 1979	WP/IO	CVW-5	
20 Aug to 14 Sep 1979	WP	CVW-5	
30 Sep to 20 Feb 1979	WP/IO	CVW-5	
14 Jul to 26 Nov 1980	WP/IO	CVW-5	
23 Feb to 5 Jun 1981	WP/IO	CVW-5	
26 Jun to 16 Jul 1981	WP	CVW-5	
3 Sep to 6 Oct 1981	WP	CVW-5	
26 Apr to 18 Jun 1982	WP	CVW-5	
14 Sep to 11 Dec 1982	WP/IO/NorPac	CVW-5	
2 Jun to 8 Aug 1983	WP	CVW-5	
25 Oct to 11 Dec 1983	WP	CVW-5	
28 Dec to 23 May 1984	WP/IO	CVW-5	
15 Oct to 12 Dec 1984	WP	CVW-5	
1 Feb to 28 Mar 1985	WP	CVW-5	
10 Jun to 14 Oct 1985	WP/IO	CVW-5	
15 Nov to 12 Dec 1985	WP	CVW-5	
17 Jan to 30 Mar 1986	WP	CVW-5	
9 Jan 1987 to 20 Mar 1987	WP	CVW-5	
23 Apr 1987 to 13 Jul 1987	WP	CVW-5	
15 Oct 1987 to 12 Apr 1988	WP/IO	CVW-5	
18 Oct 1988 to 9 Nov 1988	WP	CVW-5	
21 Jan 1989 to 24 Feb 1989	WP	CVW-5	
27 Feb 1989 to 9 Apr 1989	WP	CVW-5	
31 May to 25 Jul 1989	WP	CVW-5	
15 Aug to 11 Dec 1989	WP/IO	CVW-5	
25 Jan to 6 Apr 1990	WP	CVW-5	
2 Oct 1990 to 17 Apr 1991	WP/IO/PG	CVW-5	*Desert Storm*
10 Aug to 22 Aug 1991	Hawaii	CVW-5	
28 Aug to 14 Sep 1991	Return to Conus	CVW-14	

***Franklin D. Roosevelt* (CVA-42, CV-42)**
Class: *Midway*
Homeport: NS Mayport, FL
Comm: 27 Oct 45 as CVB-42, r/d CVA-42 1 Oct 52, r/d CV-42 30 Jun 75, decom. 30 Sep 77

14 Sep 1973 to 17 Mar 1974	Med	CVW-6
3 Jan to 16 Jul 1975	Med	CVW-6
4 Oct 1976 to 21 Apr 1977	Med	CVW-19

"FDR" made all but one of her extended deployments to the Mediterranean Sea, and saw combat only on her one trip to Vietnam in 1966. She was never rebuilt to the extent that sister ships *Midway* or *Coral Sea* were, which resulted in her being the first of her class to be retired. (Indeed, late in her life some crewmen referred to the FDR as the "Filthy, Dirty, and Rusty.") The "Rosey" made its last deployment with Lemoore-based CVW-19, coincidentally on its last deployment as well. This novel deployment also featured a squadron of Marine AV-8A *Harriers* onboard. The ship was decommissioned on 30 Sep 1977, stricken the following day, and sold for scrap on 1 Apr 1978.

***Coral Sea* (CVA-43)**
Class: *Midway*
Homeports: Alameda (1974-83) Norfolk (1983-90)
Comm: 1 Oct 47 as CVB-43, r/d CVA-43 1 Oct 52, r/d CV-43 30 Jun 75, decom 26 Apr 90.

5 Dec 1974 to 2 Jul 1975	WestPac	CVW-15	*Mayaguez rescue*
15 Feb to 5 Oct 1977	WestPac	CVW-15	
13 Nov 1979 to 11 Jun 1980	WP/IO	CVW-14	*Eagle Claw*
20 Aug 1981 to 23 Mar 1982	WP/IO	CVW-14	
21 Mar 1983 to 12 Sep 1983	World	CVW-14	
2 Oct 1985 to 19 May 1986	Med	CVW-13	*Prairie Fire, El Dorado Canyon*
29 Sep 1987 to 28 Mar 1988	Med	CVW-13	
31 May 1989 to 30 Sep 1989	Med	CVW-13	

The "Coral Maru" started out the seventies assigned to the Pacific Fleet. She was transferred to the Atlantic Fleet in 1983 via a westerly world cruise. The ship's seven deployments to Vietnam, and involve-

Coral Sea is anchored at Saint Thomas, Virgin Islands, on 22 Feb '89. From the look of things, the Air Department is carrying out maintenance on cat two, and Liberty Call is yet to be called away. CVW-13 aircraft from VFA-132, -137, and VA-55 and -65 are visible on the bow. *America* rides at anchor ahead with Air Wing-One onboard. (U.S. Navy, PHC B.J. Wallace)

ment in crises off Cambodia, Iran, and Libya make *Coral Sea* the most combat experienced member of her class. Tabbed "The Ageless Warrior" late in her life, the ship's three final deployments were to the Med with the new CVW-13. She was the second of her class to be retired, was decommissioned in a 26 April 1990 ceremony, stricken four days later, and sold for scrap.

Forrestal (CVA-59, CV-59, AVT-59)

Class: *Forrestal*
Homeports: NAF Mayport, FL 1973-92, NAS Pensacola, FL Feb 1992
Comm: 1 Oct 55, r/d CV-59 30 Jun 75, r/d AVT-16 5 Feb 92, decom. 11 Sep 93

11 Mar 1974 to 11 Sep 1974	Med	CVW-17	Cyprus Crisis
5 Mar 1975 to 22 Sep 1975	Med	CVW-17	
July 1976	Bicentennial	CVW-17	New York Naval Review
4 Apr 1978 to 26 Oct 1978	Med/NL	CVW-17	
27 Nov 1979 to 7 May 1980	Med	CVW-17	
2 Mar 1981 to 15 Sep 1981	Med	CVW-17	
8 Jun 1982 to 16 Nov 1982	Med/IO	CVW-17	
2 Jun 1986 to 10 Nov 1986	Med	CVW-6	
28 Aug to 9 Oct 1987	NorLant	CVW-6	
25 Apr 1988 to 7 Oct 1988	Med/IO/NL	CVW-6	
4 Nov 1989 to 12 Apr 1990	Med	CVW-6	
30 May 1991 to 21 Dec 1991	Med	CVW-6	

The *Forrestal* was known fleet wide as the "FID," which came from the ship's "First In Defense" motto. (James Forrestal having been the country's first Secretary of the Department of Defense.) As the world's first "Supercarrier," she redefined the type and was, arguably, as significant to naval construction as the British battleship *Dreadnought*, the big difference being her launching did not set off a round of duplication wörld wide. The ship signaled that the United States would spend the money required to maintain the naval dominance it had acquired during WWII and into the new Cold War.

The ship made ten deployments to the Mediterranean Sea and IO from 1974 with two different Air Wings. The 1974 deployment was highlighted by CVW-17's coverage of civilian evacuees from Cyprus while Greece and Turkey fought over the island. In 1976 she was the flagship for the Bicentennial Naval Review in New York harbor with a slightly modified air wing composition (see CVW-17). In late 1990 the ship and air wing went through an accelerated series of work-ups with the intent of leaving CONUS in March to join *Desert Storm*. The end of the war delayed what would prove to be the ship's final deployment until May.

After returning from her last cruise the ship was redesignated AVT-59, and was moved to Pensacola, FL, to replace *Lexington* as the Navy's dedicated training carrier. Six months later the ship entered the Philadelphia Naval Shipyard for a major overhaul that would make it better suited to the training mission. Changing DOD policy led to the cessation of the work prior to completion, with the ship being decommissioned and stricken on 11 Sep 1993. Initially placed in storage at Philadelphia, the vessel was subsequently moved to Newport, RI, where it sits today.

FID ended her career with only one significant combat deployment, that being the disastrous 1967 cruise to Vietnam that ended with the fire that killed 134 members of the ship's company. That experience led to the grim and widely known fleet nickname "Forest Fire." As the world's first true supercarrier she probably deserved better.

Saratoga (CVA-60, CV-60)

Class: *Forrestal*
Homeport: Mayport
Comm: 14 Apr 56, r/d CV-60 30 Jun 72, decom. 20 Aug 94

27 Sep 1974 to 19 Mar 1975	Med	CVW-3	
6 Jan to 28 Jul 1976	Med	CVW-3	
11 Jul to 23 Dec 1977	Med	CVW-3	
3 Oct 1978 to 5 Apr 1979	Med	CVW-3	
10 Mar to 27 Aug 1980	Med	CVW-3	
2 Apr to 20 Oct 1984	Med	CVW-17	
26 Aug 1985 to 16 Apr 1986	Med/IO	CVW-17	*Prairie Fire*
5 Jun to 17 Nov 1987	Med	CVW-17	
7 Aug 1990 to 28 Mar1991	Med/RS	CVW-17	*Desert Shield/ Storm*
6 May to 6 Nov 1992	Med	CVW-17	
12 Jan to 24 June 1994	Med	CVW-17	

Saratoga spent most of her career making deployments to the Med, with only one trip to the Pacific Ocean, and Vietnam, in 1972. She was the second carrier to hold the name *Saratoga*, the first one being CV-3. She was the first attack carrier redesignated as a "Multi-Purpose Carrier" (CV) in 1972. The 1985-86 Med cruise included involvement in the two-day *Prairie Fire* operation off Libya. Her 1990-91 participation in *Desert Storm* marked the ship's second, and last, extended combat deployment.

Saratoga's 23 year (1957-1980) marriage with CVW-3 is the longest carrier/wing affiliation in Navy history. In 1980 "Super Sara" was the first carrier to enter the Service Life Extension Program (SLEP) at the Philadelphia Naval Shipyard. After being released in 1983 the ship had CVW-17 assigned, which remained with her for the next decade. In 1990 *Saratoga* relieved *Eisenhower* in the Red Sea during *Desert Shield*. All of her subsequent *Desert Storm* operations were flown out of the Red Sea as well, with CVW-17 losing three of the five Navy aircraft shot down by enemy fire during the war. "Sara's" 344,664th, and final, trap came on 23 Jun 1994, when a VS-27 S-3B came aboard. The ship was decommissioned at Mayport on 22 Aug 1994 (20 Aug ceremony) after making 23 extended deployments, and towed to Philadelphia to join the inactive fleet. She was subsequently moved to Newport, RI, to await her fate.

Ranger (CVA-61, CV-61)

Class: *Forrestal*
Homeport: North Island
Comm: 10 Aug 57, r/d CV-61 30 Jun 72, Decom: 10 Jul 93

7 May to 18 Oct 1974	WP	CVW-2
30 Jan to 7 Sep 1976	WP/IO	CVW-2
21 Feb to 22 Sep 1979	WP	CVW-2
10 Sep 1980 to 5 May 1981	WP/IO	CVW-2
7 Apr to 19 Oct 1982	WP/IO	CVW-2
15 Jul 1983 to 29 Feb 1984	CA/WP/IO	CVW-9
18 Aug to 20 Oct 1986	NP Surge	CVW-2

2 Mar to 29 Apr 1987	NP/WP Surge	CVW-2	
14 Jul to 29 Dec 1987	WP/IO	CVW-2	
24 Feb to 24 Aug 1989	WP/IO	CVW-2	
8 Dec 90 to 8 Jun 1991	WP/IO/PG	CVW-2	*Desert Storm*
1 Aug 92 to 31 Jan 1993	WP/IO	CVW-2	

Ranger was called the "Top Gun of the Pacific Fleet" long before the movie came out. CVA-61 was the second carrier to be named *Ranger*, after CV-4. She was the first "super carrier" deployed to the Pacific Fleet (in 1959), made 22 WestPacs, and had more combat experience (7 Vietnam deployments and *Desert Storm*) than her three sisters put together. The 1983 deployment started out with a swing by Central America, specifically as a show of force against Sandanista Nicaragua. The 1986 and 1987 deployments were in an experimental "surge" mode, testing a carrier's and air wing's ability to deploy frequently for shorter periods without normal 12 month turnaround. "Surge Ops" were terminated after it was determined that continuous high tempo operations required to maintain readiness were unnecessarily hard on both equipment and men.

"Danger *Ranger*" was never SLEP'ed, and became the first of her class to be retired. Late in her life she gained something of an overstated reputation for having boiler room fires. Her 330,683rd, and last, trap was a VF-124 *Tomcat* on 11 Mar '93. She was decommissioned on 10 Jul 1993, and placed in reserve at Bremerton, WA.

***Independence* (CV-62)**

Class: *Forrestal*

Homeports: Norfolk 1973-1988 , North Island 1988-1991 , Yokosuka 1991-2000

Comm: CVA-62 10 Jan 59, r/d CV-62 28 Feb 73, decom 30 Sep 98

21 Jun 1973 to 19 Jan 1974	Med	CVW-7	
19 Jul 1974 to 21 Jan 1975	Med	CVW-7	
15 Oct 1975 to 5 May 1976	Med/NL	CVW-7	
31 Mar 1977 to 21 Oct 1977	Med	CVW-7	
28 Jun 1979 to 14 Dec 1979	Med	CVW-6	
19 Nov 80 to 10 Jun 1981	SL/IO/Med	CVW-6	
7 Jun 1982 to 22 Dec 1982	Med	CVW-6	
18 Oct 1983 to 11 Apr 1984	Carib/Med/ NL	CVW-6	Grenada, Lebanon
16 Oct 1984 to 19 Feb 1985	Med/IO	CVW-6	
15 Aug to 8 Oct 1988	Horn	CVW-17	
1988	(no cruise)	CVW-10	
23 Jun 1990 to 20 Dec 1990	WP/IO/PG	CVW-14	*Desert Shield*
5 Aug to 11 Sep 1991	Japan transfer	CVW-14/5	
15 Apr 92 to 13 Oct 1992	WP/IO/PG	CVW-5	
15 Feb to 23 Mar 1993	WP	CVW-5	
11 May to 1 Jul 1993	WP	CVW-5	
17 Nov 1993 to 17 Mar 1994	WP/IO/PG	CVW-5	
19 Jul to 29 Aug 1994	WP	CVW-5	
19 Aug to 18 Nov 1995	WP/IO/PG	CVW-5	
5 Mar to 24 Mar 1996	WP	CVW-5	
15 Feb to 10 Jun 1997	WP/IO/PG	CVW-5	
23 Jan to 6 Jun 1998	WP	CVW-5	
7 to 18 Jul 1998	Hawaii	CVW-5	turnover with *Kitty Hawk*
July 1998	CONUS	(CVW-2)	

"Indy" spent the first part of her career making routine trips to the Mediterranean, as well as one deployment to Vietnam. The 1983-84 cruise was highlighted by combat operations in Grenada and Lebanon. From Apr 1985 to May 1988 she went through the Service Life Extension Program (SLEP) at the Philadelphia Naval Shipyard, and was subsequently assigned to the Pacific Fleet. After bringing a partial Air Wing 17 around the Horn in 1988 the ship was assigned the new CVW-10, which was disestablished prior to making any deployments.

In 1989 *Indy* was available to help film the movie "Flight of the Intruder," where VA-165 A-6Es were borrowed from CVW-9, given pseudo-VA-196 markings, and filmed operating along VA-122 A-7s,

Kitty Hawk is shown here on 16 Dec 1977 while conducting UNREP with *Sacramento* (AOE-1) and the cruiser *England* (CG-22). She carries a typical "CV concept" air wing, with 54 aircraft from CVW-11 being spotted on deck. (U.S. Navy, PH1 A.E. Legare)

as well as F-4 and A-3 hulks craned aboard to achieve something of a 1972 look.

CVW-14 was assigned to the ship in 1989, and the 1990 cruise was dominated by *Operation Desert Shield*. In August 1991 *Independence* turned over with the *Midway*, becoming the Navy's sole forward deployed carrier. *Indy* swapped air wings with *Midway* in Pearl Harbor, and proceeded to her new homeport with CVW-5. She subsequently made frequent sorties to the Pacific region and the Indian Ocean. The ship left Japan on 7 July 1998, and conducted a formal turnover as the forward deployed carrier by *Kitty Hawk* off Pearl Harbor on 18 July. For her return trip *Indy* was accompanied by a composite wing made up of elements of CVW-2, -8, and -9 under CAG-2. Returning to CONUS, CV-62 was decommissioned at Bremerton on 30 Sep.

***Kitty Hawk* (CV-63)**

Class: *Kitty Hawk*

Homeport: NAS North Island, CA; 1974-1998 Yokusuka Japan; Aug 1998 to c.

Comm: 29 Apr 61, r/d CV-63 29 Apr 73

23 Nov 1973 to 9 Jul 1974	WP/IO	CVW-11	
21 May 1975 to 15 Dec 1975	WP	CVW-11	
25 Oct 1977 to 15 May 1978	WP	CVW-11	
30 May 1979 to 25 Feb 1980	WP/IO	CVW-15	
1 Apr 1981 to 23 Nov 1981	WP/IO	CVW-15	
13 Jan to 1 Aug 1984	WP/IO	CVW-2	
24 Jul to 21 Dec 1985	WP/IO	CVW-9	
3 Jan to 29 Jun 1987	World	CVW-9	travel to SLEP
18 Oct 1991-11 Dec 1991	Horn	CVW-15	return from SLEP
3 Nov 1992 to 3 May 1993	WP/IO/PG	CVW-15	
24 Jun to 22 Dec 1994	WP/IO/PG	CVW-15	
11 Oct 1996 to 11 Apr 1997	WP/IO/PG	CVW-11	
May to July 1998	Hawaii	(CVW-2)	
18 Jul to 11 Aug 1998	Japan	CVW-5	
2 Mar to 25 Aug 1999	WP/IO/PG	CVW-5	

"The Hawk" was the lead ship in what was considered by many to be an "improved *Forrestal*" class of ships, and was named for the North Carolina location of the Wright Brothers' first flight. She was a Pacific-Fleet vet, having made seven deployments to Vietnam between 1964 and 1973. In 1987 the Hawk made an around-the-world cruise via Western Pacific, Indian Ocean, Red Sea, and Med. The ship underwent SLEP at Philadelphia, PA, Jan 1988 to Aug 1990, with an announcement initially made that she would replace *Lexington* as the training carrier based in Pensacola. Plans changed, however, and she returned to San Diego via the Horn in late 1991. Aircraft from the *Kitty Hawk* launched strikes into Iraq on the night of 13 Jan 1993 during *Operation Southern Watch*. The *Hawk* replaced the *Independence* as the forward deployed carrier in 1998, with CVW-5 coming aboard off Pearl Harbor on 18 July. It had conducted a very short work-up period off San Diego in May/June before moving West. The portion between California and Hawaii was covered by a composite wing made up of portions of Air Wing-2, -8, and -9 under CAG-2. The ship arrived in Yokosuka on 11 Aug.

***Constellation* (CVA-64, CV-64)**

Class: *Kitty Hawk*

Homeports: North Island, CA

Comm: 27 Oct 61, r/d CV-64 30 Jun 75, Decom: 7 Aug 2003

21 Jun to 22 Dec 1974	WP/IO/PG	CVW-9	
12 Apr to 21 Nov 1977	WP	CVW-9	
26 Sep 1978 to 17 May 1979	WP	CVW-9	
26 Feb to 15 Oct 1980	WP/IO	CVW-9	
20 Oct 1981 to 23 May 1982	WP/IO	CVW-9	
21 Feb to 24 Aug 1985	WP/IO	CVW-14	
11 Apr to 13 Oct 1987	WP/IO	CVW-14	
1 Dec 1988 to 1 Jun 1989	WP/IO	CVW-14	
16 Sep to 19 Oct 1989	NorPac	CVW-14	
12 Feb to 7 Apr 1990	Horn	CVW-9	travel to SLEP
27 May to 22 Jul 1993	Horn	CVW-2	return from SLEP
10 Nov 94 to 10 May 1995	WP/IO	CVW-2	
1 Apr to 1 Oct 1997	WO/IO/PG	CVW-2	
18 Jun to 18 Dec 1999	WP/PG	CVW-2	

"Connie," self-styled as "America's Flagship," made all of her major deployments to the Western Pacific/Indian Ocean region since commissioning. After heavy Vietnam service, she made the first deployment of an American supercarrier into the Persian Gulf in 1974, 18 years prior to *Desert Storm*. From December 1982 to 1984 the ship went through a major overhaul at Bremerton, WA. Among other things she was configured to be the first ship to take F/A-18 *Hornets* onboard. The 1987 deployment was made during a short period of reduced

Holding one of the most illustrious ship names in Navy history, *Enterprise* is shown here while underway off San Diego on 28 Mar '84 while conducting work-ups with CVW-11. The ship is not long out of the Bremerton shipyards, after having her distinctive block island structure heavily modified. (Robert Lawson)

funding, and featured "Flight from Anchor" ("flancher") operations, where aircraft were launched and recovered while the ship was anchored in the center of Diego Garcia harbor. While they proved it could be done, the additional stress on airframes, and a general "*Why are we doing this*?" attitude, led to an end to this novel change in carrier operations.

After three WestPacs with CVW-14 "Connie" headed for SLEP, with an eastward transit around the Horn, and entered the Philadelphia Naval Shipyard in July 1990. After a shakedown with CVW-17 off Puerto Rico, the ship returned to the Pacific Fleet again via the Horn, with portions of CVW-2 embarked. In spite of the expensive SLEP work, "Connie" made only five more deployments (two coming after 2000) before being decommissioned on 7 August 2003 at North Island, and stored at Bremerton, WA.

Enterprise (CVAN-65, CVN-65)

Class: *Enterprise*
Homeport: Alameda 1974-1990, (Newport News 1990-1992) Norfolk 11/92
Comm: 25 Nov 61, r/d CVN-65 30 Jun 75

Dates	Area	Air Wing	Operation
17 Sep 1974 to 20 May 1975	WP/IO	CVW-14	*Eagle Pull*
30 Jul 1976 to 28 Mar 1977	WP/IO	CVW-14	
4 Apr to 30 Oct 1978	WP/IO	CVW-14	
Late 1978	(no cruise)	CVW-11	
1 Sep 1982 to 28 Apr 1983	NP/WP	CVW-11	
30 May to 20 Dec 1984	WP/IO/NP	CVW-11	
15 Jan to 12 Aug 1986	WP/IO/MED	CVW-11	
25 Oct to 24 Nov 1987	NorPac	CVW-11	
5 Jan to 3 July 1988	WP/IO/NP	CVW-11	
17 Sep 1989 to 16 Mar 1990	World	CVW-11	
28 Jun to 20 Dec 1996	Med/RS/PG	CVW-17	
6 Nov 1998 to 6 May 1999	Med/RS/PG	CVW-3	*Desert Fox*

Enterprise was the only nuclear powered carrier in the Pacific Fleet until the arrival of *Carl Vinson* in 1982. She carries on the name of the previous *Enterprise* (CV-6), which had the greatest combat record of an aircraft carrier in history. The 1974 cruise was notable as the first F-14 deployment in the Navy, and included participation in *Operation Eagle Pull*, the evacuation of Saigon. The ship was used to transport Marine CH-53A/D helicopters back to CONUS at the end of the deployment, along with CVW-14. She was assigned CVW-11 in late 1978 for a short period (with several aircraft so marked), but made no deployment prior to going into the yards. The wing would move to *America* and make two deployments to the Med, while *Enterprise* underwent a comprehensive overhaul at Bremerton, WA, from Jan '79 to 1982 that led to major visual changes to its trademark block superstructure, as the distinctive flat SPS-32 and -33 radar arrays (which she shared with cruiser *Long Beach*, CG-9) were replaced by standard SPS-48/49 systems. It was during work ups for the 1986 deployment that the ship was used to film the flight deck sequences for the movie "Top Gun." In 1986 the ship became the first nuclear powered warship to transit the Suez Canal when it left station in the Indian Ocean and relieved Atlantic Fleet carriers off Libya. Due to diplomatic pressure from Egypt, *Enterprise* returned to the IO via the Straits of Gibraltar and the Cape of Good Hope. In early 1991 *Enterprise* went on blocks again, this time for refueling, at Newport News, VA, after a westerly world cruise. Her home port officially changed to *Norfolk* when complete, and she deployed again in 1996 with CVW-17 embarked. A subsequent cruise with CVW-3 featured participation in Operation *Desert Fox*, with the "Big E" launching 281 sorties during the event.

In spite of a widespread sea story that refuses to die, the *Enterprise* continues to operate with a unique eight reactor design ("the story" persists, incorrectly, that she was converted to two reactors at some point). Even with the high operating costs driven by her engineering configuration, the "Big E" remains a vital member of the fleet, as well as one of the most illustrious names afloat.

America (CVA-66, CV-66)

Class: *Kitty Hawk*
Homeport: Norfolk, VA
Comm: 23 Jan 65, r/d CV-66 30 Jun 75, decom 9 Aug 96

Dates	Area	Air Wing	Operation
5 Jun 1972 to 24 Mar 1973	Med	CVW-8	
3 Jan 1974 to 3 Aug 1974	Med	CVW-8	
6 Sep 1974 to 12 Oct 1974	NoLant	CVW-8	
15 Apr 1976 to 25 Oct 1976	Med	CVW-6	
10 Jun 1977 to 19 Jul 1977	So Lant	CVW-6	
29 Sep 1977 to 25 Apr 1978	Med	CVW-6	
13 Mar 1979 to 22 Sep 1979	Med	CVW-11	
14 Apr 1981 to 12 Nov 1981	SoLant/Med/IO	CVW-11	
23 Aug 1982 to 30 Oct 1982	NL/Med/Carib	CVW-1	
8 Dec 1982 to 2 Jun 1983	Med/IO	CVW-1	
24 Apr to 14 Nov 1984	Med/IO	CVW-1	
10 Mar to 10 Sep 1986	Med	CVW-1	*Prairie Fire*
8 Feb 89 to 3 Apr 1989	NoLant	CVW-1	
11 May to 10 Nov 1989	Med/IO	CVW-1	
28 Dec 1990 to 18 Apr 1991	Med/RS/PG	CVW-1	*Desert Storm*
21 Aug to 11 Oct 1991	NorLant	CVW-1	
2 Dec 1991 to 6 Jun 1992	Med/RS/IO	CVW-1	
11 Aug 1993 to 5 Feb 1994	Med	CVW-1	
12 Sep to 22 Oct 1994	Caribbean/Haiti	US Army	
Uphold Democracy			
28 Aug 95 to 24 Feb 1996	Med/RS/PG	CVW-1	*Deliberate Force*

Commissioned in 1965, *America's* name was frequently abbreviated "USA" in official use. Over its 31 year career, the ship would see more combat than any other Atlantic-fleet carrier between Korea and 2001. She made two deployments to Vietnam (in 1970 and 1972), and was involved in combat off Libya in 1986, and Iraq in 1991. *America* was the only carrier in *Desert Storm* to operate from both the Red Sea and Persian Gulf. In 1994 USA hosted elements of the Army's 160th SOAR for its involvement in operations off Haiti. The ship's last deployment included combat operations between 9 and 30 Sep 1995 in support of NATO in Operation *Deliberate Force*.

Her 1979 and 1981 cruises were notable in the use of a West Coast air wing for Mediterranean deployments. On 6 May 1981 the ship transited the Suez Canal enroute to the Red Sea and Indian Ocean, becoming the first U.S. carrier to "do the ditch" since the 1967 "Six Day War."

Never SLEP'ed, the *America* was retired in 1996, and placed in storage at Philadelphia, PA. In spite of attempts to save the ship as a museum, she was eventually sunk in the Atlantic in 2005 in what was described as an evaluation of carrier protection systems.

John F. Kennedy (CVA-67, CV-67)

Class: *John F. Kennedy*
Homeport: Norfolk, Mayport
Comm: 7 Sep 68, r/d CV-67 29 Apr 73

28 Jun 1975 to 27 Jan 1976	Med	CVW-1	
2 Sep to 9 Nov 1976	NorLant	CVW-1	
15 Jan 1977 to 1 Aug 1977	Med	CVW-1	
29 Jun 1978 to 8 Feb 1979	Med	CVW-1	
4 Jan to 14 Jul 1982	Med/IO	CVW-3	
25 May to 1 Jul 1983	NorLant	CVW-3	
27 Sep 1983 to 2 May 1984	SL/Med	CVW-3	Lebanon
18 Aug 1986 to 3 Mar 1987	Med	CVW-3	
2 Aug 1988 to 1 Feb 1989	Med	CVW-3	
15 Aug 1990 to 28 Mar 1991	Med/RS	CVW-3	*Desert Storm*
7 Oct 1992 to 7 Apr 1993	Med	CVW-3	
29 Apr to 28 Oct 1997	Med/RS/PG	CVW-8	
17 Sep 1999 to 17 Mar 2000	Med/RS/PG	CVW-1	

Known as the "Big John," or just "JFK," the *Kennedy* is similar to the earlier *Kitty Hawk* design, although she is generally considered her own class. The ship is also notable as the last non-nuclear powered carrier built for the Navy. Christened for the assassinated 35th President of the United States, the vessel's name insures that it is frequently used to represent the Navy in formal functions and port calls at places like New York and Boston.

JFK was the only Vietnam-era supercarrier to not see action in that war. In Feb 1974 the ship participated in the final carrier qualification for Grumman TF-9J *Cougars*, these coming from Pensacola's Training Squadron Four (VT-4). Her 1975-76 cruise was the first deployment for the S-3 type, and marked the initial appearance of the F-14 and E-2C types in the Mediterranean. *Kennedy* first saw combat off Lebanon in 1984, where CVW-3 lost one A-6E. On 4 Jan 1989 a section of VF-32 F-14As flying from *Kennedy* engaged and shot down two Libyan MiG-23 aircraft. During *Operation Desert Storm*, she operated exclusively from the Red Sea, while also making the final deployment for the A-7 *Corsair II* in the Navy.

The ship entered a two-year overhaul at the Philadelphia Naval Shipyard in 1993, and subsequently moved to Mayport in September 1995. She replaced *Saratoga* at that Florida port, and became what was described as a "Reserve Operational Carrier," where a significant portion of the crew was to be made up of Reservists. The Navy initially stated that the ship would be used for Reserve and Training Command duties, while also being available for emergency deployments. Manning and maintenance issues complicated this plan, as did the Navy's continued need for a twelfth fully deployable flight deck. The ship's "reserve" status lasted not much more than eighteen months, as by April 1997 JFK sailed to the Med again with a largely regular navy crew.

In one of the more significant ship collisions of the period, the *Kennedy* struck the cruiser *Belknap* (CG-26) while underway in the Med on the night of 22 Nov 1975. Six men were killed in the mishap, and the cruiser would have to be towed back to the U.S. for four years of repairs before it was able to resume service. Among the changes instituted due to this incident was the installation of the "crunch pole" (also called by some a "Belknap mast") on the starboard side forward on all carriers, so that the ship's navigation lights (and therefore direction of movement) would be less ambiguous to other vessels.

Nimitz (CVAN-68, CVN-68)

Class: *Nimitz*
Homeport: Norfolk (5/75 to 12/86), Bremerton (7/87-9/97), Newport News (3/98-on)
Comm: 3 May, 1975, r/d CVN-68 30 Jun 75

16 Jul to 24 Sep 1975	Carib/NL	CVW-8	
7 Jul 1976 to 7 Feb 1977	Med	CVW-8	
1 Dec 1977 to 20 Jul 1978	Med/IO	CVW-8	
10 Sep 1979 to 26 May 1980	Med/IO	CVW-8	*Eagle Claw*
3 Aug 1981 to 12 Feb 1982	Med	CVW-8	Libya
10 Nov 1982 to 20 May 1983	Med	CVW-8	
8 Mar to 4 Oct 1985	Med	CVW-8	
30 Dec 1986 to 26 Jul 1987	World	CVW-8	
2 Sep 1988 to 2 Mar 1989	WP/IO	CVW-9	
15 Jun to 9 Jul 1989	NorPac	CVW-9	
25 Feb to 24 Aug 1991	WP/IO/PG	CVW-9	
2 Feb to 29 Jul 1993	WP/IO/PG	CVW-9	
27 Nov 1995 to 20 May 1996	WP/IO/PG	CVW-9	
1 Sep 1997 to 1 Mar 1998	World	CVW-9	

Nimitz is the lead ship in the most important class of warship built in the U.S. since WWII. The vessel was named for Texas native Fleet Admiral Chester Nimitz, CincPac during World War II, and later Chief of Naval Operations. She gained some fame as the main character in the 1980 movie "The Final Countdown," which placed the ship in the Pacific Ocean before it had ever been there. (Scenes showing it entering Pearl Harbor were actually filmed using *Kitty Hawk* as a stand in.) The ship transferred to the Pacific fleet via an eastward around the world cruise in 1986-87, changing homeports to Bremerton, Washington.

Nimitz was the only ship of her class to deploy with F-4, F-8, or RA-5 aircraft. During her 1980 cruise she was used as the launching platform for the abortive RH-53D *Eagle Claw* raid into Iran. The 1981 deployment was highlighted by the destruction of two Libyan SU-22 Fitter aircraft by VF-41 F-14As.

The ship has also suffered the two worst carrier landing mishaps in the Navy since Vietnam. On 26 May 1981 a VMAQ-2 EA-6B (159910) landed well right of centerline during a night recovery off the U.S. East coast, and impacted other aircraft spotted forward on the bow. The three crewmen were killed, along with 11 flight deck personnel. Two F-14As were destroyed, and 17 other Air Wing-8 aircraft damaged in the incident. On 25 Jan 1987 a VQ-2 EA-3B (144850) was lost with seven crew following an unsuccessful night barricade landing while in the Mediterranean. This mishap accelerated an eventual Navy-wide ban on all A-3 carrier operations.

At the end of her 1998 World cruise *Nimitz* pulled into Norfolk and, subsequently, went into drydock at Newport News Shipyard for her mid-life refueling, which would not be complete until June 2001.

Shakedowns

An aircraft carrier usually undertakes a "shakedown" cruise as its first significant time at sea with aircraft onboard following its commissioning, or after a major overhaul, such as SLEP. Between 1974 and 2000 these events almost always took place in the Caribbean off Puerto Rico, although *Nimitz* included a NorLant on its shakedown as well. These evolutions are largely for the training benefit of the carrier, allowing its crew and flight deck to train and test systems coming out of the yards; therefore, they are almost always made with reduced-sized air wings. Documentation of these events is spotty due to the short periods involved, and the fact that these ship/air wing combinations are not normally considered combat ready during the evolution. In many cases the wing embarked is not the CVW that is subsequently assigned for work-ups and deployment, which can lead to confusion when trying to identify photographs at a later date. This list is provided for the new construction and SLEP vessels between 1974 and 2000. The author would like to thank Mike Weeks in particular in helping fill out this section.

Forrestal	Jul-Aug 1985	CVW-6	post-SLEP
Independence	Aug-Oct 1988	CVW-17	post-SLEP
Kitty Hawk	Aug-Sep 1991	CVW-3	post-SLEP
Constellation	Mar-Apr 1993	CVW-17	post-SLEP
Nimitz	Jun-Jul 1975	CVW-8	new construction
Eisenhower	Nov-Dec 1977	CVW-1	new construction
Carl Vinson	May-Jun 82	CVW-8	new construction
T. Roosevelt	Jan-Feb 1987	CVW-1	new construction
A. Lincoln	Jan-Feb 1990	CVW-8	new construction
G. Washington	Sep-Oct 1993	CVW-7	new construction
JC Stennis	Mar 1996	CVW-8	new construction
HS Truman	Aug-Sep 98	CVW-1	new construction

CVW-8 never made a major deployment with the *Lincoln*, although a portion of it did make the ship's shakedown cruise in Jan 1990, with its aircraft suitably marked. *Bear Ace* AJ601 (161552) spreads its wings while approaching cat 3 during that evolution. (author)

***Dwight D. Eisenhower* (CVN-69)**
Class: *Nimitz*
Homeport: Norfolk, VA
Comm: 18 Oct, 1977

16 Jan to 13 July 1979	Med	CVW-7	
15 Apr to 22 Dec 1980	IO	CVW-7	
20 Aug to 7 Oct 1981	NoLant	CVW-7	
5 Jan to 13 Jul 1982	Med	CVW-7	
27 Apr to 2 Dec 1983	Med	CVW-7	
8 May to 20 Jun 1984	NoLant	CVW-7	
10 Oct 1984 to 8 May 1985	Med	CVW-7	
29 Feb to 29 Aug 1988	Med	CVW-7	
8 Mar to 12 Sep 1990	Med/RS	CVW-7	*Desert Shield*
26 Sep 1991 to 2 Apr 1992	Med/RS/PG	CVW-7	
13 to 23 Sep 1994	Caribbean	US Army	*U. Democracy*
20 Oct 1994 to 15 Apr 1995	Med/RS/PG	CVW-3	
10 Jun to 10 Dec 1998	Med/RS/PG	CVW-17	
18 Feb to 18 Aug 2000	Med/RS/PG	CVW-7	

"Ike" was ordered as CVAN-69, and changed to CVN prior to commissioning. She is named for the General of the Armies and 34th President of the United States. Her 1980 cruise to the Indian Ocean was made via the Cape of Good Hope, due to Egyptian restrictions on use of the Suez Canal by nuclear-powered vessels. The carrier went 152 days without a port call during this cruise, although her 251 day deployment wasn't in the top ten in terms of total time away from home since World War II (see sidebar). She finally made the Suez transit in 1990 enroute the Red Sea, where she provided coverage for the *Desert Shield* buildup until relieved by *Saratoga* and *Kennedy*. In 1994 the ship became the first carrier in the Atlantic Fleet to have female crew permanently assigned. On 6 June 2000 aircraft from VF-143 and VF-11 participated in strikes in Iraq as part of Operation *Southern Watch*, thus becoming the first combat weapons-delivery missions to ever be launched from the ship.

***Carl Vinson* (CVN-70)**
Class: *Nimitz*
Homeport: Alameda, CA, Bremerton (Jan 1997)
Comm: 13 Mar, 1982

1 Mar to 29 Oct 1983	World	CVW-15	
18 Oct 1984 to 25 May 1985	WestPac/IO	CVW-15	
12 Aug 1986 to 5 Feb 1987	WP/IO/NP	CVW-15	
15 Jun to 14 Dec 1988	WestPac/IO	CVW-15	
5 Sep to 8 Nov 1989	WP/NP	CVW-15	
1 Feb to 31 Jul 1990	WestPac/IO	CVW-15	
18 Feb 94 to 15 Aug 1994	WP/IO/PG	CVW-14	
14 May 96 to 14 Nov 1996	WP/IO/PG	CVW-14	
6 Nov 98 to 6 May 1999	WP/IO/PG	CVW-11	*Desert Fox*

Carl Vinson is named for the now obscure Democratic Congressman from Georgia and head of the House Naval Committee during the 1930s and '40s. He is credited with being second only to President Roosevelt in arranging the appropriations that led to the two-ocean Navy that helped win WWII. The "Distinguished Gentleman from Georgia" lived to see the ship bearing his name launched, but died prior to commissioning. The vessel has been known for years as the "Fleet Starship," or informally as the "Chuckie V" to its crew. Her first deployment was around the world from Norfolk with West Coast-based CVW-15. Since then the ship has made several cruises to the Western Pacific/Indian Ocean regions with little significant involvement in combat. On 19 Dec 1998 the ship arrived just in time to take part in the final day of Operation *Desert Fox* in Iraq. Between 1991

Longest Deployments

When the *Eisenhower* returned to the U.S. at the end of its 1980 deployment, its crew could say that they had been gone for 251 days, 152 of which were continuous, without a port call. Superlatives followed, and some press reports started making the assumption that this was the "longest since WWII," or even "longest in history." In 2003 the *Lincoln* would be away from home for 290 days and, once again, parts of the Navy press machine assumed that it was the longest carrier deployment in history. Research by historian Mike Weeks, however, shows that *Lincoln's* deployment, although much longer than the normal six month duration, ranked as only the ELEVENTH longest since the end of World War II. It certainly was the longest carrier deployment in three decades, as most of the others on this list were during Vietnam, although there are two from the 1950s, as well. What is amazing is that *Lincoln's* was the longest deployment ever for a nuclear carrier, as the other ten are all oil burners, and one (*Saipan*) was a Light Carrier (CVL) with a Marine *Skyraider* unit onboard. It's probably safe to say that most of them carried out the feat while also dealing with things like water hours (fresh water rationing), bad or no air conditioning, and no satellite TV or E-mail, not to mention having to deal with highly insensitive "Old Navy" all-male crews.

1.	*Coral Sea*	CVW-15	329 days	7 Dec 64 to 1 Nov 65	Vietnam
2.	*Midway*	CVW-5	327 days	10 Apr 72 to 3 Mar 73	Vietnam
3.	*JF Kennedy*	CVW-1	310 days	1 Dec 71 to 6 Oct 72	Med
4.	*Saratoga*	CVW-3	308 days	11 Apr 72 to 13 Feb 73	Vietnam
5.	*Tarawa*	CVG-3	298 days	12 Nov 53 to 6 Sep 54	World
6.	*BH Richard*	CVW-19	298 days	28 Jan to 21 Nov 64	WPAC
7.	*Oriskany*	CVW-19	298 days	5 Jun 72 to 30 Mar 73	Vietnam
8.	*FD Roosevelt*	CVW-6	297 days	15 Feb to 8 Dec 72	Med
9.	*Saipan*	VMA-324	295 days	28 Sep 53 to 20 Jul 54	World
10.	*America*	CVW-8	292 days	5 Jun 72 to 24 Mar 73	Vietnam
11.	*Lincoln*	CVW-14	290 days	20 Jul 02 to 6 May 03	Iraq

Big sea, little boat. While an aircraft carrier may look huge while sitting at the pier, this is how small it can look from the air—the veritable "postage stamp at sea." *Carl Vinson* conducts FRS CQ off San Diego on 29 May '93. A VF-124 F-14 is in the groove, while FRS *Hornets*, *Prowlers*, and *Tomcats* are seen on the flight deck. (author)

and 1993 *Vinson* was at Bremerton, WA, for an extensive overhaul. In 1997 the ship made the Washington shipyard her formal homeport.

***Theodore Roosevelt* (CVN-71)**
Class: *Nimitz*
Homeport: Norfolk, VA.
Comm: 25 Oct 1986.

25 Aug to 11 Oct 1988	NorLant	CVW-8	
30 Dec 1988 to 30 Jun 1989	Med	CVW-8	
28 Dec 1990 to 28 Jun 1991	Med/RS/PG	CVW-8	*Desert Storm*
11 Mar to 8 Sep 1993	Med	CVW-8/ Special MAGTF	*Deny Flight*
22 Mar to 22 Sep 1995	Med/RS/PG	CVW-8	*Deliberate Force*
25 Nov 1996 to 22 May 1997	Med/RS/PG	CVW-3	
26 Mar to 22 Sep 1999	Med/RS/PG	CVW-8	*Allied Force*

"TR" was the first of a series of *Nimitz* class carriers named for significant Presidents whose previous ships, all ballistic missile submarines (SSBNs), had been retired. CVN-71's predecessor, SSBN-600, was decommissioned on 28 Feb 1981. "The Big Stick's" second major cruise was dominated by operations in *Desert Storm*, where they began combat flights on the fourth day of the war in the Persian Gulf, after a high speed transit across the Atlantic Ocean and through the Suez Canal. She was the first nuclear carrier to ever operate in the Persian Gulf, and the only nuke to launch combat missions during the war. Following the end of hostilities she spent several weeks in the Red Sea before returning to the Med and joining *Operation Provide Comfort*, where her aircraft operated over northern Iraq in support of coalition forces protecting Kurdish tribesmen. Her 1992-93 cruise was highlighted by duty in *Operation Deny Flight*, the UN campaign in Bosnia-Herzegovina. For this deployment TR embarked the Special Marine Air ground Task Force (SPMAGTF), in addition to CVW-8. As of 2000, TR had been involved in more combat than any of her other *Nimitz*-class sisters.

***Abraham Lincoln* (CVN-72)**
Class: *Nimitz*
Homeport: Norfolk, Alameda (from 9/90), Everett (from 1/97)
Comm: 11 Nov 1989.

25 Sep to 20 Nov 1990	Horn	CVW-11
28 May to 28 Nov 1991	WP/IO/PG	CVW-11
15 Jun to 15 Dec 1993	WP/IO/PG	CVW-11
10 Apr to 9 Oct 1995	WP/IO/PG	CVW-11
11 Jun to 7 Dec 1998	WP/IO/PG	CVW-14
14 Aug 00 to 12 Feb 2001	WP/IO/PG	CVW-14

"ABE" made her shakedown cruise to the Puerto Rican op area in 1990 with CVW-8 embarked. She then had CVW-13 assigned, apparently for her trip around the Horn; however, they were replaced by AirPac's CVW-11, which would become her regular Air Wing. *Lincoln's* subsequent two extended deployments have been made to the Western Pacific\Indian Ocean, and have included operations in the Persian Gulf and off Somalia. In 1994 she became the first PacFleet carrier to embark women as a permanent part of her crew, which immediately led to members of its crew giving it the officially discouraged nickname "Babe-raham Lincoln." The previous *Abraham Lincoln*, SSBN-602, was decommissioned on 28 Feb 1981.

***George Washington* (CVN-73)**
Class: *Nimitz*
Homeport: Norfolk
Comm: 4 Jul 1992.

20 May to 17 Nov 1994	Med	CVW-7
26 Jan to 23 Jul 1996	Med/RS/PG	CVW-7
3 Oct 1997 to 3 Apr 1998	Med/RS/PG	CVW-1
27 Jun to 19 Dec 2000	Med/RS/PG	CVW-17

The "GW" gained the name of the nation's first President after the 1985 decommissioning of the previous vessel of that name, SSBN-598. The ship remained with the Atlantic Fleet after commissioning, and has made several deployments to the Med, Red Sea, and Persian Gulf.

***John C. Stennis* (CVN-74)**
Class: Nimitz
Homeport: Norfolk, North Island (from 8/98)
Comm: 9 Dec 1995

26 Feb to 26 Aug 1998	World	CVW-7
7 Jan to 3 Jul 2000	WP/IO/PG	CVW-9

The *Stennis* is yet another case of an American capital ship being named (on 19 Dec 1988) for a now obscure member of the U.S. Legislative branch, who also happened to be a significant patron of the Navy. In this case the ship's namesake was a Democratic Senator from Mississippi who was called "the Father of America's Modern Navy" by President Reagan. Stennis passed away on 23 April 1995, only eight months before "his" ship was commissioned. The ship's name also killed reported attempts by some in the Navy to name the vessel the *Thomas Jefferson*, and apply the term "Rushmore Class" to CVN-71 through 74 for the four faces carved on the South Dakota mountain. The ship's first deployment was "Around the World" with CVW-7 via the Med, Red Sea, Persian Gulf, and Pacific Ocean. CVW-9 was subsequently embarked for her second cruise.

***Harry S. Truman* (CVN-75)**
Class: Nimitz
Homeport: Norfolk
Comm: 25 Jul 1998

28 Nov 2000 to 23 May 2001	Med/PG	CVW-3

The *Truman*'s hull was originally named on 9 May 1989 as the *United States*, but the Secretary of the Navy announced on 2 Feb 1995 that it would be changed to that of the 33rd President. The ironic part of this switch is that President Truman, the old Missouri National Guard Artillery officer and WWI combat vet, was responsible for the cancellation of the original carrier *United States* (CV-58) in 1949. Truman was never noted to be a particularly strong supporter for the Navy or Marine Corps, which makes this naming even more unusual.

The *Truman* made one extended deployment in 2000 with CVW-3. If the ship goes through a normal carrier life, it may be 2050 or 2060 before it is retired.

It's widely known that Truman had no middle name, but used a simple letter "S" as a stand-alone middle initial instead. Although some Presidential historians believe that Truman reflected this by using a simple "S" (with no period), the ship chose to add the punctuation ("S."), which matches the style endorsed by his official Presidential library in Independence, MO.

The vessel's motto is "Give 'em Hell," which occasionally appears on aircraft assigned to the ship. This refers to a response to a call from a campaign crowd to "Give 'em Hell, Harry," to which the blunt speaking President responded "I'll speak the truth and they'll think its Hell!" The statement was later repeated for the press, and it ranked up with the term "The Buck Stops Here" as a defining statement for the man from Missouri.

Ronald Reagan (CVN-76)
The keel for CVN-76 was laid at Newport News on 12 Feb 1998. The vessel was named for the 40th President of the United States, and would be commissioned on 12 July 2003.

3

Carrier Air Wings (CVW)

Air Wings don't TRANSFORM. They EVOLVE.

The Carrier Air Wing (CVW) is the major aviation unit on the carrier. It is a collection of squadrons that join together and train as a team for the purpose of projecting power from the ship's decks.

The organization of these wings have undergone a continuous evolution, as the service sought to place the greatest capability at sea based on the potential threat, projected operational environment, and available budget.

As of January 1974 the Navy had 14 Attack Carrier Air Wings (CVWs, table 4). The "Attack" portion of their title, which had seprated them from the distinct Carrier ASW Air Groups (CVSGs) that operated off the ASW carriers (CVSs) through 1973, was deleted on 1 April 1976 to better describe their new function under the "CV Concept."

The two Wings that had been assigned to the "27C" ships *Oriskany* and *Hancock* were gone by 1978, CVW-19 actually making its last deployment with *Frankin D. Roosevelt*. Two new wings (CVW-10 and -13) were established during the Reagan/Lehman years, although only the latter would ever deploy. Following *Desert Storm*, both coasts stabilized at five CVWs each, and the Reserves lost one of their two.

	CVW-Atlantic Fleet	CVW-Pacific Fleet	Reserve Air Wings
1974	(6) 1,3,6,7,8,17	(8) 2,5,9,11,14,15,19,21	(2) CVWR-20, 30
1985	(7) 1,3,6,7,8,13,17	(6) 2,5,9,11,14,15	(2) 20,30
2000	(5) 1,3,7,8,17	(5) 2,5,9,11,14	(1) 20

Table 4: Carrier Air Wings 1974-2000

Carrier air power during the mid-'80s. CVW-14 rendezvous near Fallon in September 1984 for another practice Vietnam-style "Alpha Strike," which was intended to apply the maximum amount of "dumb bomb" tonnage on a selected target in the shortest amount of time. By 2000 precision guided weapons had rendered mass gaggle attacks like this largely unnecessary. Aircraft from VA-196, VF-154, VF-21, VFA-113, and VFA-25 are visible. (author)

CAG, the man

The term Carrier Air Wing (CVW) dates only to 23 December 1963, when it replaced the title Carrier Air Group (CVG). Nonetheless, it is still common to refer to a Wing as, for instance, "CAG-Two," or its commanding officer as *the* CAG, for "Commander, Air Group." Make no mistake. The man holding the honored title of CAG has, for many years, wielded power and influence well above the rank he wore.

Air Wings were traditionally commanded by Naval Aviators with the rank of Commander (O-5). These were post-command billets, with the CAG having already had command of a fleet squadron. Through this period a Naval Aviator (pilot) from either the VF or VA communities usually held the CAG position. Naval Flight Officers (NFOs) were less common as CAGs, having only been qualified to command squadrons since 1971. The first Naval Flight Officer (NFO) CAG was Cmdr. Richard "Sweat Pea" Allen, a former Naval Aviator, who commanded CVW-6 in 1979-1980. The first "career" NFO CAG was Cmdr. Tom Slater, a fighter RIO with CVW-2 1984-85.

In the mid-1980s there was a major reorganization of this critical leadership position, with the billet now being considered a "Major Warfare Commander," with the rank of Captain (O-6).[4] The elevation of the position also took the CAG out from under the Commanding Officer of the ship (where he'd been technically little more than a Department Head), and made him an equal to the ship CO under the Battle Group Commander. This new "Super CAG" had an O-5 Vice-CAG (which some wags immediately dubbed a "CAGlet") as his assistant. This was initially a non-fleet up position; in other words, the Vice did not become the CAG at the end of the tour, but moved elsewhere and into another job. Within a few years this billet was renamed Deputy CAG, and did become the stepping stone to the CAG position itself. Career fighter pilot Capt. "Bad Fred" Lewis was the first "Super CAG," taking over CVW-8 in January 1986. (Ironically, he had been COMCVW-8 once before, as a Commander.)

The "Super CAG" job opened up the position to more Naval Flight Officers, and members of communities other than fighter or attack started to be selected to take the top leadership position in the Wing. One such example was Capt. Tom Ford (CAG-11, 1984), a *Prowler* ECMO, who is believed to have been the first CAG from a squadron other than the VA/VF communities.

CAGs and their staffs are located at one of the four major jet bases through most of the period: Oceana, Cecil, Miramar, and Lemoore. By 2000 base closures and realignments had moved them all to either Oceana or Lemoore.

The Air Wing does not "own" any aircraft itself, but is assigned squadrons by their respective Type Commanders. A wing's staff members typically fly with a specific squadron from their own warfare area. CAGs themselves have been known to fly as many aircraft in their wing as they can manage qualifications for. It should be noted that the presence of a CAG's name on an aircraft's canopy rail is done out of tradition, and does not necessarily mean he's qualified to fly it—a good example being NFO CAGs, whose names are on single-seat *Hornets*.

Air Wing Configurations

The actual number of squadrons and types of aircraft assigned to an Air Wing has continually changed through the years. Air Wing configurations are influenced by a number of things, including aircraft availability, ship intermediate maintenance facilities, and community transitions. At the end of the Vietnam war, the Navy had two basic CVW configurations. *Midway* or larger carries utilized one basic format, while the two remaining *Essex* class carriers used another. Since then the service has used a variety of Air Wing organizations, while it searches for the right mix of aircraft and squadrons within the limited confines of a carrier flight deck. This evolution was demonstrated during *Operation Desert Storm*, where no two of the six CVWs deployed were exactly alike (see table 5, p 54). During the 1990s Navy also deployed two experimental "Special MAGTF" organizations, where Wings and Marine helicopter squadrons shared decks. Following *Desert Storm* the Navy started a massive reorganization of its Air Wings that would lead, in time, to the end of the Medium Attack and Fighter communities. By 2000 it was obvious that the F/A-18 would soon become the dominant aircraft on carrier flight decks, as the F-14s and S-3s went the way of the F-4s, A-7s, A-4s, and A-6s before them. As always, change is constant. It's not so much transformational—its evolutionary.

Constellation is shown underway in the South China Sea on 2 Oct 1974 with CVW-9 onboard.The ship and airwing are still in much the same form they had at the end of the Vietnam War, with two F-4J (VF-92, 96), two A-7E (VA-146, 147), and single A-6A/KA-6D (VA-165), RA-5C (RVAH-5), EA-6B (VAQ-131), and E-2B (VAW-116) squadrons. HS-6 provides the SAR helo support, and VQ-1 has two EA-3Bs present. (U.S. Navy, PHCS(AW) Robert L. Lawson)

"Typical" CVW configurations 1974-2000 (with side numbers assigned)

Note: aircraft completments listed are nominal, and can vary due to a variety of factors.

1. 1974 "Big Deck": *Midway, Forrestal, Kitty Hawk, Enterprise* classes.

2 VF squadrons	10-12 F-4 or F-14 each	100, 200 series side numbers
2 VA(L)	12 A-7 each	300, 400
1 VA(M)	12-14 A-6/KA-6	500
1 VAW	4 E-2	various
1 RVAH/VFP	3 RA-5C *OR* RF-8G	600 or 610
1 VAQ	4 EA-6B or 3 EKA-3B	610, 620, 630 or 700
1 HS	4-6 SH-3	(HC det on *Midway* class)

VAQ units were occasionally deleted due to non-availability of assets. *Midway* utilized Marine EA-6As and RF-4Bs for VAQ and VFP roles, respectively, from 1974 to 1986.

2. 1974 "Small deck": *Oriskany* and *Hancock*

2 VF	12 F-8 each	100, 200 series side numbers
3 VA	10-12 A-4 or A-7 each	300, 400, 500
VAW det	3 E-1B	010
VAQ det	3 EKA-3B	604 or 610
VFP det	3 RF-8G	600
HC det	3-4 SH-3	various

Oriskany/CVW-19 utilized A-7s, *Hancock*/CVW-21 A-4s.

This configuration, modified with the use of F-4s and a Marine AV-8A unit, and deletion of the VFP and VAQ assets was also used by *Franklin D. Roosevelt*/CVW-19 on her final deployment in 1976-77.

3. "CV Concept" (later called a "Conventional" Air Wing)

2 VF	12 F-4 or F-14 ea.	100, 200 series side numbers
2 VA(L)	12 A-7E ea.	300, 400 (later VFA/FA-18)
1 VA(M)	12-16 A-6E/KA-6D	500
1 VAQ	4 EA-6B	604, 610 or 620
1 VAW	4 E-2C	600 or 010
1 VS	10 S-3A	700 see notes for S-2 details
1 RVAH	3 RA-5C	various (deleted by 1980)
1 HS	6-8 SH-3	various

The "CV concept" was created with the demise of the dedicated ASW carrier, and coincided with the introductioin of the S-3 *Viking*. The addition of another squadron placed deck loading at a premium, which forced the VA and VF squadrons to drop 1 to 2 aircraft apiece. Even with these changes, it was normal for deploying carriers to beach a portion of their air wings at places like Cubi Point or Sigonella, Sicily, to free up additional deck space. Prior to the arrival of the Viking, both coasts experimented with placing S-2 units in CVWs. AirLant deployed single S-2 squadrons with air wings, while AirPac initially assigned an entire CVSG of three VS and two HS to CVW-11 in 1973. Space requirements lowered this to two and one, and even this overcrowded the ship. The introduction of the S-3 in 1975 quickly led to this becoming the standard Navy air wing configuration within a few years. During the '80s the A-7s were replaced by VFA squadrons with F/A-18s, and the RVAH/VFP role was taken by TARPS-equipped F-14s in the higher numbered *Tomcat* squadron. Prior to 1975, EKA-3Bs and Marine EA-6As could make up the VAQ compliment. The lack of EA-6Bs forced some carriers to deploy without a VAQ squadron up through 1985. By the late 1980s this configuration was called a "Conventional" air wing, as other variants were being tested. A modified version of this wing was identified as a "Transitional" air wing in 1989, with eight less VF and VFA airframes onboard, and two more *Intruders*. This was intended as a "transition" to the *Roosevelt*, or notional, air wing. Shortfalls in numbers of aircraft following *Desert Storm* meant that no CVWs would ever deploy with this configuration.

4. *KENNEDY* AIR WING ("The All Grumman Air Wing")

2 VF	12 F-14 ea	100, 200 series side numbers
2 VA(M)	12 A-6E/KA-6D	400, 500, 550
1 VAQ	4-5 EA-6B	604 or 620
1 VAW	4-5 E-2C	600
1 VS	10 S-3A	700
1 HS	6 SH-3	610

From 1983 to 1993 the Navy deployed two Air Wings with no light attack squadrons, and strengthened medium attack and fighter units. It was named after the first ship to deploy with the configuration, the *Kennedy*, although it was also called the "All Grumman Air Wing," even if Lockheed and Sikorsky products were also onboard.

Reasons for the wing's make up include an attempt to maximize the number of all-weather bombers onboard. There also may have been an attempt by then Secretary of the Navy John Lehman (a Naval reserve A-6 Bombardier/Navigator) to reinforce the need for an *Intruder* follow on, and to improve the Navy's hand in negotiations with McDonnell-Douglas for F/A-18 prices.

Kennedy/CVW-3 deployed three times with this configuration, and saw combat in Lebannon. *Ranger*/CVW-2 was the Pacific Fleet counterpart, and deployed as such six times, including *Desert Storm*.

5. *CORAL SEA* AIR WING

4 VFA	10-12 F/A-18 ea	later 3 VFA	100, 200, 300, 400 series side numbers
1 VA(M)	12 A-6E/KA	later 2 VA(M)	500
1 VAW	4 E-2C	600	
1 VAQ	4 EA-6B	604 or 620	
1 HS	6 SH-3H	610	

When *Coral Sea* deployed to the Med in 1985 she took the first Atlantic Fleet F/A-18s with her in a unique Air Wing made up of four *Hornet* squadrons and a single A-6 unit. The EA-6Bs did not join CVW-13 until mid-cruise, which forced an already crowded flight deck to leave 2-3 aircraft per squadron at Sigonella. The following cruise the Air Wing was modified by the deletion of one VFA, and the addition of another A-6 unit. The *Intruder* units were actually "small" in size, with eight aircraft each, for 16 total. This configuration continued for her last two cruises, and a similar version was used by *Midway*/CVW-

5 from 1986 (the second *Intruder* unit joining in 1987) through *Desert Storm*, and up to her decommissioning.

6. Notional Air Wing (*Roosevelt* Air Wing)

2 VF	9-10 F-14 ea	100, 200 series side numbers
2 VFA	12 F/A-18 ea	300, 400
2 VA(M)	9-10 A-6E ea	500, 530
1 VAW	5 E-2C	600
1 VAQ	5 EA-6B	620
1 VS	10 S-3A/B	700
1 HS	6 SH-3H	610

In the late '80s the Navy announced that the "Notional Air Wing" would be their future standard configuration. It was a reflection of the Reagan buildup years, when cost was no factor. Featuring two each VF/VFA/VAM units, and increased numbers of E-2 and EA-6B aircraft (5 in each squadron), the notional represented the largest and most versatile air force the Navy expected to place on a *Nimitz* class carrier.

Unfortunately, fiscal reality caught up with the service by the early '90s, and only *Theodore Roosevelt* embarked the Notional Air Wing. Plans to establish up to ten new A-6 units faded away, and the idea became a good example of what might have been.

Roosevelt deployed twice with the notional configuration, and showed in *Desert Storm* what it could accomplish, producing the highest number of sorties of any carrier during the war.

7. *Roosevelt* Air Wing with SPMAGTF embarked

1 VF	9-10 F-14A	100 series side numbers
3 VFA	12 F/A-18	300, 330,400
1 VA(M)	9-10 A-6E	500
1 VAW	4 E-2C	600
1 VAQ	4 EA-6B	620
1 HS	6 SH-60F	610
1 HMH(C)	6 CH-53D, 4 UH-1N	

For its 1993 deployment, the *Roosevelt* had a Marine composite helicopter squadron attached with ten aircraft, and a company of infantry on board. To make space VF-41, VA-65, and VS-24 did not make deployment, and VMFA-312 was added as a third *Hornet* squadron. Coined the Special Marine Air Ground Task Force (SPMAGTF), the Marine helicopter unit was not part of the Air Wing, but directly under the embarked Admiral, with its own full Colonel officially equal in position to CAG-8.

The plan is attributed to Commander in Chief, U.S. Atlantic Fleet (CINCLANTFLT) Adm. P.D. Miller and his staff, and it allowed a reduction in amphibious assets in the Med for significant savings in money. Officially the deployment was hailed as a great success, although operations between the two different types of aircraft were described by some who made the deployment as difficult at best, and there were open questions as to what exactly a company of Marines could be expected to accomplish, as opposed to the standard Battalion Landing Team (BLT).

America/CVW-1 deployed to the Med with a less ambitious arrangement the same year, with only four CH-46Es onboard instead of *Sea Stallions*. It would be the last of these Special MAGTFs to deploy on a carrier.

It should be noted that the Pacific Fleet counterpart, CINCPACFLT, specifically chose not to conduct such deployments with his carriers, preferring to stay with the established Amphibious Groups and their BLTs.

8. "The '90s Air Wing"

1 VF	10-14	F-14	100 series side numbers
3 VFA	10-12	FA-18	200, 300, 400
1 VAW	4-5	E-2C	600
1 VAQ	4	EA-6B	604, 620, 500
1 VS	8-10	S-3A/B	700
1 HS	6/2	SH-60F/HH-60F	610
1 VQ det	2	ES-3A	760
1 VRC det	2	C-2A	00

During the early '90s, the economic realities of the post-*Desert Storm* drawdown led the Navy to reorganize its Air Wings yet again. The A-6, with no direct replacement forthcoming, was selected for early retirement, and was replaced by a third FA-18 unit and ordnance-carrying "Bombcats." The S-3 squadron becomes the only tanker capable

CVW-1 is displayed on *John F. Kennedy* as the ship prepares for launch in 1978. The wing has a standard late-'70s "CV-concept" air wing configuration, including *Tomcats* (VF-14, -32), *Corsairs* (VA-46, -72), *Intruders* (VA-34), *Prowlers* (VAQ-133), *Vikings* (VS-32), and *Sea Kings* (HS-11). There's also an RF-8G det assigned, as the VFP-63 *Crusader* on cat 1 indicates. The only aircraft missing from this picture are VAW-125's E-2Cs. (U.S. Navy)

aircraft (until the arrival of the F/A-18E/F family in 2001), and the two F-14 units become one larger squadron with TARPS capability. Although the Navy has indicated that it plans to re-equip all ten of its remaining air wings to this configuration, as of 2000 two CVWs (7 and 8) still featured a 2 VF/ 2 VFA makeup. In addition to the "traditional" squadrons, the Navy started assigning VQ and VRC detachments directly to the Air Wing Commanders during this period. Prior to this CODs were usually assigned to the ships themselves, or were operated on a daily "as needed" basis from forward deployed units, such as VRC-50 or VR-24. However valuable the ES-3s may have been, they would not last long, as both *Shadow* squadrons were cut in the late '90s, the Battle Groups now working with land-based EP-3Es when they were available.

TF154	F-14A	F-14A+	F/A-18A	F/A-18C	A-7E	A-6E/ KA6D	EA-6B	E-2C	S-3A	S-3B	SH-3H
CV-41 (62)	0	0	30	0	0	14/4	4	4	0	0	6
CV-61 **(67)**	22	0	0	0	0	24	4	4	7	0	6
CVN-71 **(75)**	18	0	20	0	0	18	5	4	0	4	6
TF-155	F-14A	F-14A+	F/A-18A	F/A-18C	A-7E	A-6E/ KA6D	EA-6B	E-2C	S-3A	S-3B	SH-3H
CV-66 **(80)**	20	0	0	20	0	12/4	5	5	0	8	6
CV-60 **(79)**	0	19	0	18	0	14/4	4	4	0	10	6
CV-67 **(84)**	20	0	0	0	24	13/4	5	4	0	8	6

TABLE 5: CARRIER AIR WINGS: *DESERT STORM*, 1 FEB 1991

Although the Navy usually talks in terms of "standard" air wing configurations, in realilty they are in a constant state of change. This was demonstrated during *Desert Storm*, where no two of the six wings present had exactly the same make up. The three Persian Gulf ships (*TR*, *Ranger*, and *Midway*) carried the last three "dual A-6 squadron" wings, although in three different flavors, as "Notional," "All-

What's a CAG bird?

One of the more popular traditions in the Carrier Navy involves the special markings frequently placed on the aircraft that carries the name of the Air Wing Commander, or CAG. The "CAG Bird" (it is *not* a "Boss Bird"—which is an enthusiast term the Navy doesn't recognize) is, usually, the aircraft in each squadron ending with the "00" (zero-zero, or "Double nuts") modex numbers. The amount of color painted on these aircraft is usually left up to the squadrons themselves. Some units go great lengths to mark-up a single "Easter Egg," while others make little or no effort at all to distinguish these aircraft.

The traditional "CAG rainbow" that developed over the years to mark CAG birds can take many forms and colors, if it's applied at all. Some wings (such as CVW-5 or -14) seemed to use the motif more than others. During the 1980s, when low visibility markings were the rage, others dispensed with the rainbow altogether, and allowed only limited color on one aircraft in each squadron, if any.

It needs to be pointed out that these markings are largely symbolic in nature, as the presence of his name doesn't necessarily mean that the CAG is qualified to fly in the aircraft (a Naval Flight Officer CAG on a F/A-18C being a good example), or that the specific airframe is reserved for his use, as CAG will normally be assigned to fly whatever sidenumber is properly configured and spotted for the flight he's scheduled for—just like any other aircrew.

Tarsier ("Starfighter") F-4J AG200 (155532) shows full CAG markings at Miramar in May 1978, only a few months after returning from a Med cruise with CVW-7 and *Independence*. Although now marked for CVN-69, the ship would never cruise with *Phantoms*, as VF-33 and sister VF-102 soon moved to CVW-6 and back to the "Indy." The highly visible black tail and CAG star markings are fairly typical for the period. (Mick Roth)

Grumman," and "Coral Sea" configurations. In the Red Sea, *Kennedy* had the last A-7s to deploy, while *America* and *Saratoga* carried different versions of *Tomcats*. Several of the ships left S-3s at locations like Sigonella in order to make more room. *Source: Gulf War Air Power Survey*

CVW-1 AB
Formed as *Ranger* Air Group 1 Jul 38, r/d CVG-4 3 Aug 43, r/d CVAG-1 15 Nov 46, r/d CVG-1 1 Sep 48, r/d CVW-1 20 Dec 63.
Homeport: Oceana
Deployments:

28 Jun 1975 to 27 Jan 1976		***John F. Kennedy***	**Med**		
VF-14	F-14A	AB100	VAW-125	E-2C	AB720
VF-32	F-14A	AB200	VAQ-133	EA-6B	AB700
VA-46	A-7B	AB300	VS-21	S-3A	AB600
VA-72	A-7B	AB400	HS-11	SH-3D	AB000
VA-34	A-6E, KA-6D	AB500			

First cruise for S-3A and E-2C, first Med trip for F-14A. RVAH-1 made part of work ups, but did not make the deployment.

2 Sep to 9 Nov 1976		***John F. Kennedy***	**NorLant**		
VF-14	F-14A	AB100	VAW-125	E-2C	AB010
VF-32	F-14A	AB200	VAQ-133	EA-6B	AB610
VA-46	A-7E	AB300	VFP-63 det 2	RF-8G	AB600
VA-72	A-7E	AB400	VS-32	S-3A	AB700
VA-34	A-6E, KA-6D	AB500	HS-11	SH-3D	AB730

The two light attack squadrons re-equipped with A-7Es, retiring the last Cecil-based A-7Bs. An East Coast *Viking* squadron has come aboard as well, replacing California-based VS-21. RF-8s joined CVW-1 and *Kennedy*, marking the first time *Crusaders* had ever deployed with the carrier.

15 Jan to 1 Aug 1977		***John F. Kennedy***	**Med**		
VF-14	F-14A	AB100	VAW-125	E-2C	AB010
VF-32	F-14A	AB200	VAQ-133	EA-6B	AB610
VA-46	A-7E	AB300	VFP-63 det 2	RF-8G	AB600
VA-72	A-7E	AB400	VS-32	S-3A	AB700
VA-34	A-6E, KA-6D	AB500	HS-11	SH-3D	AB730

29Jun 1978 to 8 Feb 1979		***John F. Kennedy***	**Med**		
VF-14	F-14A	AB100	VAW-125	E-2C	AB010
VF-32	F-14A	AB200	VAQ-133	EA-6B	AB610
VA-46	A-7E	AB300	VFP-63 det 2	RF-8G	AB620
VA-72	A-7E	AB400	VS-32	S-3A	AB700
VA-34	A-6E, KA-6D	AB500	HS-11	SH-3D	AB730

4 Aug 1980 to 28 Mar 1981		***John F. Kennedy***	**Med**		
VF-14	F-14A	AB100	VAW-126	E-2C	AB010
VF-32	F-14A	AB200	VAQ-138	EA-6B	AB610
VA-46	A-7E	AB300	VS-32	S-3A	AB700
VA-72	A-7E	AB400	HS-11	SH-3H	AB730
VA-34	A-6E, KA-6D	AB500			

CVW-1 deploys without photo assests, the VFP-63 detachment having been removed from the wing.

23 Aug to 30 Oct 1982		***America***	**NorLant/Med/Carib**		
VF-102	F-14A, TARPS	AB100	VAW-123	E-2C	AB600
VF-33	F-14A	AB200	VAQ-135	EA-6B	AB604
VA-46	A-7E	AB300	VS-32	S-3A	AB700
VA-72	A-7E	AB400	HS-11	SH-3H	AB610
VA-34	A-6E, KA-6D	AB500			

CVW-1 moves to *America*, while two new *Tomcat* squadrons have come aboard, VF-14 and -32 having moved to CVW-6. The VAW and VAQ units are new, as well. The Air Wing 1/*America* team made an unusual three month deployment to the North Atlantic, Med. and Caribbean before returning home.

8 Dec 1982 to 2 Jun 1983		***America***	**Med/IO**		
VF-102	F-14A, TARPS	AB100	VAW-123	E-2C	AB600
VF-33	F-14A	AB200	(VAQ-136)	EA-6B	AB604)
VA-46	A-7E	AB300	VS-32	S-3A	AB700
VA-72	A-7E	AB400	HS-11	SH-3H	AB610
VA-34	A-6E, KA-6D	AB500			

Air Wing ONE was home only about five weeks before deploying again, on a regular six month trip to the Med and IO. VAQ-135 left in the interim (deploying itself with *Nimitz*/CVW-8 in November), and the wing did not have a *Prowler* unit assigned until its arrival in the IO, where VAQ-136 joined it on station. The *Gauntlets* were onboard only for the period in the Indian Ocean (6 Feb through 22 Apr,) and were on temporary loan from CVW-5 in Atsugi.

24 Apr 1984 to 14 Nov 1984		***America***	**Med/IO**		
VF-102	F-14A, TARPS	AB100	VAW-123	E-2C	AB600
VF-33	F-14A	AB200	VAQ-135	EA-6B	AB604
VA-46	A-7E	AB300	VS-32	S-3A	AB700
VA-72	A-7E	AB400	HS-11	SH-3H	AB610
VA-34	A-6E, KA-6D	AB500			

VAQ-135 has returned to CVW-1 for its 1984 deployment.

24 Aug to 9 Oct 1985		***America***	**NorLant**		
VF-102	F-14A, TARPS	AB100	VAW-123	E-2C	AB600
VF-33	F-14A	AB200	VAQ-135	EA-6B	AB604
VA-46	A-7E	AB300	VS-32	S-3A	AB700
VA-72	A-7E	AB400	HS-11	SH-3H	AB610
VA-34	A-6E, KA-6D	AB500			

10 Mar 1986 to 10 Sep 1986		***America***	**Med**		
VF-102	F-14A,TARPS	AB100	VAW-123	E-2C	AB600
VF-33	F-14A	AB200	VMAQ-2	EA-6B	AB604
VA-46	A-7E	AB300	VS-32	S-3A	AB700
VA-72	A-7E	AB400	HS-11	SH-3H	AB610
VA-34	A-6E, KA-6D	AB500			

Participated in strikes on Libya, in *Operations Prairie Fire* and *El Dorado Canyon*. VMAQ-2 det Y was assigned on a short-fused basis when VAQ-135 was deployed to *Coral Sea*/CVW-13 1 Jan 1986.

8 Feb 1989 to 3 Apr 1989		***America***	**Carib/NorLant**		
11 May 1989 to 10 Nov 1989		*America*	Med/IO		
VF-102	F-14A, TARPS	AB100	VAW-123	E-2C	AB600
VF-33	F-14A	AB200	VAQ-137	EA-6B	AB604
VFA-82	F/A-18C	AB300	VS-32	S-3A	AB700
VFA-86	F/A-18C	AB400	HS-11	SH-3H	AB610
VA-85	A-6E, KA-6D	AB500			

A-7s were replaced by *Hornets*, with VFA-82 and -86 having the first C-model F/A-18s to deploy.

28 Dec 1990 to 18 Apr 1991		***America***	**Med/RS/PG**		
VF-102	F-14A,TARPS	AB100	VAW-123	E-2C	AB600
VF-33	F-14A	AB200	VAQ-137	EA-6B	AB620
VFA-82	F/A-18C	AB300	VS-32	S-3B	AB700
VFA-86	F/A-18C	AB400	HS-11	SH-3H	AB610
VA-85	A-6E, KA-6D	AB500			

America and CVW-1 deployed at least three months early in order to participate in *Desert Storm*, where they operated from both Red Sea and Persian Gulf. They lost no aircraft in combat.

21 Aug to 11 Oct 1991		***America***	**NorLant**		
2 Dec 1991 to 6 Jun 1992		*America*	Med		
VF-102	F-14A,TARPS	AB100	VAW-123	E-2C	AB600
VF-33	F-14A	AB200	VAQ-137	EA-6B	AB620
VFA-82	F/A-18C	AB300	VS-32	S-3B	AB700
VFA-86	F/A-18C	AB400	HS-11	SH-3H	AB610
VA-85	A-6E,KA-6D	AB500			

Only four months after returning from *Desert Storm*, *America* and CVW-1 were lucky enough to be sent overseas again, this time to participate in a "critical" NATO exercise, the organization having gone almost a year without a carrier deck to work with due to *Desert Storm*. They followed up with another six-month deployment to the Med less than two months after returning from the Northern Atlantic.

11 Aug 1993 to 5 Feb 1994		***America***	**Med/IO**		
VF-102	F-14A,TARPS	AB100	VAW-123	E-2C	AB600
VFA-82	F/A-18C	AB300	VAQ-137	EA-6B	AB620
VFA-86	F/A-18C	AB400	VS-32	S-3B	AB700
VA-85	A-6E	AB500	HS-11	SH-3H	AB610
			HMM-162 det A	CH-46E	YS 00
			VRC-40 det 3	C-2A	AB

With the *Intruders* beached, CVW-1 went with a single large (14 aircraft) VF squadron, losing VF-33 for its 1993 deployment. There was no AB 200 series squadron embarked. A detachment of four Marine *Sea Knights* were also embarked as part of an experimental "Special Marine Air Ground Task Force." The ship supported NATO operations off Bosnia, as well as *Restore Hope* in Somalia.

28 Aug 1995 to 24 Feb 1996		*America*	Med/RS/PG		
VF-102	F-14B, TARPS	AB100	VAW-123	E-2C	AB600
VMFA-251	F/A-18C	AB200	VMAQ-3	EA-6B	AB620
VFA-82	F/A-18C	AB300	VS-32	S-3B	AB700
VFA-86	F/A-18C	AB400	HS-11	SH-60F/HH-60H	AB610
			VQ-6 det A	ES-3A	AB760
			VRC-40 det4	C-2A	AB

VF-102 has acquired "B" model Tomcats, and two Marine squadrons have joined the wing, as have ES-3As and SH-60s. *America* and her wing were heavily involved in combat operations over Bosnia in support of *Deny Flight* during this deployment. The Marines have joined the wing in an early version of what was later called the TacAir Integration Program. VMFA-251 adopts the empty 200 series, while VMAQ-3 has replaced the *Rooks* of VAQ-137, which had been disestablished.

3 Oct 1997-3 Apr 1998		***George Washington***	**Med/RS/PG**		
VF-102	F-14B/TARPS	AB100	VAW-123	E-2C	AB600
VMFA-251	F/A-18C	AB200	VAQ-137	EA-6B	AB620
VFA-82	F/A-18C	AB300	VS-32	S-3B	AB700
VFA-86	F/A-18C	AB400	HS-11	SH-60F/HH-60H	AB610
VQ-6 det B	ES-3A	AB760			
VRC-40 det 1	C-2A	AB			

A newly established version of VAQ-137 replaces the Marines as CVW-1's EA-6B squadron. The wing was augmented by a pair of VAQ-138 EA-6Bs (CVW-9, NG620 series) in the Persian Gulf, and kept these aircraft until they returned to Whidbey.

17 Sep 1999 to 17 Mar 2000		***John F. Kennedy***	**Med/RS/PG**		
VF-102	F-14B/TARPS	AB100	VAW-123	E-2C	AB600
VMFA-251	F/A-18C	AB200	VS-32	S-3B	AB700
VFA-82	F/A-18C	AB300	HS-11	SH-60F/HH-60H	AB610
VFA-86	F/A-18C	AB400	VRC-40 det 2	C-2A	AB
VAQ-137	EA-6B	AB500			

The *Rooks* have moved to the open 500 series for the '99-00 deployment.

CVW-2 NE

Estab. as CVBG-74 1 May 45, r/d CVBG-1 15 Nov 46, r/d CVG-2 1 Sep 48, r/d CVW-2 20 Dec 63
Homeport: Miramar, Lemoore June 1998
Carrier Air Wing TWO was one of the busiest CVWs during the Vietnam conflict, making seven deployments to South East Asia. The wing was assigned to the *Ranger* in 1967, and it would make 16 of its next 17 deployments with that valiant ship.

7 May to 18 Oct 1974		***Ranger***	**WPAC**		
VF-154	F-4J	NE100	VAW-112	E-2B	NE010
VF-21	F-4J	NE200	RVAH-13	RA-5C	NE600
VA-113	A-7E	NE300	HC-1 det 4	SH-3G	NE000
VA-25	A-7E	NE400			
VA-145	A-6A, KA-6D	NE500			

VAQ-130 det 4 worked up for deployment with EKA-3Bs marked NE610, but were withdrawn prior to departure in order to accelerate the squadron's transition to the EA-6B. This deployment was marred on 22 July when, during a firepower demonstration, a VF-21 F-4J accidentally shot down an HC-1
Sea King and its crew with a *Sidewinder* missile.

30 Jan to 7 Sep 1976		***Ranger***	**WPAC/IO**		
VF-154	F-4J	NE100	VAW-112	E-2B	NE600
VF-21	F-4J	NE200	VAQ-135	EA-6B	NE630
VA-113	A-7E	NE300	RVAH-5	RA-5C	NE610
VA-25	A-7E	NE400	HS-4	SH-3D	NE720
VA-145	A-6A, KA-6D	NE500			

In July 1976 *Ranger*/CVW-2 operated off Africa in a show of support for the Kenyan government, which was facing the threat of invasion from Idi Amin's Uganda. *Prowlers* joined the air wing, as did an HS unit.

21 Feb to 22 Sep 1979		***Ranger***	**WPAC**		
VF-154	F-4J	NE100	VAW-117	E-2B	NE600
VF-21	F-4J	NE200	VAQ-137	EA-6B	NE620
VA-113	A-7E	NE300	RVAH-7	RA-5C	NE610
VA-25	A-7E	NE400	VS-29	S-3A	NE700
VA-145	A-6E, KA-6D	NE500	HS-4	SH-3H	NE730

For the 1979 deployment, RVAH-7 would be making the last cruise for the RA-5C *Vigilante*. S-3 *Vikings* joined CVW-2, and VA-145 had transitioned to A-6Es.

At least three CAG birds are visible in this 27 July '90 shot taken on *Ranger*. *Sun King* E-2C NE600 is spotted on Cat 1 and ready to go on 27 July '90. The duty tanker—in this case *Red Griffon* S-3A NE700—is next in line for launch. Aircraft from VF-2, VAQ-131, and VA-155 (NE400) are also present. (Robert Lawson)

10 Sep 1980 to 5 May 1981		***Ranger***	**WPAC/IO**		
VF-1	F-14A	NE100	VAW-117	E-2B	NE600
VF-2	F-14A	NE200	VAQ-137	EA-6B	NE620
VA-113	A-7E	NE300	VS-37	S-3A	NE700
VA-25	A-7E	NE400	HS-2	SH-3H	NE720
VA-145	A-6E, KA-6D	NE500			

F-14A *Tomcats* from VF-1 and -2 transferred in from CVW-14, replacing the *Phantoms*.

7 Apr to 19 Oct 1982		***Ranger***	**WPAC/IO**		
VF-1	F-14A	NE100	VAW-116	E-2C	NE600
VF-2	F-14A, TARPS	NE200	VAQ-137	EA-6B	NE604
VA-113	A-7E	NE300	VS-21	S-3A	NE700
VA-25	A-7E	NE400	HS-2	SH-3H	NE610
VA-145	A-6E, KA-6D	NE500			

After over a decade of association with CVW-2, Atkrons 25 and 113 made their last deployments with A-7s, as they are pulled to become the first fleet F/A-18 *Hornet* squadrons. VF-2 gained the TARPS mission, returning nominal recon capability to CVW-2 after three years without. VS-21 replaced VS-37 as well.

13 Jan to 1 Aug 1984		***Kitty Hawk***	**WPAC/IO**		
VF-1	F-14A	NE100	VAW-116	E-2C	NE600
VF-2	F-14A, TARPS	NE200	VAQ-130	EA-6B	NE604
VA-146	A-7E	NE300	VS-38	S-3A	NE700
VA-147	A-7E	NE400	HS-2	SH-3H	NE610
VA-145	A-6E,KA-6D	NE500			

CVW-2 made one deployment in *Kitty Hawk* with new VA(L), VAQ, and VS squadrons coming aboard. The VAW-116 *Sun Kings* made the first deployment with five E-2Cs assigned, instead of the normal four. The *Red Griffins* of VS-38 became the fourth Hoover unit to deploy with CVW-2 in five years. They would be the last *Viking* unit assigned to the wing.

18 Aug to 20 Oct 1986		***Ranger***	**"Surge" NorPac/WPAC**		
2 Mar to 29 Apr 1987		***Ranger***	**"Surge" NorPac**		
VF-1	F-14A	NE100	VAW-116	E-2C	NE600
VF-2	F-14A	NE200	VAQ-131	EA-6B	NE604
VMA(AW)-121	A-6E	NE400	VS-38	S-3A	NE700
VA-145	A-6E, KA-6D	NE500	HS-14	SH-3H	NE610

Over 1985 CVW-2 was reorganized as an "All Grumman Air Wing," with two Medium attack squadrons (one of which was Marine), and no Light Attack assets. New VAQ and HS units rounded out the wing. *Ranger*/CVW-2 made two short trips to the Western Pacific over an eight month period to test the "surge" carrier concept, as compared to full 6 month deployments. High transit times, costs, and stress on crew were all given as reasons for cessation of the practice.

14 Jul to 29 Dec 1987		***Ranger***	**WPAC/IO**		
VF-1	F-14A	NE100	VAW-116	E-2C	NE600
VF-2	F-14A	NE200	VAQ-131	EA-6B	NE604
VMA(AW)-121	A-6E	NE400	VS-38	S-3A	NE700
VA-145	A-6E, KA-6D	NE500	HS-14	SH-3H	NE610

Only three months after returning from a two-month "surge" deployment *Ranger*/CVW-2 made a normal six-month West Pac/IO trip.

24 Feb to 24 Aug 1989		***Ranger***	**WPAC/IO**		
VF-1	F-14A	NE100	VAW-116	E-2C	NE600
VF-2	F-14A	NE200	VAQ-131	EA-6B	NE604
VMA(AW)-121	A-6E	NE400	VS-38	S-3A	NE700
VA-145	A-6E, KA-6D	NE500	HS-14	SH-3H	NE610

8 Dec 1990 to 8 Jun 1991		***Ranger***		**WPAC/IO/PG**	
VF-1	F-14A	NE100	VAW-116	E-2C	NE600
VF-2	F-14A, TARPS	NE200	VAQ-131	EA-6B	NE620

VA-155	A-6E	NE400	VS-38	S-3A	NE700
VA-145	A-6E	NE500	HS-14	SH-3H	NE610

The wing's Marine A-6 squadron was replaced by VA-155 on its first deployment. The wing participated in *Desert Storm*, where VF-1 killed an Iraqi MI-8/17 "Hip" helo. One VA-155 A-6E was lost, along with its crew, in combat.

1 Aug 1992 to 31 Jan 1993		***Ranger***	**WPAC/IO/PG**		
VF-1	F-14A	NE100	VAW-116	E-2C	NE600
VF-2	F-14A, TARPS	NE100	VAQ-131	EA-6B	NE620
VA-155	A-6E	NE400	VS-38	S-3A	NE700
VA-145	A-6E	NE500	HS-14	SH-3H	NE610

The 1992 deployment would prove to the last one for the *Ranger*, as well as VA-155 and S-3As. It also marked the last time a Navy carrier deployed without VFA assets embarked.

27 May to 22 Jul 1993		***Constellation***	**HORN**		
VFA-151	F/A-18C	NE300	VAW-122	E-2C	(AE)600
VFA-137	F/A-18C	NE400	VS-38	S-3B	NE700
VA-145	A-6E	NE500	HS-14	SH-3H	NE610

Constellation returned from SLEP in Philadelphia with a composite CVW-2 that included *Hornets* for the first time. The E-2 squadron was formerly assigned to now-defunct CVW-6, and apparently carried no tailcode for this trip. This was VA-145's last at sea period prior to its disestablishment.

10 Nov 1994 to 10 May 1995		***Constellation***	**WP/IO/PG**		
VF-2	F-14D, TARPS	NE100	VAW-116	E-2C	NE600
VMFA-323	F/A-18C	NE200	VAQ-131	EA-6B	NE620
VFA-151	F/A-18C	NE300	VS-38	S-3B	NE700
VFA-137	F/A-18C	NE400	HS-2	SH-60F, HH-60H	NE610
VQ-5 det D	ES-3A	NE720			
VRC-30 det2	C-2A	NE			

Following completion of a major air wing reorganization, CVW-2 had a single *Tomcat* squadron and three strike-fighter units, one of which is Marine. ES-3As have arrived, as well as SH-60s.

1 Apr to 1 Oct 1997		***Constellation***	**WP/IO/PG**		
VF-2	F-14D, TARPS	NE100	VAW-116	E-2C	NE600
VMFA-323	F/A-18C	NE200	VAQ-131	EA-6B	NE620
VFA-151	F/A-18C	NE300	VS-38	S-3B	NE700
VFA-137	F/A-18C	NE400	HS-2	SH-60F, HH-60H	NE610
VQ-5 det C	ES-3A	NE720			
VRC-30 det 3	C-2A	NE			

12 May to 15 Jun 1998		***Kitty Hawk***	**Hawaii**
Jun-July 1998	*Independence*	CONUS	

In July 1998 CVW-2 headed an effort to support the transfer of *Kitty Hawk* to Japan, to become the forward deployed carrier. The rump wing that ensued provided aircraft that helped *Kitty Hawk* complete a short work-up period off San Diego, and then acompanied it to Hawaii, where the carrier was swapped for *Independence*. CVW-8 and -9 provided aircrew and aircraft, with the whole organization coming under CAG-2. The exact composition of the "wing" is uncertain, but is known to have included upgraded F-14As, F/A-18Cs, and E-2Cs, which were turned over to CVW-5. HS-2 is believed to have been the SH-60 unit involved. The group returned to CONUS in *Indy*, presumably with the older CVW-5 cast-off airframes.

18 Jun to 18 Dec 1999		***Constellation***	**WP/IO/PG**		
VF-2	F-14D, TARPS	NE100	VAW-116	E-2C	NE600
VMFA-323	F/A-18C	NE200	VS-38	S-3B	NE700
VFA-151	F/A-18C	NE300	HS-2	SH-60F, HH-60H	NE610
VFA-137	F/A-18C	NE400	VRC-30 det 3	C-2A	NE
VAQ-131	EA-6B	NE500			

The *Lancers* moved to the open 500 series for the 1999 deployment.

CVW-3 AC

Formed as Saratoga Air Group, r/d CVG-3 25 Sep 43, r/d CVAG-3 15 Nov 46, r/d CVG-3 1 Sep 48, r/d CVW-3 20 Dec 63.
Homeports: Cecil Field, Oceana (Nov 1985)
Carrier Air Wing THREE had a unique association with *Saratoga*, having been assigned to the carrier after her commissioning in 1957, and remaining with her through one Vietnam and 16 Mediterranean deployments. VF-31 remained with the wing throughout the entire period, always holding the 100 series side numbers.

Deployments:

27 Sep 1974 to 19 Mar 1975		***Saratoga***	**Med**		
VF-31	F-4J	AC100	VAW-123	E-2C	AC730
VF-103	F-4J	AC200	VS-24	S-2G	AC610
VA-37	A-7E	AC300	RVAH-11	RA-5C	AC600
VA-105	A-7E	AC400	HS-7	SH-3H	AC700
VA-75	A-6E, KA-6D	AC500			

For its 1974 Med cruise CVW-3 tested a "CV concept" configuration, with a single S-2G *Tracker* squadron attached. There were no VAQ assets on board.

6 Jan to 28 Jul 1976		***Saratoga***	**Med**		
VF-31	F-4J	AC100	VAW-123	E-2C	AC720
VF-103	F-4J	AC200	VAQ-131	EA-6B	AC604
VA-37	A-7E	AC300	VS-22	S-3A	AC610
VA-105	A-7E	AC400	HS-7	SH-3H	AC700
VA-75	A-6E, KA-6D	AC500			

In 1976 S-3s had replaced the *Trackers*, the "Vigis" were gone, and a VAQ squadron was attached. At least two sources, including "Naval Aviation News," state that a VFP-63 detachment (either det-3 or -5, depending on the source) were on this deployment, however, there is no mention of it in the squadron history or cruise book.

11 Jul to 23 Dec 1977		***Saratoga***	**Med**		
VF-31	F-4J	AC100	VAW-123	E-2C	AC720
VF-103	F-4J	AC200	VAQ-138	EA-6B	AC600
VA-37	A-7E	AC300	VS-22	S-3A	AC620
VA-105	A-7E	AC400	HS-7	SH-3H	AC700
VA-75	A-6E, KA-6D	AC500			

No recce aircraft assigned.

3 Oct 1978 to 5 Apr 1979		***Saratoga***	**Med**		
VF-31	F-4J	AC100	VAW-123	E-2C	AC010
VF-103	F-4J	AC200	VAQ-136	EA-6B	AC614
VA-37	A-7E	AC300	RVAH-12	RA-5C	AC610

The *Tophatters* are the oldest squadron in the Navy. They used their CVW-3 CAG bird (F-14A 161855) to advertise their 75th anniversary. It's shown here at Oceana on 23 Apr 1994. (Brian Rogers)

VA-105	A-7E	AC400	VS-22	S-3A	AC700
VA-75	A-6E, KA-6D	AC500	HS-7	SH-3H	AC730

After having made a cruise with no recce aircraft onboard, CVW-3 was assigned RVAH-12, which made the last Med deployment for the RA-5C.

10 Mar to 27 Aug 1980		***Saratoga***	**Med**		
VF-31	F-4J	AC100	VAW-123	E-2C	AC600
VF-103	F-4J	AC200	VS-22	S-3A	AC700
VA-37	A-7E	AC300	HS-7	SH-3H	AC001
VA-105	A-7E	AC400			
VA-75	A-6E, KA-6D	AC500			

No EW aircraft assigned. This was CVW-3's last deployment in *Saratoga*, ending a 23 year association, the longest ship/wing pairing in Navy history.

4 Jan to 14 July 1982		***John F. Kennedy***	**Med/IO**		
VF-11	F-14A	AC100	VAW-126	E-2C	AC600
VF-31	F-14A, TARPS	AC200	VAQ-138	EA-6B	AC604
VA-37	A-7E	AC300	VS-22	S-3A	AC700
VA-105	A-7E	AC400	HS-7	SH-3H	AC610
VA-75	A-6E, KA-6D	AC500			

The transfer to the *JFK* included the introduction of F-14 *Tomcats* to CVW-3. EA-6Bs returned to the air wing as well.

25 May to 1 Jul 1983		***John F. Kennedy***	**NorLant**		
27 Sep 1983 to 2 May 1984		***John F. Kennedy***	**SL/Med**		
VF-11	F-14A	AC100	VAW-126	E-2C	AC600
VF-31	F-14A, TARPS	AC200	VAQ-137	EA-6B	AC604
VA-75	A-6E, KA-6D	AC500/510	VS-22	S-3A	AC700
VA-85	A-6E	AC540/550	HS-7	SH-3H	AC610

The first "All Grumman Air Wing," with its two A-6 squadrons in lieu of any light attack (A-7) units. The ship and air wing started the deployment with a trip to Brazil, which was followed by transit to the Med. CVW-1 participated in strikes on Lebanon (4 Dec 1983), with one VA-85 A-6E being shot down.

18 Aug 1986 to 3 Mar 1987		***John F. Kennedy***	**Med**		
VF-14	F-14A	AC100	VAW-126	E-2C	AC600
VF-32	F-14A, TARPS	AC200	VAQ-140	EA-6B	AC604
VA-75	A-6E, KA-6D	AC500/510	VS-22	S-3A	AC700
VMA(AW)-533	A-6E	AC540/550	HS-7	SH-3H	AC610
Attack Det 66	A-7E	AG/AC 300			

CVW-3 was joined by a Marine A-6 squadron and "Attack det 66," which was made up of six aircraft from VA-66, which itself was disestablished as a squadron on 1 Oct 1986. The *Corsairs* were attached by AirLant to CVW-3, specifically to provide AGM-88 HARM firing platforms. Their aircraft wore CVW-7 "AG" tailcodes for at least a part of work ups. Ironically VAQ-140, who was making its first deployment, was the first EA-6B squadron cleared to fire the weapon, as well.

Note: Between 1984 and 1987 several Cecil-based units wore CVW-3's "AC" tailcodes and open 300/400 series numbers, although they were not actually assigned to the Wing. This appears to have been authorized by LatWingLant as place holders while certain squadrons (at least VA-15, -37, -105, and VFA-15, and -87) were between CVWs, transitioning, or assigned to Marine UDP in Japan (see chapter 13).

2 Aug 1988 to 1 Feb 1989		***John F. Kennedy***	**Med**		
VF-14	F-14A	AC100	VAW-126	E-2C	AC600
VF-32	F-14A, TARPS	AC200	VAQ-130	EA-6B	AC604
VA-75	A-6E, KA-6D	AC500/510	VS-22	S-3A	AC700
VMA(AW)-533	A-6E	AC540/550	HS-7	SH-3H	AC610

In what would be the final "All Grumman" deployment to the Med, CVW-3 once again took two *Intruder* squadrons and no light attack units. VF-32 *Tomcats* shot down two Libyan MiG-23 "Floggers" on 4 Jan '89. Photographic evidence exists of at least one VMA(AW)-533 Intruder wearing a 400 series side number during the Spring of 1989, which would seem to indicate that they changed modexes just prior to leaving the wing.

15 Aug 1990 to 28 Mar 1991		***John F. Kennedy***	**Med/RS**		
VF-14	F-14A	AC100	VAW-126	E-2C	AC600
VF-32	F-14A, TARPS	AC200	VAQ-130	EA-6B	AC620
VA-46	A-7E	AC300	VS-22	S-3B	AC700
VA-72	A-7E	AC400	HS-7	SH-3H	AC610
VA-75	A-6E, KA-6D	AC500			

As of the late summer of 1990 CVW-3 was operating at a reduced pace, and its two newly attached A-7E squadrons were preparing to transition to *Hornets*. The ship had made a Fourth of July trip to take part in "Fleet Week" celebrations in Boston, and major deployment was not planned for well over a year. The Iraqi invasion of Kuwait changed everything, and the wing was put back together to take part in *Desert Shield*, and what became *Desert Storm*. VAQ-130 was increased in strength to five aircraft, which required the change to the 620 series numbers. The ship and wing would perform brilliantly in combat, in what would be the last deployment for *Corsair IIs* in the Navy.

7 Oct 1992 to 7 Apr 1993			***John F. Kennedy***	**Med**	
VF-14	F-14A	AC100	VAW-126	E-2C	AC600
VF-32	F-14A, TARPS	AC200	VAQ-130	EA-6B	AC620
VFA-37	F/A-18C	AC300	VS-22	S-3B	AC700
VFA-105	F/A-18C	AC400	HS-7	SH-3H	AC610
VA-75	A-6E	AC500	VRC-40 det 1	C-2A	AC

CVW-3 became the last AirLant wing to obtain *Hornets*, in 1992.

20 Oct 1994 to 15 Apr 1995		***Dwight D. Eisenhower***	**Med/RS/PG**		
VF-32	F-14A, TARPS	AC200	VAW-126	E-2C	AC600
VFA-37	F/A-18C	AC300	VAQ-130	EA-6B	AC620
VFA-105	F/A-18C	AC400	VS-22	S-3B	AC700
VA-75	A-6E	AC500	HS-7	SH-3H	AC610
VQ-6 det C	ES-3A	AC760			
VRC-40 det 2	C-2A	AC			

After making five deployments in *Kennedy*, CVW-3 was reassigned to the IKE, beginning a cycle that would see it in five different carriers over six years. For this deployment CVW-3 lost the *Tophatters* of VF-14, who moved to CVW-8. ES-3 *Shadows* joined the wing, for the first of three cruises.

25 Nov 1996 to 22 May 1997		***Theodore Roosevelt***	**Med/RS/PG**		
VF-32	F-14A, TARPS	AC100	VAW-126	E-2C	AC600
VMFA-312	F/A-18C	AC200	VAQ-130	EA-6B	AC620
VFA-37	F/A-18C	AC300	VS-22	S-3B	AC700
VFA-105	F/A-18C	AC400	HS-7	SH-60F, HH-60H	AC610
VQ-6 det D	ES-3A	AC			
VRC-40 det 3	C-2A	AC			

The Marines joined CVW-3 for its 1996/97 deployment as VA-75 moved to CVW-17. The helo squadron has made the change to the H-60 series as well.

6 Nov 1998 to 6 May 1999		***Enterprise***	**Med/RS/PG**		
VF-32	F-14B, TARPS	AC100	VAW-126	E-2C	AC600
VMFA-312	F/A-18C	AC200	VS-22	S-3B	AC700
VFA-37	F/A-18C	AC300	HS-7	SH-60F, HH-60H	AC610
VFA-105	F/A-18C	AC400	VQ-6 det A	ES-3A	AC760
VAQ-130	EA-6B	AC500	VRC-40 det 4	C-2A	AC

CVW-3 moved to *Enterprise* for its 1998-99 cruise, while VF-32 switched to B-model *Tomcats*.

28 Nov 2000 to 23 May 2001		***Harry S Truman***	**Med/RS/PG**		
VF-32	F-14B, TARPS	AC100	VAW-126	E-2C	AC600
VMFA-312	F/A-18C	AC200	VS-22	S-3B	AC700
VFA-37	F/A-18C	AC300	HS-7	SH-60F, HH-60H	AC610
VFA-105	F/A-18C	AC400	VRC-40 det 1	C-2A	AC

VAQ-130	EA-6B	AC500

Ending a somewhat nomadic six year period, Air Wing THREE switched to the new *Truman* in late 1999, and made the carrier's first deployment in November 2000. HST was the fifth carrier the wing had been assigned to since 1993.

CVW-5 (NF)

Estab. CVG-5 15 Feb 43, r/d CVAG-5 15 Nov 46, r/d CVG-5 1 Sep 48, r/d CVW-5 20 Dec 63.

Homeport: Atsugi, Japan

Carrier Air Wing FIVE moved to Atsugi, Japan, in 1973, along with the carrier *Midway*. For the next 18 years the duo remained joined at the hip, making frequent, short deployments to the Western Pacific and Indian Ocean areas. The close association of the *Midway*/CVW-5 team achieved a level of cohesion that became legendary, while also becoming the envy of the fleet.

The ship's 1986 major yard period in Japan allowed the wing to replace its *Phantoms* and *Corsair* IIs for new *Hornets*, while also getting ICAP II *Prowlers*. This CONUS-facilitated transition also gave the wing a rare opportunity to carry out a Fallon det, with VA-115 and VAW-115 borrowing aircraft during the event.

In 1992 the *Midway* was swapped with the *Independence*, which became the Navy's "forward deployed" carrier. The move brought F-14 *Tomcats* and S-3 *Vikings* to Japan. Eight years later, "Indy" itself was replaced by *Kitty Hawk*, which retained the Air Wing's configuration.

It was not unusual for CVW-5 squadrons to swap aircraft with other air wings visiting Japan—usually those at the end of their deployments and headed home. This allowed the wing to rotate older airframes, or obtain newer versions for their use.

The short and frequent nature of CVW-5's at sea periods makes tracking of their organization rather sporting. Although many of the ship/wing's at sea periods might be considered local operations or CQ in the U.S., they were all technically WestPac ops. The three major sources consulted in making up this section differ widely, so the author has attempted to use reported at sea periods for the ship, as well as changes in the Air Wing configuration as they are known.

29 Jan to 6 Mar 1974		***Midway***
VF-161	F-4N	NF100
VF-151	F-4N	NF200
VA-93	A-7A	NF300
VA-56	A-7A	NF400
VA-115	A-6A,B KA-6D	NF500

WP		
VAW-115	E-2B	NF010
VFP-63 det 3	RF-8G	NF600
HC-1 det 2	SH-3G	NF001

CVW-5 as it deployed from CONUS to Japan, with the Marine detachment probably joining while underway. The *Corsair* squadrons were actually converted from A-7Bs back to "As" for transfer to Japan.

18 Oct to 20 Dec 1974		***Midway***
VF-161	F-4N	NF100
VF-151	F-4N	NF200
VA-93	A-7A	NF300
VA-56	A-7A	NF400
VA-115	A-6A,B KA-6D	NF500

WP		
VAW-115	E-2B	NF010/600
VMCJ-1	det101	EA-6A RM 610
VMCJ-1	det 101	RF-4B RM 600/620
HC-1 det 2	SH-3G	001/720

The Photo-*Crusader* det has returned to California, and the Iwakuni-based Marine Composite squadron VMCJ-1 is now covering both EW and reconaissaince functions.

A VA-93 *Raven* A-7E does a touch and go on *Midway* while off Japan on 18 Aug 1984. The CAG markings for NF300 (159272) are simple, consisting of the fin cap title. (Bob Lawson)

13 Jan to 18 Feb 1975		***Midway***	**WP**		
31 Mar to 29 May 1975		***Midway***	**WP**		
4 Oct to 19 Dec 1975		***Midway***	**WP/IO**		
13 Mar to 26 Apr 1976		***Midway***	**WP**		
19 May to 22 Jun 1976		***Midway***	**WP**		
9 Jul to 4 Aug 1976		***Midway***	**WP**		
1 Nov to 17 Dec 1976		***Midway***	**WP**		
11 Jan to 1 Mar 1977		***Midway***	**WP**		
19 Apr to 5 May 1977		***Midway***	**WP**		
VF-161	F-4N	NF100	VAW-115	E-2B	NF600
VF-151	F-4N	NF200	VMAQ-2 det	EA-6A	CY 620
VA-93	A-7A	NF300	VMFP-3	det	RF-4B RF610
VA-56	A-7A	NF400	HC-1 det 2	SH-3G	NF720
VA-115	A-6A,B KA-6D	NF500			

Following the 1975 reorganization of Marine Composite squadrons, the photo and EW dets became separate squadrons. VMAQ-2 and VMFP-3 took over the duties previously held by VMCJ-1.

8 Aug to 2 Sep 1977		***Midway***	**WP**		
VF-161	F-4N/J	NF100	VAW-115	E-2B	NF600
VF-151	F-4N/J	NF200	VMAQ-2 det	EA-6A	CY 620
VA-93	A-7A	NF300	VMFP-3	det	RF-4B RF610
VA-56	A-7A	NF400	HC-1 det 2	SH-3G	NF720
VA-115	A-6E KA-6D	NF500			

As documented by the Naval History Office, the wing's FITRONS go to sea during conversion between N and J model *Phantoms*. VA-115 has re-equipped with A-6Es as well.

27 Sep to 21 Dec 1977		***Midway***	**WP/IO**		
11 Apr to 23 May 1978		***Midway***	**WP**		
9 Nov to 23 Dec 1978		***Midway***	**WP**		
11 Jan 1979 to 20 Feb 1979		***Midway***	**WP**		
7 Apr to 18 Jun 1979		***Midway***	**WP/IO**		
20 Aug to 14 Sep 1979		***Midway***	**WP**		
30 Sep 1979 to 20 Feb 1980		***Midway***	**WP/IO**		
VF-161	F-4J	NF100	VAW-115	E-2B	NF600
VF-151	F-4J	NF200	VMAQ-2 det	EA-6B	CY620
VA-93	A-7E	NF300	VMFP-3	det	RF-4B RF610
VA-56	A-7E	NF400	HC-1 det 2	SH-3G	NF720
VA-115	A-6E, KA-6D	NF500			

During 1977-78 *Midway* and CVW-5 went through a transition that saw the replacement of every jet in the wing. The fighter squadrons upgraded to F-4Js, the light attack units received A-7Es, and the *Arabs* converted to A-6Es. VMAQ-2 replaced its EA-6As with EA-6Bs in Sep 1978.

14 Jul to 26 Nov 1980		***Midway***	**WP/IO**		
VF-161	F-4J	NF100	VAW-115	E-2B	NF600
VF-151	F-4J	NF200	VAQ-136	EA-6B	NF620
VA-93	A-7E	NF300	VMFP-3	det	RF-4B RF610/110
VA-56	A-7E	NF400	HC-1 det 2	SH-3G	NF720
VA-115	A-6E, KA-6D	NF500			

The *Gauntlets* of VAQ-136 joined CVW-5 in Feb 1980, replacing the Marine detachment.

23 Feb to 5 Jun 1981	***Midway***	**WP/IO**
26 Jun to 16 Jul 1981	***Midway***	**WP**
3 Sep to 6 Oct 1981	***Midway***	**WP**
26 Apr to 18 Jun 1982	***Midway***	**WP**
14 Sep to 11 Dec 1982	***Midway***	**WP/IO/NorPac**

2 Jun to 8 Aug 1983		***Midway***	**WP**		
25 Oct to 11 Dec 1983		***Midway***	**WP**		
28 Dec to 23 May 1984		***Midway***	**WP/IO**		
VF-161	F-4S	NF100	VAW-115	E-2B	NF600
VF-151	F-4S	NF200	VAQ-136	EA-6B	NF620/604
VA-93	A-7E	NF300	VMFP-3 det	RF-4B	RF110
VA-56	A-7E	NF400	HC-1 det 2	SH-3G	NF720/610
VA-115	A-6E,KA-6D	NF500			

Six years after getting F-4Js, VF-151 and -161 upgraded again, to F-4Ss. VAQ-136 and HC-1 are reported to have changed sidenumbers in August '81 and December '82, respectively.

15 Oct to 12 Dec 1984		***Midway***	**WP**		
1 Feb to 28 Mar 1985		***Midway***	**WP**		
VF-161	F-4S	NF100	VAW-115	E-2B	NF600
VF-151	F-4S	NF200	VAQ-136	EA-6B	NF604
VA-93	A-7E	NF300	HS-12	SH-3H	NF610
VA-56	A-7E	NF400			
VA-115	A-6E,KA-6D	NF500			

The *Wyverns* of HS-12 joined CVW-5 in August 1984, replacing the HC-1 det.

10 Jun to 14 Oct 1985		***Midway***	**WP/IO**		
15 Nov to 12 Dec 1985		***Midway***	**WP**		
17 Jan to 30 Mar 1986		***Midway***	**WP**		
VF-161	F-4S	NF100	VAW-115	E-2C	NF600
VF-151	F-4S	NF200	VAQ-136	EA-6B	NF604
VA-93	A-7E	NF300	HS-12	SH-3H	NF610
VA-56	A-7E	NF400			
VA-115	A-6E,KA-6D	NF500			

VAW-115 retired the regular Navy's last E-2Bs in early 1985 and gained E-2Cs.

9 Jan 1987 to 20 Mar 1987		***Midway***	**WP**		
23 Apr 1987 to 13 Jul 1987		***Midway***	**WP**		
VFA-195	F/A-18A	NF100 (400)	VAW-115	E-2C	NF600
VFA-151	F/A-18A	NF200	VAQ-136	EA-6B	NF604
VFA-192	F/A-18A	NF300	HS-12	SH-3H	NF610
VA-115	A-6E, KA-6D	NF500			

CVW-5 takes advantage of an extended shipyard period by *Midway* to reequip with *Hornets*, with VFA-192, -195, and -151 bringing the new aircraft over from CONUS in November 1986. Its new form is as a modified *Coral Sea* air wing, with a single A-6 and three F/A-18 squadrons. VFA-195 arrived with 400 series numbers, and moved to the open 100 series. Long-serving Japan squadrons VF-161, VA-93, and VA-56 have returned to CONUS, the *Rock Rivers* getting *Hornets*, with the two Atkrons being disestablished.

15 Oct 1987 to 12 Apr 1988		***Midway***	**WP/IO**		
18 Oct 1988 to 9 Nov 1988		***Midway***	**WP**		
21 Jan 1989 to 24 Feb 1989		***Midway***	**WP**		
27 Feb 1989 to 9 Apr 1989		***Midway***	**WP**		
31 May to 25 Jul 1989		***Midway***	**WP**		
15 Aug to 11 Dec 1989		***Midway***	**WP/IO**		
25 Jan to 6 Apr 1990		***Midway***	**WP**		
2 Oct 1990 to 17 Apr 1991		***Midway***	**WP/IO/PG**	***Desert Storm***	
VFA-195	F/A-18A	NF100	VAW-115	E-2C	NF600
VFA-151	F/A-18A	NF200	VAQ-136	EA-6B	NF604
VFA-192	F/A-18A	NF300	HS-12	SH-3H	NF610
VA-185	A-6E, KA-6D	NF400			
VA-115	A-6E, KA-6D	NF500			

The *Nighthawks* of VA-185 arrived in mid-1987, with the result of having two small (nine aircraft) *Intruder* units and three *Hornet* squadrons. This was the configuration the wing took into *Desert Storm*, where it became the only wing to make it through the war without losing a single aircraft to either combat or operational mishap.

10 to 22 Aug 1991 ***Midway***		**Hawaii**			
VFA-195	F/A-18A	NF100	VAW-115	E-2C	NF600
VFA-151	F/A-18A	NF200	VAQ-136	EA-6B	NF604
VFA-192	F/A-18A	NF300	HS-12	SH-3H	NF610
VA-115	A-6E, KA-6D	NF500			

Midway's first significant at sea period following *Desert Storm* involved the return of the *Midway* to the United States. The ship and air wing met *Independence*/CVW-14 in Pearl Harbor, Hawaii, where they swapped portions of their air wings. *Midway* continued east with CVW-14, and "Indy" proceeded to Japan with CVW-5 as the Navy's new forward deployed carrier. VA-185 was disestablished about a week prior to this effort, with VA-115 largely absorbing its aircraft and personnel.

28 Aug to 11 Sep 1991		***Independence***	**transit to Japan**		
VF-154	F-14A, TARPS	NF100	VAW-115	E-2C	NF600
VF-21	F-14A	NF200	VAQ-136	EA-6B	NF620
VFA-192	F/A-18C	NF300	VS-21	S-3B	NF700
VFA-195	F/A-18C	NF400	HS-12	SH-3H	NF610
VA-115	A-6E	NF500			

CVW-5 headed back to Japan with its new carrier, as well as F-14 and S-3 squadrons, the wing finally getting a standard 2VF/2VFA/1VA(M) configuration. VFA-192 and -195 traded *Hornets* with CVW-14's units, getting C-models in the deal. Former wing member VFA-151 returned to California with *Midway*. VA-115 also used the event to send its last KA-6Ds home.

15 Apr to 13 Oct 1992		***Independence***	**WP/IO/PG**		
15 Feb to 25 Mar 1993		***Independence***	**WP**		
11 May to 1 Jul 1993		***Independence***	**WP**		
17 Nov 1993 to 17 Mar 1994		***Independence***	**WP/IO/PG**		
19 Jul to 29 Aug 1994		***Independence***	**WP**		
VF-154	F-14A, TARPS	NF100	VAW-115	E-2C	NF600
VF-21	F-14A	NF200	VAQ-136	EA-6B	NF620
VFA-192	F/A-18C	NF300	VS-21	S-3B	NF700
VFA-195	F/A-18C	NF400	HS-12	SH-3H	NF610
VA-115	A-6E	NF500			

19 Aug to 18 Nov 1995		***Independence***	**WP/IO/PG**		
VF-154	F-14A, TARPS	NF100	VAW-115	E-2C	NF600
VF-21	F-14A	NF200	VAQ-136	EA-6B	NF620
VFA-192	F/A-18C	NF300	VS-21	S-3B	NF700
VFA-195	F/A-18C	NF400	VQ-5 det 5	ES-3A	NF720
VA-115	A-6E	NF500	HS-14	SH-3H	NF610

HS-14 becomes CVW-5's helicopter unit, replacing HS-12, while also bringing new H-60s onboard. ES-3A *Shadows* joined CVW-5 as a permanent det in Atsugi.

5 Mar to 24 Mar 1996		***Independence***	**WP**		
VF-154	F-14A, TARPS	NF100	VAW-115	E-2C	NF600
VF-21	F-14A	NF200	VAQ-136	EA-6B	NF620
VFA-192	F/A-18C	NF300	VS-21	S-3B	NF700
VFA-195	F/A-18C	NF400	VQ-5 det 5	ES-3A	NF720
VA-115	A-6E	NF500	HS-14	SH-60F, HH-60H	NF610
VRC-30 det	C-2A	NF430			

A VRC-30 detachment, now assigned directly to the air wing, replaces VRC-50 support.

15 Feb to 10 Jun 1997		***Independence***	**WP**		
23 Jan to 6 Jun 1998		***Independence***	**WP/IO/PG**		
VF-154	F-14A, TARPS	NF100	VAW-115	E-2C	NF600
VFA-27	F/A-18C	NF200	VAQ-136	EA-6B	NF620
VFA-192	F/A-18C	NF300	VS-21	S-3B	NF700
VFA-195	F/A-18C	NF400	VQ-5 det 5	ES-3A	NF
HS-14	SH-60F, HH-60H	NF610			
VRC-30 det 5	C-2A	NF430			

CVW-5 loses one of its F-14 squadrons (VF-21 being disestablished) and VA-115 (moved to Lemoore for conversion to *Hornets*), while gaining another Strike-Fighter outfit, VFA-27. During the early 1998 period in the Persian Gulf, VAQ-136 was augmented with a pair of VAQ-138 EA-6Bs (NG 620 series) that cross-decked from *Nimitz* prior to its departure for home.

July 1998	***Independence***	**Hawaii**
July 1998	***Kitty Hawk***	**Japan**

Independence and CVW-5 travel to Hawaii to swap out as the forward deployed carrier with *Kitty Hawk*. They meet the *Hawk*, which is carrying a composite wing headed by CVW-2, made up largely of newer airframes bound for CVW-5. Unfortunately, specifics of this event are not well documented.

2 Mar to 25 Aug 1999		***Kitty Hawk***	**WP/IO/PG**		
11 Apr to 5 Jun 2000		***Kitty Hawk***	**WP**		
26 Sep to 20 Nov 2000		***Kitty Hawk***	**WP**		
VF-154	F-14A, TARPS	NF100	VAW-115	E-2C	NF600
VFA-27	F/A-18C	NF200	VS-21	S-3B	NF700
VFA-192	F/A-18C	NF300	HS-14	SH-60F, HH-60H	NF610
VFA-195	F/A-18C	NF400	VRC-30 det 5	C-2A	NF430
VAQ-136	EA-6B	NF500			

CVW-5 resumes its pattern of frequent ops throughout the Western Pacific and IO with its new carrier, the only significant change for the Air Wing being the movement of the *Prowler* squadron to the open 500 series during this period.

CVW-6 AE

Established CVG-17 1 Jan 43, r/d CVBG-17 22 Jan 46, r/d CVBG-5 15 Nov 46, r/d CVG-6 27 Jul 48,
r/d CVW-6 20 Dec 63, disestab. 1 Apr 92 Homeport: Oceana

Carrier Air Wing SIX began the post-Vietnam period on the smallest attack carrier in the Atlantic Fleet, with what was undoubtedly the oldest collection of aircraft, as well. Although assigned to the new CVAN *Enterprise* in 1962, after 1964 CVW-6 would never be paired with a nuke boat again. The wing made only one sustained combat deployment to Vietnam (in 1968), and participated in action in Grenada and Lebanon before becoming the only "old" (pre-1974) air wing to be disestablished in the post-*Desert Storm* drawdown.

14 Sep 1973 to 17 Mar 1974		*Franklin D. Roosevelt*	Med		
VF-41	F-4B	AE100	VAW-121	E-1B	AE 710
VA-15	A-7B	AE300	VFP-63	det 2	RF-8G AE600
VA-87	A-7B	AE400	HC-2 det	SH-3G	HU00
VA-176	A-6A,C, KA-6D	AE500			

VS-28 S-3A AE700 (159764) displays an obvious lack of CAG markings, as there is nothing showing in this view at Alameda on 19 Mar '83 to match its "double nuts" side number. Capt Jerry Breast, the title painted under the co-pilot's window, was actually CO of the *Independence* at that time. CAG "Hunyak" Andrews' name is probably on the other side. (Michael Grove)

As of January 1974, CVW-6 was making its fourth cruise in "Rosey" since 1969. Their 1973-74 deployment featured only one large (18 airframes) fighter unit in an AirLant experiment to determine if a single, larger VF was more efficient than two. VF-84 was beached, and contributed aircraft, aircrew, and personnel to a larger VF-41, with roughly half staying in Oceana for the duration of cruise. VF-41 had reverted from F-4Js to older F-4Bs for this deployment as well, probably due to a war enduced shortage of "J" airframes.

3 Jan to 16 Jul 1975		***Franklin D. Roosevelt***	**Med**		
VF-41	F-4N	AE100	VAW-121	E-1B	AE710
VF-84	F-4N	AE200	VFP-63 det 2	RF-8G	AE620
VA-15	A-7B	AE300	HC-2 det	SH-3G	HU00
VA-87	A-7B	AE400			
VA-176	A-6A,C, KA-6D	AE500			

VF-84 returned to CVW-6, and converted with VF-41 to F-4Ns for the 1975 deployment. This would be VAW-121's last trip with E-1B *Tracers*, as they would soon convert to E-2 *Hawkeyes*. West Coast RVAW-110 would replace them on Rosey's next deployment, with CVW-19.

15 Apr to 25 Oct 1976		***America***	**Med**		
VF-143	F-14A	AE100	VAW-124	E-2C	AE720
VF-142	F-14A	AE200	VAQ-137	EA-6B	AE700
VA-15	A-7E	AE300	VS-28	S-3A	AE600
VA-87	A-7E	AE400	VFP-63 det 5	RF-8G	AE710
VA-176	A-6E, KA-6D	AE500	HS-15	SH-3D	AE000

Air Wing SIX got a complete makeover when it transferred to the "big deck" *America* in 1975/76. New *Tomcats*, *Prowlers*, and *Vikings* arrived, while the Attack Squadrons received more advanced versions of their aircraft.

10 Jun to 19 Jul 1977		***America***	**SoLant**		
VF-143	F-14A	AE100	VAW-124	E-2C	AE720
VF-142	F-14A	AE200	VAQ-137	EA-6B	AE700
VA-15	A-7E	AE300	VS-28	S-3A	AE600
VA-87	A-7E	AE400	VFP-63 det 5	RF-8G	AE710
VA-176	A-6E, KA-6D	AE500	HS-15	SH-3D	AE000

25 Sep 1977 to 25 Apr 1978		***America***	**Med**		
VF-143	F-14A	AE100	VAW-124	E-2C	AE720
VF-142	F-14A	AE200	VAQ-137	EA-6B	AE700
VA-15	A-7E	AE300	VS-28	S-3A	AE600
VA-87	A-7E	AE400	HS-15	SH-3D	AE000
VA-176	A-6E, KA-6D	AE500			

Other than the loss of the VFP-63 det, CVW-6 remains essentially unchaged over two major deployments.

28 Jun to 14 Dec 1979		***Independence***	**Med**		
VF-102	F-4J	AE100	VAW-122	E-2C	AE720
VF-33	F-4J	AE200	VAQ-130	EA-6B	AE700
VA-15	A-7E	AE300	VS-28	S-3A	AE600
VA-87	A-7E	AE400	HS-15	SH-3H	AE000
VA-176	A-6E, KA-6D	AE500			

In 1978 CVW-6 moved to the *Independence*, and reverted to F-4 *Phantom IIs* to match that ship's intermediate level maintenance capability. Once again, no VFP det is assigned.

19 Nov 1980 to 19 Jun 1981		***Independence***	**Med/IO**		
VF-102	F-4J	AE100	VAW-122	E-2C	AE720
VF-33	F-4J	AE200	VAQ-131	EA-6B	AE700
VA-15	A-7E	AE300	VFP-63 det 4	RF-8G	AE616
VA-87	A-7E	AE400	VS-28	S-3A	AE600
VA-176	A-6E, KA-6D	AE500	HS-15	SH-3H	AE610

This would be the final Med deployment for the RF-8 *Crusaders*, as well as the last for F-4s in the wing.

7 Jun to 22 Dec 1982		***Independence***	**Med**		
VF-14	F-14A	AE100	VAW-122	E-2C	AE600
VF-32	F-14A, TARPS	AE200	VAQ-131	EA-6B	AE604
VA-15	A-7E	AE300	VS-28	S-3A	AE700
VA-87	A-7E	AE400	HS-15	SH-3H	AE610
VA-176	A-6E, KA-6D	AE500			

F-14s return to CVW-6, with two squadrons transferring from CVW-1. TARPS F-14As have replaced the Photo-*Crusaders*.

18 Oct 1983 to 11 Apr 1984		***Independence***	**Carib/Med/NL**		
VF-14	F-14A	AE100	VAW-122	E-2C	AE600
VF-32	F-14A, TARPS	AE200	VAQ-131	EA-6B	AE604
VA-15	A-7E	AE300	VS-28	S-3A	AE700
VA-87	A-7E	AE400	HS-15	SH-3H	AE610
VA-176	A-6E, KA-6D	AE500			

CVW-6 Participated in combat operations in Grenada and Lebanon, the latter with loss of one VA-15 A-7E.

16 Oct 1984 to 19 Feb 1985		***Independence***	**Med/RS/IO**		
VF-14	F-14A	AE100	VAW-122	E-2C	AE600
VF-32	F-14A, TARPS	AE200	VAQ-131	EA-6B	AE604
VA-15	A-7E	AE300	VS-28	S-3A	AE700
VA-87	A-7E	AE400	HS-15	SH-3H	AE610
VA-176	A-6E, KA-6D	AE500			

After only six months home the *Indy*/CVW-6 team returned to the Med, while visiting the Red Sea and IO as well.

2 Jun to 10 Nov 1986		***Forrestal***	**Med**		
VF-11	F-14A	AE100	VAW-122	E-2C	AE600
VF-31	F-14A, TARPS	AE200	VAQ-132	EA-6B	AE604
VA-37	A-7E	AE300	VS-28	S-3A	AE700
VA-105	A-7E	AE400	HS-15	SH-3H	AE610
VA-176	A-6E, KA-6D	AE500			

Air Wing SIX changed carriers again in 1986, to *Forrestal*, with which it made its final four deployments. This would be the FID's first deployment with F-14s. New VA(L) and VAQ units have also come aboard.

26 Aug to 9 Oct 1987		***Forrestal***	**NorLant**		
25 Apr to 7 Oct 1988		***Forrestal***	**Med/IO/NorLant**		
VF-11	F-14A	AE100	VAW-122	E-2C	AE600
VF-31	F-14A, TARPS	AE200	VAQ-132	EA-6B	AE604
VA-37	A-7E	AE300	VS-28	S-3A	AE700
VA-105	A-7E	AE400	HS-15	SH-3H	AE610
VA-176	A-6E, KA-6D	AE500			

CVW-17 made both a NorLant and Med deployment over a two year period. It was joined in the Med by a pair of S-3Bs from VX-1 (along with crews from VS-27) as part of an eval to test the new aircraft in an operational environment.

4 Nov 1989 to 12 Apr 1990		***Forrestal***	**Med**		
VF-11	F-14A	AE100	VAW-122	E-2C	AE600
VF-31	F-14A, TARPS	AE200	VAQ-142	EA-6B	AE604
VA-37	A-7E	AE300	VS-28	S-3A	AE700
VA-105	A-7E	AE400	HS-15	SH-3H	AE610
VA-176	A-6E, KA-6D	AE500			

FID's 1989 deployment was delayed about a month to repair damage from an electrical fire that occurred on 9 Oct. An otherwise routine Med deployment was notable as VAQ-142's one and only deployment. The light attack units were making what was originally planned to be their final deployments, as they were scheduled for disestablishment. *Desert Storm* changed things though, and VA-37 and -105 received *Hornets* after cruise, and CVW-1's VA-46 and -72 were shut down instead.

30 May to 21 Dec 1991		***Forrestal***	**Med**		
VF-11	F-14A	AE100	VAW-122	E-2C	AE600
VF-31	F-14A, TARPS	AE200	VAQ-133	EA-6B	AE620
VFA-132	F/A-18A	AE300	VS-28	S-3B	AE700
VFA-137	F/A-18A	AE400	HS-15	SH-3H	AE610
VA-176	A-6E, KA-6D	AE500			

The final deployment for both CVW-6 and *Forrestal*. Too late to take part in *Desert Storm*, the ship and air wing participated in Operation *Provide Comfort*, flying post-war support missions over Northern Iraq. The cruise would be highlighted by a *Steeljaw* E-2C that would suffer an inflight fire on 8 July off Turkey. The crew of five bailed out, and air wing aircraft subsequently shot it down via a VFA-132 *Hornet*. The wing would be disestablished on 1 Apr 1992. This trip marked the final deployments for VFA-132, VA-176, VAW-122, VS-28, and VAQ-133.

CVW-7 AG

Estab. CVG-18 20 Jul 43, r/d CVAG-7 15 Nov 46, r/d CVG-7 1 Sep 48, r/d CVW-7 20 Dec 63.
Homeport: NAS Oceana, VA

21 Jun 1973 to 19 Jan 1974		***Independence***	**Med**		
VF-102	F-4J	AG100	VAW-122	E-2B	AG720
VF-33	F-4J	AG200	RVAH-14	RA-5C	AG600
VA-66	A-7E	AG300	VAQ-130	EKA-3B	AG610 det 1
VA-12	A-7E	AG400	VS-28	S-2E	AG920
VA-65	A-6E, KA-6D	AG500	HS-5	SH-3D	AG800

S-2s deployed with CVW-7, although they would spend four months of cruise working from the beach out of Souda Bay, Crete. The EKA-3B det was cross-decked to Indy mid-cruise from *JFK*/CVW-1, apparently in order to keep some EW capability deployed during Mid-East tensions. It would be the last EKA-3B deployment to the Med.

19 Jul 1974 to 21 Jan 1975		***Independence***	**Med**		
VF-102	F-4J	AG100	VAW-122	E-2B	AG720
VF-33	F-4J	AG200	VAQ-132	EA-6B	AG700
VA-66	A-7E	AG300	RVAH-9	RA-5C	AG600
VA-12	A-7E	AG400	VS-31	S-2G	AG920/930
VA-65	A-6E, KA-6D	AG500	HS-5	SH-3D	AG800

S-2s returned for the 1974/75 deployment, and EA-6Bs joined the air wing for the first time.

A section of *Pukin Dogs* from VF-143 fly over the Fallon range for Bob Lawson's camera on 19 May 1987. AG100 has some color befitting their CAG bird, while -101 displays the subdued markings the rest of the unit's *Tomcats* wore at that time.

15 Oct 1975 to 5 May 1976		***Independence***	**NorLant/Med**		
VF-102	F-4J	AG100	VAW-117	E-2B	AG770
VF-33	F-4J	AG200	VAQ-132	EA-6B	AG710
VA-66	A-7E	AG300	RVAH-13	RA-5C	AG600
VA-12	A-7E	AG400	HS-5	SH-3D	AG800
VA-65	A-6E, KA-6D	AG500			

CVW-7 lost its VS squadron, returning to a "classic" '70s era air wing configuration. A west coast AEW unit (VAW-117) joined the wing.

31 Mar to 21 Oct 1977		***Independence***	**Med**		
VF-102	F-4J	AG100	VAW-117	E-2B	AG600
VF-33	F-4J	AG200	RVAH-12	RA-5C	AG610
VA-66	A-7E	AG300	VAQ-136	EA-6B	AG614
VA-12	A-7E	AG400	VS-31	S-3A	AG700
VA-65	A-6E, KA-6D	AG500	HS-5	SH-3D	AG730

Vigilantes made their last appearance in the Med, with RVAH-12. VAQ-136's Standard-version EA-6Bs were the last of their sub-variant to deploy. S-3s joined the air wing in the form of VS-31.

16 Jan to 13 Jul 1979		***Eisenhower***	**Med**		
VF-143	F-14A	AG100	VAW-121	E-2C	AG010
VF-142	F-14A	AG200	VAQ-138	EA-6B	AG600
VA-66	A-7E	AG300	VS-31	S-3A	AG700
VA-12	A-7E	AG400	HS-5	SH-3D	AG730
VA-65	A-6E, KA-6D	AG500			

The new nuclear carrier *Dwight D. Eisenhower* made its first deployment with CVW-7 embarked, which would be the first of ten cruises over the next twelve years for the pair. The *Phantoms* were traded for F-14s, and E-2Cs arrived.

15 Apr to 22 Dec 1980		***Eisenhower***	**IO**		
VF-143	F-14A	AG100	VAW-121	E-2C	AG010
VF-142	F-14A	AG200	VAQ-132	EA-6B	AG610
VA-66	A-7E	AG300	VS-31	S-3A	AG700
VA-12	A-7E	AG400	HS-5	SH-3H	AG730
VA-65	A-6E, KA-6D	AG500			

Ike made this Indian Ocean deployment via the Cape of Good Hope due to political concerns (later overcome) by the Egyptians about putting a nuclear carrier in the Suez Canal. The ship spent 247 of its 253 deployed days underway. VAQ-132 has replaced VAQ-138, but otherwise the wing remains the same.

20 Aug to 7 Oct 1981		***Eisenhower***	**NorLant**		
VF-143	F-14A	AG100	VAW-121	E-2C	AG600
VF-142	F-14A	AG200	VAQ-132	EA-6B	AG604
VA-66	A-7E	AG300	VS-31	S-3A	AG700
VA-12	A-7E	AG400	HS-5	SH-3H	AG730
VA-65	A-6E, KA-6D	AG500			

5 Jan to 13 Jul 1982		***Eisenhower***	**Med**		
VF-143	F-14A TARPS	AG100	VAW-121	E-2C	AG600
VF-142	F-14A	AG200	VAQ-132	EA-6B	AG604
VA-66	A-7E	AG300	VS-31	S-3A	AG700
VA-12	A-7E	AG400	HS-5	SH-3H	AG730
VA-65	A-6E, KA-6D	AG500			

After going almost five years without photo-recon capability, CVW-7 deploys with the TARPS system in VF-143's *Tomcats*.

27 Apr to 2 Dec 1983		***Eisenhower***	**Med**		
VF-143	F-14A TARPS	AG100	VAW-121	E-2C	AG600
VF-142	F-14A	AG200	VAQ-132	E-2C	AG604
VA-66	A-7E	AG300	VS-31	S-3A	AG700

VA-12	A-7E	AG400	HS-5	SH-3	AG610
VA-65	A-6E, KA-6D	AG500			

8 May to 20 Jun 1984		***Eisenhower***	**NorLant**		
10 Oct 1984 to 8 May 1985		***Eisenhower***	**Med**		
VF-143	F-14A TARPS	AG100	VAW-121	E-2C	AG600
VF-142	F-14A	AG200	VAQ-132	EA-6B	AG604
VA-66	A-7E	AG300	VS-31	S-3A	AG700
VA-12	A-7E	AG400	HS-5	SH-3H	AG610
VA-65	A-6E, KA-6D	AG500			

The 1985 deployment would mark almost six years where CVW-7 would be assigned to *Eisenhower* with the same configuration and squadrons.

29 Feb to 29 Aug 1988		***Eisenhower***	**Med**		
VF-143	F-14A, TARPS	AG100	VAW-121	E-2C	AG600
VF-142	F-14A	AG200	VAQ-140	EA-6B	AG604
VA-46	A-7E	AG300	VS-31	S-3A	AG700
VA-72	A-7E	AG400	HS-5	SH-3H	AG610
VA-34	A-6E, KA-6D	AG500			

CVW-7 changed out its Atkrons, as East Coast community transitions and squadron movements influenced other wings.

8 Mar to 12 Sep 1990		***Eisenhower***	**Med/RS**		
VF-143	F-14A+, TARPS	AG100	VAW-121	E-2C	AG600
VF-142	F-14A+	AG200	VAQ-140	EA-6B	AG604
VFA-136	F/A-18A	AG300	VS-31	S-3B	AG700
VFA-131	F/A-18A	AG400	HS-5	SH-3H	AG610
VA-34	A-6E, KA-6D	AG500			

The air wing upgraded with F-14A+ (later redesignated F-14B) and S-3Bs, and made the first deployment with those types. Two *Hornet* squadrons replaced the A-7s as well. During this deployment the ship and CVW participated in *Desert Shield.*

26 Sep 1991 to 2 Apr 1992		***Eisenhower***	**Med/RS/PG**		
VF-143	F-14B, TARPS	AG100	VAW-121	E-2C	AG600
VF-142	F-14B	AG200	VAQ-140	EA-6B	AG604
VFA-136	F/A-18C	AG300	VS-31	S-3B	AG700
VFA-131	F/A-18C	AG400	HS-5	SH-3H	AG610
VA-34	A-6E, KA-6D	AG500			

Other than the two Strike Fighter units reequipping with "C" Models, the wing retained its previous organization.

20 May to 17 Nov 1994		***George Washington***	**Med/NorLant**		
VF-143	F-14B, TARPS	AG100	VAW-121	E-2C	AG600
VF-142	F-14B	AG200	VAQ-140	EA-6B	AG620
VFA-136	F/A-18C	AG300	VS-31	S-3B	AG700
VFA-131	F/A-18C	AG400	HS-5	SH-3H	AG610
VA-34	A-6E	AG500	VQ-6 det B	ES-3A	AG760

ES-3As joined CVW-7 as the wing moved to the new carrier *George Washington.* Among other activities was participation in the 50th anniversary commemoration of the D-Day landings at Normandy, where the wing painted several aircraft with ceremonial black and white "invasion stripes."

26 Jan to 23 Jul 1996		***George Washington***	**Med/RS/PG**		
VF-143	F-14B, TARPS	AG100	VAW-121	E-2C	AG600
VFA-136	F/A-18C	AG300	VAQ-140	EA-6B	AG620
VFA-131	F/A-18C	AG400	VS-31	S-3B	AG700
VA-34	A-6E	AG500	HS-5	SH-60F, HH-60H	AG610
			VQ-6 det B	ES-3A	AG760

With the *Ghostriders* of VF-142 gone, CVW-7 deployed with a large, single F-14B squadron.

26 Feb to 26 Aug 1998		***John C. Stennis***	**World**		
VF-143	F-14B, TARPS	AG100	VAW-121	E-2C	AG600
VF-11	F-14B	AG200	VS-31	S-3B	AG700
VFA-136	F/A-18C	AG300	HS-5	SH-60F, HH-60H	AG610
VFA-131	F/A-18C	AG400	VQ-6 det C	ES-3A	AG760
VAQ-140	EA-6B	AG500	VRC-40 det 2	C-2A	AG

Stennis moved to her new California homeport via the Med, Red Sea, Persian Gulf, and Pacific Ocean. A second *Tomcat* squadron returned to round out CVW-7, and VAQ-140 became the first *Prowler* squadron to move to the open 500 series.

18 Feb to 18 Aug 2000		***Eisenhower***	**Med/PG**		
VF-143	F-14B, TARPS	AG100	VAW-121	E-2C	AG600
VF-11	F-14B	AG200	VS-31	S-3B	AG700
VFA-136	F/A-18C	AG300	HS-5	SH-60F, HH-60H	AG610
VFA-131	F/A-18C	AG400	VRC-40 det 3	C-2A	
VAQ-140	EA-6B	AG500			

CVW-7 returned to the Ike to end the decade. The wing dropped ordnance on Iraq as part of *Southern* Watch on 6 Jun 2000, becoming the first aircraft to ever engage an enemy from *Eisenhower*.

CVW-8 AJ

Estab. CVG-8 9 Apr 51, r/d CVW-8 20 Dec 1963.

Homeport: Oceana

3 Jan to 3 Aug 1974		***America***	**Med**		
VF-143	F-4J	AJ100	VAW-124	E-2B	AJ740
VF-142	F-4J	AJ200	RVAH-1	RA-5C	AJ600
VA-82	A-7C	AJ300	VAQ-133	EA-6B	AJ610
VA-86	A-7C	AJ400	HC-2 det 66	SH-3G	AJ000
VA-35	A-6E, KA-6D	AJ500			

Pacific Fleet F-4 squadrons joined *America* and CVW-8 for their 1974 Med deployment. VAQ-133 made the first EA-6B cruise in the Med, as well. VA-82 and -86 were the only squadrons to ever deploy with the A-7C version.

6 Sep to 12 Oct 1974		***America***	**NorLant**		
VF-213	F-4J	NH100	VAW-126	E-2B	AA760
VF-103	F-4J	AC200	RVAH-1	RA-5C	AJ600
VA-82	A-7C	AJ300	VMCJ-1 det B	EA-6A	CY620
VA-86	A-7C	AJ400	HC-2 det 66	SH-3G	AJ000
VA-35	A-6E, KA-6D	AJ500			

About a month after returning home from the Med, the *America*/CVW-8 team made a trip to the Northern Atlantic with an unusual assortment of squadrons, including three from other airwings, and a Marine EW detachment. This would be the final sustained at sea period for the A-7C *Corsair II*.

VA-65's CAG bird, AJ500 (161675), is prepared for launch on TR while deployed in the Red Sea during the post *Desert Storm* period on 4 Apr 1991. It was the only *Tiger* aircraft that wore the squadron's trademark orange paint at that time. (author)

16 Jul to 24 Sep 1975		*Nimitz*	**Carib/NorLant**		
VF-31	F-4J	AC100	VAW-116	E-2B	AJ710
VMFA-333	F-4J	AJ120/130	VAQ-130	EA-6B	AJ610
VA-82	A-7E	AJ300	HS-15	SH-3D	AJ000
VA-86	A-7E	AJ400			
VA-35	A-6E, KA-6D	AJ500			

CVW-8 made *Nimitz's* first major underway period away from Conus with another curious mix of squadrons, including F-4J units from CVW-3 and the Marines, as well as a West Coast E-2 unit. VAQ-130 was making its first deployment as a *Prowler* unit. This at sea period was also part of *Nimitz's* shakedown routine, which marks one of the few times this kind of post-construction activity entailed an overseas deployment.

7 Jul 1976 to 7 Feb 1977		*Nimitz*	**Med**		
VMFA-333	F-4J	AJ100	VAW-116	E-2B	AJ010
VF-74	F-4J	AJ200	RVAH-9	RA-5C	AJ600
VA-82	A-7E	AJ300	VAQ-130	EA-6B	AJ610
VA-86	A-7E	AJ400	HC-2 det	SH-3G	HU
VA-35	A-6E, KA-6D	AJ500			

Nimitz's first Med deployment was made with a Marine F-4 unit, as well as a West Coast E-2 squadron. This would be the only six-month (or longer) deployment for a *Nimitz* class ship with *Phantom IIs* onboard.

1 Dec 1977 to 20 Jul 1978		*Nimitz*	**Med/NorLant**		
VF-41	F-14A	AJ100	VAW-112	E-2B	AJ010
VF-84	F-14A	AJ200	RVAH-6	RA-5C	AJ600
VA-82	A-7E	AJ300	VAQ-135	EA-6B	AJ610
VA-86	A-7E	AJ400	VS-24	S-3A	AJ700
VA-35	A-6E, KA-6D	AJ500	HS-9	SH-3D	AJ730

For *Nimtz's* second major deployment, the wing brought aboard F-14s and S-3s, as well as new VAW, VAQ, and RVAH units. Heavy-Six was actually on its last deployment prior to being disestablished.

10 Sep 1979 to 26 May 1980		*Nimitz*	**Med/IO**		
VF-41	F-14A	AJ100	VAW-112	E-2B	AJ010
VF-84	F-14A	AJ200	VFP-63 det 5	RF-8G	AJ600
VA-82	A-7E	AJ300	VAQ-134	EA-6B	AJ610
VA-86	A-7E	AJ400	VS-24	S-3A	AJ700
VA-35	A-6E, KA-6D	AJ500	HS-9	SH-3H	AJ730

It was during work-ups that the ship and air wing would be used to film the movie "Final Countdown."

The 1979-80 deployment would feature the only appearance by RF-8G *Crusaders* on a *Nimitz* class carrier. Det 5 would actually cross-deck to *Coral Sea* on 17 Apr, and return to California with CVW-14's det 2.

While in the IO on 24 April 1980, the ship was used as a launching point for eight RH-53Ds as part of Operation *Eagle Claw*. Six would be lost in the operation, two would return. Although CVW-8 was prepared to fly missions over Iran to support the hostage rescue mission, it was not required. Most, if not all, of the squadrons painted distinctive stripes on their wings for this operation.

29 Aug to 17 Oct 1980		*Nimitz*	**NorLant**		
3 Aug 1981 to 12 Feb 1982		*Nimitz*	**Med**		
VF-41	F-14A	AJ100	VAW-124	E-2C	AJ010
VF-84	F-14A	AJ200	VMAQ-2 det Y	EA-6B	AJ610
VA-82	A-7E	AJ300	VS-24	S-3A	AJ700
VA-86	A-7E	AJ400	HS-9	SH-3H	AJ730
VA-35	A-6E, KA-6D	AJ500			

After five years a Norfolk-based E-2 unit was assigned to CVW-8 again. The sole Marine EA-6B squadron supplied a detachment for this cruise as well. During workups, on 26 May 1981 a VMAQ-2 *Prowler* crashed during night CQ. The crew of three was killed, as were 11 deck crew, making this the worst carrier landing mishap since Vietnam.

10 Nov 1982 to 20 May 1983		***Nimitz***	**Med**		
VF-41	F-14A	AJ100	VAW-124	E-2C	AJ010
VF-84	F-14A TARPS	AJ200	VAQ-135	EA-6B	AJ604
VA-82	A-7E	AJ300	VS-24	S-3A	AJ700
VA-86	A-7E	AJ400	HS-9	SH-3H	AJ610
VA-35	A-6E, KA-6D	AJ500			

VAQ-135 replaces the Marine *Prowler* unit, the *Black Ravens* getting the task only two weeks after returning home from a six-month deployment with CVW-1 and *America*.

8 Mar to 4 Oct 1985		***Nimitz***	**Med**		
VF-41	F-14A	AJ100	VAW-124	E-2C	AJ600
VF-84	F-14A, TARPS	AJ200	VAQ-138	EA-6B	AJ604
VA-82	A-7E	AJ300	VS-24	S-3A	AJ700
VA-86	A-7E	AJ400	HS-9	SH-3H	AJ610
VA-35	A-6E, KA-6D	AJ500			

Yet another new VAQ has joined the air wing, with the *Yellowjackets* replacing the *Black Ravens*.

15 Aug to 15 Oct 1986		**Nimitz**	**NorLant**		
VF-41	F-14A	AJ100	VAW-124	E-2C	AJ600
VF-84	F-14A, TARPS	AJ200	VAQ-138	EA-6B	AJ604
VA-82	A-7E	AJ300	VS-24	S-3A	AJ700
VA-86	A-7E	AJ400	HS-9	SH-3H	AJ610
VA-35	A-6E, KA-6D	AJ500			

30 Dec 1986 to 26 Jul 1987		***Nimitz***	**World**		
VF-41	F-14A	AJ100	VAW-124	E-2C	AJ600
VF-84	F-14A, TARPS	AJ200	VAQ-138	EA-6B	AJ604
VA-82	A-7E	AJ300	VS-24	S-3A	AJ700
VA-86	A-7E	AJ400	HS-9	SH-3H	AJ610
VA-35	A-6E, KA-6D	AJ500			

An otherwise successful deployment was marred on 25 January when a VQ-2 EA-3B (144850, JQ12) was lost with seven crewmen while trying to execute a night barricade arrestment on *Nimitz*.

25 Aug to 11 Oct 1988		***T.Roosevelt***	**NorLant**		
VF-41	F-14A	AJ100	VAW-124	E-2C	AJ600
VF-84	F-14A, TARPS	AJ200	VAQ-141	EA-6B	AJ620
VFA-15	F/A-18A	AJ300	VS-24	S-3A	AJ700
VFA-87	F/A-18A	AJ400	HS-9	SH-3H	AJ610
VA-35	A-6E	AJ500/510			
VA-36	A-6E	AJ520/530			

After 12 years of association with the *Nimitz*, CVW-8 moved to the new carrier *Theodore Roosevelt*, while also switching to F/A-18s at the same time. The wing was reformed as the first "Notional Air Wing," with two squadrons each of F-14, F/A-18, and A-6E. It would be the only one created, and would make two Med deployments with this mold. VA-36 was established as the wing's second *Intruder* unit, and a new *Prowler* squadron also joined the wing.

30 Dec 1988 to 30 Jun 1989		***T. Roosevelt***	**Med**		
VF-41	F-14A	AJ100	VAW-124	E-2C	AJ600
VF-84	F-14A, TARPS	AJ200	VAQ-141	EA-6B	AJ620
VFA-15	F/A-18A	AJ300	VS-24	S-3A	AJ700
VFA-87	F/A-18A	AJ400	HS-9	SH-3H	AJ610
VA-35	A-6E	AJ500/510			
VA-36	A-6E	AJ520/530			

28 Dec 1990 to 28 Jun 1991		***T.Roosevelt***	**Med/RS/PG**		
VF-41	F-14A	AJ100	VAW-124	E-2C	AJ600
VF-84	F-14A, TARPS	AJ200	VAQ-141	EA-6B	AJ620
VFA-15	F/A-18A	AJ300	VS-24	S-3B	AJ700
VFA-87	F/A-18A	AJ400	HS-9	SH-3H	AJ610
VA-65	A-6E	AJ500/510			
VA-36	A-6E	AJ520/530			

CVW-8 exchanged VA-35 for VA-65, and participated in *Desert Storm*, flying more sorties than any other carrier/air wing team while losing one A-6E, and its crew of two, to enemy action.

11 Mar to 8 Sep 1993		***T.Roosevelt***	**Med/RS**		
VF-84	F-14A, TARPS	AJ200	VAW-124	E-2C	AJ600
VFA-15	F/A-18C	AJ300	VAQ-141	EA-6B	AJ620
VMFA-312	F/A-18C	AJ330	HS-3	SH-60F,HH-60H	AJ610
VFA-87	F/A-18C	AJ400	HMH-362 (rein)	CH-53D, UH-1N	YL00
VA-36	A-6E	AJ500	VRC-40 det 2	C-2A	AJ

CVW-8 and TR deployed with a "Special MAGTF," which included a CH-53 composite unit and a Company of Marines. The Marines were not actually assigned to the wing, but were a separate and equal entity. HMH-362 (reinforced) was assigned as the senior Marine unit, bringing its CH-53Ds onboard, along with UH-1Ns assigned from HMLA-167. To make room for the Marines three Navy squadrons (VF-41, VS-24, and VA-65) were beached. Results from this experiment were mixed, and not repeated in CVW-8. The wing and ship were heavily involved in *Deny Flight/Provide Promise* over the former Yugoslavia during this deployment.

22 Mar to 22 Sep 1995		***T. Roosevelt***	**Med/RS/PG**		
VF-41	F-14A, TARPS	AJ100	VAW-124	E-2C	AJ600
VMFA-312	F/A-18C	AJ330	VAQ-141	EA-6B	AJ620
VFA-15	F/A-18C	AJ300	VS-24	S-3B	AJ700
VFA-87	F/A-18C	AJ400	HS-3	SH-60F, HH-60H	AJ610
VQ-6 det D	ES-3A	AJ760			
VRC-40 det3	C-2A	AJ			

The helos did not return for the 1995 deployment, although VMFA-312 was retained. VS-24 came back and, with VA-36 disestablished, CVW-8 moved to a single F-14/three FA-18 configuration for its 1995 deployment. VF-41 replaced the *Jolly Rogers*, gaining TARPS aircraft for the first time. The wing was heavily involved in operations over Bosnia and Operation *Deny Flight* during this deployment. VAQ-141 was augmented by two aircraft from Reserve VAQ-209, which carried AJ626 and 627 side numbers. The *Shadowhawks* actually spent a good deal of time land-based out of Aviano at the order of European Command, in order to provide EW support for USAF and NATO forces while the ship was not on station. VAQ-141 and the -209 det were sent back to CONUS ahead of the carrier, and arrived home on 17 Sept.

29 Apr to 28 Oct 1997		***JF Kennedy***	**Med/RS/PG**			
VF-41	F-14A, TARPS	AJ100	VAW-124	E-2C	AJ600	
VF-14	F-14A	AJ200	VAQ-141	EA-6B	AJ620	
VFA-15	F/A-18C	AJ300	VS-24	S-3B	AJ700	
VFA-87	F/A-18C	AJ400	HS-3	SH-60F, HH-60H	AJ610	VQ-6 det A
ES-3A	AJ760					
VRC-40 det 4	C-2A	AJ				

CVW-8 returned to two *Tomcat* squadrons for its 1987 deployment, while also switching to *JFK*.

26 Mar to 22 Sep 1999		***T. Roosevelt***	**Med/RS/PG**		
VF-41	F-14A, TARPS	AJ100	VAW-124	E-2C	AJ600
VF-14	F-14A	AJ200	VS-24	S-3B	AJ700
VFA-15	F/A-18C	AJ300	HS-3	SH-60F, HH-60H	AJ610
VFA-87	F/A-18C	AJ400	VRC-40 det 1	C-2A	AJ
VAQ-141	EA-6B	AJ500			

Returning to T.R, CVW-8 participated in *Operation Allied Force* before heading for the Persian Gulf and *Southern Watch* duties.

CVW-9 NG

Estab. CVG-9 26 Mar 52, r/d CVW-9 20 Dec 63, Homeport: Lemoore

21 Jun to 22 Dec 1974		*Constellation*	WP/IO/PG		
VF-96	F-4J	NG100	VAW-116	E-2B	NG010
VF-92	F-4J	NG200	RVAH-5	RA-5C	NG600
VA-146	A-7E	NG300	VAQ-131	EA-6B	NG610
VA-147	A-7E	NG400	HS-6	SH-3D	NG730
VA-165	A-6A, KA-6D	NG500			

"Connie" became the first "Supercarrier" to enter the Persian Gulf on this deployment. VF-92 and -96 were making their last deployments.

12 Apr to 21 Nov 1977		***Constellation***	**WP**		
VF-211	F-14A	NG100	VAW-126	E-2C	NG600
VF-24	F-14A	NG200	VFP-63 det 1	RF-8G	NG610
VA-146	A-7E	NG300	VAQ-132	EA-6B	NG620
VA-147	A-7E	NG400	VS-21	S-3A	NG700
VA-165	A-6E, KA-6D	NG500	HS-6	SH-3D	NG720

F-14s and S-3s joined CVW-9 for the 1977 deployment, and East Coast VAW-126 brought its new E-2Cs over from Norfolk. RF-8Gs have replaced the *Vigilantes* in the photo role.

26 Sep 1978 to 17 May 1979		***Constellation***	**WP/IO**		
VF-211	F-14A	NG100	VAW-126	E-2C	NG600
VF-24	F-14A	NG200	VFP-63 det 3	RF-8G	NG610
VA-146	A-7E	NG300	VAQ-132	EA-6B	NG620
VA-147	A-7E	NG400	VS-37	S-3A, US-3A	NG700
VA-165	A-6E, KA-6D	NG500	HS-6	SH-3H	NG720

VS-37 has the sole US-3A assigned for deployment to support the ship in the Indian Ocean.

26 Feb to 15 Oct 1980		***Constellation***	**WP/IO**		
VF-211	F-14A	NG100	VAW-116	E-2C	NG600
VF-24	F-14A	NG200	VFP-63 det 3	RF-8G	NG610
VA-146	A-7E	NG300	VS-38	S-3A	NG700
VA-147	A-7E	NG400	HS-6	SH-3H	NG720
VA-165	A-6E, KA-6D	NG500			

The *Sun Kings* have replaced VAW-126 as the wing's E-2 squadron. No EA-6B unit was assigned due to a lack of available squadrons.

Red Griffon S-3A NG700 (160159) is shown seconds before being shot from *Constellation's* cat 3 in March 1980. The "Hoover" displays a full "CAG rainbow" in all of its glory. (Rick Burgess)

20 Oct 1981 to 23 May 1982		***Constellation***	**WP/IO**		
VF-211	F-14A, TARPS	NG100	VAW-112	E-2C	NG600
VF-24	F-14A	NG200	VAQ-134	EA-6B	NG604
VA-146	A-7E	NG300	VS-38	S-3A	NG700
VA-147	A-7E	NG400	HS-8	SH-3H	NG610
VA-165	A-6E, KA-6D	NG500			

On what would be *Connie's* last deployment with CVW-9, VF-211 introduced the TARPS pod, which allowed the RF-8Gs to be beached. The wing also hosted its third E-2 squadron in as many cruises.

15 Jul 1983 to 29 Feb 1984		***Ranger***	**Cent America/WP/IO**		
VF-211	F-14A, TARPS	NG100	VAW-112	E-2C	NG600
VF-24	F-14A	NG200	VAQ-138	EA-6B	NG604
VA-192	A-7E	NG300	VS-33	S-3A	NG700
VA-195	A-7E	NG400	HS-8	SH-3H	NG610
VA-165	A-6E, KA-6D	NG500			

CVW-9 switched to *Ranger* for one deployment, and brought aboard two new A-7 squadrons. The ship started cruise by swinging by Nicaragua, where it made its presence known to the ruling Sandinista Government.

24 Jul to 21 Dec 1985		***Kitty Hawk***	**WP/IO**		
VF-211	F-14A, TARPS	NG100	VAW-112	E-2C	NG600
VF-24	F-14A	NG200	VAQ-130	EA-6B	NG604
VA-146	A-7E	NG300	VS-33	S-3A	NG700
VA-147	A-7E	NG400	HS-2	SH-3H	NG610
VA-165	A-6E, KA-6D	NG500			

Moving to *Kitty Hawk* for the first of two deployments, CVW-9 welcomed back VA-146 and -147.

3 Jan to 29 Jun 1987		***Kitty Hawk***	**World**		
VF-211	F-14A, TARPS	NG100	VAW-112	E-2C	NG600
VF-24	F-14A	NG200	VAQ-130	EA-6B	NG604
VA-146	A-7E	NG300	VS-33	S-3A	NG700
VA-147	A-7E	NG400	HS-2	SH-3H	NG610
VA-165	A-6E, KA-6D	NG500			

The *Hawk* made a west coast to east coast around-the-world cruise in order to make a date for SLEP conversion. CVW-9 remains essentially unchanged.

2 Sep 1988 to 2 Mar 1989		***Nimitz***	**WP/IO**		
VF-211	F-14A, TARPS	NG100	VAW-112	E-2C	NG600
VF-24	F-14A	NG200	VAQ-138	EA-6B	NG604
VA-146	A-7E	NG300	VS-33	S-3A	NG700
VA-147	A-7E	NG400	HS-2	SH-3H	NG610
VA-165	A-6E, KA-6D	NG500			

After two deployments in *Kitty Hawk* CVW-9 moves to *Nimitz*, with a new EA-6B unit assigned.

15 Jun to 9 Jul 1989		***Nimitz***	**NorPac**		
VF-211	F-14A, TARPS	NG100	VAW-112	E-2C	NG600
VF-24	F-14A	NG200	VAQ-138	EA-6B	NG604
VA-146	A-7E	NG300	VS-33	S-3A	NG700
(VA-147	*A-7E/FA-18*	*NG400)*	HS-2	SH-3H	NG610
VA-165	A-6E, KA-6D	NG500			

The *Argonauts*, although assigned to CVW-9, did not make this trip due to F/A-18 transition.

12 Feb to 7 Apr 1990		***Constellation***	**Horn**		
VF-33	F-14A	AB200	VAW-112	E-2C	NG600
VFA-82	F/A-18C	AB300	VAQ-138	EA-6B	NG604
VA-165	A-6E, KA-6D	NG500	VS-33	S-3A	NG700
			HS-75	SH-3H	NW or NG

A highly modified CVW-9 acompanied "Connie" as she moved from San Diego to Philadelphia for SLEP. Single east coast VF and VFA squadrons from CVW-1 were used, while the wing's own units upgraded their equipment. A reserve HS unit made the trip, as HS-2 converted to *Seahawks*.

25 Feb to 24 Aug 1991		***Nimitz***	**WP/IO/PG**		
VF-211	F-14A+, TARPS	NG100	VAW-112	E-2C	NG600
VF-24	F-14A+	NG200	VAQ-138	EA-6B	NG620
VFA-146	F/A-18C	NG300	VS-33	S-3A	NG700
VFA-147	F/A-18C	NG400	HS-2	SH-60F/HH-60H	NG610
VA-165	A-6E, KA-6D	NG500			

Nimitz and CVW-9 arrive in the Persian Gulf after the end of *Desert Storm* as the only Pacific Fleet carrier to operate F-14A+ (F-14B) type. The wing's light attack units are now flying strike fighters, and HS-2 is taking the SH-60F on its first deployment.

2 Feb to 29 Jul 1993		***Nimitz***	**WP/IO/PG**		
VF-211	F-14A, TARPS	NG100	VAW-112	E-2C	NG600
VF-24	F-14A	NG200	VAQ-138	EA-6B	NG620
VFA-146	F/A-18C	NG300	VS-33	S-3B	NG700
VFA-147	F/A-18C	NG400	HS-2	SH-60F/HH-60H	NG610
VA-165	A-6E, KA-6D	NG500			

The Fitrons have reverted to F-14As after the Navy decides to place all F-14A+ (F-14B) types on the East Coast. VA-165 is making the final deployment with KA-6D as well.

27 Nov 1995 to 20 May 1996		***Nimitz***	**WP/IO/PG**		
VF-211	F-14A, TARPS	NG100	VAW-112	E-2C	NG600
VF-24	F-14A	NG200	VAQ-138	EA-6B	NG620
VFA-146	F/A-18C	NG300	VS-33	S-3B	NG700
VFA-147	F/A-18C	NG400	HS-8	SH-60F, HH-60F	NG610
VA-165	A-6E	NG500	VQ-5 det C	ES-3A	NG720
VRC-30 det4	C-2A	NG			

1 Sep 1997 to 1 Mar 1998		***Nimitz***	**WP/IO/PG**		
VF-211	F-14A, TARPS	NG100	VAW-112	E-2C	NG600
VMFA-314	F/A-18C	NG200	VAQ-138	EA-6B	NG620
VFA-146	F/A-18C	NG300	VS-33	S-3B	NG700
VFA-147	F/A-18C	NG400	HS-8	SH-60F, HH-60F	NG610
VQ-5 det D	ES-3A	NG720			
VRC-30 det 4	C-2A	NG			

VF-24 and VA-165 have been disestablished, and a Marine *Hornet* unit has come aboard. Nimitz/CVW-9 left the Persian Gulf without *Prowlers*, as VAQ-138 transferred its aircraft to *Independence*/ CVW-5/ VAQ-136 and *G.Washington*/ CVW-1/ VAQ-137 to increase the number of EA-6Bs available to 5th Fleet during a time of tension with Iraq. After about two months the 138 aircrew that were left flew back to CONUS via commercial aviation, while the aircraft came home with their new squadrons.

7 Jan to 3 Jul 2000		***JC Stennis***	**WP/IO/PG**		
VF-211	F-14A, TARPS	NG100	VAW-112	E-2C	NG600
VMFA-314	F/A-18C	NG200	VS-33	S-3B	NG700
VFA-146	F/A-18C	NG300	HS-8	SH-60F, HH-60F	NG610
VFA-147	F/A-18C	NG400	VRC-30 det 4	C-2A	NG
VAQ-138	EA-6B	NG500			

CVW-10 NM

Estab. 7 Nov 1986 disestab. 1 Jun 1988 Homeport: Miramar

Air Wing TEN was formed as the fourteenth air wing in the Navy, and the West Coast counterpart to CVW-13. It was the second CVW-10, the first one being an East Coast organization disestablished in November 1969. Although intended for the carrier *Independence*, it survived less than a year before fiscal realities and personnel shortages forced it into history. CVW-10 never deployed, and all but one of its squadrons (VA-155) were disestablished. CVW-10 does not appear to have ever had a second VFA or a VAQ assigned, although several units were mentioned for both slots. The wing's "NM" tailcode had been assigned to CVW-19 up to 1977 and, more recently, by LatWingPac for squadrons between carrier assignments.

<1986-1987>	**(*Independence*)**	**no cruise**			
VF-191	F-14A	NM100	VAW-111	E-2C	NM600
VF-194	F-14A	NM200	(NONE)	EA-6B	(NM604)
(NONE)	———	(NM300)	VS-35	S-3A	NM700
VFA-161	F/A-18A	NM400	HS-16	SH-3H	NM610
VA-155	A-6E, KA-6D	NM500			

CVW-11 NH

Estab. CVG-11 10 Nov 42, r/d CVAG-11 15 Nov 46, r/d CVG-11 1 Sep 48, r/d CVW-11 20 Dec 63.

Homeport: Miramar, Lemoore (July 1997)

23 Nov 1973 to 9 Jul 1974		***Kitty Hawk***	**WP/IO**		
VF-213	F-4J	NH100	VAW-114	E-2B	NH010
VF-114	F-4J	NH200	RVAH-7	RA-5C	NH600
VA-192	A-7E	NH300	VAQ-136	EA-6B	NH610
VA-195	A-7E	NH400	VS-37	S-2G	NH700
VA-52	A-6A, KA-6D	NH500	VS-38	S-2G	NH710
	HS-4	SH-3D	NH720		

Operating under the "CV Concept," *Kitty Hawk* and CVW-11 had a crowded flight deck, with two S-2 *Tracker* squadrons attached to its normal wing. In order to clear up deck space, the ship would have to operate with a substantial detachment at Cubi Point for most of the cruise.

21 May to 15 Dec 1975		***Kitty Hawk***	**WP**		
VF-213	F-4J	NH100	VAW-114	E-2B	NH010
VF-114	F-4J	NH200	RVAH-6	RA-5C	NH600
VA-192	A-7E	NH300	VAQ-136	EA-6B	NH610
VA-195	A-7E	NH400	VS-37	S-2G	NH700
VA-52	A-6E, KA-6D	NH500	VS-38	S-2G	NH710
HS-8	SH-3D	NH720			

Kitty Hawk makes its second "CV concept" deployment with *Trackers* embarked. This would be the last U.S. Navy cruise for the pugnacious "Stoof." VA-52 has graduated to A-6Es, and a new RVAH is aboard.

25 Oct 1977 to 15 May 1978		***Kitty Hawk***	**WP**		
VF-114	F-14A	NH100	VAW-122	E-2C	NH605
VF-213	F-14A	NH200	RVAH-7	RA-5C	NH610
VA-192	A-7E	NH300	VAQ-131	EA-6B	NH620
VA-195	A-7E	NH400	VS-33	S-3A, US-3A	NH700
VA-52	A-6E, KA-6D	NH500	HS-8	SH-3H	NH720

E-2Cs and S-3s have come aboard, while *Tomcats* have replaced the *Phantoms*. East coast VAW-122 has introduced E-2Cs to the Air Wing as well.

13 Mar to 22 Sep 1979		***America***	**Med**		
VF-114	F-14A	NH100	VAW-124	E-2C	NH600
VF-213	F-14A	NH200	VFP-63 det 4	RF-8G	NH610
VA-192	A-7E	NH300	VAQ-131	EA-6B	NH620
VA-195	A-7E	NH400	VS-33	S-3A	NH700
VA-95	A-6E, KA-6D	NH500	HS-12	SH-3H	NH740

CVW-11 was temporarily assigned to *Enterprise* in late 1978 (with a number of aircraft being suitably marked), only to be re-assigned to Norfolk based *America*, becoming the second AirPac CVW to deploy on an AirLant carrier since the end of Vietnam, *FDR*/CVW-19 being the other such team. The E-2 squadron came from AirLant, while the rest were Pacific Fleet squadrons. The *Green Lizards* have swapped air wings with VA-52, which moved to CVW-15.

14 Apr to 12 Nov 1981		***America***	**Med/IO**		
VF-114	F-14A	NH100	VAW-123	E-2C	NH600
VF-213	F-14A, TARPS	NH200	VAQ-133	EA-6B	NH620
VA-192	A-7E	NH300	VS-33	S-3A	NH700
VA-195	A-7E	NH400	HS-12	SH-3H	NH740
VA-95	A-6E, KA-6D	NH500			

CVW-11 made its second consecutive deployment in *America*. The ship became the first carrier to transit the Suez Canal since the 1967 "Three Day War." A third successive Norfolk based E-2 unit has been assigned for this deployment.

1 Sep 1982 to 23 Mar 1983		***Enterprise***	**WP/IO**		
VF-114	F-14A	NH100	VAW-117	E-2C	NH600
VF-213	F-14A, TARPS	NH200	VAQ-133	EA-6B	NH604
VA-22	A-7E	NH300	VS-37	S-3A	NH700
VA-94	A-7E	NH400	HS-6	SH-3H	NH610
VA-95	A-6E, KA-6D	NH500			

Switching back to the Pacific Fleet and *Enterprise*, CVW-11 gets two new A-7 units, as VA-192 and 195 transition to *Hornets*. New E-2 and H-3 units join as well.

30 May to 20 Dec 1984		***Enterprise***	**WP/IO**		
VF-114	F-14A	NH100	VAW-117	E-2C	NH600
VF-213	F-14A, TARPS	NH200	VAQ-133	EA-6B	NH604
VA-22	A-7E	NH300	VS-21	S-3A	NH700
VA-94	A-7E	NH400	HS-6	SH-3H	NH610
VA-95	A-6E, KA-6D	NH500			

CVW-11 takes on a new S-3 unit, while VAQ-133 makes the last EA-6B EXCAP deployment in the Navy.

15 Jan to 12 Aug 1986		***Enterprise***	**WP/IO/Med/SL**		
VF-114	F-14A	NH100	VAW-117	E-2C	NH600
VF-213	F-14A, TARPS	NH200	VAQ-133	EA-6B	NH604
VA-22	A-7E	NH300	VS-21	S-3A	NH700
VA-94	A-7E	NH400	HS-6	SH-3H	NH610
VA-95	A-6E, KA-6D	NH500			

Enterprise was used to film the flight deck scenes for the 1986 movie "Top Gun" during work-ups in 1985. The "Big E," with CVW-11 embarked, left the Indian Ocean, and proceeded through the Suez in a rare visit by a Pacific Fleet carrier to the 6th Fleet. The air wing remained unchanged from the previous deployment.

25 Oct to 24 Nov 1987		***Enterprise***	**NorPac**		
VF-114	F-14A	NH100	VAW-117	E-2C	NH600
VF-213	F-14A, TARPS	NH200	VAQ-133	EA-6B	NH604
VA-22	A-7E	NH300	VS-21	S-3A	NH700
VA-94	A-7E	NH400	HS-6	SH-3H	NH610
VA-95	A-6E, KA-6D	NH500			

5 Jan to 3 Jul 1988		***Enterprise***	**WP/IO**		
VF-114	F-14A	NH100	VAW-117	E-2C	NH600
VF-213	F-14A, TARPS	NH200	VAQ-135	EA-6B	NH620
VA-22	A-7E	NH300	VS-21	S-3A	NH700
VA-94	A-7E	NH400	HS-6	SH-3H	NH610
VA-95	A-6E, KA-6D	NH500			

Enterprise and CVW-11 participate in *Praying Mantis* against Iran during this cruise. VAQ-135 makes the first deployment with five EA-6Bs embarked, forcing the move to the NH620 series.

17 Sep 1989 to 16 Mar 1990		***Enterprise***	**World**		
VF-114	F-14A	NH100	VAW-117	E-2C	NH600
VF-213	F-14A, TARPS	NH200	VAQ-135	EA-6B	NH604

VA-22	A-7E	NH300	VS-21	S-3A	NH700
VA-94	A-7E	NH400	HS-6	SH-3H	NH610
VA-95	A-6E, KA-6D	NH500			

CVW-11 makes its last deployment in *Enterprise*, which is returning to the east coast for refueling. VAQ-135 has reverted to a four aircraft configuration, and moved back to the 604 to 607 series.

25 Sep to 20 Nov 90		***Abraham Lincoln***	**Horn**		
VF-114	F-14A	NH100	VAW-117	E-2C	NH600
VF-213	F-14A TARPS	NH200	VAQ-135	EA-6B	NH620
VFA-305	F/A-18A	ND400	VS-29	S-3A	NH700
VA-95	A-6E, KA-6D	NH500	HS-17	SH-3H	NH/AK61X

CVW-11 accompanied its new carrier *Abraham Lincoln* while it transited around the Horn. Reserve VFA-305, with elements of VFA-303 attached, covered for the wing's two VA squadrons, which were in transition to the *Hornet* themselves. CVW-13's HS-17 replaced HS-6 for this event as well for what would be its last at sea period prior to disestablishment.

28 May to 28 Nov 1991		***Abraham Lincoln***	**WP/IO/PG**		
VF-114	F-14A	NH100	VAW-117	E-2C	NH600
VF-213	F-14A, TARPS	NH200	VAQ-135	EA-6B	NH620
VFA-22	F/A-18C	NH300	VS-29	S-3A	NH700
VFA-94	F/A-18C	NH400	HS-6	SH-60F, HH-60H	NH610
VA-95	A-6E, KA-6D	NH500			

Lincoln makes its first extended deployment with CVW-11 embarked. *Hornets* have replaced the *Corsairs* in the wing.

15 Jun to 15 Dec 1993		***Abraham Lincoln***	**WP/IO/PG**		
VF-213	F-14A, TARPS	NH100	VAW-117	E-2C	NH600
VMFA-314	F/A-18A	NH200	VAQ-135	EA-6B	NH620
VFA-22	F/A-18C	NH300	VS-29	S-3B	NH700
VFA-94	F/A-18C	NH400	HS-6	SH-60F, HH-60H	NH610
VA-95	A-6E	NH500			

The legendary VF-114 *Aardvarks* have been disestablished and replaced in kind by a Marine *Hornet* unit.

10 Apr to 9 Oct 1995		***Abraham Lincoln***	**WP/IO/PG**		
VF-213	F-14A, TARPS	NH100	VAW-117	E-2C	NH600
VFA-22	F/A-18C	NH300	VAQ-135	EA-6B	NH620
VFA-94	F/A-18C	NH400	VS-29	S-3B	NH700
VA-95	A-6E	NH500	HS-6	SH-60F, HH-60H	NH610
VQ-5 det B	ES-3A	NH720			
VRC-30 det3	C-2A	NH			

The Marines have been dropped, and the 200 series numbers are vacant for WestPac '95.

11 Oct 1996 to 11 Apr 1997		***Kitty Hawk***	**WP/IO/PG**		
VF-213	F-14D, TARPS	NH100	VAW-117	E-2C	NH600
VFA-97	F/A-18A	NH200	VAQ-135	EA-6B	NH620
VFA-22	F/A-18C	NH300	VS-29	S-3B	NH700
VFA-94	F/A-18C	NH400	HS-6	SH-60F, HH-60H	NH610
VQ-5 det B	ES-3A	NH720			
VRC-30 det 2	C-2A	NH			

Shifting back to an oil-burning carrier, CVW-11 adds a third VFA with the retirement of the A-6E. VFA-97 has joined the wing with A-model *Hornets*, as CVW-11 becomes the first wing to deploy with mixed versions of the F/A-18. The *Black Lions* have re-equipped with F-14Ds, as well.

6 Nov 1998 to 6 May 1999		***Carl Vinson***	**WP/IO/PG**		
VF-213	F-14D, TARPS	NH100	VAW-117	E-2C	NH600
VFA-97	F/A-18A	NH200	VS-29	S-3B	NH700

VFA-22	F/A-18C	NH300	HS-6	SH-60F, HH-60H	NH610
VFA-94	F/A-18C	NH400	VQ-5 det C	ES-3A	NH720
VAQ-135	EA-6B	NH500	VRC-30 det 2	C-2A	NH

CVW-13 AK ***Guardians***

Estab. 1 Mar 1984 disestab. 1 Jan 1991 Homeport: Oceana

Air Wing THIRTEEN was the first new CVW in the Navy since the 1966 establishment of CVW-17. There was a previous CVG-13 during the jet age, being formed in Aug 1961, and surviving only fourteen months before being disestablished. The new wing adopted the patch of the previous group, and was assigned to the *Coral Sea*, which had recently arrived in the Atlantic Fleet. The ship/wing team introduced the F/A-18A *Hornet* to the Mediterranean, and made three deployments before it was cut in the post *Desert Storm* period. The wing's "AK" tailcode was previously used by CVW-10, which was disestablished in November 1969. CVW-13 was unique, in that it had a recognized air wing nickname, the *Guardians*.

2 Oct 1985 to 19 May 1986		***Coral Sea***	**Med**		
VFA-131	F/A-18A	AK100	VAW-127	E-2C	AK600
VFA-132	F/A-18A	AK200	VAQ-135	EA-6B	AK620 (Jan. 1986)
VMFA-314	F/A-18A	AK300	HS-17	SH-3H	AK610
VMFA-323	F/A-18A	AK400			
VA-55	A-6E, KA-6D	AK500			

CVW-13 made up the original "Coral Sea Air Wing," with four VFAs and a single VA(M) unit assigned. The original plan was for it to get four equally new Navy Strike-Fighter units attached. Only two were up and ready in time for deployment, so two Marine Fighter-Attack squadrons were "borrowed" from El Toro's 3rd MAW to fill the deck. The other two squadrons (VFA-136 and -137) would join the wing for later deployments. The VA(M), VAW, and HS units were also established specifically for this wing, and would see it through its short, six-plus year life.

Air Wing-13 was the last CVW that did not have a *Prowler* unit attached, largely due to limitations of the ship's small deck. Nontheless, after combat with Libya became a distinct possibility, VAQ-135 was pulled out of CVW-1 on 1 Jan 1986 to join CVW-13 mid-cruise with five aircraft, three of which were normally onboard at any one time. An air wing beach det was kept at Sigonella to free up deck space on the ship, with aircraft being rotated through as the deployment progressed. The *Guardians* were heavily involved in Operations *Prairie Fire* and *El Dorado Canyon* during this deployment.

29 Sep 1987 to 28 Mar 1988		***Coral Sea***	**Med**		
VFA-131	F/A-18A	AK100	VAW-127	E-2C	AK600
VFA-136	F/A-18A	AK300	VAQ-133	EA-6B	AK604
VFA-137	F/A-18A	AK400	HS-17	SH-3H	AK610
VA-55	A-6E	AK500			
VA-65	A-6E	AK510			

For its second deployment CVW-13 was modified by dropping one Strike Fighter unit, while adding a second small *Intruder* squadron (VA-65). New VFA-136 and -137 joined the organization for their first deployments, while -132 and the Marines left. VAQ-133 brought ICAP II EA-6Bs into the air wing as well.

31 May to 30 Sep 1989		***Coral Sea***	**Med**		
VMFA-451	F/A-18A	AK100	VAW-127	E-2C	AK600
VFA-132	F/A-18A	AK200	VAQ-133	EA-6B	AK604
VFA-137	F/A-18A	AK400	HS-17	SH-3H	AK610
VA-55	A-6E	AK500			
VA-65	A-6E	AK510			

On its third and final trip to the Med, CVW-13 brought the Marines back into the fold, as well as the *Privateers*. VFA-136 has moved to CVW-7, hence the open 300 series. Following the last cruise in *Coral Sea* CVW-13 floated between available decks, and would be associated with both *Kitty Hawk* and *Abraham Lincoln* during 1990, although it would deploy with neither (the wing did conduct a short CQ peiod with *Lincoln* in Aug 1990). By the end of that year CVW-13 had been declared excess to the needs of the Navy, and it was disestablished in January 1991. VA-55, VAW-127, and HS-17 would go with it. VFA-132, VFA-137, VAQ-133, and VA-65 would find at least temporary employment elsewhere. Of these only 137 would survive past 1992.

CVW-14 NK

CVG-101 estab. from Naval Reserve units 1 Aug 50, r/d CVG-14 4 Feb 53, r/d CVW-14 20 Dec 1963.
Homeport: Miramar, Lemoore (Feb 1998)

17 Sep 1974 to 20 May 1975		***Enterprise***	**WP/IO**		
VF-1	F-14A	NK100	VAW-113	E-2B	NK600
VF-2	F-14A	NK200	RVAH-12	RA-5C	NK610
VA-97	A-7E	NK300	VAQ-137	EA-6B	NK620
VA-27	A-7E	NK400	HS-2	SH-3D	NK700
VA-196	A-6A, KA-6D	NK500			

As of 1974 CVW-14 was the most modern and capable air wing in the Navy. VF-1 and VF-2 were making the first *Tomcat* deployments in the Navy, and VAQ-137 was on its first cruise since being established. CVW-14 provided air cover over Saigon, Vietnam, during *Eagle Pull*.

30 Jul 1976 to 28 Mar 1977		***Enterprise***	**WP/IO**		
VF-1	F-14A	NK100	VAW-113	E-2B	NK600
VF-2	F-14A	NK200	RVAH-1	RA-5C	NK610
VA-97	A-7E	NK300	VAQ-134	EA-6B	NK620
VA-27	A-7E	NK400	VS-29	S-3A	NK700
VA-196	A-6E, KA-6D	NK500	HS-2	SH-3D	NK720

S-3 *Vikings* joined CVW-14 for the Bi-centennial deployment.

4 Apr to 30 Oct 1978		***Enterprise***	**WP/IO**		
VF-1	F-14A	NK100	VAW-113	E-2B	NK600
VF-2	F-14A	NK200	RVAH-1	RA-5C	NK610
VA-97	A-7E	NK300	VAQ-134	EA-6B	NK620
VA-27	A-7E	NK400	VS-38	S-3A	NK700
VA-196	A-6E, KA-6D	NK500	HS-2	SH-3D	NK720

Other than a new "Hoover" unit, Air Wing FOURTEEN remained the same for its 1978 WestPac, which would prove to be its last in *Enterprise*.

30 Sep 1979 to 20 Feb 1980		***Coral Sea***	**WP/IO**		
VMFA-323	F-4N	NK100	VAW-113	E-2B	NK600
VMFA-531	F-4N	NK200	VFP-63 det 2	RF-8G	NK620
VA-97	A-7E	NK300	HC-1 det 3	SH-3G	NK720
VA-27	A-7E	NK400			
VA-196	A-6E, KA-6D	NK500			

Even the Marines could get into the CAG markings act. In 1979 two El Toro based VMFAs joined CVW-14 in *Coral Sea* for a trip to the Western Pacific and Indian Ocean. VMFA-323 *Death Rattler* NK100 sits at El Toro in November of that year with a suitably striped serpent. (Michael Grove)

Moving from the Pacific Fleet's largest flight deck to the smallest, Marine F-4 units provided the Wing's fighter cover, and Photo-*Crusaders* came aboard. The ship and wing stood by to provide support for the ill-fated *Operation Eagle Claw* while off Iran. Vivid "invasion stripes" were painted on air wing aircraft for the abortive op. VFP-63's det 2 was joined by det 5, off *Nimitz*, on 17 Apr, and rode the ship home to California.

20 Aug 1981 to 23 Mar 1982		***Coral Sea***	**WP/IO**		
VF-154	F-4N	NK100	VAW-113	E-2B	NK600
VF-21	F-4N	NK200	VFP-63 det 2	RF-8G	NK115
VA-97	A-7E	NK300	HC-1 det 3	SH-3G	NK610
VA-27	A-7E	NK400			
VA-196	A-6E, KA-6D	NK500			

VF-154 and VF-21 were originally equipped with F-4Ss for this deployment, but swapped airframes with reserve VF-301 and -302 in order to get F-4Ns and their slower approach speeds, which were more suited to *Coral Sea*. VFP-63 was aboard for the last *Crusader* deployment. Note: VS-21's S-3As wore CVW-14's "NK" code for at least two short periods in 1980 and '83, but apparently only as a temporary measure, as it did not deploy with *Coral Sea*.

21 Mar to 12 Sep 1983		***Coral Sea***	**WORLD**		
VF-154	F-4N	NK100	VAW-113	E-2B	NK600
VF-21	F-4N	NK200	HS-12	SH-3H	NK610
VA-97	A-7E	NK300			
VA-27	A-7E	NK400			
VA-196	A-6E, KA-6D	NK500			

The "Ageless Warrior" made an around-the-world cruise with CVW-14 embarked, via the Indian Ocean, Med, and Caribbean. HS-12 has replaced the HC SAR detachment. While in the Caribbean the ship was joined for a short period by a detachment of F-4Ns from the Dallas Reserves of VF-202. This trip marked the final deployment for CONUS-based *Phantoms* and E-2Bs, although both continued in Japan off *Midway*/CVW-5.

21 Feb to 24 Aug 1985		***Constellation***	**WP/IO**		
VF-154	F-14A, TARPS	NK100	VAW-113	E-2C	NK600
VF-21	F-14A	NK200	VAQ-139	EA-6B	NK604
VFA-113	F/A-18A	NK300	VS-37	S-3A	NK700
VFA-25	F/A-18A	NK400	HS-8	SH-3H	NK610
VA-196	A-6E, KA-6D	NK500			

Joining "Connie" as she came out of the yards, CVW-14 had transformed with F-14s and the first *Hornets* in the Navy. F-14s, E-2Cs, a new EA-6B unit, and S-3s again made CVW-14 the most modern air wing in the Navy, at least for a short period.

11 Apr to 13 Oct 1987		***Constellation***	**WP/IO**		
VF-154	F-14A, TARPS	NK100	VAW-113	E-2C	NK600
VF-21	F-14A	NK200	VAQ-139	EA-6B	NK604
VFA-113	F/A-18A	NK300	VS-37	S-3A	NK700
VFA-25	F/A-18A	NK400	HS-8	SH-3H	NK610
VA-196	A-6E, KA-6D	NK500			

CVW-14's 1987 deployment was during a time of tight money for ship's fuel oil; therefore, the ship anchored at Diego Garcia for a period and conducted "Flanchor Ops" (Flight at Anchor), where they launched and recovered aircraft while the ship swung on its chain. The unusual concept was hard on aircraft, and considered of little real training value compared to the risk, and not continued.

1 Dec 1988 to 1 Jun 1989		***Constellation***	**WP/IO**		
VF-154	F-14A, TARPS	NK100	VAW-113	E-2C	NK600
VF-21	F-14A	NK200	VAQ-139	EA-6B	NK604
VFA-113	F/A-18A	NK300	VS-37	S-3A	NK700
VFA-25	F/A-18A	NK400	HS-8	SH-3H	NK610
VA-196	A-6E, KA-6D	NK500			

16 Sep to 19 Oct 1989		***Constellation***	**NorPac**		
VF-154	F-14A, TARPS	NK100	VAW-113	E-2C	NK600
VF-21	F-14A	NK200	VAQ-139	EA-6B	NK604
VFA-113	F/A-18A/C	NK300	VS-37	S-3A	NK700
VFA-25	F/A-18A/C	NK400	HS-8	SH-3H	NK610
VA-196	A-6E, KA-6D	NK500			

Connie goes north with CVW-14, and the VFAs take a mixed bag of *Hornets* with them during transition.

23 Jun to 20 Dec 1990		***Independence***	**WP/IO/PG**		
VF-154	F-14A, TARPS	NK100	VAW-113	E-2C	NK600
VF-21	F-14A	NK200	VAQ-139	EA-6B	NK604
VFA-113	F/A-18C	NK300	VS-37	S-3A	NK700
VFA-25	F/A-18C	NK400	HS-8	SH-3H	NK610
VA-196	A-6E	NK500			

Transferring to the *Independence*, CVW-14 participated in *Desert Shield*. Its Strike-Fighter squadrons had fully transitioned to "C" model *Hornets* as well.

5 to 22 Aug 1991	***Independence***	**Hawaii**			
VF-154	F-14A, TARPS	NK100	VAW-113	E-2C	NK600
VF-21	F-14A	NK200	VAQ-139	EA-6B	NK604
VFA-113	F/A-18C	NK300	VS-21	S-3A	NK700
VFA-25	F/A-18C	NK400	HS-8	SH-3H	NK610
VA-196	A-6E	NK500			

CVW-14 accompanied "Indy" as she executed the 1991 "Swapex" with *Midway*. The two ships met in Pearl Harbor and swapped out portions of their air wings. *Independence* headed to Japan with CVW-5 to become the Navy's forward deployed carrier, while CVW-14 returned to the U.S. with *Midway*.

28 Aug to 14 Sep 1991		***Midway***	**Return to CONUS**		
VFA-151	F/A-18A	NF/NK200	VAW-113	E-2C	NK600
VFA-113	F/A-18A	NK300	VAQ-139	EA-6B	NK604
VFA-25	F/A-18A	NK400	HS-8	SH-3H	NK610
VA-196	A-6E, KA-6D	NK500			

Midway came back to the Continental U.S. for the first time in 18 years with a highly modified air wing composition. CVW-14's *Tomcats* and *Vikings* had transferred to CVW-5 in Hawaii, while its two *Hornet* units traded their newer F/A-18Cs for VFA-192/195's A-models. VFA-151 also came home with the ship, and would move on to CVW-2. The wing's "new" *Hornets* received only limited markings for the transit home. All three Strike-Fighter units would get Cs before their next deployments. Although VA-196 had already transferred its last KA-6Ds, it did return to the U.S. with former VA-115 tankers.

18 Feb to 15 Aug 1994		***Carl Vinson***	**WP/IO/PG**		
VF-11	F-14D	NK100	VAW-113	E-2C	NK600
VF-31	F-14D, TARPS	NK200	VAQ-139	EA-6B	NK620
VFA-113	F/A-18C	NK300	VS-35	S-3B	NK700
VFA-25	F/A-18C	NK400	HS-8	SH-60F, HH-60H	NK610
VA-196	A-6E	NK500	VQ-5 det B	ES-3A	NK720

Now in *Carl Vinson*, CVW-14 received new F-14D and S-3B squadrons, as well as H-60s.

14 May to 14 Nov 1996		***Carl Vinson***	**WP/IO/PG**		
VF-11	F-14D	NK100	VAW-113	E-2C	NK600
VF-31	F-14D, TARPS	NK200	VAQ-139	EA-6B	NK620
VFA-113	F/A-18C	NK300	VS-35	S-3B	NK700
VFA-25	F/A-18C	NK400	HS-4	SH-60F, HH-60H	NK610
VA-196	A-6E	NK500	VQ-5 det D	ES-3A	NK

HS-8 was replaced by HS-4 prior to CVW-14's second deployment in *Vinson*.

11 Jun to 7 Dec 1998		***Abraham Lincoln***	**WP/IO/PG**		
VF-31	F-14D, TARPS	NK100	VAW-113	E-2C	NK600
VFA-115	F/A-18C	NK200	VAQ-139	EA-6B	NK620
VFA-113	F/A-18C	NK300	VS-35	S-3B	NK700
VFA-25	F/A-18C	NK400	HS-4	SH-60F, HH-60H	NK610
VQ-5 det B	ES-3A	NK720			
VRC-30 det 1	C-2A	NK			

CVW-14 moved to *Lincoln*, lost its *Intruders* and a *Tomcat* unit (the *Red Rippers*, who moved to CVW-7), while gaining a third F/A-18 squadron—the *Eagles* of VFA-115, which had just converted from *Intruders*.

14 Aug 2000 to 12 Feb 2001		***Abraham Lincoln***	**WP/IO/PG**		
VF-31	F-14D TARPS	NK100	VAW-113	E-2C	NK600
VFA-115	F/A-18C	NK200	VAQ-139	EA-6B	NK620
VFA-113	F/A-18C	NK300	VS-35	S-3B	NK700
VFA-25	F/A-18C	NK300	HS-4	SH-60F/HH-60H	NK610
VRC-30 det 1	C-2B	NK			

The second deployment in *Lincoln* included the same squadrons, with the exception of the ES-3 detachment, which had been retired.

CVW-15 NL

Estab. CVG-15 5 Apr 51, r/d CVW-15 30 Dec 63, disestab. 31 Mar 95. Homeport: Miramar

5 Dec 1974 to 2 Jul 1975		***Coral Sea***	**WP**		
VF-51	F-4N	NL100	RVAW-110 det 3	E-1B	NL010
VF-111	F-4N	NL200	VFP-63 det 5	RF-8G	NL610
VA-22	A-7E	NL300	HC-1 det 3	SH-3G	NL000
VA-94	A-7E	NL400			
VA-95	A-6A, KA-6D	NL500			

Air Wing FIFTEEN started the period with the Pacific Fleet's second F-4N deployment. The wing flew combat in support of the rescue of the SS *Mayaguez* off Cambodia during this cruise.

15 Feb to 5 Oct 1977		***Coral Sea***	**WP**		
VF-191	F-4J	NL100	VAW-114	E-2B	NL600
VF-194	F-4J	NL200	VFP-63 det 3	RF-8G	NL610
VA-22	A-7E	NL300	VMAQ-2 det A/B	EA-6A	CY620
VA-94	A-7E	NL400	HC-1 det 3	SH-3G	NL000
VA-95	A-6E, KA-6D	NL500			

VF-191 and 194, recently converted from F-8s, made their only *Phantom* deployment with CVW-15 in 1977. They would be disestablished soon after returning to Miramar. E-2s were assigned to the wing, and EA-6A *Intruders* joined in WestPac. The Marines used two different detachments, each spending about half the cruise with the ship.

Two East Coast A-7E squadrons joined Miramar based CVW-15 for their 1983 cruise in *Carl Vinson*. The *Gunslingers* of VA-105 had an appropriately marked CAG bird at the Wing's Fallon det in October 1982. NL300 (159970) is shown waiting its turn for the fuel pits with a practice AGM-45 *Shrike* missile. (Michael Grove)

30 May 1979 to 25 Feb 1980		***Kitty Hawk***	**WP/IO**		
VF-51	F-14A	NL100	VAW-114	E-2C	NL600
VF-111	F-14A	NL200	VFP-63 det 1	RF-8G	NL610
VA-22	A-7E	NL300	VAQ-135	EA-6B	NL620
VA-94	A-7E	NL400	VS-21	S-3A, US-3A	NL700
VA-95	A-6E, KA-6D	NL500	HS-8	SH-3H	NL720

Moving to a big deck carrier, CVW-15 gained F-14s, E-2Cs, EA-6Bs, and S-3s.

1 Apr to 23 Nov 1981		***Kitty Hawk***	**WP/IO**		
VF-51	F-14A	NL100	VAW-114	E-2C	NL600
VF-111	F-14A	NL200	VFP-63 det 1	RF-8G	NL610
VA-22	A-7E	NL300	VAQ-135	EA-6B	NL604
VA-94	A-7E	NL400	VS-29	S-3A	NL700
VA-95	A-6E, KA-6D	NL500	HS-4	SH-3H	NL730

Air Wing-15 changed its ASW units prior to the 1981 deployment, as VS-29 and HS-4 came aboard.

1 Mar to 29 Oct 1983		***Carl Vinson***	**World**		
VF-51	F-14A	NL100	VAW-114	E-2C	NL600
VF-111	F-14A	NL200	VAQ-134	EA-6B	NL604
VA-37	A-7E	NL300	VS-29	S-3A	NL700
VA-105	A-7E	NL400	HS-4	SH-3H	NL610
VA-52	A-6E, KA-6D	NL500			

CVW-15 joined "Starship *Vinson*" as she sailed from Norfolk to Alameda with a new group of Atkrons. Initially CVW-11 and -15 swapped A-7 squadrons, with VA-192/195 joining Air Wing Fifteen. They were moved on to CVW-9, and two Cecil-based *Corsair* units joined Whidbey's VA-52 to provide the wing's attack punch for cruise.

18 Oct 1984 to 25 May 1985		***Carl Vinson***	**WP/IO**		
VF-51	F-14A	NL100	VAW-114	E-2C	NL600
VF-111	F-14A	NL200	VAQ-134	EA-6B	NL604
VA-97	A-7E	NL300	VS-29	S-3A	NL700
VA-27	A-7E	NL400	HS-4	SH-3H	NL610
VA-52	A-6E, KA-6D	NL500			

CVW-15 returned to PacFlt A-7 units as VA-97 and -27 transferred over from CVW-14, which was transitioning to *Hornets*.

12 Aug 1986 to 5 Feb 1987		***Carl Vinson***	**WP/IO/Norpac**		
VF-51	F-14A	NL100	VAW-114	E-2C	NL600
VF-111	F-14A	NL200	VAQ-134	EA-6B	NL604
VA-97	A-7E	NL300	VS-29	S-3A	NL700
VA-27	A-7E	NL400	HS-4	SH-3H	NL610
VA-52	A-6E, KA-6D	NL500			

After spending Christmas in Australia, the 1986-1987 deployment ended with two weeks of operations in the Bering Sea between Alaska and the Soviet Union. Weather proved frightful, with 18 foot seas, -25°F degree wind chill, and heavy snow encountered. In spite of conducting flight operations in intermittent zero ceiling /zero visibility conditions, the wing flew without a single mishap, although things reportedly got exciting at times.

15 Jun to 14 Dec 1988		***Carl Vinson***	**WP/IO**		
VF-51	F-14A	NL100	VAW-114	E-2C	NL600
VF-111	F-14A	NL200	VAQ-134	EA-6B	NL604
VA-97	A-7E	NL300	VS-29	S-3A	NL700
VA-27	A-7E	NL400	HS-4	SH-3H	NL610
VA-52	A-6E, KA-6D	NL500			

5 Sep 1989 to 8 Nov 1989		***Carl Vinson***	**WP/NorPac**		
VF-51	F-14A	NL100	VAW-114	E-2C	NL6001
VF-111	F-14A	NL200	VAQ-134	EA-6B	NL604

VA-97	A-7E	NL300	VS-29	S-3A	NL700
VA-27	A-7E	NL400	HS-4	SH-3H	NL610
VA-52	A-6E, KA-6D	NL500			

1 Feb to 31 Jul 1990		***Carl Vinson***	**WP/IO**		
VF-51	F-14A	NL100	VAW-114	E-2C	NL600
VF-111	F-14A	NL200	VAQ-134	EA-6B	NL604
VA-97	A-7E	NL300	VS-29	S-3A	NL700
VA-27	A-7E	NL400	HS-4	SH-3H	NL610
VA-52	A-6E, KA-6D	NL500			

The 1990 *Vinson*/CVW-15 deployment ended six remarkable years where the ship/Air Wing structure remained essentially unchanged. After making the final PacFlt *Corsair II* deployment VA-27 and -97 would alter the mix by transitioning to F/A-18s, while the wing moved to another carrier.

18 Oct 1991-11 Dec 1991		***Kitty Hawk***	**Horn**		
VF-51	F-14A	NL100	VAW-114	E-2C	NL600
VF-111	F-14A	NL200	VAQ-134	EA-6B	NL620
VFA-97	F/A-18A	NL300	VS-37	S-3A	NL700
VFA-27	F/A-18A	NL400	HS-4	SH-60F, HH-60H	NL610
VA-52	A-6E, KA-6D	NL500			

Leaving *Vinson* behind after six deployments, CVW-15 moved to *Kitty Hawk*. CVW-15 squadrons received *Hornets* in 1990-91, along with SH-60s. VS-37 joined the wing as well, and it accompanied the *Hawk* on its post-SLEP trip around the Horn for San Diego.

3 Nov 1992 to 3 May 1993		***Kitty Hawk***	**WP/IO/PG**		
VF-51	F-14A	NL100	VAW-114	E-2C	NL600
VF-111	F-14A	NL200	VAQ-134	EA-6B	NL620
VFA-97	F/A-18A	NL300	VS-37	S-3B	NL700
VFA-27	F/A-18A	NL400	HS-4	SH-60F/HH-60H	NL610
VA-52	A-6E, KA-6D	NL500			

The *Kitty Hawk* and CVW-15 initially provided aircraft to support *Restore Hope* off Somalia. Turning north, the wing sent 20 aircraft ahead to Dhahran, Saudi Arabia, where they were made available for Central Command tasking for *Southern Watch*. The aircraft returned to the *Hawk* after seven days, and on 13 January the air wing participated in strikes on Iraq in response to provocative acts by Sadaam Hussein.

24 Jun to 22 Dec 1994		***Kitty Hawk***	**WP/IO/PG**		
VF-51	F-14A	NL100	VAW-114	E-2C	NL600
VF-111	F-14A	NL200	VAQ-134	EA-6B	NL620
VFA-97	F/A-18A	NL300	VS-37	S-3A	NL700
VFA-27	F/A-18A	NL400	HS-4	SH-60F, HH-60H	NL610
VA-52	A-6E	NL500	VQ-5 det C	ES-3A	NL720

By now self-styled as the "Wolfpack," Carrier Air Wing FIFTEEN made its final deployment in 1994. It was disestablished in March 1995, along with VF-51, VF-111, VA-52, VAW-114, and VS-37.

AA300 is a VFA-83 F/A-18C (163509) shown at Fallon in Oct 1991. The special tail markings on this CAG bird fit well with the *Rampagers'* ram's head logo, and are a popular motif adopted from the Navy's trade school located at Annapolis, Maryland. The aircraft also carries a "Battle E" award ribbon, as well as a very subtle indication under the cockpit that the unit has won the Estocin Award as the top VFA squadron in the Navy in 1990, Michael Estocin having been an A-4 pilot with VA-192, KIA in April 1967, and posthumously awarded the Medal of Honor for flight over North Vietnam. (Michael Grove)

CVW-17 AA

Estab. 1 Nov 66. Homeport: Oceana, Cecil Field (Jun 1980), Oceana (Sep 1994)

As of 1974, CVW-17 was the youngest air wing in the Navy, having been established only in 1966, and making all of its deployments in *Forrestal*. The wing's tailcode was normally carried in a distinctive "Alpha-Alpha" form, with a lightning bolt connecting the two letters.

11 Mar to 11 Sep 1974		***Forrestal***	**Med**		
VF-11	F-4J	AA100	VAW-126	E-2B	AA760
VF-74	F-4J	AA200	RVAH-6	RA-5C	AA600
VA-83	A-7E	AA300	HS-3	SH-3D	AA000
VA-81	A-7E	AA400			
VA-85	A-6E, KA-6D	AA500			

As of 1974, CVW-17 had a standard air wing configuration of two VF, two VA(L), and a single VA(M). Only EW support was missing. In July the ship and air wing provided cover during the evacuation of U.S. citizens from Cyprus, while Greece and Turkey fought over the island.

5 Mar to 22 Sep 1975		***Forrestal***	**Med**		
VF-11	F-4J	AA100	VAW-111	E-2B	AA700
VF-74	F-4J	AA200	VAQ-134	EA-6B	AA610
VA-83	A-7E	AA300	RVAH-7	RA-5C	AA600
VA-81	A-7E	AA400	HS-3	SH-3D	AA000
VA-85	A-6E, KA-6D	AA500			

For its 1975 Med deployment CVW-17 used a Pacific Fleet E-2 unit, and was joined by EA-6Bs.

4 July 1976	***Forrestal***	**International Naval Review**			
VF-11	F-4J	AA100	VAW-(?)	E-2	(AA700)
VMFA-451	F-4J	AA200	RVAH-12	RA-5C	AA600
VA-83	A-7E	AA300	HS-3	SH-3D	AA000
VA-81	A-7E	AA400			
VA-85	A-6E, KA-6D	AA500			

Forrestal and CVW-17 were selected to represent the Navy at the Bi-Centennial Naval Review in New York Harbor on 4 July 1976. A Marine F-4 unit replaced VF-74, which was assigned to CVW-8 in *Nimitz* for its initial deployment. The author has not been able to identify what, if any, E-2 unit supported this event.

4 Apr to 26 Oct 1978		***Forrestal***	**Med/NorLant**		
VF-11	F-4J	AA100	VAW-116	E-2B	AA010
VF-74	F-4J	AA200	VAQ-130	EA-6B	AA610
VA-83	A-7E	AA300	VS-30	S-3A	AA700
VA-81	A-7E	AA400	HS-3	SH-3D	AA000
VA-85	A-6E, KA-6D	AA500			

The *Be-Devilers* re-joined CVW-17 for its 1978 deployment to the Med. The wing would also make do without a dedicated photo-recon capability until the arrival of F-14 TARPS several years ahead.

27 Nov 1979 to 7 May 1980		***Forrestal***	**Med**		
VF-11	F-4J	AA100	VAW-125	E-2C	AA010
VF-74	F-4J	AA200	VAQ-133	EA-6B	AA610
VA-83	A-7E	AA300	VS-30	S-3A	AA700
VA-81	A-7E	AA400	HS-3	SH-3H	AA000
VA-85	A-6E, KA-6D	AA500			

2 Mar to 15 Sep 1981		***Forrestal***	**Med**		
VMFA-115	F-4J	AA100	VAW-125	E-2C	AA010
VF-74	F-4J	AA200	VAQ-130	EA-6B	AA610
VA-83	A-7E	AA300	VS-30	S-3A	AA700
VA-81	A-7E	AA400	HS-3	SH-3H	AA730
VA-85	A-6E, KA-6D	AA500			

The Marines return in the form of the *Silver Eagles* of VMFA-115 and their *Phantoms* for the wing's 1981 trip to the Med, as VF-74 goes through F-4S transition.

8 Jun to 16 Nov 1982		***Forrestal***	**Med**		
VF-74	F-4S	AA100	VAW-125	E-2C	AA600
VF-103	F-4S	AA200	VAQ-130	EA-6B	AA604
VA-83	A-7E	AA300	VS-30	S-3A	AA700
VA-81	A-7E	AA400	HS-3	SH-3H	AA610
VA-85	A-6E, KA-6D	AA500			

Forrestal's 1982 deployment would prove to be the only appearance of carrier-based Navy F-4Ss to the Med, with VF-74 and VF-103 doing the honors. The *Sluggers* reported to CVW-17 after transition with the AA100 series numbers, but swapped with the *Be-Devilers* prior to the Fallon det. VF-74 switched to the 100 series side numbers, and changed the color of the tail trim from yellow to the appropriate red at the same time.

2 Apr to 20 Oct 1984		***Saratoga***	**Med**		
VF-74	F-14A	AA100	VAW-125	E-2C	AA600
VF-103	F-14A, TARPS	AA200	VMAQ-2 det X	EA-6B	AA604
VA-83	A-7E	AA300	VS-30	S-3A	AA700
VA-81	A-7E	AA400	HS-3	SH-3H	AA610
VMA(AW)-533	A-6E, KA-6D	AA500			

After having spent its first 17 years on one carrier, a 1983 move to *Saratoga* also gave the wing a chance to reequip its FITRONS with *Tomcats*. Marine *Intruder* and *Prowler* units were assigned as well.

26 Aug 1985 to 16 Apr 1986		***Saratoga***	**Med/IO**		
VF-74	F-14A	AA100	VAW-125	E-2C	AA600
VF-103	F-14A, TARPS	AA200	VAQ-137	EA-6B	AA604
VA-83	A-7E	AA300	VS-30	S-3A	AA700
VA-81	A-7E	AA400	HS-3	SH-3H	AA610
VA-85	A-6E, KA-6D	AA500			

The *Black Falcons* of VA-85 returned to the wing after a cruise with CVW-3. VAQ-137 introduced the ICAP II version of the EA-6B to the fleet during this deployment. On 19 Oct 1985 F-14s, E-2s, and tankers were involved in the aerial intercept of an Egypt Air Boeing 737 that was carrying terrorists who had been involved in the seizure of the ship *Achille Lauro*, and the murder of an American citizen. The ship and air wing also participated in Operation *Prairie Fire* off Libya in March 1986.

5 Jun to 17 Nov 1987		***Saratoga***	**Med**		
VF-74	F-14A	AA100	VAW-125	E-2C	AA600
VF-103	F-14A, TARPS	AA200	VAQ-137	EA-6B	AA604
VA-83	A-7E	AA300	VS-30	S-3A	AA700
VA-81	A-7E	AA400	HS-3	SH-3H	AA610
VA-85	A-6E, KA-6D	AA500			

15 Aug to 8 Oct	**1988**	***Independence***	**Horn**		
VFA-131	F/A-18A	AA100	VAW-125	E-2C	AA600
VF-103	F-14A, TARPS	AA200	VS-30	S-3B	AA700
VA-155	A-6E, KA-6D	AA500	HS-3	SH-3H	AA610

A truncated version of CVW-17 accompanied *Indy* as it made its post-SLEP move to the West Coast. Whidbey-based VA-155 joined the wing for the trip, as did CVW-13's VFA-131. Both units carried the wing's "AA" markings for the duration.

7 Aug 1990 to 28 Mar 1991		***Saratoga***	**Med/RS**		
VF-74	F-14A+	AA100	VAW-125	E-2C	AA600
VF-103	F-14A+, TARPS	AA200	VAQ-132	EA-6B	AA604
VFA-83	F/A-18C	AA300	VS-30	S-3B	AA700
VFA-81	F/A-18C	AA400	HS-3	SH-3H	AA610
VA-35	A-6E, KA-6D	AA500			

Saratoga and CVW-17 participated in *Desert Shield/Desert Storm* operations from the Red Sea with the combat loss of an F/A-18C, A-6E, and F-14A+.

6 May to 6 Nov 1992		***Saratoga***	**Med**		
VF-74	F-14B	AA100	VAW-125	E-2C	AA600
VF-103	F-14B, TARPS	AA200	VAQ-132	EA-6B	AA604
VFA-83	F/A-18C	AA300	VS-30	S-3B	AA700
VFA-81	F/A-18C	AA400	HS-9	SH-3H	AA610
VA-35	A-6E, KA-6D	AA500	VX-1 det A	ES-3A	JA770

CVW-17 was selected to test the new ES-3A *Shadow* aircraft during its 1992 Med cruise. A detachment from VX-1 supplied two of the aircraft, which joined the ship in September. The F-14A+ *Tomcats* have now received the designation F-14B. HS-9 has joined the wing in a swap with CVW-8. It would be the last deployment for the *Sea Griffons*.

12 Jan to 24 Jun 1994		***Saratoga***	**Med**		
VF-103	F-14B	AA200	VAW-125	E-2C	AA600
VFA-83	F/A-18C	AA300	VAQ-132	EA-6B	AA620
VFA-81	F/A-18C	AA400	VS-30	S-3B	AA700
VA-35	A-6E	AA500	HS-15	SH-60F, HH-60H	AA610
VQ-6 det A	ES-3A	AA760			

CVW-17 lost a *Tomcat* squadron, VF-74 being disestablished. There was no 100 series squadron for this deployment, which would be the last for *Saratoga*. HS-15 joined, along with its SH-60s.

28 Jun to 20 Dec 1996		***Enterprise***	**Med/RS/PG**		
VF-103	F-14B, TARPS	AA200	VAW-125	E-2C	AA600
VFA-83	F/A-18C	AA300	VAQ-132	EA-6B	AA620
VFA-81	F/A-18C	AA400	VS-30	S-3B	AA700
VA-75	A-6E	AA500	HS-15	SH-60F, HH-60H	AA610
VQ-6 det C	ES-3A	AA760			

VF-103 changed its name from the *Sluggers* to the *Jolly Rogers* in October 1995. VA-75 was making the last cruise of the A-6 *Intruder*. It would be disestablished soon after returning to CONUS. VF-103 made the first *Tomcat* deployment with LANTIRN pods.

10 Jun to 10 Dec 1998		***Dwight D Eisenhower***	**Med/RS/PG**		
VF-103	F-14B, TARPS	AA100	VAW-125	E-2C	AA600
VFA-34	F/A-18C	AA200	VAQ-132	EA-6B	AA620
VFA-83	F/A-18C	AA300	VS-30	S-3B	AA700
VFA-81	F/A-18C	AA400	HS-15	SH-60F, HH-60H	AA610
VQ-6 det D	ES-3A	AA760			
VRC-40 det 3	C-2A	AA			

Having lost its Medium Attack squadron, CVW-17 took a third *Hornet* unit, VFA-34, with VF-103 moving to the AA100 series.

21 Jun to 18 Dec 2000		***George Washington***	**Med/RS/PG**		
VF-103	F-14B, TARPS	AA100	VAW-125	E-2C	AA600
VFA-34	F/A-18C	AA200	VS-30	S-3B	AA700
VFA-83	F/A-18C	AA300	HS-15	SH-60F, HH-60H	AA610
VFA-81	F/A-18C	AA400	VRC-40 det		
VAQ-132	EA-6B	AA500			

The VF-51 *Screaming Eagles* made the last deployment of *Franklin D. Roosevelt*, as well as CVW-19. They returned to Miramar, where this picture was taken, to await transition to *Tomcats*. This picture of NM100 (F-4N 152326) at Miramar was actually taken that December, after the wing had been disestablished. What appears to be a MiG kill star on the splitter plate is something of a mystery, as neither this airframe, nor the name on the canopy rail (RADM "Ted" Fellowes, the Miramar fighter wing commander at that time) are listed an any Vietnam MiG killer lists the author has seen. (Mick Roth)

CVW-19 NM

Estab. CVG-19 15 Aug 43, r/d CVAG-19 15 Nov 46, r/d CVG-19 1 Sep 48, r/d CVW-19 20 Dec 63, disestab. 30 Jun 77. Homeport: Lemoore

Air Wing Nineteen had a distinguished record from the Vietnam war, with eight deployments in three carriers. As of 1974 it was on yet another WestPac in the 27C *Oriskany*. The wing/ship team would make one more trip to WestPac before the "O-Boat" was decommissioned. Afterwards a heavily reorganized CVW-19 made a single deployment to the Mediterranean for *Franklin Roosevelt's* final deployment.

18 Oct 1973 to 5 Jun 1974		***Oriskany***	**WPAC**		
VF-191	F-8J	NM100	VAW-111 det 6	E-1B	NM010
VF-194	F-8J	NM200	VFP-63 det 4	RF-8G	NM600
VA-153	A-7B	NM300	VAQ-130 det 3	EKA-3B	NM614
VA-215	A-7B	NM400	HC-1 det 1	SH-3G	NM000
VA-155	A-7B	NM500			

The 1973/74 deployment would prove to be the last for the EKA-3B, as the *Zappers* canceled a later detachment (to *Ranger*/CVW-2) and moved to Whidbey Island to transition to *Prowlers*.

16 Sep 1975 to 3 Mar 1976		***Oriskany***	**WPAC**		
VF-191	F-8J	NM100	RVAW-110 det 4	E-1B	NM010
VF-194	F-8J	NM200	VFP-63 det 4	RF-8G	NM600
VA-153	A-7B	NM300	HC-1 det 4	SH-3G	NM700
VA-215	A-7B	NM400			
VA-155	A-7B	NM500			

This trip to WestPac would be the last deployment for U.S. Navy F-8 *Crusaders* in their fighter form. VFP-63 would continue to deploy photo birds for another four years. Fitrons 191 and 194 would return to Miramar, and transition to *Phantom IIs* afterwards. The West Coast E-2 RAG supplied the AEW det for this trip.

4 Oct 1976 to 21 Apr 1977		***Franklin D. Roosevelt***	**Med**		
VF-51	F-4N	NM100	RVAW-110 det 4	E-1B	NM010
VF-111	F-4N	NM200	HC-1 det 3	SH-3G	NM720
VA-153	A-7B	NM300			
VA-215	A-7B	NM400			
VA-155	A-7B	NM500			
VMA-231	AV-8A	NM600			

In one of the odder air wing configurations of the period, West Coast CVW-19 was reorganized to make *Roosevelt's* last deployment to the Med. Two *Phantom* units joined the air wing, as did the first VSTOL jet squadron to ever accompany a CV, as Cherry Point-based VMA-231 brought 14 *Harriers* onboard. The experimental configuration was a result of an Air Lant order (27-77) that directed the investigation of V/STOL aircraft in a CV environment. In order to make room for the *Harriers* the VF and VA units took only ten aircraft apiece, with three E-1Bs and four helos making up the rest of the air wing. With deck space at a premium, no recon or EW dets were embarked. RVAW-110, which had started placing its last E-1s into storage, quickly found three "Fudds" to form a new det 4 to cover this deployment.

Results of the deployment were mixed, with the *Harriers* proving remarkably versatile in operation, but shorter legged than their conventional counterparts, generally following a "last to launch/first to recover" schedule that led to a normal 1 hour 15 minute cycle time, or a quarter hour shorter than the rest of the air wing. Bomb loads were also reduced, particularly when compared to the *Corsairs* onboard, and CAP stations were limited to about 100 nm from the ship, about half that of the *Phantoms*. Nonetheless, the deployment showed that, with some effort and original thinking, conventioinal and V/STOL aircraft could co-exist on the same ship. In any event, the mixture would not be re attempted.

The axe fell after the ship's return, as *Roosevelt* went to the scrappers, while CVW-19 and the three Atkrons were disestablished. VF-51 and 111 got *Tomcats* and a new life, while the "Willy Fudds," having made their last deployment after almost twenty years of service, returned to the Arizona desert. By the year 2000 only VMA-231 survived, as an AV-8B unit.

CVW-21 NP

Estab. CVG-21 1 Jul 55, r/d CVW-21 20 Dec 63, disestab. 12 Dec 1975 Homeport: Lemoore

CVW-21 was another wing with a valorous combat record, having been a "small deck" specialist during the Vietnam conflict. It was the last "classic" 27C wing of two *Crusader* and three *Skyhawk* squadrons. As of 1974 CVW-21 was returning home from WestPac. It would deploy one more time before being disestablished.

8 May 1973 to 8 Jan 1974		***Hancock***	**WPAC/IO**		
VF-211	F-8J	NP100	VAW-111 det 2	E-1B	NP01X
VF-24	F-8J	NP200	VAQ-135/130 det 5	EKA-3B	NP610
VA-212	A-4F	NP300	VFP-63 det 1	RF-8G	NP600
VA-164	A-4F, TA-4F	NP400	HC-1 det 3	SH-3G	NP000
VA-55	A-4F	NP500			

Each of the three A-4 units specialized in a specific air-to-ground weapon. VA-212 was the AGM-62 *Walleye* glide bomb unit, VA-55 handled AGM-45 *Shrike* missiles for the "Iron Hand" role, and VA-164 were the laser guided bomb specialists, with two-seat TA-4Fs being assigned to use the hand-held laser designator. The "Whale" det was transferred to VAQ-130 mid-cruise, as VAQ-135's home squadron moved to Whidbey Island for *Prowler* transition.

18 Mar to 20 Oct 1975		***Hancock***	**WPAC**		
VF-211	F-8J	NP100	RVAW-110 det 6	E-1B	NP010
VF-24	F-8J	NP200	VFP-63 det 6	RF-8G	NP610
VA-212	A-4F	NP300	HC-1 det 1	SH-3G	NP000
VA-164	A-4F, TA-4F	NP400			
VA-55	A-4F	NP500			

CVW-21 made the last A-4 *Skyhawk* deployment in the U.S. Navy, as all of its Atkrons would be disestablished afterwards, as was the Air Wing itself. The Fighter squadrons transitioned to *Tomcats*, and the ship was decommissioned.

CVW-21 was the last Air Wing to deploy with A-4 *Skyhawks*. VA-164's NP400 is appropriately attired in CAG markings at Lemoore in December 1975, the unit's last month. (Michael Grove)

Reserves

The Navy created two reserve carrier air wings in April 1970 that were organized roughly along the lines of fleet wings, the one major exception being that they never had VS units assigned. Their structure remained relatively stable through the years, with their squadrons going through aircraft transitions as newer airframes became available from the fleet. CVWR-30 and most of its squadrons were disestablished during the post-*Desert Storm* force reductions. While the CVWRs conducted periodic visits to ships for carrier qualifications, neither wing ever deployed overseas as a complete unit. They are shown here at ten year intervals. See individual squadrons for details.

CVWR-20 AF

Estab. 1 April 1970 Homeport: Cecil, Atlanta (Oct 1996)

CVWR-20 was originally established with five attack squadrons and no fighter units attached. VF-201 and -202 were initially assigned to CVWR-30 for a short period (where they wore that wing's ND tailcodes), and joined the CVWR-20 only after VA-209 (A-4L, Glenview) and VA-210 (A-4C, South Weymouth) were disestablished during the spring of 1971. CVWR-20 also took over control of the two non-carrier deploying reserve adversary units during the '90s, both of which adopted the "AF" tailcode upon their assignment. Land based VFC-12 joined the wing in October 1992, followed by VFC-13 in June 1994. This was done to place all Reserve tactical squadrons under one administrative command. The wing's "Alpha Foxtrot" (AF) code was used by CVG/CVW-6 between 1956 and 1965, but was changed to "Alpha Echo" (AE) when, according to one story, a visiting VIP assumed that it meant the airplanes belonged to the Air Force. CVWR-20 would still use the code throughout, however.

July 1974

VF-201	F-8J	AF100	Dallas	VFP-206	RF-8G	AF630	Washington
VF-202	F-8K	AF200	Dallas	VAW-207	E-1B	AF010	Norfolk
VA-203	A-7A	AF300	Jacksonville	VAQ-208	KA-3B	AF650	Alameda
VA-204	A-4L	AF400	Memphis				
VA-205	A-4L	AF500	Atlanta				

CVWR-20 was behind its west coast counterpart in terms of modernization in mid-1974, as it still had *Crusaders* assigned, as well as A-4s. *Phantoms* arrived in 1976, and the last *Skyhawk* unit received *Corsairs* in 1978.

July 1984

VF-201	F-4N	AF100	Dallas	VFP-206	RF-8G	AF630	Washington
VF-202	F-4N	AF200	Dallas	VAW-78	E-1B	AF010	Norfolk
VA-203	A-7E	AF300	Cecil	VAK-208	KA-3B	AF610	Alameda
VA-204	A-7B	AF400	N.Orleans	VAQ-209	EA-6A	AF700	Norfolk
VA-205	A-7E	AF500	Atlanta				

By 1984 CVWR-20 was about a decade behind the times, with older airframes still assigned almost across the board. Only the two Atkrons flying A-7Es were still in daily use with the fleet.

July 1994

VF-201	F-14A	AF100	Dallas	VAW-78	E-2C	AF600	Norfolk
VF-202	F-14A	AF200	Dallas	VAQ-209	EA-6B	AF604	Washington
VFA-203	F/A-18A	AF300	Cecil				
VFA-204	F/A-18A	AF400	N.Orleans	VFC-12 *	FA-18A/B		Oceana
VA-205	A-6E	AF500	Atlanta	VFC-13 *	FA-18A/B		Fallon

With the exception of a VS squadron, CVWR-20 looks much like a regular navy wing as of mid-1994.

The "Whales," *Phantoms*, and *Corsairs* are gone, while *Tomcats*, *Hornets*, *Prowlers*, *Hawkeyes*, and attack *Intruders* have come aboard. The Reserves' two VFC outfits have been assigned to the wing for administrative purposes, and were not suitable for carrier operations. (*= non carrier deployable)

Dec 2000

VFA-201	F/A-18A	AF100	Ft Worth	VAW-77 *	E-2C	AF00	Atlanta
VFA-203	F/A-18A	AF300	Atlanta	VAW-78	E-2C	AF600	Norfolk
VFA-204	F/A-18A	AF400	New Orleans	VFC-12*	FA-18A/B		Oceana
VAQ-209	EA-6B	AF500	Washington	VFC-13*	F-5E/F		Fallon

CVWR-20 was reduced in size during the mid-'90s, as its intended role became less deployment as a coherent unit, and more a supplier of individual squadrons as needed by the fleet. VF-202 and VA-205 are gone, VF-201 has converted to Hornets, and VFA-203 has moved to Atlanta. A new VAW has been established in Georgia to support land-based counter-drug operations. The two adversary units remain as well. (*= non carrier deployable)

CVWR-30 ND
Estab. 1 Apr 1970 Disestab. 31 Dec 1994
Homeport: Alameda

July 1974

VF-301	F-4B	ND100	Miramar	VFP-306	RF-8G	ND600	Washington
VF-302	F-4B	ND200	Miramar	VAW-307	E-1B	ND010	North Island
VA-303	A-7A	ND300	Alameda	VAQ-308	KA-3B	ND630	Alameda
VA-304	A-7A	ND400	Alameda				
VA-305	A-7A	ND500	Pt Mugu				

VF-301 and -302 joined the wing in the summer of 1971, replacing VF-201 and -202, which moved to CVWR-20. The wing's F-8s and A-4s had already been replaced by *Phantoms* and *Corsairs*, making it, with the exception of a VA(M) unit, not much less capable than a Regular Navy CVW. The wing's "November Delta" (ND) tailcode was almost always applied in a very clever fashion, with a stylized letter "N" being applied over a "Delta" (triangle) shape.

July 1984

VF-301	F-4N	ND100	Miramar	VFP-306	RF-8G	ND600	Washington
VF-302	F-4N	ND200	Miramar	VAW-88	E-2B	ND010	North Island
VFA-303	(A-7E)	ND300	Lemoore	VAK-308	KA-3B	ND630	Alameda
VA-304	A-7B	ND400	Alameda	VAQ-309	EA-6A	ND610	Whidbey Is.
VA-305	A-7B	ND500	Pt Mugu				

By 1984 CVWR-30 had an EW unit assigned, as well as E-2Bs and "newer" *Phantoms* (Ns being remodeled Bs). VA-303 has moved to Lemoore and been redesignated, but has not received any *Hornets* yet.

1994 (at disestablishment)

VF-301	F-14A	ND100	Miramar	VAW-88	E-2C	ND010	Miramar
VF-302	F-14A	ND200	Miramar	VAQ-309	EA-6B	ND604	Whidbey Is.
VFA-303	F/A-18A	ND300	Lemoore				
VFA-305	F/A-18A	ND400	Pt Mugu				
VA-304	A-6E	ND500	Alameda				

At the time of disestablishment CVWR-30 closely resembled a regular navy air wing, with only S-3s missing.

While not a CAG bird, A-7B ND410 shows the unique "November Delta" tailcode used by CVWR-30, as well as the vivid orange markings applied to VA-304 *Corsairs* during the period. It also wears a Meritorious Unit Commendation ribbon behind the intake. A-7B 154549 is at Fallon in May 1980. (Michael Grove)

CVSGR

Two Reserve Carrier Anti-Submarine Groups (CVSGRs) were formed in 1970 in parallel with the CVWRs. The end of the distinct ASW carriers and groups in the regular Navy (the last three, CVSG-53, -56, and -59, were disestablished in June 1973) meant that their Reserve counterparts would not last long. Both Groups were shut down in 1976, although the HS and VAW squadrons survived with other organizations. Each CVSGR had six squadrons: three VS (with Grumman *Trackers*), two HS (Sikorsky *Sea Kings*), and one VAW (E-1B *Tracers*). They also had a small ASW-Fighter unit (VSF) assigned for protection, with A-4Cs and, later, F-8s assigned. The two Reserve ASW Air Groups were never well documented, and lived their short lives in relative obscurity. See individual squadron listings for details.

CVSGR-70	**AW**	**established 1 May 70**	**disest. Jun 1976**				
VS-71	S-2E	AW100	Lakehurst	VAW-78	E-1B	AW010	Norfolk
VS-72	S-2E	AW200	Norfolk	HS-74	SH-3D	AW400	So Weymouth
VS-73	S-2E	AW300	Detroit	HS-75	SH-3D	AW500	Lakehurst
(VSF-76	A-4C	AW600	New Orleans)				

-VSF-76 received F-8Hs in 1971 and was disestablished in Sep 1973, joining VSF-86 to become VC-13.

CVSGR-80	**NW**	**established 1 May 70**	**r/d HelWingRes Jun 1976**				
VS-81	S-2E	NW100	North Island	VAW-88	E-1B	NW010	North Isl.
VS-82	S-2E	NW200	Alameda	HS-84	SH-3D	NW400	North Isl.
VS-83	S-2E	NW300	Whidbey Isl.	HS-85	SH-3D	NW500	Alameda
(VSF-86	A-4C	NW600	NewOrleans)				

-VS-81 was originally based at NAS Los Alimitos CA and moved to North Island in 1971.
-CVSGR-80 was reorganized into a new Functional Wing, Helicopter Wing Reserve (HelWingsRes).
-VSF-86 received F-8Hs in 1971 and was disestablishd in Sep 1973, becoming the basis for VC-13.

4

Fighter Squadrons (VF)

"When you meet another pilot, don't bother asking him what he drives. If he flies fighters he'll definitely let you know.... If he doesn't, why embarrass him?"

- Old fighter pilot's saying

They were the MiG killers of the Vietnam war, the stuff of legends and movies, and their crews flew manly aircraft with the names *Phantom* and *Crusader*. Their social affairs were also of legend—while nobody talked about flying into Lemoore for Happy Hour, most of the Fleet (and a good portion of the Marines and Air Force) knew that the Oceana Officer's Club was the place to be after work on a Friday. The Miramar O'Club on Wednesday nights grew to epic status as "WOXOF,"[5] whose "bogey rich environment" was portrayed with at least some accuracy in the movie "Top Gun."

After hours activities aside, Miramar proudly wore the appellation of "Fightertown," with a huge sign by the runway for all to see. Oceana followed suit, with large letters on a prominent hangar spelling "Fighter Country." There was no doubt at either location where you were, or what their business and passion was all about.

As of January 1974 there were 28 Fighter Squadrons in the Regular Navy, with the fighter communities based at Oceana (AirLant) and the Pacific Fleet's Miramar. 22 squadrons flew the F-4 *Phantom II*, four the F-8 *Crusader*, and two were preparing to make the first deployment with the new F-14A *Tomcat*.

The quartet of remaining F-8 *Crusader* squadrons flew the self-styled "Last of the Gunfighters" out of Miramar. It was a truly legendary aircraft that achieved the best air-to-air kill ratio (6:1) of all U.S. fighters over the entire Vietnam war. The 'Sader was not without its faults, however, including a gun system that had a tendency to jam when you needed it most (under heavy G-force), and limited rearward visibility. The type's fearsome reputation really came from its highly skilled and motivated pilots, who truly believed they were the last real practitioners of dogfighting in the U.S. military. Many of these same men also reveled in a somewhat macabre fashion in the type's high carrier landing mishap rate, which only increased the "manly" reputation of the aircraft and the aircrew who flew it. The F-8 would make its final deployment in the fighter role from an American carrier in 1976.

The McDonnell-Douglas F-4 *Phantom II* series rates as one of the true classic airframes of Naval Aviation. First deployed in the early '60s as a fleet interceptor in the mold of the F3H *Demon* that proceeded it, the Navy developed the type into a very capable fighter-bomber aircraft that was, with improved crew training, able to succeed in the MiG-filled skies over Vietnam. (Indeed, according to author Marshall Michel, in his superb book *Clashes*, during the penultimate stage of the air war of Vietnam, during Linebacker I and II in late 1972, the Navy achieved a 6:1 ratio with its *Phantoms*, while the Air Force managed only 2:1).

The Grumman F-14 *Tomcat* was the Navy's premier fighter aircraft between 1974 and the end of the Millennium. The F-14 was the longest serving of all the fabled Grumman line of Cats, and would see over 30 years of carrier duty. Here a VF-21 F-14A prepares to launch from *Constellation's* cat 1 while in the Western Pacific in May 1985. (author)

Four versions of the *Phantom* served in the fleet between 1974 and 1986. Two Oceana units (VF-41, -84) were still in F-4Bs as of January 1974, while two sisters (VF-14, -32) were turning in their "Bravos" while awaiting *Tomcats*. VF-51 and -111 had Bs at Miramar, while the pair forward deployed in *Midway* (VF-151, -161) had F-4Ns, which were modified Bs. The remaining *Phantom* squadrons flew the F-4J, with slatted-wing -Ss (upgraded Js) coming in 1980.

Introduced to VF-124 in 1973, the Grumman F-14 *Tomcat* would remain the Navy's leading fighter aircraft for the next thirty plus years and, in many ways, become the very symbol of Naval Aviation through the period. The type's long range, powerful AWG-9 radar and AIM-54 *Phoenix* missiles[6] provided defense for the fleet as a more-than-fitting successor to the legendary *Phantom*. The type was known Navy-wide as the "Turkey," not for a lack of fighting ability, but for the way it looked while coming aboard the boat—with its wide wing span and flapping horizontal stabilizer "tail feathers."

The *Tomcat* first deployed with two new units (VF-1 and -2) in 1974. *Phantom* and *Crusader* squadrons transitioned to F-14s through the '70s and early '80s, so that by November 1982, when *Forrestal* returned from the Med, only the two *Midway*-class decks were left with F-4s. They would both get F/A-18 Strike-Fighters for their fighter complement by 1986, with the last *Phantoms* finally being beached.

The underpowered F-14A was followed by the F-14A+ (38 new, 47 modified "A"s), which arrived at Oceana in 1987, and was later renamed F-14B.[7] They first went to sea with CVW-7 (VF-142, VF-143) in 1990. The even better F-14D (37 new, 18 former "As") deployed with CVW-14 (VF-11 and -31) four years later. Initial plans placed F-14Bs on both coasts, but that soon changed for support reasons, and by 1992 the four "B" units were at Oceana, while the quartet of "D" squadrons could be found at Miramar. The final F-14D was delivered on 10 July 1992, ending *Tomcat* production at 712 airframes.

Combat for the *Tomcat* included well publicized air-to-air encounters with Muammar al-Qaddafi's Air Force (results: U.S. Navy 4, Libya 0), and a single helo kill during *Desert Storm*. F-14 crews chafed at the bit during *Storm*, as the USAF was believed by many fighter crews to keep the lucrative CAP stations to themselves, which resulted in Air Force F-15Cs shooting down 33 Iraqi aircraft during the war. There were also stories that the long and recently ended war with Iran had led Iraqi fighter pilots to both respect and fear the F-14, and that the mere scent of a *Tomcat's* AWG-9 radar in the area would start Iraqi aircraft running in the opposite direction, usually right into USAF hands. One *Saratoga* F-14A+ was lost during the war while protecting a *Prowler*. The pilot was recovered, while the RIO became a POW.

By 1990 the community that at one time bragged "Not a pound for air-to-ground" had learned the error of its ways, and was hanging ordnance from their "Bombcats." Four years later *Toms* were dropping precision weapons—GBU-16 laser guided bombs, with the help of other laser-equipped aircraft for designation. LANTIRN ("Low Altitude Navigation/Targeting Infra Red Night" pod) came in 1995, which gave the aircraft a FLIR and laser targeting system that was better than what the F/A-18 possessed. With a little training the F-14 Radar Intercept Officers (RIOs) became passable Bombardier-Navigators (B/Ns), and the *Tomcat* quickly became the premier precision weapon delivery platform in the Air Wing. The fighters couldn't have timed things better, as the retirement of the entire medium attack (A-6) community had led to a major gap in precision weapon delivery capability in the fleet that the F-14s filled nicely.

The end of the dedicated RA-5C and RF-8G reconnaissance units in the early 1980s led to yet another new trick for the F-14, as *Tomcat* squadrons took up the photo-reconnaissance mission for the fleet. VF-84 and -211 were the first to deploy with the Tactical Air Reconnaissance Pod System (TARPS) in 1981. Each air wing subsequently deployed with three or four TARPS-wired airframes, with the higher numbered squadron getting the mission. Although later F-14Ds were all configured for the pod, only one unit in the air wing would actually conduct the mission due to the training and additional manning required.

By December 1991 there were still 24 regular Navy VF units, and all but one of the Air Wings deployed with a pair of *Tomcat* units (*Midway* still having *Hornets*). Airframe attrition and a high-level decision to not proceed with upgrades past the D-model placed the handwriting on the wall for the *Tomcat*, so starting in 1993 the Navy reduced the number of VF units by half. Squadrons started being disestablished, and most air wings deployed with single, slightly larger (typically 14 aircraft) F-14 outfits and, as available, a third F/A-18 unit.

In 1996 the reduction in community size and concurrent BRAC action led to the unthinkable, as Miramar was transferred to the Marines (who moved down from El Toro and Santa Ana), while the surviving Pacific Fleet fighter units were transferred to Oceana, thereby placing all of the Regular Navy Fitrons at one location for the first time in history. By 2000 there were only 12 VFs remaining in the Navy, made up of four A, five B, and three D units. Two AirLant CVWs (-7 and -8) still had a pair of fighter outfits, with the rest having three *Hornet* squadrons, along with the solo VF unit.

As of the writing of this book, the last VF is scheduled to be gone by 2007, having transitioned to the new F/A-18E or F as Strike-Fighter units, thus ending over 80 years of fighter squadrons in carrier duty. It should be noted that, to its everlasting credit, the service is going well out of its way to keep some of its most historic squadrons, such as the *Tomcatters* and *Tophatters*, alive through this transition.

Naval Reserves

The four Reserve VF units were formed with F-8 *Crusaders* in 1970-71. Within two years they had started getting F-4Bs, with the *Crusaders* being completely replaced by 1976. F-4Ns and -Ss followed, in 1975 and 1980 respectively. The Sierra models actually came to CVWR-30 in an odd piece of luck, when CVW-14 found out that its "new" F-4Ss were judged unsuitable for deployment in *Coral Sea* due to higher landing speeds. Regular squadrons VF-21 and -154 therefore traded their newly modified F-4Ss with VF-301 and -302, getting their F-4Ns in the deal. (It needs to be said that there are some fighter aircrew that would tell you that the lighter "N" was the better aircraft—so who got the best end of this deal is a matter of opinion!)

The first Reserve F-14s arrived in 1984, although both of CVWR-30's Fitrons were disestablished in a plan that also axed VF-202 to bring CVWR-20 down to one fighter squadron in 1994. Fighting-201, the final Reserve FitRon, was redesignated a VFA only five years later.

VF-1 ***Wolfpack*** **Miramar**

F-14A (F-14D)

Estab. 14 Oct 1972, disestab 30 Sep 1993 (1 Jul ceremony)

17 Sep 74 to 20 May 75	*Enterprise*	WP/IO	F-14A	NK100	
30 Jul 76 to 28 Mar 77	*Enterprise*	WP/IO	F-14A	NK100	
4 Apr to 30 Oct 78	*Enterprise*	WP/IO	F-14A	NK100	
10 Sep 80 to 4 May 81	*Ranger*	WP/IO	F-14A	NE100	
7 Apr to 19 Oct 82	*Ranger*	WP/IO	F-14A	NE100	
13 Jan to 1 Aug 84	*Kitty Hawk*	WP/IO	F-14A	NE100	
18 Aug 86 to 20 Oct 86	*Ranger*	NP/WP surge	F-14A	NE100	
3 Mar to 29 Apr 87	*Ranger*	WP surge	F-14A	NE100	
14 Jul to 29 Dec 87	*Ranger*	WP/IO	F-14A	NE100	
24 Feb to 24 Aug 89	*Ranger*	WP/IO	F-14A	NE100	
8 Dec 90 to 8 Jun 91	*Ranger*	WP/IO/PG	F-14A	NE100	*Desert Storm*
1 Aug 92 to 31 Jan 93	*Ranger*	WP/IO/PG	F-14A	NE100	

Fighting-1 was formed in 1972, specifically to be one of the first two F-14 squadrons in the Navy. The *Wolfpack* is the fifth distinct unit to bear the VF-1 designation, and designed an original and dramatic logo and nickname that did not relate to any of the four previous squadrons designated VF-1. The squadron made the first *Tomcat* deployment in *Enterprise* in 1974, where they participated as cover for Operation *Frequent Wind*, the final evacuation of Vietnam. They switched to CVW-2 in 1979, and made their final nine deployments with that organization. The squadron's main claim to fame during *Desert Storm* was as the only F-14 unit to make an air-to-air kill, the squadron commander (and RIO) Cdr. Ron McElraft being involved in the destruction of an unlucky Iraqi MI-8 helicopter on 6 Feb 1991. VF-1 was selected for transition to the F-14D in 1993, along with VF-2, and began transition only to be disestablished the following September.

VF-2 ***Bounty Hunters*** **Miramar, Oceana**

F-14A, F-14A TARPS, F-14D, F-14D TARPS

Established 14 Oct 1972

17 Sep 74 to 20 May 75	*Enterprise*	WP/IO	F-14A	NK200
30 Jul 76 to 28 Mar 77	*Enterprise*	WP/IO	F-14A	NK200
4 Apr to 30 Oct 78	*Enterprise*	WP/IO	F-14A	NK200
10 Sep 80 to 4 May 81	*Ranger*	WP/IO	F-14A	NE200
7 Apr to 19 Oct 82	*Ranger*	WP/IO	F-14A, TARPS	NE200
13 Jan to 1 Aug 84	*Kitty Hawk*	WP/IO	F-14A, TARPS	NE200
18 Aug 86 to 20 Oct 86	*Ranger*	NP/WP surge	F-14A, TARPS	NE200
3 Mar to 29 Apr 87	*Ranger*	WP surge	F-14A, TARPS	NE200
14 Jul to 29 Dec 87	*Ranger*	WP/IO	F-14A, TARPS	NE200

The *Wolfpack* of VF-1 was the only *Tomcat* squadron to be credited with an air-to-air "kill" during Desert Storm, NE103 (162603) and its crew dispatching an Iraqi MI-8 helo on 6 Feb '91. The aircraft is shown here five days prior to the event while tanking over the North Gulf from a 19th Air Refueling Wing KC-135R. The victorious *Tomcat* would itself be lost on 26 June 2000, while with VF-211. (author)

24 Feb to 24 Aug 89	*Ranger*	WP/IO	F-14A, TARPS	NE200	
8 Dec 90 to 8 Jun 91	*Ranger*	WP/IO/PG	F-14A, TARPS	NE200	*D Storm*
1 Aug 92 to 31 Jan 93	*Ranger*	WP/IO/PG	F-14A, TARPS	NE200	
10 Nov 94 to 10 May 95	*Constellation*	WP/IO/PG	F-14D, TARPS	NE100	
1 Apr to 1 Oct 97	*Constellation*	WP/IO/PG	F-14D, TARPS	NE100	
18 Jun to 17 Dec 99	*Constellation*	WP/IO/PG	F-14D, TARPS	NE100	

VF-2 was formed along with VF-1 as the first two *Tomcat* squadrons in the Navy. As opposed to its sister squadron, Fighting-2 adopted a logo and some characteristics of the third VF-2 (of five), which had served in *Langley* (CV-1) during the 1920s. As the CVW-2 TARPS squadron VF-2 survived the post *Desert Storm* drawdown, and converted to F-14Ds in 1993-94. On 9 Sept 1999 a VF-2 *Tomcat* fired an AIM-54 *Phoenix* at a fleeing Iraqi MiG-23 *Flogger* over Southern Iraq. This appears to have been the second, and last, time the U.S. Navy shot the missile in combat.

VF-11 **_Red Rippers_** **Oceana, Miramar, Oceana**

F-4J, F-14A, F-14D, F-14B

Established VF-43 1 Sep 1950, r/d VF-11 16 Feb 1959

11 Mar to 11 Sep 74	*Forrestal*	Med	F-4J	AA100
5 Mar to 22 Sep 75	*Forrestal*	Med	F-4J	AA100
July 1976	*Forrestal*	Bi-Centennial	F-4J	AA100
4 Apr to 26 Oct 78	*Forrestal*	Med/NorLant	F-4J	AA100
27 Nov 79 to 7 May 80	*Forrestal*	Med	F-4J	AA100
4 Jan to 14 Jul 82	*JF Kennedy*	IO	F-14A	AC100
27 Sep 83 to 2 May 84	*JF Kennedy*	Med	F-14A	AC100
2 Jun to 10 Nov 86	*Forrestal*	Med	F-14A	AE100
25 Apr to 7 Oct 88	*Forrestal*	Med/IO/NL	F-14A	AE100
4 Nov 89 to 12 Apr 90	*Forrestal*	Med	F-14A	AE100
30 May to 21 Dec 91	*Forrestal*	Med	F-14A	AE100
18 Feb to 15 Aug 94	*Carl Vinson*	WP/IO/PG	F-14D	NK100
14 May to 14 Nov 96	*Carl Vinson*	WP/IO/PG	F-14D	NK100
26 Feb to 26 Aug 98	*JC Stennis*	World	F-14B	AG200
18 Feb to 18 Aug 00	*Eisenhower*	Med/RS/PG	F-14B	AG200

The *Red Rippers* own one of the truly classic insignias of aviation, with the boar's head motif coming off of the Gordon's gin bottle. Nonetheless, this version of VF-11 dates only from the 16 Feb 1959 redesignation of VF-43, which dispensed with its previous *Fighting Falcons* identity to adopt the logo and nickname of the previous *Red Ripper* squadron, which dated from 1927, and had expired a day earlier. Confusing histories aside, the *Rippers* were a fixture at Oceana for years, having flown *Phantoms* and all three versions of the *Tomcat*. In March 1992 the *Rippers*, along with VF-31, moved to sunny California, where they became the first squadrons to receive the new F-14D. The *Rippers* subsequently returned to Oceana in December 1996, and re-equipped with F-14Bs.

The *Red Rippers* were one of the first two F-14D squadrons in the fleet, gaining the "Delta" in 1992. NK106 is shown conducting CQ on *Abraham Lincoln* on 18 Oct 1992 in very subdued markings. They would deploy with CVW-14 in *Carl Vinson* the following year. (author)

VF-14	***Tophatters***	**Oceana**		
F-14A				

Established as Air Detachment, Pacific Fleet Sep 1919, r/d VT-5, 15 Jun 1920, r/d VP-4-1 7 Sep 1921, r/d VF-4 23 Sep 1921, r/d VF-1 1 Jul 1922, r/d VF-1B 1 Jul 1927, r/d VB-2B 1 Jul 1934, r/d VB-3 1 Jul 1937, r/d VB-4 1 Jul 1939, r/d VS-41 15 Mar 1941, r/d VB-41 1 Mar 1943, r/d VB-4 4 Aug 1943, r/d VA-1A 15 Nov 1946, r/d VA-14 2 Aug 1948, r/d VF-14 15 Dec 1949.

28 Jun 75 to 27 Jan 76	*JF Kennedy*	Med	F-14A	AB100
2 Sep to 9 Nov 76	*JF Kennedy*	NorLant	F-14A	AB100
15 Jan to 1 Aug 77	*JF Kennedy*	Med	F-14A	AB100
29 Jan 78 to 8 Feb 79	*JF Kennedy*	Med	F-14A	AB100
4 Aug 80 to 28 Mar 81	*JF Kennedy*	Med	F-14A	AB100
7 Jun to 22 Dec 82	*Independence*	Med	F-14A	AE100
18 Oct 83 to 11 Apr 84	*Independence*	Med/IO	F-14A	AE100
16 Oct 84 to 11 Apr 85	*Independence*	Carib/Med	F-14A	AE100
18 Aug 86 to 3 Mar 87	*JF Kennedy*	Med	F-14A	AC100
2 Aug 88 to 1 Feb 89	*JF Kennedy*	Med	F-14A	AC100
15 Aug 90 to 28 Mar 91	*JF Kennedy*	Med/RS	F-14A	AC100 *D.Storm*
7 Oct 92 to 7 Apr 93	*JF Kennedy*	Med/RS	F-14A	AC100
29 Apr to 28 Oct 97	*JF Kennedy*	Med/RS/PG	F-14A	AJ200
26 Mar to 22 Sep 99	*T Roosevelt*	Med/RS/PG	F-14A	AJ200 *A. Force*

VF-14 is THE oldest aviation squadron in the Navy, having existed under multiple designations since 1919. The *Tophat* insignia is another Naval Aviation classic, having adorned Naval aircraft since the 1920s, under the name *High Hatters*. The squadron has gone through at least fifteen different designations, ten of which were prior to WWII. Its roles have included torpedo (VT), Scout (VS), bombing (VB), and attack (VA), as well as fighter. As of 1974, the *Tophatters* were completing transition from the F-4B to the *Tomcat*. Their 1975-76 deployment marked the first for the type in the Atlantic Fleet. They would serve with four wings (1, 6, 3, 8) over the next 25 years. During the 1999 deployment the unit participated in *Allied Force*, where it dropped 350 laser guided bombs and almost 400,000 lbs of ordnance. One *Tophatter Tomcat* crew was given credit for destroying 26 Serbian aircraft located in an underground hangar facility with a single laser guided bomb.

VF-21	***Freelancers***	**Miramar, Atsugi**		
F-4J, F-4S, F-4N, F-14A				

Estab. VF-81 2 Mar 1944, r/d VF-13A 15 Nov 1946, r/d VF-131 2 Aug 1948, r/d VF-64 15 Feb 1950, r/d VF-21 1 Jul 1959. disestab. 31 Jan 1996

7 May to 18 Oct 74	*Ranger*	WP	F-4J	NE200
30 Jan to 7 Sep 76	*Ranger*	WP	F-4J	NE200
21 Feb to 22 Sep 79	*Ranger*	WP	F-4J	NE200
1980	(*Coral Sea*)	no cruise	F-4S	NK200
20 Aug 81 to 23 Mar 82	*Coral Sea*	WP/IO	F-4N	NK200
21 Mar to 12 Sep 83	*Coral Sea*	WP/IO	F-4N	NK200
21 Feb to 24 Aug 85	*Constellation*	WP/IO	F-14A	NK200
11 Apr to 13 Oct 87	*Constellation*	WP/IO	F-14A	NK200
1 Dec 88 TO 1 Jun 89	*Constellation*	WP/IO	F-14A	NK200
16 Sep 89 to 19 Oct 89	*Constellation*	NorPac	F-14A	NK200
23 Jun to 20 Dec 90	*Independence*	WP/IO/PG	F-14A	NK200
5 to 22 Aug 91	*Independence*	Hawaii	F-14A	NK200
28 Aug to 11 Sep 91	*Independence*	to Japan	F-14A	NF200
Sep 1991 to 1996	*Independence*	Fwd deployed	F-14A	NF200

VF-21 was flying F-4Js as of 1974. In December 1979 VF-21 (and VF-154) moved to CVW-14 in *Coral Sea*, and received the fleet's first newly modified F-4Ss; however, the aircraft's higher landing speed cut safety margins below acceptable limits on the older ship's arresting gear. Both units subsequently traded aircraft with Reserve VF-301/302, and flew older (and slower landing) F-4Ns for their last two *Phantom* deployments. By 1983 VF-21 and VF-154 were the last two regular *Phantom* units at Miramar, and they received their first *Tomcats* in December. During the 1974 *Ranger* deployment the unit was involved in the accidental shoot-down of an HC-1 SH-3G. In 1987 a *Freelancer Tomcat* fired *Sparrow* missiles at what was believed to have been an Iranian aircraft in the Strait of Hormuz, although there has been a fair amount of confusion as to what actually happened during the incident. In late 1991 VF-21 transferred to CVW-5, becoming one of the first two F-14 units assigned to Japan. The *Freelancers* made multiple West Pac and IO deployments for the next five years, before being disestablished.

VF-24 *Red Checkertails, Fighting Renegades* **Miramar**
F-8J, F-14A, F-14A+
Estab. VF-211 1 Jun 1955, r/d VF-24 9 Mar 1959. disestab. 31 Aug 1996

8 May 73 to 8 Jan 74	*Hancock*	WP/IO	F-8J	NP200
18 May to 29 Oct 75	*Hancock*	WP/IO	F-8J	NP200
12 Apr to 21 Nov 77	*Constellation*	WP	F-14A	NG200
26 Sep 78 to 17 May 79	*Constellation*	WP/IO	F-14A	NG200
26 Feb to 15 Oct 80	*Constellation*	WP/IO	F-14A	NG200
20 Oct 81 to 23 May 82	*Constellation*	WP/IO	F-14A	NG200
15 Jul 83 to 28 Feb 84	*Ranger*	SoPac/WP/IO	F-14A	NG200
24 Jul 85 to 21 Dec 85	*Kitty Hawk*	WP/IO	F-14A	NG200
3 Jan to 29 Jun 87	*Kitty Hawk*	World	F-14A	NG200
2 Sep 88 to 2 Mar 89	*Nimitz*	WP/IO	F-14A	NG200
15 Jun to 9 Jul 89	*Nimitz*	NorPac	F-14A	NG200
25 Feb to 24 Aug 91	*Nimitz*	WP/IO/PG	F-14A+	NG200
2 Feb to 29 Jul 93	*Nimitz*	WP/IO/PG	F-14A	NG200
27 Nov 95 to 20 May 96	*Nimitz*	WP/IO/PG	F-14A	NG200

Fighting Twenty Four was established as VF-211 in 1955 as an FJ-3 day-fighter squadron, and subsequently transitioned to *Crusaders*, while also swapping designations with VF-24 *Checkmates* in March 1959. Their histories have been confused ever since. The *Checkertails* were in the second pair of AirPac FitRons to get *Tomcats*, trading in their F-8J *Crusaders* in 1976. The *Renegade* name became much more associated with the unit as time went on. The squadron received F-14A+ aircraft in 1990, and took them on a single WestPac deployment before the decision was made to base all of the type (now called the F-14B) at Oceana. The squadron flew two more deployments with F-14As before being disestablished in August 1996.

VF-31 ***Tomcatters*** **Oceana, Miramar, Oceana**
F-14A, F-14A TARPS, F-14D TARPS
Estab. VF-1B 1 Jul 35, combined with VF-8B and r/d VF-6 1 Jul 37, r/d VF-3 15 Jul 43, r/d VF-3A 15 Nov 46, r/d VF-31 7 Aug 48.

27 Sep 74 to 19 Mar 75	*Saratoga*	Med	F-4J	AC100	
16 Jul to 24 Sep 75	*Nimitz*	Carib/NorLant	F-4J	AC100	CVW-8
6 Jan to 28 Jul 76	*Saratoga*	Med	F-4J	AC100	
11 Jul to 23 Dec 77	*Saratoga*	Med	F-4J	AC100	
3 Oct 78 to 5 Apr 79	*Saratoga*	Med	F-4J	AC100	
10 Mar to 27 Aug 80	*Saratoga*	Med	F-4J	AC100	
4 Jan to 14 Jul 82	*JF Kennedy*	Med/IO	F-14A, TARPS	AC200	
27 Sep 83 to 2 May 84	*JF Kennedy*	Med	F-14A, TARPS	AC200 Lebanon	
2 Jun to 10 Nov 86	*Forrestal*	Med	F-14A, TARPS	AE200	
25 Apr to 7 Oct 88	*Forrestal*	Med/IO/NL	F-14A, TARPS	AE200	
4 Nov 89 to 12 Apr 90	*Forrestal*	Med	F-14A, TARPS	AE200	
30 May to 21 Dec 91	*Forrestal*	Med	F-14A, TARPS	AE200	

VF-31 transitioned from *Phantoms* to *Tomcats* in 1981. Brand new TARPS-configured F-14A AC214 (161150) sits at Pensacola on 17 Apr 1981. The distinctive black nose markings, a carry over from F-4s, earned the unit the nickname "flying pencils" among some at Oceana. (author)

18 Feb to 15 Aug 94	*Carl Vinson*	WP/IO/PG	F-14D, TARPS	NK200
14 May to 14 Nov 96	*Carl Vinson*	WP/IO/PG	F-14D, TARPS	NK200
11 Jun to 7 Dec 98	*Lincoln*	WP/IO/PG	F-14D, TARPS	NK100
14 Aug 2000 to 12 Feb 2001	*Lincoln*	WP/IO/PG	F-14D, TARPS	NK100

VF-31 is another Fighter Squadron with a classic logo, this being Felix the Cat carrying an old fashioned lighted bomb. The squadron was flying F-4Js with CVW-3 as of 1974, and continued in the *Phantom* through 1980-81. F-14As and the TARPS mission arrived in 1981. The squadron's participation in opposed photo missions over Lebanon in 1983 helped lead to the 6 Dec '83 strikes by *Kennedy* and *Independence* aircraft in that country. After spending over 24 years with CVW-3 the squadron transferred to Air Wing Six and *Forrestal*. In July 1992 VF-31 (with VF-11) moved to Miramar, where they joined CVW-14 as one of the first two fleet F-14D units. The *Tomcatters* made two deployments from California before moving back to Oceana again in November 1996.

VF-32 ***Swordsmen, Gypsies*** **Oceana**

F-14A, F-14A TARPS, F-14B, F-14B TARPS

Estab. VBF-3 1 Feb 45, r/d VF-4A 15 Nov 46, r/d VF-32 7 Aug 48

28 Jun 75 to 27 Jan 76	*JF Kennedy*	Med	F-14A	AB200
2 Sep to 9 Nov 76	*JF Kennedy*	NorLant	F-14A	AB200
15 Jan to 1 Aug 77	*JF Kennedy*	Med	F-14A	AB200
29 Jan 78 to 8 Feb 79	*JF Kennedy*	Med	F-14A	AB200
4 Aug 80 to 28 Mar 81	*JF Kennedy*	Med	F-14A	AB200
7 Jun to 22 Dec 82	*Independence*	Med	F-14A, TARPS	AE200
18 Oct 83 to 11 Apr 84	*Independence*	Med/IO	F-14A, TARPS	AE200 *G/L*
16 Oct 84 to 11 Apr 85	*Independence*	Carib/Med	F-14A, TARPS	AE200
18 Aug 86 to 3 Mar 87	*JF Kennedy*	Med	F-14A, TARPS	AC200
2 Aug 88 to 1 Feb 89	*JF Kennedy*	Med	F-14A, TARPS	AC200
15 Aug 90 to 28 Mar 91	*JF Kennedy*	Med/RS	F-14A, TARPS	AC200
DStorm				
7 Oct 92 to 7 Apr 93	*JF Kennedy*	Med/RS	F-14A, TARPS	AC200
20 Oct 94 to 15 Apr 95	*Eisenhower*	Med/RS/PG	F-14A, TARPS	AC200
25 Nov to 22 May 97	*T Roosevelt*	Med/RS/PG	F-14A, TARPS	AC100
6 Nov 98 to 6 May 99	*Enterprise*	Med/RS/PG	F-14B, TARPS	AC100
28 Nov 00 to 23 May 01	*HS Truman*	Med/RS/PG	F-14B, TARPS	AC100

The *Swordsmen* started the period undergoing transition as one of the first two F-14A units in AirLant (along with VF-14). The unit's official nickname was frequently mixed with its "Gypsy" callsign, with the title "Gypsy Swordsmen" being used as well, with an appropriately attired twin-tailed feline decorating the tails of their *Tomcats* from mid-1982. Two "Gypsy" *Tomcats* scored the last two Libyan kills in January 1989 when they downed two MiG-23 "Floggers" while over the Gulf of Sidra. The unit flew opposed TARPS photo missions over Grenada and Lebanon during the 1983 deployment, as well as seeing extensive duty during *Desert Storm*.

VF-33 ***Tarsiers, Starfighters*** **Oceana**

F-4J, F-14A

Estab. VF-33 12 Oct 48, disestab. 1 Oct 1993

21 Jun 73 to 19 Jun 74	*Independence*	Med	F-4J	AG200	
19 Jul 74 to 21 Jan 75	*Independence*	Med	F-4J	AG200	
15 Oct 75 to 5 May 76	*Independence*	NL/Med	F-4J	AG200	
31 Mar 77 to 21 Oct 77	*Independence*	Med	F-4J	AG200	
28 Jun to 14 Dec 79	*Independence*	Med	F-4J	AE200	
19 Nov 80 to 10 Jun 81	*Independence*	Med/IO	F-4J	AE200	
23 Aug to 30 Oct 82	*America*	NL/Med/Carib	F-14A	AE200	
8 Dec 82 to 2 Jun 83	*America*	Med/IO	F-14A	AB200	
24 Apr to 14 Nov 84	*America*	Med/IO	F-14A	AB200	
10 Mar to 10 Sep 86	*America*	Med	F-14A	AB200	
8 Feb to 3 Apr 89	*America*	NorLant	F-14A	AB200	
11 May to 10 Nov 89	*America*	Med/IO	F-14A	AB200	
12 Feb to 7 Apr 90	*Constellation*	HORN	F-14A	AB200	CVW-9
28 Dec 90 to 18 Apr 91	*America*	Med/RS/PG	F-14A	AB200	*Desert Storm*
2 Dec 91 to 6 Jun 92	*America*	Med	F-14A	AB200	

VF-33 dates back to 1948, and managed to last for 45 years without being redesignated once. They flew *Corsairs*, *Furys*, *Tigers*, and *Phantoms* before gaining *Tomcats* in 1981. The distinctive *Tarsier* patch, which had been used by the squadron since the early-1950s, featured a seemingly fierce creature's head with wings, as opposed to the real Tarsier, a smallish, and generally very shy nocturnal South East Asian mammal. The logo was worn by actor Tom Skerritt's character "Viper" in the movie "Topgun," as well as by the unit's Operations Officer, "Jester." This fact notwithstanding, the unit ditched the insignia and name in 1987 when the squadron Commander elected to go with the unit's *Starfighter* callsign as its new nickname and design. Nonetheless, a version of the *Tarsier* logo (known within the Oceana F-14 community as the "Monkey patch") did appear late in the squadron's days as a sort of alternate design for rebellious junior officers. In 1990 the unit joined CVW-9 for a short trip around the Horn in *Constellation*. VF-33 participated in *Desert Storm* as a member of CVW-1.

VF-41 **_Black Aces_** **Oceana**

F-4B, F-4N, F-14A, F-14A TARPS

Estab. 1 Sep 50.

14 Sep 73 to 17 Mar 74	*FD Roosevelt*	Med	F-4B	AE100	
3 Jan to 26 Jul 75	*FD Roosevelt*	Med	F-4N	AE100	
1 Dec 77 to 20 Jul 78	*Nimitz*	Med/NorLant	F-14A	AJ100	
10 Sep 79 to 26 May 80	*Nimitz*	Med/IO	F-14A	AJ100	
3 Aug 81 to 12 Feb 82	*Nimitz*	Med	F-14A	AJ100	Libya
10 Nov 82 to 20 May 83	*Nimitz*	Med	F-14A	AJ100	
8 Mar to 4 Oct 85	*Nimitz*	Med	F-14A	AJ100	
30 Dec 86 to 26 Jul 87	*Nimitz*	World	F-14A	AJ100	
25 Aug to 11 Oct 88	*T Roosevelt*	NorLant	F-14A	AJ100	
30 Dec 88 to 30 Jun 89	*T Roosevelt*	Med	F-14A	AJ100	
28 Dec 90 to 28 Jun 91	*T Roosevelt*	Med/RS/PG	F-14A	AJ100	*D Storm*
22 Mar to 22 Sep 95	*T Roosevelt*	Med/RS/PG	F-14A, TARPS	AJ100	
29 Apr to 28 Oct 97	*JF Kennedy*	Med/RS/PG	F-14A, TARPS	AJ100	
26 Mar to 22 Sep 99	*T Roosevelt*	Med/RS/PG	F-14A, TARPS,	AJ100	*A. Force*

The *Black Aces* were flying the oldest *Phantoms* in the fleet as of January 1974, and were underway in *Franklin Roosevelt* as the only fighter squadron in CVW-6 having been directed to make the deployment as a large (18 airframe) unit in an AirLant experiment. They transitioned to F-4Ns that same year, and returned to the Med for a final *Phantom* deployment in 1975 as a normally sized outfit. The *Aces* received F-14As in 1975-76, and retained the type for the next 25 years. On August 16, 1981, the squadron bagged two Libyan Sukhoi-22s while on deployment in *Nimitz*. The squadron participated in *Desert Storm* in 1991 from *Theodore Roosevelt*. The *Aces* missed TR's 1993 Med deployment in order to make room for the Special MAGTAF. They gained TARPS aircraft during this period, and rejoined CVW-8 for subsequent deployments as a large (14 airframe) squadron. On 5 Sep '95 VF-41 claimed the title as the first F-14 to expend bombs in combat when they dropped 1000lb LGBs while using a VFA-87 *Hornet* to illuminate the target. The *Black Aces'* 1997 deployment featured 13 *Tomcats*, five of which were TARPS configured, and another five LANTIRN capable.

VF-43 **_Challengers_** **Oceana**

A-4E/F, TA-4F/J, T-38A, F-5E/F, T-2C, F-21A, F-16N, TF-16N

Estab. VF-74A 1 May 45, r/d VF-74 1 Aug 45, r/d VF-1B 15 Nov 46, r/d VF-21 1 Sep 48, r/d VA-43 1 Jul 59, r/d VF-43 1 Jun 73, disestab. 1 July 1994

VF-43 was a fleet unit flying F11F-1 *Tigers* in CVG-4 when, in July 1959, it became a replacement unit within the newly formed RCVG-4. The squadron would in time become the Oceana based instrument training squadron and, subsequently, one of the first dedicated adversary outfits flying *Skyhawks* and *Talons*. F-5E/F *Tiger IIs* followed from the mid-'70s. VF-43 became the primary Navy operator of the Israeli built and supported F-21A *Kfir*, which it flew from April 1985 to April 1988. F-16Ns arrived on loan from VF-45 in 1988 to replace the *Kfirs*. The squadron also provided "out of control flight" training in the North American T-2C *Buckeye*, where aircrew were trained in spin recovery techniques. As of early 1989 VF-43 was assigned six A-4E, three A-4F, four TA-4J, four T-2C, and six F-16Ns. VF-43 was disestablished 1 July 1994 as part of the massive post *Desert Storm* cutbacks.

VF-45; see VA-45, chapter 5

VF-51 **_Screaming Eagles_** **Miramar**

F-4B, F-4N, F-14A

Est. VF-1 15 Feb 43, r/d VF-5 15 Jul 43, r/d VF-5A 15 Nov 46, r/d VF-51 16 Aug 48, disestab. 31 Mar 1995 (16 Feb ceremony)

5 Dec 74 to 2 Jul 75	*Coral Sea*	WP	F-4N	NL100
4 Oct 76 to 21 Apr 77	*FD Roosevelt*	Med	F-4N	NM100

30 May 79 to 25 Feb 80	*Kitty Hawk*	WP/IO	F-14A	NL100	
1 Apr to 23 Nov 81	*Kitty Hawk*	WP/IO	F-14A	NL100	
1 Mar to 29 Oct 83	*Carl Vinson*	World	F-14A	NL100	
18 Oct 84 to 25 May 85	*Carl Vinson*	WP/IO	F-14A	NL100	
12 Aug 86 to 5 Feb 87	*Carl Vinson*	WP/IO	F-14A	NL100	
15 Jun to 14 Dec 88	*Carl Vinson*	WP/IO	F-14A	NL100	
5 Sep to 8 Nov 89	*Carl Vinson*	WP/NorPac	F-14A	NL100	
1 Feb to 31 Jul 90	*Carl Vinson*	WP/IO	F-14A	NL100	
18 Oct to 11 Dec 91	*Kitty Hawk*	Horn	F-14A	NL100	
3 Nov 92 to 3 May 92	*Kitty Hawk*	WP/IO/PG	F-14A	NL100	
24 Jun to 22 Dec 94	*Kitty Hawk*	WP/IO	F-14A	NL100	

VF-51 was the oldest Fitron on the West Coast, having been established as *Fighting-One* in Feb 1943. The VF-51 designation came in 1948, and the squadron had a distinguished record in *Panthers*, *Cougars*, *Furies*, and *Crusaders* prior to gaining *Phantoms* in 1969. The unit started the period with F-4Bs, and quickly transitioned to F-4Ns. The squadron joined CVW-15 after *Tomcat* transition in 1978, and stayed with the Air Wing until it was shut down in 1995.

VF-74 **Be-Devilers** **Oceana**

F-14A, F-14A+ (F-14B)

Est. VBF-20 16 Apr 45, r/d VF-10A 15 Nov 46, r/d VF-92 12 Aug 48, r/d VF-74 15 Jan 50, disestab. 30 April 1994

11 Mar 74 to 11 Sep 74	*Forrestal*	Med	F-4J	AA200	
5 Mar to 22 Sep 75	*Forrestal*	Med	F-4J	AA200	
7 Jul 76 to 7 Feb 77	*Nimitz*	Med	F-4J	AJ200	
4 Apr to 26 Oct 78	*Forrestal*	Med/NorLant	F-4J	AA200	
27 Nov 79 to 7 May 80	*Forrestal*	Med	F-4J	AA200	
2 Mar to 15 Sep 81	*Forrestal*	Med	F-4J	AA200	
8 Jun to 16 Nov 82	*Forrestal*	Med	F-4S	AA100	
2 Apr to 20 Oct 84	*Saratoga*	Med	F-14A	AA100	
26 Aug 85 to 16 Apr 86	*Saratoga*	Med/IO	F-14A	AA100	
5 Jun to 17 Nov 87	*Saratoga*	Med	F-14A	AA100	
7 Aug 90 to 28 Mar 91	*Saratoga*	Med/RS	F-14A+	AA100	*D.Storm*
6 May to 6 Nov 92	*Saratoga*	Med	F-14B	AA100	

VF-74 flew *Corsairs*, *Cougars*, and *Skyrays* before becoming the Atlantic Fleet's first F4H-1 (F-4B) *Phantom II* unit in 1961. The *Be-Devilers*, along with VF-103, flew the last *Phantoms* in Oceana, starting 1974 in F-4Js, and transitioning to F-4Ss for one deployment in 1981-82. The squadron was assigned to CVW-17 for the entire period, except for a short trip with CVW-8 and *Nimitz*, where they were paired with VMFA-333. F-14A *Tomcats* arrived in 1983, which were replaced by F-14A+ (F-14B) in 1988. On 19 Oct 1985 the unit participated in the capture of the *Achille Lauro* hijackers. The squadron flew in *Desert Storm* in 1991, and was disestablished after only one further deployment.

VF-84 **Jolly Rogers** **Oceana**

F-4B, F-4N, F-4J, F-14A, F-14A TARPS

Est. VA-86 1 Jul 55, r/d VF-84 1 Jul 55, disestab. 1 Oct 1995

1974	——	(no cruise)	F-4B	AE200	
3 Jan to 26 Jul 75	*FD Roosevelt*	Med	F-4N	AE200	
1 Dec 77 to 20 Jul 78	*Nimitz*	Med/NorLant	F-14A	AJ200	
10 Sep 79 to 26 May 80	*Nimitz*	Med/IO	F-14A	AJ200	
3 Aug 81 to 12 Feb 82	*Nimitz*	Med	F-14A TARPS	AJ200	
10 Nov 82 to 20 May 83	*Nimitz*	Med	F-14A TARPS	AJ200	
8 Mar to 4 Oct 85	*Nimitz*	Med	F-14A TARPS	AJ200	
30 Dec 86 to 26 Jul 87	*Nimitz*	World	F-14A TARPS	AJ200	
25 Aug to 11 Oct 88	*T Roosevelt*	NorLant	F-14A TARPS	AJ200	
30 Dec 88 to 30 Jun 89	*T Roosevelt*	Med	F-14A TARPS	AJ200	
28 Dec 90 to 28 Jun 91	*T Roosevelt*	Med/RS/PG	F-14A TARPS	AJ200	*D Storm*
11 Mar to 8 Sep 93	*T Roosevelt*	Med	F-14A TARPS	AJ200	

Few units in the history of Naval Aviation can boast the immediate recognition that VF-84 had. Their skull and crossbones image has been carried on the tail of their aircraft since they received F-4 *Phantoms* in 1965. Since then they have seen combat in Vietnam and *Desert Storm*, been featured in a movie ("The Final Countdown"), and even disparaged by the Soviet press. VF-84's use of the *Jolly Roger* image dates only from 1959, when the unit adopted the logo and traditions of VF-61, which had been disestablished on 1 April. Fighting 61 was the actual lineal descendent of the original and legendary *Jolly Rogers* of VF-17, which had flown F4U *Corsairs* in the Solomon Islands during WWII. VF-84 started 1974 as one of the last two F-4B units in AirLant (along with VF-41). They did not make the 1973-74 cruise with CVW-6 in *Roosevelt*, being directed to remain at Oceana while the *Black Aces* deployed as a large (18 airframe) squadron. VF-84 "loaned" six aircraft, six aircrew, and 100 enlisted men to beef up VF-41 while retaining six F-4Bs at Oceana. F-4Ns arrived in June 1964, which they flew for one deployment before transitioning to F-14s. The unit operated *Tomcats* for 15 years before being disestablished in October, 1995. With the end of VF-84, the *Sluggers* of VF-103 were "offered" the opportunity to adopt the *Jolly Roger* nickname, logo, and traditions, and did so the day after VF-84 expired.

VF-92 *Silver Kings* **Miramar**
F-4J
Est. VF-92 23 Mar 52, r/d VF-54 1 Jun 62, r/d VF-92 15 Oct 63, disestab 12 Dec 1975

21 Jun to 22 Dec 74	*Constellation*	WP/IO	F-4J	NG200

VF-92 was, along with partner VF-96, shut down after making only one post-Vietnam cruise. The squadron was also known by their "Silver Kite" callsign.

VF-96 ***Fighting Falcons*** **Miramar**
F-4J
Reserve VF-791 activated 20 Jul 50, r/d VF-142 4 Feb 53, r/d VF-96 1 Jun 62, disestab. 1 Dec 1975

21 Jun to 22 Dec 74	*Constellation*	WP/IO	F-4J	NG100

The leading Navy MiG-killing squadron of the Vietnam War (with eight), VF-96 was rewarded by the Navy for its historical feat by being sent into oblivion after making only one post-war cruise.

VF-101 ***Grim Reapers*** **Oceana (Key West, Miramar)** **FRS**
F-4B, F-4N, F-4J, F-4S, F-14A, F-14A+ (F-14B), F-14D, F-14 TARPS, A-4E, TA-4J, T-34C
VF-101 estab. 1 May 52

VF-101 has been training Navy fighter crews on the East Coast since 1958. The squadron carries on the traditions, name, and logo of the legendary VF-10 *Grim Reapers* of WWII, which was disestablished in 1945. In 1958 it was pulled from fleet duty as an F4D unit, and became the AirLant "all-weather" VF training unit at Key West. F3H *Demons* and F3D *Skyknights* were also assigned, and new F4H *Phantom IIs* arrived in 1962. In 1971 the unit was moved to Oceana, while leaving a detachment at Key West to teach air combat maneuvering. F-14A *Tomcats* arrived in Dec 1975, with that type quickly becoming the dominant program, so much so that in Aug 1977 the F-4 portion, along with its KW det, was spun off as VF-171.

The *Reapers* ACM det at Key West also included A-4 *Skyhawks* for use as opponents. Another detachment ("Det D") was placed at Miramar in 1994 to provide training for the F-14D squadrons, all of which were West Coast based at that time. The first improved *Tomcat*, the awkwardly designated F-14A+, arrived at the RAG on 11 Apr 1988. On 12 Sept 1990 VF-101 became the first non-test unit to drop bombs from the *Tomcat*. VF-101 historically wore AD100 series numbers. In the mid-nineties VF-101 started applying the markings of dead *Tomcat* squadrons (such as VF-74 and -114) to a number of their aircraft as a method of honoring the memory of these recently departed units.

Don't let the markings confuse you—this is a VF-101 F-14B (161432, AD114) at Oceana on 17 Sep '94. The insignia and paint honor the memory of the VF-74 *Be-Devilers*, and was one of several aircraft painted with the heraldry of departed *Tomcat* squadrons by the FRS during this period. (Brian Rogers)

VF-102 ***Diamondbacks*** **Oceana**

F-4J, F-14A, F-14A TARPS

Estab. VA-36 1 Jul 55, r/d VF-102 1 Jul 55 (same day)

21 Jun 73 to 19 Jun 74	*Independence*	Med	F-4J	AG100	
19 Jul 74 to 21 Jan 75	*Independence*	Med	F-4J	AG100	
15 Oct 75 to 5 May 76	*Independence*	NL/Med	F-4J	AG100	
31 Mar 77 to 21 Oct 77	*Independence*	Med	F-4J	AG100	
28 Jun to 14 Dec 79	*Independence*	Med	F-4J	AE100	
19 Nov 80 to 10 Jun 81	*Independence*	Med/IO	F-4J	AE100	
23 Aug to 30 Oct 1982	*America*	NL/Med/Carib	F-14A TARPS	AB100	
8 Dec 82 to 2 Jun 83	*America*	Med/IO	F-14A, TARPS	AB100	
24 Apr to 14 Nov 84	*America*	Med/IO	F-14A, TARPS	AB100	
10 Mar to 10 Sep 86	*America*	Med	F-14A, TARPS	AB100	
8 Feb to 3 Apr 89	*America*	NorLant	F-14A, TARPS	AB100	
11 May to 10 Nov 89	*America*	Med/IO	F-14A, TARPS	AB100	
28 Dec 90 to 18 Apr 91	*America*	Med/RS/PG	F-14A, TARPS	AB100	*D Storm*
2 Dec 91 to 6 Jun 92	*America*	Med	F-14A, TARPS	AB100	
11 Aug 93 to 5 Feb 94	*America*	Med/IO	F-14A, TARPS	AB100	
28 Aug 95 to 24 Feb 96	*America*	Med/RS/PG	F-14B, TARPS	AB100	
3 Oct 97 to 3 Apr 98	*G Washington*	Med/RS/PG	F-14B, TARPS	AB100	
15 Sep 99 to 19 Mar 00	*JF Kennedy*	Med/RS/PG	F-14B, TARPS	AB100	

The *Diamondbacks* were established in 1955 as an attack squadron, and redesignated as VF-102 the same day. They were a night-fighter outfit with *Banshees* and *Skyrays* before getting some of the first F-4Bs in the Atlantic Fleet. *Tomcats* were assigned from 1981, and improved F-14Bs came in 1994. The squadron participated in *Desert Storm* as a member of CVW-1.

VF-103 ***Sluggers, Jolly Rogers*** **Oceana**

F-4J, F-4S, F-14A, F-14A TARPS, F-14A+ , F-14A+ TARPS (F-14B, F-14B TARPS)

Estab. 1 May 52

6 Sep to 12 Oct 74	*America*	NorLant	F-4J	AC200	CVW-8
27 Sep 74 to 19 Mar 75	*Saratoga*	Med	F-4J	AC200	
6 Jan to 28 Jul 76	*Saratoga*	Med	F-4J	AC200	
11 Jul to 23 Dec 77	*Saratoga*	Med	F-4J	AC200	
3 Oct 78 to 5 Apr 79	*Saratoga*	Med	F-4J	AC200	
10 Mar to 27 Aug 80	*Saratoga*	Med	F-4J	AC200	
8 Jun to 16 Nov 82	*Forrestal*	Med	F-4S	AA200	
2 Apr to 20 Oct 84	*Saratoga*	Med	F-14A TARPS	AA200	
26 Aug 85 to 16 Apr 86	*Saratoga*	Med/IO	F-14A TARPS	AA200	
5 Jun to 17 Nov 87	*Saratoga*	Med	F-14A TARPS	AA200	
15 Aug to 8 Oct 88	*Independence*	Horn	F-14A TARPS	AA200	
7 Aug 90 to 28 Mar 91	*Saratoga*	Med/RS	F-14A+ TARPS	AA200	*D.Storm*
6 May to 6 Nov 92	*Saratoga*	Med	F-14B TARPS	AA200	
12 Jan to 24 Jun 94	*Saratoga*	Med	F-14B TARPS	AA200	
28 Jun to 20 Dec 96	*Enterprise*	Med/RS/PG	F-14B TARPS	AA200	
10 Jun to 10 Dec 98	*Eisenhower*	Med/RS/PG	F-14B TARPS	AA100	
21 Jun to 19 Dec 00	*G Washington*	Med/RS/PG	F-14B TARPS	AA100	

Even though VF-103 was assigned to CVW-3, they made a short trip to the Northern Atlantic with CVW-8 and *America* in 1974 before returning to their "home" wing. The *Sluggers* shared with stablemate VF-74 the distinction of making the last AirLant F-4 deployment, in what was also the only trip to the Med for the F-4S model. The squadron initially wore AA100 series numbers after receiving the F-4S, but moved to AA200 prior to deployment. *Tomcats*, along with the TARPS mission, came in 1983. VF-103 suffered the only *Tomcat* loss of *Desert Storm*, on 21 Jan 1991. Although the *Sluggers* had a long history of their own, on 29 Sep 1995 a ceremony was held as the squadron adopted the name, traditions, and Bones[8] of the VF-84 *Jolly Rogers*, which had been disestablished the previous day. The squadron was the first Night Vision Goggle (NVG) qualified F-14 unit (in 1995), and the fleet test squadron for the F-14 LANTIRN "Bombcat" in spring 1995 for the rapid advancing effort. It subsequently received the first deployable LANTIRN targeting pods in the community during the Spring of 1996, and introduced the *Tomcat*-LANTIRN combination during Operation *Southern Watch* missions the following December.

The *Sundowners* of VF-111 were famed for their sharks teeth and "setting sun" tail markings. NL214 (150475) is an F-4N at Fallon in May 1976, and also features the unit's take on Bicentennial markings, which celebrated the nation's 200th birthday. The squadron's next deployment would actually be with CVW-19 in *Franklin D. Roosevelt*. (Michael Grove).

VF-111 ***Sundowners*** **Miramar**

F-4B, F-4N, F-14A, F-14A TARPS

Estab. VA-156 4 Jun 56, r/d VF-111 20 Jan 59, disestab. 31 March 1995 (16 Feb ceremony)

5 Dec 74 to 2 Jul 75	*Coral Sea*	WP	F-4N	NL200
4 Oct 76 to 21 Apr 77	*FD Roosevelt*	Med	F-4N	NM200
30 May 79 to 25 Feb 80	*Kitty Hawk*	WP/IO	F-14A	NL200
1 Apr to 23 Nov 81	*Kitty Hawk*	WP/IO	F-14A	NL200
1 Mar to 29 Oct 83	*Carl Vinson*	World	F-14A TARPS	NL200
18 Oct 84 to 25 May 85	*Carl Vinson*	WP/IO	F-14A TARPS	NL200
12 Aug 86 to 5 Feb 87	*Carl Vinson*	WP/IO	F-14A TARPS	NL200
15 Jun to 14 Dec 88	*Carl Vinson*	WP/IO	F-14A TARPS	NL200
5 Sep to 8 Nov 89	*Carl Vinson*	WP/NorPac	F-14A TARPS	NL200
1 Feb to 31 Jul 90	*Carl Vinson*	WP/IO	F-14A TARPS	NL200
18 Oct to 11 Dec 91	*Kitty Hawk*	Horn	F-14A TARPS	NL200
3 Nov 92 to 3 May 92	*Kitty Hawk*	WP/IO/PG	F-14A TARPS	NL200
24 Jun to 22 Dec 94	*Kitty Hawk*	WP/IO	F-14A TARPS	NL200

The *Sundowners* bore another famous insignia, and carried the traditions of a previous VF-111, which traced a history back to World War II's VF-11. The lineage of the original *Sundowner* squadron ended with the disestablishment of the first VF-111 on 19 January 1959. A new Fighting-111 was designated the following day (from F11F flying VA-156), and it immediately adopted the *Sundowner* logo and traditions for its use. The squadron logo, which originally portrayed a pair of F4F *Wildcats* shooting a Japanese sun into the ocean, is a true Navy classic, and the unit's aircraft tails portrayed setting sun's rays for many years. Shark's teeth showed up on the unit's F-8 *Crusaders* in the early 1960s, and continued through on *Phantoms* and *Tomcats*. The dramatic teeth motif did vanish for a period in 1984-85 when the Miramar wing strictly enforced new TPS-related paint regulations, which technically don't allow nose markings. VF-111 flew F-4Bs as of Jan '74, and then F-4Ns through 1977, when they transitioned to F-14As, which they retained until disestablished with CVW-15 in 1995.

VF-114 ***Aardvarks*** **Miramar**

F-4J, F-14A

Estab. VBF-119 20 Jan 45, r/d VF-20A 15 Nov 46, r/d VF-192 24 Aug 48, r/d VF-114 15 Feb 50, disestab. 30 Apr 1993

23 Nov 73 to 9 Jul 74	*Kitty Hawk*	WP/IO	F-4J	NH200
21 May to 15 Dec 75	*Kitty Hawk*	WP	F-4J	NH200
25 Oct 77 to 15 May 78	*Kitty Hawk*	WP	F-14A	NH100
13 Mar to 22 Sep 79	*America*	Med	F-14A	NH100
14 Apr to 12 Nov 81	*America*	Med/IO	F-14A	NH100
1 Sep to 23 Mar 82	*Enterprise*	WP/IO	F-14A	NH100
30 May to 20 Dec 84	*Enterprise*	WP/IO	F-14A	NH100
15 Jan to 12 Aug 86	*Enterprise*	WP/IO/Med/SL	F-14A	NH100
25 Oct to 24 Nov 1987	*Enterprise*	NorPac	F-14A	NH100

The *Pacemakers* ofVF-121 were the *Phantom* RAG at Miramar for almost 20 years. F-4J NJ154 (157259) catches its breath on a rain dampened ramp at Cannon AFB, NM, in August 1976. The Arrow title on the fin tip is probably the call sign of the pilot whose name is painted on the canopy rail. (John Pouch)

5 Jan to 3 Jul 88	*Enterprise*	WP/IO	F-14A	NH100	*P.Mantis*
17 Sep 89 to 16 Mar 90	*Enterprise*	WP/IO	F-14A	NH100	
25 Sep to 20 Nov 90	*Lincoln*	Horn	F-14A	NH100	
28 May to 28 Nov 91	*Lincoln*	WP/IO/PG	F-14A	NH100	

The *Aardvarks* were one of the more colorful units at Miramar, wearing orange flight suits in peacetime long after everyone else had gone to green. Their name comes from the anteater character in Johnny Hart's "B.C." comic strip, and dates from the early 1960s when, according to the commonly accepted story, the Junior Officers of the squadron picked it by acclimation when they dumped the previous *Executioner* logo and nickname. The vivid orange critter was known to show up just about anywhere on base, being painted on the hold short line of the runway, or in the Officer's Club parking lot. They were flying F-4Js in 1974, and transitioned to *Tomcats* in 1976. The *Aardvarks* made nine West Pac or Med deployments with CVW-11 and F-14s before being disestablished.

VF-121 ***Pacemakers*** **Miramar** **FRS**

F-4B, F-4J, F-4S

Reserve VF-781 activated 1950, r/d VF-121 4 Feb 53, disestablished 30 Sep 1980

Fighting-121 had been the AirPac "all-weather" RAG since 1959, having flown the F3H *Demon* (until 1963) and F4H *Phantom II* (since 1960). The *Pacemakers* became a tremendously important training unit, being heavily involved in developing tactics that turned the *Phantom* into a successful fighter aircraft in Vietnam. In 1969 VF-121 began a special Air Combat Maneuvering curriculum that would split off in July 1972 to become the Navy Fighter Weapons School (NFWS), better known as "Topgun." In December 1980 former members of the squadron manned the "VF-121 Transition Support Detachment," which flew 13 "new" F-4S *Phantoms* overseas to join CVW-5's fighter squadrons. Five former VF-151 and VF-161 F-4Js were returned to California by the det, which would be the final act by the unit. With its demise, Oceana based VF-171 took over all F-4 FRS duties in the Navy.

VF-124 ***Gunfighters*** **Miramar** **FRS**

F-14A, F-14A TARPS, F-14D, T-34C

Est. VF-53 16 Aug 48, r/d VF-124 11 Apr 58, disestab. 30 Sept 1994

The *Gunfighters* had been the Pacific Fleet's "day fighter" RAG, and flew F-8 *Crusaders* until conversion to the F-14 in 1972-73. The unit continued that function until it was disestablished in 1994. From 1973 to 1976 Marines were assigned to VF-124 as the service began, and then canceled, its own F-14A transition. F-14Ds arrived in November 1990, in a decision that put the "Deltas" on the West Coast and the "Bravos" at Oceana. The squadron initially used the NJ400 series, and moved to NJ100 side numbers in 1992.

VF-126 ***Fighting Seahawks, Bandits*** **Miramar** **FRS**

TA-4F/J, A-4E/F/M, T-2C, T-38A, F-5E/F, F-16N, TF-16N

Est. VA-126 6 Apr 56, r/d VF-126 15 Oct 65 disestab.. 1 Apr 1994

VF-126 was the West Coast counterpart to VF-43, being the Miramar "instrument RAG" for many of its years before becoming a dedicated adversary unit following Vietnam. The *Seahawks* were actively involved in ACM training through most of the Vietnam War, as their TA-4s had been used since the mid-1960s to simulate bandits for the co-located F-4 and F-8 units. Their contributions helped lead to the formation of the formal *Topgun* program.

T-2Cs were assigned from January 1978 to conduct out-of-control (spin) flight training within the Miramar fighter community. Improved adversary aircraft (A-4Fs) came three months later. In 1981 the unit changed its nickname to *Bandits*, which was more befitting its new primary mission. As of 1982 squadron strength was set at three A-4F, eleven TA-4J, and a trio of T-2Cs. Supersonic aircraft arrived in the fall

Before they were the *Bandits*, VF-126 went by the *Fighting Seahawks* as the Miramar instrument RAG. They became involved in DACM training during the Vietnam War, as their TA-4 *Skyhawks* proved to be excellent MiG-17 simulators. When this picture was taken, in Feb '77, the instrument role was still the primary one though; note the training hood stowed in the aft cockpit of TA-4J NJ605 (153518) at Cannon AFB, NM. (John Pouch)

of 1982 in the form of three F-5Es and a single T-38A. A-4Ms were operated for a short period from 1992. Between 1985 and 1987 the unit's Commanding Officer was Randy "Duke" Cunningham, the Navy's only pilot ace from Vietnam and, as of 2005, a Republican Congressman from Oceanside, CA, who resigned his office after facing federal bribery charges. The *Bandits* were disestablished 1 Apr '94.

VFA-127; See VA-127, Chapter 5

VF-142 — ***Ghostriders*** — **Miramar, Oceana**

F-4J, F-14A, F-14B

Est. VF-193 24 Aug 48, r/d VF-142 15 Oct 63, disestab 30 Apr 1995

3 Jan to 3 Aug 74	*America*	Med	F-4J	AJ200	
15 Apr to 25 Oct 76	*America*	Med	F-14A	AE200	
10 Jun to 19 Jul 77	*America*	NorLant	F-14A	AE200	
25 Sep 77 to 25 Apr 78	*America*	Med	F-14A	AE200	
16 Jan to 13 Jul 79	*Eisenhower*	Med	F-14A	AG200	
15 Apr 80 to 22 Dec 80	*Eisenhower*	IO	F-14A	AG200	
20 Aug to 7 Oct 81	*Eisenhower*	NorLant	F-14A	AG200	
5 Jan to 13 Jul 82	*Eisenhower*	Med	F-14A	AG200	
27 Apr to 2 Dec 83	*Eisenhower*	Med	F-14A	AG200	
8 May to 20 Jun 84	*Eisenhower*	NorLant	F-14A	AG200	
10 Oct 84 to 8 May 85	*Eisenhower*	Med	F-14A	AG200	
29 Feb to 29 Aug 88	*Eisenhower*	Med	F-14A	AG200	
8 Mar to 12 Sep 90	*Eisenhower*	Med/RS	F-14A+	AG200	*D.Shield*
26 Sep 91 to 2 Apr 92	*Eisenhower*	Med	F-14B	AG200	
20 May to 17 Nov 94	*G Washington*	Med	F-14B	AG200	

The *Ghostriders* had been a Pacific fleet unit since establishment in 1948. The unit flew *Corsairs*, *Banshees*, and *Demons* before gaining *Phantom IIs* in 1964. They made seven deployments to Vietnam in three carriers. In 1973 VF-142 (and sister VF-143) was assigned to Atlantic Fleet CVW-8 for a 1974 cruise in *America*, after which they moved permanently to Oceana, where they began training for the F-14A. The squadron then made 14 deployments in the A and B (A+) models before being disestablished. For reasons known only to the Oceana VF community, the *Ghostriders* were also known as the "Goats."

VF-143 — ***Pukin' Dogs*** — **Miramar, Oceana**

F-4J, F-14A, F-14A TARPS, F-14B, F-14B TARPS

Reserve VF-871 activated 20 Jul 50, r/d VF-123 4 Feb 53, r/d VF-53 12 Apr 58, r/d VF-143 20 Jun 62

3 Jan to 3 Aug 74	*America*	Med	F-4J	AJ100
15 Apr to 25 Oct 76	*America*	Med	F-14A	AE100
10 Jun to 19 Jul 77	*America*	NorLant	F-14A	AE100
25 Sep 77 to 25 Apr 78	*America*	Med	F-14A	AE100
16 Jan to 13 Jul 79	*Eisenhower*	Med	F-14A	AG100
15 Apr 80 to 22 Dec 80	*Eisenhower*	IO	F-14A	AG100
20 Aug to 7 Oct 81	*Eisenhower*	NorLant	F-14A	AG100

5 Jan to 13 Jul 82	*Eisenhower*	Med	F-14A, TARPS	AG100	
27 Apr to 2 Dec 83	*Eisenhower*	Med	F-14A, TARPS	AG100	
8 May to 20 Jun 84	*Eisenhower*	NorLant	F-14A, TARPS	AG100	
10 Oct 84 to 8 May 85	*Eisenhower*	Med	F-14A, TARPS	AG100	
29 Feb to 29 Aug 88	*Eisenhower*	Med	F-14A, TARPS	AG100	
8 Mar to 12 Sep 90	*Eisenhower*	Med/RS	F-14A+ TARPS	AG100	*D.Shield*
26 Sep 91 to 2 Apr 92	*Eisenhower*	Med	F-14B, TARPS	AG100	
20 May to 17 Nov 94	*G Washington*	Med	F-14B, TARPS	AG100	
26 Jan to 23 Jul 96	*G Washington*	Med/RS/PG	F-14B, TARPS	AG100	
26 Feb to 26 Aug 98	*JC Stennis*	World	F-14B, TARPS	AG100	
18 Feb to 18 Aug 00	*Eisenhower*	Med/PG	F-14B, TARPS	AG100	

Bearing one of the more unusual and notorious nicknames in the fleet, the *Pukin' Dogs'* title dates from 1958, when the *Blue Racers* of VF-123 were redesignated VF-53. The CO wanted a new logo to go with the change, and a design was approved that featured a snarling black panther with wings (called a griffin, even if standard mythology features a lion) over a blue shield. A group of Junior Officers were so impressed with the new logo that they made a paper maché representation of the beast and presented it at a squadron party. One of the wives stated that the crouching winged panther logo looked like a hound throwing up, or a "Puking Dog." Slightly modified the name stuck, and in time completely replaced the previous title. The new name quickly became a mark of honor, and was soon recognized fleet-wide. Not everyone liked the title, though; some thought it juvenile, unprofessional, and embarrassing for the Navy. In 1994 a Vice Admiral in the chain of command gave the squadron a direct order to stop using their chosen nickname, while also strongly suggesting they become the "Griffins." Instead, the squadron became just the *Dogs* until that Flag Officer retired in 1996, upon which it became *Pukin' Dogs* yet again.

As of 1974 VF-143 was a Miramar-based outfit flying *Phantoms*. They made a deployment with Atlantic Fleet CVW-8 in *America*, and then actually moved to Oceana for F-14 transition. VF-143 continued through 2000 with deployments in CVW-6 and CVW-7, and was involved in *Desert Shield*.

VF-151, VFA-151 ***Vigilantes*** **Atsugi, Lemoore**

F-4B, F-4N, F-4J, F-4S, F/A-18A

Est. VF-23 6 Aug 48, r/d VF-151 23 Feb 1959, r/d VFA-151 1 Jun 86

1974 to 1977	*Midway*	Fwd Deployed	F-4N	NF200	
1977 to 1980	*Midway*	Fwd Deployed	F-4J	NF200	
1980 to 1986	*Midway*	Fwd Deployed	F-4S	NF200	
1986 to 1991	*Midway*	Fwd Deployed	F/A-18A	NF200	*D. Storm*
10 to 22 Aug 91	*Midway*	Hawaii	F/A-18A	NF200	
28 Aug to 14 Sep 91	*Midway*	CONUS	F/A-18A	NF/NK200	
29 May to 22 Jul 93	*Constellation*	Horn	F/A-18C	NE300	
10 Nov 94 to 10 May 95	*Constellation*	WP/IO/PG	F/A-18C	NE300	
1 Apr to 1 Oct 97	*Constellation*	WP/IO/PG	F/A-18C	NE300	
18 Jun to 17 Dec 99	*Constellation*	WP/IO/PG	F/A-18C	NE300	

The *Vigilantes* were one of two forward-deployed *Phantom* units in *Midway* for twelve years before converting to *Hornets* in 1986. The December 1980 transition from F-4Js to F-4S was made in Japan, with aircraft flown over by former members of VF-121. The squadron made the last fleet carrier launch of a U.S. Navy *Phantom*, from *Midway*, on 25 Mar '86. The *Vigilantes* subsequently underwent *Hornet* transition at Lemoore, and returned to Japan and CVW-5. In 1991 the unit ended its stay in the far east, and returned to CONUS in *Midway* as a temporary member of CVW-14. They transitioned to the "C" model *Hornet* and to CVW-2, where it has remained since. While at Lemoore in 1991-92 some of its "A" models were noted with NM300 series markings, denoting assignment to the Lemoore Wing.

In 1986 *Midway's* CVW-5 went through a wholesale transition, trading its *Phantoms* and *Corsairs* for three squadrons of *Hornets*. With VAQ-136 also in country to pick up new EA-6Bs, the wing took the rare opportunity to conduct an Air Wing Fallon det, with VAW-115 and VA-115 borrowing aircraft to participate. *Vigilante* F/A-18A NF204 (162896) is shown at Fallon in Oct '86 during that evolution. (Michael Grove)

VF-154	***Black Knights***	**Miramar, Atsugi**		
F-4J, F-4S, F-4N, F-14A, F-14A TARPS				
Reserve VF-837 activated 1 Feb 51, r/d VF-154 4 Feb 53.				
7 May to 18 Oct 74	*Ranger*	WP	F-4J	NE100
30 Jan to 7 Sep 76	*Ranger*	WP	F-4J	NE100
21 Feb to 22 Sep 79	*Ranger*	WP	F-4J	NE100
1980	(*Coral Sea*)	no cruise	F-4S	NK100
20 Aug 81 to 23 Mar 82	*Coral Sea*	WP/IO	F-4N	NK100
21 Mar to 12 Sep 83	*Coral Sea*	WP/IO	F-4N	NK100
21 Feb to 24 Aug 85	*Constellation*	WP/IO	F-14A, TARPS	NK100
11 Apr to 13 Oct 87	*Constellation*	WP/IO	F-14A, TARPS	NK100
1 Dec 88 to 1 Jun 89	*Constellation*	WP/IO	F-14A, TARPS	NK100
16 Sep 89 to 19 Oct 89	*Constellation*	NorPac	F-14A, TARPS	NK100
23 Jun to 20 Dec 90	*Independence*	WP/IO/PG	F-14A, TARPS	NK100 *D.Shield*
5 to 22 Aug 91	*Independence*	Hawaii	F-14A, TARPS	NK100
28 Aug to 11 Sep 91	*Independence*	to Japan	F-14A, TARPS	NF100
Sep 91 to Dec 2000	*Independence*	Fwd deployed	F-14A, TARPS	NF100

The *Black Knights* have been teamed with VF-21 since 1966, and followed a similar path as the *Freelancers*, being reequipped with F-4Ss in 1980, only to have to trade them to the reserves five months later for older F-4Ns that were more compatible with *Coral Sea's* smaller deck and arresting gear. *Tomcats* arrived in 1984, and the squadron subsequently made multiple deployments to WestPac with the type. In August 1991 the *Knights* joined CVW-5 and moved to Japan with *Independence*. See CVW-5 in chapter 2 for detailed at sea period listings.

VF-161, VFA-161	***Chargers, Rock Rivers***	**Atsugi, Lemoore**		
F-4B, F-4N, F-4J, F-4S, F/A-18A				
Est. VF-161 1 Sep 60, r/d VFA-161 1 June 1986		disestab. 1 Apr 1988		
1974 to 1977	*Midway*	Fwd Deployed	F-4N	NF100
1977 to 1980	*Midway*	Fwd Deployed	F-4J	NF100
1980 to 1986	*Midway*	Fwd Deployed	F-4S	NF100
(1986)	(*Midway*)	no cruise	F/A-18A	NF100
(1987-1988)	(*Independence*)	no cruise	F/A-18A	NM400

The *Chargers* were also known by their radio callsign "Rock River." VF-161 dated from 1960, when it was established as the all-weather fighter unit in the new CVW-16. In 1965 the squadron retired the fleet's last F3H-2 *Demons*, transitioned to F-4Bs, and made six deployments to Vietnam while achieving six MiG kills. In 1974 the unit moved to Japan with CVW-5, and became one of the last two deploying *Phantom* units in the Navy. After returning to CONUS in 1986 VFA-161 reequipped with *Hornets*, and was eventually assigned to the new CVW-10 after initially wearing CVW-5 markings on their FA-18s. They would be the only FA-18 unit attached to the new wing before it was disbanded. The squadron was disestablished on 1 Apr 1988.

CVW-14's two fighter units were assigned newly modified F-4Ss in 1980, only to soon find out that the slatted-wing *Phantoms* were considered just a bit "too hot" for landing for *Coral Sea's* flight deck, particularly in potential emergency situations. VF-154 and -21 therefore traded Miramar Reserve squadrons VF-301 and -302 for their older, and slightly slower, F-4Ns, and subsequently made two deployments with them. *Black Knight* F-4S is at Andrews AFB in Nov 1980. (Rick Burgess)

VF-171	***Aces***	**Oceana, Key West**	**FRS**	
F-4J, F-4N, F-4S, A-4E, TA-4J				
Estab. 8 Aug 1977	disestab. 1 Jun 1984			

The *Aces* were formed in 1977 to take over the *Phantom* training role from VF-101, which continued as an F-14 RAG. The unit was assigned a number that had last belonged to a former fleet F2H *Banshee* unit disestablished in 1958. They also adopted a logo that was loosely based on the original unit's design. The *Aces'* home base was at Oceana, where students went through the majority of the training syllabus. VF-171 also took over the *Grim Reapers'* permanent air combat maneuvering training detachment at Key West, along with its dedicated A-4 *Skyhawk* adversary aircraft. As of 1981 the det had ten F-4N, three A-4Es, and a TA-4J assigned, all of which carried distinctive markings and insignia signifying its unique status. The det retired its last F-4Ns in late 1982, with F-4Js and -Ss being used in Key West subsequently. The squadron initially retained VF-101's AD100 series for its aircraft, but soon shifted to AD-200 side numbers, while the Key West aircraft were numbered from AD250. When VF-171 was disestablished VMFAT-101 took over what little Navy *Phantom* training that remained.

VF-191 (1)	***Satan's Kittens***	**Miramar**		
F-8J, F-4J				
Estab. VF-19 15 Aug 43, r/d VF-19A 15 Nov 46, r/d VF-191 24 Aug 48, disestab. 1 Mar 1978				
18 Oct 73 to 5 Jun 74	*Oriskany*	WP/IO	F-8J	NM100
16 Sep 75 to 3 Mar 76	*Oriskany*	WP	F-8J	NM100
15 Feb to 5 Oct 77	*Coral Sea*	WP	F-4J	NL100

VF-191 was one of the last two regular Navy VF units to be equipped with the F-8 *Crusader*. When the squadron transitioned to *Phantoms* in 1976 it announced it had gone 28 months without an F-8 mishap, which was quite an accomplishment in *Crusaders*. The *Kittens* made only one deployment in F-4s before being disestablished.

VF-191 (2)	***Satin's Kittens/Hellcats***	**Miramar**		
F-14A				
Estab. 1 Dec 1986	disestab. 30 Apr 1988			
(1987-88)	(*Independence*)	no cruise	F-14A	NM100

The second VF-191 was established in 1986 as a charter member of the new CVW-10. The squadron adopted the logo and traditions of the previous unit. As with sister VF-194, it was disestablished without deploying.

VF-194 (1)	***Legendary Red Lightnings***		**Miramar**	
F-8J, F-4J				
Estab. VF-91 26 Mar 52, r/d VF-194 1 Aug 63, disestab. 30 Apr 1978				
18 Oct 73 to 5 Jun 74	*Oriskany*	WP/IO	F-8J	NM200
16 Sep 75 to 3 Mar 76	*Oriskany*	WP	F-8J	NM200
15 Feb to 5 Oct 77	*Coral Sea*	WP	F-4J	NL200

Paired with VF-191, Fighting-194 was another experienced *Crusader* squadron, although they managed to make eight deployments to Vietnam with no aerial victories. The *Red Lightnings* were noted for their habit of transmitting the squadron's signature "Hud'n Hud'n" call on the radio whenever they entered the traffic pattern at Miramar. The normal response was for another squadron to key the mike and say "And no MiGs," to remind them of that fact. They made one deployment with *Phantoms* before being disestablished in 1978.

The *Legendary Red Lightings* started flying Vought's F-8 *Crusader* in 1960, and in 1976 became one of the last pair (with VF-191) to deploy with the fighter version. F-8J NM211 comes aboard *Oriskany* during the final cruise. The squadron's unique "Hud'n Hud'n" call is prominently displayed on the upraised wing center section. (Pete Clayton)

VF-194 (2)	***Legendary Red Lightnings***		**Miramar**	
F-14A (F-14A TARPS)				
Established 1 Dec 1986	disestablished 30 Apr 1988			
(1987-88)	(Independence)	no cruise	F-14A	NM200

The 1986 version of VF-194 adopted the name, logo, and traditions of the previous squadron, as well as the "Hud'n Hud'n" call. The response remained "And still no MiGs." As with the other CVW-10 units, the second VF-194 made no deployments before being disestablished.

VF-201, VFA-201 *Hunters* **Dallas, Ft Worth** **Naval Reserve**

F-8H, F-4N, F-4S, F-14A, F/A-18A

Estab. 25 Jul 70, r/d VFA-201 1 Jan 1999

As of 1974 the *Hunters* were assigned to CVWR-20, after having been part of CVWR-30 for a very short period in 1970-71. According to one former squadron member, the *Hunters* title was picked because the unit's initial core came from F-8 equipped VF-162, which had the same name. The *Hunters* relinquished their *Crusaders* for *Phantoms* in 1976, the F-4S arrived in 1984, and *Tomcats* took over during 1987. In March 1983 the unit (with VF-202) deployed 18 F-4Ns to Sigonella, Sicily, for a three-week period in a rare overseas trip by a reserve fighter squadron. The squadron retired the last Navy Reserve F-4N on 29 Feb 1984. They became the sole surviving reserve Fitron in 1994, and moved to NAS JRB Ft Worth in 1998. In January 1999 the unit transitioned to F/A-18A *Hornets* and retired their *Tomcats*, the last in the Reserves. VF-201 wore AF100 series side numbers

VF-202 *Superheats* **Dallas** **Naval Reserve**

F-8H, F-4N, F-4S, F-14A, F-14A TARPS

Estab. 1 Jul 70, disestab. 31 Dec 1994 (9 Jul 94 ceremony)

VF-202 followed sister VF-201 from F-8s to F-4Ns (1976), to the F-4S (1983), and on to F-14As (1987), while it also assumed the duties as a TARPS squadron. The unit was disestablished in December 1994. The *Superheats* had the distinction of making the last F-4 trap in the Navy, 18 Oct '86, on *America*. In early 1983 the unit made a three-week deployment to Sigonella, Sicily, and placed a detachment aboard *Coral Sea* with CVW-14 for a period of operations in the Caribbean at the end of that ship's 1983 Around-the-World cruise. VF-202 was disestablished in 1994 as part of the reserve's post-*Desert Storm* reorganization.

VF-211 *Fighting Checkmates* **Miramar, Oceana (8/96)**

F-8J, F-14A, F-14A TARPS, F-14A+, F-14A+ TARPS

Estab. VB-74 1 May 45, r/d VA-1B 15 Nov 46, r/d VA-24 1 Sep 48, r/d VF-24 1 Dec 49, r/d VF-211 9 Mar 59.

8 May 73 to 8 Jan 74	*Hancock*	WP/IO	F-8J	NP100
18 May to 29 Oct 75	*Hancock*	WP/IO	F-8J	NP100
12 Apr to 21 Nov 77	*Constellation*	WP	F-14A	NG100
26 Sep 78 to 17 May 79	*Constellation*	WP/IO	F-14A	NG100
26 Feb to 15 Oct 80	*Constellation*	WP/IO	F-14A	NG100
20 Oct 81 to 23 May 82	*Constellation*	WP/IO	F-14A, TARPS	NG100
15 Jul 83 to 28 Feb 84	*Ranger*	SoPac/WP/IO	F-14A, TARPS	NG100
24 Jul 85 to 21 Dec 85	*Kitty Hawk*	WP/IO	F-14A, TARPS	NG100
3 Jan to 29 Jun 87	*Kitty Hawk*	World	F-14A, TARPS	NG100
2 Sep 88 to 2 Mar 89	*Nimitz*	WP/IO	F-14A, TARPS	NG100
15 Jun to 9 Jul 89	*Nimitz*	NorPac	F-14A, TARPS	NG100
25 Feb to 24 Aug 91	*Nimitz*	WP/IO/PG	F-14A+, TARPS	NG100
2 Feb to 29 Jul 93	*Nimitz*	WP/IO/PG	F-14A, TARPS	NG100
27 Nov 95 to 20 May 96	*Nimitz*	WP/IO/PG	F-14A, TARPS	NG100
1 Sep 97 to 1 Mar 98	*Nimitz*	WP/IO/PG	F-14A, TARPS	NG100
7 Jan to 3 Jul 00	*JC Stennis*	WP/IO/PG	F-14A, TARPS	NG100

VF-211 was the most successful F-8 squadron, and second placed Navy fighter unit overall in Vietnam, killing seven MiGs during the war. The *Checkmates* were a veteran day-fighter outfit that flew *Corsairs*, *Panthers*, *Cougars*, *Furys*, and *Tigers* before getting *Crusaders* in 1959-60. Transitioning to *Tomcats* in 1974 along with VF-24, the squadron subsequently made fourteen deployments with CVW-9 in five different carriers. VF-211 made the first deployment to WestPac with the TARPS pod in 1981. In 1990 the unit was equipped with F-14A+ (F-14B) *Tomcats*, only to lose them after only one deployment when the decision was made to place all "Bs" on the East Coast. VF-211 stayed with CVW-9 even after its move to Oceana in August 1996.

VF-213 ***Black Lions*** **Miramar, Oceana**

F-4J, F-14A, F-14A TARPS, F-14D, F-14D TARPS

Estab. 22 Jun 55

6 Sep to 12 Oct 74	*America*	NorLant	F-4J	NH100	CVW-8
23 Nov 73 to 9 Jul 74	*Kitty Hawk*	WP/IO	F-4J	NH100	
21 May to 15 Dec 75	*Kitty Hawk*	WP	F-4J	NH100	
25 Oct 77 to 15 May 78	*Kitty Hawk*	WP	F-14A	NH200	
13 Mar to 22 Sep 79	*America*	Med	F-14A	NH200	
14 Apr to 12 Nov 81	*America*	Med/IO	F-14A	NH200	
1 Sep to 23 Mar 82	*Enterprise*	WP/IO	F-14A TARPS	NH200	
30 May to 20 Dec 84	*Enterprise*	WP/IO	F-14A TARPS	NH200	
15 Jan to 12 Aug 1986	*Enterprise*	WP/IO/Med/SL	F-14A TARPS	NH200	
25 Oct to 24 Nov 1987	*Enterprise*	NorPac	F-14A TARPS	NH200	
5 Jan to 3 Jul 88	*Enterprise*	WP/IO	F-14A TARPS	NH200 *P.Mantis*	
17 Sep 89 to 16 Mar 90	*Enterprise*	WP/IO	F-14A TARPS	NH200	
25 Sep to 20 Nov 90	*Lincoln*	Horn	F-14A, TARPS	NH200	
28 May to 28 Nov 91	*Lincoln*	WP/IO/PG	F-14A, TARPS	NH200	
15 Jun to 15 Dec 93	*Lincoln*	WP/IO	F-14A, TARPS	NH100	
10 Apr to 8 Oct 95	*Lincoln*	WP/IO/PG	F-14A, TARPS	NH100	
11 Oct 96 to 11 Apr 97	*Kitty Hawk*	WP/IO/PG	F-14A, TARPS	NH100	
6 Nov 98 to 6 May 99	*Carl Vinson*	WP/IO/PG	F-14D, TARPS	NH100	

The *Black Lions* (who also frequently display their nickname as one word, *Blacklions*) were long time residents of CVW-11, having been assigned to the air wing in 1964. They were established in 1955 as the night-fighter element of CVG-21, and flew *Banshees*, *Skyrays*, and *Demons* before getting F-4s. In 1974 the squadron was temporarily attached to CVW-8 to fill out *America's* trip to Norway for a NATO exercise. In 1999 the *Lions* were involved in combat while carrying out Operation *Southern Watch* duties. Two VF-213 *Tomcats* fired AIM-54 *Phoenix* missiles, unsuccessfully, at Iraqi MiG-25 "Foxbats" on 5 January, in what was reportedly the missile's first combat use in U.S. history. VF-213 was the last Miramar-based Fitron to move to Oceana, officially arriving on 10 April 1997.

VF-301 ***Devil's Disciples*** **Miramar** **Naval Reserve**

F-8J, F-4B, F-4N, F-4S, F-14A

Estab. 1 Oct 70, disestab. 31 Dec 1994

Dating from October 1970, VF-301 was assigned to CVWR-30 and wore the ND100 series numbers. F-4Bs were assigned in 1974, and F-4Ns arrived in 1978. In 1980 the squadron (and sister VF-302) traded aircraft with regular units VF-154 and VF-21, gaining the F-4S in the process. The *Phantoms* were phased out from October 1984 with the arrival of F-14As.

VF-301's "Triple Sticks" (side number 111) starts its takeoff roll at Miramar on 21 Feb 1982. Judging from the lack of external stores, this event will probably be a short ACM event—but as fighter pilots are eager to tell you, "45 minutes of fighter time is worth twice that much in any other aircraft." The non-standard paint scheme was one of several so called "Heater-Ferris" designs applied to CVWR-30 F-4Ss during this period. (Bob Lawson)

VF-302 ***Stallions*** **Miramar** **Naval Reserve**
F-8K, F-4B, F-4N, F-4S, F-14A, F-14A TARPS
Estab. 21 May 71, disestab. 31 Dec 1994
The *Stallions* were the second FitRon in CVWR-30, and wore the ND200 series in the air wing. The *Crusaders* gave way to F-4Bs in 1973, which were in turn replaced by F-4Ns in 1975. F-4S *Phantoms* arrived from CVW-14 in 1980 (see VF-301 and VF-154 for details), and in 1985 VF-302 transitioned to F-14A and TARPS aircraft (from May '86). The squadron was disestablished in December 1994 along with the rest of its wing in the post *Desert Storm* draw down.

Navy Fighter Weapons School (NFWS, *Topgun*)
While *Topgun* (officially one word—not two, as in the movie or, curiously, as painted on the side of their Miramar hangar) was a command, it was not quite a squadron; yet it exercised an influence over the entire Navy/Marine VF community that completely belied its size.

Topgun was the name applied to a special course started 3 March 1969 at Miramar F-4 RAG VF-121 to teach advanced ACM tactics. It became a separate detachment in January 1972 as the Navy Fighter Weapons School (NFWS), and was formally established as a distinct command on 21 July '72. A-4Es were initially assigned as stripped-down "Mongoose" aircraft, to simulate sub-sonic opponents, like the MiG-17. T-38As arrived in 1973, bringing supersonic capability to the unit. New F-5Es and -Fs came in 1975, as dedicated dissimilar adversary aircraft.

Initial classes included both air-to-air as well as air-to-ground training. The latter was soon dropped, as the school became an ACM specialized organization.

The school's results are well documented, and do not need to be repeated here, and its success led to the establishment of an entire adversary subculture within the Navy/Marine VF community.

The NFWS runs a five-week fighter course, with fleet Squadron Commanders being given "billets," or slots, for *Topgun* classes that they select crews to attend. Units have to provide their own aircraft and flight money ("Optar") to get through the school. As of 1980 students received 75 classroom and 40 flight hours in the course.

Topgun is the final authority within the service in advanced fighter training and tactics, and became the blueprint for other "post-graduate" schools established in other communities. In 1976 the school added a "Topscope" course to teach advanced intercept tactics to E-2 and ship radar operators. Two years later it was blended into the regular fighter syllabus, allowing these critical individuals to train alongside the aircrew they would control.

As of Jan 1974 *Topgun* had only seven aircraft assigned: five T-38As and a pair of A-4Es. By the fall of 1982 *Topgun* owned five F-5Es, three F-5Fs, four A-4Es, and one A-4F. F-16Ns were introduced on 17 June 1987, replacing the F-5s, which moved to the adversary units. The *Falcons* were flown hard, and retired in Jan 1995 after only eight years of service. They were in turn replaced by former fleet F/A-18s and F-14s. A small number of A-4Ms were assigned in the early '90s,but the long serving and faithful *Skyhawks* all departed in May 1994. By Jan '95 the inventory stood at sixteen FA-18A/Bs and five F-14As. NFWS moved from Miramar to Fallon in June 1996, where it joined "Strike U" to form the Naval Strike & Air Warfare Center (NSAWC), where *Topgun* survives as a very influential department.

The Navy's most numerous adversary aircraft for many years was the Douglas *Skyhawk*, which gained a measure of public exposure as the bogie aircraft in the movie "Top Gun." Here a trio of NFWS A-4Es sit on the Miramar ramp in November 1985. The lead "Scooter," marked for the Marines, is 150023. (author)

Adversaries

Following Vietnam, the Navy jumped enthusiastically into the adversary mission (don't say "Aggressor"—that's an Air Force term) as "Dissimilar Air Combat Maneuvering" (DACM) became the mantra for fighter training. The unqualified combat results of the *Topgun* program, as well as certain other activities, led the Navy to turn a number of "support" squadrons into Adversary units, whose mission was to provide opponents for fleet squadrons in a variety of training situations.

The Navy's adversary program is managed by the Navy Fighter Weapons School (NFWS), otherwise known as *Topgun*. Adversary pilots and instructors are trained and certified by *Topgun*, and instructed to use foreign force tactics and weapons envelopes against fleet aircraft. More importantly, they are also taught to be real instructors, who can professionally recreate engagements during a post-flight debrief to get specific training points across to students, instead of using the more traditional disorganized (and frequently contentious) "I shot you first" chalkboard arguments that had long been the norm.

Topgun's primary course was, and is, a specialized program for selected fleet aircrews. Squadrons are given "slots" to send crews with their aircraft for an intense five-week course in ACM and fighter tactics. Upon graduation, these aircrew become "patch wearers" who return to their squadrons as the resident experts in the field. As can be imagined, competition to attend the school is intense, and selection is usually a sign of superior airmanship and ability. The school is also instrumental in developing new tactics for the air-to-air business, and is considered one of the leading such locations in the world.

Beyond the "Graduate Level" training that *Topgun* provided for select aircrew, the fleet needed locally based aircraft to help train squadrons during the periods between deployments. From the late 1970s the Navy developed units to provide dissimilar ACM opponents at the four "Master Jet Bases" for squadron-level training.

The four "Instrument RAGs" based at Oceana, Cecil, Miramar, and Lemoore were obvious candidates, as all flew A-4 *Skyhawks*, and they became the basis for the formal fleet adversary program of the late 1970s. Fleet Composite (VC) units were also trained for the mission, allowing deployed squadrons to have access to well trained adversary support, as well.

Supersonic aircraft from the Air Force, in the form of T-38s and F-5s soon appeared, the latter in 1975. These aircraft frequently wore foreign inspired or unusual camouflage paint jobs, as well as the insignia of potential opponent nations. T-2C "fighter guppies" were assigned to VF-43 and -126 to provide "out of control" (spin) training for aircrew at both Miramar and Oceana, as well as occasionally representing light-strike jets, such as Galebs or Macchis. By the mid-'80s the dissimilar ACM program was going full bore, with serious senior-officer support. The program's high water mark would be about 1989, when 148 airframes were flying Navy-wide in the adversary role.

There was no debate that the adversary units were effective, but they were also expensive to operate. Odd aircraft types (particularly the F-21A *Kfirs*), safety concerns, and "different priorities" conspired against the program, and in the end the service decided that dissimilar Regular Navy ACM units were a luxury it could no longer afford.

All four of the dedicated Regular Navy adversary units were disestablished following *Desert Storm*, while two Reserve composite-fighter units (VFC-12 and -13) survived. The reserves at NAS Dallas also flew a small group of *Skyhawks* in the adversary role for a short period from September 1987 and into 1994. Officially they operated under the title of Operations Maintenance Division (OMD) NAS Dallas, with four A-4Ms. Reserve F/A-18 units filled in, as well and did good work, even if their *Hornets* were little different from the fleet units they faced. In the end the DACM program wasn't quite what it used to be, as by 2001 only VFC-13 and VMFT-401 were left as true "dissimilar" Navy/Marine adversary units.

Formal Navy/Marine Adversary Units

VF-43	Oceana	1975 to 1994	A-4, F-21, F-16, F-5, T-2, T-38
VA/VF-45	Cecil/Key West	1975 to 1996	A-4, F-16, F-5
VF-126	Miramar	1972 to 1994	A-4, F-16, T-2, F-5, T-38
VA/VFA-127	Lemoore/Fallon	1975 to 1996	A-4, F-5
VC/VFC-12	Oceana	current	A-4, F/A-18,
VC/VFC-13	Miramar/Fallon	current	A-4, F/A-18, F-5
NFWS	Miramar/Fallon	current	A-4, F-5, T-38, F-14, F-18
VF-101/171	det Key West	1974 to 84	A-4
OMD Dallas	Dallas	1987 to 94	A-4M, TA-4J
VMFT-401	Yuma	1987 to cur.	F-21A, F-5

See VF and VA squadron listings for more unit details

Adversary Squadron Strength: January 1985

VF-45	10 TA-4J, 3 A-4E, 1 T-39D (admin support)
VF-43	12 F-21A, 5 A-4E, 4 TA-4J, 4 T-2C
VF-126	12 TA-4J, 4 A-4F, 3 F-5E, 1 T-38, 4 T-2C
VA-127	4 A-4F, 1 TA-4F, 8 TA-4J
NFWS	5 F-5E, 3 F-5F, 4 A-4E, 1 A-4F
VC-12	10 TA-4J, 2 A-4F, 2 A-4E
VC-13	10 TA-4J, 4 A-4E

The ultimate adversary aircraft of the late 1980s were the Navy's F-16Ns, which were the lightest *Fighting Falcons* built, and therefore possessed a reputation as being the "hottest" of their type in the world. 22 single seat and four two-seaters were acquired by the service and operated by *Topgun*, VF-43, VF-45, and VF-126. The Navy rode them hard, and had to retire the lot by 1995. Several, their lives spent, ignobly ended up as targets in the desert. TF-16N AD05, from VF-43, is shown on a photo mission over the Fallon range on 23 Apr '90 with Bob Lawson, editor and chief photographer of "The Hook" magazine, in the back seat. (author)

Among the most notable adversary aircraft operated by the Navy was the F-21 *Kfir*, 12 of which were leased from Israel between April 1985 and April 1988, and operated by VF-43. The exotic *Kfir* had a mixed reputation, being expensive to operate, as well as having short legs and no radar. They were replaced in VF-43 by the cheaper and more flexible F-5 *Tiger II* series. Yuma based Marine Reserve unit VMFT-401 received 13 other "Lion Cubs," and flew them until 1989. (999728, Fallon, Nov '86. Michael Grove)

Northrop's F-5 series proved to be the Navy's first really successful supersonic dissimilar adversary, replacing a small number of T-38 *Talons* from 1975. VFA-127's F-5E NJ741 (741545) is a former USAF aircraft, and carries North Korean markings on its tail at Fallon in March 1994. The insignias of other potential opponents were carried on other squadron aircraft during the same period. A group of Miramar based F-5s, painted black with red stars, masqueraded as "MiG-28s" in the movie "Top Gun." (Michael Grove)

The Navy never used the A-4M in its light attack units, but the service did fly a limited number as adversaries for a short period of time. The Reserves had a small force at NAS Dallas between 1987 and 1994. 7D02 (158189) is at Fallon in August '88. (Michael Grove)

5

Attack Squadrons (VA) Strike Fighter Squadrons (VFA)

"Fighter Pukes make movies. Attack Pilots make history."

So went the bumper sticker, which was based on the belief at places like Whidbey, Oceana, Lemoore, and Cecil Field that, while the VF guys got the glory (particularly in movies like "Top Gun"), it was Attack Aviation that carried the load, punished the enemy, and won wars.

Navy carrier-based Attack squadrons had long been divided into three groups: Heavy, Medium, and Light. The first category was formally designated VAH, and flew A-3 *Skywarriors* and A-5 *Vigilantes* from 1956, up until the last unit was either redesignated or disestablished in 1971. The latter two categories both used the VA title, with Medium Attack (A-1s and A-6s) being informally called "VA(M)" within the service, while Light Attack (flying A-4s and A-7s) was also frequently called "VA(L)." They were distinct communities in almost all ways, with separate bases and type wings to support them, as well as different personalities. Although there were notable exceptions, by the end of Vietnam most "big deck" carrier air wings carried a single Medium attack unit and two light attack squadrons, while "Small deck" (*Essex*-class) carriers typically carried three light attack units.[9]

As of January 1974 there were 30 light attack squadrons in the regular Navy—three units still flew the A-4 *Skyhawk*, while 27 operated four different versions of the A-7 Corsair (two with As, five Bs, two Cs, and the balance in Echoes). Twelve Medium attack squadrons flew the A-6 *Intruder*, one unit for each of the air wings in *Midway*-class or larger ships.

The *Skyhawk* was a legendary platform that had carried a good portion of the attack load for the Navy during Vietnam. The last three fleet A-4 squadrons were all equipped with F-models modified with more powerful J-52-P-408 engines. All three units were disestablished with CVW-21 in 1975. Once replaced in the Air Wing, the *Skyhawk* continued to provide valuable service with adversary units, Composite Squadrons, Training Command, and the *Blue Angels*. The remarkable A-4 managed to survive in the Navy inventory nine years after its replacement (the A-7) had been completely retired.

The *Corsair* was another workhorse, and although it never quite got the accolades the *Skyhawk* did (in particular, the type never had the "fun to fly" reputation of the A-4), it could carry a lot of ordnance a long distance and, in the Echo-version, probably possessed the most

Between 1983 and 1996 the F/A-18 *Hornet* series became the primary strike aircraft in the Navy. Here a trio of VFA-87 *Golden Warriors* fly off the wing of an EA-6B while off the coast of Egypt on 13 Jan '91. The following day they would proceed with *Theodore Roosevelt* through the Suez Canal. A week later they would be at war over Iraq. (author)

accurate iron bombing system of its day. The A-7 proved to be a worthy design, and lasted at sea until 1991, even if both TF-30 (A-7A/B/C) and TF-41 (A-7E) powered versions were generally considered to be underpowered behind the boat due to slow engine response. That being said, the all-time (as of 2005) U.S. Navy carrier landing leader, Capt John "Lites" Leenhouts, made most of his 1,645 traps in *Corsairs*.

First deployed in 1967, the A-7 continued to improve as it matured. In mid-1979 the type gained the AAR-45 FLIR pod, with VA-81 and VA-146 getting the first ones. Each *Corsair*-equipped air wing would typically deploy with one of its two VA(L) squadrons wired to carry the pod. Other known FLIR pod-carrying units included VA-22, 37, 66, 72, 86, 93, 97, 105, and 192. The A-7 also introduced the AGM-88 High Speed Anti-Radiation Missile (HARM) into fleet service, with -146 getting the missile in 1983. VA-83 claimed the first combat use of the weapon during 1986 operations off Libya.

The last major *Corsair II* version, the two-seat TA-7C, started arriving at the RAGs in June 1978, and proved valuable as a trainer and test bird. VA-46 and -72 made the final A-7 deployment in 1990-91, and performed with distinction in *Desert Storm*. The type was rapidly retired from all service after the Gulf War, with the last airframe being retired at Pt Mugu in November 1994.

In 1983 the F/A-18A *Hornet* entered the scene, with the stated goal of replacing all of the A-7 Light Attack squadrons, as well as the F-4 fighter units left on *Midway*-class ships. The type had begun in 1974 when CNO issued formal operational requirements for what was called the VFAX. Given the VFA designation, this new community was initially called "Fighter Attack," along the lines of Marine VMFA units. The title was changed to "Strike Fighter" on 25 Mar 1983, while retaining the VFA designation, and that was how they entered the fleet. The sexy new aircraft was subject to a good bit of hyperbole upon its introduction, including the occasional "never been done before" press releases about this "new concept" that mixed the two missions. Historically, VFA units actually had a precedent with the numerous Fighter-Bomber (VBF) squadrons that were established late in World War II with F4U *Corsairs* and F6F *Hellcats* as dual-role units.

The F/A-18A was (and is) a superb design that was advertised for its ability to combine fighter and attack missions "equally" in one platform, hence the Navy-sponsored (and the non DOD-recognized) "/" (slash) in the designation. The *Hornet* was a big step up for the former light attack community, being a supersonic platform with excellent air-to-air capability, as well as a very accurate air-to-ground system. Its primary, and widely reported, deficiency was "short range," and although it had nowhere near the legs of the A-7, it was really never any worse than the *Phantom*. (As stated by one former F-4 driver, "these *Corsair* guys just have to learn they can't rage around in blower for an hour.") It didn't take the fleet long to figure out the type's strengths, however, and the decision to move from the slow, but steady *Corsair* was obviously the right one.

Pacific Fleet light attack and strike fighter units were based in Lemoore, California, throughout this period. In the Atlantic Fleet these units were located at Cecil Field, Florida, until 1989-99, when the base was closed, and all but two of the remaining VFAs and the Type Wing moved to Oceana, Virginia. The remaining pair of squadrons was placed at MCAS Beaufort, SC, in an act that probably had had more to do with political issues (public concerns about noise and base loading at Oceana) than operational necessity.

Medium attack squadrons were based at Oceana (Atlantic Fleet) and Whidbey Island (Pacific Fleet). As stated before, the Navy had 12 squadrons flying the rugged and battle proven A-6 *Intruder* series as of 1974, with one squadron assigned each "big deck" Air Wing. The A-6A that saw sterling service in Vietnam was followed by the A-6E (1974), A-6E TRAM (1978), and A-6E SWIP (1990), each version increasing the type's capabilities. The KA-6D was also deployed as the fleet's standard tanker, with four or five attached to most units. With four external fuel tanks the KA-6 had 23,600 lbs (3,522 gallons) of JP-5 available for transfer. (as opposed to an A-7E, with 13,100 lbs/1,955 gal, or an A-4F with 9,800 lbs/1,463 gal).

Through a period of growth when John Lehman (an A-6 B/N in the Reserves) was Secretary of the Navy, four more A-6 squadrons were established, bringing the community to an apogee of 16 deployable units in 1987, and plans were made for more, with a goal of placing two *Intruder* outfits in every wing. Two Marine A-6 squadrons went to sea as well, and the new A-12 *Avenger* II was earmarked as an *Intruder* replacement.

The good times lasted only about six years though, as the A-12 was canceled, as were potential A-6F and A-6G follow-ons. To the surprise of many, the service decided after *Desert Storm* to close out the entire medium attack community while seeking cheaper alternatives. The *Intruder* line closed at Bethpage in January 1992 with the delivery of the 708th, and final, A-6. That bird (164385) would only survive until 8 Sep 1993, as it was lost in a supreme act of buffoonery when a VA-95 pilot tried to "surprise" a squadron mate (161682) through a "thump maneuver," where he would rapidly fly underneath the other aircraft, and then pull up right in front of him. Both aircraft ended up at the bottom of the Persian Gulf after the resulting collision—all four aircrew ejected successfully.

The Navy went from 16 Medium Attack units in 1990 to zero in only eight years, with the mission now being carried largely by F-14 *Tomcats* with the LANTIRN pod. As of 2000 a larger, improved version of the *Hornet*, the F/A-18F *Super Hornet*, was on the way to carry out the mission as well.

Naval Reserve

Eight A-4 equipped Atkrons were established in 1970 as part of the massive reorganization of the Naval Air Reserves. Six remained at the start of 1974, all being light attack units with either *Skyhawks* or *Corsairs*. In 1988 the first of two A-7 squadrons transitioned to A-6 *Intruders*, returning the Medium Attack mission to the reserves years after the retirement of its last A-1 *Skyraiders*.

In 1984 the first Reserve A-7 unit received F/A-18A *Hornets* and became a Strike-Fighter squadron. This placed the Navy's newest aircraft in the Reserves prior to the first fleet cruise, and when there were still 20 Regular Navy A-7 units deploying. Touted as part of the "Total Force" concept, where the Reserves would fly the same aircraft as the Regulars, it also raised the emotional question at Lemoore and Cecil as to why "non-deploying" units were getting the "newest and best" aircraft ahead of carrier-based squadrons that would be the first to go into combat.

Controversy aside, by 1992 the Reserves had four VFA and two VA(M) units in two air wings that, with the exception of VS units, closely mirrored fleet organization. Among other missions, the reserve VFAs provided vital support in the bogey role when regular adversary units were being disestablished.

Following *Desert Storm* the Reserves got the axe, along with the Regulars, as they lost half of their VFAs and both of their Medium Attack squadrons. By 1998 only VFA-203 and -204 survived. A year later Dallas-based VF-201 traded in its *Tomcats* for F/A-18As, thereby returning a third Strike Fighter squadron to the Reserves.

VA-12 *Ubangis, Clinchers* **Cecil Field**

A-7E

Estab. VBF-4 12 May 45, r/d VF-2A 15 Nov 46, r/d VF-12 2 Aug 48, r/d VA-12 1 Aug 55

disestab. 1 Oct 1986

21 Jun 73 to 19 Jan 74	*Independence*	MED	A-7E	AG400
19 Jul 74 to 21 Jan 75	*Independence*	MED	A-7E	AG400
15 Oct 75 to 5 May 76	*Independence*	MED/NorLant	A-7E	AG400
31 Mar to 21 Oct 77	*Independence*	MED	A-7E	AG400
16 Jan to 13 Jul 79	*Eisenhower*	MED	A-7E	AG400
15 Apr to 22 Dec 80	*Eisenhower*	MED	A-7E	AG400
20 Aug to 7 Oct 81	*Eisenhower*	NorLant	A-7E	AG400
5 Jan 82 to 13 Jul 82	*Eisenhower*	MED	A-7E	AG400
27 Apr 83 to 2 Dec 83	*Eisenhower*	MED	A-7E	AG400
10 Oct 84 to 8 May 85	*Eisenhower*	MED	A-7E	AG400

VA-12 was known by a number of names, including *Ubangis, Clinchers* (based on their tactical callsign), and by the motto "Kiss of Death," which comes from their insignia. The squadron flew A-7Es with CVW-7 from 1971 until their end in 1986. VA-12 was one of only four Cecil-based *Corsair* units that did not transition to *Hornets*. The VA-12 designation was scheduled to return to use in the late 1980s as an A-6 unit at Oceana. Budget realities forced the cancellation of these plans, however.

VA-15, VFA-15 *Valions* **Cecil Field, Oceana**

A-7B, A-7E, F/A-18A, F/A-18C

Estab. VA-67 1 Aug 68, r/d VA-15 2 Jun 69, r/d VFA-15 1 Oct 1986

14 Sep 73 to 17 Mar 74	*F.D. Roosevelt*	MED	A-7B	AE300	
3 Jan to 16 Jul 75	*F.D. Roosevelt*	MED	A-7B	AE300	
15 Apr to 25 Oct 76	*America*	MED	A-7E	AE300	
10 Jun to 19 Jul 77	*America*	SoLant	A-7E	AE300	
25 Sep 77 to 25 Apr 78	*America*	MED	A-7E	AE300	
28 Jun to 14 Dec 79	*America*	MED	A-7E	AE300	
19 Nov 80 to 10 Jun 81	*Independence*	MED/IO	A-7E	AE300	
7 Jun to 22 Dec 82	*Independence*	MED	A-7E	AE300	
18 Oct 83 to 11 Apr 84	*Independence*	Carib/Med	A-7E	AE300	Grenada Lebanon
16 Oct 84 to 19 Feb 85	*Independence*	MED/IO	A-7E	AE300	
1 Dec 85 to 13 Jun 86	MAG-12	Iwakuni	A-7E	AC300	(not in CVW-3)
25 Aug 88 to 11 Oct 88	*T.Roosevelt*	NLANT	F/A-18A	AJ300	
30 Dec 88 to 30 Jun 89	*T.Roosevelt*	MED	F/A-18A	AJ300	
28 Dec 90 to 28 Jun 91	*T.Roosevelt*	MED/RS/PG	F/A-18A	AJ300	*Desert Storm*
11 Mar to 8 Sep 93	*T.Roosevelt*	MED/RS	F/A-18C	AJ300	
22 Mar to 22 Sep 95	*T. Roosevelt*	MED/RS/PG	F/A-18C	AJ300	
29 Apr to 28 Oct 97	*J.F.Kennedy*	MED/RS/PG	F/A-18C	AJ300	
26 Mar to 22 Sep 99	*T.Roosevelt*	MED/RS/PG	F/A-18C	AJ300	*Allied Force*

The squadron's nickname is derived from the term "V.A.-Lions." The *Valions* were originally VA-67, which was one of the first A-7A units in the Atlantic Fleet. They were redesignated on 2 Jun '69 for the specific purpose of retaining the original VA-15's name, logo, and traditions at Cecil Field. The first VA-15 had dated from 1942, and was disestablished in 1 Jun '69. The "new" *Valions* started the period as an A-7B squadron in CVW-6, and transitioned to A-7Es in 1975.

The 1983-84 cruise included combat action in Grenada (*Urgent Fury*), where they flew 143 CAS sorties, and delivered over 40 bombs, and almost 19,000 rounds of 20mm. Several months later they were involved in the strikes on Syrian targets in Lebanon, where they flew eight sorties. CAG-6, Cdr. Ed Andrews, was shot down while flying a *Valion* aircraft, while the squadron XO was hit by an IR-guided SAM and still successfully recovered on *Independence*. In 1985 the squadron made a six month deployment with Marine Aircraft Group 12 in Iwakuni, Japan, while temporarily wearing CVW-3's "AC" code, although not assigned to the wing. Gaining *Hornets* in June 1986, the unit kept the

AC300 series for a short period before joining CVW-8, where they have remained ever since. They were heavily involved in Operation *Desert Storm* from *Theodore Roosevelt*. The squadron moved to Oceana, VA, on 1 Jan 1999.

VA-22, VFA-22 ***Fighting Red Cocks*** **Lemoore**
A-7E, F/A-18C
Estab. VF-63 27 Jul 48, r/d VA-63 Mar 56, r/d VA-22 1 Jul 59, r/d VFA-22 4 May 1990

5 Dec 74 to2 Jul 75	*Coral Sea*	WPAC	A-7E	NL300 *Mayaguez*
15 Feb to 5 Oct 77	*Coral Sea*	WPAC	A-7E	NL300
30 May 79 to 25 Feb 80	*Kitty Hawk*	WPAC	A-7E	NL300
1 Apr to 23 Nov 81	*Kitty Hawk*	WPAC	A-7E	NL300
1 Sep 82 to 28 Apr 83	*Enterprise*	WPAC	A-7E	NH300
30 May to 20 Dec 84	*Enterprise*	WPAC/IO	A-7E	NH300
15 Jan to 12 Aug 86	*Enterprise*	WP/IO/MED/SL	A-7E	NH300
25 Oct to 24 Nov 1987	*Enterprise*	NorPac	A-7E	NH300
5 Jan to 3 Jul 88	*Enterprise*	WPAC/IO	A-7E	NH300 *P.Mantis*
17 Sep 89 to 16 Mar 90	*Enterprise*	World	A-7E	NH300
28 May to 28 Nov 91	*Lincoln*	WPAC/IO	F/A-18C	NH300
15 Jun to 15 Dec 93	*Lincoln*	WPAC/IO	F/A-18C	NH300
10 Apr to 9 Oct 95	*Lincoln*	WP/IO/PG	F/A-18C	NH300
11 Oct 96 to 11 Apr 97	*Kitty Hawk*	WP/IO/PG	F/A-18C	NH300
6 Nov 98 to 6 May 99	*Carl Vinson*	WP/IO/PG	F/A-18C	NH300

The *Red Cocks* were WestPac vets, having made five combat deployments to Vietnam with *Skyhawks* prior to conversion to A-7s in 1970. They were involved in combat during the *Mayaguez* rescue (1975) and *Praying Mantis* (1988). Transitioning to *Hornets* in 1990, the *Red Cocks* spent the rest of the period on a succession of WestPac cruises with CVW-11.

"YCBARC"—so the VA-22 squadron motto goes—"You Can't Beat a Red Cock." A smart looking division of *Red Cock Corsairs* is shown over Fallon on 15 May '87 while working up with CVW-11. The squadron would be heavily involved in Operation *Praying Mantis* during the following deployment. (Bob Lawson)

VA-25, VFA-25 ***Fist of the Fleet*** **Lemoore**

A-7E, F/A-18A, F/A-18C

Est. VT-17 1 Jan 43, r/d VA-6B 15 Nov 46, r/d VA-65 27 Jul 48, r/d VA-25 1 Jul 59, r/d VFA-25 1 Jul 83

7 May to 18 Oct 74	*Ranger*	WP	A-7E	NE400	
30 Jan to 7 Sep 76	*Ranger*	WP/IO	A-7E	NE400	
21 Feb to 22 Sep 79	*Ranger*	WP	A-7E	NE400	
10 Sep 80 to 4 May 81	*Ranger*	WP/IO	A-7E	NE400	
7 Apr to 19 Oct 82	*Ranger*	WP/IO	A-7E	NE400	
21 Feb to 24 Aug 85	*Constellation*	WP/IO	F/A-18A	NK400	
11 Apr to 13 Oct 87	*Constellation*	WP/IO	F/A-18A	NK400	
1 Dec 88 to 1 Jun 89	*Constellation*	WP/IO	F/A-18A	NK400	
16 Sep to 19 Oct 89	*Constellation*	NorPac	F/A-18A/C	NK400	
23 Jun to 20 Dec 90	*Independence*	WP/IO/PG	F/A-18C	NK400	*Desert Shield*
5 to 22 Aug 91	*Independence*	Hawaii	F/A-18C	NK400	
28 Aug to 14 Sep 91	*Midway*	Swapex	F/A-18A	(NK)400	
18 Feb to 14 Aug 94	*Carl Vinson*	WP/IO/PG	F/A-18C	NK400	
14 May to 14 Nov 96	*Carl Vinson*	WP/IO/PG	F/A-18C	NK400	
11 Jun to 7 Dec 98	*Lincoln*	WP/IO/PG	F/A-18C	NK400	
14 Aug 00 to 12 Feb 01	*Lincoln*	WP/IO/PG	F/A-18C	NK400	

The *Fists* were famed as the last single-seat Navy A-1 *Skyraider* unit to see combat in Vietnam, in 1968. Converting directly to *Corsairs*, VA-25 flew the type for over two decades before becoming the second fleet F/A-18A *Hornet* unit. They have subsequently deployed only with CVW-14. In Aug 1991 the *Fists* were involved in the transfer of *Independence* to Japan, meeting the *Midway* in Hawaii. The squadron (along with sister VFA-113) traded their C-model *Hornets* with CVW-5 units, and returned to CONUS with *Midway* and F/A-18As. On 17 May 1995 the *Fists'* Commanding Officer, Joseph Kleefisch, was killed, along with his passenger, Rear Admiral James Prout (Commander Cruiser Destroyer Group THREE), when the VFA-125 F/A-18D they were in (163492, NJ323) crashed in northern New Mexico. Admiral Prout, a surface warrior, was being given a familiarization ride in the *Hornet* at the time.

CVW-14 got the first *Hornets*, in 1983. Here early block F/A-18As from VFA-25 and -113 approach the waist cats on *Constellation* while off San Diego on 10 May 1984. (author)

VA-27, VFA-27 ***Royal Maces, Chargers*** **Lemoore, Atsugi**
A-7E, F/A-18A, F/A-18C
Est. VA-27 1 Sep 67, r/d VFA-27 24 Jan 1991

17 Sep 74 to 20 May 75	*Enterprise*	WP/IO	A-7E	NK400
30 Jul 76 to 28 Mar 77	*Enterprise*	WP/IO	A-7E	NK400
4 Apr 78 to 30 Oct 78	*Enterprise*	WP/IO	A-7E	NK400
30 Sep 79 to 20 Feb 80	*Coral Sea*	WP/IO	A-7E	NK400
20 Aug 81 to 23 Mar 82	*Coral Sea*	WP/IO	A-7E	NK400
21 Mar to 12 Sep 83	*Coral Sea*	World	A-7E	NK400
18 Oct 84 to 25 May 85	*Carl Vinson*	WP/IO	A-7E	NL400
12 Aug 86 to 5 Feb 87	*Carl Vinson*	WP/IO	A-7E	NL400
15 Jun to 14 Dec 88	*Carl Vinson*	WP/IO	A-7E	NL400
5 Sep to 8 Nov 89	*Carl Vinson*	WP/NorPac	A-7E	NL400
1 Feb to 31 Jul 90	*Carl Vinson*	WP/IO	A-7E	NL400
18 Oct to 11 Dec 91	*Kitty Hawk*	Horn	F/A-18A	NL400
3 Nov 92 to 3 May 93	*Kitty Hawk*	WP/IO/PG	F/A-18A	NL400
24 Jun to 22 Dec 94	*Kitty Hawk*	WP/IO	F/A-18A	NL400
1996 to 1998	*Independence*	Fwd Deployed	F/A-18C	NF200
1998 to 2000	*Kitty Hawk*	Fwd Deployed	F/A-18C	NF200

Originally established in 1967 as one of Lemoore's first two fleet A-7 units (VA-97 being the other), the *Maces* flew *Corsairs* until 1990, when it transitioned to *Hornets*. The *Royal Mace* title dates from the unit's 1967 origins, and lasted until 1991, when the unit's *Charger* callsign was used as a nickname until they were returned to *Royal Mace* by a new CO in 1996. The squadron received F/A-18Cs in 1995, and moved to Japan in June 1996, where they joined CVW-5 to take the place of the wing's second F-14 squadron, VF-21.

VA-34, VFA-34 ***Blue Blasters*** **Oceana, Cecil, Oceana**
A-6E, A-6E TRAM, A-6E SWIP, KA-6D, F/A-18C
Est. VA-34 1 Jun 69, r/d VFA-34 30 Sep 1996

28 Jun 75 to 27 Jan 76	*John F. Kennedy*	Med	A-6E, KA	AB500	
2 Sep to 9 1976	*John F. Kennedy*	NorLant	A-6E, KA	AB500	
15 Jan to 1 Aug 77	*John F. Kennedy*	Med	A-6E, KA	AB500	
29 Jun 78 to 8 Feb 79	*John F. Kennedy*	Med	A-6E, KA	AB500	
4 Aug 80 to 28 Mar 81	*John F. Kennedy*	Med	A-6E, KA	AB500	
23 Aug to 30 Oct 82	*America*	Med/NorLant	A-6E TRAM, KA	AB500	
8 Dec 82 to 2 Jun 83	*America*	Med/IO	A-6E TRAM, KA	AB500	
24 Apr to 14 Nov 84	*America*	Carib/Med/IO	A-6E TRAM, KA	AB500	
24 Aug to 9 Oct 1985	*America*	NorLant	A-6E TRAM, KA	AB500	
10 Mar to 10 Sep 86	*America*	Med	A-6E TRAM, KA	AB500	Libya
29 Feb to 29 Aug 88	*Eisenhower*	Med	A-6E TRAM, KA	AG500	

A *Royal Mace Corsair II* takes a wire on *Coral Sea* in December 1981. NK402 wears an early, and very austere, version of TPS which featured a lighter shade of gray on the bottom surfaces than was later used. (Bob Lawson)

8 Mar to 12 Sep 90	*Eisenhower*	Med/RS	A-6E TRAM, KA	AG500	*Desert Shield*
26 Sep to 2 Apr 92	*Eisenhower*	Med	A-6E TRAM, KA	AG500	
20 May to 17 Nov 94	*G. Washington*	Med/RS/PG	A-6E SWIP	AG500	
26 Jan to 23 Jul 96	*G. Washington*	Med/RS/PG	A-6E SWIP	AG500	
10 Jun to 10 Dec 98	*Eisenhower*	Med/RS/PG	F/A-18C	AA200	
21 Jun to 18 Dec 00	*G. Washington*	Med/RS/P	F/A-18C	AA200	

The *Blasters* were established in 1970 using the insignia and traditions of a previous A-4 unit. The squadron never deployed to Vietnam with *Intruders*, although they would participate in action off Libya in 1986. In 1996 VA-34 became one of only two *Intruder* squadrons to transition to *Hornets*, being transferred to Cecil in September of that year as VFA-34. The *Blasters* returned to Oceana in March 1999, along with the rest of the Strike Fighter Wing.

VA-35 ***Black Panthers*** **Oceana**

A-6A, A-6E, A-6E TRAM, A-6E SWIP, KA-6D

Est. VB-3B 1 Jul 34, r/d VB-4 1 Jul 37, r/d VB-3 1 Jul 39, r/d VA-3A 15 Nov 46, r/d VA-34 7 Aug 48, r/d VA-35 15 Nov 50, disestab. 31 Jan 1995 (24 Jan ceremony)

3 Jan to 3 Aug 74	*America*	Med	A-6E, KA	AJ500	
6 Sep to 12 Oct 74	*America*	NorLant	A-6E, KA	AJ500	
16 Jul to 24 Sep 75	*Nimitz*	Carib/NorLant	A-6E, KA	AJ500	
7 Jul 76 to 7 Feb 77	*Nimitz*	Med	A-6E, KA	AJ500	
1 Dec 77 to 20 Jul 78	*Nimitz*	Med/NorLant	A-6E, KA	AJ500	
10 Sep 79 to 26 May 80	*Nimitz*	Med/ SL/IO	A-6E TRAM, KA	AJ500	
29 Aug to 17 Oct 1980	*Nimitz*	NorLant	A-6E TRAM, KA	AJ500	
3 Aug 81 to 12 Feb 82	*Nimitz*	Med	A-6E TRAM, KA	AJ500	
10 Nov 82 to 20 May 83	*Nimitz*	Med	A-6E TRAM, KA	AJ500	
8 Mar to 4 Oct 85	*Nimitz*	Med	A-6E TRAM, KA	AJ500	
15 Aug to 16 Oct 1986	*Nimitz*	NorLant	A-6E TRAM, KA	AJ500	
30 Dec 86 to 26 Jul 87	*Nimitz*	World	A-6E TRAM, KA	AJ500	
25 Aug to 11 Oct 88	*T. Roosevelt*	Med	A-6E TRAM, KA	AJ500	
7 Aug 90 to 28 Mar 91	*Saratoga*	Med/RS	A-6E TRAM, KA	AA500	*Desert Storm*
6 May to 6 Nov 92	*Saratoga*	Med	A-6E SWIP, KA	AA500	
12 Jan to 24 Jun 94	*Saratoga*	Med	A-6E SWIP	AA500	

The *Black Panthers* were one of the more distinguished squadrons in Navy history, having been originally established in 1934 as Bombing Squadron THREE Baker (VB-3B). The unit, through successive designations, would see combat in four major wars. In 1991 the squadron participated in *Desert Storm* with CVW-17, where it lost one aircraft and had another heavily damaged. The squadron's battle honors included Midway, Eastern Solomons, Guadalcanal, Iwo Jima, Korea, Vietnam, and *Desert Storm*. For whatever reason, the Navy did not have a place for this illustrious unit in the early 1990s draw down, preferring to retain several Strike Fighter squadrons with lineages only a fraction as significant.

The *Black Panthers* had among the most memorable—and best looking—markings in *Intruder* history. AJ501 (160996) taxis at Fallon in January 1981 with a load of Mk.82s and a practice LGB. (Michael Grove)

VA-36	***Roadrunners***	**Oceana**			
A-6E TRAM, A-6E SWIP					
established 6 Mar 1987	disestablished 31 Mar 94 (11 March ceremony)				
25 Aug to 11 Oct 88	*T.Roosevelt*	NorLant	A-6E TRAM	AJ500	
30 Dec 88 to 30 Jun 89	*T.Roosevelt*	Med	A-6E TRAM	AJ530	
28 Dec 90 to 28 Jun 91	*T.Roosevelt*	Med/RS/PG	A-6E TRAM	AJ530	*Desert Storm*
11 Mar to 8 Sep 93	*T.Roosevelt*	Med/RS	A-6E SWIP	AJ500	

The *Roadrunners* were the second of the new '80s era *Intruder* squadrons established at Oceana. The *Roadrunner* title was adopted from an earlier VA-36, a Cecil Field based A-4 *Skyhawk* unit that had disestablished on 1 Aug 1970. Attempts to use the original outfit's insignia, based on the Warner Brothers' cartoon character, were officially disapproved (cartoons not being allowed in new naval insignia since Vietnam), so the squadron designed a motif depicting a more realistic looking bird grappling with a snake. VA-36 made only four deployments before being disestablished; however, its 1990-91 deployment included significant combat in *Desert Storm*, during which the unit lost one aircraft and its crew to enemy fire.

VA-37, VFA-37	***(Raging) Bulls***	**Cecil Field, Oceana**		
A-7E, F/A-18C				
Est. VA-37 1 Jul 67, r/d VFA-37 28 Nov 1990 (15 Nov ceremony)				
27 Sep 74 to 19 Mar 75	*Saratoga*	Med	A-7E	AC300
6 Jan to 28 Jul 76	*Saratoga*	Med	A-7E	AC300
11 Jul to 23 Dec 77	*Saratoga*	Med	A-7E	AC300
3 Oct 78 to 5 Apr 79	*Saratoga*	Med	A-7E	AC300
10 Mar to 27 Aug 80	*Saratoga*	Med	A-7E	AC300
4 Jan to 14 Jul 82	*JF Kennedy*	IO	A-7E	AC300
1 Mar to 29 Oct 83	*Carl Vinson*	World	A-7E	NL300
1 Dec 84 to 14 Jun 85	MAG-12	Iwakuni	A-7E	AC300 (not in CVW-3)
2 Jun to 10 Nov 86	*Forrestal*	Med	A-7E	AE300
25 Apr to 7 Oct 88	*Forrestal*	Med	A-7E	AE300
4 Nov 89 to 12 Apr 90	*Forrestal*	Med/IO/NL	A-7E	AE300
30 May to 21 Dec 91	*Forrestal*	Med	A-7E	AE300
7 Oct 92 to 7 Apr 93	*JF Kennedy*	Med	F/A-18C	AC300
20 Oct 94 to 15 Apr 95	*Eisenhower*	Med/RS/PG	F/A-18C	AC300
25 Nov 96 to 22 May 97	*T Roosevelt*	Med/RS/PG	F/A-18C	AC300
6 Nov 98 to 6 May 99	*Enterprise*	Med/RS/PG	F/A-18C	AC300
28 Nov 00 to 23 May 01	*HS Truman*	Med/RS/PG	F/A-18C	AC300

The *Bulls* made multiple trips to the Med with A-7Es and, in 1983, made an around the world trip in *Carl Vinson* with West Coast based CVW-15. In 1984 they relieved VA-105 in Iwakuni, Japan, in support of the Marines. They wore CVW-3 "AC" tailcodes during this deployment, even if they were not assigned to that wing. Their final four Corsair II deployments would be with CVW-6 and *Forrestal*. VA-37 (along with sister VA-105) were on the chopping block in 1991, along with CVW-6 when *Desert Storm* forced VA-46 and -72 to deploy again with *Corsairs*. The *Bulls* and *Gunslingers* took their place in the *Hornet* transition schedule and survived, while the *Clansmen* and *Blue Hawks* did not. VA/VFA-37 has used two logos, one a snorting bull's head that dates from the unit's 1967 establishment, and another that is based on the Schlitz Malt Liquor logo that appears frequently, but does not appear to have ever been officially approved by CNO. The squadron's move from Cecil Field to Oceana occurred in April 1999.

VA-42	***Green Pawns, Thunderbolts***	**Oceana**	**FRS**
A-6A, A-6C, A-6E, A-6E TRAM, A-6E SWIP, KA-6D, TC-4C			
Est. VF-42 1 Sep 50, r/d VA-42 1 Nov 53,	disestablished 30 Sep 1994		

The East Coast *Intruder* training squadron. A former fleet AD outfit, VA-42 was one of the initial readiness squadrons, becoming the AirLant *Skyraider* RAG in 1958. It subsequently became the first *Intruder* training squadron in 1963. After three decades of training A-6 crews and maintainers for the fleet they changed their name to *Thunderbolts* (in 1992), adopting the name and traditions of the recently disestablished VA-176, thereby abandoning the logo and traditions of the *Green Pawn* line, which went back to 1950. The new image lasted only two years before the unit was disestablished. VA-42 maintained a Medium Attack Weapons Detachment at El Centro, CA, along with VA-128 from the 1980s. The TC-4Cs (also called "Ticks") were heavily modified Grumman *Gulfstreams* that were used for crew training by the A-6 RAGs. Jan 1974 squadron strength was 13 A-6Es, 1 A-6A, 2 A-6Cs, and 3 TC-4Cs.

VA-45, VF-45 *Blackbirds* **Cecil, Key West FRS**

A-4E/F, TA-4F/J, F-16N, TF-16N, F/A-18A, F-5E/F, T-39D

Est. VA-45 15 Feb 63, r/d VF-45 7 Feb 1985 disest. 31 Mar 1996

The third VA-45, this version was established in February 1963, specifically to become the instrument training squadron for Cecil Field. VA-45 adopted the insignia and traditions of the second Atkron-45, which had flown AD *Skyraiders* from 1950. The nickname and squadron motto "4 and 20" reportedly came from the number of Regular and Reserve Navy officers assigned to the unit during Korea.

VA-45 initially flew F9F-8T *Cougars* and, from the mid-'60s, TA-4 *Skyhawks*. Like its Oceana sister (VF-43), the unit moved into the adversary role, which made up a good deal of its flight time as of its 1980 move to Key West. A single T-39D was maintained by the squadron for use by a local Key West staff. By 1984 the adversary mission had completely replaced their previous instrument role, and on 7 Feb '85 they were redesignated VF-45. As of early 1989 the squadron stable was made up of eight A-4Es, four TA-4Js, ten F-16Ns, and two TF-16Ns, with six F-5E/Fs due that summer. A small number of *Hornets* replaced the F-16s in 1995. The *Blackbirds* officially disestablished on 31 Mar '96 with an 8 March ceremony at Key West.

VA-46 *Clansmen* **Cecil Field**

A-7B, A-7E

Est. VA-46 24 May 55	disestab.	30 Jun 1991	(23 May ceremony)		
28 Jun 75 to 27 Jan 76	*JF Kennedy*	Med	A-7B	AB300	
2 Sep to 9 Nov 76	*JF Kennedy*	Med	A-7B	AB300	
15 Jan to 1 Aug 77	*JF Kennedy*	Med	A-7B	AB300	
29 Jun 78 to 8 Feb 79	*JF Kennedy*	Med	A-7E	AB300	
4 Aug 80 to 28 Mar 81	*JF Kennedy*	Med	A-7E	AB300	
23 Aug to 30 Oct 1982	*America*	NL/Med/Carib	A-7E	AB300	
8 Dec 82 to 2 Jun 83	*America*	Med/IO	A-7E	AB300	
24 Apr to 14 Nov 84	*America*	Med/IO	A-7E	AB300	
10 Mar to 10 Sep 86	*America*	Med	A-7E	AB300	
29 Feb to 29 Aug 88	*Eisenhower*	Med	A-7E	AG400	
15 Aug 90 to 28 Mar 91	*JF Kennedy*	Med/RS	A-7E	AC300	*Desert Storm*

VA-46's nickname comes from the Scottish heritage of the unit's first CO, Cdr. Clifford McDougal, with widely differing variations of his family tartan gracing the unit's aircraft ever since. The squadron, along with stable mate VA-72, flew the last fleet A-7Bs on the east coast, and were scheduled for transition to F/A-18s in 1990, when they deployed in *Kennedy* with CVW-3 to what became *Desert Storm*. After a highly successful combat deployment VA-46 and -72, the final two Light Attack squadrons in the Navy, were disestablished.

VA-52 *Knightriders* **Whidbey Island**

A-6A, A-6E, A-6E TRAM, A-6E SWIP, KA-6D

Reserve VF-884 act. 20 Jul 50, r/d VF-144 4 Feb 53, r/d VA-52 23 Feb 59, disestab. 31 Mar 1995 (17 Mar ceremony)

23 Nov 73 to 9 Jul 74	*Kitty Hawk*	WP, IO	A-6A/B, KA	NH500
21 May to 15 Dec 75	*Kitty Hawk*	WP	A-6E, KA	NH500
25 Oct 77 to 5 May 78	*Kitty Hawk*	WP	A-6E, KA	NH500
30 May 79 to 25 Feb 80	*Kitty Hawk*	WP, IO	A-6E, KA	NL500
1 Apr to 23 Nov 81	*Kitty Hawk*	WP, IO	A-6E, KA	NL500
1 Mar to 29 Oct 83	*Carl Vinson*	World	A-6E TRAM, KA	NL500
18 Oct 84 to 24 May 85	*Carl Vinson*	WP, IO	A-6E TRAM, KA	NL500
12 Aug 86 to 5 Feb 87	*Carl Vinson*	WP, IO	A-6E TRAM, KA	NL500
15 Jun to 14 Dec 88	*Carl Vinson*	WP, IO	A-6E TRAM, KA	NL500
5 Sep to 8 Nov 89	*Carl Vinson*	NorPac	A-6E SWIP, KA	NL500
1 Feb to 31 Jul 90	*Carl Vinson*	WP/IO	A-6E SWIP, KA	NL500
18 Oct to 11 Dec 91	*Kitty Hawk*	Horn	A-6E SWIP, KA	NL500
3 Nov to 3 May 93	*Kitty Hawk*	WP/IO/PG	A-6E SWIP, KA	NL500
24 Jun to 22 Dec 94	*Kitty Hawk*	WP/IP/PG	A-6E SWIP	NL500

VA-52 was a distinguished unit, having come from the Korean-War activation of Olathe, Kansas, based VF-884, the legendary *Bitter Birds*. The unit flew F4U-4s and, subsequently, F9Fs before becoming a medium attack squadron with AD *Skyraiders*. In 1959 they adopted the *Knightriders* title, along with the peculiar logo of a fully armored knight riding a sea turtle, leading to the casual names "turtle hurders" and "turtle beaters." VA-52 made seven deployments to Vietnam, three in *Skyraiders* and four in *Intruders*. On 23 Jan 1993 VA-52 participated in strikes on Iraq which may well have been the final use of the *Intruder* to drop ordnance. Their 45 year history came to an end in 1995.

VA-55 (1) — ***Warhorses*** — **Lemoore**

A-4F

Est. VT-5 15 Feb 43, r/d VA-6A 15 Nov 46, r/d VA-55 16 Aug 48, disestab. 12 Dec 1975

8 May 73 to 8 Jan 74	*Hancock*	WPAC	A-4F	NP500
18 Mar to 20 Oct 75	*Hancock*	WPAC	A-4F	NP500

The *Warhorses* were one of the last three fleet A-4 *Skyhawk* units. The unit was the CVW-21 "Iron Hand" specialist, with APS-70 equipped A-4F aircraft.

VA-55 (2) — ***Warhorses*** — **Oceana**

A-6E TRAM, A-6E SWIP, KA-6D

Estab. 7 Oct 83 — disestab. 1 Jan 91 (22 Feb ceremony)

2 Oct 85 to 19 May 86	*Coral Sea*	Med	A-6E TRAM, KA	AK500	Libya action
29 Sep 87 to 28 Mar 88	*Coral Sea*	Med	A-6E TRAM	AK500	
31 May to 30 Sep 89	*Coral Sea*	Med	A-6E SWIP	AK500	

Established as the first new AirLant *Intruder* unit during the mid-'80s build up. Adopted the nickname and traditions of a Lemoore-based A-4 squadron disestablished in 1975. VA-55 joined the newly formed CVW-13, and participated in Operations *Prairie Fire* and *El Dorado Canyon* against Libya on its first deployment. For the following two deployments VA-55 was joined in Air Wing 13 by VA-65. VA-55 was disestablished prior to the start of *Desert Storm*, with many of its men transferring to other squadrons deployed to the combat zone

VA-56 — ***Champions*** — **Atsugi**

A-7A, A-7E

Est. 4 Jun 56 — disestab. 31 Aug 1986

1974 to 1977	*Midway*	Fwd Deployed	A-7A	NF400
1977 to 1986	*Midway*	Fwd Deployed	A-7E	NF400

The "Champs" moved to Atsugi, Japan, in 1973, and spent the next 13 years flying *Corsairs* from the *Midway* with CVW-5. The squadron had actually flown A-7Bs, and converted back to A-7As prior to their move overseas. When time came to transition the Air Wing to *Hornets*, VA-56 joined its sister squadron VA-93 and exited into history.

VA-65 — ***(Fighting) Tigers*** — **Oceana**

A-6A, A-6E, A-6E TRAM, A-6E SWIP, KA-6D

Est. VT-74 1 May 45, r/d VA-2B 15 Nov 46, r/d VA-25 1 Sep 48, r/d VA-65 1 Jul 59, disestab. 31 Mar 92 (26 Mar ceremony)

21 Jun 73 to 19 Jan 74	*Independence*	Med	A-6E, KA	AG500
19 Jul 74 to 21 Jan 75	*Independence*	Med	A-6E, KA	AG500
15 Oct 75 to 5 May 76	*Independence*	Med	A-6E, KA	AG500
31 Mar to 21 Oct 77	*Independence*	Med	A-6E, KA	AG500
16 Jan to 13 Jul 79	*Eisenhower*	Med	A-6E, KA	AG500

As of 1974, only the *Midway's* two light attack squadrons flew A-7As in the fleet. VA-56 and VA-93 operated the type until replaced by Echos in 1977. Both squadrons were disestablished in 1986. "Champ" NF402 is on final to Atsugi on 18 Dec 1975. Following years of service with the U.S. Navy, 153188 would end up with the Portuguese Air Force. (Toshiki Kudo)

15 Apr to 22 Dec 80	*Eisenhower*	IO	A-6E TRAM, KA	AG500	
20 Aug to 7 Oct 81	*Eisenhower*	NorLant	A-6E TRAM, KA	AG500	
5 Jan to 13 Jul 82	*Eisenhower*	Med	A-6E TRAM, KA	AG500	
27 Apr to 2 Dec 83	*Eisenhower*	Med	A-6E TRAM, KA	AG500	
8 May to 20 Jun 84	*Eisenhower*	Med	A-6E TRAM, KA	AG500	
10 Oct to 8 May 85	*Eisenhower*	Med	A-6E TRAM, KA	AG500	
29 Sep 87 to 28 Mar 88	*Coral Sea*	Med	A-6E TRAM	AK510	
31 May to 30 Sep 89	*Coral Sea*	Med	A-6E TRAM	AK510	
28 Dec to 28 Jun 91	*T.Roosevelt*	Med/RS/PG	A-6E TRAM	AJ 530	*Desert Storm*

The *Tigers* were another of the early east coast *Intruder* units, having transitioned from A-1s in 1965. After three combat deployments to Vietnam, the squadron spent 15 years in CVW-7 before moving to CVW-13 in 1985. The *Tigers* participated in two "Dual A-6 Wings": with VA-55 in *Coral Sea* (1986-89), and with VA-36 in *Theodore Roosevelt* (1989-1991). They performed with distinction in *Desert Storm*, where the squadron was credited with sinking 22 Iraqi Naval boats. VA-65 was beached following *Desert Storm* in order to make room for Marine helicopters in an experimental fixed wing/rotary wing deployment for *Roosevelt*. It was disestablished within the year. The *Tigers* were known for years for their "hi-viz" insignia orange markings on their *Intruders*, as well as their somewhat un-manly assigned radio callsign of "Cupcake." In the early 1980s a Commanding Officer went to the trouble to officially change the callsign to the more bellicose "Fighting Tiger," which they retained until the end.

VA-66 ***Waldos, Waldomen*** **Cecil Field**

A-7E

Reserve VF-671 act. 1 Feb 51, r/d VF-81 4 Feb 53, r/d VA-66 1 Jul 55, disestab. 1 Oct 1986

21 Jun 73 to 19 Jan 74	*Independence*	Med	A-7E	AG400
19 Jul 74 to 21 Jan 75	*Independence*	Med	A-7E	AG400
15 Oct 75 to 5 May 76	*Independence*	Med/NorLant	A-7E	AG400
31 Mar to 21 Oct 77	*Independence*	Med	A-7E	AG400
16 Jan to 13 Jul 79	*Eisenhower*	Med	A-7E	AG400
15 Apr to 22 Dec 80	*Eisenhower*	Med	A-7E	AG400
20 Aug to 7 Oct 81	*Eisenhower*	NorLant	A-7E	AG400
5 Jan 82 to 13 Jul 82	*Eisenhower*	Med	A-7E	AG400
27 Apr 83 to 2 Dec 83	*Eisenhower*	Med	A-7E	AG400
10 Oct 84 to 8 May 85	*Eisenhower*	Med	A-7E	AG400
18 Aug 86 to 3 Mar 87	*JF Kennedy*	Med	A-7E	AG/AC300 *Attack Det 66*

The *Waldos* spent most of the period flying A-7E *Corsairs* with CVW-7. By mid-1986 the formation of four new *Hornet* units in AirLant had made VA-66 and sister squadron VA-12 superfluous, so both were marked for extinction. In a surprise move, AirLant directed VA-66 to form "Attack Det 66" (the "Grumman Defenders"), a six aircraft detachment to deploy with *Kennedy* and CVW-3's "All Grumman Air Wing." The

The *Waldos* of Atkron-66 supplied a six-plane detachment to CVW-3 in early 1986 to support the otherwise "All-Grumman Air Wing" for its Med deployment in *Kennedy*. The squadron took its time to remark its aircraft, as shown here with A-7E AG302 during workups in May '86, which still carries the tailcode and ship name from its previous assignment. *Intruders* from VA-75 and VMA-(AW)-533 are also shown, spotted in the "six pack" area. (Rick Burgess)

det was organized specifically to provide platforms that could carry the AGM-88 HARM anti-radiation missile in the wing, since their A-6Es were limited to the obsolescent AGM-45 *Shrike*. The det marked their squadron's official disestablishment date while underway in *Kennedy*, with a ceremony featuring a 21 gun salute while Cdr. Richard Marquis threw a rubber chicken (representing the squadron logo) overboard. The det itself was disestablished 31 Mar 1987, ending the *Waldo's* 34 year history.

VA-72 ***Blue Hawks*** **Cecil Field**

A-7B, A-7E

Est. VBF-18 25 Jan 45, r/d VF-8A 15 Nov 46, r/d VF-72 28 Jul 48, r/d VA-72 3 Jan 56, disestab. 30 Jun 1991 (23 May ceremony)

28 Jun 75 to 27 Jan 76	*JF Kennedy*	Med	A-7B	AB400	
2 Sep to 9 Nov 76	*JF Kennedy*	Med	A-7B	AB400	
15 Jan to 1 Aug 77	*JF Kennedy*	Med	A-7B	AB400	
29 Jun 78 to 8 Feb 79	*JF Kennedy*	Med	A-7E	AB400	
4 Aug 80 to 28 Mar 81	*JF Kennedy*	Med	A-7E	AB400	
23 Aug to 30 Oct 82	*America*	NL/Med/Carib	A-7E	AB400	
8 Dec 82 to 2 Jun 83	*America*	Med/IO	A-7E	AB400	
24 Apr to 14 Nov 84	*America*	Med/IO	A-7E	AB400	
10 Mar to 10 Sep 86	*America*	Med	A-7E	AB400	
29 Feb to 29 Aug 88	*Eisenhower*	Med	A-7E	AG400	
15 Aug 90 to 28 Mar 91	*JF Kennedy*	Med/RS	A-7E	AC400	*Desert Storm*

VA-72 dated from 1945, and was the first A4D *Skyhawk* unit in the fleet. They were paired with VA-46 throughout this period, and made the last deployments in both the A-7B and A-7E. As with the *Clansmen*, VA-72's participation in *Desert Storm* cost them the chance to transition to *Hornets*, with both units being disestablished soon after returning from the war.

VA-75 ***Sunday Punchers*** **Oceana**

A-6A, A-6E, A-6E TRAM, A-6E SWIP, KA-6D

Est. VB-18 20 Jul 43, r/d VA-7A 15 Nov 46, r/d VA-74 27 Jul 48, r/d VA-75 15 Feb 50, disestab. 31 Mar 97 (28 Feb ceremony)

27 Sep 74 to 19 Mar 75	*Saratoga*	Med	A-6E, KA	AC500	
6 Jan to 28 Jul 76	*Saratoga*	Med	A-6E, KA	AC500	
11 Jul to 23 Dec 77	*Saratoga*	Med	A-6E, KA	AC500	
3 Oct 78 to 5 Apr 79	*Saratoga*	Med	A-6E, KA	AC500	
10 Mar to 27 Aug 80	*Saratoga*	Med	A-6E, KA	AC500	
4 Jan to 14 Jul 82	*J.F. Kennedy*	Med	A-6E TRAM, KA	AC500	
25 May to 1 Jul 83	*J.F. Kennedy*	NorLant	A-6E, TRAM, KA	AC500	
27 Sep 83 to 2 May 84	*J.F. Kennedy*	Med	A-6E, TRAM,KA	AC500	Lebanon
18 Aug 86 to 3 Mar 87	*J.F. Kennedy*	Med	A-6E, TRAM,KA	AC500	
2 Aug 88 to 1 Feb 89	*J.F. Kennedy*	Med	A-6E, SWIP, KA	AC500	
15 Aug 90 to 28 Mar 91	*J.F. Kennedy*	Med/RS	A-6E, SWIP, KA	AC500	*Desert Storm*
7 Oct 92 to 7 Apr 93	*J.F. Kennedy*	Med	A-6E, SWIP, KA	AC500	
20 Oct 94 to 15 Apr 95	*Eisenhower*	Med/RS/PG	A-6E SWIP	AC500	
28 Jan to 20 Dec 96	*Enterprise*	Med/RS/PG	A-6E SWIP	AA500	

VA-75 accumulated a superb service record over 53 years of duty. It was the first A-6 unit in the fleet, taking the type directly into combat off *Independence* in 1965. The *Punchers* were probably the penultimate Oceana-based *Intruder* unit, participating in three Vietnam deployments, as well as action over Lebanon in 1983, and in *Desert Storm*. After having flown with CVW-3 since 1968, VA-75 made the final *Intruder* cruise with CVW-17. What was left of the squadron conducted the final carrier operations for the A-6 type on 12 March 1997, almost two weeks after disestablishment. Its final two aircraft were flown to the Arizona desert on 19 March.

VA-81, VFA-81 ***Sunliners*** **Cecil Field, Oceana**

A-7E, F/A-18C

Est. VA-66 1 Jul 55, r/d VA-81 1 Jul 59, r/d VFA-81 4 Feb 1988

11 Mar to 11 Sep 74	*Forrestal*	Med	A-7E	AA400
5 Mar to 22 Sep 75	*Forrestal*	Med	A-7E	AA400
July 1976	*Forrestal*	Bi-Centennial	A-7E	AA400
4 Apr to 26 Oct 78	*Forrestal*	Med/NL	A-7E	AA400
27 Nov 79 to 7 May 80	*Forrestal*	Med	A-7E	AA400

2 Mar to 15 Sep 81	*Forrestal*	Med	A-7E	AA400	
8 Jun to 16 Nov 82	*Forrestal*	Med	A-7E	AA400	
2 Apr to 20 Oct 84	*Saratoga*	Med	A-7E	AA400	
26 Aug 85 to 16 Apr 86	*Saratoga*	Med/IO	A-7E	AA400	*Prairie Fire*
5 Jun 87 to 17 Nov 87	*Saratoga*	Med	A-7E	AA400	
7 Aug 90 to 28 Mar 91	*Saratoga*	Med/RS	F/A-18C	AA400	*Desert Storm*
6 May to 6 Nov 92	*Saratoga*	Med	F/A-18C	AA400	
12 Jan to 24 Jun 94	*Saratoga*	Med	F/A-18C	AA400	
28 Jun to 20 Dec 96	*Enterprise*	Med/RS/PG	F/A-18C	AA400	
10 Jun to 10 Dec 98	*Eisenhower*	Med/RS/PG	F/A-18C	AA400	
21 Jun to 19 Dec 00	*G Washington*	Med/RS/PG	F/A-18C	AA400	

"*Who Said Sunliners?*" VFA-81 started the period in A-7Es and converted to *Hornets* in 1988, along with sister VFA-83. The two units had been a matched paired since 1960, and were unique as being the only surviving former light attack units that had not made at least one deployment to Vietnam. In mid-1979 VA-81 became the first A-7 unit to be equipped with the AAR-45 podded FLIR pod system. The 1985-86 trip to the Med included combat operations during *Prairie Fire*, where the *Sunliners* shot AGM-88 HARMs at Libyan SA-5 sites. The squadron was heavily involved in *Desert Storm*, where it shot down two Iraqi MiG-21s and lost one aircraft itself, to a MiG-25. VFA-81 moved to Oceana in December 1989.

VA-82, VFA-82 — ***Marauders*** — **Cecil Field, Beaufort**

A-7C, A-7E, F/A-18C

Est. VA-82 1 May 67, r/d VFA-82 15 Jul 1987

3 Jan to 3 Aug 74	*America*	Med	A-7C	AJ300	
6 Sep to 12 Oct 74	*America*	NorLant	A-7C	AJ300	
16 Jul to 24 Sep 75	*Nimitz*	Carib/NL	A-7E	AJ300	
7 Jul 76 to 7 Feb 77	*Nimitz*	Med	A-7E	AJ300	
1 Dec 77 to 20 Jul 78	*Nimitz*	Med/NL	A-7E	AJ300	
10 Sep 79 to 26 May 80	*Nimitz*	Med/IO	A-7E	AJ300	
3 Aug 81 to 12 Feb 82	*Nimitz*	Med	A-7E	AJ300	
10 Nov 82 to 29 May 83	*Nimitz*	Med	A-7E	AJ300	
8 Mar to 4 Oct 85	*Nimitz*	Med	A-7E	AJ300	
30 Dec 86 to 26 Jul 87	*Nimitz*	World	A-7E	AJ300	
8 Feb to 3 Apr 89	*America*	NorLant	F/A-18C	AB300	
11 May to 10 Nov 89	*America*	Med/IO	F/A-18C	AB300	
12 Feb to 7 Apr 90	*Constellation*	Horn	F/A-18C	AB300	CVW-9
28 Dec 90 to 18 Apr 91	*America*	Med/RS/IO	F/A-18C	AB300	*Desert Storm*
2 Dec 91 to 5 Jun 92	*America*	Med	F/A-18C	AB300	
11 Aug 93 to 5 Feb 94	*America*	Med/IO	F/A-18C	AB300	
28 Aug 95 to 24 Feb 96	*America*	Med/RS/PG	F/A-18C	AB300	
3 Oct 97 to 3 Apr 98	*G Washington*	Med/RS/PG	F/A-18C	AB300	
15 Sep 99 to 19 Mar 00	*JF Kennedy*	Med/PG	F/A-18C	AB300	

The *Marauders* were one of only two fleet Atkrons to fly the peculiar A-7C variant (this being an E airframe with the A/B's TF-30 engine), sister VA-86 being the other. Transitioning to A-7Es in 1974 and then to *Hornets* in 1987, the squadron has since been a member of CVW-1, with whom it participated in *Desert Storm*. In 1990 the squadron accompanied *Constellation* as it transited to the East Coast via the Horn for its scheduled SLEP. The *Marauders* (with VFA-86) were the first units to receive F/A-18Cs, which came in December 1987. In June 1999 VFA-82 became one of two AirLant VFAs to be based with the Marines at Beaufort, SC.

VA-83, VFA-83 — ***Rampagers*** — **Cecil Field, Oceana**

A-7E, F/A-18C

Reserve VF-916 activated 1 Feb 51, r/d VF-83 4 Feb 53, r/d VA-83 1 Jul 55, r/d VFA-83 1 Mar 1988

11 Mar to 11 Sep 74	*Forrestal*	Med	A-7E	AA300
5 Mar to 22 Sep 75	*Forrestal*	Med	A-7E	AA300
July 1976	*Forrestal*	Bi-Centennial	A-7E	AA300
4 Apr to 26 Oct 78	*Forrestal*	Med/NL	A-7E	AA300
27 Nov 79 to 7 May 80	*Forrestal*	Med	A-7E	AA300
2 Mar to 15 Sep 81	*Forrestal*	Med	A-7E	AA300

8 Jun to 16 Nov 82	*Forrestal*	Med	A-7E	AA300	
2 Apr to 20 Oct 84	*Saratoga*	Med	A-7E	AA300	
26 Aug 85 to 16 Apr 86	*Saratoga*	Med/IO	A-7E	AA300	*Prairie Fire*
5 Jun 87 to 17 Nov 87	*Saratoga*	Med	A-7E	AA300	
7 Aug 90 to 28 Mar 91	*Saratoga*	Med/RS	F/A-18C	AA300	*Desert Storm*
6 May to 6 Nov 92	*Saratoga*	Med	F/A-18C	AA300	
12 Jan to 24 Jun 94	*Saratoga*	Med	F/A-18C	AA300	
28 Jun to 20 Dec 96	*Enterprise*	Med/RS/PG	F/A-18C	AA300	
10 Jun to 10 Dec 98	*Eisenhower*	Med/RS/PG	F/A-18C	AA300	
21 Jun to 19 Dec 00	*G Washington*	Med/RS/PG	F/A-18C	AA300	

VA-83, like sister VA-81, never made a deployment to Vietnam, instead making multiple Cold War trips to the Med during the war. *Corsairs* replaced *Skyhawks* in 1970, and *Hornets* followed in 1988. The "Rammies" participated in *Desert Storm* with CVW-17. On 25 January 1985 the *Rampagers* fired the first AGM-88 HARM by a fleet squadron.

VA-85 **_Black Falcons_** **Oceana**

A-6E, A-6E TRAM, A-6E SWIP, KA-6D

Reserve VA-859 activated 1 Feb 51, r/d VA-85 4 Feb 53, disestab. 30 Sep 94 (22 Sep ceremony)

11 Mar to 11 Sep 74	*Forrestal*	Med	A-6E, KA	AA500	
5 Mar to 22 Sep 75	*Forrestal*	Med	A-6E, KA	AA500	
July 1976	*Forrestal*	Bi-centennial	A-6E, KA	AA500	
4 Apr to 26 Oct 78	*Forrestal*	Med	A-6E, KA	AA500	
27 Nov 79 to 7 May 80	*Forrestal*	Med	A-6E, KA	AA500	
2 Mar to 15 Sep 81	*Forrestal*	Med	A-6E, KA	AA500	
8 Jun to 16 Nov 82	*Forrestal*	Med	A-6E TRAM, KA	AA500	
25 May to 1 Jul 83	*J.F. Kennedy*	NorLant	A-6E, TRAM, KA	AC540/550	
27 Sep 83 to 2 May 84	*J.F.Kennedy*	Med	A-6E TRAM, KA	AC540/550	Lebanon
26 Aug 85 to 16 Apr 86	*Saratoga*	Med, IO	A-6E TRAM, KA	AA500	*Prairie Fire*
5 Jun to 17 Nov 87	*Saratoga*	Med	A-6E TRAM, KA	AA500	
8 Feb to 3 Apr 89	*America*	NorLant	A-6E TRAM, KA	AB500	
11 May to 10 Nov 89	*America*	Med/RS/IO	A-6E TRAM, KA	AB500	
28 Dec 90 to 18 Apr 91	*America*	Med/RS/PG	A-6E TRAM, KA	AB500	*Desert Storm*
2 Dec 91 to 6 Jun 92	*America*	Med	A-6E TRAM, KA	AB500	
11 Aug 93 to 5 Feb 94	*America*	Med	A-6E SWIP	AB500	

The *Black Falcons* were the second fleet A-6 squadron, and made four successive Vietnam cruises in less than five years, a record for Atlantic Fleet squadrons. The price for this intense tempo, however, was eleven *Intruders* and 13 men, three of which were commanding officers. The *Black Falcons* participated in retaliatory strikes into Lebanon on 4 Dec 1983, with the loss of one aircraft. During its 1985-86 deployment in *Saratoga* the unit was involved in *Prairie Fire* strikes against Libyan patrol boats. In 1990-91 the *Black Falcons* flew from *America* in Operation *Desert Storm*, flying combat missions from both the Red Sea and Persian Gulf. At the time of its disestablishment VA-85 had completed 43 years of active service.

The KA-6D was the Navy's standard tanker aircraft for over 20 years. AA521 (152893) belongs to VA-85, and is shown sitting on the alert pad at Key West on 5 July 1980 while backing up fighters covering a carrier conducting Training Command CQ in the area. (author)

VA-86, VFA-86 *Sidewinders* **Cecil Field, Beaufort**

A-7C, A-7E, F/A-18C

Reserve VF-921 activated 1 Feb 51, r/d VF-84 4 Feb 53, r/d VA-86 1 Jul 55, r/d VFA-86 15 Jul 1987

3 Jan to 3 Aug 74	*America*	Med	A-7C	AJ400	
6 Sep to 12 Oct 74	*America*	NorLant	A-7C	AJ400	
16 Jul to 24 Sep 75	*Nimitz*	Carib/NL	A-7E	AJ400	
7 Jul 76 to 7 Feb 77	*Nimitz*	Med	A-7E	AJ400	
1 Dec 77 to 20 Jul 78	*Nimitz*	Med/NL	A-7E	AJ400	
10 Sep 79 to 26 May 80	*Nimitz*	Med/IO	A-7E	AJ400	
3 Aug 81 to 12 Feb 82	*Nimitz*	Med	A-7E	AJ400	
10 Nov 82 to 29 May 83	*Nimitz*	Med	A-7E	AJ400	
8 Mar to 4 Oct 85	*Nimitz*	Med	A-7E	AJ400	
30 Dec 86 to 26 Jul 87	*Nimitz*	World	A-7E	AJ400	
8 Feb to 3 Apr 89	*America*	NorLant	F/A-18C	AB400	
11 May to 10 Nov 89	*America*	Med/IO	F/A-18C	AB400	
28 Dec 90 to 18 Apr 91	*America*	Med/RS/IO	F/A-18C	AB400	*Desert Storm*
2 Dec 91 to 5 Jun 92	*America*	Med	F/A-18C	AB400	
11 Aug 93 to 5 Feb 94	*America*	Med/IO	F/A-18C	AB400	
28 Aug 95 to 24 Feb 96	*America*	Med/RS/PG	F/A-18C	AB400	
3 Oct 97 to 3 Apr 98	*G Washington*	Med/RS/PG	F/A-18C	AB400	
15 Sep 99 to 19 Mar 00	*JF Kennedy*	Med/PG	F/A-18C	AB400	

VA-86 was originally a Reserve squadron from NAS St Louis, MO, being activated during the Korean War. The 1979-80 deployment in *Nimitz* was highlighted by the abortive rescue attempt of American hostages in Tehran, Iran. VA-86, along with other squadrons in CVW-8, applied orange/black recognition markings to their aircrafts' starboard wings. The *Sidewinders* were unique, in that they left the stripes on their *Corsairs* until well after their return to Cecil Field. *Hornets* replaced *Corsairs* in 1987, and the squadron distinguished itself during *Desert Storm* as a member of CVW-1. A squadron A-7 was used in a barricade sequence for the 1980 movie "The Final Countdown." VFA-86's official move to MCAS Beaufort, SC, occurred on 1 Jan 1999.

VA-87, VFA-87 *Golden Warriors* **Cecil Field, Oceana**

A-7B, A-7E, F/A-18A, F/A-18C

Estab. VA-87 1 Feb 68, r/d VFA-87 1 May 1986

14 Sep 73 to 17 Mar 74	*F.D. Roosevelt*	MED	A-7B	AE400	
3 Jan to 16 Jul 75	*F.D. Roosevelt*	MED	A-7B	AE400	
15 Apr to 25 Oct 76	*America*	MED	A-7E	AE400	
10 Jun to 19 Jul 77	*America*	SoLant	A-7E	AE400	
25 Sep 77 to 25 Apr 78	*America*	MED	A-7E	AE400	
28 Jun to 14 Dec 79	*America*	MED	A-7E	AE400	
19 Nov 80 to 10 Jun 81	*Independence*	MED/IO	A-7E	AE400	
7 Jun to 22 Dec 82	*Independence*	MED	A-7E	AE400	
18 Oct 83 to 11 Apr 84	*Independence*	CARIB/Med	A-7E	AE400	Grenada/Lebanon
16 Oct 84 to 19 Feb 85	*Independence*	MED/IO	A-7E	AE400	
25 Aug 88 to 11 Oct 88	*T.Roosevelt*	NLANT	F/A-18A	AJ400	
30 Dec 88 to 30 Jun 89	*T.Roosevelt*	MED	F/A-18A	AJ400	
28 Dec 90 to 28 Jun 91	*T.Roosevelt*	MED/RS/PG	F/A-18A	AJ400	*Desert Storm*
11 Mar to 8 Sep 93	*T.Roosevelt*	MED/RS	F/A-18C	AJ400	
22 Mar to 22 Sep 95	*T. Roosevelt*	MED/RS/PG	F/A-18C	AJ400	
29 Apr to 28 Oct 97	*J.F.Kennedy*	MED/RS/PG	F/A-18C	AJ400	
26 Mar to 22 Sep 99	*T.Roosevelt*	MED/RS/PG	F/A-18C	AJ400	*Allied Force*

VA-87 was one of the first AirLant A-7 units, being established with the type in 1968. The squadron flew *Corsairs* for 18 years before starting *Hornet* transition in 1986. They wore CVW-3 "AC400" markings for a short while before joining CVW-8. VFA-87 has subsequently been involved in *Desert Storm* and over Bosnia. Their *Hornets* occasionally display their alternate nickname *Battle Cry* on their external fuel tanks.

VA-93 — ***Blue Blazers, Ravens*** — **Atsugi**

A-7A, A-7E

Est VF-93 26 Mar 52, r/d VA-93 15 Sep 56, disestab. 31 Aug 1986

1974 to 1977	*Midway*	Fwd Deployed	A-7A	NF300	
1977 to 1986	*Midway*	Fwd Deployed	A-7E	NF300	

VA-93 had a distinguished record dating from 1952, which included seven trips to Vietnam while flying A-4 *Skyhawks* and A-7 *Corsair IIs*. The unit moved to Japan with *Midway*/CVW-5 in 1973, and remained there in a forward deployed status until 1986, when it was disestablished. A-7Es replaced A-7As (the fleet's last) in April 1977. (See the listings for CVW-5 for a detailed list of at sea periods.) The squadron had used the *Blue Blazers* nickname through Vietnam, but adopted its "Raven" callsign as a new title by the mid-'70s.

VA-94, VFA-94 — ***Mighty Shrikes*** — **Lemoore**

A-7E, F/A-18C

Est. VF-94 26 Mar 52, r/d VA-94 1 Aug 58, redesig. VFA-94 28 Jun 1990

5 Dec 74 to2 Jul 75	*Coral Sea*	WPAC	A-7E	NL400 *Mayaguez*	
15 Feb to 5 Oct 77	*Coral Sea*	WPAC	A-7E	NL400	
30 May 79 to 25 Feb 80	*Kitty Hawk*	WPAC	A-7E	NL400	
1 Apr to 23 Nov 81	*Kitty Hawk*	WPAC	A-7E	NL400	
1 Sep 82 to 28 Apr 83	*Enterprise*	WPAC	A-7E	NH400	
30 May to 20 Dec 84	*Enterprise*	WPAC/IO	A-7E	NH400	
15 Jan to 12 Aug 1986	*Enterprise*	WP/IO/Med/SL	A-7E	NH400	
25 Oct to 24 Nov 1987	*Enterprise*	NorPac	A-7E	NH400	
5 Jan to 3 Jul 88	*Enterprise*	WPAC/IO	A-7E	NH400	*Praying Mantis*
17 Sep 89 to 16 Mar 90	*Enterprise*	World	A-7E	NH400	
28 May to 28 Nov 91	*Lincoln*	WPAC/IO	F/A-18C	NH400	
15 Jun to 15 Dec 93	*Lincoln*	WPAC/IO	F/A-18C	NH400	
10 Apr to 9 Oct 95	*Lincoln*	WP/IO/PG	F/A-18C	NH400	
11 Oct 96 to 11 Apr 97	*Kitty Hawk*	WP/IO/PG	F/A-18C	NH400	
6 Nov 98 to 6 May 99	*Carl Vinson*	WP/IO/PG	F/A-18C	NH400	

The *Shrikes* date from 1952, and made seven deployments to Vietnam in *Skyhawks* and *Corsairs*. The unit helped in the *Mayaguez* rescue in 1975, and participated in *Praying Mantis* from *Enterprise* in 1988, where they helped sink the Iranian FFL *Sahand*.

VA-95 — ***Green Lizards*** — **Whidbey Island**

A-6A, A-6E, KA-6D

Est. VA-95 1 Apr 72, disestab. 31 Oct 95 (18 Nov ceremony)

5 Dec 74 to 2 Jul 75	*Coral Sea*	WP, SEA	A-6A, KA	NL500 *Mayaguez*	
15 Feb to 5 Oct 77	*Coral Sea*	WP	A-6E, KA	NL500	
13 Mar to 22 Sep 79	*America*	Med	A-6E, KA	NH500	
14 Apr to 12 Nov 81	*America*	Med, IO	A-6E TRAM, KA	NH500	
1 Sep 82 to 23 Mar 83	*Enterprise*	NP, WP, IO	A-6E TRAM, KA	NH500	
30 May to 20 Dec 84	*Enterprise*	WP, IO	A-6E TRAM, KA	NH500	
15 Jan to 12 Aug 1986	*Enterprise*	WP/IO/Med/SL	A-6E TRAM, KA	NH500	
25 Oct to 24 Nov 87	*Enterprise*	NorPac	A-6E TRAM, KA	NH500	
5 Jan to 3 Jul 88	*Enterprise*	WP, IO, Iran	A-6E, TRAM, KA	NH500	*P. Mantis*

NL500 (159574) is a *Green Lizard*, as the marking on the centerline tank suggests. The A-6E is at Fallon in May 1978. (Michael Grove)

17 Sep 89 to 16 Mar 90	*Enterprise*	World	A-6E, TRAM, KA	NH500
9-11/90	*A.Lincoln*	Horn	A-6E SWIP, KA	NH500
28 May to 28 Nov 91	*A.Lincoln*	WP, IO, PG	A-6E SWIP, KA	NH500
15 Jun to 15 Dec 93	*A.Lincoln*	WP, IO	A-6E SWIP	NH500
10 Apr to 9 Oct 95	*A.Lincoln*	WP, IO, PG.	A-6E SWIP	NH500

The *Lizards* were the last of the Vietnam era *Intruder* squadrons to be established at Whidbey, and made one deployment in the combat area, supporting the clearing of minefields in Operation *End Sweep*. On their second cruise the unit participated in *Frequent Wind*, the evacuation of Saigon, and the re-capture of the *SS Mayaguez*. From 1979 to 1981 the unit made two deployments to the Med and/or IO with CVW-11 in *America*. The latter cruise also included A-6E TRAM aircraft. The *Lizards* played center stage in 1988's Operation *Praying Mantis* against Iranian Naval units, and were largely responsible for the sinking of the light frigate *Sahand*, the largest man-of-war to be sunk by the A-6 type.

VA-97, VFA-97	***Warhawks***	**Lemoore**		
A-7E, F/A-18A				
Est. VA-97 1 Jun 67, r/d VFA-97 24 Jan 91				
17 Sep 74 to 20 May 75	*Enterprise*	WP/IO	A-7E	NK300
30 Jul 76 to 28 Mar 77	*Enterprise*	WP/IO	A-7E	NK300
4 Apr 78 to 30 Oct 78	*Enterprise*	WP/IO	A-7E	NK300
30 Sep 79 to 20 Feb 80	*Coral Sea*	WP/IO	A-7E	NK300
20 Aug 81 to 23 Mar 82	*Coral Sea*	WP/IO	A-7E	NK300
21 Mar to 12 Sep 83	*Coral Sea*	World	A-7E	NK300
13 Oct 84 to 24 May 85	*Carl Vinson*	NP/WP/IO	A-7E	NL300
12 Aug 86 to 5 Feb 87	*Carl Vinson*	NP/WP/IO	A-7E	NL300
15 Jun to 14 Dec 88	*Carl Vinson*	WP/IO	A-7E	NL300
5 Sep 89 to 8 Nov 89	*Carl Vinson*	NP/WP	A-7E	NL300
1 Feb 90 to 31 Jul 90	*Carl Vinson*	WP/IO	A-7E	NL300
18 Oct to 11 Dec 91	*Kitty Hawk*	Horn	F/A-18A	NL300
3 Nov 2 to 3 May 93	*Kitty Hawk*	WP/IO/PG	F/A-18A	NL300
24 Jun to 22 Dec 94	*Kitty Hawk*	WP/IO/PG	F/A-18A	NL300
11 Oct 96 to 11 Apr 97	*Kitty Hawk*	WP/IO/PG	F/A-18A	NH200
6 Nov 98 to 6 May 99	*Carl Vinson*	WP/IO/PG	F/A-18A	NH200

VA-97 was one of the first A-7 units in the Navy, being established with the type in 1967. The *Warhawks* converted to the *Hornet* in 1990-91, and deployed with CVW-15 until 1995. The squadron subsequently moved to CVW-11, where it operated F/A-18As alongside a pair of "C" model units (VFA-22 and -94). VFA-97 would be the last fleet unit to operate the straight Alpha-version of the *Hornet* (into 2004), although so-called F/A-18A+ *Hornets* would return later with Reserve and Marine units.

The AAR-45 FLIR pod was introduced to the A-7E in 1979, and provided the type at least a modicum of night vision capability. VA-97's NL301 (160540) is shown at Corpus Christi on 14 Apr 1984, not long after the squadron had moved from CVW-14 to -15. (Phil Friddell)

VA-105, VFA-105 *Gunslingers* **Cecil Field, Oceana**

A-7E, F/A-18C

Est. 4 Mar 68, r/d VFA-105 17 Dec 1990

27 Sep 74 to 19 Mar 75	*Saratoga*	Med	A-7E	AC400
6 Jan to 28 Jul 76	*Saratoga*	Med	A-7E	AC400
11 Jul to 23 Dec 77	*Saratoga*	Med	A-7E	AC400
3 Oct 78 to 5 Apr 79	*Saratoga*	Med	A-7E	AC400
10 Mar to 27 Aug 80	*Saratoga*	Med	A-7E	AC400
4 Jan to 14 Jul 82	*JF Kennedy*	IO	A-7E	AC400
1 Mar to 29 Oct 83	*Carl Vinson*	World	A-7E	NL400
2 Jun to 17 Dec 84	MAG-12	Iwakuni	A-7E	AC400 (not in CVW-3)
2 Jun to 10 Nov 86	*Forrestal*	Med	A-7E	AE400
25 Apr to 7 Oct 88	*Forrestal*	Med	A-7E	AE400
4 Nov 89 to 12 Apr 90	*Forrestal*	Med/IO/NL	A-7E	AE400
30 May to 21 Dec 91	*Forrestal*	Med	A-7E	AE400
7 Oct 92 to 7 Apr 93	*JF Kennedy*	Med	F/A-18C	AC400
20 Oct 94 to 15 Apr 95	*Eisenhower*	Med/RS/PG	F/A-18C	AC400
25 Nov 96 to 22 May 97	*T Roosevelt*	Med/RS/PG	F/A-18C	AC400
6 Nov 98 to 6 May 99	*Enterprise*	Med/RS/PG	F/A-18C	AC400
28 Nov 00 to 23 May 01	*HS Truman*	Med/RS/PG	F/A-18C	AC400

The *Gunslingers* were an early Cecil-based A-7 unit, being established in 1968. They made multiple Med deployments with CVW-3 before taking a world cruise with the new *Carl Vinson* as a part of Pacific Fleet CVW-15. They followed that with a six-month deployment to Japan as the first Navy A-7 unit to work for the Marines as part of their Unit Deployment Plan. In April 1985 the unit moved to CVW-6, and subsequently made the *Forrestal's* last four deployments before transitioning to *Hornets* in 1992. The unit moved to Oceana April 1999.

VFA-106 *Gladiators* **Cecil Field, Oceana, (Fallon)** **FRS**

F/A-18A,B,C,D, T-34C

Estab. 27 Apr 84.

The *Gladiators* were the second Navy *Hornet* FRS, and adopted the nickname and a modified logo from the previous VA-106, a fleet A-4 *Skyhawk* unit, which was disestablished November 1969. The first student class was started in October 1985, and graduated March 1986. The unit moved to Oceana in May 1999. Normal modex for A/C models is AD300, B/D is AD400. A permanent training detachment was established at Fallon in March 1987. It was combined with the co-located VFA-125 det in 1994 to become the Strike Fighter Weapons Detachment Fallon. The T-34C "Turbo Weenie" was used as a hack for a variety of utility purposes.

VA-113, VFA-113 *Stingers* **Lemoore**

A-7E, F/A-18A, F/A-18C

Est. VF-113 15 Jul 48, r/d VA-113 Mar 56, r/d VFA-113 25 Mar 1983

7 May to 18 Oct 74	*Ranger*	WP	A-7E	NE300	
30 Jan to 7 Sep 76	*Ranger*	WP/IO	A-7E	NE300	
21 Feb to 22 Sep 79	*Ranger*	WP	A-7E	NE300	
10 Sep 80 to 4 May 81	*Ranger*	WP/IO	A-7E	NE300	
7 Apr to 19 Oct 82	*Ranger*	WP/IO	A-7E	NE300	
21 Feb to 24 Aug 85	*Constellation*	WP/IO	F/A-18A	NK300	
11 Apr to 13 Oct 87	*Constellation*	WP/IO	F/A-18A	NK300	
1 Dec 88 to 1 Jun 89	*Constellation*	WP/IO	F/A-18A	NK300	
16 Sep to 19 Oct 89	*Constellation*	NorPac	F/A-18A/C	NK300	
23 Jun to 20 Dec 90	*Independence*	WP/IO/PG	F/A-18C	NK300	*Desert Shield*
5 to 22 Aug 91	*Independence*	Hawaii	F/A-18C	NK300	
28 Aug to 14 Sep 91	*Midway*	Swapex	F/A-18A	(NK)300	
18 Feb to 14 Aug 94	*Carl Vinson*	WP/IO/PG	F/A-18C	NK300	
14 May to 14 Nov 96	*Carl Vinson*	WP/IO/PG	F/A-18C	NK300	
11 Jun to 7 Dec 98	*Lincoln*	WP/IO/PG	F/A-18C	NK300	
14 Aug 00 to 12 Feb 01	*Lincoln*	WP/IO/PG	F/A-18C	NK300	

VFA-113 has been matched with VA/VFA-25 since 1970. They were the first fleet VFA unit, and one of the first two F/A-18A *Hornet* units to deploy (in *Constellation* in 1985). After participating in Desert Shield, the unit accompanied Indy/CVW-14 and participated in the "swapex" of Japan-based carriers. VFA-113 traded its late-model F/A-18Cs for CVW-5 F/A-18As and returned home with *Midway*. The squadron received new C-model *Hornets*, and subsequently cruised with CVW-14 in *Carl Vinson* and *Lincoln*.

VA-115, VFA-115 ***Arabs, Eagles*** **Atsugi, Lemoore**
A-6A, A-6E, KA-6D, F/A-18C
Est. VT-11 10 Oct 42, r/d VA-12A 15 Nov 46, r/d VA-115 15 Jul 48, inactive Aug 67 to 1 Jan 70, r/d VFA-115 30 Sep 1996

1/74-9/77	*Midway*	forward deployed	A-6A, B, KA	NF500
9/77-1980	*Midway*	forward deployed	A-6E, KA	NF500
1980-8/91	*Midway*	forward deployed	A-6E TRAM, KA	NF500
8/91-1993	*Independence*	forward deployed	A-6E TRAM	NF500
1993 to 3/96	*Independence*	forward deployed	A-6E SWIP	NF500
11 Jun to 7 Dec 98	*Lincoln*	WP/IO/PG	F/A-18C	NK200
14 Aug 00 to 12 Feb 01	*Lincoln*	WP/IO/PG	F/A-18C	NK200

VA-115's historical nickname was *Arabs* (pronounced A'-rab), which was initially used by the *Intruder* unit. Political considerations, however, led to the unit's adopting the less sensitive *Eagle* title in March 1978. In 1973 the squadron moved with its air wing to Japan, where for the remainder of its existence it made numerous cruises throughout the Pacific and Indian Ocean areas as part of the Navy's unofficial "Foreign Legion." The squadron retired the final A-6As in the Navy in 1977, with at least some of the aircraft returning to CONUS on the decks of amphibious ships. From 1979 to 1984 VA-115 was the Pacific Fleet's repository of Standard ARM capable A-6Bs and AWG-21 equipped A-6Es. The squadron was reduced in size to nine aircraft in 1987 when VA-185 joined it in CVW-5, and as such it fought in *Desert Storm*. In 1991 VA-185 was disestablished, and -115 absorbed most of the command, raising its assigned strength back to 15 aircraft. The *Eagles* lasted in Japan until 1996, when they returned to the U.S. and were redesignated VFA-115, becoming the only Pacific Fleet *Intruder* unit to transition to another aircraft. After making two deployments with F/A-18Cs with CVW-14 the squadron would become the fleet's first F/A-18E *Super Hornet* unit.

VA-122 ***Flying Eagles*** **Lemoore** **FRS**
A-7E, A-7C, TA-7C, T-28B/C, O-2A, T-39D
Est. VC-35 25 May 50, r/d VA(AW)-35 1 Jul 56, r/d VA-122 29 Jun 56, disestab. 31 May 1991 (6 Apr ceremony)
Formerly known as *Corsair College*, VA-122 had been AirPac's A-7 RAG since November 1966. Between June 1988 and 1991 the unit handled *Corsair* training duties for both coasts. The squadron was disestablished in 1991 at the end of the Navy's A-7 era, with their last Carrier Qualification for new A-7 pilots occurring in February 1991. The squadron was assigned a variety of support aircraft through the years, including O-2As, T-28s, and at least one T-39D. Normal tailcode was NJ200 series, although one T-39D wore a squadron oriented NJ122.

VFA-122 ***Flying Eagles*** **Lemoore** **FRS**
F/A-18E, F/A-18F, F/A-18C
Established 1 Oct 98 (15 Jan 1999 ceremony)
The *Flying Eagles* name returned to Lemoore seven years after VA-122 had been disestablished. Although the unit adopted the name and traditions of the previous squadron, it does not retain the lineage, as it is officially considered a separate organization. The squadron also picked a modified version of the old insignia, with a generic bald eagle flying over a patriotically colored shield. VFA-122 was formed to be the new F/A-18E/F *Super Hornet* RAG, although it utilized a small number of F/A-18Cs as the new aircraft were being delivered. Its first F/A-18E/Fs

The *Rough Raiders* flew a large number of training sorties out of their Fallon detachment. Here F/A-18A NJ510 climbs out of the Nevada base with a load of Mk.76 practice bombs on its MERs in June 1986. The "student" in this case is a Marine Captain transitioning from *Phantoms*. This aircraft (161747) would be sent to the desert at AMARC in Nov 1995, and stricken in July 2001. (author)

were accepted by the unit on 17 Nov 1999. Although officially called *Super Hornets*, the type quickly became known in the fleet by the name "Rhino." Aircraft carry NJ200 series markings. The first fleet *Super Hornet* squadron would be VFA-115, who received their initial F/A-18Es in 2001.

VA-125 ***Rough Raiders*** **Lemoore** **FRS**
A-7A, A-7B
Reserve VA-923 activated 29 Jul 50, r/d VA-125 4 Feb 53, disestab. 1 Oct 1977
VA-125 was the former AirPac A-4 *Skyhawk* FRS until 1970, when it took over the duties of training pilots and maintenance personnel in the TF-30 powered versions of the *Corsair* for the West Coast. The 1977 end of the last five Pac-fleet A-7A/B units (VA-56, -93, -153, -155, and -215) quickly led to the demise of the *Rough Raiders* as well. As of January 1974 the unit held ten A-7As and seven A-7Bs. The squadron was assigned NJ500 series numbers.

VFA-125 ***Rough Raiders*** **Lemoore, (Fallon) FRS**
F/A-18A, F/A-18B, F/A-18C, F/A-18D, A-7E, O-2A, T-34C
Est. 13 Nov 80
Formed as the Navy's first F/A-18 Hornet FRS, VFA-125 adopted the name and traditions of the former VA-125. The unit also initially used the former VA-125 "torch and atom" insignia, but later developed a different logo that featured a pirate with a knife in his teeth. The squadron was originally designated as Fighter-Attack Squadron-125 (VFA), which followed the lines of Marine VMFA units. On 25 March 1983 the title was changed Navy-wide to Strike-Fighter Squadron with no change in the VFA designation. Since that time the unit has trained both Navy and Marine crew and maintenance personnel in the A/B/C/D versions of the *Hornet*. A few A-7Es were utilized early in the squadron's history until a sufficient number of *Hornets* were delivered. O-2As were adopted from VA-122 in 1986 to perform range spotting functions at the Fallon ranges. These were replaced by T-34Cs in 1990. Squadron *Hornets* started in the NJ500 series, but moved to the 300 nose numbers in 1992. A permanent forward detachment was formed at Fallon in December 1983, which allowed more intensive student training on the Nevada ranges without the costs and time involved in transit to and from Lemoore. The det was combined with the east coast RAG VFA-106 in 1994 to form the Strike-Fighter Weapons Detachment Fallon.

VA-127, VFA-127 ***Royal Blues, Cylons, Desert Bogeys*** **Lemoore, Fallon** **FRS**
TA-4F, TA-4J, A-4E, A-4F, F-5E, F-5F, T-38A/B, F/A-18A
Est. VA-127 15 Jun 62, r/d VFA-127 1 Mar 1987, disestab. 31 Mar 1996.
As of 1974 the *Royal Blues* held two roles, being the sole A-4 *Skyhawk* FRS, as well as being the instrument squadron at Lemoore for the AirPac light attack community. In November 1975 the squadron was designated an adversary training unit, and in October 1983 the instrument training mission was completely dropped. The squadron was redesignated a Strike Fighter Squadron as VFA-127 on 1 Mar '87, and moved to NAS Fallon, NV, the following October to be closer to the ranges they usually worked in. The odd title *Cylon* came in 1981 from the enemy robots in the cheesy science fiction TV show "Battlestar Gallactica." The latest name, *Desert Bogeys*, was certainly more appropriate, and needed a lot less explanation than *Cylon*. VA/VFA-127 used a diverse variety of aircraft in the ACM training role, with the A-4s being supplemented by T-38s, F-5s (9/87), and F/A-18A/Bs in March 1992. The squadron was disestablished in 1996 during the post *Desert Storm* force reductions. Aircraft carried NJ700 series numbers for years, which were frequently shortened to the last two digits during the adversary years, as they were painted to represent Soviet style "bort" numbers.

VA-128 ***Golden Intruders*** **Whidbey Island** **FRS**
A-6A, A-6E, A-6E TRAM, A-6E SWIP, KA-6D, TC-4C
Est. 1 Sep 67, disestab. 30 Sep 1995 (29 Sep ceremony)
The West Coast A-6 FRS, VA-128 was established from the A-6 portion of the Whidbey A-3 FRS VAH-123. It took over the duties of training Marine *Intruder* crews in October 1986, and became the sole A-6 training squadron in Sept 1994 when VA-42 was disestablished. VA-128 aircraft were assigned NJ800 series numbers until 1992, when they switched to the VA(M) fleet-standard 500 series. As of Jan 1974 squadron strength was 19 A-6A, 2 A-6E, and a trio of TC-4Cs.

VFA-131 ***Wildcats*** **Lemoore, Cecil Field, Oceana**
F/A-18A, F/A-18C
Est. VFA-131 3 Oct 83

2 Oct 85 to 19 May 86	*Coral Sea*	Med	F/A-18A	AK100	Libya
29 Sep 87 to 28 Mar 88	*Coral Sea*	Med	F/A-18A	AK100	
15 Aug to 8 Oct 88	*Independence*	Horn	F/A-18A	AA100	
8 Mar to 12 Sep 90	*Eisenhower*	Med	F/A-18A	AG400	*Desert Shield*
26 Sep 91 to 2 Apr 92	*Eisenhower*	Med	F/A-18C	AG400	

20 May to 17 Nov 94	*G Washington*	Med	F/A-18C	AG400
26 Jan to 23 Jun 96	*G Washington*	Med/RS/PG	F/A-18C	AG400
26 Feb to 26 Aug 98	*JC Stennis*	World	F/A-18C	AG400
18 Feb to 18 Aug 00	*Eisenhower*	Med	F/A-18C	AG400

The *Wildcats* were the first of four new *Hornet* squadrons established for CVW-13 in the mid-'80s. They were formed in Lemoore, and trained at VFA-125 before moving to Cecil Field in February 1985 (with a 3 Oct '85 official date) prior to their first deployment. The new squadron saw action off Libya on its first deployment, and accompanied *Coral Sea*/CVW-13 on their second Med cruise. Other than a short stay with CVW-17 while it took a trip around the Horn with "Indy," the *Wildcats* have been with CVW-7 ever since.

VFA-132 *Privateers* **Lemoore, Cecil Field, Oceana**

F/A-18A

Estab. 3 Jan 1984 disestab. 1 June 92

2 Oct 85 to 19 May 86	*Coral Sea*	Med	F/A-18A	AK200	Libya
5 Oct 87 to 28 Apr 88	MAG-15	Iwakuni JA	F/A-18A	AK200	
31 May 89 to 30 Sep 88	*Coral Sea*	Med	F/A-18A	AK200	
30 May to 21 Dec 91	*Forrestal*	Med	F/A-18A	AE300	

VFA-132 holds the unique distinction of being the only deploying Navy Strike Fighter squadron that had been disestablished up to 2000. VFA-132 was formed at Lemoore, and moved to Cecil Field with sister VFA-131 in February 1985. The unit was one of the two new F/A-18 outfits that made CVW-13's first deployment, and participated in action off Libya in 1986. In 1987 the squadron was assigned to Marine Aircraft Group 11 in Japan under that service's six-month Unit Deployment Plan. It returned to CVW-13 for its final deployment, and then made CVW-6's last cruise as well before leaving the service's roles. In one of the more memorable squadron incidents, a VFA-132 shot down a wayward VAW-122 E-2C with 20mm cannon fire on 8 July 1991. The *Hawkeye* had suffered an inflight fire that forced the crew to bail out. The *Hornet* shot it down over water to keep it from flying into Syria, or some other excitable country.

VFA-136 *Knighthawks* **Lemoore, Cecil Field, Oceana**

F/A-18A, F/A-18C

Estab. 1 Jul 1985

29 Sep 87 to 28 Mar 88	*Coral Sea*	Med	F/A-18A	AK300
8 Mar to 12 Sep 90	*Eisenhower*	Med	F/A-18A	AG300
26 Sep 91 to 2 Apr 92	*Eisenhower*	Med	F/A-18C	AG300
20 May to 17 Nov 94	*G Washington*	Med	F/A-18C	AG300
26 Jan to 23 Jun 96	*G Washington*	Med/RS/PG	F/A-18C	AG300
26 Feb to 26 Aug 98	*JC Stennis*	World	F/A-18C	AG300
18 Feb to 18 Aug 00	*Eisenhower*	Med	F/A-18C	AG300

VFA-136 was the third of four new *Hornet* units that were originally planned to fill out CVW-13 for its first deployment, but was one of the pair that were delayed, reportedly due to a lack of personnel. (VFA-137 was the other). Oddly numbered out of sequence (VFA-133 and -134 would have made more sense), the two squadrons were established in time for *Coral Sea*/CVW-13's second deployment, which they made with the only slightly older VFA-131. The *Knighthawks* subsequently moved with the *Wildcats* to CVW-7. VFA-136 was the third, and last, "new" *Hornet* unit to be formed on the West Coast, and moved to Cecil prior to deployment. The unit subsequently moved to Oceana.

VFA-137 *Kestrels* **Cecil Field, Lemoore**

F/A-18A, F/A-18C

Estab. 1 Jul 1985

29 Sep 87 to 28 Mar 88	*Coral Sea*	Med	F/A-18A	AK400
31 May to 30 Sep 89	*Coral Sea*	Med	F/A-18A	AK400
30 May to 21 Dec 91	*Forrestal*	Med	F/A-18A	AE300
29 May to 22 Jul 93	*Constellation*	Horn	F/A-18C	NE400
10 Nov 94 to 10 May 95	*Constellation*	WP/IO/PG	F/A-18C	NE400
1 Apr to 1 Oct 97	*Constellation*	WP/IO/PG	F/A-18C	NE400
18 Jun to 17 Dec 99	*Constellation*	WP/IO/PG	F/A-18C	NE400

The last of the four CVW-13 F/A-18 squadrons to be formed, VFA-137 adopted a more elegant title for the Sparrow Hawk as their nickname. VFA-137 made two deployments with CVW-13, and one in *Forrestal* with CVW-6 before moving to Lemoore in October 1992 for assignment to CVW-2. Squadron aircraft have been known to carry the title "Fleet Falcons" on their external tanks, apparently for those who don't know what a Kestrel is.

VA-145	***Swordsmen***	**Whidbey Island**			
A-6A, A-6E, A-6E TRAM, A-6E SWIP, KA-6D					
Reserve VA-702 activated 20 Jul 50, r/d VA-145 4 Feb 53,		disestab. 1 Oct 93 (13 Oct ceremony			
7 May to 18 Oct 74	*Ranger*	WP	A-6A, KA	NE500	
30 Jan to 7 Sep 76	*Ranger*	WP/IO	A-6A, KA	NE500	
21 Feb to 22 Sep 79	*Ranger*	WP	A-6E, KA	NE500	
10 Sep 80 to 4 May 81	*Ranger*	WP/IO	A-6E, KA	NE500	
7 Apr to 19 Oct 82	*Ranger*	WP/ IO	A-6E TRAM, KA	NE500	
13 Jan to 1 Aug 84	*Kitty Hawk*	WP/ IO	A-6E TRAM, KA	NE500	
18 Aug to 20 Oct 86	*Ranger*	WP surge	A-6E TRAM, KA	NE500	
3 Mar to 29 Apr 87	*Ranger*	WP surge	A-6E TRAM, KA	NE500	
14 Jul to 29 Dec 87	*Ranger*	WP/ IO	A-6E TRAM	NE500	
24 Feb to 24 Aug 89	*Ranger*	WP/ IO	A-6E SWIP	NE500	
8 Dec 90 to 8 Jun 91	*Ranger*	WP/ IO/ PG	A-6E SWIP	NE500	*D.Storm*
1 Aug 92 to 31 Jan 93	*Ranger*	WP/IO/ PG	A-6E SWIP	NE500	
29 May to 22 Jul 93	*Constellation*	Horn	A-6E SWIP	NE500	

VA-145 was the last Whidbey-based *Intruder* unit to deploy with A-6As, with Echoes arriving in 1976, A-6E TRAMs in Nov 1981, and the Pacific Fleet's first SWIPs in 1988. In 1984-85 the unit became the last location for Pacific Fleet AWG-21/Standard ARM capable A-6Es. Participated in dual A-6 wing configurations with both the Marine (VMA-AW-121) and Navy (VA-155) squadrons. From 1986 to 1987 VA-145 accompanied *Ranger* and CVW-2 as they carried out short "surge" operations to the Western and Northern Pacific operations areas. The squadron was heavily involved in *Desert Storm* from *Ranger*, and made two subsequent deployments before being disestablished.

VA-146, VFA-146	***Blue Diamonds***	**Lemoore**		
A-7E, F/A-18C				
Est. VA-147 1 Feb 56	r/d VFA-147 21 Jul 1989			
21 Jun to 22 Dec 74	*Constellation*	WP/IO	A-7E	NG300
12 Apr to 21 Nov 77	*Constellation*	WP	A-7E	NG300
26 Sep 78 to 17 May 79	*Constellation*	WP/IO	A-7E	NG300
26 Feb to 15 Oct 80	*Constellation*	WP/IO	A-7E	NG300
20 Oct 81 to 23 May 82	*Constellation*	WP/IO	A-7E	NG300
13 Jan to 1 Aug 84	*Kitty Hawk*	WP/IO	A-7E	NE300
24 Jul 85 to 21 Dec 85	*Kitty Hawk*	WP/IO	A-7E	NG300
3 Jan 87 to 29 Jun 87	*Kitty Hawk*	World	A-7E	NG300
2 Sep 88 to 2 Mar 89	*Nimitz*	WP/IO	A-7E	NG300
15 Jun to 9 Jul 89	*Nimitz*	NorPac	A-7E	NG300
25 Feb to 24 Aug 91	*Nimitz*	WP/IO/PG	F/A-18C	NG300
2 Feb to 29 Jul 93	*Nimitz*	WP/IO/PG	F/A-18C	NG300

Resting for a short spell at Cannon AFB, New Mexico, in August 1976, this VA-146 *Blue Diamond* (NG310, 159648) carries full-color markings that are essentially the same the squadron wore in Vietnam. (John Pouch)

27 Nov 95 to 20 May 96	*Nimitz*	WP/IO/PG	F/A-18C	NG300
1 Sep 97 to 1 Mar 98	*Nimitz*	WP/IO/PG	F/A-18C	NG300
7 Jan to 3 Jul 00	*JC Stennis*	WP/IO/PG	F/A-18C	NG300

The *Blue Diamonds* were another '50s era light attack outfit that flew Grumman *Cougars* and North American *Furies* in its past. The unit made seven deployments to Vietnam in *Skyhawks* and *Corsairs*, and transitioned to *Hornets* in 1989. All but one of its deployments since 1968 have been with CVW-9. In 1983 VA-146 became the first squadron to be qualified to carry the AGM-88 HARM.

VA-147, VFA-147 ***Argonauts*** **Lemoore**

A-7E, F/A-18C

Est. VA-147 1 Feb 67, r/d 20 Jun 1989

21 Jun to 22 Dec 74	*Constellation*	WP/IO	A-7E	NG400
12 Apr to 21 Nov 77	*Constellation*	WP	A-7E	NG400
26 Sep 78 to 17 May 79	*Constellation*	WP/IO	A-7E	NG400
26 Feb to 15 Oct 80	*Constellation*	WP/IO	A-7E	NG400
20 Oct 81 to 23 May 82	*Constellation*	WP/IO	A-7E	NG400
13 Jan to 1 Aug 84	*Kitty Hawk*	WP/IO	A-7E	NE400
24 Jul 85 to 21 Dec 85	*Kitty Hawk*	WP/IO	A-7E	NG400
3 Jan 87 to 29 Jun 87	*Kitty Hawk*	World	A-7E	NG400
2 Sep 88 to 2 Mar 89	*Nimitz*	WP/IO	A-7E	NG400
25 Feb to 24 Aug 91	*Nimitz*	WP/IO/PG	F/A-18C	NG400
2 Feb to 29 Jul 93	*Nimitz*	WP/IO/PG	F/A-18C	NG400
27 Nov 95 to 20 May 96	*Nimitz*	WP/IO/PG	F/A-18C	NG400
1 Sep 97 to 1 Mar 98	*Nimitz*	WP/IO/PG	F/A-18C	NG400
7 Jan to 3 Jul 00	*JC Stennis*	WP/IO/PG	F/A-18C	NG400

Also called the "Argos" and "Jasons," VA-147 was the first A-7 unit to deploy (in 1967), and has been paired with VA-146 since 1970. It has made multiple deployments with CVW-9, and one with CVW-2. VA-147 did not make a Jun-Jul '89 North Pacific trip with CVW-9/*Nimitz* due to its *Hornet* transition.

VFA-151; See VF-151, Chapter 4

VA-153 ***Blue Tail Flies*** **Lemoore**

A-7B

Reserve VF-831 activated 1 Feb 51, r/d VA-153 4 Feb 53, disestab. 30 Sep 1977

18 Oct 73 to 5 Jun 74	*Oriskany*	WPAC	A-7B	NM300
16 Sep 75 to 3 Mar 76	*Oriskany*	WPAC	A-7B	NM300
4 Oct 76 to 21 Apr 77	*F.D. Roosevelt*	MED	A-7B	NM300

The *Flies*' odd name comes from the Korean War, when two of the unit's battle damaged F9F-5 *Panthers* were mated to form one usable airframe. The front portion was anodized natural metal, while the aft half was Navy blue. Comparisons between the aircraft and an insect featured in the popular song "Jimmy Crack Corn" led to the squadron title. In time the unit painted the rear of its aircraft a light blue color to match the name. The squadron made three deployments following Vietnam before being disestablished as one of the last AirPac A-7B units to deploy.

VA-155 (1) ***Silver Foxes*** **Lemoore**

A-7B

Estab. VT-153 26 Nov 45, r/d VA-16A 15 Nov 46, r/d VA-155 14 Jul 48, disest. 30 Sep 1977

18 Oct 73 to 5 Jun 74	*Oriskany*	WPAC	A-7B	NM500
16 Sep 75 to 3 Mar 76	*Oriskany*	WPAC	A-7B	NM500
4 Oct 76 to 21 Apr 77	*F.D. Roosevelt*	MED	A-7B	NM500

The *Foxes*, in company with its CVW-19 stable mates VA-153 and VA-215, made three post-Vietnam deployments before being disestablished.

VA-155 (2) ***Silver Foxes*** **Whidbey Island**

A-6E TRAM, A-6E SWIP, KA-6D

Estab. 1 Sep 87 (4 Sep ceremony) disestab. 30 Apr 93

(none)	(—)	no cruise	A-6E TRAM, KA	NM500
15 Aug to 8 Oct 88	*Independence*	Horn	A-6E TRAM, KA	AA500

8 Dec 90 to 8 Jun 91	*Ranger*	WP/IO/PG	A-6E TRAM	NE400	*D.Storm*
1 Aug 92 to 31 Jan 93	*Ranger*	WP/IO/PG	A-6E SWIP	NE400	

VA-155 replaced VA-185 in the newly formed CVW-10, but never deployed with the short lived air wing. On 1 May 1988 the *Foxes* became the only Whidbey *Intruder* squadron to ever be assigned to an east coast air wing, as it replaced VA-85 in CVW-17. The same year, a portion of the unit joined the wing as it accompanied *Independence* around the Horn to its post-SLEP homeport of North Island, CA. In October 1989 the *Foxes* moved to Pacific fleet CVW-2, where they joined VA-145 in a dual Intruder Air Wing. The squadron's first extended deployment included combat operations in Operation *Desert Storm*, where it flew 647 sorties and dropped 2,289,910 pounds of ordnance, while losing one aircraft and its crew. VA-155 was equipped with A-6E SWIP *Intruders* upon return to Whidbey, which it flew on its second and final overseas cruise.

VFA-161: See VF-161, Chapter 4.

VA-164 **_Ghostriders_** **Lemoore**

A-4F, TA-4F

Estab.

1 Sep 60, disestab. 2 Dec 1975

8 May 73 to 8 Jan 74	*Hancock*	WPAC	A-4F, TA-4F	NP400
18 Mar to 20 Oct 75	*Hancock*	WPAC	A-4F, TA-4F	NP400

VA-164 was one of the last three fleet A-4F units in the Navy. The squadron deployed in *Hancock* as the Laser Guided Bomb (LGB) specialist, with the two-seat TA-4Fs being used with hand-held laser designators.

VA-165 **_Boomers_** **Whidbey Island**

A-6E, A-6E TRAM, A-6E SWIP, KA-6D

Estab. 1 Sep 60, disestab. 30 Sep 96

21 Jun to 22 Dec 74	*Constellation*	WP/IO/PG	A-6A, KA	NG500
12 Apr to 21 Nov 77	*Constellation*	WP	A-6E, KA	NG500
26 Sep 78 to 17 May 79	*Constellation*	WP/IO	A-6E, KA	NG500
26 Feb to 15 Oct 80	*Constellation*	WP/IO	A-6E, KA	NG500
20 Oct 81 to 23 May 82	*Constellation*	WP/IO	A-6E TRAM, KA	NG500
15 Jul 83 to 29 Feb 84	*Ranger*	WP/IO	A-6E TRAM, KA	NG500
24 Jul to 21 Dec 85	*Kitty Hawk*	WP/IO	A-6E TRAM, KA	NG500
3 Jan to 29 Jun 87	*Kitty Hawk*	World	A-6E TRAM, KA	NG500
2 Sep 88 to 2 Mar 89	*Nimitz*	WP/IO	A-6E TRAM, KA	NG500
15 Jun to 9 Jul 89	*Nimitz*	NorPac	A-6E TRAM, KA	NG500
12 Feb to 7 Apr 90	*Constellation*	Horn	A-6E TRAM, KA	NG500
25 Feb to 24 Aug 91	*Nimitz*	WP/IO/PG	A-6E TRAM, KA	NG500
2 Feb to 29 Jul 93	*Nimitz*	WP/IO/PG	A-6E SWIP, KA	NG500
27 Nov 95 to 20 May 96	*Nimitz*	WP/IO/PG	A-6E SWIP	NG500

The *Boomers* dated from 1960, when they were established as the AD (A-1) squadron for the new CVG-16. The 1983 deployment in *Ranger* included a short period off Central America during political unpleasantries with the Nicaraguan Sandinistas. In 1989 the squadron was picked to participate in the movie version of "Flight of the Intruder," with operations on *Independence*, and several aircraft painted in markings representing VA-196 in 1972. The 1990 cruise on *Constellation* involved only a portion of the unit, as it accompanied the ship's post-SLEP transfer from the west to east coast. The 1993 deployment in *Nimitz* was the final cruise for the KA-6D type.

VA-174 **_Hell Razors_** **Cecil Field** **FRS**

A-7A, A-7B, A-7C, A-7E, TA-7C, T-39D

Estab. VB-81 1 Mar 44, r/d VA-13A 15 Nov 46, r/d VA-134 2 Aug 48, r/d VF-174 15 Feb 50, r/d VA-174 1 Jul 66, disestab. 30 June 1988

VA-174 was the Atlantic Fleet F-8 RAG as VF-174 until 1966, when it became the first A-7 training squadron in the Navy. The unit carried out training duties for the east coast light attack community until its disestablishment in 1988. The *Hell Razors* were, necessarily, a large squadron, and 1974 strength was 21 A-7Es, 14 A-7Bs, 5 A-7Cs, 2 A-7As, and a sole T-39D used for admin support. A/B/C models lasted until around 1977, when VA-72 and -46 transitioned to E-models. Two-seat TA-7Cs arrived in June 1978. The squadron's most famous alumnus is, without doubt, Cdr. John McCain, the former POW, and later U.S. Senator (R-AZ) and Presidential aspirant, who served as squadron Commanding Officer between July 1976 and July 1977. A detachment was kept at NAS El Centro for many years. VA-174 aircraft normally wore AD400 series side numbers.

VA-176	***Thunderbolts***	**Oceana**			
A-6A, A-6E, A-6E TRAM, A-6E SWIP, KA-6D					
Estab. VA-176 1 Jun 55,	disestab. 30 Oct 92 (18 Sep ceremony)				
14 Sep 73 to 17 Mar 74	*F.D.Roosevelt*	Med	A-6A/C, KA	AE500	
3 Jan to 16 Jul 75	*F.D.Roosevelt*	Med	A-6A/C, KA	AE500	
15 Apr to 25 Oct 76	*America*	Med	A-6E, KA	AE500	
10 Jun to 19 Jul 77	*America*	Med	A-6E, KA	AE500	
29 Jun to 14 Dec 79	*Independence*	Med	A-6E, KA	AE500	
19 Nov 80 to 19 Jun 81	*Independence*	Med/IO/SoLant	A-6E, KA	AE500	
7 Jun to 22 Dec 82	*Independence*	Med	A-6E TRAM, KA	AE500	
18 Oct 83 to 11 Apr 84	*Independence*	Carib/Med/NL	A-6E TRAM, KA	AE500	Gren/Leb
19 Oct 84 to 19 Feb 85	*Independence*	Med	A-6E TRAM, KA	AE500	
2 Jun to 10 Nov 86	*Forrestal*	Med	A-6E TRAM, KA	AE500	
26 Aug to 9 Oct 87	*Forrestal*	NorLant	A-6E TRAM, KA	AE500	
25 Apr to 7 Oct 88	*Forrestal*	Med/IO/NL	A-6E TRAM, KA	AE500	
4 Nov 89 to 12 Apr 90	*Forrestal*	Med	A-6E TRAM, KA	AE500	
30 May to 21 Dec 91	*Forrestal*	Med	A-6E SWIP, KA	AE500	

VA-176 was the fifth, and last, Atlantic Fleet *Intruder* squadron organized during the Vietnam period. It had been the last single-seat A-1 *Skyraider* unit on the east coast, and even had a MiG-17 kill to its credit during combat in Vietnam. The squadron operated largely out of the Mediterranean with CVW-6 for the next 21 years, and saw limited combat operations during the Invasion of Grenada and strikes on Lebanon in 1983-84. The *Thunderbolts* were unique among the older A-6 units, in that they made every deployment with the same Air Wing. They were also the only *Intruder* unit to deploy in *Franklin D. Roosevelt*. VA-176 was the first squadron to deploy with the KA-6D, and the first Oceana *Intruder* unit to be disestablished during the post *Desert Storm* draw down; however, its name and insignia lived on as the RAG VA-42 adopted both in 1992.

VA-185	***Nighthawks***	**Whidbey, Atsugi**		
A-6E TRAM, KA-6D				
Estab. 1 Dec 86	disestab. 30 Aug 91 (6 Aug ceremony at Atsugi)			
Sep 87 to Aug /91	*Midway*	fwd deployed	A-6E TRAM, KA	NF400

The shortest lived of all *Intruder* squadrons; VA-185 was formed with the intent of being a charter member of CVW-10, but was instead transferred to Japan in September 1987 to join CVW-5 in *Midway*. The *Nighthawks* became a small, nine aircraft squadron, with seven bombers and two tankers normally assigned. The unit participated in *Desert Storm*, but was disestablished soon afterwards, with VA-115 functionally absorbing the unit, as CVW-5 became a single *Intruder* wing again. VA-185 flew over 14,000 hours in its four years and nine months, without loss of a single aircraft or aircrew in peace or war.

The *Nighthawks* of VA-185 were the shortest lived *Intruder* unit, flying for less than five years. NF401 (157025) is seen here over Clover Valley in Washington on 1 Aug 1987 a few weeks before they moved to join CVW-5 in Japan. (author)

VA-192, VFA-192 ***World Famous Golden Dragons*** **Lemoore, Atsugi**
A-7E, F/A-18A, F/A-18C
Est. VF-153 26 Mar 45, r/d VA-15A 15 Nov 46, r/d VA-151 15 Jul 48, r/d VF-192 15 Feb 50, r/d VA-192 15 Mar 56, r/d VFA-192 10 Jan 1986

23 Nov 73 to 9 Jul 74	*Kitty Hawk*	WP/IO	A-7E	NH300
21 May to 15 Dec 75	*Kitty Hawk*	WP	A-7E	NH300
25 Oct 77 to 15 May 78	*Kitty Hawk*	WP	A-7E	NH300
13 Mar to 22 Sep 79	*America*	Med	A-7E	NH300
14 Apr to 12 Nov 81	*America*	Med,IO	A-7E	NH300
Jan to Aug 1982	(none)	(no cruise)	A-7E	NL300
15 Jul to 29 Feb 83	*Ranger*	SoPac/WP/IO	A-7E	NG300
4 Jun to 14 Dec 85	MAG-12	Iwakuni	A-7E	NM300
1986 to 1991	*Midway*	fwd deployed	F/A-18A	NF300 *Desert Storm*
1991 to 1997	*Independence*	fwd deployed	F/A-18C	NF300
1997 to 2000	*Kitty Hawk*	fwd deployed	F/A-18C	NF300

The *Golden Dragons* have a distinguished record dating from 1945. Their F9F-5 *Panthers* were used as the primary aircraft for the classic 1954-55 movie "Bridges of Toko-Ri." VA-192 made seven deployments to Vietnam in *Skyhawks*, where squadron member Lt.Cdr Mike Estocin was awarded a posthumous Medal of Honor for actions against North Vietnamese targets in April 1967. The squadron made multiple deployments with CVW-11, and was assigned to CVW-15 for a short period in 1982 before joining Air Wing Nine. In 1985 they made a six-month deployment with MAG-12 in Iwakuni, Japan, wearing ComLatWingPac's "NM" code. Converting to *Hornets* in 1986, the squadron moved to Japan and joined the *Midway*/CVW-5 team, with whom it participated in *Desert Storm*. VA-192 has also been known for years as the "World Famous Golden Worms."

VA-195, VFA-195 ***Dambusters*** **Lemoore, Atsugi**
A-7E, F/A-18A, F/A-18C
Est. VT-19 15 Aug 43, r/d VA-20A 15 Nov 46, r/d VA-195 24 Aug 48, r/d VFA-195 1 Apr 1985

23 Nov 73 to 9 Jul 74	*Kitty Hawk*	WP/IO	A-7E	NH400
21 May to 15 Dec 75	*Kitty Hawk*	WP	A-7E	NH400
25 Oct 77 to 15 May 78	*Kitty Hawk*	WP	A-7E	NH400
13 Mar to 22 Sep 79	*America*	Med	A-7E	NH400
14 Apr to 12 Nov 81	*America*	Med,IO	A-7E	NH400
Jan to Oct 1982	(none)	(no cruise)	A-7E	NL400
15 Jul to 29 Feb 83	*Ranger*	SoPac/WP/IO	A-7E	NG400
1986 to 1991	*Midway*	fwd deployed	F/A-18A	NF400/100 *Desert Storm*
1991 to 1997	*Independence*	fwd deployed	F/A-18C	NF400
1997 to 2000	*Kitty Hawk*	fwd deployed	F/A-18C	NF400

The *Dambusters* received their nickname from a torpedo attack against the Hwachon Dam in North Korea in May 1951. They were another veteran PacFlt squadron, having flown AD *Skyraiders* in Korea, and then making seven deployments to Vietnam in *Skyhawks* and *Corsair IIs*. In 1982 the unit was assigned for a short time to CVW-15 before moving on to Air Wing Nine. Following conversion to the *Hornet*, VFA-195 moved to Japan with sister VFA-192. The squadron arrived in Japan wearing the NF400 series, and was quickly switched to the open 100 series in CVW-5, which they wore for the remainder of their time with *Midway*. They would subsequently be moved back to the 400 series when F-14 *Tomcats* arrived in the wing.

VA-196 ***Main Battery*** **Whidbey Island**
A-6A, A-6E, A-6E TRAM, A-6E SWIP, KA-6D
Est. VF-153 15 Jul 48, r/d VF-194 15 Feb 50, r/d VA-196 4 May 55, disest. 21 Mar 97 (28 Feb ceremony)

14 Sep 74 to 20 May 75	*Enterprise*	WP, IO	A-6A, KA	NK500
30 Jul 76 to 28 Mar 77	*Enterprise*	WP, IO	A-6E, KA	NK500
4 Apr to 30 Oct 78	*Enterprise*	WP, IO	A-6E, KA	NK500
30 Sep 79 to 20 Feb 80	*Coral Sea*	WP, IO	A-6E, KA	NK500
20 Aug 81 to 23 Mar 82	*Coral Sea*	WP,IO	A-6E, KA	NK500
21 Mar to 12 Sep 83	*Coral Sea*	WP,IO	A-6E, KA	NK500
21 Feb to 24 Aug 85	*Constellation*	WP,IO	A-6E TRAM, KA	NK500
11 Apr to 13 Oct 87	*Constellation*	WP,IO	A-6E TRAM, KA	NK500
1 Dec 88 to 1 Jun 89	*Constellation*	WP, IO	A-6E TRAM, KA	NK500
16 Sep to 19 Oct 89	*Constellation*	NorPac	A-6E TRAM, KA	NK500

23 Jun to 20 Dec 90	*Independence*	WP,IO,PG	A-6E SWIP	NK500	*Desert Shield*
5 to 22 Aug 91	*Independence*	Hawaii	A-6E SWIP	NK500	
28 Aug to 14 Sep 91	*Midway*	Swapex	A-6E SWIP, KA	NK500	
18 Feb to 15 Aug 94	*Carl Vinson*	WP,IO,PG	A-6E SWIP	NK500	
14 May to 14 Nov 96	*Carl Vinson*	WP,IO,PG	A-6E SWIP	NK500	

VA-196's historical nickname (*The Main Battery*) refers to the squadron being the primary weapon of the carrier air wing, and dates from its days in A-1 *Skyraiders*. The secondary nickname *Milestone* was the unit's radio call sign, and was used interchangeably with *Main Battery* for many years. In addition, the squadron frequently used "Devil" for an abbreviated radio callsign, based on its logo. VA-196 was the first Pacific Fleet *Intruder* unit, and the last to be disestablished. The squadron made five deployments to Vietnam, while also losing more aircraft in South East Asia than any other *Intruder* unit. A-6E TRAMs arrived in 1984, SWIPs in 1990. Other major operations VA-196 was involved with include the aborted release of the Iranian hostages in 1982, and *Desert Shield* in 1990. In 1991 the Milestones were involved in the *Independence/Midway* "Swapex," with the squadron returning to the U.S. from Hawaii with VA-115's old aircraft, including KA-6Ds. Squadron member Steven Coontz immortalized the aircraft in his novel *The Flight of the Intruder*, which was made into a movie using VA-165 aircraft. VA-196 became the final Pacific Fleet *Intruder* unit, with its last carrier operations being conducted on *Carl Vinson* in the Strait of San Juan de Fuca in February 1997.

VFA-201: see VF-201, chap 7.

VA-203, VFA-203 — ***Blue Dolphins*** — **Jacksonville, Cecil Field, Atlanta** — **Naval Reserve**

A-4L, A-7A, A-7B, A-7E, F/A-18A
Estab. VA-203 1 Jul 70, r/d VFA-203 1 Oct 1989

The *Blue Dolphins* were formed at Jacksonville, and moved to Cecil in December 1977. Starting with *Skyhawks*, they acquired *Corsairs* in April 1974, A-7Bs in Aug 1977, and A-7Es in Sep 1983. On 1 Oct 1989 the squadron was redesignated as a Strike-Fighter (VFA) squadron, with *Hornets* arriving the month afterwards. With the closure of Cecil Field, the unit moved to NAS Atlanta in Oct 1996. Assigned tailcode and modex have been AF300.

VA-204, VFA-204 — ***(Terciopelos) River Rattlers*** — **Memphis, New Orleans** — **Naval Reserve**

A-4C/L, A-7B, A-7E, F/A-18A
Estab.
VA-204 1 Jul 70, r/d 1 May 1991 (13 Apr ceremony)

VA-204 started at Memphis, TN, with at least two sources stating their initial name was *Terciopelos*, which is an obscure Central American venomous snake. Before long the name appears to have been changed to the more easily explained *River Rattlers*. In January 1978 the unit moved to New Orleans, LA. A-7B *Corsairs* replaced the *Skyhawks* in Mar 1978, and A-7Es arrived in Jun 1986. F/A-18As were assigned from March 1991, with the last *Corsair II*, which was also the last A-7 in the Reserves, leaving on 8 March. On 1 May 1991 the unit became VFA-204. In 2000 the unit deployed eight aircraft to Andersen AFB, Guam, in order to provide adversary support for CVW-5, which was flying off *Kitty Hawk*. The highly unusual trip ended with the squadron carrying out day carrier qualifications on the *Hawk*. Assigned tailcode and modex are AF400.

A VA-203 A-7B (AF306, 154452) flies formation off a VAQ-33 *Skywarrior* near the Dry Tortugas on 12 Aug 1981. A *Firebird* EA-6A and another *Blue Dolphin* are nearby. (author)

VA-205 ***Green Falcons*** **Atlanta** **Naval Reserve**

A-4L, A-7B, A-7E, A-6E TRAM, A-6E SWIP, KA-6D

Est. VA-205 1 Jul 70, disestab. 31 Dec 94 (25 Sep ceremony)

Located at Atlanta throughout its life, VA-205 started as a light attack unit with *Skyhawks*. A-7Bs arrived in Sep 1975, and were replaced by A-7Es in June 1984. In Aug 1990 the unit transitioned to *Intruders*, and became the Medium attack component of CVWR-20. Assigned tailcode and modex were AF500.

VA-212 ***Rampant Raiders*** **Lemoore**

A-4F

Est. VF-212 20 Jun 55, r/d VA-212 1 Apr 56, disestab. 12 Dec 1975

8 May 73 to 8 Jan 74	*Hancock*	WPAC	A-4F	NP300	Vietnam
18 Mar to 20 Oct 75	*Hancock*	WPAC	A-4F	NP300	

VA-212 was originally an F7U *Cutlass* squadron that quickly transitioned to FJ-4B *Furies*, and then A4Ds. It was another battle hardened unit, having made seven combat deployments to Vietnam with *Skyhawks*. The *Raiders* made one more trip to WestPac after the war with CVW-21 and *Hancock* before being disestablished. The *Raiders* were CVW-21's *Walleye* TV-guided bomb specialists. The squadron's rampant lion insignia was reportedly based on the L...wenbrau beer logo.

VA-215 ***Barn Owls*** **Lemoore**

A-7B

Est. VA-215 1 Mar 68, disestab. 30 Sep 1977

18 Oct 73 to 5 Jun 74	*Oriskany*	WPAC	A-7B	NM400
16 Sep 75 to 3 Mar 76	*Oriskany*	WPAC	A-7B	NM400
4 Oct 76 to 21 Apr 77	*F.D. Roosevelt*	MED	A-7B	NM400

The *Barn Owls* were established at Lemoore as an early A-7 unit, and adopted the name and logo of a previous A-1 *Skyraider* outfit. By 1974 they were a member of CVW-19, and made three deployments after Vietnam: two in *Oriskany*, and a solo trip in *Franklin D. Roosevelt* to the Med. It was one of the final three A-7B squadrons in AirPac.

VA-303, VFA-303 ***Golden Hawks*** **Alameda, Lemoore** **Naval Reserve**

A-7A, A-7B, F/A-18A

Est. VA-303 1 Jul 70, r/d 1 Jan 1984, disestab. 31 Dec 1994

25 Sep to 20 Nov 1990	*Lincoln*	Horn	F/A-18A (ND300)	CVW-11

A light attack unit in CVWR-30, VA-303 was equipped with A-7As until Aug 1977, when B-model *Corsairs* arrived. On 1 Jan 1984 the unit was redesignated VFA-303, and was moved to Lemoore for *Hornet* transition as part of the "Total Force" concept, where parts of the Reserves moved to new aircraft before most of the fleet. It would not be until October 1985 that the squadron actually received its first F/A-18s, the unit having used VFA-125 birds up to that point. In 1990, a portion of the unit joined VFA-305 in supporting the transfer of the *Abraham Lincoln* to the Pacific Fleet. Assigned tailcode and modex was ND300.

CVW-21 and *Hancock* had the last deploying *Skyhawk* units in the Navy. All three squadrons were disestablished in December 1975. VA-212 A-4F NP312 is shown at Lemoore that same month. 154992 would subsequently become a *Blue Angel*, and be lost with its pilot at Niagara Falls, NY, on 13 July 1985 after colliding with a teammate. (Michael Grove)

Seven reserve Strike-Fighter units received F/A-18As, and several also had a single F/A-18B attached. VFA-305's two-seater (ND414, 161711) is shown while conducting CQ on *Carl Vinson* on 31 May 1993. The *Lobos* would be disestablished the following year. (author)

VA-304 *Firebirds* **Alameda** **Naval Reserve**
A-7A, A-7B, A-6E, A-6E TRAM, A-6E SWIP, KA-6D
Est. VA-304 1 Jul 70, disestab. 31 Dec 94 (17 Sep ceremony)
No major deployments. VA-304 started as a light attack unit in CVWR-30 with A-4Cs, which were replaced by A-7As in 1971. These were replaced successively by A-7Bs (Sep '77) and A-7Es (Sep '86) before the unit became the first Reserve A-6 squadron, in July 1988. Originally assigned the ND400 tailcode and modex, the squadron assumed the normal Medium-attack 500 series shortly after acquiring *Intruders*.

VA-305, VFA-305 *Hackers, Lobos* **Pt. Mugu** **Naval Reserve**
A-7A, A-7B, F/A-18A
Est. VA-305 1 Jul 70, r/d VFA-305 1 Jan 87, (18 Jan ceremony) distab. 31 Dec 1994
25 Sep to 20 Nov 1990 *Lincoln* Horn F/A-18A ND400 CVW-11
Formed as the third light attack unit in CVWR-30 in 1970, VA-305 changed its nickname to the *Lobos* in 1974. A-7As gave way to B-models in 1978, and in 1987 VFA-205 became a Strike-Fighter squadron. VFA-205 joined CVW-11 for a short period in 1990 to accompany *Abraham Lincoln* as it transited from the Atlantic to Pacific fleets. This was advertised as the first time a Reserve Squadron had been assigned to a Regular Navy Air Wing since the massive 1970 reorganization of the Reserves. Originally assigned the tailcode and modex ND500, it subsequently swapped side numbers with VA-304, and moved to ND400 around 1989.

NSWC: Naval Strike Warfare Center 1984-96
NSAWC: Naval Strike & Air Warfare Center
1996-current ("Strike U")
Drive one hour east of Reno, Nevada, on highway U.S. 50 ("America's Loneliest Road"), and you come to Fallon, Nevada, a little town whose population is said to be 7500, not counting the local jack rabbits, mule deer, rattlesnakes, and even motorists who blow through without stopping.

Five miles further southeast of town is Naval Air Station Fallon, home to the Naval Strike & Air Warfare Center (NSAWC), the single most important aviation training facility in the entire U.S. Navy.

Fallon's training area covers over 1500 square miles of central Nevada desert, and includes four bombing ranges under a heavily instrumented flight area. The base has long been home for pre-cruise Air Group and Wing training detachments, and is, traditionally, the first time in a work-up cycle when the entire air wing meets for combined operations. RAGs and Training Command squadrons also use the base and its ranges for honing their skills. Some units, the Lemoore replacement units in particular, kept permanent or semi-permanent detachments here, which allowed for focused syllabus work away from the distractions of home.

What is now called NSAWC (pronounced as one word, "en'-soc") dates from the early 1980s, when then Secretary of the Navy John Lehman ordered that a permanent training organization be formed to develop a center for Naval strike aviation that would have the same impact that *Topgun* had had on the fighter community. On 27 April 1984 a "Strike University" was formed at Lemoore to begin the task. This group was transferred to Fallon on 8 May, and on 15 Sep 1984 it was formally established as the **Naval Strike Warfare Center** (NSWC), which quickly became known as "Strike U."

The initial 21 officer staff moved into a beat-up old wooden building on the base and went to work. Six aircraft came as well: two each A-6E, F/A-18, and A-7E. By 1994 the command had eight *Hornets*, three *Intruders*, and three *Sea Kings*. F-14s and H-60s would arrive later.

NSWC quickly developed a baseline training syllabus for carrier air wing training. Up to then each Air Wing pretty much set its own schedule and priorities for its visits to Fallon. "Strike U" also established standardized training and qualification standards for strike leads and other warfare commanders. The two to three week CVW training period became a comprehensive and intense training period for everyone concerned. Many other areas that had previously been hit-or-miss affairs, like threat training and tactics development, were conducted here as well.

Air Wings were also introduced to previously under-represented warfare areas, such as Special Warfare, surface ship ("Blackshoe") operations, and Combat Search and Rescue. Strike lead and senior leadership syllabuses were established to teach advanced carrier warfare. Experienced flyers were brought in to become instructors, and orders to teach at "Strike U" quickly became a highly sought after ticket for many aviators. The staff, largely hand picked and based on community reputations, grew to include ship drivers, SEALS, and Air Force and Army members to better reflect the joint nature of modern warfare.

The Navy poured millions of dollars into Fallon, and vastly improved things like billeting and the support establishment, as well as the ranges. A 35,000 square foot training building was also built with state of the art instructional facilities in it. Two large new hangars were erected for the use of visiting wings, as well as fuel pits, improved bomb farms, and a third runway. An extensive electronic warfare range was established with realistic threat simulators. A Tactical Air Combat Training System (TACTS) was set up to provide real-time flight information, as well as post-flight mission analysis. VFA-127 moved onto the base in 1987, providing a permanent adversary unit for use on the ranges. Reserve VFC-13 would replace them nine years later.

By *Desert Storm* "Strike U" was an institution, and a lead member of the so-called "Desert Four"—the quartet of critical tactics development and training organizations in Naval Aviation (Miramar's *Topgun*, China Lake/VX-5, and the Marines' MAWTS-1 at Yuma).

On 11 July 1996 the **Naval Strike & Air Warfare Center** was established to formally merge NSWC and the two Miramar schools, *Topgun* and *Topdome* (CAEWS: Carrier Airborne Early Warning School) into one centralized "Aviation Center of Excellence" for the Navy at Fallon. As such, NSAWC continues these units' previous roles, as well as overseeing the syllabus development at local type training schools like Whidbey's Electronic Attack Weapons School (EAWS) and Strike Fighter Weapons Schools at both Oceana and Lemoore.

As of 2000 the organization was headed by a Rear Admiral who reported to the Chief of Naval Operations.[10] By now there were over 500 people assigned, including 130 officers and 280 enlisted.

NSAWC's influence on Naval Aviation cannot be understated. Its ability in performing its job should be judged by the combat success of Naval Aviation since its opening.

COMPRONS

Composite Squadrons (VC, or COMPRON) have gone through a number of forms over the years, with the "Composite" mission description changing at least three times since the start of World War II. Comprons initially flew TBM *Avengers* and FM *Wildcats* off escort carriers (CVEs) for Anti Submarine Warfare (ASW) or amphibious invasion support. From the late '40s they became special mission squadrons that supplied detachments to carriers for ASW, photo, electronic warfare, airborne early warning, night fighter, and attack, as well as other special mission areas. All of these units were redesignated between 1952 and 1956, and provided the basis for what became the VS, VFP, VAQ, VAW, and VAH communities.

What we now call Comprons were originally titled Utility (VU) squadrons. They were renamed in 1965, with the VC designation returning to denote their multi-role, fleet support mission. VCs were assigned to major training locations to provide mundane activities that included target sleeve towing, radar calibration, and range support. During the early 1960s these units flew a variety of airframes cast off from the fleet, including F-8A/B *Crusaders*, F-6A *Skyrays*, and early A-4 *Skyhawk* variants. By the mid-1980s most of the VC units were flying later versions of the A-4 *Skyhawk*, as well as H-3 *Sea Kings*, S-2 *Trackers*, and even P-2 *Neptunes*. From the mid-to-late '70s they also adopted the adversary mission, which most took on with gusto. Guantanimo VC-10 was also assigned a secondary

A TA-4J from Gitmo's Compron-Ten (JH10, 154315) is typical of the *Skyhawks* used worldwide by the Navy's composite squadrons. It's shown at Key West on 20 Sep '80. (author).

combat role to provide air defense and close air support to the base in the event of a Cuban attack, and periodically loaded up bombs and AIM-9 *Sidewinders* on their TA-4s to train for that mission.

Budget realities from the 1980s led to the Navy taking a serious look at finding other ways to carry out the Composite mission. The first two VCs to go were Miramar-based VC-7 and VC-2 at Oceana, both being disestablished in 1980, with their missions being covered by co-located Reserve units, or contractors flying Lear Jets or other similar aircraft. The post-*Desert Storm* drawdown led to the end of the remaining units. Puerto Rico's VC-8 would be the last one, being disestablished in 2003.

Regular Navy Composite Squadrons and 1974 aircraft

UA	VC-1	Barber's Point	A-4E, US-2, SH-3G, DP-2E	disestablished. 30 Sep 92
JE	VC-2	Oceana, Jax	A-4C/E,TA-4J, US-2,TS-2	disestablished 30 Sep 80
UE	VC-5	Naha, Cubi Point	A-4E, US-2, SH-3, DP-2E	disestablished 31 Aug 92
UC	VC-7	Miramar	A-4C, TA-4J	disestablished 30 Sep 80
GF	VC-8	Roosevelt Roads	A-4C,US-2,SH-3,DP-2E, EP-2H	disestablished 30 Sep 03
JH	VC-10	Guantanimo Bay	F-8K, US-2	disestablished 15 Aug 93

Reserve Composite Squadrons

JY, AF	VC-12	Detroit, Oceana	r/d VFC-12	22 Apr 88
UX, ND, AF	VC-13	N.Orleans, Miramar, Fallon	r/d VFC-13	22 Apr 88

Two VC units were formed in 1973 in the Naval Reserve. VC-12 was established with A-4L *Skyhawks* at NAF Detroit, while at New Orleans VC-13 was organized with F-8H *Crusaders* by the combination of two Anti-Submarine Fighter units, VSF-76 and -86. The *Fighting Omars* of VC-12 moved to NAS Oceana in 1975, where they quickly became an adversary unit, and were reequipped with A-4E/F and TA-4Js. In 1988 they were redesignated Fighter-Composite Squadron Twelve (VFC-12). The *Skyhawks* gave way to *Hornets* in 1993, which remained their mission aircraft into the 21st century.

The *Saints* of Compron-Thirteen transitioned to A-4Ls from April 1974, and moved to Miramar in February 1976. TA-4Js (1976) and A-4E/Fs (1983) were assigned as the squadron assumed a primary adversary role, supporting ComFitAEWWingPac *Tomcats* and *Phantoms*. As of the spring of 1989 they flew 14 *Skyhawks*, with a mix of TA-4Js and A-4Fs assigned. On 22 April 1988 the unit was redesignated VFC-13. FA-18A/B *Hornets* were assigned, and the *Skyhawks* retired in August 1993. In March-April 1996 they moved to Fallon, NV, in order to support Air Wing training, and took over VFA-127's F-5E/F *Tiger IIs* to carry out the work. The 1996 disestablishment of VFA-127 left the *Saints* as the only dedicated adversary squadron based at Fallon. The squadron wore unique UX tailcodes for years before joining CVWR-30 (ND code), and then CVWR-20 (AF) for administrative purposes.

The RAGS

The role of training aircrew and maintenance personnel for fleet duty falls to the Fleet Readiness Squadrons (FRS), which are also universally known as RAGs.[11] The RAG title comes from "Readiness Air Group," a term that has actually been obsolete since 23 December 1963, when the term Wing replaced Group in Navy terminology. The use of "RAG" has never waned, however, even over 40 years later, and it remains largely interchangeable with the term FRS in normal usage.

The RAG concept, at least in its modern form, dates from the advent of high performance jets to the fleet in the mid-1950s. Mishap rates were high and getting worse, and there was no standardized method of training nugget Naval Aviators coming out of Training Command in the hot new aircraft of the period. The existing path was for a freshly minted pilot to head directly to his fleet squadron, where he was typically handed a flight manual and told to study it prior to his first flight. Although some squadrons did this better than others, it was realized that a saner way had to be found to prepare new pilots for the fleet.

In the mid-'50s Moffett-based Composite Squadron-3 (VC-3) began to offer specialized training in a variety of new high-performance platforms (including the FJ, F3H, F4D, and F7U series) as Fleet Introduction Training for hand-picked individuals, who would then take their new knowledge into deploying units. VC-3, which became the first VF(AW)-3 in July 1956, showed that specialized type instruction was indeed the path to greater safety, and the Navy made plans to provide formal introductory instruction in all fleet aircraft.

In April 1958 two Air Groups (CVG-4 and CVG-12) were pulled from the fleet, and they became the basis for the new Readiness Carrier Air Groups (RCVGs). It is from these units that the RAG structure came that exists to this day (and why most of the AirPac FRSs are numbered in the 120 series). Over time there generally became one FRS on each coast for each type of aircraft in the fleet.

The Readiness Groups (RCVGs), which became Wings (RCVWs) in 1963, survived until December 1970, when they were disestablished, with the squadrons being assigned directly to Type Commanders under AirLant or AirPac supervision.

Under the RAG system, new Naval Aviators and NFOs would be assigned to an FRS after earning their "Wings of Gold." They would then go through a formal syllabus, where they obtained a NATOPS qualification in their aircraft, which is a rough Navy equivalent of a civilian type rating. Experienced aircrew returning to the fleet would

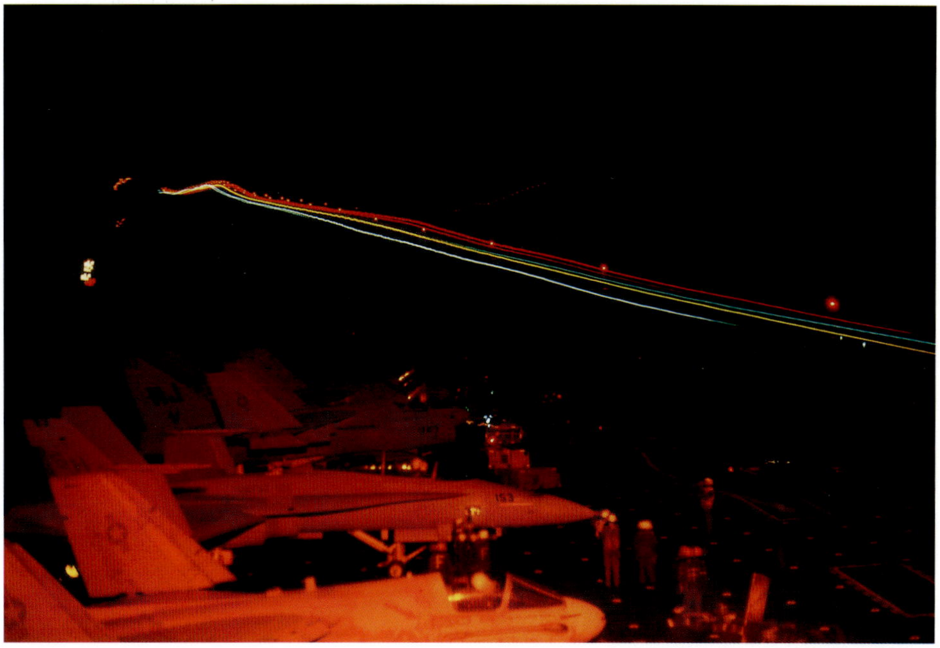

Although day carrier qualified in Training Command, the first time a Naval Aviator "sees the boat" at night is in the RAG. A replacement pilot's successful night qualification usually marks his graduation as a "nugget" fleet aviator. This time exposure was taken on *Independence* on 26 Aug 1989, and shows a VFA-125 F/A-18 during a night approach. At least two other *Hornets* are visible in the pattern—the F/A-18's red tail strobes standing out in the dark. The blob of white and red lights astern are from the planeguard frigate trailing the "Bird Farm." Replacement pilots from VA-122 and VMFAT-101 wait on the sidelines for their "turn in the barrel." (author)

also go through a shorter version of the program as well. Along with flight instruction, the RAGs also provide critical FRAMP training for enlisted maintenance personnel.

Each of the four Navy "Master Jet Bases" also had what was called an "Instrument RAG" attached to provide the annual instrument flight training required for all aviators. This program was a holdover from the 1950s, when the service spread night and foul weather carrier operations to the entire wing, and not just select units and aircrew.

VA-127's 1975 course was typical for the instrument squadrons. A newly minted "nugget" Ensign would receive a nine flight/18 hour syllabus prior to starting the *Corsair* RAG at Lemoore, almost all "under the bag" in the back seat of a TA-4. Fleet aviators would return to -127 for an annual refresher program that could include up to four hops, while requalifing for their "instrument card." Improvements in simulators, as well as the costs associated with flight, led the Navy to move a lot of this training indoors during the late 1970s, which allowed the Instrument RAGs to become dedicated adversary units.

Up to the 1990s, the Navy generally kept separate FRS for each type on each coast. Post *Desert-Storm* draw downs have led to only one training squadron per aircraft type, with roughly half of the squadrons subsequently being disestablished.

The RAGs are absolutely critical for fleet training. Development of the RAG concept is generally considered one of the three major influences on flight safety in post WWII tailhook aviation, ranking along the Naval Aviation Training & Operational Procedure Standardization (NATOPS) program, and the development of large angle-decked carriers with modernized launch and landing systems.

The two "Hummer" replacement squadrons took over the training duties for the similar C-2 *Greyhound* in 1985. Here one of each from VAW-110 is seen during CQ on *Indy* while off San Diego on 27 Aug '89. The COD over the ramp is a wee bit low, and seems to be trolling for a one-wire. (author)

VF-124 was the initial *Tomcat* RAG, getting its first "Turkeys" in 1972. One of their F-14As takes the two wire on *Indy* on 29 Aug '89 during CQ off San Diego. (author)

Carrier Aircraft Fleet Readiness Squadrons: July 1974

AirLant			AirPac		
VA-42	Oceana	A-6	VF-121	Miramar	F-4
VF-43	Oceana	instruments	VA-122	Lemoore	A-7E
VA-45	Cecil Field	instruments	VF-124	Miramar	F-14
VF-101	Oceana	F-4, F-14	VA-125	Lemoore	A-7A/B
VA-174	Cecil Field	A-7B/E	VF-126	Miramar	instruments
RVAW-120	Norfolk	E-2	VA-127	Lemoore	instruments
RVAH-3	Albany	RA-5C	VA-128	Whidbey Is.	A-6
VS-30	Quonset Pt.	S-2	VAQ-129	Whidbey Is.	EA-6B
HS-1	Jacksonville	SH-3	RVAW-110	North Is.	E-1, E-2
			VS-41	North Is.	S-3
			HS-10	North Is.	SH-3
			NARU	Alameda	A-3

The mighty "Whale" dominated the flight deck. While in the late 1950s and early '60s up to 10 would deploy with heavy attack squadrons, by the mid-'70s getting more than two on a carrier seemed to take an act of Congress. The *Firebirds* were the fifth, and final, A-3 *Skywarrior* FRS, and carried out carrier work with TA-3Bs up through 1989, as they trained pilots for VQ-1 and VQ-2. GD24 is shown headed for the bow cats on *Nimitz* on 14 Aug '80 during carrier qualifications. (author)

The Navy and Marines share three *Hornet* FRSs, with replacement pilots from both services going to VFA-106, -125, and VMFAT-101. Here three *Gladiator* F/A-18As and a single B are seen over the western desert on 22 May '87. They all carry the "Marines" title on their starboard side, befitting their dual service training role. (Bob Lawson)

As of 1974 most of the warfare communities had two RAGs, with one on each coast. There were single FRSs for the smaller *Vigilante*, *Skywarrior*, *Viking*, and *Prowler* communities. The A-3 duties were actually carried out by the Naval Air Reserve Unit (NARU) at Alameda, a role they only held until 1977, when the mission was transferred back to the Regulars at Norfolk's VAQ-33.

VS-30 was wrapping up its S-2 replacement duties, and would become a fleet S-3 squadron within a year. There were also four instrument RAGs—two on each coast as well, although the adversary role was rapidly increasing in importance. The E-2 community was alone in using the "R for readiness" designation (as in RVAW) for its RAGs. This lasted until 1983, when they were redesignated as "straight" VAWs. Within the *Vigilante* community, of course, the letter R in RVAH meant reconnaissance.

Several of the squadrons listed also had admin support aircraft assigned. See each of the individual squadron listings for more details on specific units.

Carrier Aircraft Fleet Readiness Squadrons: July 2000

AirLant			AirPac		
VF-101	Oceana	F-14A/B/D	VAQ-129	Whidbey Is.	EA-6B
VFA-106	Oceana	F/A-18A/BC/D	VFA-122	Lemoore	(F/A-18E/F)
VAW-120	Norfolk	E-2, C-2	VFA-125	Lemoore	F/A-18A/B/C/D
			HS-10	North Is.	SH-60F, HH-60H
			VS-41	North Is.	S-3B
	VMFAT-101	Miramar	F/A-18A/B/C/D		

By the end of 2000, the Navy had greatly reduced the number of FRSs it operated, with every community other than the F/A-18s having gone to a single site. The *Hornets* had three RAG locations, as Marine VMFAT-101 also trained Navy personnel, just as VFA-106 and -125 had Marine students. Newly established VFA-122 was still in the process of accepting its first F/A-18E/F *Super Hornets*, and had not yet started formal training.

At one time the Navy had four dedicated instrument training squadrons, with one being located at each of the "Master Jet Bases." These units conducted aircrew instrument refresher training with TA-4Js. VA-45 serviced the Atlantic Fleet's light attack community out of Cecil Field. A *Blackbird Skyhawk* taxis here at Corpus Christi, TX, on 9 Nov '79—note the instrument hood stowed in the aft cockpit. AD611 also carries a buddy store on centerline, although tanking was not a mission these units were typically known for. By the early 1980s the instrument role had been largely transferred to the mission FRSs, and the "instrument RAGs" had become adversary units. This aircraft (153460) would be lost while flying with TraWing-3 on 4 May 1983. (author)

6

Airborne Early Warning, Logistics (VAW, VRC)

"Frankly, I'd trade both of your aircraft for one Navy E-2"
- Navy Squadron Commander and strike package lead to an Air Force E-3 AWACS Lt Col. at a *Red Flag* exercise, Nellis AFB, NV, 1990.

Airborne Early Warning squadrons (VAW)
Although usually considered "support" squadrons, the Navy's Airborne Early Warning (AEW) units have long been the glue that tied the rest of the air wing together. The U.S. Navy invented the modern AEW business late in WWII, when it paired TBM *Avengers* with the APS-20 radar under Project *Cadillac*. Although they wouldn't see combat in that war, the Navy progressed through several "W for early warning" derivatives of the AD *Skyraider* (including the AD-3W, AD-4W, and AD-5W) before introducing the Grumman WF-2 *Tracer* in 1959. Also known with affection as the "Willy Fudd" or "Stoof with a Roof," the E-1B, as it was redesignated in 1962, served ably through Vietnam until its 1977 retirement.

The Navy first deployed the E-2A *Hawkeye* in 1966, and it overcame serious early developmental problems to become a superb system that remains in production over 40 years later. The "Hummer," so-called because of its filling-rattling turbo-prop resonance, has set the world standard for its warfare area ever since. It has been sold to seven countries, and has been produced in larger numbers than any other AEW platform in history. They have proved absolutely invaluable in the areas of fleet defense and strike control, and the community remains the Navy's experts in the area of command, control, and communications. When the E-2 *Hawkeye* series is finally retired (whenever that is), the type will hold the title as longest serving carrier aircraft in history.

Modern Airborne Early Warning (VAW) squadrons were formed in 1956, when the Navy took its two AEW-mission Composite squadrons VC-11 and VC-12 and renamed them VAW-11 and -12. These units provided three or four aircraft detachments to Pacific and Atlantic carriers, respectively, until April 1967, when their dets became distinct, four-aircraft squadrons for each air wing. The resulting community expansion led to the current arrangement, where Atlantic Fleet units are numbered in the 120 series, while Pacific Fleet squadrons are found in the 110s. Since then there have been at least 18 Regular and five Reserve VAW squadrons formed to carry out the mission. The East Coast VAW community has been based at Norfolk, Virginia, throughout its existence, while their AirPac counterparts have moved sequentially from North Island to Miramar (1975) and Pt Mugu (1998).

As of 1974, the E-2B was the most common variant of the *Hawkeye*, being assigned to nine squadrons that were supported by two FRSs. Two fleet E-1B units, as well as the AirPac RAG, still covered the 27Cs and two of the *Midway* class decks. The E-2C had been introduced by Norfolk's VAW-123 in late 1973; however, in an odd bit of logistical planning, the Pacific Fleet carriers were the first equipped to support the "C," so several Norfolk E-2C units made Westpacs, while four California-based B-squadrons deployed to the Med. It was not until 1983 that all CONUS E-2 units were equipped with the "C" model. Since then the type has gone through several incremental changes (also called "spirals" in Pentagonese) that have

Bluetail E-2C AG600 (160703) is shown in flight near Fallon on 19 May '87 in a dramatic photo taken by Bob Lawson.

led to descriptive terms like E-2C+ ("E-2C PLUS"), "Group I," and "Group II." The specifics of these modifications really require a separate book to explain, so all will be referred to as simply E-2Cs in this work.

Along with normal carrier duty, VAW squadrons have been heavily used in the counter-drug mission, typically sending detachments to places like Roosevelt Roads, PR, to work with U.S. Customs, the Drug Enforcement Agency (DEA), and the Coast Guard. Some units have also been shore based for short periods to Keflavik, Iceland, where they spelled USAF E-3 *Sentries* by conducting NATO and NORAD AEW duties.

E-2 squadrons have used a bewildering array of nicknames through the years, which has made accurate tracking of their identities a real challenge. Some use formal nicknames, while others have adopted tactical call signs for the same purpose. Squadron insignias have also changed frequently. VAW-117 has gone through at least four name changes over 25 years, and the Norfolk RAG (VAW-120) has had three different official insignias. VAW-124's famed and non-politically correct "Bear Aces" logo featuring a female derriere was all but the official design for many years, even if Washington, DC, never approved it as such. In 1985 VAW-113 changed their familiar *Black Eagle* (which some squadron members called the "soul parrot") design to a modish double-headed eagle motif (the "psychedelic chicken"), which only lasted two cruises before a new CO brought back the original design. Other examples are listed under specific squadrons.

Naval Reserves

The Reserves formed four VAW units with E-1Bs in 1970, one for each of their CVWRs and CVSGRs. When the two ASW groups were disestablished in 1975, their two early warning squadrons were re-equipped with E-2Bs, and they replaced the two CVWR outfits, which were disestablished. A fifth reserve unit was established for land-based counter-drug operations in 1995.

VAW-77 — ***Night Wolves*** — **Atlanta** — **Naval Reserve**

E-2C

Estab. 1 Oct 1995

Formed in 1995 specifically as a non-carrier based unit for the purpose of conducting counter-drug operations. Assigned the AF 00 tailcode.

VAW-78 — ***Fighting Escargot*** — **Norfolk** — **Naval Reserve**

E-1B, E-2B, E-2C

Estab. 1 Jul 1970

VAW-78 was formed with E-1Bs in 1970 as part of CVSGR-70. In 1975, when the rest of the group was being disestablished, the Naval Reserve decided to re-equip both VAW-78 and its West Coast CVSGR-80 counterpart VAW-88 with *Hawkeyes*, and move them to the Reserve Carrier Air Wings CVWR-20 and -30. VAW-78 received the first Reserve E-2Cs in April 1983. The whimsically named *Escargot*, which came from the "shell" above their original "Willy Fudds," have been the AEW component of CVWR-20 for over a quarter century now.

VAW-88 — ***Cotton Pickers*** — **North Island, Miramar** — **Naval Reserve**

E-1B, E-2B, E-2C

Estab. 1 Jun 1970, disestab. 31 Dec 1994

The *Cotton Pickers* followed the same path as VAW-78, being the only fixed-wing survivors of CVSGR-80, and replacing the E-1B unit in CVWR-30 (VAW-307) in 1975. The *'Pickers* retired the last E-2B in service (151724, ND012) on 24 Sep '86, as they transitioned to the E-2C. They were disestablished with the balance of their wing in 1994.

RVAW-110, VAW-110 — ***Firebirds*** — **North Island, Miramar** — **FRS**

E-1B, E-2B, E-2C, TE-2A, TE-2C, C-2A

Estab. RVAW-110 20 Apr 67, r/d VAW-110 1 May 1983 disestab. 30 Sep 1994

18 Oct 73 to 5 Jun 74	*Oriskany*	E-1B	WP/IO	NM010	det 6	from VAW-111
5 Dec 74 to 2 Jul 75	*Coral Sea*	E-1B	WP	NL 010	det 3	
18 Mar 75 to 20 Oct 75	*Hancock*	E-1B	WP	NP 010	det 6	
16 Sep 75 to 3 Mar 76	*Oriskany*	E-1B	WP	NM 010	det 4	
4 Oct 76 to 21 Apr 77	*F.D. Roosevelt*	E-1B	Med	NM 010	det 4	

The AirPac AEW training squadron, the peculiar "RVAW" designation dates from the squadron's 1967 establishment, where the "R" was assumed to stand for "Replacement."[12] The squadron would retain this title until redesignated VAW-110 in May 1983. In 1974 both FRSs took over the duties of completing the training of prospective Naval Flight Officers (NFOs) in the AEW business, which allowed training squadron VT-86 to retire the EC-121 *Warning Stars* it had used in that role for years. The unit moved from North Island to Miramar in July 1975, where it joined FitAEWWingPac. Aircraft were assigned the "TT" tailcode, which they wore until 1980, when they switched to the West Coast standard "NJ" RAG code.

RVAW-110 provided the last E-1B detachments to the fleet after assuming that role from VAW-111 on 29 Mar '74, gaining two detachments in the deal. They continued deploying "Fudd" dets until retiring the type from deployed service in 1977. The E-2C arrived in April 1980, and from December 1980 the squadron took over Pacific Fleet C-2 training from VRC-30. VAW-110 was disestablished in September 1994 when the Navy decided to center all E-2 training at VAW-120 in Norfolk.

In a really peculiar piece of immortality, director Tony Scott chose to use VAW-110's blue and red "diving bird" insignia for the fictional "VF-1" in the movie "Top Gun," and it became the patch worn by "Maverick" (Tom Cruise) and "Goose" (Anthony Andrews) as they took on "MiG-28s" and Naval Authority. VAW-110's insignia would be later modified slightly and adopted by the East Coast RAG, VAW-120.

VAW-111 (1)	***(Grey Berets, Hunters) Seabats***		**North Island, Miramar**			
E-1B, E-2B						
Estab. 1 Apr 67	Disestab. 1 Jun 77 July					
8 May 73 to 8 Jan 74	*Hancock*	E-1B	WP	NP010	det 2	
18 Oct 73 to 5 Jun 74	*Oriskany*	E-1B	WP/IO	NM010	det 6	to RVAW-110
5 Mar to 22 Sep 75	*Forrestal*	E-2B	Med	AA700		

Formed in 1967 to provide all E-1B *Tracer* detachments to the Pacific Fleet. The original nickname refers to the appearance of the E-1's radome. It, and *Hunters*, appears to have been in use prior to 1974, as subsequent documents use only the *Seabat* nickname. The squadron transitioned to E-2Bs in 1974, with RVAW-110 making the final deployments for the "Fudd." The last two dets were transferred to the RAG 29 Mar '74. The first *Seabat* E-2B arrived in August '74. VAW-111 made only one full squadron deployment with *Hawkeyes*, to the Med in Feb. They were detached from CVW-17 on 25 June '76, and remained at Miramar for another year before being disestablished.

VAW-111 (2)	***Sea Bats***	**Miramar**		
E-2C				
Estab. 1 Oct 1986	disestab. 30 Apr 1988			
(1987-88)	*Independence*	(no cruise)	E-2C	NM600

Established with CVW-10 in 1986, the second version of VAW-111 made no deployments before being disestablished.

VAW-112	***Golden Hawks***	**North Island, Miramar, Pt Mugu**		
E-2B, E-2C				
Estab. 20 Apr 1967				
7 May to 18 Oct 74	*Ranger*	WP	E-2B	NE010
30 Jan to 7 Sep 76	*Ranger*	WP/IO	E-2B	NE600
1 Dec 77 to 20 Jul 78	*Nimitz*	Med/NL	E-2B	AJ010
10 Sep 79 to 26 May 80	*Nimitz*	Med/IO	E-2B	AJ010
20 Oct 81 to 23 May 82	*Constellation*	WP/IO	E-2C	NG600
15 Jul 83 to 29 Feb 84	*Ranger*	SoPac/WP/IO	E-2C	NG600
24 Jul to 21 Dec 85	*Kitty Hawk*	WP/IO	E-2C	NG600
3 Jan to 29 Jun 87	*Kitty Hawk*	World	E-2C	NG600
2 Sep 88 to 2 Mar 89	*Nimitz*	WP/IO	E-2C	NG600
12 Feb to 7 Apr 90	*Constellation*	Horn	E-2C	NG600
15 Jun 89 to 9 Jul 90	*Nimitz*	NorPac	E-2C	NG600

A section of VAW-112 *Golden Hawk* E-2Cs are shown low over the Sierra Nevadas on 30 May 1981, not long after the squadron had transitioned from B-models. (Bob Lawson)

25 Feb to 24 Aug 91	*Nimitz*	WP/IO/PG	E-2C	NG600	
2 Feb to 29 Jul 93	*Nimitz*	WP/IO/PG	E-2C	NG600	
27 Nov 95 to 20 May 96	*Nimitz*	WP/IO/PG	E-2C	NG600	
1 Sep 97 to 1 Mar 98	*Nimitz*	WP/IO/PG	E-2C	NG600	
7 Jan to 3 Jul 00	*JC Stennis*	WP/IO/PG	E-2C	NG600	

After having been established in 1967, VAW-112 was inactive between May 1970 and July 1973, and made its "return engagement" deployment in *Ranger* in 1974. From 1977 to 1980 the squadron was assigned to AirLant's CVW-8, where it made the second and third deployments of the new nuke carrier *Nimitz*. The unit returned to the Pacific Fleet in 1981, and transitioned to E-2Cs. It's been assigned to CVW-9 ever since.

VAW-113 ***Black Eagles*** **North Island, Miramar, Pt Mugu**

E-2B, E-2C

Estab. 30 Apr 1967

17 Sep 74 to 20 May 75	*Enterprise*	WP/IO	E-2B	NK600	
30 Jul 76 to 27 Mar 77	*Enterprise*	WP/IO	E-2B	NK600	
4 Apr to 30 Oct 78	*Enterprise*	WP/IO	E-2B	NK600	
30 Sep 79 to 20 Feb 80	*Coral Sea*	WP/IO	E-2B	NK600	
20 Aug 81 to 23 Mar 82	*Coral Sea*	WP/IO	E-2B	NK600	
21 Mar to 12 Sep 83	*Coral Sea*	WP/IO	E-2B	NK600	
21 Feb to 24 Aug 85	*Constellation*	WP/IO	E-2C	NK600	
11 Apr to 13 Oct 87	*Constellation*	WP/IO	E-2C	NK600	
1 Dec 88 to 1 Jun 89	*Constellation*	WP/IO	E-2C	NK600	
16 Sep to 10 Oct 89	*Constellation*	NorPac	E-2C	NK600	
23 Jun to 20 Dec 90	*Independence*	WP/IO/PG	E-2C	NK600	*Desert Shield*
5 to 22 Aug 91	*Independence*	Hawaii	E-2C	NK600	
28 Aug to 14 Sep 91	*Midway*	Swapex	E-2C	NK600	
18 Feb to 15 Aug 94	*Carl Vinson*	WP/IO/PG	E-2C	NK600	
14 May to 14 Nov 96	*Carl Vinson*	WP/IO/PG	E-2C	NK600	
11 Jun to 7 Dec 98	*Lincoln*	WP/IO/PG	E-2C	NK600	
14 Aug 00 to 12 Feb 01	*Lincoln*	WP/IO/PG	E-2C	NK600	

The *Black Eagles* are unusual for a West Coast squadron, in that they have made all of their deployments with a single air wing, and never deployed on an AirLant ship. They were the last CONUS-based E-2B unit in the service, finally getting E-2Cs in 1984. The 1991 trip to Hawaii and back was part of the "swapex" between *Midway* and *Independence*.

VAW-114 ***Hormel Hogs*** **North Island, Miramar**

E-2B, E-2C

Estab. 20 Apr 1967, Disestab. 31 March 1995

23 Nov 73 to 9 Jul 74	*Kitty Hawk*	WP/IO	E-2B	NH010
21 May to 15 Dec 75	*Kitty Hawk*	WP	E-2B	NH010
15 Feb to 5 Oct 77	*Coral Sea*	WP	E-2B	NL600
30 May 79 to 25 Feb 80	*Kitty Hawk*	WP/IO	E-2C	NL600
1 Apr to 23 Nov 81	*Kitty Hawk*	WP/IO	E-2C	NL600
1 Mar 83 to 29 Oct 83	*Carl Vinson*	World	E-2C	NL600
18 Oct 84 to 25 May 85	*Carl Vinson*	WP/IO	E-2C	NL600
12 Aug 86 to 5 Feb 87	*Carl Vinson*	WP/IO	E-2C	NL600
15 Jun to 14 Dec 88	*Carl Vinson*	WP/IO	E-2C	NL600
5 Sep to 8 Nov 89	*Carl Vinson*	WP/IO	E-2C	NL600
1 Feb to 31 Jul 90	*Carl Vinson*	WP/IO	E-2C	NL600
18 Oct to 11 Dec 91	*Kitty Hawk*	Horn	E-2C	NL600
3 Nov 92 to 3 May 93	*Kitty Hawk*	WP/IO/PG	E-2C	NL600
24 Jun to 22 Dec 94	*Kitty Hawk*	WP/IO/PG	E-2C	NL600

VAW-114 drew upon its "Hormel" callsign, with its meat packing company connotation, and combined it with a version of the University of Arkansas' "Razorback" image to form its nickname, the *Hormel Hogs*. In June 1978 they became the first Miramar-based E-2C squadron. The colorful *Hogs* were the only "old" E-2 unit disestablished in the post *Desert Storm* draw down, disappearing into history along with a majority of CVW-15.

VAW-115 ***Sentinels, Liberty Bells*** **Atsugi**

E-2B, E-2C

Estab. 20 Apr 67

Jan 1974 to Sum-1975	*Midway*	forward deployed	E-2B	NF010
Sum 1975 to Spr 1985	*Midway*	forward deployed	E-2B	NF600
Spr 1985 to August 1991	*Midway*	forward deployed	E-2C	NF600 *D. Storm*
Aug 91 to Jul 98	*Independence*	forward deployed	E-2C	NF600
Jul 98 to 2001	*Kitty Hawk*	forward deployed	E-2C	NF600

VAW-115 is the sole "forward deployed" VAW unit, being attached to CVW-5 throughout the period covered in this book. (See the CVW-5 listings in chapter 2 for specific at sea periods.) The *Liberty Bells* were the last E-2B squadron in the regular Navy, turning in their "Bravos" around March 1985. In 1991 the unit participated in Operation *Desert Storm*.

VAW-116 ***Sun Kings*** **North Island, Miramar, Pt Mugu**

E-2B, E-2C

Estab. 20 Apr 1967

21 Jun to 22 Dec 74	*Constellation*	WP/IO	E-2B	NG	
16 Jul to 24 Sep 75	*Nimitz*	Carib/NL	E-2B	AJ710	
7 Jul 76 to 7 Feb 77	*Nimitz*	Med	E-2B	AJ010	
4 Apr to 26 Oct 78	*Forrestal*	Med	E-2B	AA010	
26 Feb to 14 Oct 80	*Constellation*	WP/IO	E-2C	NG600	
7 Apr to 19 Oct 82	*Ranger*	WP/IO	E-2C	NE600	
13 Jan to 1 Aug 84	*Kitty Hawk*	WP/IO	E-2C	NE600	
18 Aug to 20 Oct 86	*Ranger*	NorPac	E-2C	NE600	
3 Mar to 29 Apr 87	*Ranger*	NP/WP	E-2C	NE600	
14 Jul to 29 Dec 87	*Ranger*	WP/IO	E-2C	NE600	
24 Feb to 24 Aug 89	*Ranger*	WP/IO	E-2C	NE600	
9 Dec 90 to 8 Jun 91	*Ranger*	WP/IO/PG	E-2C	NE600	*Desert Storm*
1 Aug 92 to 31 Jan 93	*Ranger*	WP/IO/PG	E-2C	NE600	
29 May to 22 Jul 93	*Constellation*	Horn	E-2C	NE600	
10 Nov 94 to 10 May 95	*Constellation*	WP/IO/PG	E-2C	NE600	
1 Apr to 1 Oct 97	*Constellation*	WP/IO/PG	E-2C	NE600	
18 Jun to 17 Dec 99	*Constellation*	WP/IO/PG	E-2C	NE600	

The *Sun Kings* made four deployments in the mid to late 1970s with E-2Bs, three of which were with Atlantic Fleet carriers and air wings. After transitioning to "Cs" they have made multiple trips to West Pac, all but one with CVW-2. The 1990-91 deployment was punctuated by Operation *Desert Storm*.

VAW-117 ***Gamecocks, Wallbangers, Lemurs, Nighthawks*** **Miramar, Pt Mugu**

E-2B, E-2C

Established 1 July 1974

15 Oct 75 to 5 May 76	*Independence*	Med	E-2B	AG770	
31 Mar to 21 Oct 77	*Independence*	Med	E-2B	AG600	
21 Feb to 22 Sep 79	*Ranger*	WP	E-2B	NE600	
10 Sep 80 to 4 May 81	*Ranger*	WP/IO	E-2B	NE600	
1 Sep 82 to 23 Mar 83	*Enterprise*	WP/IO	E-2C	NH600	
30 May to 20 Dec 84	*Enterprise*	WP/IO	E-2C	NH600	
15 Jan to 12 Aug 1986	*Enterprise*	WP/IO/Med/SL	E-2C	NH600	
25 Oct to 24 Nov 87	*Enterprise*	NorPac	E-2C	NH600	
5 Jan to 3 Jul 88	*Enterprise*	WP/IO	E-2C	NH600	*P. Mantis*
17 Sep 89 to 16 Mar 90	*Enterprise*	WP/IO	E-2C	NH600	
25 Sep to 20 Nov 90	*Lincoln*	Horn	E-2C	NH600	
28 May to 28 Nov 91	*Lincoln*	WP/IO/PG	E-2C	NH600	
15 Jun to 15 Dec 93	*Lincoln*	WP/IO/PG	E-2C	NH600	
10 Apr to 9 Oct 95	*Lincoln*	WP/IO/PG	E-2C	NH600	
11 Oct 96 to 11 Apr 97	*Kitty Hawk*	WP/IO/PG	E-2C	NH600	
6 Nov 98 to 6 May 99	*Carl Vinson*	WP/IO/PG	E-2C	NH600	

VAW-117 was established in 1974, and made its first two deployments to the Mediterranean as part of an AirLant CVW. Since then the squadron has made a succession of deployments to the Western Pacific and Indian Ocean areas. The 1988 deployment in Enterprise included action during Operation *Praying Mantis*.

VAW-117 has gone through a number of nicknames, and at least three logos. The original *Gamecock* insignia was used with the *Wallbanger* tactical call sign until 1978, when they adopted the Lemur—a small, nocturnal, and generally unobtrusive creature with big eyes—as their image. By 1984 the cute fuzzy animal was gone, replaced by a new name (*Nighthawks*) and insignia with a generic flying bird motif. VAW-117 was the last Miramar-based *Hawkeye* unit to move to Pt. Mugu, officially arriving on 6 Nov '98.

RVAW-120, VAW-120 *Cyclones, Grey Hawks* **Norfolk**
E-2B, E-2C, TE-2A, TE-2C, C-2A
Estab. RVAW-120 1 Jul 1967, r/d VAW-120 1 May 1983
The AirLant E-2 RAG since 1967, many of the comments about RVAW/VAW-110 apply to 120 as well. The C-2 training role arrived in July 1985, which led to a new name combining both types of aircraft (*Greyhounds* and *Hawkeyes*), and an equally new logo. The original design featured a hawk flying over an open book, which reflected "By the book" FRS training. It was replaced in 1986 by a blazing sun device with a hawk and silhouettes of both platforms. By 2004 the unit had changed again, and adopted the slightly modified insignia of the old West Coast RAG, VAW-110. Originally assigned a "GE" tailcode, the unit adopted the AirLant "AD" FRS tailcode in 1980.

VAW-121 *Palmettos, Griffons, Bluetails,* **Norfolk**
E-1B, E-2B, E-2C
Estab. 1 Apr 1967

14 Sep 73 to 17 Mar 74	*FD Roosevelt*	Med	E-1B	AE710
3 Jan to 16 Jul 75	*FD Roosevelt*	Med	E-1B	AE710.
16 Jan to 13 Jul 79	*Eisenhower*	Med	E-2C	AG010
15 Apr to 22 Dec 80	*Eisenhower*	IO	E-2C	AG010
20 Aug to 7 Oct 81	*Eisenhower*	NL	E-2C	AG600
5 Jan to 13 Jul 82	*Eisenhower*	Med	E-2C	AG600
27 Apr to 2 Dec 83	*Eisenhower*	Med	E-2C	AG600
8 May to 20 Jun 84	*Eisenhower*	Med	E-2C	AG600
10 Oct 84 to 8 May 85	*Eisenhower*	Med	E-2C	AG600
29 Feb to 29 Aug 88	*Eisenhower*	Med	E-2C	AG600
8 Mar to 12 Sep 90	*Eisenhower*	Med/RS	E-2C	AG600
26 Sep 91 to 2 Apr 92	*Eisenhower*	Med	E-2C	AG600
20 May to 17 Nov 94	*G Washington*	Med	E-2C	AG600
26 Jan to 23 Jul 96	*G Washington*	Med/RS/PG	E-2C	AG600
26 Feb to 26 Aug 98	*JC Stennis*	World	E-2C	AG600

A handful of E-2As were rebuilt into TE-2Cs, which were used for pilot training. 148712 was actually the fifth *Hawkeye* built, and folds its wings after trapping on *Nimitz* on 14 Aug '80. The squadron still carries its unique GE tailcode, as well as its original RVAW title at this time. A rendition of the Meritorious Unit Commendation (MUC) ribbon is painted below the unit insignia. (author)

18 Feb to 18 Aug 00	*Eisenhower*	Med/RS/PG	E-2C	AG600	

The *Bluetails* started out the period as the only Atlantic Fleet E-1B squadron, and made two deployments with the "Fudd" before being held in inactive status for a three year period. The squadron was re-manned in 1977, and assigned new E-2C *Hawkeyes* for assignment to CVW-7, where it has remained ever since. The *Palmetto* name dates from their tactical call sign while an E-1 unit. *Griffon* is the formal nickname, and relates to the squadron insignia; however, *Bluetail*, a latter callsign, has become the unit's most widely used title.

VAW-122 — ***Hummergators, Steeljaws*** — **Norfolk**

E-2B, E-2C

Estab. 1 Apr 1967, disestab. 31 Mar 1996 (15 Mar ceremony)

21 Jul 73 to 19 Jan 74	*Independence*	Med	E-2B	AG720	
19 Jul 74 to 21 Jan 75	*Independence*	Med	E-2B	AG720	
25 Oct 77 to 15 May 78	*Kitty Hawk*	WPAC	E-2C	NH605	
28 Jun to 14 Dec 79	*Independence*	Med	E-2C	AE720	
19 Nov 80 to 10 Jun 81	*Independence*	Med/IO	E-2C	AE720	
7 Jun to 22 Dec 82	*Independence*	Med	E-2C	AE600	
18 Oct 83 to 11 Apr 84	*Independence*	Med	E-2C	AE600	Grenada/Lebanon
16 Oct 84 to 19 Feb 85	*Independence*	Med/IO	E-2C	AE600	
2 Jun 86 to 10 Nov 86	*Forrestal*	Med	E-2C	AE600	
25 Apr 88 to 7 Oct 88	*Forrestal*	Med/IO/NL	E-2C	AE600	
4 Nov 89 to 12 Apr 90	*Forrestal*	Med	E-2C	AE600	
30 May 91 to 21 Dec 91	*Forrestal*	Med	E-2C	AE600	
29 May to 22 Jul 93	*Constellation*	Horn	E-2C	(-) 600	(with CVW-2)

VAW-122's initial nickname was *Hummergators*, which referred to both the squadron's E-2 "Hummer" aircraft, and the standard fighter data link of the day, which went by the title "Alligator." The unit was the last Norfolk based VAW to deploy with E-2Bs, and made two Med cruises before joining CVW-11 in *Kitty Hawk* in 1977 with new E-2Cs for a deployment to the Western Pacific. Around 1980 the squadron took advantage of the late-'70s craze over the movie "Jaws" to replace the unique, if somewhat odd, *Hummergator* nickname with their *Steeljaw* callsign. The unit simultaneously adapted the logo of the World Hockey Association's Los Angeles Sharks for their new insignia, although the Navy did not officially recognize the new design until 1985. The *Steeljaws* continued to deploy with CVW-6 until that wing was disestablished. Its last deployment in *Forrestal* was notable, in that the unit lost an E-2C (161343) on 8 July '91 to in-flight engine fire, the crew of five bailing out successfully. The aircraft was subsequently shot down by a VFA-132 *Hornet*, undoubtedly as a "hazard to navigation." The squadron subsequently operated in a land-based counter-narcotics role until 1993, when it joined portions of CVW-2 as it accompanied *Constellation* on her post-SLEP cruise around the Horn. Returning home, VAW-122 continued the counter-drug mission to places like Guantanimo, Panama, Curacao, and Puerto Rico until disestablished in 1996. The squadron's aircraft were wearing the E-2 wing's old GE tailcode at the end.

VAW-123 — ***Screwtops*** — **Norfolk**

E-2C

Estab. 1 Apr 1967

27 Sep 74 to 19 Mar 75	*Saratoga*	E-2C	Med	AC730	
6 Jan to 28 Jul 76	*Saratoga*	E-2C	Med	AC730	
11 Jul to 23 Dec 77	*Saratoga*	E-2C	Med	AC720	
3 Oct 78 to 5 Apr 79	*Saratoga*	E-2C	Med	AC010	
10 Mar to 27 Aug 80	*Saratoga*	E-2C	Med	AC010	
14 Apr to 12 Nov 81	*America*	E-2C	Med/IO	NH600	
23 Aug to 30 Oct 1982	*America*	E-2C	NL/Med/Carib	AB600	
8 Dec 82 to 2 Jun 83	*America*	E-2C	Med/IO	AB600	
24 Apr to 14 Nov 84	*America*	E-2C	Med/IO	AB600	
10 Mar to 19 Sep 86	*America*	E-2C	Med	AB600	Libya ops
8 Feb to 3 Apr 89	*America*	E-2C	NorLant	AB600	
11 May to 10 Nov 89	*America*	E-2C	Med/IO	AB600	
28 Dec 90 to 18 Apr 91	*America*	E-2C	Med/RS/PG	AB600	*Desert Storm*
2 Dec 91 to 6 Jun 92	*America*	E-2C	Med	AB600	
11 Aug 93 to 5 Feb 94	*America*	E-2C	Med/RS/PG	AB600	

28 Aug 95 to 24 Feb 96	*America*	E-2C	Med/RS/PG	AB600	
3 Oct 97 to 3 Apr 98	*G Washington*	E-2C	Med/RS/PG	AB600	
15 Sep 99 to 19 Mar 00	*JF Kennedy*	E-2C	Med/RS/PG	AB600	

VAW-123 was the first E-2C squadron in the Navy, acquiring the type in Nov 1973. The unit made multiple trips to the Med and IO, once with West Coast-based CVW-11. The *Screwtops* are famed for the spiral design they have painted on the tops of the radomes.

VAW-124 — ***Bulls Eye Hummers, Bear Aces*** — **Norfolk**

E-2B, E-2C

Estab. 1 Sep 1967

3 Jan to 3 Aug 74	*America*	E-2B	Med	AJ740	
15 Apr to 25 Oct 76	*America*	E-2C	Med	AE720	
10 Jun to 19 Jun 77	*America*	E-2C	SoLant	AE720	
25 Sep 77 to 25 Apr 78	*America*	E-2C	Med	AE720	
13 Mar to 22 Sep 79	*America*	E-2C	Med	NH600	
3 Aug 81 to 12 Feb 82	*Nimitz*	E-2C	Med	AJ010	
10 Nov 82 to 20 May 83	*Nimitz*	E-2C	Med	AJ010	
8 Mar to 4 Oct 85	*Nimitz*	E-2C	Med	AJ600	
30 Dec 86 to 26 Jul 87	*Nimitz*	E-2C	World	AJ600	
25 Aug to 11 Oct 88	*T Roosevelt*	E-2C	NorLant	AJ600	
30 Dec 88 to 30 Jun 89	*T Roosevelt*	E-2C	Med	AJ600	
28 Dec 90 to 28 Jun 91	*T Roosevelt*	E-2C	Med/RS/PG	AJ600	*Desert Storm*
11 Mar to 8 Sep 93	*T Roosevelt*	E-2C	Med/RS	AJ600	
22 Mar to 22 Sep 95	*T Roosevelt*	E-2C	Med/RS/IO	AJ600	
29 Apr to 28 Oct 97	*JF Kennedy*	E-2C	Med/RS/PG	AJ600	
26 Mar to 22 Sep 99	*T Roosevelt*	E-2C	Med/RS/PG	AJ600	

VAW-124 spent the period in four air wings and on five carriers, all in the Atlantic Fleet, although the 1979 deployment was to the Med with Pacific Fleet CVW-11. The *Bulls Eye Hummer* title was replaced by a name that officially referred to the squadron's ability to direct the interception of Soviet TU-95 "Bear" aircraft. Nonetheless, the unit is perhaps best known for its unofficial insignia, with a woman's bare bottom featured on their earlier bulls-eye ("dart board") design, and their "Bear Aces" name with its obvious double entendre.

VAW-125 — ***Ringmasters, Torchbearers, Tiger Tails*** — **Norfolk**

E-2B, E-2C

Estab. 1 Oct 1968

28 Jun 75 to 27 Jan 76	*JF Kennedy*	E-2C	Med	AB750	
2 Sep to 9 Nov 76	*JF Kennedy*	E-2C	Med	AB750	
15 Jan to 1 Aug 77	*JF Kennedy*	E-2C	Med	AB750	
29 Jun 78 to 8 Feb 79	*JF Kennedy*	E-2C	Med	AB010	
27 Nov 79 to 7 May 80	*Forrestal*	E-2C	Med	AA010	
2 Mar to 15 Sep 81	*Forrestal*	E-2C	Med	AA010	
8 Jun to 16 Nov 82	*Forrestal*	E-2C	Med	AA600	
2 Apr to 20 Oct 84	*Saratoga*	E-2C	Med	AA600	
26 Aug 85 to 16 Apr 86	*Saratoga*	E-2C	Med/IO	AA600	
5 Jun to 17 Nov 87	*Saratoga*	E-2C	Med	AA600	
15 Aug to 8 Oct 88	*Independence*	E-2C	Horn	AA600	
7 Aug 90 to 28 Mar 91	*Saratoga*	E-2C	Med/RS	AA600	*Desert Storm*
6 May to 6 Nov 92	*Saratoga*	E-2C	Med	AA600	
12 Jan to 24 Jun 94	*Saratoga*	E-2C	Med	AA600	
28 Jun to 20 Dec 96	*Enterprise*	E-2C	Med/RS/PG	AA600	
10 Jun to 10 Dec 98	*Eisenhower*	E-2C	Med/RS/PG	AA600	
21 Jun to 19 Dec 00	*G Washington*	E-2C	Med/RS/PG	AA600	

VAW-125 was the east coast's first E-2B unit (in 1970), and the second to receive E-2Cs, going through transition in 1974. They used at least three nicknames between 1974 and 2000. During *Desert Storm* a *Tiger Tail* aircraft provided initial warning and control to a division of VFA-81 *Hornets* that led to the downing of a pair of MiG-21s.

VAW-126 ***Closeouts, Sea Hawks*** **Norfolk**

E-2B, E-2C

Estab. 1 Apr 1969

11 Mar to 6 Sep 74	*Forrestal*	E-2B	Med	AA760	
6 Sep to 3 Oct 74	*America*	E-2B	NorLant	AA760	with CVW-8
12 Apr to 21 Nov 77	*Constellation*	E-2C	WP	NG600	
26 Sep 78 to 17 May 79	*Constellation*	E-2C	WP/IO	NG600	
4 Aug 80 to 28 Mar 81	*JF Kennedy*	E-2C	Med	AB600	
25 May to 1 Jul 83	*JF Kennedy*	E-2C	Med	AB600	
4 Jan to 14 Jul 82	*JF Kennedy*	E-2C	IO	AC600	
27 Sep 83 to 2 May 84	*JF Kennedy*	E-2C	Med	AC600	
18 Aug 86 to 3 Mar 87	*JF Kennedy*	E-2C	Med	AC600	
2 Aug 88 to 1 Feb 89	*JF Kennedy*	E-2C	Med	AC600	
15 Aug 90 to 28 Mar 91	*JF Kennedy*	E-2C	Med/RS	AC600	*Desert Storm*
7 Oct 92 to 7 Apr 93	*JF Kennedy*	E-2C	Med	AC600	
20 Oct 94 to 15 Apr 95	*Eisenhower*	E-2C	Med/RS/PG	AC600	
25 Nov to 22 May 97	*T Roosevelt*	E-2C	Med/RS/PG	AC600	
6 Nov 98 to 6 May 99	*Enterprise*	E-2C	Med/RS/PG	AC600	
28 Nov 00 to 23 May 01	*HS Truman*	E-2C	Med/RS/PG	AC600	

VAW-126 had their 1974 deployment increased by a month, as the squadron cross-decked from the *Forrestal* to the *America* to support a pick-up version of CVW-8 for a NATO exercise. Returning home, they transitioned to E-2Cs and introduced the type to the Pacific Fleet with a pair of deployments in *Constellation*.. The squadron changed its name to the *Seahawks* in 1979, *Closeout* probably having been the unit's tactical call sign.

VAW-127 ***Seabats*** **Norfolk**

E-2C

Estab. 2 Sep 83 disestab. 30 Sep 91

2 Oct 85 to 19 May 86	*Coral Sea*	E-2C	Med	AK600	Libya raids
29 Sep 87 to 28 Mar 88	*Coral Sea*	E-2C	Med	AK600	
31 May 89 to 30 Sep 89	*Coral Sea*	E-2C	Med	AK600	

Formed in 1983 as a member of the new CVW-13, VAW-127 made only three deployments before it was disestablished. It performed with distinction during combat against Libya during its first cruise. The squadron adopted a name and insignia very similar to the original AirLant AEW unit, VAW-12.

VAW-207 **Norfolk** **Naval Reserve**

E-1B

Estab. 1 Jul 1970 Disestab. 1 Sep 1974

An original part of CVWR-20, VAW-207 was disestablished in favor of VAW-78 in 1974 after having served for five years. Normal squadron strength was four E-1Bs. No squadron nickname appears for either VAW-207 or -307 in their official historical records.

VAW-307 **North Island** **Naval Reserve**

E-1B

Estab. 1 Jul 1970 Disestab. 1 Sep 74

Formed as a charter member of CVWR-30 in 1970, VAW-307 was disestablished only four years later when it was replaced in the wing by VAW-88. The squadron lost one aircraft (147232) that was forced to ditch on 13 July '72. Amazingly, the "Fudd" floated, and it was towed to land by a ship, although salt water damage resulted in a strike assessment.

Fleet Tactical Support Squadrons, Fleet Logistics Support Squadrons (VRC/VR)

"The COD is overhead with 800 pounds of mail"

- Carrier announcement of immeasurable morale value

The Navy's logistic support squadrons technically come in both land based (VR) and carrier-capable (VRC) flavors, although at least two units carried out both functions. Known throughout the fleet as CODs (for Carrier On-board Delivery), these aircraft rarely get much press, but they provide essential service to the fleet by expediting people, mail, and high priority cargo. These unheralded units deserve a lot of credit for routinely operating large aircraft safely on and off carriers while carrying over 20 passengers at a time, which is a remarkable achievement by any standard.

Initially called Fleet Tactical Support Squadrons, they became Fleet Logistics Support Squadrons, with no change in designation, on 1 April 1976.

As of 1974 the Navy had four VR/VRC units providing COD services on a regional basis (one each East Coast, West Coast, Med, and Western Pacific). These units used Grumman C-1A *Traders* and C-2A *Greyhounds* to ply their business, which included passengers, critical parts, and all important mail delivery. Most were also assigned land based logistical support aircraft, such as C-130s and/or T-39s, for theater support. Each carrier typically had a C-1 assigned as well for its own use, but as these were attached to the carrier itself and not the air wing, they will not be detailed here.

The reciprocating-engined *Traders* were beached through the late '80s, as Avgas was removed from the carriers, with the last one (146048, assigned to *Lexington*) being retired in September 1988. In the early 1990s the four COD squadrons were reduced to two, and a C-2 det was assigned directly to the Air Wing, with their aircraft carrying CVW tailcodes while deployed.

The C-1 could carry seven passengers, as well as up to 3500 pounds of mail or cargo. The C-2 has an aft cargo ramp and a cavernous cargo hold that could take up to five tons of palletized cargo (up to and including jet engines), or a skid with 26 passenger seats on it. Flying in a *Greyhound* is not an enjoyable experience for most tailhook aviators, who don't like being stuffed in a dark hole while sitting backwards in an uncomfortable seat with only two tiny windows to look out of. Nonetheless, a ride in the COD remained the quickest way to or from the beach from the boat, and could be either an "E-ticket ride," or stark terror, particularly for non-aviators.

Six US-3A "Miss Piggys" were modified from S-3A *Vikings* and attached to VRC-50 for mail, high priority cargo, and passenger service to serve Arabian Sea carriers from Diego Garcia, BIOT. The first of these (157998) was converted by Lockheed in September 1975. The US-3A had all of its ASW gear removed, and could carry over 4000lbs of cargo, as well as three crew and five passengers. As an aside, there were no ejection seats installed as, of course, it would have been considered bad form for the pilots to jump out on their passengers for whatever reason.

The initial US-3A was flown by AirPac VS squadrons in WestPac and IO from September 1976 through March 1982, with transfers usually being conducted in theater. The "host" squadron would provide maintenance and aircrew for the bird. At least two of these units (VS-33 and VS-38) actually painted the aircraft in full squadron markings (as NH712 and NK712, respectively). The airframe was also used as a ship's COD on at least two boats (*Midway* and *Constellation*) before moving to VRC-50. Around 1980 she was given a simple overall white scheme with an American flag on the tail, while retaining the 712 side number.

Dubbed "Miss Piggy" after the Muppets character, in February 1981 the US-3A proved its value as a long range COD asset, hauling

The first US-3A bounced around the Pacific Fleet for several years before being assigned to VRC-50, where it was joined by five sisters. 157998 is shown at Cubi Point, PI, in October 1979, while assigned to the *Midway* as a COD. The small oval window behind the cockpit and lack of wingtip antennas is the quick visual reference for this type. The large cargo pods could be carried by all S-3s. These ones carry U.S. Postal Service stickers, as well as lettering that states "In COD we trust." (Rick Burgess)

passengers, high priority cargo, and mail between Diego Garcia and carriers operating in the Arabian Sea. Five more S-3As were converted to US-3As by NARF Alameda from April 1982, and all would be assigned to VRC-50 at Cubi Point. Although most, if not all, received Muppets related names and nose art (including "Kermit" and "Gonzo"), they still collectively retained the "Miss Piggy" title. The US-3As served admirably until transferred to VS-41 for a short period of time in 1994 before heading for retirement in the Arizona desert.

The Navy's other VR squadrons, those that operated land-based transports exclusively, are beyond the scope of this book.

VR-24 ***World's Biggest Little Airline, Lifting Eagles*** **Naples/Rota, Sigonella**
C-1A, C-2A, CT-39, C-130F, RH-53D JM tailcode
Estab. 1 Sep 1948 disestab. 31 Jan 93 (29 Jan ceremony)
VR-24 provided COD and other freight and passenger hauling services to 6th Fleet carriers in the Mediterranean. In January 1976, after years of being based at both Naples and Rota (and with detachments all over the Med), it moved to Sigonella, while changing its nickname at about the same time. As of 1980 squadron strength included three CT-39G, four C-130F, six C-1A, five C-2A, and three RH-53D, which were used in the vertical lift role. In 1984 the C-1s were retired, and the C-130s were spun off to become VR-22. The squadron itself was disestablished in 1993, as VRC-40 COD detachments attached directly to the Air Wings started deploying to cover the mission for Atlantic Fleet carriers.

VR-30, VRC-30 ***Providers*** **Alameda, North Island**
C-1A, C-2A, CT-39, UC-12B RW tailcode
Estab. VR-30 1 Oct 1966, r/d VRC-30 1 Oct 1978
VRC-30 provides COD services for the operations areas off San Diego, as well as VIP flights for AirPac. Since 1988 it has sent C-2 detachments to all deploying AirPac airwings, as well. C-1s were replaced by C-2s by late 1981, and VRC-30 became the sole Greyhound unit in AirPac with the Oct 1994 disestablishment of VRC-50. The squadron was named the C-12 FRS for the Navy in October 1980. Detachment 5 was established at Atsugi, Japan, in Aug 1994 to support CVW-5.

VRC-40 ***Rawhides*** **Norfolk**
C-1A, C-2A, CT-39E JK tailcode
Estab. VRC-40 1 Jul 1960
The *Rawhides* were the Atlantic Fleet counterpart to VRC-30. The squadron went by the title "Cod Fish Airlines" in earlier times. As of Jan 1974 the squadron rostered 11 C-1As. Transition from the C-1A to the C-2A was complete in 1986. VRC-40 has been providing AirLant CVWs with C-2 detachments since the early 1990s.

VRC-30 provided COD service to carriers off the West Coast. Here a C-1A prepares to start on *Constellation* prior to its return flight to North Island on 16 Mar 1986. At this time *Traders* usually deck launched (without a catapult), as the carriers tried to discourage use of the bridle style catapult system. (author)

A *Foo Dog* C-2A *Greyhound* is over *Constellation's* ramp on 20 Apr 1985 while in the IO. Mail Call for the crew is not far away. (author)

VRC-50 *Foo Dogs* **Cubi Point, Andersen AFB**
C-1A, C-2A, US-3A, CT-39E, C-130F RG tailcode
Estab. 1 Oct 1966 disestablished 7 Oct 1994

The *Foo Dogs* flew a variety of aircraft throughout the Pacific region from their home in the Philippines. As of 1977 squadron inventory stood at three C-130F, two CT-39E, six C-1A, and seven C-2A. Between 1981 and '94 the squadron was the sole operator of the five US-3A "Miss Piggys," which were primarily used between D-Gar and carriers in the Gulf of Oman and Persian Gulf. During *Desert Storm* the squadron used Fujairah, UAE, as a forward base for C-2 flights, where they connected with Military Airlift Command activities. On 1 Aug 1992 the squadron moved from the Philippines to Andersen AFB, Guam, partially as a result of the eruption of Mt Pinatubo and its impact on U.S. operations in the PI, as well as the general withdrawal of U.S. forces from the country. They were disestablished only two years later.

7

Electronic Warfare, Tanking (VAQ, VAK, VQ)

"When you jam a radar you're working against the operator as much as the machine. The best jamming is when the guy behind the scope doesn't even realize his picture is being denied." - Prowler ECMO

Tactical Electronic Warfare/ Electronic Attack Squadrons (VAQ) The Navy's "Q for electronic countermeasures" title for aircraft dates from 1945, while the actual use of the VAQ (Tactical Electronic Warfare, or TACELRON) squadron designation was only initiated in 1968. Prior to that year, active jamming "radio countermeasures" was an niche mission, and folded into the VAW role or, as in Korea, sprinkled among attack units. By the late '60s the proliferation of threat radar systems and, particularly, deadly surface-to-air missiles (SAMs) had established an unarguable need for a separate EW community.

As of 1974 the six-year old community was only 24 months into the *Prowler* era, with five deployable units trying to cover 12 air wings, two squadrons in training, and one Alameda-based "Whale" squadron making its last deployments.[13]

39 EKA-3Bs had been modified at Alameda from KA-3B *Skywarrior* tankers from 1967 to replace the Navy's obsolete EA-1F "Queer Spads" still fighting in Vietnam. Not to be confused with the seven-man, ELINT-mission EA-3B, the EKA-3B possessed a powerful array of jammers operated by a three-man (one pilot, two NFOs) crew. The aircraft also had 20,400 lbs (3,045 gallons) of fuel available for aerial refueling through its internal hose-drum unit. The EKA-3B proved to be an interim EW aircraft, as it served only seven years before being completely replaced by the EA-6B.

Grumman built 170 *Prowlers* between 1969 and 1991, making it the most numerous dedicated electronic warfare aircraft ever procured by the U.S. military. 164403, the final airframe, was delivered on 29 July 1991, and lasted a decade before it suffered a massive engine failure/fire and crashed off North Carolina on 21 Nov 2001 while assigned to VMAQ-1.

Prowler squadrons spent most of the '70s and early '80s spread thin while jumping between Air Wings. This shortfall was so severe that several carriers deployed without EW assets during the period. The most extreme example of this constant rotation was VAQ-135 which, in 1982, was allowed only two weeks home between six-month deployments to the Med. It would not be until 1985 that every CVW had a VAQ assigned to it.

A VAQ-129 ICAP I executes a section takeoff from Whidbey's runway 25 on 13 May 1987. The gear is coming up and, passing 185 knots, the lead aircraft will give the signal to retract the flaps. NJ921 (158649) is being flown by instructor Lt. George "Rockhead" Rockwell, who would later rise to command VR-61. A replacement ECMO is in the right seat. The back end is occupied by a solo student in the ECMO-2 seat. (author)

In 1998 the EA-6B assumed the duties as the only tactical radar jamming platform for the entire Department of Defense when the USAF retired the last of its EF-111A *Ravens*. Four new "expeditionary" *Prowler* squadrons were established to cover this mission (see sidebar).

From April to June 1999 Navy *Prowlers* operated "Electronic Attack Wing Aviano" alongside the Air Force's 31st FW/AEW at Aviano, Italy. This temporary, and unofficial, organization was built from a core of EA-6Bs and crews from VAQ-138, -140, and -209, and also included volunteers from a number of other units and schoolhouses, such as VAQ-129, Electronic Attack Weapons School, and Strike U. Characterized as a *Prowler* "Rainbow Coalition," the wing carried out combat operations against the former Yugoslavia during Operation *Allied Force*. The collocated Marine EA-6B units remained largely independent through the same operation, at their insistence.

Squadron titles were changed from Tactical Electronic Warfare Squadrons (TACELRON) to Electronic Attack Squadrons (VAQRON) on 30 March 1998, although the VAQ designation remained unchanged. It should be noted that VMAQs did not make a similar change, choosing instead to retain the "Marine Tactical Electronic Warfare Squadron" title, something that even "official" sources have occasionally missed.

The EA-6B deployed in four major variants between 1974 and 2001: Standard (std), Expanded Capability (EXCAP), Improved Capability (initially just ICAP, later ICAP I), and Improved Capability II (ICAP II), which includes the Block 82, 86, and 89 sub-variants. The type's criticality to joint warfare was demonstrated in both *Desert Storm* and over Bosnia, when other aircraft were not allowed to enter threat envelopes without jamming or other SEAD aircraft in support.

VAQ units normally deployed with only four airframes, and began the period using a number of different modex series that were usually assigned at the Air Wing level. They could be found wearing 610, 620, 630, and 700 numbers, with the individual aircraft typically being numbered from, say, 610 through 613. By 1982 the 604 series was adopted as the VAQ standard, with aircraft being numbered above the E-2s as 604 through 607. In 1985 some units moved to the 620 series (620 through 624) in anticipation of five aircraft, although some of these outfits still deployed with only four. In 1997-98 VAQ units were moved Navy-wide to the 500 series numbers (500 to 503) vacated by the end of the *Intruder* community.

VAQ-128 *Fighting Phoenix* **Whidbey Island**

EA-6B

established 1 Oct 1997

Sep to Dec 98	4404th Wg	Prince Sultan SA	EA-6B	ICAP II	NL670	*Southern Watch*
Dec 99 to Mar 00	39th AEW	Incirlik TU	EA-6B	ICAP II	NL510	*Northern Watch*
Oct 00 to Jan 01	39th AEW	Incirlik TU	EA-6B	ICAP II	NL510	*Northern Watch*

VAQ-128 was the last expeditionary EA-6B squadron to be formed, with its title, name (including the former VA-128 "fenix" callsign), and logo referring specifically to the former A-6 *Intruder* RAG, although officially it is a completely unrelated unit. The squadron made land-based deployments in support of Combatant Commanders overseas.

VAQ-129 *Vikings* **Whidbey Island** **FRS**

EA-6B

Established VAH-10 1 May 60, r/d VAQ-129 1 Sep 70

VAQ-129 began the decade as a deploying EKA-3B squadron with two detachments at sea; however, the unit had already been identified as the new EA-6B RAG with deliveries beginning in 1971. VAQ-132 was the first squadron to go through the new syllabus, with VAQ-131 following. By mid-1974 the squadron had eight aircraft assigned, and was supporting five four-plane fleet squadrons (VAQ-131, -132, -133, -134, -136), with two more in training (VAQ-130 and -135). The *Vikings* increased in size with the community, with its typical strength around 18 airframes. The Marines arrived for training in 1977, and by 1998 the *Prowler* family stood at its zenith: 16 Navy (10 fleet, 4 expeditionary, 1 reserve, 1 FRS) and four Marine squadrons. VAQ-129 used the former VAQWING-13 "TR" tailcode until about 1974, when it switched to the standard AirPac FRS "NJ" markings. Side numbers were originally in the 900 series, and moved to 650 to 699 (1992) and 500 series (1999) to more closely match fleet numeration.

VAQ-130 *Zappers* **Alameda, Whidbey Island**

EKA-3B, KA-3B, TA-3B, EA-6B

Estab. VAW-13 1 Sep 59 r/d VAQ-130 1 Oct 68

8 May 73 to 8 Jan 74	*Hancock*	WP/IO	EKA-3B	NP610	det 5
1973 to 19 Jan 74	*Independence*	Med	EKA-3B	AG610	det 1
18 Oct 73 to 5 Jun 74	*Oriskany*	WP/IO	EKA-3B	NM 610	det 3
(1974)	(*Ranger*)	(no cruise)	EKA-3B	NE610	det 4
15 Jul to 24 Sep 75	*Nimitz*	Carib/NL	EA-6B std	AJ610	
7 Jul 76 to 7 Feb 77	*Nimitz*	Med	EA-6B std	AJ610	
4 Apr to 26 Oct 78	*Forrestal*	Med/NorLant	EA-6B ICAP I	AA610	
28 Jun to 14 Dec 79	*Independence*	Med	EA-6B ICAP I	AE700	
2 Mar to 15 Sep 81	*Forrestal*	Med	EA-6B ICAP I	AA610	

8 Jun to 16 Nov 82	*Forrestal*	Med	EA-6B ICAP I	AA604	
13 Jan to 1 Aug 84	*Kitty Hawk*	WP/IO	EA-6B ICAP I	NE604	
24 Jul to 21 Dec 85	*Kitty Hawk*	WP/IO	EA-6B ICAP I	NG604	
3 Jan to 29 Jun 87	*Kitty Hawk*	World	EA-6B ICAP II	NG604	
2 Aug 88 to 1 Feb 89	*JF Kennedy*	Med	EA-6B ICAP II	AC604	
15 Aug 90 to 28 Mar 91	*JF Kennedy*	Med/RS	EA-6B ICAP II	AC620	*Desert Storm*
7 Oct 82 to 7 Apr 93	*JF Kennedy*	Med	EA-6B ICAP II	AC620	
Aug to Sep 1993	Aviano IT	NATO	EA-6B ICAP II	AC620	*Deny Flight*
20 Oct 94 to 15 Apr 95	*Eisenhower*	Med/RS/PG	EA-6B ICAP II	AC620	
25 Nov 96 to 22 May 97	*T Roosevelt*	Med/RS/PG	EA-6B ICAP II	AC620	
6 Nov 98 to 6 May 99	*Enterprise*	Med/RS/PG	EA-6B ICAP II	AC500	*Desert Fox*
28 Nov 00 to 23 May 01	*HS Truman*	Med/RS/PG	EA-6B ICAP II	AC500	

The *Zappers* are the oldest Navy tactical jamming squadron in existence, tracing their lineage back to VAW-13's establishment in 1959. Since then they have been in combat with EA-1F and EKA-3B aircraft, as well as EA-6B *Prowlers*. As of January 1974 the *Zappers* had three *Skywarrior* dets underway, with a fourth working up for a summer deployment with *Ranger*/CVW-2. *Hancock's* det actually started out as a part of VAQ-135, but transferred to the *Zappers* in August 1973. Det 1 had been in the Med since April 1973, having deployed with JFK/CVW-1 before cross-decking to *Indy* at some point in order to keep EW capability in the area during the '73 Arab-Israeli conflict. The *Ranger* det was pulled from the wing just prior to cruise, making det 3, in *Oriskany*, the last EKA-3B deployment in the Navy. The move also signaled the end of VAQ-130's other role as the A-3 FRS, which transferred to NARU Alameda.

VAQ-130 moved to Whidbey, and started EA-6B transition as the last of the original six A-3 flying VAQ squadrons to do so. Initially equipped with Standard *Prowlers*, the unit joined CVW-8 and deployed to the Med in *Nimitz*. Since then the squadron has made numerous deployments to both coasts, and saw combat in *Desert Storm* and *Desert Fox*. In 1993 the *Zappers* made a short land-based deployment to Italy to support NATO operations over Bosnia as part of *Deny Flight*.

VAQ-131 *Lancers* **Whidbey Island**

EA-6B

Reserve VP931 act.2 Sep 1950. r/d VP-57 4 Feb 1953, r/d VAH-4 3 Jul 1956, r/d VAQ-131 1 Nov 68.

21 Jun to 22 Dec 74	*Constellation*	WP/IO/PG	EA-6B	Std	NG610	
6 Jan to 28 Jun 76	*Saratoga*	Med	EA-6B	EXCAP	AC604	
25 Oct 77 to 15 May 78	*Kitty Hawk*	WP	EA-6B	EXCAP	NH620	
13 Mar to 22 Sep 79	*America*	Med	EA-6B	ICAP I	NH620	
19 Nov 80 to 19 Jun 81	*Independence*	Med/IO	EA-6B	ICAP I	AE700	
7 Jun to 22 Dec 82	*Independence*	Med	EA-6B	ICAP I	AE604	
18 Oct 83 to 11 Apr 84	*Independence*	Med	EA-6B	ICAP I	AE604	
16 Oct 84 to 19 Feb 85	*Independence*	Med/RS/IO	EA-6B	ICAP I	AE604	
18 Aug to 20 Oct 86	*Ranger*	NorPac/WPac	EA-6B	ICAP II	NE604	
3 Mar to 29 Apr 87	*Ranger*	NorPac	EA-6B	ICAP II	NE604	
14 Jul to 29 Dec 87	*Ranger*	WP/IO	EA-6B	ICAP II	NE604	
24 Feb to 24 Aug 89	*Ranger*	WP/IO	EA-6B	ICAP II	NE604	
8 Dec 90 to 8 Jun 91	*Ranger*	WP/IO	EA-6B	ICAP II	NE620	*Desert Storm*
1 Aug 92 to 31 Jan 93	*Ranger*	WP/IO/PG	EA-6B	ICAP II	NE620	
10 Nov 94 to 10 May 95	*Constellation*	WP/IO/PG	EA-6B	ICAP II	NE620	
Nov, Dec 1996	31st FW	Aviano Italy	EA-6B	ICAP II	NE620	
1 Apr to 1 Oct 97	*Constellation*	WP/IO/PG	EA-6B	ICAP II	NE620	
Jun to Aug 98	4404th AEW(P)	Prince Sultan SA	EA-6B	ICAP II	NE500	
26 Jun to 11 Jul 99	MAG 12	Iwakuni, JA	EA-6B	ICAP II	NE500	
11 Jul to 17 Dec 99	*Constellation*	WP/IO/PG	EA-6B	ICAP II	NE500	

Dating from 1950, the *Lancers* are the oldest squadron in the VAQ community, although they've only been in the jamming business since 1968, when they received EKA-3Bs. They were the second EA-6B unit to deploy, and have subsequently been equipped with every version of *Prowler*. The squadron participated in combat operations over Grenada (*Urgent Fury*) and Lebanon during their 1983-84 deployment, and with five aircraft in *Desert Storm*. In 1996 they deployed to Aviano, Italy, to cover Operation *Deny Flight* operations. The squadron spent the summer of 1998 in Saudi Arabia on temporary duty supporting a Provisional Air Force Air Expeditionary Wing (AEW(P)). In 1999 the *Lancers* proceeded CVW-2 and *Constellation* to West Pac, and spent three weeks at Iwakuni, Japan, prior to joining the ship and air wing on deployment.

VAQ-132 *Scorpions* **Whidbey Island**
EA-6B
Est. VAH-2 1 Nov 55, r/d VAQ-132 1 Nov 68

19 Jul 74 to 21 Jan 75	*Independence*	Med	EA-6B	EXCAP	AE700	
15 Oct 75 to 5 May 76	*Independence*	NL/Med	EA-6B	EXCAP	AE710	
12 Apr to 21 Nov 77	*Constellation*	WP	EA-6B	EXCAP	NG620	
26 Sep 78 to 17 May 79	*Constellation*	WP/IO	EA-6B	EXCAP	NG620	
15 Apr to 22 Dec 80	*Eisenhower*	IO	EA-6B	ICAP I	AG610	
20 Aug to 7 Oct 81	*Eisenhower*	NL	EA-6B	ICAP I	AG604	
5 Jan to 13 Jul 82	*Eisenhower*	Med	EA-6B	ICAP I	AG604	
27 Apr to 2 Dec 83	*Eisenhower*	Med	EA-6B	ICAP I	AG604	
8 May to 20 Jun 84	*Eisenhower*	NorLant	EA-6B	ICAP I	AG604	
10 Oct 84 to 8 May 85	*Eisenhower*	Med	EA-6B	ICAP I	AG604	
2 Jun to 10 Nov 86	*Forrestal*	Med	EA-6B	ICAP I	AE604	
25 Apr to 7 Oct 88	*Forrestal*	Med/IO/NL	EA-6B	ICAP I	AE604	
7 Aug 90 to 28 Mar 91	*Saratoga*	Med/RS	EA-6B	ICAP II	AA604	*Desert Storm*
6 May to 6 Nov 92	*Saratoga*	Med	EA-6B	ICAP II	AA604	
12 Jan to 24 Jun 94	*Saratoga*	Med	EA-6B	ICAP II	AA620	
28 Jun to 20 Dec 96	*Enterprise*	Med/RS/PG	EA-6B	ICAP II	AA620	
10 Jun to 10 Dec 98	*Eisenhower*	Med/RS/PG	EA-6B	ICAP II	AA620	
Mar to Jul 99	363rd AEW	Prince Sultan SA	EA-6B	ICAP II	AA500	
21 Jun to 18 Dec 00	*G Washington*	Med/RS/PG	EA-6B	ICAP II	AA500	

The "Arachnids" were the first EA-6B unit to deploy (in *America* in 1972), and have subsequently flown every *Prowler* version. They were heavily engaged in *Desert Storm* from *Saratoga*. In 1999 they made a four-month deployment to Saudi Arabia to cover *Southern Watch* commitments.

VAQ-133 (1) *Wizards* **Whidbey Island**
EA-6B
Est. 4 Mar 69, disestab. 1 Jun 1992

3 Jan to 3 Aug 74	*America*	Med	EA-6B	EXCAP	AJ610
28 Jun 75 to 27 Jan 76	*JF Kennedy*	Med	EA-6B	EXCAP	AB700
15 Jan to 1 Aug 77	*JF Kennedy*	Med	EA-6B	EXCAP	AB610
29 Jun to 8 Feb 79	*JF Kennedy*	Med	EA-6B	EXCAP	AB610
27 Nov 79 to 7 May 80	*Forrestal*	Med	EA-6B	EXCAP	AA610
14 Apr to 12 Nov 81	*America*	Med/IO	EA-6B	EXCAP	NH620
1 Sep 82 to 23 Mar 83	*Enterprise*	WP/IO	EA-6B	EXCAP	NH604
30 May to 20 Dec 84	*Enterprise*	WP/IO	EA-6B	ICAP II	NH604
15 Jan to 12 Aug 1986	*Enterprise*	WP/IO/Med/SL	EA-6B	ICAP II	NH604
29 Sep 87 to 28 Mar 88	*Coral Sea*	Med	EA-6B	ICAP II	AK604
31 May to 30 Sep 89	*Coral Sea*	Med	EA-6B	ICAP II	AK604
30 May to 21 Dec 91	*Forrestal*	Med	EA-6B	ICAP II	AE620

The *Wizards* were the fourth fleet EA-6B unit to deploy, and the first to the Med. They would also make the first and last EXCAP deployments. In spite of their many years of service, the first VAQ-133 never participated in sustained combat operations as a *Prowler* squadron. In late 1986 they were moved to CVW-13, becoming their first permanently assigned VAQ unit. (VAQ-135 having been temporarily assigned during the previous cruise.) When it became apparent in 1989 that CVW-13 was to be shut down, VAQ-133 was switched to CVW-6, and VAQ-142 became the unit sacrificed. The move only bought the *Wizards* an additional deployment and two years before they too were disestablished.

VAQ-133 (2) *Wizards* **Whidbey Island**
EA-6B
Estab 1 Apr 1996

Jan to Jun 97	MAG 12	Iwakuni, JA	EA-6B	ICAP II	NL630
Jul to Dec 98	39th AEW	Incirlik, TU	EA-6B	ICAP II	NL530
Mar to Apr 99	363rd AEW	Prince Sultan SA	EA-6B	ICAP II	NL530
Apr to Jul 00	363rd AEW	Prince Sultan SA	EA-6B	ICAP II	NL530

The second VAQ-133 was formed as an expeditionary unit in the spring of 1996, adopting the name, logo, and traditions of its predecessor. It has subsequently made multiple land-based deployments.

VAQ-134 ***Garudas*** **Whidbey Island**
EA-6B
Estab. 17 Jun 69

5 Mar to 22 Sep 75	*Forrestal*	Med	EA-6B	EXCAP	AA610
30 Jul 76 to 28 Mar 77	*Enterprise*	WP/IO	EA-6B	EXCAP	NK620
4 Apr to 30 Oct 78	*Enterprise*	WP/IO	EA-6B	ICAP I	NK620
10 Sep 79 to 26 May 80	*Nimitz*	Med/IO	EA-6B	ICAP I	AJ610
20 Oct 81 to 23 May 82	*Constellation*	WP/IO	EA-6B	ICAP I	NG604
1 Mar to 29 Oct 83	*C Vinson*	World	EA-6B	ICAP I	NL604
18 Oct 84 to 25 May 85	*C Vinson*	WP/IO	EA-6B	ICAP I	NL604
12 Aug 86 to 5 Feb 87	*C Vinson*	WP/IO	EA-6B	ICAP I	NL604
15 Jun to 14 Dec 88	*C Vinson*	WP/IO	EA-6B	ICAP I	NL604
5 Sep to 8 Nov 89	*C Vinson*	WP/NorPac	EA-6B	ICAP I	NL604
1 Feb to 31 Jul 90	*C Vinson*	WP/IO	EA-6B	ICAP II	NL604
18 Oct to 11 Dec 91	*Kitty Hawk*	Horn	EA-6B	ICAP II	NL604
3 Nov 92 to 3 May 93	*Kitty Hawk*	WP/IO/PG	EA-6B	ICAP II	NL620
24 Jun to 22 Dec 94	*Kitty Hawk*	WP/IO/PG	EA-6B	ICAP II	NL620
May to Nov 96	MAG 12	Iwakuni, JA	EA-6B	ICAP II	NL620
Dec 97 to Jun 98	39th AEW	Incirlik TU	EA-6B	ICAP II	NL640
23 Feb to 7 Mar 99	31st AEW	Aviano, IT	EA-6B	ICAP II	NL640
24 Mar to 22 Apr 99	31st AEW	Aviano, IT	EA-6B	ICAP II	NL640
Jun to Sep 99	39th AEW	Incirlik TU	EA-6B	ICAP II	NL540
Jul to Oct 00	363rd AEW	Prince Sultan SA	EA-6B	ICAP II	NL540

Named after an Indonesian deity, the *Garudas* were another former "Whale" unit moved to Whidbey for *Prowlers*. The curious choice of nicknames reportedly came about when the first CO flew the Asian airline of the same name in 1969, and he subsequently decided to use it for his new outfit's title. The unit would survive the shut-down of CVW-15 in 1995, and became the first expeditionary unit in VAQWING, subsequently making several trips overseas in support of Joint operations. They retained the CVW tailcode, which became the *de facto* code used for all subsequent "concrete" *Prowler* units. In 1999 the unit made two short trips to Aviano, although they were not present for what became *Allied Force*.

VAQ-135 ***Black Ravens*** **Whidbey Island**
EA-6B
Estab. 15 May 69

30 Jan to 7 Sep 76	*Ranger*	WP/IO	EA-6B	Std	NE630	
1 Dec 77 to 20 Jul 78	*Nimitz*	Med/NL	EA-6B	ICAP I	AJ610	
30 May 79 to 25 Feb 80	*Kitty Hawk*	WP/IO	EA-6B	ICAP I	NL620	
1 Apr to 23 Nov 81	*Kitty Hawk*	WP/IO	EA-6B	ICAP I	NL604	
23 Aug to 30 Oct 82	*America*	NL/Med/Carib	EA-6B	ICAP I	AB604	
10 Nov 82 to 20 May 83	*Nimitz*	Med	EA-6B	ICAP I	AJ604	
24 Apr to 14 Nov 84	*America*	Med/RS/IO	EA-6B	ICAP I	AB604	
2 Oct 85 to 19 May 86	*Coral Sea*	Med	EA-6B	ICAP I	AK620	Libya
25 Oct to 24 Nov 87	*Enterprise*	NorPac	EA-6B	ICAP I	NH604	
5 Jan to 3 Jul 88	*Enterprise*	WP/IO	EA-6B	ICAP I	NH620	*Praying Mantis*
17 Sep 89 to 16 Mar 90	*Enterprise*	World	EA-6B	ICAP II	NH604	
25 Sep to 20 Nov 90	*Lincoln*	Horn	EA-6B	ICAP II	NH620	
28 May to 28 Nov 91	*Lincoln*	WP/IO/PG	EA-6B	ICAP II	NH620	
15 Jun to 15 Dec 93	*Lincoln*	WP/IO/PG	EA-6B	ICAP II	NH620	
10 Apr to 9 Oct 95	*Lincoln*	WP/IO/PG	EA-6B	ICAP II	NH620	
6 Nov 98 to 6 May 99	*C Vinson*	WP/IO/PG	EA-6B	ICAP II	NH500	*Desert Fox*
May to Aug 00	39th AEW	Incirlik, TU	EA-6B	ICAP II	NH500	

The *Black Ravens* were the next-to-last EKA-3B unit to move to Whidbey for *Prowler* transition, transferring in 1973, and making its first *Prowler* deployment about three years later. Although the *Black Ravens* had always used an insignia featuring a blackbird, its nickname was only officially adopted after arrival at Whidbey, and actually came from one of the squadron's A-3 detachments (the Alameda unit using its *Homebrew* callsign as a nickname between 1969 and 1973). They made the first EA-6B ICAP cruise, in 1977, on a deployment that also saw the loss of their Skipper, CDR Pete Rodderick, along with his three crewmembers, when the aircraft left the *Nimitz* on a routine day event and never returned. In 1982 the squadron came home in October, only to deploy for another Med cruise two weeks later in *Nimitz*, which was undoubtedly the shortest turnaround in *Prowler* history. On New Years Eve 1986 they were ordered to the Mediterranean to join CVW-13 mid-cruise in *Coral Sea*. Because it was alerted to move on such short notice only two of the squadron's five aircraft were actually its own, as VAQs-132, -138, and -139 all contributed singles to make the commitment. Only three were usually kept onboard the ship, however, due to space limitations, the others being kept at Sigonella. They subsequently performed with distinction in combat off Libya. For the 1988 deployment the Ravens provided jamming support for CVW-11 aircraft and other naval units involved in Operation *Praying Mantis* in the Persian Gulf. The 1998 cruise included combat in Operation *Desert Fox*. In 2000 the squadron deployed to Incirlik, Turkey, on a temporary basis in the expeditionary role in support of *Northern Watch*. The *Black Raven* insignia has gone through three changes, initially featuring a hook-nosed fowl with a largely solid wing. In the early-1980s the unit softened up the bird's beak, and by 1985 the wing had been feathered as well, making the creature look somewhat more like a black canary than a true raven.

VAQ-136	***Gauntlets***	**Whidbey Island, Atsugi**				
EA-6B						
Estab. 6 Apr 1973						
23 Nov 73 to 9 Jul 74	*Kitty Hawk*	WP/IO	EA-6B	Std	NH610	
21 May to 15 Dec 75	*Kitty Hawk*	WP	EA-6B	Std	NH610	
31 Mar to 21 Oct 77	*Independence*	Med	EA-6B	Std	AG614	
3 Oct 78 to 5 Apr 79	*Saratoga*	Med	EA-6B	ICAP I	AC614	
Mar 80 to Nov 86	*Midway*	fwd deployed	EA-6B	ICAP I	NF620/604	
6 Feb to 22 Apr 83	*America*	IO	EA-6B	ICAP I	AB604	see note
Nov 86 to Aug 91	*Midway*	fwd deployed	EA-6B	ICAP II	NF620/604	*D Storm*
10 to 22 Aug 91	*Midway*	Hawaii	EA-6B	ICAP II	NF604	
28 Aug to 11 Sep 91	*Independence*	Japan	EA-6B	ICAP II	NF620	
Sep 91-July 98	*Independence*	fwd deployed	EA-6B	ICAP II	NF620	
Jul 98-2000	*Kitty Hawk*	fwd deployed	EA-6B	ICAP II	NF500	

VAQ-136 shows up in official documents as early as 1971 as a projected Alameda-based EKA-3B unit, but it would not be established until 1973 as the first EA-6B squadron without an A-3 background. VAQ-136 made the last deployment in the Standard version *Prowler* and, in 1979, moved to Atsugi, Japan, to join CVW-5 as the only forward deployed EA-6B unit. The *Gauntlets* were subsequently involved in *Desert Storm* off *Midway*. The 1983 deployment in *America* was a temporary assignment to CVW-1, where the squadron joined the carrier on station, and returned to Japan at the end of the ship's IO tour. During the 1998 visit to the Persian Gulf in *Independence* VAQ-136 was augmented with two EA-6Bs and aircrew from VAQ-138, off *Nimitz*.

VAQ-137 (1)	***Rooks***	**Whidbey Island**			
EA-6B					
Estab.	14 Dec 1973	Disestab. 30 Sep 1994			
17 Sep 74 to 20 May 75	*Enterprise*	WP/IO	EA-6B	EXCAP	NK620
15 Apr to 25 Oct 76	*America*	Med	EA-6B	EXCAP	AE700
10 Jun to 19 Jul 77	*America*	SoLant	EA-6B	EXCAP	AE700

As of January 1980, when this picture was taken at Fallon, there were only nine fleet Prowler units covering 12 air wings. Three VAQs still flew the EXCAP version of the EA-6B at this time, including VAQ-137, pictured here. The *Rooks* had a thing for checkerboards, as their speed brakes and even crew helmets indicate. This aircraft (159582) would be lost with its crew of three near Norfolk in Oct '81 while assigned to VAQ-138. (Michael Grove)

25 Sep 77 to 25 Apr 78	*America*	Med	EA-6B	EXCAP	AE700	
21 Feb to 22 Sep 79	*Ranger*	WPac	EA-6B	EXCAP	NE620	
10 Sep 80 to 4 May 81	*Ranger*	WP/IO	EA-6B	EXCAP	NE620	
7 Apr to 19 Oct 82	*Ranger*	WP/IO	EA-6B	EXCAP	NE604	
25 May to 1 Jul 83	*JF Kennedy*	NorLant	EA-6B	EXCAP	AC604	
27 Sep to 2 May 84	*JF Kennedy*	Med	EA-6B	EXCAP	AC604	*Lebanon*
26 Aug 85 to 16 Apr 86	*Saratoga*	Med/IO	EA-6B	ICAP II	AA604	*Prairie Fire*
5 Jun to 17 Nov 87	*Saratoga*	Med	EA-6B	ICAP II	AA604	
8 Feb to 3 Apr 89	*America*	NorLant	EA-6B	ICAP II	AB604	
11 May to 10 Nov 89	*America*	Med/RS/IO	EA-6B	ICAP II	AB604	
28 Dec 90 to 18 Apr 91	*America*	Med/RS/IO	EA-6B	ICAP II	AB620	*Desert Storm*
2 Dec 91 to 6 Jun 92	*America*	Med	EA-6B	ICAP II	AB620	
11 Aug 93 to 5 Feb 94	*America*	Med/RS/PG	EA-6B	ICAP II	AB620	

The eighth fleet *Prowler* unit adopted a Northwest Indian image of a rook—another name for a raven—as its logo. VAQ-137 had considerable combat experience for one of the later squadrons, having participated in strikes on Lebanon and Libya, as well as being heavily involved in *Desert Storm*. It was the first ICAP II unit to deploy, in Aug '85. The unit made sixteen deployments before it was disestablished in December 1994 as part of an agreement where the Marines put VMAQ-3 in CVW-1.

VAQ-137 (2) ***Rooks*** **Whidbey Island**
EA-6B
Estab. 1 Oct 1996

3 Oct 97 to 3 Apr 98	*G Washington*	Med/RS/PG	EA-6B	ICAP II	AB620
15 Sep 99 to 19 Mar 00	*JF Kennedy*	Med/RS/PG	EA-6B	ICAP II	AB500

In a curious circumstance, the VAQ-137 designation was resurrected in 1996 to become an expeditionary squadron, but when a change in policy sent VMAQ-3 back to the Marines, it allowed the new edition of VAQ-137 to "return" to its old air wing. Although the unit has no officially recognized connection with the previous -137, the new squadron adopted the logo and traditions of the original *Rooks*, thereby returning one of the more colorful legacies to Whidbey Island. The squadron was augmented during the Persian Gulf portion of the 1998 deployment by two VAQ-138 aircraft, and apparently returned to Whidbey with six EA-6Bs.

VAQ-138 ***Yellow Jackets*** **Whidbey Island**
EA-6B
Estab. 27 Feb 1976

15 Jan to 13 Jul 79	*Eisenhower*	Med	EA-6B	Std	AG600
11 Jul to 23 Dec 77	*Saratoga*	Med	EA-6B	EXCAP	AC600
4 Aug 80 to 28 Mar 81	*JF Kennedy*	Med	EA-6B	EXCAP	AB610
4 Jan to 14 Jul 82	*JF Kennedy*	Med/IO	EA-6B	EXCAP	AC604
15 Jul 83 to 29 Feb 84	*Ranger*	SP/WP/IO	EA-6B	EXCAP	NG604
8 Mar to 4 Oct 85	*Nimitz*	Med	EA-6B	ICAP I	AJ604
30 Dec 86 to 26 Jul 87	*Nimitz*	World	EA-6B	ICAP I	AJ604
2 Sep 88 to 2 Mar 89	*Nimitz*	WP/IO	EA-6B	ICAP I	NG604
15 Jun to 9 Jul 89	*Nimitz*	WP/IO	EA-6B	ICAP I	NG604

A VAQ-138 *Yellowjacket* EA-6B banks to the right while flying over southern Utah, 23 Apr 1992. The pilot is Lcdr. Todd Zecchin, who would later command the squadron. (author)

25 Feb to 24 Aug 91	*Nimitz*	WP/IO/PG	EA-6B	ICAP II	NG620	
2 Feb to 29 Jul 93	*Nimitz*	WP/IO/PG	EA-6B	ICAP II	NG620	
27 Nov 95 to 20 May 96	*Nimitz*	WP/IO/PG	EA-6B	ICAP II	NG620	
Nov 96 to Jan 97	MAG 12	Iwakuni JA	EA-6B	ICAP II	NG620	
1 Sep 97 to 1 May 98	*Nimitz*	WP/IO/PG	EA-6B	ICAP II	NG620 see notes	
14 Apr to 29 Jun 99	31st AEW	Aviano, IT	EA-6B	ICAP II	NG620	*Allied Force*
7 Jan to 3 Jul 00	*JC Stennis*	WP/IO/PG	EA-6B	ICAP II	NG500	

The '*Jackets* were established as the ninth fleet EA-6B unit in 1976, and made 13 major deployments over the following 24 years. The squadron's name came from the unit's first Commanding Officer, who adopted the mascot of his alma mater, Georgia Tech University. In 1996-97 the *Yellow Jackets* deployed to Japan to support MAG-12. When the *Nimitz* left the Persian Gulf at the end of the 1998 deployment, VAQ-138 sent its aircraft and aircrew to two other carriers in order to provide additional EA-6B support for possible action against Iraq. *George Washington* (CVW-1/VAQ-137) and *Independence* (CVW-5/VAQ-136) each got two *Yellowjacket* aircraft. After about two months on their adopted carriers, the '*Jackets* aircrew flew home via commercial aviation, while their aircraft remained. VAQ-138 would not see sustained combat until 1999, when they deployed to Aviano, IT, in a temporary land-based role during Operation *Allied Force* as part of the ad hoc "Electronic Attack Wing Aviano" with VAQ-140 and -209.

VAQ-139 ***Cougars*** **Whidbey Island**

EA-6B

Estab. 1 Jul 1983

21 Feb to 24 Aug 85	*Constellation*	WP/IO	EA-6B ICAP I NK604	
11 Apr to 13 Oct 87	*Constellation*	WP/IO	EA-6B ICAP I NK604	
1 Dec 88 to 1 Jun 89	*Constellation*	WP/IO	EA-6B ICAP II NK604	
16 Sep to 19 Oct 89	*Constellation*	WP/IO	EA-6B ICAP II NK604	
23 Jun to 20 Dec 90	*Independence*	WP/IO/PG	EA-6B ICAP II NK604	*Desert Shield*
5 to 22 Aug 91	*Independence*	Hawaii	EA-6B ICAP II NK604	
28 Aug to 14 Sep 91	*Midway*	Swapex	EA-6B ICAP II NK604	
18 Feb to 15 Aug 94	*C Vinson*	WP/IO/PG	EA-6B ICAP II NK620	
14 May to 14 Nov 96	*C Vinson*	WP/IO/PG	EA-6B ICAP II NK620	
11 Jun to 7 Dec 98	*Lincoln*	WP/IO/PG	EA-6B ICAP II NK620	
14 Aug 00 to 12 Feb 01	*Lincoln*	WP/IO/PG	EA-6B ICAP II NK620	

The *Cougars* logo is "borrowed" from the Mercury car company, while the background color was originally Carolina blue. In Feb 2000 the squadron skipper changed the official color to a darker shade of blue. VAQ-139 has been assigned to CVW-14 since its 1983 establishment. Although the unit participated in *Desert Shield*, it had not seen sustained combat operations by 2000.

VAQ-140 ***Patriots*** **Whidbey Island**

EA-6B

Estab. 1 Oct 1985

18 Aug 86 to 3 Mar 87	*JF Kennedy*	Med	EA-6B	ICAP II	AC604	
29 Feb to 29 Aug 88	*Eisenhower*	Med	EA-6B	ICAP II	AG604	
8 Mar to 12 Sep 90	*Eisenhower*	Med/RS	EA-6B	ICAP II	AG604	
26 Sep 91 to 2 Apr 92	*Eisenhower*	Med	EA-6B	ICAP II	AG604	
20 May to 12 Sep 90	*Eisenhower*	Med/RS	EA-6B	ICAP II	AG604	*Desert Shield*
26 Sep 91 to 2 Apr 92	*Eisenhower*	Med	EA-6B	ICAP II	AG604	
20 May to 17 Nov 94	*G Washington*	Med/NorLant	EA-6B	ICAP II	AG620	
26 Jan to 23 Jul 96	*G Washington*	Med/RS/PG	EA-6B	ICAP II	AG620	
26 Feb to 26 Aug 98	*JC Stennis*	World	EA-6B	ICAP II	AG500	
13 Apr to 29 Jun 99	31st AEW	Aviano, IT	EA-6B	ICAP II	AG500	*Allied Force*
18 Feb to 18 Aug 00	*Eisenhower*	Med/PG	EA-6B	ICAP II	AG500	

VAQ-140 was notable as the first EA-6B unit to deploy with HARM-capable *Prowlers*, in 1986. After making its first deployment with CVW-3, the squadron has been assigned only to CVW-7 ever since. In 1997 the squadron became the first EA-6B unit to move to the 500 series side numbers, which had been open since the departure of the *Intruder* community. Although heavily involved in *Desert Shield*, the *Patriots* did not see sustained combat operations until being part of the ad hoc "Electronic Attack Wing Aviano" during Operation *Allied Force* in 1999.

VAQ-141 ***Shadowhawks*** **Whidbey Island**

EA-6B

Estab. 1 Jul 1987

25 Aug to 11 Oct 88	*T Roosevelt*	NorLant	EA-6B	ICAP II	AJ620	
30 Dec 88 to 30 Jun 89	*T Roosevelt*	Med	EA-6B	ICAP II	AJ620	
28 Dec 90 to 28 Jun 91	*T Roosevelt*	Med/RS/PG	EA-6B	ICAP II	AJ620	*Desert Storm*
11 Mar to 8 Sep 93	*T Roosevelt*	Med/RS	EA-6B	ICAP II	AJ620	*Deny Flight*
22 Mar to 22 Sep 95	*T Roosevelt*	Med/RS/PG	EA-6B	ICAP II	AJ620	
29 Apr to 28 Oct 97	*JF Kennedy*	Med/RS/PG	EA-6B	ICAP II	AJ620	
26 Mar to 22 Sep 99	*T Roosevelt*	Med/RS/PG	EA-6B	ICAP II	AJ500	*Allied Force*

The *Shadowhawks'* name and basic logo was drafted at a bar by the unit's first CO, Cdr. Arboth "Arb" Rylant. The unit's second deployment involved *Desert Storm*, and it has subsequently seen combat in *Deny Flight* and *Allied Force*. The squadron size was increased to six aircraft in 1993 for *Deny Flight* through the addition of two aircraft and crews from VAQ-209 (which carried AJ626 and 627 side numbers). The unit spent a good deal of the 1993 deployment land-based at Aviano, Italy, in support of NATO operations over Bosnia. It returned home ahead of the carrier, arriving NAF Washington on 17 Sep, and proceeding to Whidbey on the 18th.

VAQ-142 (1) ***Grim Watchdogs*** **Whidbey Island**

EA-6B

Estab	1 Jun 1988	disestab. 1 Jul 1991			
4 Nov 89 to 12 Apr 90	*Forrestal*	Med	EA-6B	ICAP II	AE604
1990-91	——	(none)	EA-6B	ICAP II	AK604

The squadron's unusual nickname came from the unit's first CO, CDR "Whiskey Bob" Hamilton, who used one of the titles of his first squadron, VS-27. The *Watchdogs* made only one deployment, with CVW-6 in *Forrestal*, before they swapped air wings with VAQ-133, which was in the doomed CVW-13, in an attempt to keep the community favored *Wizards* alive. The plan largely backfired, as -133 didn't last much longer, being disestablished with CVW-6, while -142's organization became the basis for the "new" VAQ-35.

VAQ-142 (2) ***Gray Wolves*** **Whidbey Island**

EA-6B

Established 1 Apr 1997

Mar to Jun 98	4404th WG(P)	Prince Sultan SA	EA-6B	ICAP II	NL620	
Aug to Sep 98	4404th WP(P)	Prince Sultan SA	EA-6B	ICAP II	NL520	
Dec 98 to Mar 99	363rd AEW	Prince Sultan SA	EA-6B	ICAP II	NL520	*Desert Fox*
Sep to Dec 99	39th AEW	Incirlik TU	EA-6B	ICAP II	NL520	
Aug to Oct 00	39th AEW	Incirlik TU	EA-6B	ICAP II	NL520	

In what was essentially the third version of this squadron, the second VAQ-142 was brought back as an expeditionary unit, and has made a series of deployments to garden spots throughout the world in support of joint requirements. The unit's participation in *Desert Fox* strikes marked the first major use of an "expeditionary" *Prowler* unit in combat. The squadron initially adopted a modified version of the original VAQ-142/VAQ-35 logo (with the bloated dog's head now over a starry background), with the latter squadron's nickname, spelled slightly differently. At some point the "fat dog" design was ditched in favor of an unimaginative new insignia with a crude looking dog's head (which one former CO described as a "Mad Collie") in front of a generic lightning bolt. Curiously, as of 2001 the Naval History Office, the official keeper of squadron insignia for the service, still recognized the "star spangled dog" version as their only real insignia.

VAQ-209 ***Star Warriors*** **Norfolk, Washington** **Naval Reserve**

EA-6A, EA-6B

Established 1 Oct 1977

C. 95	*T Roosevelt*	Med	EA-6B	ICAP II	AJ62X	augment VAQ-141
6 Jun to 6 July 1998	39th AEW	Incirlik	EA-6B	ICAP II	AF620	*Northern Watch*
13 Apr to 29 Jun 1999	31st AEW	Aviano	EA-6B	ICAP II	AF620	augment VAQ-138/140
Mar to May 2000	39th AEW	Incirlik	EA-6B	ICAP II	AF500	*Northern Watch*

When VMAQ-2 converted from EA-6As to EA-6B *Prowlers* in 1977, the electric *Intruders* were made available to the Reserves, with VAQ-209 being established in October of that year. Using a logo featuring the helmet of Darth Vader, the *Star Warriors* were formed at Norfolk with EA-6As as part of CVWR-20. They moved to NAF Washington in May 1990 and converted to EA-6Bs. The 1994 disestablishment of VAQ-309 left -209 as the only *Prowler* squadron in the Naval Reserve. The increased demand for joint EA-6B support at deployed locations led to the unit being deployed as both a complete unit, or in an augmentation role for other squadrons on an annual basis from 1998. The 1995 deployment involved two aircraft and 27 personnel attached to VAQ-141 and CVW-8 for four months. As such, they were the first carrier-based naval reserve squadron to actually deploy for combat operations since Korea. The 1998 deployment involved three aircraft for 30 days to cover *Northern Watch* commitments. In 1999 -209 sent two aircraft and 78 personnel to Aviano, where they joined "Attack Wing Aviano" for further combat operations over the former Yugoslavia. The squadron returned to Turkey in 2000 with four aircraft for 45 days as part of Operation *Northern Watch*. VAQ-209 EA-6As wore AF700 codes. Their EA-6Bs were normally coded AF620 and AF500.

VAQ-309 ***Axemen*** **Whidbey Island** **Naval Reserve**
EA-6A, EA-6B
Established Dec 1979 disestablished 31 Dec 94 (Sep ceremony)
The *Axemen* were formed in 1979 to provide electronic warfare capability within CVWR-30. The squadron flew EA-6A *Intruders* until they were replaced by block-86 *Prowlers* from 2 Dec 1989. The squadron was shut down along with its wing in 1994. Tailcodes were normally ND610 and 620.

Joint Prowlers

Following *Desert Storm*, the Department of Defense was under a great deal of Congressional pressure to place certain aviation mission areas under single-service control. Among these areas were strategic reconnaissance, transport, and tactical radar jamming. It was the last one that was actually chosen for consolidation.

As of the mid-1990s, the Air Force was operating a fleet of about 40 EF-111A *Ravens*, while the Navy and Marines had roughly 100 EA-6B *Prowlers* in service, with about 20 other aircraft in storage. When comparing the two aircraft, the *Raven* featured much greater speed and range than the *Prowler*, but only carried an ALQ-99 tactical jamming system that was most comparable to the mid-seventies EA-6B ICAP I design. A comprehensive "Systems Improvement Program" (SIP), which would have given the aircraft a system superior to that installed in the EA-6B at that time, only needed funding to start. For a variety of reasons, however, the Air Force didn't seem to be nearly as interested in the tactical EW business as the Navy was, and the SIP was canceled. In particular, many senior officers in the USAF believed that exotic stealth technology had made support radar jamming unnecessary.

In comparison, the Navy had continually upgraded the EA-6B, with successive versions being designated ICAP II Block 82, Block 86, and Block 89, with Block 89A pending. The service had placed the AGM-88 HARM anti-radiation missile on the aircraft in the mid-'80s, while the Air Force, with its influential *Wild Weasel* force, had refused to arm the *Raven*. For these reasons, and for some others left unsaid, the EA-6B was truly the better mission platform.

A mid-'90s study by the Joint Chiefs of Staff concurred that in almost all ways the EA-6B was the better EW aircraft, and that tactics could mitigate the range and speed issues. It was also determined that, if they had to go to only one type, the Air Force's smaller *Raven* force would not be able to cover all DoD commitments, while the EA-6B fleet, which could be brought up to 120 airframes, could do the job. The *Prowler* got the nod, and the *Raven* was forced into early retirement in the Arizona desert.

As their part of the bargain, the Navy agreed to establish five new "Joint" squadrons that would support deployed Air Force Air Expeditionary Wings (AEWs). These units would not normally carrier qualify, and would follow a different training track than their Air Wing brethren. Four Air Force aircrew (one pilot, three navigators) would be assigned to each of these squadrons to provide them with "light blue suit" expertise.

While called "Joint" squadrons, they remained Navy units under Navy organization, chain of command, and regulations. (Contrary to reports that lingered for years, there were never any "Air Force *Prowler* squadrons.") Unit assignments and tasking would be driven by a periodic meeting held by the JCS, where the Unified Commands (largely Pacific, European, and Central Commands) sat down and determined where and when these assets would be rotated to. Little noticed was that the four Marine EA-6B squadrons (VMAQ-1 to 4) and the sole remaining reserve unit (VAQ-209) were also involved, as they became part of the expeditionary mix, meaning nine squadrons were available for normal "concrete" deployment.

Deployed locations were initially established at Prince Sultan AB, Al Kharj, Saudi Arabia (for Central Command and Operation *Southern Watch*); Incirlik AB in Turkey (European Command, *Northern Watch*), and Iwakuni, Japan (Pacific Command). MCAS Iwakuni continued as a normal location in support of the 3rd MAW as well. In time *Prowlers* would also soon be sent to Aviano AB in northeast Italy for operations involving the former Yugoslavia.

The *Garudas* of VAQ-134, available following the disestablishment of CVW-15, were picked to be the first "joint" unit, and it made the initial expeditionary deployment to MCAS Iwakuni, Japan, in May 1996. Three other squadrons (VAQ-133, -142, and -128) were eventually established for the role, while the fifth intended unit, a new VAQ-137, was instead assigned to CVW-1 to replace VMAQ-3. The long-promised "fifth squadron" (VAQ-143 *Cobras*) waited several years for enough people and airframes to be created. Although finally scheduled for establishment in FY2002, it would never actually be activated.

Fleet units have been temporarily assigned to the "concrete" mission as well, often in the middle of their carrier work-up cycle. By April 1998 EA-6Bs had completely replaced the EF-111A, and the last of the *Ravens* were in the boneyard. Since that time, land based *Prowlers* have been heavily involved in combat worldwide, and are now considered a critical warfighting aircraft.

Southern Watch EA-6B joint support deployments: 1998 to 2001 **Prince Sultan AB, Saudi Arabia**

Mar to Jun 1998	VAQ-142	block 82	NL620	
Jun to Aug 1998	VAQ-131	block 86	NE620	- temp from CVW-2
Aug, Sep 1998	VAQ-142	block 82	NL520	
Sep to Dec 1998	VAQ-128	block 82	NL570	
Dec 98 to Mar 99	VAQ-142	block 82	NL520	
Mar Jul 1999	VAQ-132	block 86	AA500	- temp from CVW-17
July 1999 to Apr 2000: no units assigned				
Apr to July 2000	VAQ-133	block 82	NL530	
July to Oct 2000	VAQ-134	block 82	NL540	
Oct 00 to Jan 01	VMAQ-1	block 82	CB	

EA-6Bs replaced USAF EF-111A *Ravens* at PSAB in March 1998, in support of *Southern Watch*. They were assigned to the 4404th Wing (Provisional) until September 1998, when it was replaced by the 363rd Air Expeditionary Wing (AEW). The period between July 1999 and April 2000 was "gapped" to allow the Navy/Marine *Prowler* force to recover from the strain of combat operation in *Allied Force*.

Northern Watch EA-6B joint support deployments: 1998 to 2001 **Incirlik, Turkey**

Dec 97 to Jun 98	VAQ-134	block 82	NL640	
Jun, Jul 98	VAQ-209	block 82	AF620	
Jul to Dec 98	VAQ-133	block 82	NL630	
Dec 98 to Jul 99	VMAQ-1	block 82	CB	- moved to Aviano 3-4/99
Jun 99 to Sep 99	VAQ-134	block 82	NL540	
Sep to Dec 99	VAQ-142	block 82	NL520	
Dec 99 to Mar 00	VAQ-128	block 82	NL570	
Mar 00 to May 00	VAQ-209	block 82	AF500	
May 00 to Aug 00	VAQ-135	block 86	NH500	- temp. from CVW-11
Aug 00 to Oct 00	VAQ-142	block 82	NL520	
Oct 00 to Jan 01	VAQ-128	block 82	NL570	

EA-6Bs replaced USAF EF-111A *Ravens* at Incirlik, Turkey, in December 1997 to support the 39th AEW and *Northern Watch*. Reserve unit VAQ-209 covered the requirement twice, as did the Marines, once. Without EA-6B support, *Northern Watch* flights over Iraq were largely suspended in Mar/Apr '99.

EA-6B joint support detachments: Aviano, Italy.

Aug to Sep 93	VAQ-130	block 86	AC620	
Aug to Sep 93	VAQ-141	block 86	AJ620	off CVN-71
Sep 95	VMAQ-1	block 82	CB	
Mar 96 to Feb 97	VMAQ-2	block 82	CY	
Sep 96 to Feb 97	VMAQ-4	block 82	RM	
Feb to Sep 97	VMAQ-3	block 82	MD	
Feb, Mar 99	VAQ-134	block 82	NL640	- 3 weeks, returned to Whidbey
Feb to Jul 99	VMAQ-2	block 82	CY	
Mar, Apr 99	VAQ-134	block 82	NL640	- 4 wks, pers. returned to Whidbey
Mar, Apr 99	VMAQ-1	block 82	CB	- deployed from Incirlik 5 weeks
Mar to Jun 99	VMAQ-4	block 82	RM	
Apr to Jun 99	VAQ-140	block 86	AG500	- temp from CVW-7
Apr to Jun 99	VAQ-138	block 86	NG500	- temp from CVW-9
Apr to Jun 99	VAQ-209	block 86	AF500	- 2 aircraft augment

Land-based EA-6Bs started supporting operations over the former Yugoslavia in August 1993, and involved a healthy mix of expeditionary, fleet, reserve, and Marine units. Aviano was an "as needed" deployment location, with three distinct periods of activity. The 1999 period involved up to 29 EA-6Bs at one time, and was run through two largely independent "squadrons," one Marine and one Navy. The Navy unit was called, unofficially, "Electronic Attack Wing Aviano," and was commanded for a period by the Commodore of VaqWingPac, Captain (later Rear Admiral) John Cryer. Aircraft, aircrew, and maintenance support were combined for the operation. Additional aircrew were obtained from VAQ-129, the Whidbey EW school, and NSAWC for what was described as a "Prowler Rainbow Coalition." *Allied Force* strained EA-6B operations to a point that it forced the Joint Chiefs of Staff to suspend EA-6B participation in *Southern Watch* in Saudi Arabia for nine months afterwards.

FEWSG

The Fleet Electronic Warfare Support Group (FEWSG) was formed at Norfolk in 1969 to organize and manage electronic adversary operations during fleet exercises. From 1970 the Group had its own squadron to perform the majority of its missions, and two others followed in time.

Most FEWSG aircraft were configured with special jamming gear and radar simulators that mimicked Soviet equipment that might be faced in an anti-ship attack. Their crews were trained in Soviet tactics, and they could be very successful in their mission, often to the point of exasperation among those receiving their attention. Chaff laying and radar jamming were both heavy and effective. Communications jamming and intrusion were particular specialties of the NC-121K and ERA-3B aircraft. The "Connie's" enlisted crew in particular carried a load of eight track tapes to play everything from Russian folk songs to screeching hard rock over fleet circuits. Their music selection was rarely appreciated.

FEWSG was frequently augmented by VC or fleet units who could act as additional targets during fleet exercises. The group's success, and demands for its services, led to the formation of VAQ-34 and -35, which eventually made it a true "wing."

VAQ-33's original "Golf Delta" tailcode was retained, and in time it became a Group code, with -33, -34 and -35 being numbered in the 100, 200, and 300 series, respectively.

In addition to its three squadrons, FEWSG also controlled a pair of contractor-operated, Navy-marked Boeing EB-47E jamming aircraft through 1977, when they were replaced by two NKC-135As that flew under the "Nucar" ("new-car") callsign. These two platforms were the largest aircraft operated by the Navy for many years. A single EC-24A—a modified civil Douglas DC-8-54F—supplemented the Boeings in 1984. The entire force was retired by the end of 1998.

FEWSG was redesignated the Fleet Tactical Readiness Group (FTRG) on 1 April 1992, just prior to its "air force" going away. The "electronic aggressor" role was picked up by the Reserves and fleet VAQ units, but it would never be at the level, or originality, seen during the 1980s and early '90s.

VAQ-33 ***Firebirds*** **Norfolk/Oceana, Key West**

ERA-3B, TA-3B, KA-3B, A-3B, F-4B, F-4J, EF-4B, EF-4J, TA-4J, EA-6A, TA-7C, NC-121K, P-3A, P-3B, EP-3A, EP-3J

Tailcode: GD X or 1X until March 1983, then GD100 series.

Estab. VC-33 31 May 1949, r/d VA(AW)-33 2 Jul 56, r/d VAW-33 30 Jan 59, r/d VAQ-33 1 Feb 68.

Disestab. 1 Oct 1993

As of the late '60s VAQ-33 was a carrier-based squadron deploying EA-1F detachments to Atlantic Fleet carriers from Quonset Point, RI. In 1970 it came under the control of FEWSG, moved to Norfolk, and became the prototype "electronic adversary" operation, in effect a composite squadron flying an eclectic mix of aircraft as the opposing side during fleet exercises. The *Night Hawk* title used by the original unit was replaced by a new logo and *Firebird* nickname, at the same time as the new jet crowd replaced the previous prop flyers in the ready room.

Squadron operations depended on fleet demand, with the schedule being driven by who needed what training where. It could entail a solo EA-4F making runs on a warship off the coast, to full-squadron deployments to places like Roosevelt Roads and Miramar. Out of area operations were also made, to places like Norway, Japan, Canada, and Hawaii. On at least one occasion, in 1975, the unit's EA-4Fs were transported to and from a Hawaii exercise on the flight deck of a carrier, being craned on and off, since they were no longer suitable for carrier operations.

Skywarrior FRS duties were assumed in 1977 from NARU Alameda, and five TA-3Bs were assigned for that role, the ERAs (called "Warbirds" within the unit) being too heavy to be used as trainers. Originally based on the old seaplane ramp at Norfolk, the squadron opened a permanent detachment at Oceana (with its longer runways) in 1978 for A-3 training and F-4 operations. In 1980 the squadron moved to the former RA-5C

At one time FEWSG had a stable of eight ERA-3B *Skywarriors*, evenly divided between VAQ-33 and -34. Two *Flashbacks* are shown here off San Diego on 14 Jan 1986 during a "Hey Rube" fighter training exercise. The quartet of EW Operators in these aircraft are preparing to give the fighters fits with their radar and communications jamming. (author)

Vigilante hangar in Key West, where it served until disestablished in Oct 1993. VAQ-33 carried out the last A-3 carrier qualification on 25 Aug 1989 under the guise of instructor proficiency, and retired the type from Naval service in a 27 Sep '91 ceremony. The seemingly ageless "Whale" would continue to fly as a test bed airframe with several defense contractors.

Full description of the many aircraft the squadron owned and how they were modified would take more space than is available here. Two EW modified A-3Bs were used until 1972, when the four ERA-3Bs began to arrive. The *Phantoms* specialized as high-speed threat presentations, and were retired in 1981, largely due to high costs associated with their use. The *Constellation* (practically nobody in the squadron called it by its official military name, *Warning Star)* was replaced in 1983 by a P-3A that was subsequently modified for the FEWSG mission as an EP-3A. At least three more *Orions* would arrive later with two becoming EP-3Js. The EA-4Fs/TA-4Js were replaced by TA-7Cs that never received the formal modifications to make them EA-7Ls, like sister squadron VAQ-34 possessed.

The *Firebirds* lost five aircraft over 23 years of FEWSG duty, including an A-3B, ERA-3B, two EA-4Fs, and an EA-6A. Six aircrew were killed in these mishaps. The 22 May 1985 loss of EA-4F 154655 at North Island, CA, was believed to involve the first ejection of a female (Lt. Katherine "KC" Cullen) from a Navy jet in history.

Befitting their unique mission, the *Firebirds* went through an almost continual state of aircraft rotation. In 1974 they had four ERA-3B, four EA-4F, one EF-4B, and one NC-121K. By 1980 they stabled four ERA-3B, five TA-3B, three EA-4F, one TA-4J, four EA-6A, and the single NC-121K. At the end, the *Firebirds* operated seven EA-6As and three *Orions*.

VAQ-33 was something of a flying circus, which remained a unique squadron manned by a colorful and memorable group of personnel through its history.

VAQ-34 ***Flashbacks, Aggressors*** **Point Mugu, Lemoore**
ERA-3B, KA-3B, UA-3B, EA-3B, EA-7L, TA-7C, F/A-18A, F/A-18B
Estab 1 March 1983 Disestab 1 Oct 1993 (5 Oct ceremony)

In 1983 FEWSG doubled in size, as VAQ-34 was established at Pt Mugu. Although ostensibly formed to cover west coast operations (with VAQ-33 taking the Atlantic Fleet), the two squadrons frequently operated together on major exercises. Four RA-3Bs were pulled from the boneyard and modified to ERA-3B standards for the squadron, and six TA-7Cs were reconfigured as EA-7Ls. A single KA-3B made up the remainder of the squadron's fleet, although solo EA and UA-3Bs (a modified RA-3B) were also operated at times. The retirement of the "Whales" and *Corsairs* in 1991 led to the use of eight early-block *Hornets*, and a move to Lemoore in June 1992.

VAQ-34 would have a thing with unintentional ejections from its aircraft over its ten year history. On 19 July 1990 a pilot and NFO left EA-7L 156743 without warning while flying at altitude over California. Three years later, on 6 July 1993, the squadron XO and a Lt.Cdr back-seater were ejected from their F/A-18B while it was rolling out on the runway at Lemoore at the end of a flight. All four aircrew and the *Hornet* (161733) survived. The *Corsair* was a loss.

The squadron reportedly used the nickname *Electric Horsemen* for a short period before its *Flashback* callsign became command's preferred handle. In 1987 the unit changed its logo and nickname to reflect its "electronic aggressor" mission, and the *Aggressor* nickname took root. Aircraft markings were modified accordingly to give them a Soviet appearance, with red stars and large red nose numbers.

VAQ-35 ***Grey Wolves*** **Whidbey Island**
EA-6B
Estab 14 Aug 1991 (1 Jul ceremony) Disestab 1 Oct 1993 (7 Oct ceremony)

The 1991 retirement of the ERA-3B resulted in a substantial reduction in FEWSG's jamming capacity. A temporary surplus of EA-6B airframes led to the establishment of VAQ-35 at Whidbey Island as the third, and last, member of the FEWSG stable to fill the gap. The squadron was established in August 1991 from the remains of recently disestablished VAQ-142. The new unit adopted parts of -142's past, including a modified version of their dog's head insignia, although they dumped the largely unpopular *Grim Watchdog* title for *Grey Wolves*. VAQ-35 lasted at Whidbey only about two years before being disestablished with the rest of FEWSG in the post *Desert Storm* drawdown. Like its sister squadrons, VAQ-35 participated in exercises worldwide during its short life, with at least 42 such detachments being conducted. The squadron was notable, in that it was the first land-based Navy EA-6B unit, and the largest "fleet" unit in the community, with up to eight *Prowlers* assigned at any one time. The squadron's name and traditions would return to Whidbey in 1997 as the new VAQ-142 *Gray Wolves*, using slightly different spelling.

Aerial Refueling Squadrons (VAK)

"It used to be the F-8s and RA-5s that scared everyone at the boat. Now it's just us." - A-3 community LSO, 1981.

A *Jockey* KA-3B has just been chocked on Whidbey Island's transient line with its drag parachute billowing in October 1987. The bomb bay doors and belly hatch are open, while the plane captain watches things through the upper hatch. The "Whale's" twin J-57 engines produced a distinctive howling sound while at idle that was hard to mistake for any other aircraft. (author)

VAQ/VAK-208 ***Jockeys*** **Alameda** **Naval Reserve**
KA-3B
Estab. VAQ-208 31 Jul 70, r/d VAK-208 1 Oct 79, disestab. 30 Sep 89

VAQ/VAK-308 ***Griffins*** **Alameda** **Naval Reserve**
KA-3B
Estab. as VAQ-308 2 May 1970, r/d VAK-308 1 Oct 1979, disestab. 30 Sep 1988.

VAQ-208 was established as part of CVWR-20, while sister squadron VAQ-308 was assigned to CVWR-30. In spite of the VAQ title, the squadrons' primary missions were always aerial refueling, pathfinding (providing navigation leads for long-range transits by tactical aircraft), and logistics support. Both initially received KA-3B aircraft, with the apparent goal to eventually assign EKA-3Bs; however, no Navy Location & Allowance Lists show any EKA-3B aircraft ever being assigned to either VAQ-208 or its sister -308. Indeed, many of their KA-3Bs were actually redesignated EKAs that had the EW gear removed. By 1979 the EKA-3B was out of the inventory, and both Reserve Air Wings had EA-6A units assigned, so -208 and -308 were themselves redesignated as the Navy's first ever "Tankrons" (VAKs) to better reflect their primary mission.

Both units proved to be among the most traveled of the Reserve squadrons of this period, as they supported numerous fleet operations worldwide. Both units participated in Operation *Nickel Grass*, which involved the rapid transfer of Navy A-4s to Israel during the 1973 "Yom Kippur War." On 1 Aug 1975 a VAQ-208 KA-3B set what was said to be a new nonstop flight record for carrier-based jets when it flew a 13-hour, 6100 mile non-stop mission between Rota, Spain, and its home base in Alameda.

Both units supported deployed carriers on a short-term basis, including work with the *Enterprise* in the Bay of Bengal in 1971-72, *Kennedy* in the Northern Atlantic (1972), and *Independence* in the Med (1974). Carrier operations frequently involved use as a "Fast COD," with cargo pallets installed in the bomb bays. As late as 1988 VAK-308 deployed aircraft to Sigonella, Sicily, to support NATO exercises.

Both squadrons were normally assigned four "Whales" apiece. VAQ/VAK-208 used, sequentially, AF650, 610, and 520 series numbers. VAQ/VAK-308 wore ND630 and 520 numbers.

Naval Air Reserve Unit, Alameda **Alameda** **Naval Reserve**
TA-3B, RA-3B 6G
Of the many Naval Air Reserve Units (NARUs), Alameda needs to be mentioned here, as it was the Navy's A-3 *Skywarrior* replacement training unit between 1974 and 1977. With the end of the Vietnam War, the Navy assumed that the retirement of the "Whale" was close, so when dual fleet/FRS unit VAQ-130 moved to Whidbey for EA-6B transition in June 1974, the RAG function fell to the Alameda Reserves. Before long it became obvious that the A-3 still had many years left in it, and that the Reserves were not really manned or organized to produce a regular flow of replacement aircrew and maintenance troops to VQ-1, VQ-2, and VAQ-33, as well as the remaining VIP and test units still flying the type. The role moved to VAQ-33 at Norfolk in October 1977, who also gained the TA-3Bs at the same time. NARU Alameda aircraft wore 6G tailcodes.

Fleet Air Reconaisance (VQ)

"In God we trust. All others we monitor."
- VQ community saying.

The Navy's VQ community conducts surveillance missions of a normally sensitive nature, and prefers to remain out of the public spotlight as much as possible. Among its publicly-released roles is to "...provide real-time signals intelligence to tactical commanders for air, surface, and ground operations."

As of 1974, the two battle group-oriented VQ squadrons in the Navy were VQ-1 and -2, which provided land and carrier based support with EP-3 and EA-3 aircraft.[14]

VQ EA-3B *Skywarriors* ("Whales") deployed to the carriers on a regular basis, although they were not always considered part of the air wing, and frequently wore their own unique tailcodes. The EA-3B dets could be one or two aircraft, depending on mission requirements, and didn't always remain on a ship for the entire cruise. The official order to beach the "Whale" occurred on 31 Dec 1988, almost two years after a night landing mishap on *Nimitz* that took the lives of seven members of VQ-2. VAQ-33, the FRS, continued to day CQ TA-3Bs on a periodic basis through Aug 1989 for contingency and proficiency reasons. With the loss of the EA-3B, the Navy would gap the carrier-based VQ mission until the arrival of the ES-3A *Shadow*.

The Navy converted 16 S-3A *Vikings* into ES-3As, and established two new squadrons for the type. Although officially named the *Shadow*, the ES-3 also continued the "Hoover's" vacuum cleaner reference with the unofficial (and clever) handle of "Electrolux". Each squadron had a nominal strength of eight aircraft, and attached two-aircraft detachments to deploying carrier air wings. The first ES-3 detachment to move out was VQ-5's det A, which was forward deployed in *Independence* in Nov 1993. A "typical" ES-3 det would consist of two aircraft, four pilots, four NFOs, five enlisted aircrew, and about 25 maintenance personnel, the remaining support being provided by the air wing's assigned S-3 unit.

The *Shadow* possessed excellent mission systems operated by highly specialized crew, but the type was not always used to its ability, and it frequently ended up overhead the ship as "just another tanker." The entire community was shut down after less than eight years of service. The official position was that the aircraft needed expensive upgrades in order to meet new requirements. The result was the end of the carrier-based VQ mission, as the Navy decided to rely on land-based and other platforms. The last ES-3A was retired on 10 Aug 1999.

Unfortunately, the nomadic and low key nature of the VQ-1 and -2 "Whale" dets makes their movement and assignments difficult to track. Therefore no attempt will be made here to record them. On the other hand, ES-3 detachments were well documented, and are provided here.

EA-3B is perched on *Constellation's* "finger" just aft of a lowered elevator four during the ship's 1985 WestPac. By this time the squadron routinely used air wing tailcodes (CVW-14's NK here) instead of the unit's own "Peter Rabbit" (PR) code. This "Whale" also carries a small notation on the tail that states "On loan from the Smithsonian Institution." (author)

VQ-1 ***World Watchers*** **Agana**
EA-3B, RA-3B, TA-3B, VA-3B tailcode PR
Estab. 1 Jun 55

VQ-1 operated both land based (EP-3) and carrier based (EA-3) detachments from Agana, Guam, throughout the Pacific and Indian Ocean regions. It provided EA-3B detachments to deployed carriers from 1974 through 1988, and has continued to fly EP-3s since. RA-3Bs and the Heavy Photo mission were adopted from co-located VAP-61 when that squadron disestablished in 1971. All RA-3Bs were transferred by the mid-'70s. A single admin support TA-3B or similar VA-3B were also usually assigned.

VQ-1 suffered three major A-3 mishaps after Vietnam. One EA-3B (146450) was lost off *Ranger* on 4 Aug 1982, with the loss of six of seven men onboard. EA-3B 144854 crashed at Miramar while conducting practice night carrier landings in June '87, killing two. The VA-3B (142672) went down off Guam on 23 Jan 1985, killing the squadron Commander, an EP-3 pilot, along with seven other men.

VQ-2 ***Batmen*** **Rota**
EA-3B, TA-3B, UA-3B tailcode JQ
Estab. 1 Sep 55

VQ-2 flew both land based (EP-3) and carrier based (EA-3) missions from its Rota, Spain, home throughout Europe and the Mediterranean. Single non-mission A-3s (TA-3B or UA-3B) were also on strength for admin support duties. VQ-2 provided EA-3B detachments to deployed carriers from 1974 through 1988. The loss of a VQ-2 EA-3B (JQ12, 144850) on *Nimitz* with seven men on 25 Jan 1987 accelerated the end of A-3 *Skywarrior* carrier operations Navy wide. During 1991 VQ-2 supported Operation *Desert Storm* with a two aircraft detachment to Riyadh, Saudi Arabia, after which the "Whales" were retained for shore based operations until being retired the following October. The squadron continues in its primary mission with EP-3Es to this day.

VQ-5 ***Sea Shadows*** **Agana, North Island**
ES-3A
Estab. 15 Aug 1991. Disestab. 30 July 1999 (4 June ceremony)

VQ-5 typically deployed two aircraft detachments to deploying carriers. The squadron moved from Guam to California between Aug 1994 and Jan 1995 in order to be co-located with the rest of the Pacific Fleet S-3 community. VQ-5 routinely supported operations over Iraq during *Operation Southern Watch*, and strikes during *Desert Fox*. A permanent Detachment 5 was assigned to Misawa, Japan, to support CVW-5 on both *Independence* and *Kitty Hawk*. The unit deployed fifteen detachments during its short history.

Nov 1993 to Mar 1994	*Independence*	CVW-5	WP/IO/PG	det A
Feb to Aug 1994	*Carl Vinson*	CVW-14	WP/IO/PG	det B
Jun to Dec 1994	*Kitty Hawk*	CVW-15	WP/IO/PG	det C
Nov 1994 to May 1995	*Constellation*	CVW-2	WP/IO/PG	det D
Apr to Oct 1995	*Lincoln*	CVW-11	WP/IO/PG	det B
Nov 1995 to May 1996	*Nimitz*	CVW-9	WP/IO/PG	det C

The ES-3A returned unique and valuable ELINT capability to the battle group that had been lost with the retirement of the EA-3B. Nonetheless, the fact it was usually burdened with a refueling store, and ended up overhead as "just another tanker," says volumes for how it was actually viewed by many air wing and flag staffs. VQ-5 det B ES-3A (NK727, 159404) is shown here during CQ on *Lincoln* on 16 Feb '98 with a VAW-113 *Black Eagle* E-2C turning alongside. (Mark Morgan)

May to Nov 1996	*Carl Vinson*	CVW-14	WP/IO/PG	det D
Oct 1996 to Apr 1997	*Kitty Hawk*	CVW-11	WP/IO/PG	det B
Apr to Oct 1997	*Constellation*	CVW-2	WP/IO/PG	det C
Sep 1997 to Mar 1998	*Nimitz*	CVW-9	WP/IO/PG	det D
Jun to Dec 1998	*Lincoln*	CVW-14	WP/IO/PG	det B
Nov 1998 to May 1999	*Carl Vinson*	CVW-11	WP/IO/PG	det C
1994 to 1997	*Independence*	CVW-5	WP/IO	det 5 forward deployed
1997 to 1999	*Kitty Hawk*	CVW-5	WP/IO	det 5 forward deployed

VQ-6 ***Black Ravens*** **Cecil Field, Jacksonville**

ES-3A

Estab. 5 Aug 1991 Disestab.30 Sep 1999 (26 Aug ceremony)

Like its West Coast counterpart, the *Black Ravens* provided signals intelligence to deploying carriers. Although established in 1991, the first *Shadow* was not delivered until August the following year. The *Ravens* (which adopted the same name as much-older EA-6B equipped VAQ-135) moved to nearby Jacksonville with the rest of the Atlantic-Fleet S-3 community when Cecil was closed in 1998. VQ-6 covered 13 deployments during its short history with four, two-aircraft detachments. It provided support for Operations *Southern Watch* and *Desert Fox*.

Jan to Jun 1994	*Saratoga*	CVW-17	Med	det A
Jun to Nov 1994	*G.Washington*	CVW-7	Med	det B
Nov 1994 to Apr 1995	*Eisenhower*	CVW-3	Med/PG	det C
Apr to Sep 1995	*Roosevelt*	CVW-8	Med/PG	det D
Sep 1995 to Feb 1996	*America*	CVW-1	Med/PG	det A
Jan to Jul 1996	*G.Washington*	CVW-7	Med/PG	det B
Jul to Dec 1996	*Enterprise*	CVW-17	Med/PG	det C
Dec 1996 to May 1997	*Roosevelt*	CVW-3	Med/PG	det D
Apr 1997 to Oct 1997	*J.F. Kennedy*	CVW-8	Med/PG	det A
Oct 1997 to Apr 1998	*G.Washington*	CVW-1	Med/PG	det B
Feb to Aug 1998	*J.C. Stennis*	CVW-7	World	det C
Jun to Dec 1998	*Eisenhower*	CVW-17	Med/PG	det D
Nov 1998 to May 1999	*Enterprise*	CVW-3	Med/PG	det A

8

Photo-Recon (RVAH/VFP)

"No matter where we go, the first thing the Admiral seems to want is pictures." - Anonymous Staff Officer

Reconnaissance Heavy Attack Squadrons (RVAH)

At the start of 1974, the entire Navy RVAH community (10 fleet squadrons and one FRS) was based at NAS Albany, GA, under the administrative control of Commander, Reconnaissance Attack Wing ONE (CRAW-1). The "Heavy Recon" units were the first in the Navy to routinely deploy to both coasts from one central location, which they had done since the introduction of the RA-5C *Vigilante* in the mid-'60s. Originally based at NAS Sanford, FL, the "Vigi" force moved to NAS Albany, GA (the former Turner AFB), in 1968. The entire community relocated again, to NAS Key West, FL, during 1974, where it remained until its 1978 demise.

All but two of the RVAH squadrons were descended from A-3 Heavy Attack (VAH) units. Within the VAH community, Atlantic Fleet units from Sanford were odd-numbered, while Pacific Fleet squadrons, located at Whidbey Island, were even numbered. RVAH-6 was the only original Whidbey-based *Skywarrior* unit to move east for *Vigilante* conversion, while RVAH-12 and -14 were established specifically as RA-5C squadrons at Sanford. The *Bats* of Heavy-13 were established with A3D-2s at Sanford, and moved to Whidbey before returning to Sanford for *Vigilante* transition.

To further add to the distinctive nature of the wing, all CRAW-1 squadrons were assigned distinctive tailcodes, starting with the letter "G," which were normally carried only by the FRS (RVAH-3) and, occasionally, units between air wings.

By 1974 shortages in airframes had forced RVAH squadrons to deploy with only three aircraft. Units were attached to air wings on *Forrestal*-class or larger carriers due to their size and landing speed, *Midway* and *Essex* class attack carriers normally carrying a VFP-63 RF-8G detachment in lieu of *Vigilantes*. The small number of squadrons resulted in units being transferred between Air Wings on a routine basis. Only rarely did *Vigilante* units make consecutive cruises on the same ship.

By any definition, the RA-5C was a remarkable platform. It was the Navy's fastest fleet aircraft in a combat configuration, routinely besting its fighter escort in both speed and endurance. The type's eye watering numbers came at the expense of landing characteristics, where its size and high approach speeds could make it a real handful to bring back aboard the boat.

The *Vigilante's* recon sensors were world class, and pushed the level of technology in the areas of infra-red, wet-film photography,

The *Sea Dragons* of RVAH-3 were the only RAG the *Vigilante* community ever had. GJ301 (156625) sits at Key West in April 1979, about four months before the unit was disestablished. (Michael Grove)

and even laser warning. At least one former CAG called the type "the finest conventional recon platform in the U.S. military" (the Air Force's SR-71 obviously being considered "unconventional" in this discussion!)

By the mid-'70s the Navy could no longer afford the luxury of a dedicated photo-recon platform on its decks. The type's complex systems, parts availability, and airframe attrition all conspired against it, and the first squadron (RVAH-14) was disestablished in May 1974. RF-8G detachments began to replace the "Vigi" on some of the big decks, and by 1979 all of the Heavy Recon squadrons were gone, with the final flight by a *Vigilante* being made on 20 Nov. The RA-5C was finally replaced in name, if not mission capability, by TARPS equipped F-14s. The Navy will be hard pressed to ever have a more strikingly beautiful aircraft in its inventory.

RVAH-1 *Smokin' Tigers* **Albany, Key West (8/74)**
RA-5C tailcode GH
Estab. VAH-1 1 Nov 55, r/d RVAH-1 1 Sep 64, Disest. 19 Jan 1979

1/74-8/74	*America*	MED	RA-5C	AJ60X
7/76-3/77	*Enterprise*	WP	RA-5C	NK61X
4/78-10/78	*Enterprise*	WP	RA-5C	NK61X

Notes: The *Tigers* had been the first A-3 *Skywarrior* unit to deploy, and one of only two squadrons to deploy with the initial attack version of the *Vigilante* (A3J-1/A-5A). They made ten deployments with the RA-5C, including four to Vietnam.

RVAH-3 *Sea Dragons* **Albany, Key West (1/74)** **FRS**
RA-5C, TA-3B, TA-4J tailcode: GJ
Estab. VAH-3 15 Jun 56, r/d RVAH-3 1 Jul 64, disestab. 17 Aug, 1979.
The *Vigilante* Fleet Readiness Squadron (FRS) throughout its life. TA-3B *Skywarriors* and TA-4 *Skyhawks* were utilized for navigator radar training, admin duties, and as chase planes for early RA-5C pilot training flights. The unit moved to Key West in January 1974, with a squadron strength of 8 RA-5Cs, 2 TA-3Bs, and a pair of TA-4Js.

RVAH-5 *Savage Sons* **Albany, Key West (1/74)**
RA-5C tailcode: GK
Estab. VC-5 9 Sep 48, r/d VAH-5 1 Nov 55, r/d RVAH-5 1 Mar 64, disestab, 30 Sep 1977

6/74-12/74	*Constellation*	WESTPAC	RA-5C	NG60X
1/76-9/76	*Ranger*	WESTPAC	RA-5C	NE61X

Operated the RA-5C from 1964 through 1976, making nine deployments. The *Sons* made the first deployment with the RA-5C, in 1964, with *Ranger* and CVW-9 in Vietnam. The squadron was also known as the "Mushmouths," based on their original patch from their A-3 days bearing the cartoon depiction of an African native's head. Banned for obvious reasons, the squadron developed a new logo featuring the silhouette of an American Indian in full headdress. However the older name persisted, and as late as 1969 a version of the older logo could be found peering over tail markings on squadron aircraft. Moved to Key West January 1974.

RVAH-6 *Fleurs* **Albany, Key West (9/74)**
RA-5C tailcode: GS
Estab. VC-6, 6 Jan 50, r/d VAH-6 1 Jul 56, r/d RVAH-6 23 Sep 65, disestab 20 Oct 1978

3-9/74	*Forrestal*	Med	RA-5C	AA600
5-12/75	*Kitty Hawk*	WestPac	RA-5C	NH600
12/77-7/78	*Nimitz*	Med	RA-5C	AJ600

Using a *fleur de lis* as an insignia, the squadron's title is French for "flower," which led to no small amount of ribbing from other "Vigi" units. The *Fleurs* made eight total RA-5C deployments, and were the last RVAH to deploy on a *Nimitz* class CVN. The squadron moved to Key West September 1974.

RVAH-7 *Peacemakers of the Fleet* **Albany, Key West (7/74)**
RA-5C tailcode: GL
Estab. VC-7 10 Aug 50, r/d VAH-7 1 Nov 55, r/d RVAH-7 1 Dec 64, disestab. 28 Sep, 1979

11/73-7/74	*Kitty Hawk*	WestPac	RA-5C	NH600
3-9/75	*Forrestal*	Med	RA-5C	AA600
10/77-5/78	*Kitty Hawk*	WestPac	RA-5C	NH610
2/79-9/79	*Ranger*	WestPac	RA-5C	NE610

The second of two operational A-5A squadrons, the *Peacemakers* made three deployments with the attack version, and ten with the RA-5C. They made the final fleet "Vigi" deployment, and were the last RVAH squadron in the Navy. Moved to Key West July 1974.

The last "Vigi" squadron to deploy was RVAH-7. AA603 (156639) has stopped for gas at Cannon AFB, NM, in August 1976. The squadron still has three years and two deployments to go before being disestablished. (John Pouch)

RVAH-9 ***Hoot Owls*** **Albany, Key West (1/74)**
RA-5C tailcode: GM
Estab. VC-9 15 Jan 53, r/d VAH-9 1 Nov 55, r/d RVAH-9 3 Jun 64, disestab. 30 Sep 1977

7/74-1/75	*Independence*	Med	RA-5C	AG60X
7/76-2/77	*Nimitz*	Med	RA-5C	AJ60X

The "Hooters" made nine *Vigilante* deployments, all but two to the Med.

RVAH-11 ***Checkertails*** **Albany, Key West ('74)**
RA-5C tailcode: GN
Estab. VC-8 3 Dec 51, r/d VAH-11 1 Nov 55, r/d RVAH-11 1 Jul 66, disestab. 1 June 1975

9/74-3/75	*Saratoga*	Med	RA-5C	AC600

The *Checkertails* were the second "Vigi" unit to disestablish following Vietnam. They made seven RA-5C deployments, four of which were to South East Asia.

RVAH-12 ***Speartips*** **Albany, Key West (1/74)**
RA-5C tailcode: GP
Estab. RVAH-12 1 Jul 65, disestab. 2 Jul, 1979

9/74-5/75	*Enterprise*	WestPac	RA-5C	NK600
1976	*Forrestal*	Naval Review	RA-5C	AA600
3-10/77	*Independence*	Med	RA-5C	AG600
10/78-2/79	*Saratoga*	Med	RA-5C	AC60X

The *Speartips* were the first "Vigi" unit that did not have an A-3 background. Made the last Vigilante cruise to the Mediterranean. Moved to Key West January 1974. RVAH-12 joined CVW-17 in late 1975, and supported the wing for a short series of work ups and the 1976 Bi-Centennial Naval Review. They transferred to CVW-7 in Oct '76, and made two more Med deployments before being disestablished in July '79.

RVAH-13 ***Bats*** **Albany, Key West (4/74)**
RA-5C tailcode: GR
Estab. VAH-13 3 Jan 61, r/d RVAH-13 1 Nov 64, disestab. 30 June 1976

5-10/74	*Ranger*	WestPac	RA-5C	NE60X
10/75-4/76	*Independence*	Med	RA-5C	AG60X

The *Bats* were formed at Sanford in 1961 with A3D-2s, and quickly moved to the West Coast with the new carrier *Constellation*. After three short years at Whidbey the unit returned to Florida in 1964 for *Vigilante* transition. The *Bats* made eight RA-5C deployments. Their insignia is derived from the Bacardi Rum label.

RVAH-14 ***Eagle Eyes*** **Albany**
RA-5C tailcode: GQ
Estab. 1 Feb 1968 disestab. 1 May, 1974

6/73-1/74	*Independence*	Med	RA-5C	AG60X

The shortest lived *Vigilante* unit, RVAH-14 made only four cruises to the Med before becoming the first RVAH to be disestablished. The *Eagle Eyes* were the only *Vigilante* squadron that did not move to Key West.

Light Photographic Squadrons (VFP)

The VFP community was made up of a single Regular Navy outfit (VFP-63) out of Miramar and a pair of Reserve units (VFP-206, -306) based at NAF Washington. The "Fightin' Photos" and their RF-8s established an enviable record, and actually outlasted the RA-5C *Vigilante* in the photo mission, but only by about three years.

VFP-63 ***Eyes of the Fleet*** **Miramar** **(FRS)**
RF-8G, F-8H, F-8J Tailcode: PP
Estab. as VC-61 20 Jan 49, r/d VFP-61 2 Jul 56, r/d VCP-63 1 Jul 59, r/d VFP-63 1 Jul 61
Disestab. 30 Jun 1982 (11 Jun 82 ceremony)

8 May 73 to 8 Jan 74	*Hancock*	WP/IO	RF-8G	NP600	det 1
14 Sep 73 to 17 Mar 74	*FD Roosevelt*	Med	RF-8G	AE600	det 2
18 Oct 73 to 5 Jun 74	*Oriskany*	WP/IO	RF-8G	NM600	det 4
29 Jan to 6 Mar 74	*Midway*	WP	RF-8G	NF600	det 3
5 Dec 74 to 2 Jul 75	*Coral Sea*	WP	RF-8G	NL600	det 5
3 Jan to 16 Jul 75	*FD Roosevelt*	Med	RF-8G	AE600	det 2
18 Mar to 20 Oct 75	*Hancock*	WP	RF-8G	NP600	det 1
16 Sep to 3 Mar 76	*Oriskany*	WP	RF-8G	NM600	det 4
15 Apr to 25 Oct 76	*America*	Med	RF-8G	AE710	det 5
2 Sep to 9 Oct 76	*JF Kennedy*	NorLant	RF-8G	AB600	det 2
15 Jan to 1 Aug 77	*JF Kennedy*	Med	RF-8G	AB620	det 2
15 Feb to 5 Oct 77	*Coral Sea*	WP	RF-8G	NL610	det 3
12 Apr to 21 Nov 77	*Constellation*	WP	RF-8G	NG610	det 1
10 Jun to 19 Jul 77	*America*	SoLant	RF-8G	AE710	det 5
25 Sep 77 to 25 Apr 78	*America*	Med	RF-8G	AE710	det 5
29 Jun 78 to 8 Feb 79	*JF Kennedy*	Med	RF-8G	AB620	det 2
26 Sep 78 to 17 May 79	*Constellation*	WP/IO	RF-8G	NG610	det 3
13 Mar 79 to 25 Feb 80	*America*	Med	RF-8G	NH610	det 4
30 May 79 to 25 May 80	*Kitty Hawk*	WP/IO	RF-8G	NL610	det 1
10 Sep 79 to 26 May 80	*Nimitz*	IO	RF-8G	AJ600	det 5
det 5 cross-decked to *Coral Sea* 17 Apr 80 and joined det 2 to return to CONUS					
30 Sep 79 to 20 May 80	*Coral Sea*	WP/IO	RF-8G	NK620	det 2
26 Feb to 15 Oct 80	*Constellation*	WP/IO	RF-8G	NG610	det 3
19 Nov 80 to 10 Jun 81	*Independence*	Med/IO	RF-8G	AE616	det 4
1 Apr 81 to 23 Nov 81	*Kitty Hawk*	WP/IO	RF-8G	NL115	det 1
20 Aug 81 to 23 Mar 82	*Coral Sea*	WP/IO	RF-8G	NK115	det 2

Detachments listed are verified through official squadron records. There appears to have been dets provided to other carriers at times, but squadron records only show dets leaving or returning from "major" deployments to the Western Pacific, Mediterranean, or Indian Ocean.

Miramar's VFP-63 provided the last RF-8G detachments to carriers. The final trip to the Med was conducted by det 4, who deployed in Indy with CVW-7 in 1980-81. Here AG618 (144618) taxis at Fallon in May '80. (Michael Grove)

VFP-63 had a long and illustrious history, having, in one form or another, provided photo dets to Pacific Fleet carriers since 1949. They deployed "P" versions of the *Panther*, *Banshee*, *Cougar*, *Skywarrior*, and *Crusader*, and saw heavy combat in Korea and Vietnam. The unit lost 20 aircraft in the later war, along with seven pilots killed. The type's last combat appears to have been with det 5 in 1975, when its aircraft made opposed runs over mainland Cambodia during the *Mayaguez* rescue.

The unit had been the only deploying RF-8 outfit since the January 1968 disestablishment of its East Coast counterpart, VFP-62, with most detachments having three aircraft. Up through 1976 the RF-8G was used on *Midway* and *Essex* class ships, with the RA-5Cs covering the "big deck" *Forrestal* and later carriers. In 1976 Photo-*Crusaders* started making deployments in the larger ships again as the *Vigilante* community wound down. Demand outstripped availability, with the result being several carrier/air wings cruised without dedicated photo-recon support. Nonetheless, the RF-8 would deploy for another six years before the last det returned home to Miramar, in 1982.

In September 1972 VFP-63 became the sole F-8 FRS, taking the mission over from VF-124, which was transitioning to the new F-14 *Tomcat*. Specialized VF syllabus events to train crews for the last four *Crusader* fighter units continued until July 1975, although F-8Js were retained in the squadron until October 1980 as additional non-mission airframes for VFP pilot training. Squadron strength as of mid-1979 was 24 RF-8G and 5 F-8J. New pilot training was completed in January 1981 with the graduation of LTJG John Dugene, who made the final deployment with det 2 in *Coral Sea*. The squadron's last RF-8G was transferred to MASDC on 28 May 1982, about two weeks before the disestablishment ceremony.

Squadron aircraft normally used a "PP" tailcode when in CONUS and air wing codes while deployed. While home at Miramar, VFP-63 came under the control of FitAEWWingPac.

VFP-206 ***Hawkeyes*** **Washington** **Naval Reserve**
RF-8G
Estab . 1 Jun 1970disestab. 29 Mar 1987
VFP-206 was attached to CVWR-20, and was one of two Reserve RF-8 units; the *Hawkeyes* would be the last U.S. military operator of the legendary *Crusader*, being disestablished in Mar 1987. The squadron made the last cats and traps of U.S. Navy *Crusaders* in October 1986 on *America*. Squadron aircraft carried at least three sets of side numbers over the years, moving from AF630 to 600, and finally 700.

VFP-306 ***Photomasters*** **Washington** **Naval Reserve**
RF-8G
Estab. 1 Jun 1970 disestab. 9 Sep 1984
Assigned to CVWR-30, VFP-306 operated for 14 years. ND600 series numbers were carried by the squadron throughout its existence.

VFP-63 operated fighter F-8s along with its photo birds up through October 1980 for use as pilot trainers. F-8J PP102 (150297) waits at Miramar's hold short prior to take off on 16 Feb '79. (Bob Lawson).

A Reserve RF-8G from VFP-206 calls at Glenview, IL, on 17 July 1986. AF602 (146882) carries Tactical Paint Scheme with very subdued markings. The squadron would disestablish in March of the following year, closing the book on U.S. Navy *Crusader* operations. (author)

9

Air Antisubmarine Squadrons (VS) Sea Control Squadrons (VS)

"Nobody seems to understand what we do out here. Sometimes we can't get the time of day out of the Flag staff. But have a Soviet sub show up in the area and see how many friends we have." - S-3 aviator to the author, USS *Constellation*, 1985

The Navy's carrier-based anti-submarine warfare (ASW) force ended the Vietnam War at the end of the S-2 era, and on the cusp of the S-3 age.

Fleet S-2 units were based at Quonset Point, RI, and North Island, CA. The *Viking* initially went into North Island and Cecil Field, which coincided with closure of the Rhode Island base.

Grumman's S-2 had a lot of character. It was known affectionately throughout the Navy as the "Stoof," which was derived from its pre-1962 S2F designation, as well as by a lot of other titles, one of the better of which being "two T-28s flying formation with a garbage truck." The *Tracker* was indeed the heart and soul of the VS community, and its decidedly unglamorous piston-slapping, oil dripping, unpressurized image was in stark contrast to the pointy-nosed, afterburning, go-fast "Jet Navy" on the attack carriers. In '70s terms, it was like comparing your sister to Raquel Welch. Sure, Sis had her points, but who would you rather see in a bathing suit contest?

For about twenty years the Navy operated distinct ASW Groups (formally called CVSGs from 1960), made up of S-2 and SH-3 squadrons. The development of the "CV concept" led to the retirement of the special ASW groups, and movement of the VS and HS units to the big deck "attack" carriers. Along with the additional aircraft, the "new" CVs had ASW Operations Centers (ASWOCs) added to monitor the undersea battle. Five *Tracker* squadrons deployed with CVs prior to the *Viking's* arrival in the early '70s to test this concept, using both S-2Es and Gs.

Initial results were mixed, in that the addition of up to two more squadrons to the carrier led to overcrowding on the ship and flight deck. Some Air Wings left CONUS with their ASW assets, only to deposit them at Sigonella or Cubi for the majority of cruise, while the jets went out and did their "attack carrier" thing. Other wings tried to make it work with varied results, particularly since attack and fighter crews often had trouble understanding ASW ("Awful Slow Warfare") and its nuances. The uncertainties and tedium of chasing an unseen enemy with no immediate feedback like gun camera film or a bomb spot had the unwanted effect of frequently placing the VS crews in something of a "back of the bus" situation with their other air wing brethren. Nonetheless the die was cast, and by the end of 1975 every carrier in the fleet had dropped the "Attack" portion of their CVA/CVAN title for the CV/CVN designation.

A section of *Top Cats* head to the Fallon ranges with a load of Mk.82 500lb bombs on 19 May 1987. AG705 wears the original gray and white paint, while wingman -706 is in TPS. (Bob Lawson)

First introduced on 20 Feb 1974, the Lockheed S-3 *Viking* changed the entire face of the VS community. Known universally as the "Hoover" from its distinctive vacuum-cleaner like engine noise, the S-3 was to have been an important step towards making the "CV concept" work in the mid to late 1970s. In the end, however, the Navy dropped their primary mission, gave them a new name ("Sea Control"), and taught them a few new tricks while headed for the demise of the entire community.

The first S-3 squadron to deploy was VS-21, a North Island unit that went to the Med in *John F. Kennedy* with CVW-1 in 1975-76. S-2 units quickly transitioned to the new aircraft so that, by 1980, every air wing on *Forrestal*-class CVs or larger had "Hoovers" attached (*Midway*-class carriers never having S-3 squadrons assigned).

West Coast squadrons were based at North Island, while the East Coast home for *Vikings* was Cecil Field until 1999-2000, when they moved down the road to the P-3 and helo base at Jacksonville.

Pacific Fleet units generally rotated between carriers until the mid-'80s, while Atlantic Fleet S-3 squadrons normally stayed with one air wing for their entire lives.

Whatever the merits of their platform, within the air wing the S-3 community frequently suffered from a Rodney Dangerfield "Don't get no respect" image. Early policy (which was continued from S-2s) placed two rated Naval Aviators in the front seats, with a single NFO and Enlisted ASW Operator in the back. Lack of flight time and traps for junior pilots developed into significant morale problems within the community which led, from 1988, to the reduction of pilots by 1/2, and the training of NFOs to man the front right seat as tactical coordinators and navigators. Even with this change the VS business was often misunderstood within some Air Wings and at times its members seemed to be stuck in a cycle of proving their worth to the staffs and their peers.

The S-3A was replaced by the S-3B, which first flew on 13 Sep 1984, and went to the fleet from 1989. Improvements in the type included AGM-84 *Harpoon* anti-ship missile, APS-137 Inverse Synthetic Aperture Radar (ISAR), ALE-39 chaff buckets and improved ALR-76 ESM system. The East Coast started conversion in 1988, and the west coast followed from October 1990. The first "Bravo" deployment would be made by VS-31, with Air Wing Seven in 1990. The final "A" model cruise would occur with VS-38 three years later.

In 1998 the "Hoover" also started carrying an air-refueling store under its port wing, with VS-37 being the first unit to deploy with the capability. It was this mission for which the type became really critical, particularly after the retirement of the A-6 *Intruder* series in the mid to late 1990s.

Desert Storm proved to be the *Vikings'* actual "baptism of fire," and the type proved valuable in patrolling the northern Arabian Gulf for Iraqi shipping, as well as ESM platforms augmenting the EA-6Bs. At least one Iraqi boat was sunk by VS-32 during the war, when the pilot dropped three Mk.82 bombs, as well as his D-704 buddy store on the target. In another incident a VS-24 S-3B managed to bolter on *Midway*, which the crew had somehow mistaken for the somewhat larger *Theodore Roosevelt*. It was only on downwind for their second pass when they realized their mistake in basic ship identification, and they sheepishly departed the *Midway's* pattern to find the right boat. The *Scouts* of VS-24 also claimed to be the first S-3 unit to drop bombs on a land target during the war, when they dumped a load of Mk.82s on an Iraqi AAA battery on the Al Faw peninsula.

In 16 Sep 1993 the community's units were renamed Sea Control Squadrons (SEACONRONs), although they retained the VS designation. The type's excellent ISAR, long loitering capability, and diverse weapons load (including, but not limited to, *Harpoon*, *Maverick*, rockets, torpedoes, and bombs) made the type a superb patrol and surveillance asset. Unfortunately, as time went on, it frequently seemed as if the tanking mission overrode all others. As a gas passer the "Hoover" was well suited to handle the departure and recovery mission over the carrier, but the design's low top end speed made it largely unsuitable as a mission tanker, as it was unable to keep up with F/A-18 *Hornet* strike groups.

The post *Desert Storm* period saw the formation of one new squadron (VS-35), while three were disestablished (VS-27, -28, and 37). The community dropped to one RAG (VS-41), and the S-3B equipped all air wings. Nonetheless, the type lost its ASW mission, along with all of its superb enlisted AW aircrewmen, in 1999-2000, with the carrier-protection mission being taken over completely by submarines, helicopters and, at least theoretically, shore-based P-3s. Squadron size was reduced to six aircraft in 1992, only to be increased back to eight a year later, largely to provide tanking platforms with the impending retirement of the A-6 series.

The "War Hoover's" superb crews continued to excel at the "sea control" role, and gamely carried out the decidedly unglamorous tanker mission, as well. No matter how well they did their work though, by 2000 it was obvious that the entire community would be extinct within a decade. It has been said by more than one observer that VS deserved better.

A single *Viking* (157996) was rebuilt as a KS-3A in the late 1970s with an internal hose-drum refueling unit to test the platform as a dedicated tanker. Although the aircraft served until 1984 with VS-41, in the end the Navy decided to modify fleet aircraft for buddy store use. The KS-3A was rebuilt into a US-3A, and was lost with two VRC-50 pilots while conducting a practice emergency approach at Cubi Point on 20 Jan '89.

The ES-3A *Shadow* derivative is covered under the VQ part of chapter 7. The US-3A "Miss Piggy" series can be found with the VRC section in chapter 6.

VS-21 ***Redtails*** **North Island, Atsugi**

S-2E, S-2G, S-3A, S-3B

Estab. CVEG-41 26 Mar 45, r/d CVEG-1 15 Nov 46, r/d VC-21 1 Sep 48, r/d VS-21 23 Apr 50

28 Jun 75 to 27 Jan 76	*JF Kennedy*	Med	S-3A	AB600
12 Apr to 21 Nov 77	*Constellation*	WP	S-3A	NG700
30 May 79 to 25 May 80	*Kitty Hawk*	WP/IO	S-3A	NL700
(1980)	——	no cruise	S-3A	NK700

An NK tailcode on an S-3A wouldn't normally turn heads, but in this case CVW-14 is matched to the *Coral Sea*, which had no *Vikings* assigned. VS-21 carried the code twice during the early 1980s, but did not deploy with the wing until 1991. NK710 (160569) sits at Key West on 29 Nov 1980. 1979 must've been good for the outfit, as the aircraft displays a Battle "E" and Isbell Trophy ("A"), as well as a "Golden Wrench" award. (author)

7 Apr to 19 Oct 1982	*Ranger*	WP/IO	S-3A	NE700	
(1983)	——	no cruise	S-3A	NK700	
30 May to 20 Dec 84	*Enterprise*	WP/IO	S-3A	NH700	
15 Jan to 12 Aug 1986	*Enterprise*	WP/IO/Med/SL	S-3A	NH700	
25 Oct to 24 Nov 87	*Enterprise*	NorPac	S-3A	NH700	
5 Jan to 3 Jul 88	*Enterprise*	WP/IO	S-3A	NH700	
17 Sep 89 to 16 Mar 90	*Enterprise*	World	S-3A	NH700	
5 to 22 Aug 1991	*Independence*	Hawaii	S-3B	NK700	'swapex'
Aug 1991 to 1999	*Independence*	fwd deployed	S-3B	NF700	
1999 to 2001	*Kitty Hawk*	fwd deployed	S-3B	NF700	

VS-21 is one of the more notable *Viking* units for a number of reasons. The *Redtails* were the initial fleet S-3 squadron, accepting their first *Vikings* in June 1974. They also were the first to go to sea with the type, making a Med deployment in *Kennedy* in 1975-76. 25 years later they remain the only North Island-based VS unit to deploy with an East Coast Air Wing. VS-21 deployed with more air wings (7) than any other *Viking* unit. It appears to have been assigned to CVW-14 at least three times, but only deployed with that wing once, for the *Indy/Midway* Hawaiian "swapex." The periods where they wore the "NK" code in 1980 and 1983 appear to have been as placeholders only, as the wing was assigned to the *Coral Sea*, which did not deploy with "Hoovers." The squadron moved to Atsugi, Japan, in 1991 with *Independence*, and joined CVW-5, making it the only forward deployed VS squadron. See CVW-5 listings in chapter 3 for more detailed information on deployments from Japan.

VS-22 ***Checkmates, Vidars*** **Cecil Field, Jacksonville**

S-2E, S-2G, S-3A, S-3B

Estab. VS-22 18 May 60

6 Jan to 28 Jul 76	*Saratoga*	Med	S-3A	AC620	
11 Jul to 23 Dec 1977	*Saratoga*	Med	S-3A	AC620	
3 Oct 78 to 5 Apr 79	*Saratoga*	Med	S-3A	AC700	
10 Mar to 27 Aug 80	*Saratoga*	Med	S-3A	AC700	
4 Jan to 14 Jul 82	*JF Kennedy*	Med/IO	S-3A	AC700	
25 May to 1 Jul 83	*JF Kennedy*	NorLant	S-3A	AC700	
27 Sep 83 to 2 May 84	*JF Kennedy*	Med	S-3A	AC700	
18 Aug 86 to 3 Mar 87	*JF Kennedy*	Med	S-3A	AC700	
2 Aug 88 to 1 Feb 89	*JF Kennedy*	Med	S-3A	AC700	
15 Aug 90 to 28 Mar 91	*JF Kennedy*	Med/RS	S-3B	AC700	*Desert Storm*
7 Oct 92 to 7 Apr 93	*JF Kennedy*	Med	S-3B	AC700	
20 Oct 94 to 15 Apr 95	*Eisenhower*	Med/RS/PG	S-3B	AC700	
25 Nov 96 to 22 May 97	*T Roosevelt*	Med/RS/PG	S-3B	AC700	
6 Nov 98 to 6 May 99	*Enterprise*	Med/RS/PG	S-3B	AC700	
28 Nov 99 to 23 May 01	*HS Truman*	Med/RS/PG	S-3B	AC700	

VS-22 used its *Vidar* callsign as an alternate nickname. As of 1974 it was still an S-2 unit, and moved, without aircraft, to North Island to transition to the *Viking*. The squadron was in place at Cecil by mid-1975, and made their initial S-3A Med deployment in *Saratoga*. The squadron never left CVW-3, and followed the wing as it moved through six different carriers.

The ALE-37 chaff buckets aft of the wheel wells quickly mark this "Hoover" as an S-3B, which replaced the S-3A in the fleet between 1988 and 1993. The *Viking* also took on the tanking mission during the same period. VS-24's AJ705 is shown here over Fallon on 19 Apr '90 with the hose extended from its buddy store. The *Scout* has its FLIR turret extended so the crew can watch what's going on behind it. (author)

VS-24	***Scouts***	**Cecil Field, Jacksonville**			
S-2E, S-2G, S-3A, S-3B					
Estab. VS-24 25 May 1960					
27 Sep 74 to 19 Mar 75	*Saratoga*	Med	S-2G	AC610	
1 Dec 77 to 20 Jul 78	*Nimitz*	Med/NL	S-3A	AJ700	
10 Sep 79 to 26 May 80	*Nimitz*	Med/IO	S-3A	AJ700	
3 Aug 81 to 12 Feb 82	*Nimitz*	Med	S-3A	AJ700	
10 Nov 82 to 20 May 83	*Nimitz*	Med	S-3A	AJ700	
8 Mar to 4 Oct 85	*Nimitz*	Med	S-3A	AJ700	
20 Dec 86 to 26 Jul 86	*Nimitz*	World	S-3A	AJ700	
25 Aug to 11 Oct 88	*T Roosevelt*	NorLant	S-3A	AJ700	
30 Dec 90 to 28 Jun 91	*T Roosevelt*	Med/RS/PG	S-3B	AJ700	*Desert Storm*
11 Mar to 8 Sep 93	*T Roosevelt*	Med/RS	S-3B	AJ700	
22 Mar to 22 Sep 95	*T Roosevelt*	Med/RS/PG	S-3B	AJ700	
29 Apr to 28 Oct 97	*JF Kennedy*	Med/RS/PG	S-3B	AJ700	
26 Mar to 22 Sep 99	*T Roosevelt*	Med/RS/PG	S-3B	AJ700	

Also known as the "Duty Cats" for their irreverent alternate patch, which featured a beat-up looking black feline with a lightning bolt hitting it in the rear end. VS-24 made one "CV concept" cruise with S-2s before transitioning to *Vikings*. Although several squadron S-3As were initially marked for CVW-17 (AA) in 1975, the squadron has served with CVW-8 ever since 1976, and participated in *Desert Storm*. During DS a VS-24 S-3B dropped a load of MK.82 bombs on a AAA site on Iraq's Al Faw peninsula, apparently making it the first of its type to ever drop bombs over land. CAG-8 congratulated the crew, and then, with concern for the aircraft's vulnerability, promptly banned the squadron from ever going over the beach again. On 4 July 1980 the squadron was involved in a tragedy when a child was inadvertently ejected from one of their *Vikings* (159769) while the aircraft was on display at an airshow at NAS Willow Grove, PA. The child was killed, and the S-3 community was promptly forbidden from opening cockpits to viewing during public displays.

VS-27	***Sea Wolves***	**Cecil Field**	**FRS**

S-3A, S-3B

Estab. 30 Jan 1987 (22 Jan ceremony) Disestab. 30 Sep 1994. (29 Sep ceremony)

VS-27 was formed in 1987 from the VSSU (see below) as the East Coast S-3 Fleet Readiness Squadron. This was the second VS-27, as the original unit was disestablished in June 1973. VS-27 initiated training in the S-3B type, with the first one arriving in Nov 1987. The squadron was disestablished in September 1994, with VS-41 becoming the sole S-3 FRS yet again. The *Wolves* used the traditional AirLant RAG "AD" tailcode on its aircraft. Official Navy documents dated December '83 state that the second VS FRS was originally scheduled to be designated VS-40; however, by 1987 the title had changed to VS-27.

VS-28	***Hukkers, Gamblers***	**Cecil Field, Jacksonville**		
S-2E, S-2G, S-3A, S-3B				
Estab. 1 Jun 60	disestablished	1 Oct 92		
21 Jun 73 to 19 Jan 74	*Independence*	Med	S-2E	AG920
15 Apr to 25 Oct 76	*America*	Med	S-3A	AE600
10 Jun to 19 Jul 77	*America*	SoLant	S-3A	AE600
25 Sep 77 to 25 Apr 78	*America*	Med	S-3A	AE600

28 Jun to 14 Dec 79	*Independence*	Med	S-3A	AE600	
19 Nov 80 to 19 Jun 81	*Independence*	Med/IO	S-3A	AE700	
7 Jun to 22 Dec 82	*Independence*	Med	S-3A	AE700	
18 Oct 83 to 11 Apr 84	*Independence*	Med	S-3A	AE700	Grenada
16 Oct 84 to 19 Feb 85	*Independence*	Med/RS/IO	S-3A	AE700	
2 Jun to 10 Nov 86	*Forrestal*	Med	S-3A	AE700	
25 Apr to 7 Oct 88	*Forrestal*	Med/IO/NL	S-3A	AE700	
4 Nov 89 to 12 Apr 90	*Forrestal*	Med	S-3A	AE700	
30 May to 21 Dec 91	*Forrestal*	Med	S-3B	AE700	

The squadron's original name was *Hukkers*, which changed in 1985 to *Gamblers*. Equipped with Grumman S-2s as of 1974, the unit was taking part in a "CV concept" deployment with *Independence*/CVW-7, although the unit, which was augmented with crews from VS-22, actually was beached at Souda Bay, Crete, between September and January '74. They returned home, and moved temporarily to North Island for transition to the *Viking*. During *Urgent Fury* the *Gamblers* were used for sea surveillance missions around the island of Grenada. The squadron made only one deployment with the S-3B before being disestablished, along with CVW-6.

VS-29 ***Dragonfires*** **North Island**

S-2E, S-2G, S-3A, S-3B

Estab. VS-29 1 Apr 60

30 Jul 76 to 28 Mar 77	*Enterprise*	WP/IO	S-3A	NK700
21 Feb to 22 Sep 79	*Ranger*	WP	S-3A	NE700
1 Apr to 23 Nov 81	*Kitty Hawk*	WP/IO	S-3A	NL700
1 Mar to 29 Oct 83	*Carl Vinson*	World	S-3A	NL700
18 Oct 84 to 25 May 85	*Carl Vinson*	WP/IO	S-3A	NL700
12 Aug 86 to 5 Feb 87	*Carl Vinson*	WP/IO	S-3A	NL700
15 Jun to 14 Dec 88	*Carl Vinson*	WP/IO	S-3A	NL700
5 Sep to 8 Nov 89	*Carl Vinson*	NorPac	S-3A	NL700
1 Feb to 31 Jul 90	*Carl Vinson*	WP/IO	S-3A	NL700
28 May to 28 Nov 91	*Lincoln*	WP/IO/PG	S-3A	NH700
15 Jun to 15 Dec 93	*Lincoln*	WP/IO/PG	S-3B	NH700
10 Apr to 9 Oct 95	*Lincoln*	WP/IO/PG	S-3B	NH700
6 Nov 98 to 6 May 99	*Carl Vinson*	WP/IO/PG	S-3B	NH700

VS-29 made the first Pacific Fleet deployment with the *Viking*, making the 1976 cruise with CVW-14 in *Enterprise*. They subsequently deployed with two other air wings before settling with CVW-11. During 1975 the squadron's S-3s initially carried the NS code of defunct CVSG-53.

VS-30 ***Diamondcutters*** **Cecil Field, Jacksonville (FRS)**

S-2E, S-2G, S-3A, S-3B

Reserve VS-801 activated 9 Apr 51, r/d VS-30 4 Feb 53

4 Apr to 26 Oct 78	*Forrestal*	Med/NL	S-3A	AA700	
27 Nov 79 to 7 May 80	*Forrestal*	Med	S-3A	AA700	
2 Mar to 15 Sep 81	*Forrestal*	Med	S-3A	AA700	
8 Jun to 16 Nov 82	*Forrestal*	Med	S-3A	AA700	
2 Apr to 20 Oct 84	*Forrestal*	Med	S-3A	AA700	
26 Aug 85 to 16 Apr 86	*Saratoga*	Med/RS/IO	S-3A	AA700	
5 Jun to 17 Nov 87	*Saratoga*	Med	S-3A	AA700	
15 Aug to 8 Oct 88	*Independence*	Horn	S-3B	AA700	
7 Aug 90 to 28 Mar 91	*Saratoga*	Med/RS	S-3B	AA700	*Desert Storm*
6 May to 6 Nov 92	*Saratoga*	Med	S-3B	AA700	
12 Jun to 24 Jun 94	*Saratoga*	Med	S-3B	AA700	
28 Jun to 20 Dec 96	*Enterprise*	Med/RS/PG	S-3B	AA700	
10 Jun to 10 Dec 98	*Eisenhower*	Med/RS/PG	S-3B	AA700	
21 Jun to 18 Dec 00	*G Washington*	Med/RS/PG	S-3B	AA700	

VS-30 was the sole S-2 FRS as of 1974, having moved to Florida from Quonset Point in Sept '73. The last "Stoof" class, made up largely of Peruvian Navy flight crew, graduated in Oct 1975. VS-30 officially became a fleet squadron in Jan 1976, and transitioned to the S-3A. The unit has deployed with only one air wing with *Vikings*, that being CVW-17. They were the first squadron to deploy with the improved S-3B, taking part in a trip around the Horn with *Independence* in 1988 and, subsequently, to *Desert Storm*. in *Saratoga*.

VS-31 ***Top Cats*** **Cecil Field, Jacksonville**
S-2E, S-2G, S-3A, S-3B
Estab. VC-31 28 Sep 48, r/d VS-31 20 Apr 51.

19 Jul 74 to 21 Jan 75	*Independence*	Med	S-2G	AG920	
31 Mar to 21 Oct 77	*Independence*	Med	S-3A	AG700	
16 Jan to 13 Jul 79	*Eisenhower*	Med	S-3A	AG700	
15 Apr to 22 Dec 80	*Eisenhower*	IO	S-3A	AG700	
20 Aug to 7 Oct 81	*Eisenhower*	NorLant	S-3A	AG700	
5 Jan to 13 Jul 82	*Eisenhower*	Med	S-3A	AG700	
27 Apr to 2 Dec 83	*Eisenhower*	Med	S-3A	AG700	
8 May to 20 Jun 84	*Eisenhower*	NorLant	S-3A	AG700	
10 Oct 84 to 8 May 85	*Eisenhower*	Med	S-3A	AG700	
29 Feb to 29 Aug 88	*Eisenhower*	Med	S-3A	AG700	
8 Mar to 12 Sep 90	*Eisenhower*	Med/RS	S-3B	AG700	*Desert Shield*
26 Sep 91 to 2 Apr 92	*Eisenhower*	Med	S-3B	AG700	
20 May to 17 Nov 94	*G Washington*	Med/NL	S-3B	AG700	
26 Jan to 23 Jul 96	*G Washington*	Med/RS/PG	S-3B	AG700	
26 Feb to 26 Aug 98	*JC Stennis*	World	S-3B	AG700	
18 Feb to 18 Aug 00	*Eisenhower*	Med/RS/PG	S-3B	AG700	

VS-31 made a single "CV concept" trials cruise with "Stoofs" before transitioning to *Vikings*. The squadron has been assigned to CVW-7 throughout. For a short period in 1974 they used a two-digit side number ("AG XX") series before moving to the now-standard 700 series. VS-31 was the last unit to have enlisted ASW operators, transferring their final such aircrew on 24 Mar '99.

VS-32 ***Norsemen, Maulers*** ***Cecil Field, Jacksonville***
S-2E, S-3A, S-3B
Estab. VC-32 31 May 49, r/d VS-32 20 Apr 50

15 Jan to 1 Aug 77	*JF Kennedy*	Med	S-3A	AB700	
29 Jun to 8 Feb 79	*JF Kennedy*	Med	S-3A	AB700	
4 Aug 80 to 28 Mar 81	*JF Kennedy*	Med	S-3A	AB700	
23 Aug to 30 Aug 82	*America*	NL/Med/Carib	S-3A	AB700	
8 Dec 82 to 2 Jun 83	*America*	Med/IO	S-3A	AB700	
24 Apr to 14 Nov 84	*America*	Med/IO	S-3A	AB700	
10 Mar to 10 Sep 86	*America*	Med/IO	S-3A	AB700	
8 Feb to 3 Apr 89	*America*	NorLant	S-3A	AB700	
11 May to 10 Nov 89	*America*	Med/IO	S-3A	AB700	
28 Dec 90 to 18 Apr 91	*America*	Med/RS/PG	S-3B	AB700	*Desert Storm*
2 Dec 91 to 6 Jun 92	*America*	Med	S-3B	AB700	
11 Aug 93 to 5 Feb 94	*America*	Med/RS/PG	S-3B	AB700	
28 Aug 95 to 24 Feb 96	*America*	Med/RS/PG	S-3B	AB700	
3 Oct 97 to 3 Apr 98	*G Washington*	Med/RS/PG	S-3B	AB700	
15 Sep 99 to 19 Mar 00	*JF Kennedy*	Med/RS/PG	S-3B	AB700	

Famed in *Desert Storm* for being the first S-3 unit to sink an enemy boat, although with a trio of Mk.82 bombs and a D-704 buddy store that also left the aircraft (AB705, 159765). The squadron were initially called the *Norsemen*, but changed to the *Maulers* during the period.

VS-33 ***Screwbirds*** ***North Island***
S-2G, S-3A, S-3B, US-3A
Estab. VS-33 1 Apr 60

25 Oct 77 to 15 May 78	*Kitty Hawk*	WP	S-3A, US-3A	NH700
13 Mar to 22 Sep 79	*America*	Med	S-3A	NH700
14 Apr to 12 Nov 81	*America*	Med/IO	S-3A	NH700
15 Jul 83 to 29 Feb 84	*Ranger*	SoPac/WP/IO	S-3A	NG700

24 Jul to 21 Dec 85	*Kitty Hawk*	WP/IO	S-3A	NG700
3 Jan to 29 Jun 87	*Kitty Hawk*	World	S-3A	NG700
2 Sep 88 to 2 Mar 89	*Nimitz*	WP/IO	S-3A	NG700
15 Jun to 9 Jul 89	*Nimitz*	NorPac	S-3A	NG700
12 Feb to 7 Apr 90	*Constellation*	Horn	S-3A	NG700
25 Feb to 24 Aug 91	*Nimitz*	WP/IO/PG	S-3A	NG700
2 Feb to 29 Jul 93	*Nimitz*	WP/IO/PG	S-3B	NG700
27 Nov 95 to 20 May 96	*Nimitz*	WP/IO/PG	S-3B	NG700
1 Sep 97 to 1 Mar 98	*Nimitz*	WP/IO/PG	S-3B	NG700
7 Jan to 3 Jul 00	*Nimitz*	WP/IO/PG	S-3B	NG700

VS-33 possesses one of the more colorful names and logos in Naval Aviation, that of a sad looking feathered creature with a machine screw run through it. The title apparently dates from the '60s, as an S-2 unit when they felt they were getting the wrong end of too many bad deals. The squadron was assigned to CVW-11 in 1973, with the intention of deploying with S-2Gs, but was pulled prior to the '73-74 cruise due to overcrowding on the ship. VS-33 deployed with the first US-3A COD in 1977-78 on a trial basis.

VS-35 (1) ***Boomerangs*** **North Island**
(no aircraft)
Established 1 Oct 76 Disestablished 30 Mar 77

In 1976 the Navy established a new *Viking* squadron at North Island, which adopted the name and insignia of a previous S-2 unit that had disestablished in 1973. Confounded by budget and airframe constraints, the second VS-35 never received an aircraft, and was disestablished only five months later.

VS-35 (2) ***Boomerangs*** ***North Island***
S-3A
Established 3 Mar 1987 Disestablished 1 Jun 1988

The third VS-35 lived and died as a charter member of CVW-10. The third version of the *Boomerangs* was nominally assigned with the wing to "Indy," and had aircraft, but lasted only 15 months before being disestablished.

(1987-88)	*Independence*	(no cruise)	S-3A	NM700

VS-35 (3) ***Blue Wolves*** ***North Island***
S-3A, S-3B
Established 4 Apr 1991

18 Feb to 15 Aug 94	*Carl Vinson*	WP/IO/PG	S-3B	NK700
14 May to 14 Nov 96	*Carl Vinson*	WP/IO/PG	S-3B	NK700
11 Jun to 7 Dec 98	*Lincoln*	WP/IO/PG	S-3B	NK700
14 Aug 00 to 12 Feb 01	*Lincoln*	WP/IO/PG	S-3B	NK700

The fourth version of VS-35 faired better than the previous three, being formed during the community S-3B transition, and surviving into the 21st Century. Initially assigned "A" models, the squadron would transition to "Bs" from January 1993. Although occurring after the scope of

The *Boomerangs* of VS-35 were established with CVW-10 in 1987, becoming the third unit to hold that designation. They lasted only about 15 months before going away with their wing. A fourth VS-35 would be formed in April 1991. S-3A NM711 from the third unit is shown while conducting CQ on *Enterprise* in Sept 1987. (author)

While HS-1 was nominally the east coast H-3 RAG, they did pull planeguard duties on occasion. AR724 (148970) is an SH-3D flaring to land on *Nimitz* after covering an FRS CQ period on the ship on 14 Aug 1980. (author)

Naval Reserves

The Reserves had four HS units as of 1974, all having been formed four years previously to put two in each CVSGR. By 1995 only one (HS-75) remained in its original form, with two others becoming LAMPS squadrons, and the fourth an HC outfit.

HS-1 ***Sea Horses*** **Jacksonville** **FRS**

SH-3D, SH-3G, SH-3H, SH-60F

Estab. 3 Oct 51, Disestab. 30 Jun 1997 (28 May ceremony)

The East Coast carrier-based ASW helicopter replacement training squadron, HS-1 occasionally supported carrier detachments off the East Coast. The squadron used the "AR" tailcode, which was shared with VS-30 when it too was a training unit. HS-1 received *Seahawks* in 1990 to transition Atlantic Fleet units to the new helo. Late in its life HS-1 advertised that it was typically training 75 pilots, 80 aircrew, 300 rescue swimmers, and 400 maintainers a year. The school house was closed in 1997 when all HS FRS duties were centered at HS-10 in California.

HS-2 ***Golden Falcons*** **Imperial Beach, North Island**

SH-3D, SH-3H, SH-60F, HH-60F

Estab. 7 Mar 1952

7 Sep 74 to 20 May 75	*Enterprise*	SH-3D	WP/IO	NK700
30 Jul 76 to 28 Mar 77	*Enterprise*	SH-3D	WP/IO	NK720
4 Apr to 30 Oct 78	*Enterprise*	SH-3D	WP/IO	NK720
10 Sep 80 to 4 May 81	*Ranger*	SH-3H	WPAC/IO	NE720
7 Apr to 19 Oct 82	*Ranger*	SH-3H	WPAC/IO	NE610
13 Jan to 1 Aug 84	*Kitty Hawk*	SH-3H	WPAC/IO	NE610
24 Jul to 21 Dec 85	*Kitty Hawk*	SH-3H	WPAC/IO	NG610
3 Jan to 29 Jun 87	*Kitty Hawk*	SH-3H	WPAC/IO	NG610
2 Sep 88 to 2 Mar 89	*Nimitz*	SH-3H	WPAC/IO	NG610
15 Jun to 9 Jul 89	*Nimitz*	SH-3H	WPAC/IO	NG610
25 Feb to 24 Aug 91	*Nimitz*	SH-60F, HH-60H	WP/IO/PG	NG610
2 Feb to 2 Jul 93	*Nimitz*	SH-60F, HH-60H	WP/IO/PG	NG610
10 Nov 94 to 10 May 95	*Constellation*	SH-60F, HH-60H	WP/IO/PG	NE610
1 Apr to 1 Oct 97	*Constellation*	SH-60F, HH-60H	WP/IO/PG	NE610
July 1998	*Kitty Hawk*	SH-60F, HH-60H	Hawaii	NE610
July 1998	*Independence*	SH-60F, HH-60H	CONUS	NE610
18 Jun to 17 Dec 99	*Constellation*	SH-60F, HH-60H	WP/IO/PG	NE610

HS-2 deployed with three air wings (14, 2, and 9), and made the first deployment with the SH-60F series aircraft, in 1991. In 1998 HS-2 appears to have accompanied the *Kitty Hawk* with a composite CVW-2 to Hawaii to conduct the swap out for the forward deployed carrier. It returned to CONUS in *Indy*.

Along with the anti-submarine SH-60Fs that arrived in the early to mid-1990s, the HS squadrons also deployed with a pair of HH-60H helos. Specially configured to conduct Combat SAR, these aircraft have also proven to be invaluable in supporting special operations forces. HS-4 HH-60H NL616 (163792) is at Fallon in August 1992. (Michael Grove)

HS-3 ***Tridents*** **Jacksonville**
SH-3D, SH-3H, SH-60F, HH-60F
Estab. 18 Jun 1952

11 Mar to 11 Sep 74	*Forrestal*	SH-3D	Med	AA000
5 Mar to 22 Sep 75	*Forrestal*	SH-3D	Med	AA000
July 1976	*Forrestal*	SH-3D	Bi-Centennial	AA000
4 Apr to 26 Oct 78	*Forrestal*	SH-3D	Med/NL	AA000
27 Nov 79 to 7 May 80	*Forrestal*	SH-3H	Med	AA000
2 Mar to 15 Sep 81	*Forrestal*	SH-3H	Med	AA730
8 Jun to 16 Nov 82	*Forrestal*	SH-3H	Med	AA610
2 Apr to 20 Oct 84	*Saratoga*	SH-3H	Med	AA610
26 Aug 85 to 16 Apr 86	*Saratoga*	SH-3H	Med/IO	AA610
5 Jun to 17 Nov 87	*Saratoga*	SH-3H	Med	AA610
15 Aug to 8 Oct 88	*Independence*	SH-3H	Horn	AA610
7 Aug 90 to 28 Mar 91	*Saratoga*	SH-3H	Med	AA610
6 May to 6 Nov 92	*Saratoga*	SH-3H	Med	AA610
11 Mar to 8 Sep 93	*T.Roosevelt*	SH-60F, HH-60H	Med/RS	AJ610
22 Mar to 22 Sep 95	*T.Roosevelt*	SH-60F, HH-60H	Med/RS	AJ610
29 Apr to 28 Oct 97	*JF Kennedy*	SH-60F, HH-60H	Med/RS/PG	AJ610
26 Mar to 22 Sep 99	*T Roosevelt*	SH-60F, HH-60H	Med/RS/PG	AJ610

The *Tridents* deployed with CVW-17 until receiving the first AirLant SH-60F *Seahawks* in 1992, and joining CVW-8 in the *Roosevelt*.

HS-4 ***Black Knights*** **Imperial Beach, North Island**
SH-3D, SH-3H, SH-60F, HH-60F
Estab. 30 Jun 1952

23 Nov 73 to 9 Jul 74	*Kitty Hawk*	SH-3D	WPAC/IO	NG720
30 Jun to 7 Sep 76	*Ranger*	SH-3D	WPAC	NE720
21 Feb to 22 Sep 79	*Ranger*	SH-3H	WPAC	NE730
1 Apr to 23 Nov 81	*Kitty Hawk*	SH-3H	WP/IO	NL730
1 Mar to 29 Oct 83	*Carl Vinson*	SH-3H	World	NL610
18 Oct 84 to 25 May 85	*Carl Vinson*	SH-3H	WP/IO	NL610
12 Aug 86 to 5 Feb 87	*Carl Vinson*	SH-3H	WP/IO	NL610
15 Jun to 14 Dec 88	*Carl Vinson*	SH-3H	WP/IO	NL610
5 Sep to 8 Nov 89	*Carl Vinson*	SH-3H	WP/NorPac	NL610
1 Feb to 31 Jul 90	*Carl Vinson*	SH-3H	WP/IO	NL610
18 Oct to 11 Dec 91	*Kitty Hawk*	SH-60F	Horn	NL610
3 Nov 92 to 3 May 93	*Carl Vinson*	SH-60F, HH-60H	WP/IO/PG	NL610

VS-37 and its Stoofs joined CVW-11 in 1973, and made two deployments in *Kitty Hawk* before transitioning to S-3s. The *Sawbucks* would be the last VS unit to fly S-2s in the Navy. Two S-2Gs are depicted here motoring serenely along off the Philippines in July 1975. (Doug Siegfried)

this book, VS-35 would gain fame on 6 May 2003 when one of its aircraft was used to fly President George W. Bush onto the *Abraham Lincoln* off San Diego.

VS-37 ***Sawbucks*** ***North Island***

S-2G, S-3A, S-3B, US-3A

Estab. 24 Jun 1953 from Reserve squadron VS-871 Disestablished 31 Mar 1995

23 Nov 73 to 9 Jul 74	*Kitty Hawk*	WP/IO	S-2G	NH700
21 May to 15 Dec 75	*Kitty Hawk*	WP	S-2G	NH700
26 Sep 78 to 17 May 79	*Constellation*	WP/IO	S-3A	NG700
10 Sep 80 to 4 May 81	*Ranger*	WP/IO	S-3A	NE700
1 Sep 82 to 23 Mar 83	*Enterprise*	WP/IO	S-3A	NH700
21 Feb to 24 Aug 85	*Constellation*	WP/IO	S-3A	NK700
11 Apr to 13 Oct 87	*Constellation*	WP/IO	S-3A	NK700
1 Dec 88 to 1 Jun 89	*Constellation*	WP/IO	S-3A	NK700
16 Sep to 19 Oct 89	*Constellation*	NorPac	S-3A	NK700
23 Jun to 20 Dec 90	*Independence*	WP/IO/PG	S-3A	NK700
18 Oct to 11 Dec 91	*Kitty Hawk*	Horn	S-3A	NL700
3 Nov 92 to 3 May 93	*Kitty Hawk*	WP/IO/PG	S-3B	NL700
24 Jun to 22 Dec 94	*Kitty Hawk*	WP/IO/PG	S-3B	NL700

VS-37 was the last S-2 unit in the Regular Navy, and made two "Stoof" deployments in CVs prior to *Viking* conversion. The *Sawbucks* retired their last S-2G (152374) on 29 Aug 1976. In 1988 they became the first S-3 unit to deploy with aerial refueling capability. VS-37 would be the first "old" S-3 squadron to be disestablished, being shutdown along with CVW-15.

VS-38 ***Red Griffons ("Claw Clan")*** ***North Island***

S-2G, S-3A, S-3B

Reserve VC-892 activated 20 Jul 50, r/d VS-892 4 Aug 50, r/d VS-38 4 Feb 53

23 Nov 73 to 9 Jul 74	*Kitty Hawk*	WP/IO	S-2G	NH710	
21 May to 15 Dec 75	*Kitty Hawk*	WP	S-2G	NH710	
4 Apr to 30 Oct 78	*Enterprise*	WP/IO	S-3A	NK700	
26 Feb to 15 Oct 80	*Constellation*	WP/IO	S-3A	NG700	
20 Oct 81 to 23 May 82	*Constellation*	WP/IO	S-3A	NG700	
13 Jan to 1 Aug 84	*Kitty Hawk*	WP/IO	S-3A	NE700	
18 Aug to 20 Oct 86	*Ranger*	NP/WP	S-3A	NE700	
3 Mar to 29 Apr 87	*Ranger*	NP	S-3A	NE700	
14 Jul to 29 Dec 87	*Ranger*	WP/IO	S-3A	NE700	
24 Feb to 24 Aug 89	*Ranger*	WP/IO	S-3A	NE700	
8 Dec 90 to 8 Jun 91	*Ranger*	WP/IO/PG	S-3A	NE700	*Desert Storm*
1 Aug 92 to 31 Jan 93	*Ranger*	WP/IO/PG	S-3A	NE700	
29 May to 22 Jul 93	*Constellation*	Horn	S-3B	NE700	
10 Nov 94 to 10 May 95	*Constellation*	WP/IO/PG	S-3B	NE700	
1 Apr to 1 Oct 97	*Constellation*	WP/IO/PG	S-3B	NE700	
18 Jun to 17 Dec 99	*Constellation*	WP/IO/PG	S-3B	NE700	

Prior to the adoption of the buddy-store capability in the *Viking* force, the Navy modified a single S-3A with an internally mounted hose-drum unit. The sole KS-3A (157996) spent several years in test duty before ending up with VS-41 as their RA751. It's shown here as a tanker at Moffett Field in Mar'79. The airframe would subsequently be modified to US-3A "Miss Piggy" standards, and be lost with two VRC-50 crew at Cubi Point in Jan '89. (Rick Burgess)

The *Red Griffons* made the last deployment with the S-3A in 1992-93. They transitioned to the S-3B in time for their 1993 trip around Cape Horn with *Constellation*. The squadron was also known by the title "Claw Clan," which referred to a memorable 1960 squadron incident where one of their S-2s launched from a carrier in heavy seas. Right at the moment the aircraft left the bow a large green-water wave ("claw") came up and consumed the "Stoof." Everybody held their breath until the Grumman product emerged, and continued its climb out. The legend of the "Claw Clan" was born that day.

VS-41 ***Shamrocks*** ***North Island*** **FRS**
S-2G, S-3A, S-3B, US-3A, KS-3A
Estab. VS-41 30 Jun 60.
The *Shamrocks* were the long-serving AirPac S-2 replacement squadron, and they kept that role in the S-3 era. They were the sole S-3 FRS from the aircraft's first delivery (20 Feb 1974) until VS-27 was formed in 1987, and then afterwards when VS-27 was disestablished seven years later. VS-41 operated the sole KS-3A, as well as at least one of the "Miss Piggy" US-3As for short periods. Squadron aircraft carried the old carrier-ASW training tailcode of "RA" until 1979, when it adopted the standard "NJ" code for AirPac carrier RAGs.

VSSU **Air Anti-Submarine Support Unit**
Sea Wolves Cecil Field FRS
First aircraft 1982 Established as VS-27 22 Jan 1987
As the *Viking* community grew, it became necessary to establish a training unit on the East Coast. VSSU was an established organization that had been providing trainer and ASW staff support for Cecil Field units since 1975. In 1982 the unit had its first S-3A assigned, and it was conducting local type familiarization and flight training that did not require the complete "Category 1" syllabus for new crews. VSSU aircraft used the tailcode ("AR") of the former AirLant carrier-based ASW training squadrons. By 1987 the "support unit" had grown in size to warrant its establishment as a second dedicated "Hoover" RAG, and it became VS-27.

Reserves
The Navy formed six S-2E squadrons in 1970 as part of the massive reorganization of the Naval Air Reserve Forces. These units were assigned to the two Reserve Carrier ASW Air Groups (CVSGRs), and would last only six years before joining these organizations in oblivion. As with their respective groups, they never received much press, and things like their nicknames and operational records are largely unknown. With no S-3 *Vikings* ever going to the "Weekend Warriors," their end would make them the last aircraft-equipped VS units in the Reserves. A Squadron Augmentation Unit (SAU) would be later established to organize and train reserve aircrew and maintenance personnel to, as their name implies, augment regular S-3 units in times of crisis, although they owned no aircraft themselves.

Between 1982 and 1987 the VS Support Unit (VSSU) operated as a "mini-RAG" to provide training for the East Coast S-3 community at Cecil Field. It became the basis for VS-27. AR15 (160415) sits at Pensacola on 1 Oct'82 (author)

24 Jun to 22 Dec 94	*Carl Vinson*	SH-60F, HH-60H	WP/IO/PG	NL610
14 May to 14 Nov 96	*Carl Vinson*	SH-60F, HH-60H	WP/IO/PG	NK610
11 Jun to 7 Dec 98	*Lincoln*	SH-60F, HH-60H	WP/IO/PG	NK610
14 Aug 00 to 12 Feb 01	*Lincoln*	SH-60F, HH-60H	WP/IO/PG	NK610

HS-4 made numerous deployments to WestPac in both *Sea Kings* and *Seahawks*.

HS-5 *Night Dippers* **Jacksonville**

SH-3D, SH-3H, SH-60F, HH-60F

Estab. 3 Jan 1956

21 Jun 73 to 19 Jan 74	*Independence*	SH-3D	Med	AG800
19 Jul 74 to 21 Jan 75	*Independence*	SH-3D	Med	AG800
15 Oct 75 to 5 May 76	*Independence*	SH-3D	Med	AG800
31 Mar to 21 Oct 77	*Independence*	SH-3D	Med	AG730
16 Jan to 13 Jul 79	*Eisenhower*	SH-3D	Med	AG730
15 Apr to 22 Dec 80	*Eisenhower*	SH-3H	IO	AG730
20 Aug to 7 Oct 81	*Eisenhower*	SH-3H	NLANT	AG730
5 Jan to 13 Jul 82	*Eisenhower*	SH-3H	Med	AG730
27 Apr to 2 Dec 83	*Eisenhower*	SH-3H	Med	AG610
8 May to 29 Jun 84	*Eisenhower*	SH-3H	NLANT	AG610
10 Oct 84 to 8 May 85	*Eisenhower*	SH-3H	Med	AG610
29 Feb to 29 Aug 88	*Eisenhower*	SH-3H	Med	AG610
8 Mar to 12 Sep 90	*Eisenhower*	SH-3H	Med/RS	AG610
26 Sep 91 to 2 Apr 92	*Eisenhower*	SH-3H	Med	AG610
20 May to 17 Nov 94	*G Washington*	SH-3H	Med/NL	AG610
26 Jan to 23 Jul 96	*G Washington*	SH-60F, HH-60H	Med/RS/PG	AG610
26 Feb to 26 Aug 98	*JC Stennis*	SH-60F, HH-60H	World	AG610
18 Feb to 18 Aug 00	*Eisenhower*	SH-60F, HH-60H	MED/RS/PG	AG610

The *Night Dippers* have been assigned to CVW-7 since 1972. Transition to SH-60s came in 1995.

HS-6 *Indians* **Imperial Beach, North Island**

SH-3D, SH-3H, SH-60F, HH-60F

Estab. 1 Jun 1956

21 Jun to 22 Dec 74	*Constellation*	SH-3D	WPAC/IO/PG	NG730
12 Apr to 21 Nov 77	*Constellation*	SH-3D	WP	NG720
26 Sep 78 to 17 May 79	*Constellation*	SH-3H	WP/IO	NG720
26 Feb to 15 Oct 80	*Constellation*	SH-3H	WP/IO	NG720
1 Sep 82 to 23 Mar 83	*Enterprise*	SH-3H	WP/IO	NH610
30 May to 20 Dec 84	*Enterprise*	SH-3H	WP/IO	NH610
15 Jan to 12 Aug 1986	*Enterprise*	SH-3H	WP/IO/Med/SL	NH610
25 Oct to 24 Nov 87	*Enterprise*	SH-3H	NorPac	NH610
5 Jan to 3 Jul 88	*Enterprise*	SH-3H	WP/IO	NH610

The Sikorsky SH-60F *Seahawk* arrived in the fleet in 1991 to replace the veteran *Sea Kings*. HS-6's NE617 is shown here departing *Lincoln* on 17 Oct 1992. (author)

17 Sep 89 to 16 Mar 90	*Enterprise*	SH-3H	World	NH610	
28 May to 28 Nov 91	*A.Lincoln*	SH-60F, HH-60H	WP/IO/PG	NH610	
15 Jun to 15 Dec 93	*A.Lincoln*	SH-60F, HH-60H	WP/IO/PG	NH610	
10 Apr to 9 Oct 95	*A.Lincoln*	SH-60F, HH-60H	WP/IO/PG	NH610	
11 Oct 96 to 11 Apr 97	*Kitty Hawk*	SH-60F, HH-60H	WP/IO/PG	NH610	
6 Nov 98 to 6 May 99	*Carl Vinson*	SH-60F, HH-60H	WP/IO/PG	NH610	

The *Indians* made multiple deployments to the Western Pacific with CVW-9 and -11. They transitioned to H-60s in 1990.

HS-7 ***Shamrocks, Dusty Dogs*** **Jacksonville**

SH-3D, SH-3H, SH-60F, HH-60F

Estab	15 Dec 1969				
27 Sep 74 to 19 Mar 75	*Saratoga*	SH-3H	Med	AC700	
6 Jan to 28 Jul 76	*Saratoga*	SH-3H	Med	AC000	
11 Jul to 23 Dec 77	*Saratoga*	SH-3H	Med	AC700	
3 Oct 78 to 5 Apr 79	*Saratoga*	SH-3H	Med	AC730	
10 Mar to 27 Aug 80	*Saratoga*	SH-3H	Med	AC730	
4 Jan to 14 Jul 82	*JF Kennedy*	SH-3H	Med	AC610	
25 May to 1 Jul 83	*JF Kennedy*	SH-3H	Med	AC700	
27 Sep 83 to 2 May 84	*JF Kennedy*	SH-3H	Med	AC700	
18 Aug 86 to 3 Mar 87	*JF Kennedy*	SH-3H	Med	AC610	
2 Aug 88 to 1 Feb 89	*JF Kennedy*	SH-3H	Med	AC610	
14 Aug 90 to 28 Mar 91	*JF Kennedy*	SH-3H	Med/RS	AC610	*DStorm*
7 Oct 92 to 7 Apr 93	*JF Kennedy*	SH-3H	Med	AC610	
13 to 23 Sep 1994	*Eisenhower*	SH-3H	Caribbean	AC610	Haiti
20 Oct 94 to 15 Apr 95	*Eisenhower*	SH-3H	Med/RS/PG	AC610	
25 Nov 96 to 22 May 97	*T Roosevelt*	SH-60F, HH-60H	Med/RS/PG	AC610	
6 Nov 98 to 6 May 99	*Enterprise*	SH-60F, HH-60H	Med/RS/PG	AC610	
28 Nov 99 to 23 May 00	*HS Truman*	SH-60F, HH-60H	Med/RS/PG	AC610	

With a formal nickname of the *Shamrocks*, HS-7 has long used its *Dusty Dog* callsign as an alternate title. The squadron had moved to Jacksonville from Quonset Point in 1973. HS-7 spent the entire 1974-2000 period with CVW-3, participating in *Desert Storm* and *Uphold Democracy*. They transitioned to H-60s in 1995-96.

HS-8 ***Eightballers*** **Imperial Beach, North Island**

SH-3D, SH-3H, SH-60F, HH-60F

Estab. 1 Nov 1969

21 May to 15 Dec 75	*Kitty Hawk*	SH-3D	WP	NH720
25 Oct 77 to 15 May 78	*Kitty Hawk*	SH-3H	WP	NH720
30 May 79 to 25 Feb 80	*Kitty Hawk*	SH-3H	WP/IO	NL610
20 Oct 81 to 23 May 82	*Constellation*	SH-3H	WP/IO	NG610
15 Jul 83 to 29 Feb 84	*Ranger*	SH-3H	SoPac/WP/IO	NG610
21 Feb to 24 Aug 85	*Constellation*	SH-3H	WP/IO	NK610
11 Apr to 13 Oct 87	*Constellation*	SH-3H	WP/IO	NK610
1 Dec 88 to 1 Jun 89	*Constellation*	SH-3H	WP/IO	NK610
16 Sep to 19 Oct 89	*Constellation*	SH-3H	NorPac	NK610
23 Jun to 20 Dec 90	*Independence*	SH-3H	WP/IO/PG	NK610
18 Feb to 15 Aug 94	*Carl Vinson*	SH-60F, HH-60H	WP/IO/PG	NK610
27 Nov 95 to 20 May 96	*Nimitz*	SH-60F, HH-60H	WP/IO/PG	NG610
1 Sep 97 to 1 Mar 98	*Nimitz*	SH-60F, HH-60H	WP/IO/PG	NG610
7 Jan to 3 Jul 2000	*JC Stennis*	SH-60F, HH-60H	WP/IO/PG	NG610

HS-8 deployed with four different air wings over 25 years, and transitioned to the H-60 in 1993.

HS-9 ***Sea Griffons*** **Jacksonville**

SH-3D, SH-3H

Estab. 4 June 1976	disestab. 30 Apr 1993			
1 Dec 77 to 20 Jul 78	*Nimitz*	SH-3H	Med/NL	AJ730

10 Sep 79 to 26 May 80	*Nimitz*	SH-3H	Med/IO	AJ730	
29 Aug to 17 Oct 1980	*Nimitz*	SH-3H	NorLant	AJ730	
3 Aug 81 to 12 Feb 82	*Nimitz*	SH-3H	Med	AJ730	
10 Nov 82 to 20 May 83	*Nimitz*	SH-3H	Med	AJ610	
8 Mar to 4 Oct 85	*Nimitz*	SH-3H	Med	AJ610	
30 Dec 86 to 26 Jul 87	Nimitz	SH-3H	Med	AJ610	
25 Aug to 11 Oct 88	*T.Roosevelt*	SH-3H	NorLant	AJ610	
30 Dec 88 to 30 Jun 89	*T.Roosevelt*	SH-3H	Med	AJ610	
28 Dec 90 to 28 Jun 91	*T.Roosevelt*	SH-3H	Med/RS/PG	AJ610	*D.Storm*
6 May to 6 Nov 1992	*Saratoga*	SH-3H	Med	AA610	

Squadron aircraft were featured in several sequences during the 1980 movie "The Final Countdown." The *Griffons* lost out during the post-*Desert Storm* shuffle of units undergoing SH-60 transition, and were disestablished in 1993 after a final deployment with *Saratoga*/CVW-17.

HS-10 *Taskmasters, Warhawks* **Imperial Beach, North Island FRS**

SH-3D, SH-3H, SH-60F, HH-60H
Estab. 27 Jun 1957
The AirPac HS training squadron—moved from NALF Imperial Beach, CA, to North Island in December 1976. The unit switched from SH-3 to SH-60F training in mid to late 1989, while also changing with the squadron nickname. HS-10 used the "RA" tailcode for West Coast carrier-based ASW replacement units.

HS-11 *Dragonslayers* **Jacksonville**

SH-3D, SH-3H, SH-60F, HH-60F
Estab. 27 Jun 1957

28 Jun 75 to 27 Jan 76	*JF Kennedy*	SH-3D	Med	AB000	
15 Jan to 1 Aug 77	*JF Kennedy*	SH-3D	Med	AB000	
39 Jun 79 to 8 Feb 79	*JF Kennedy*	SH-3D	Med	AB730	
4 Aug 80 to 28 Mar 81	*JF Kennedy*	SH-3H	Med	AB730	
23 Aug to 30 Oct 82	*America*	SH-3H	Med/NL	/Carib	AB610
8 Dec 82 to 2 Jun 83	*America*	SH-3H	Med/IO	AB610	
24 Apr to 14 Nov 84	*America*	SH-3H	Med/IO	AB610	
10 Mar to 19 Sep 86	*America*	SH-3H	Med	AB610	
8 Feb to 3 Apr 89	*America*	SH-3H	NorLant	AB610	
11 May to 10 Nov 89	*America*	SH-3H	Med/IO	AB610	
28 Dec 90 to 18 Apr 91	*America*	SH-3H	Med/RS/PG	AB610	*D Storm*
2 Dec 91 to 6 Jun 92	*America*	SH-3H	Med	AB610	
11 Aug 93 to 5 Feb 94	*America*	SH-3H	Med/RS/PG	AB610	
28 Aug 95 to 24 Feb 96	*America*	SH-60F, HH-60H	Med/RS/PG	AB610	
3 Oct 97 to 3 Apr 98	*G. Washington*	SH-60F, HH-60H	Med/RS/PG	AB610	
15 Sep 99 to 19 Mar 00	*JF Kennedy*	SH-60F, HH-60H	Med/RS/PG	AB610	

HS-11 spent the entire period assigned to CVW-1, and participated in *Desert Storm*. They traded in their *Sea Kings* for H-60s in 1994.

HS-12 *Wyverns* **North Island, Atsugi**

SH-3D, SH-3H
Estab. 15 July 1977 disestab. 30 Nov 94

13 Mar to 22 Sep 79	*America*	SH-3H	Med	NH740
14 Apr to 12 Nov 81	*America*	SH-3H	Med/IO	NH740
21 Mar to 12 Sep 83	*Coral Sea*	SH-3H	World	NK610
15 July 1984 to Aug 91	*Midway*	SH-3H	fwd deployed	NF610
10 to 22 Aug 91	*Midway*	SH-3H	Hawaii	NF610
28 Aug to 11 Sep 91	*Independence*	SH-3H	Japan	NF610
Sep 91 to Sep 1994	*Independence*	SH-3H	fwd deployed	NF610

HS-12 was the first west coast unit to get the SH-3H. The *Wyverns* were real global travelers, having made two deployments from North Island to the Med and IO, a world tour with *Coral Sea*, and then were forward deployed with *Midway/Independence* and CVW-5 from 1984 to 1994. They were the first HS unit attached to *Midway*, where they replaced a SAR detachment from HC-1. HS-12 was replaced in CVW-5 in September 1994 by HS-14 and its SH-60s. Returning to CONUS, the *Wyverns* were disestablished after about 17 years of service.

HS-14	***Chargers***	**North Island, Atsugi**		
SH-3D, SH-3H, SH-60F, HH-60F				
Estab.10 Jul 1984				
18 Aug to 20 Oct 86	*Ranger*	SH-3H	WPAC	NE610
3 Mar to 29 Apr 87	*Ranger*	SH-3H	WPAC	NE610
14 Jul to 29 Dec 87	*Ranger*	SH-3H	WPAC/IO	NE610
24 Feb to 24 Aug 89	*Ranger*	SH-3H	WPAC/IO	NE610
8 Dec 90 to 8 Jun 91	*Ranger*	SH-3H	WPAC/IO/PG	NE610
1 Aug 92 to 31 Jan 93	*Ranger*	SH-3H	WPAC/IO/PG	NE610
27 May to 22 Jul 1993	*Constellation*	SH-3H	Horn	NE610
Aug/Sep 1994 to 1997	*Independence*	SH-60F,HH-60H	fwd deployed	NF610
1997 to 1999	*Independence*	SH-60F, HH-60H	fwd deployed	NF610
1999 to 2000	*Kitty Hawk*	SH-60F, HH-60H	fwd deployed	NF610

On 15 Oct 1992 HS-14 became the first U.S. Navy squadron to land an aircraft on a Soviet warship, when one of their SH-3Hs visited the *Udaloy*-class destroyer *Admiral Vinogradov*. The squadron moved to Japan in the Autumn of 1994 to replace HS-12, and introduce the H-60 type to CVW-5.

HS-15	***Red Lions***	**Jacksonville**		
SH-3D, SH-3H, SH-60F, HH-60F				
Estab. 29 Oct 1971				
15 Jun to 15 Sep 75	*Nimitz*	SH-3D	NLANT	AJ000
15 Apr to Oct 76	*America*	SH-3D	Med	AE000
10 Jun to 19 Jul 77	*America*	SH-3D	Med	AE000
25 Sep 77 to 25 Apr 78	*America*	SH-3D	Med	AE000
28 Jun to 14 Dec 79	*Independence*	SH-3H	Med	AE000
19 Nov 80 to 19 Jun 81	*Independence*	SH-3H	Med	AE610
7 Jun to 22 Dec 82	*Independence*	SH-3H	Med	AE610
18 Oct 83 to 11 Apr 84	*Independence*	SH-3H	Med	AE610
16 Oct 84 to 19 Feb 85	*Independence*	SH-3H	Med/RS/IO	AE610
2 Jun to 10 Nov 86	*Independence*	SH-3H	Med	AE610
25 Apr to 7 Oct 88	*Forrestal*	SH-3H	Med/IO/NL	AE610
4 Nov 89 to 12 Apr 90	*Forrestal*	SH-3H	Med	AE610
30 May to 21 Dec 91	*Forrestal*	SH-3H	Med	AE610
12 Jan to 24 Jun 94	*Saratoga*	SH-60F, HH-60H	Med	AA610
28 Jun to 20 Dec 96	*Enterprise*	SH-60F, HH-60H	Med/RS/PG	AA610
10 Jun to 10 Dec 98	*Eisenhower*	SH-60F, HH-60H	Med/RS/PG	AA610
21 Jun to 18 Dec 00	*G Washington*	SH-60F, HH-60H	Med/RS/PG	AA610

HS-15 was established at Lakehurst, NJ, in 1971 as part of "Sea Control" concept, where it deployed with *Guam* (LPH-9) as it tested its role as an "Interim Sea Control Ship," where a small-deck ship with AV-8A *Harriers* and ASW helos was evaluated as a partial CV replacement. The unit moved to Jacksonville in November 1973, and became a conventional HS squadron, deploying first as part of *Nimitz's* shakedown cruise to NorLant. It subsequently moved to CVW-6, where it remained through 1991-92. H-60s arrived in the Spring of 1992 with the squadron moving to CVW-17.

HS-16	***Nighthawks***	**North Island**		
SH-3H				
Estab. 10 Mar 1987	disestab. 1 Jun 1988			
(1987-88)	*(Independence)*	SH-3H	no cruise	NM610

Formed as part of the short-lived Carrier Air Wing TEN, HS-16 existed only about 15 months, and made no major deployments.

HS-17	***Neptune's Raiders***	**Jacksonville**		
SH-3H				
Estab. 4 April 1984	disestab. 30 Jun 1991 (2 Jul ceremony)			
2 Oct 85-19 May 86	*Coral Sea*	SH-3H	MED	AK610
29 Sep 87-28 Mar 88	*Coral Sea*	SH-3H	MED	AK610
31 May -30 Sep 89	*Coral Sea*	SH-3H	MED	AK610

25 Sep to 20 Nov 90 *Lincoln* SH-3H Horn NH/AK610 CVW-11
HS-17 was established specifically as a member of the new CVW-13 in 1984. After making three deployments with CVW-13 the squadron covered the East-to-West movement of the *Abraham Lincoln* with CVW-11 around the Horn of South America before being disestablished.

HS-74 ***Demon Elves*** **South Weymouth** **Naval Reserve**
SH-3A, D, G, H
Estab. 1 Jul 70, r/d HSL-74 1 Jan 85
A charter member of CVSGR-70, HS-74 was originally based at Quonset Point, and moved to Massachusetts in 1973. It transferred to HELWINGRES in 1976. It converted to SH-2F aircraft with a designation change to denote the LAMPS mission in 1985.

HS-75 ***Emerald Knights*** **Lakehurst, Jacksonville** **Naval Reserve**
SH-3A, D,G, H, SH-60F
Estab. . 1 Jul 70,
12 Feb to 7 Apr 90 *Constellation* Horn SH-3H NW CVW-9
Formed as part of CVSGR-70, and transferred to HelWingRes with normal duties to support CVWR-20. HS-75 joined CVW-9 and *Constellation* while it made the trip from San Diego to Philadelphia in 1990. The squadron moved to Jacksonville in Oct 1985, and transitioned to SH-60F in 2000, while remaining the only Reserve HS unit.

HS-84 ***Thunderbolts*** **North Island** **Naval Reserve**
SH-3A, D, G, H
Estab. 1 Jul 70 r/d HSL-84 1 Mar 1984.
The *Thunderbolts* were established as a part of CVSGR-80, and subsequently transferred to HELWINGRES. They were redesignated a LAMPS squadron in March 1984, and converted to the SH-2F.

HS-85 ***Golden Gaters*** **Alameda, North Island** **Naval Reserve**
SH-3A, D, G, H
Estab. 1 Jul 70 r/d HC-85 1 Oct 94.
HS-85 was formed as part of CVSGR-80, and subsequently transferred to HELWINGRES. They moved in Nov 1993 to North Island, and were redesignated a combat support squadron late the following year. Among their other duties, HS-85 periodically supported Canadian Forces ships out of British Columbia. Their aircraft were also used to portray HS-4 *Sea Kings* during the recovery scenes in the movie "Apollo 13."

The reserves had four SH-3 units at one time. Among other duties, Alameda based HS-85 provided periodic helo support for the Canadian forces oiler HMCS *Provider*, as the Canadian Navy did not have helicopters of its own on the west coast at this time. SH-3D NW506 is shown visiting *Constellation* 21 July 1984. (author)

Please forgive me if I say a couple of things about the helo guys. On 25 Oct 1984 I ejected from an EA-6B while the plane was leaving "Connie's" angle deck. We were about 80 miles off the big island of Hawaii, and I went into the water along the carrier's port side. I was not even out of my chute before I saw our "Eight-Baller" SH-3H NK610 smokin' around the corner, and hell bent to pick me and my three buddies out of the water. Talk about an Angel—two minutes after ejection they were overhead, and the swimmer was coming down the line to me.

Professional?—these guys spend hours upon hours motoring around monotonously in starboard delta, and then, *BAM*!, the alarm goes off, and they jump into action. The helo types never seem to get the credit they deserve for the work they do for the rest of the Air Wing. Thanks Guys for being there.

During *Desert Storm* there was a day where I came back from a combat mission in *Prowlers* after having done the usual jamming mission. It was another counter for an Air Medal—but nothing really memorable, at least that mission. After debrief I accompanied my crew into the "Dirty Shirt" for lunch, where we sat with a pair of pilots from HS-9. We compared notes—and they proceeded to talk about hunting mines, and then mentioned their latest event, where they worked with a SEAL team doing unspecified work "over the beach." The HAC shrugged his shoulders and gave me a quick "just another day in the office" look to end the story. He wasn't bragging—he didn't need to. What we were doing—at least that day—paled to what our rotary wing brethren were up to. And we had no idea.

On another occasion in October 1988 I was Officer in Charge (OinC) for a VAQ-129 FRS CQ det in *Ranger*. It was late at night, and I was down in the Carrier Air Traffic Control Center (CATCC), acting as the *Prowler* representative while we conducted night CQ for replacement pilots.

We were about halfway through the night as I recall, when somebody—the CATCC officer, maybe the boss—asked "Has anyone seen the planeguard helo?" Calls went out on the radio for the helo that was supposed to be in starboard delta. There was nothing but silence in response.

It was gone.

At some time during our nights' work—nobody knew exactly when—our HS-14 *Sea King* had gone into the water. We stopped other operations and started the SAR, hoping that we could find something. We didn't, and four men were dead. We don't know what happened to them—perhaps they had a massive equipment failure, maybe they "just flew into the water." We'll never know. God be with you, Gentlemen. ***RJM***

Helicopter Combat Support (HC)

The HC community was made up of a small number of squadrons that provided detachments to ships to carry out many of the mundane support tasks required of helicopters. Two units, HC-1 and HC-2, provided Search and Rescue (SAR) dets to deploying carriers from the 1940s and through the Vietnam War. HS squadrons began to take over the role as part of the "CV Concept" post war, and by the late 1970s only carriers of the *Midway* class were still deploying with HC detachments onboard. The last carrier to deploy with a dedicated HC det was *Midway*, in 1984. The normal aircraft during this period was the Sikorsky SH-3G, a specialized SAR variant of the ASW helo.

HC-1	***Pacific Fleet Angels***	**Imperial Beach, North Island**				
SH-3A/G, CH-53E, MH-53E						
Estab. as HU-1 1 Apr 48, r/d HC-1		1 Jul 65	disestab. 29 Apr 1994			
8 May 73 to 8 Jan 74	*Hancock*	SH-3G	WP/IO	CVW-21	NP000	det 3
18 Oct 73 to 5 Jun 74	*Oriskany*	SH-3G	WP	CVW-19	NM000	det 1
7 May to 18 Oct 74	*Ranger*	SH-3G	WP	CVW-2	NE600	det 4
5 Dec 74 to 2 Jul 75	*Coral Sea*	SH-3G	WP	CVW-15	NL720	det 3
18 Mar to 20 Oct 75	*Hancock*	SH-3G	WP	CVW-21	NP000	det 1
16 Sep 75 to 3 Mar 76	*Oriskany*	SH-3G	WP	CVW-19	NM700	det 4
4 Oct 76 to 21 Apr 77	*FD Roosevelt*	SH-3G	Med	CVW-19	NM720	det 3
15 Feb to 5 Oct 77	*Coral Sea*	SH-3G	WP	CVW-15	NL720	det 4

The background is unmistakably San Francisco, which means HC-1's SH-3G NK721 is turning at NAS Alameda, homeport for *Coral Sea*. HC-1 still provided SAR dets to the two remaining *Midway* class carriers at this time, 24 Jan 1981. (author)

30 Sep 79 to 20 Feb 80	*Coral Sea*	SH-3G	WP/IO	CVW-14	NK720	det 3
30 Aug 81 to 23 Mar 82	*Coral Sea*	SH-3G	WP/IO	CVW-14	NK610	det 3
Jan 1974 to May 84	*Midway*	SH-3G	fwd deployed CVW-5	NF610/720	det 2	

HC-1 provided SAR detachments to carriers through 1984, and carried on another decade by providing other support activities to fleet units off California. In its previous guise of HU-1 the unit had been conducting the same duties since the introduction of helicopters in the late 1940s. The *Angels* also flew CH-53Es in the Vertical Replenishment role off California in its later days, and became the SH-3 FRS when HS-10 converted to the SH-60F in mid-1989. HC-1 "home guard" helos normally wore the squadron's own "UP" tailcode. Detachment 2 was forward deployed with *Midway* and CVW-5 from 1973 through 1984. The squadron moved from Ream Field at Imperial Beach to North Island with the rest of the Pacific Fleet helicopter units in 1976.

HC-2 (1) *Fleet Angels* **Jacksonville**

SH-3G

Established as HU-2 1 Apr 48, r/d HC-2 1 Jul 65 disestab. 30 Sep 1977

14 Sep 73 to 17 Mar 74	*FD Roosevelt*	SH-3G	Med	CVW-6	AE000	det 42
3 Jan to 3 Aug 74	*America*	SH-3G	Med	CVW-8	AJ000	det 66
6 Sep to 12 Oct 74	*America*	SH-3G	NLANT	CVW-8	AJ000	det 66
3 Jan to 16 Jul 75	*FD Roosevelt*	SH-3G	Med	CVW-6	AE000	det 42
7 Jul 76 to 7 Feb 77	*Nimitz*	SH-3G	Med	CVW-8	AJ730	det 68

The Atlantic Fleet carrier-based SAR unit was HC-2, which had been based at Lakehurst, NJ, until 1973, when it moved to Jax. Like HC-1, they were replaced in the CV search and rescue role by HS units. A new, and historically distinct, HC-2 was established at Norfolk on 1 Apr 1987. HC-2 was assigned the "HU" tailcode.

HC-16 ***Bullfrogs*** **Pensacola** **FRS**

HH-46A, UH-1N, SH/UH-3G

Estab. 1 Nov 74, r/d HC-16 20 May 77 disestab. 1 Apr 1994

HC-16 operated under Chief of Naval Air Training (CNATRA) as HCT-16 until 1977, when it was moved to AirLant control. The squadron was the Navy training unit for station helicopters, while also providing planeguard support for *Lexington* and other carriers off Florida as necessary. HC-16 was assigned the BF tailcode.

Other Helicopter Combat Support Squadrons

Other squadrons in the HC community, such as those that specialize in Vertical Replenishment, although critical, are beyond the scope of this book, as they are rarely, if ever, assigned directly to Carrier Air Wings. HC-3, -6, and -7 were all established 1 Sep 1967.

HC-2 (second)	Norfolk	VH/SH-3, CH-53E	VIP and utility, estab. 4/87
HC-3	North Island	CH-46D, HH-46A/D	Vertical replenishment (FRS)
HC-4	Sigonella	CH-53E, MH-53E	Vertical replenishment. Estab. 5/83
HC-5	Agana	HH-46A/D	Vertical replenishment. Estab 2/84
HC-6	Norfolk	CH-46D	Vertical replenishment.
HC-7	North Island	HH-3A	Combat SAR, Dist. 6/75
HC-8	Norfolk	CH-46D	Vertical Replenishment. Estab. 12/84
HC-9	North Island	HH-3A	Combat SAR (Naval Reserve), Est. 8/75, Dist. 7/90
HC-11	North Island	CH-46D	Vertical Replenishment. Estab. 10/77

HSL, HAL, HM, and HCS squadrons are not covered in this work.

11

Marine Carrier Deployments 1974-2001

"Some people spend an entire lifetime wondering if they've made a difference. The Marines don't have that problem."
- attributed to President Ronald Reagan

Marine fixed wing aircraft have spent more time at sea on carriers than most people realize. Tailhook equipped "Devil Dog" biplanes were on the *Lexington* (CV-2) and *Saratoga* (CV-3) in the 1930s, and their aircraft saw combat from Navy flightdecks in WWII, Korea, and Vietnam. Even though this tradition continued with the end of the war in South East Asia, the appearance of Marine aircraft on carriers was still considered something of an oddity through most of the 1980s, and into the '90s. Up to 1993, the assignment of Marine squadrons to Navy Air Wings was generally thought of as a temporary thing, and it frequently meant they were filling in for unavailable Navy units.

On 9 Jan 1993 the Secretary of the Navy directed that one VMAQ and two Marine VMFA squadrons be integrated into Carrier Air Wings. VMFA-312, -314, and VMAQ-3 subsequently went to sea, and others soon followed, although the *Prowler* unit lasted only one cruise before being beached again in favor of a Navy sister. Other Fighter-Attack squadrons would follow, but only on an irregular basis.

It would not be until 2000 that Marine carrier participation was formally codified as the "TacAir Integration Plan," where every CVW would, in time, have a Marine VMFA unit assigned to replace a Navy counterpart. At the same time a small number of Navy VFAs would start to deploy to Japan as part of the Marine Unit Deployment Plan (UDP). "The plan" would, theoretically, have placed every single-seat Marine *Hornet* unit in a Navy CVW within a few years, leaving only the two-seated F/A-18D squadrons to deploy from beach locations. Substantial increases in operational requirements in the post-9/11 environment would mean that, by 2004, this widely advertised "transformational" program still involved only four air wings, however.

Marine fixed-wing units normally carry the tailcodes of their assigned air wings on their aircraft once on cruise. Some delay applying these markings until late in the work-up cycle, using instead their normally assigned distinct Marine tailcodes, which are listed with each squadron. Units assigned to MAG-31 used a group-directed "BM" ("Beaufort Marines") code in lieu of squadron codes for a period in the 1990s.

The following listings cover only those Marine units that deployed in Navy carriers as part of CVWs, and does not include the normal Marine UDP to Japan, or other land based activities that these squadrons or similar units carried out between 1974 and 2001.

CVW-17 lost VF-11 in 1980, and gained VMFA-115 for *Forrestal's* 1981 Med deployment. A *Silver Eagle* F-4J (AA107, 155787) is shown here conducting CQ on *Nimitz* on 13 Aug '80 in preparation for that event. For many of the squadron's pilots this was the first time they'd flown aboard the boat since training command. (author)

VMA-231 was the only AV-8A *Harrier* unit to ever deploy as part of a Carrier Air Wing. NM602 (159241) approaches the *Franklin Roosevelt* during that ship's 1977 deployment with CVW-19. (Pete Clayton)

Attack (VMA)

VMA-231	***Ace of Spades***	**MCAS Cherry Point, NC**		**CG tailcode**
10/76-5/77	*FD Roosevelt*	AV-8A	Med	NM600

In 1976 the Navy decided to experiment with a V/STOL squadron onboard one of its carriers. VMA-231, one of only three AV-8A *Harrier* units in the Fleet Marine Force, was subsequently tasked to take its aircraft onboard *Franklin Roosevelt* in what was that ship's final trip to the Med. The squadron's 14 aircraft joined a modified CVW-19 (which also had 20 F-4Ns and 30 A-7Bs assigned) for the deployment. The outfit was detached from FDR on 27 November, when it flew aboard *Guam* (LPH-9), and accompanied the ship through the Suez Canal to participate in Kenyan Independence Day celebrations off Mombassa. It returned to CV-42 on 3 Jan 1977, and stayed onboard through the end of cruise. There have been no subsequent deployments by V/STOL aircraft in Navy CVWs, Marine *Harrier* units going back to their normal six aircraft detachments as part of the Air Combat Element (ACE) on Amphibious Assault Ships (LPHs, LHAs, or LHDs).

All Weather Attack [VMA (AW)]

VMA(AW)-533	***Night Hawks***	**MCAS Cherry Point, NC**		**ED tailcode**
2 Apr to 24 Oct 84	*Saratoga*	Med	A-6E, KA-6D	AA500
18 Aug 86 to 3 Mar 87	*JF Kennedy*	Med	A-6E	AC540/550
2 Aug 88 to 1 Feb 89	*JF Kennedy*	Med	A-6E	AC540/550

VMA(AW)-121	***Green Knights***	**MCAS El Toro, CA**		**VK tailcode**
18 Aug to 20 Oct 86	*Ranger*	NP/WP	A-6E	NE400
3 Mar to 29 Apr 87	*Ranger*	NorPac	A-6E	NE400
14 Jul to 29 Dec 87	*Ranger*	WP/IO	A-6E	NE400

Two Marine *Intruder* units, one from each coast, joined carrier air wings during the period covered. VMA(AW)-533 made three deployments, one in *Saratoga* as the only Medium Attack asset onboard, and two in *Kennedy*, where it was matched with a Navy A-6 squadron in a so-called "All Grumman Air Wing." The squadron's use of KA-6Ds in 1984 made it only the second Marine unit to operate the type, after VMA(AW)-224 in 1972. Although 533 deployed with AC540 and 550 side numbers, there is photographic evidence that shows at least one of their aircraft being marked in the AC400 series during early 1989, apparently after their last deployment, but before they returned to Marine operational control. VMA(AW)-121 was also in a "dual A-6 Air Wing," and was paired with VA-145 in CVW-2 for almost three years.

Two Marine *Intruder* units deployed on carriers between 1974 and 2001. The *Green Knights* of VMA(AW)-121 were assigned to CVW-2 in *Ranger* for five years. NE401 (161688) is shown at Fallon in Sept 1988. (Michael Grove)

The *Checkerboards* joined CVW-8 in 1992, and made five deployments by 2001. F/A-18C AJ337 (164273) is at Fallon in October 1992. (Michael Grove)

Fighter-Attack (VMFA)

VMFA-115	***Silver Eagles***	**MCAS Beaufort, SC**		**VE tailcode**
2 Mar to 15 Sep 81	*Forrestal*	Med	F-4J	AA 100

VMFA-115 made one deployment in FID with F-4Js in the early 1980s, being paired in CVW-17 with VF-74.

VMFA-251	***Thunderbolts***	**MCAS Beaufort, SC**		**DW tailcode**
28 Aug 95 to 24 Feb 96	*America*	Med/RS/PG	F/A-18C	AB 200
3 Oct 97 to 3 Apr 98	*G Washington*	Med/RS/PG	F/A-18C	AB 200
15 Sep 99 to 19 Mar 00	*JF Kennedy*	Med/RS/PG	F/A-18C	AB 200

The *Thunderbolts* made three trips to the Med in five years, all with CVW-1. Their association with the wing would continue into 2001.

VMFA-312	***Checkerboards***	**MCAS Beaufort, SC**		**DR tailcode**
11 Mar to 8 Sep 93	*T Roosevelt*	Med/RS	F/A-18C	AJ 330
22 Mar to 22 Sep 95	*T Roosevelt*	Med	F/A-18C	AJ 330
25 Nov 96 to 22 May 97	*T Roosevelt*	Med/RS/PG	F/A-18C	AC 200
6 Nov 98 to 6 May 99	*Enterprise*	Med/RS/PG	F/A-18C	AC 200
28 Nov 00 to 23 May 01	*HS Truman*	Med/IO	F/A-18C	AC 200

The *Checkerboards* were no strangers to carrier duty, having flown combat with F4U *Corsairs* off Light (CVL) and Escort (CVE) Carriers during the Korean War. In 1993 they became an early member of what was later called the TacAir Integration Program. They were the first Marine C-model F/A-18 squadron to deploy with a carrier air wing. The unit was used as the basis for the "312 *Werewolf* Squadron," commanded by "Bull" Meechum (actor Robert Duvall) in the 1979 movie "The Great Santini," with its *Phantoms* being featured in several flight scenes.

VMFA-314	***Black Knights***	**MCAS El Toro and Miramar, CA**		**VW tailcode**	
2 Oct 85 to 19 May 86	*Coral Sea*	Med	F/A-18A	AK 300	Libya
15 Jun to 15 Dec 93	*Lincoln*	WP/IO/PG	F/A-18A	NH 200	
1 Sep 97 to 1 Mar 98	*Nimitz*	WP/IO/PG	F/A-18C	NG 200	
7 Jan to 3 Jul 00	*JC Stennis*	WP/IO/PG	F/A-18C	NG 200	

As one of the first three Marine *Hornet* units, the *Black Knights* deployed in Norfolk-based *Coral Sea* with CVW-13 in 1985-86, taking part in action off Libya during the deployment. Three subsequent cruises with Pacific Fleet units were made during the following years. VMFA-314 was the *Hornet* unit featured in the science fiction movie "Independence Day," with actor Will Smith portraying the hero Naval Aviator.

VMFA-323	***Death Rattlers***	**MCAS El Toro and Miramar, CA**		**WS tailcode**	
30 Sep 79 to 20 Feb 80	*Coral Sea*	WP/IO	F-4N	NK 100	
2 Oct 85 to 19 May 86	*Coral Sea*	Med	F/A-18A	AK 400	Libya
10 Nov 94 to 10 May 95	*Constellation*	WP/IO	F/A-18C	NE 200	
1 Apr to 1 Oct 97	*Constellation*	WP/IO	F/A-18C	NE 200	
18 Jun to 17 Dec 99	*Constellation*	WP/IO	F/A-18C	NE 200	

The "Snakes" deployed in *Coral Sea* from both coasts, once in *Phantoms*, and later again in *Hornets*. The squadron was a regular member of CVW-2 between 1994 and 1999.

The *Warlords* of VMFA-451 were assigned to the CVW-17/*Forrestal* team for what turned out to be a short period in 1975-76, while normally assigned VF-74 was making a deployment with the new carrier *Nimitz*. AA206 (F-4J 155521) was one of the last in CVW-17 markings, and is shown at Beaufort, SC, on 17 Mar '77. The nose number is in the normal Marine single or double digit presentation, while the air wing's -206 still appears on the tail. (author)

VMFA-333	***Shamrocks***	**MCAS Beaufort, SC**		**DN tailcode**
16 Jul to 24 Sep 75	*Nimitz*	NorLant	F-4J	AJ 120/130
7 Jul 76 to 7 Feb 77	*Nimitz*	Med	F-4J	AJ 200

Phantom flying "Trip Trey" had a history of going to sea, having made two previous carrier deployments to Vietnam, as well as one to the Med. In 1975 it participated in work-ups and the first deployments of the new nuclear carrier *Nimitz*, being paired in CVW-8 with VF-74. The unit transitioned to *Hornets* in 1987, and deactivated in March 1992 after participating in *Desert Storm* as a land based unit.

VMFA-451	***Warlords***	**MCAS Beaufort, SC**		**VM tailcode**	
July 1976	*Forrestal*	(No cruise)	F-4J	AA 200	bi-centennial
30 May to 30 Sep 89	*Coral Sea*	Med	F/A-18A	AK 100	

VMFA-451 was assigned to CVW-17 for roughly a year between late 1975 and late 1976. The unit replaced VF-74 while it was attached to CVW-8 for a cruise in *Nimitz*. While the *Warlords* didn't make a major deployment with the wing, they did accompany the *Forrestal* for at least two trips to the Puerto Rican op area, as well as the International Naval Review in New York Harbor on 4 July 1976. After conversion to *Hornets* the unit deployed as the only Marine unit in CVW-13 for *Coral Sea's* last deployment. Six years after participating in *Desert Storm* from Shaikh Isa, Bahrain, the squadron was deactivated.

VMFA-531	***Grey Ghosts***	**MCAS El Toro CA**		**EC tailcode**
30 Sep 79 to 20 Feb 80	*Coral Sea*	WP/IO	F-4N	NK 200

The *Ghosts* joined the *Death Rattlers* for the 79/80 deployment in *Coral Sea*, where the Marines provided all of the fighter coverage for CVW-14. The cruise included the very near prospect of flying combat against the Iranian Air Force in support of the aborted hostage rescues during Operation *Eagle Claw*. VMFA-531 was deactivated in March 1992.

VMFAT-101 ***Sharpshooters*** **MCAS El Toro, Miramar** **SH tailcode** **FRS**

101 was the Marine F-4 RAG based at Yuma, Arizona, through May 1987, when it moved to El Toro to become the third Navy/Marine Hornet FRS. The unit keeps its Marine structure and commanding officer, but normally has a Navy Executive Officer assigned. A significant number of its students are usually Navy Officers, as well. The squadron has operated F/A-18A, B, C, and D versions, as well as a few T-34C support birds.

Composite

VMCJ-1	***Golden Hawks***	**MCAS Iwakuni, JA**		**RM tailcode**
5/74-8/75	*Midway*	fwd deployed	RF-4B	RM 610
1/74-8/75	*Midway*	fwd deployed	EA-6A	RM 610

A year after the 1973 arrival of the *Midway*/CVW-5 team in Japan, Iwakuni-based VMCJ-1 began to support the ship and air wing with a photo-recon/ EW det. labeled "Detachment 101." The RF-4Bs replaced a det of VFP-63 RF-8Gs, while the "Electric *Intruders*" supplanted VAQ-130 EKA-3Bs. VMCJ-1 was deactivated in 1975 when the Corps reorganized its EW and photo assets into separate squadrons.

With no RF-8s based in Japan and RA-5s too big to operate off of *Midway*, the Marines provided photo-recon support for CVW-5 out of the 3rd MAW at Iwakuni. VMFP-3 flew RF-4Bs from the carrier between 1976 and 1984. RF610 (157342) displays the carrier's name at Cubi Point in October 1979. (Rick Burgess)

Photo Reconnaissance (VMFP)

VMFP-3	***Eyes of the Corps***	**MCAS El Toro CA**		**RF tailcode**
10/76-1981	*Midway*	fwd deployed	RF-4B	RF 610
1981-6/84	*Midway*	fwd deployed	RF-4B	NF/RF 110

In 1975 the Corps reorganized its three Composite (VMCJ) squadrons into distinct photo-recon and electronic warfare units, VMFP-3 and VMAQ-2. "P-3" supported *Midway*/CVW-5 with photo-*Phantom* dets on six month temporary duty from its California home.

Tactical Electronic Warfare (VMAQ)

VMAQ-2	***Playboys, Panthers***	**MCAS Cherry Point, NC**		**CY tailcode**	
6 Sep to 12 Oct 74	*America*	NorLant	EA-6A	CVW-8	CY det
9/75-8/78	*Midway*	fwd deployed	EA-6A	CVW-5	CY610 dets
15 Feb to 5 Oct 77	*Coral Sea*	WestPac	EA-6A	CVW-15	CY610 dets A/B
9/78-2/80	*Midway*	fwd deployed	EA-6B	CVW-5	CY 610 dets
3 Aug to 12 Feb 82	*Nimitz*	Med	EA-6B	CVW-8	AJ 610 det Y
2 Apr to 20 Oct 84	*Saratoga*	Med	EA-6B	CVW-17	AA 604 det X
10 Mar to 10 Sep 86	*America*	Med	EA-6B	CVW-1	AB 620 det Y

North Carolina based VMAQ-2 assumed the Corps' airborne EW mission from the three Composite squadrons in September 1975. Six month detachments continued to support VMCJ-1's previous EA-6A requirement on the *Midway* at the same time. EA-6Bs arrived in 1978, and four-plane squadron dets (designated X, Y, and Z) deployed with CVW-5 until replaced by VAQ-136 in 1980. "Q-2" has made three subsequent carrier deployments, all to the Med. The 1986 cruise in *America* was as a short fused replacement of VAQ-135, which had been pulled from CVW-1 to join *Coral Sea* and CVW-13 off Libya. The *Playboy* det subsequently provided critical jamming support for U.S. Air Force and Navy raids into Libya. The battle tested squadron was pressured into changing its famous nickname subsequent to the 1991 Tailhook affair, and has since been known as the *Panthers* and *Death Jesters*, although the Playboy Bunny logo still shows up periodically on flight suits as a form of Junior Officer rebellion.

VMAQ-3	***Moon Dogs***	**MCAS Cherry Point, NC**		**MD tailcode**
28 Aug 95 to 24 Feb 96	*America*	Med/PG	EA-6B	AB 620

In 1993 the Navy and Marines agreed to replace one embarked VAQ squadron with a Marine equivalent. CVW-1 was selected, and VAQ-137 disestablished to make room for VMAQ-3. The *Moon Dogs* made a single deployment to the Med, where they were heavily involved in Operation *Deny Flight* before the decision was reversed, returning VMAQ-3 to the normal Marine UDP cycle, their place being taken by a newly established version of VAQ-137. For a portion of the cruise the squadron placed aircraft on the beach at Aviano, where they flew support alongside VAQ-131, which had been deployed to the Italian base, as well.

Heavy Helicopter (HMH)

HMH-362	*Ugly Angels*	MCAS New River, NC	YL tailcode	
11 Mar to 8 Sep 93	*T.Roosevelt*	Med/RS	CH-53D, UH-1N	YL 00

For its third major deployment, the "Teddy" *Roosevelt* carried a company of Marine Infantry, as well as a mixed squadron of helicopters and a reduced size CVW-8. HMH-362 was the Air Combat Element (ACE), or senior aviation component of a "Special MAGTF" concept, where a carrier would replace an Amphibious Group in the Med. Eight CH-53Ds and four UH-1Ns (from HMLA-167) made the deployment. The Marines onboard were officially separate and equal to CVW-8, with their own Colonel reporting directly to the Battle Group Commander. Although officially called a success, most reports also concluded that large rotary wing aircraft do not mix well with a carrier air wing's cyclic operations, and the *Roosevelt* reverted to a standard configuration for its next deployment.

Medium Helicopter (HMM)

HMM-162	*Golden Eagles*	MCAS New River, NC	YS tailcode	
11 Aug 93 to 5 Feb 94	*America*	Med/IO	CH-46E	YS 00 Det A

The Marines deployed a det of four *Sea Knights* alongside CVW-1 on a "routine" Med cruise in another "Special MAGTF" experiment. Once again, it was said that operational problems involved with trying to mix the dissimilar type aircraft led to this being the last such deployment.

Navy Units on Marine UDP

The Unit Deployment Plan (UDP) is the Marines' periodic rotation of squadrons from CONUS to the 1st Marine Air Wing in Japan and Okinawa. During the early to late 1980s a number of Navy attack squadrons made six-month UDP deployments to MCAS Iwakuni, Japan, where they were assigned to a Marine Aircraft Group (MAG) for tasking. The Attack (VA) squadrons replaced Marine A-4M units over two years, while the sole VFA unit spelled a Leatherneck F-4S outfit while they transitioned to *Hornets*.

These five deployments were considered somewhat out of the ordinary when they occurred. In 2000 the formal Tactical Air Integration Program (TAIP) was released, where the Navy agreed to send strike fighter units to Japan under Marine operational command on a regular basis. It would not be until 2004 when VFA-97 would make the first of these trips.

In terms of markings, VFA-132 retained its previous Air Wing tailcode, while VA-15, -37, and 105 wore CVW-3's AC code, although they were not assigned to that wing at that time. VA-192 adopted the former CVW-19 "NM" code that was being used at that time by LatWingPac for units between Air Wings.

VA-105	2 Jun 84-17 Dec 84	A-7E	MAG-12	AC 400
VA-37	1 Dec 84-14 Jun 85	A-7E	MAG-12	AC 300
VA-192	4 Jun 85-14 Dec 85	A-7E	MAG-12	NM 300
VA-15	1 Dec 85-13 Jun 86	A-7E	MAG-12	AC 300
VFA-132	5 Oct 87-28 Apr 88	F/A-18A	MAG-15	AK 200

Five Navy squadrons deployed in support of the Marines between 1984 and 1988. AC301 is a VA-37 A-7E (157453) at Cubi Point on 2 Apr 1985, while assigned to Iwakuni-based MAG-12, as the "Globe, Anchor, and Eagle" on the tailpipe indicates. (author)

12

Type and Functional Wings

"We're from the Wing and are here to help you."
- Typical opening line at the start of TypeWing administrative inspection.

As with any large bureaucracy, the Navy has a complex corporate structure to control all of its moving parts. As compared to the Air Force or Marines, which have comparatively straightforward command relationships (the Air Force using a direct-line Major Command, Wing, Group, Squadron structure for most flying units), the Navy's organizational tree is a bewildering array of trunks, branches, offshoots, and dead ends that can easily confound the casual observer (not to mention many in the service, as well).

There are two parallel command structures in Naval Aviation, these being operational and administrative. Each has its own assigned functions, and frequently involves completely separate organizational structures.

On top of the heap is the Type Commander, who is the senior aviation officer on each coast. His Operational commanders include Carrier Group Commanders (which won't be covered here) and Carrier Air Wing Commanders (CAGs, covered in chapter 3). The administrative command chain is carried out through the Functional and Type Wings, which are usually arranged by like type aircraft and location.

The Navy designates both Operational and Administrative Control for most flying units, using the shortened titles OPCON and ADCON. In most cases carrier based units use their Carrier Air Wings (CVWs) as their OPCON. The CVW provides flying money (Operating Target, or OPTAR), and drives the operational schedule. ADCON is usually given to the local type wing, as it provides higher level administrative support, and holds most inspection authority.

Changes in mission areas and aircraft types led to multiple reorganizations through the years, and have made tracking these organizations difficult at times. To make comprehension even more sporting for the outsider, the Navy assigns short Plain Language Addresses (PLADs) to units, which are shortened versions of formal titles for message traffic routing purposes. (The worst one undoubtedly being Fighter Medium Attack Airborne Early Warning Wing U.S. Atlantic Fleet, FitMatAEWWingLant, which was, mercifully, changed to Tactical Wings US Atlantic Fleet after about 2 years of use.) These names, such as ComNavAirLant, are typically spoken as words in daily conversation, and used interchangeably with the formal title. PLADs can be spelled out in official correspondence in ALL CAPITALS, as well as an acronym (almost all of these organizations being pronounced in normal conversation as a word).

As stated before, at the top of the organization is the **Type Commander**, with one being assigned to each coast. Between 1974 and 2001 Commander Naval Air Forces Pacific Fleet and Commander Naval Air Forces Atlantic Fleet were Vice Admirals (O-9) who "owned" all of the aircraft carriers and functional wings in their respective oceans. ComNavAirLant also goes by the names CNAL and AirLant, while ComNavAirPac is also referred to as CNAP or AirPac. (Note that these should not be confused with the name Navair, which refers to Naval Air Systems Command, the organization that oversees the design and procurement of the service's aircraft.)

This system was changed in October 2001, with AirPac also becoming Commander, Naval Air Force, the "owner" of all Naval Avia-

The "November Mike" tailcode was used by two Air Wings: CVW-19 (1956 to 1978) and CVW-10 (1986-88). Between 1980 and 1986 the Light Attack Wing at Lemoore used it for squadrons assigned to them while they were between air wings, in transition, or with the Marines in Japan. At the very least VA/VFA-113, -192, -195, and VF/VFA-151 used the code during this period. The *Dambusters* of VFA-195 were in the process of moving from *Corsairs* to *Hornets* when this picture was taken at Miramar on 13 Jan '86. They would subsequently move to Japan and join CVW-5. (author)

tion units, with AirLant becoming a two-star position underneath him. This change was made to bring both coasts under a single, senior commander for a variety of reasons, including standardization of training, safety, and other issues. A full description of this change is beyond the scope of this book.

Functional Wings (Funcwings) are a level down from the Type Commanders, and usually had an O-7 (either Rear Admiral, Lower Half, RDML, or Commodore Admiral, COMO) in command. He might have been the next senior in command of Type Wings underneath him, or could simply act as a large Type Wing (as in ComMatVAQWingPac). All of the carrier-aircraft related "Func Wings" were disestablished or downgraded from 1992, when the Navy decided it had to move more Flag officers to the Pentagon and Joint billets in order to compete with the other services. Some of these wings had unofficial names that were widely known within the service. For example, Whidbey's ComMatVAQWingPac was known locally as "VacuumPac," and Miramar's ComFitAEWWingPac also went by "Fit-Fudd," which was a combination of Fighter, and the unofficial name for the E-1 *Tracer*, the "Willy Fudd."

Beneath the functional wings are the **Type Wings**, which is a Captain who controls land based intermediate maintenance functions, administrative inspections, and other mundane support activities for a group of like aircraft. An example would be LatWingPac, based at Lemoore, who was in charge of all such activities for Pacific Fleet A-7 units. Type wings also control the Fleet Readiness Squadrons for the type of aircraft associated with the wing. Although wearing the rank of Captain, this individual is usually referred to by the honorary title "Commodore" (see sidebar). Type Wings normally came under Functional Wings until the early 1990s, when most were reassigned to come directly under the Type Commander (AirLant or AirPac).

All wing organizations precede their title with the word "Commander." For example, Helicopter Wings U.S. Atlantic Fleet would also be known as ComHelWingsLant in normal usage. The "Commander" title has been dropped in the following functional and type listings for the purpose of simplicity. The following information contains only carrier-related command elements. Keeping within the scope of this book, patrol, and logistical wings are not included.

Commander, Naval Air Forces U.S. Atlantic Fleet (ComNavAirLant)
Norfolk. Vice Admiral position, in charge of all aviation activities on the East Coast, under Commander, US Atlantic Fleet.

FUNCWINGS

Sea Based Antisubmarine Warfare Wings US Atlantic Fleet — Jacksonville
Helicopter Wings US Atlantic Fleet — HelWingsLant — Jacksonville
r/d 1986, disestab. 30 Sep 92.
controlled HSWing-ONE and HelSeaConWingsLant-ONE and THREE (HSL units)

Strike Fighter Wings US Atlantic Fleet — StrkFitWingsLant — Cecil Field
Est. 1 Oct 1986, d. 30 Sep 1992
Controlled Cecil Field type wings (LatWing ONE and SeaStrikeWing ONE)

Fighter Medium Attack Airborne Early Warfare Wings US Atlantic Fleet,
Tactical Wings US Atlantic Fleet — TacWingsLant — Oceana
r/d from FitMatAEWWing 27 Apr 89, d. 30 Sep 1992
Controlled Oceana/Norfolk type wings (FitWing ONE, MatWing ONE, CAEWW-12)

TYPEWINGS

Commander, Light Attack Wing-ONE — LatWing-ONE — Cecil Field
Strike Fighter Wing US Atlantic Fleet — StrkFitWingLant — Cecil Field, Oceana
East Coast light attack (A-7) and Strike Fighter units. r/d SFWL 12 Aug 1993. Moved to Oceana 1999.

CVW-15 was disestablished in 1995, and its EA-6B unit, VAQ-134, became the first "expeditionary" *Prowler* squadron, leaving carrier duty to support joint operations ashore world wide. The unit retained its old wing's NL tailcode, which subsequently became the defacto code for ComVaqWingPac (CVWP) and all following "concrete" *Prowler* units. Somewhat confusing things here is the fact that the now land based *Garudas* were placing the names of their former carriers on their aircraft at this time—which explains the *Ranger* title four years after the ship had been decommissioned! NL640 (160787) sits on the Whidbey ramp on 26 Nov 1997. (author)

Air Anti Submarine Wing One AirAntiSubWing ONE Cecil Field
Sea Strike Wing One SeaStrikeWing ONE Cecil Field
Sea Control Wing US Atl. Flt. SeaConWingLant Cecil Field, Jax
East Coast S-3 squadrons. r/d SSW-1 May 87, r/d SCWLant Apr 93, moved Sep 97

Reconnaissance Heavy Attack Wing ONE ReconHatWing ONE Albany, Key West
All RA-5C squadrons. Moved to Key West 1974. Disestablished 7 Jan 80. (two months after the last *Vigilante* had left Key West)

Medium Attack Wing -ONE MatWing ONE Oceana
Attack Wing US Atlantic Fleet AtkWingLant Oceana
East Coast A-6 squadrons. R/d 2 Aug 93. Attack Wing Lant disestab. 1 Apr 97.

Fighter Wing -ONE FitWing-ONE Oceana
Fighter Wing US Atlantic Fleet FitWingLant Oceana
East Coast F-4 and F-14 squadrons. Redesignated 9 Jul 93.

Airborne Early Warning Wing TWELVE AEWWING-12 Norfolk
Airborne Early Warning Wing US Atlantic Fleet AEWWingLant Norfolk
East Coast E-1 and E-2 squadrons. R/D 1 Sep 93

Helicopter Anti-Submarine Wing ONE HSWing-ONE Jacksonville
Helicopter Anti-Submarine Wing US Atlantic Fleet HSWingLant Jacksonville
East Coast SH-3 squadrons: est. 1 Apr 73, r/d 5 Aug 93

Commander, Naval Air Forces U.S. Pacific Fleet (COMNAVAIRPAC)
North Island, CA. Vice Admiral position, in charge of all aviation activities on the West Coast.

FUNCTIONAL WINGS
Antisubmarine Warfare Wing US Pacific Fleet ASWWingPac North Island
West Coast S-3s, H-3s, H-2s
d. 30 Sep 1993, broken up into separate Type Wings.

Fighter Airborne Early Warning Wing US Pacific Fleet FitAEWWingPac Miramar
West Coast F-4, F-8, RF-8, F-14, E-1 and E-2 squadrons e. 1974. d. 30 Sep 1993. Broken up into separate wings. Locally known as "FitFudd", a combination of "fighter" and (Willy) "Fudd", a nickname for the E-1B *Tracer*.

Medium Attack Tactical Electronic Warfare Wing US Pac. Flt. MatVAQWingPac
Whidbey Island
West Coast A-6 and all EA-6B activities. Locally known as "VacuumPac". D. 1 Feb 93. Broken into separate wings.

TYPE WINGS
Attack Wing US Pacific Fleet MatWingPac Whidbey Island
West Coast A-6 squadrons. Estab. 1 Sep 93, D. 30 Apr 97.

Electronic Combat Wing US Pacific Fleet VAQWingPac Whidbey Island
Electronic Attack Wing US Pacific Fleet VAQWingPac
All Navy EA-6B squadrons. Estab. 1 Sep 93, r/d 30 Mar 98.
Air Pac initially tried to stick VAQWing with the PLAD TacElWingsPac in 1993. It was changed to VAQWing at Whidbey's request soon after establishment.

Light Attack Wing US Pacific Fleet LatWingPac Lemoore
Strike Fighter Wing US Pacific Fleet StrkFitWingPac Lemoore
West Coast A-7 squadrons with a Rear Admiral until 1 June 1993.
West Coast F/A-18 squadrons. r/d 15 Apr 91. Was a Functional wing

Fighter Wing US Pacific Fleet FitWingPac Miramar
West Coast F-14 squadrons. Estab. 1 Sep 93, Disestab. 31 Jan 97.

Carrier Airborne Early Warning Wing-ELEVEN CAEWW-11 North Island
West Coast E-1 and E-2 units. Moved to Miramar in 1974 and merged with FitWing to form FitAEWWingPac.

Airborne Early Warning Wing Pacific Fleet AEWWingPac Miramar, Pt Mugu
West Coast E-2 squadrons. Estab. 1 Aug 93, moved 1 Jul 98.

Air Antisubmarine Wing US Pacific Fleet AirASWWingPac North Island
Sea Control Wing Pacific Fleet SeaConWingPac North Island
West Coast S-3 squadrons., est. 22 Apr 93

Helicopter Anti-Submarine Wing US Pacific Fleet HSWingPac North Island
West Coast SH-3 squadrons est. 1 Jul 93

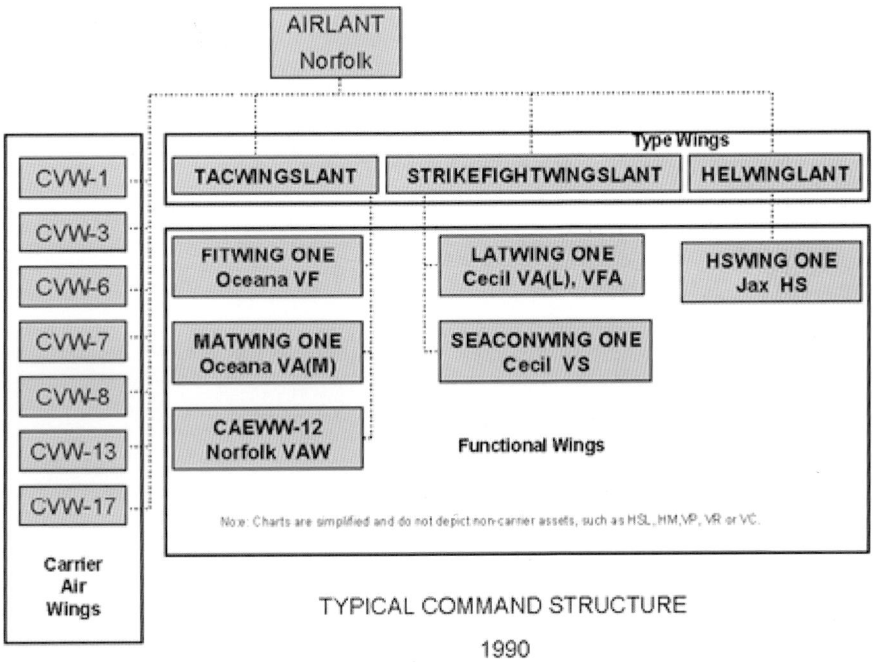

TYPICAL COMMAND STRUCTURE

1990

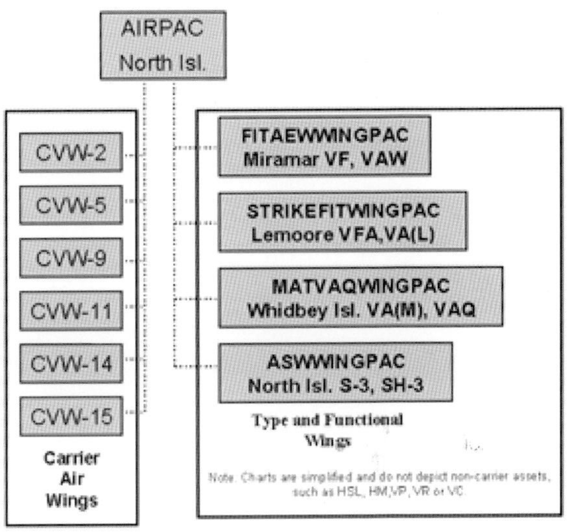

What the heck is a Commodore?

The Navy's senior officer rank structure has caused no small amount of confusion over the years, largely due to the service's hidebound sense of tradition in this area, and desire to not have a true one-star flag rank for officers for most of the period.

Prior to 1950, the rank of Commodore was equivalent to an Army Brigadier General (pay grade O-7); however, obscure tradition dictated that this be used only in wartime. In 1950 the Navy "retired" the Commodore rank again, and started promoting suitable Captains (O-6) directly to Rear Admiral (lower half), where they would wear two stars while being paid at the O-7 rate. He could subsequently be promoted to Rear Admiral (upper half), which would still be only two stars in rank, while being paid as an O-8, making him equivalent to an Army Major General.

During this period the term Commodore remained as an honorary title bestowed upon Captains who "owned" wings or other unified groups of aircraft on land. In other words, the Commander of a Type Wing would be called a Commodore, although his rank was Captain. (Note that the term was NEVER used for the commander of a carrier air group or wing, as he ***ALWAYS*** goes by the title CAG.)

This changed in 1982, with the passage of the DOPMA Act in the U.S. Congress, which directed the Navy to use the one-star rank with the title of Commodore Admiral, which was abbreviated as COMO. This was done as much to soothe the other services, which never appreciated the fact that new Navy admirals were automatically senior to their one-stars after promotion. The name was shortened to just Commodore only a year later, largely because a lot of people thought "Commodore Admiral" sounded silly.

It only took four years before tradition won out again, as the formal Commodore rank survived only until 1986, when the Navy went back to calling the O-7 rank Rear Admiral (lower half), which was abbreviated RDML, while O-8s became, yet again, Rear Admiral (upper half), or RADMs. Since the lower half rank now actually wore one-star insignia, the other services didn't really care what the Navy called them, and the term Commodore returned yet again as a title for land based wing commanders with the rank of Captain.

Type Wing Commanders usually go by the title of Commodore, even if they wear the rank of Captain. The somewhat anonymous TA-4J (AD600 153461) pictured here belongs to VA-45 at Key West on 16 July 1980. It carries the name of "Snuffy" Smith, the Commander of Cecil Field's LATWING-ONE. The lettering is largely symbolic, and a mark of respect—the number of times the Commodore actually flew this aircraft probably could be counted on one hand, if ever. AD600 also wears a stylized Safety "S" award and an adversary paint job, although it also carries an instrument hood in the rear cockpit befitting the *Blackbird's* other primary mission at the time. (author)

13

Bases

"Pardon Our Noise: It's a Sound of Freedom."
- Sign alongside highway 20, Whidbey Island, WA

Naval Air Stations/Naval Air Facilities/Carrier Bases in CONUS
The Navy gives its bases descriptive titles that provide some sort of idea as to what warfare community the facility works in. Aviation locations are usually called Naval Air Stations (NAS), Naval Air Facility (NAF—a small NAS with less support), Outlying Field (OLF—a small practice field with very limited facilities and no permanent units), or Naval Auxiliary Landing Field (NALF, or just ALF—similar to an OLF). Bases with ships are usually called Naval Stations (NS), while Marine bases will have the letter "M" precede the remainder of the title. Bases "owned" by the test and evaluation part of the Navy have used a bewildering variety of names over the years that cannot be described in a simple fashion—see individual locations for more information.

As opposed to the Air Force, where "AFB" follows the title, the term "Naval Air Station" (NAS) *always* precedes the actual name, although this arrangement is frequently (and incorrectly) reversed in casual use (as in, it's NAS Oceana, not "Oceana NAS"). In 1994 at least three Naval Reserve bases were given the clunky title "Naval Air Station Joint Reserve Base" (NAS JRB) to denote Navy bases with other services' reserve units onboard as tenants. Curiously, when Navy or Marine units are tenants on USAF facilities, the JRB title is not used, and they are usually given separate names, such as NAS Atlanta or NAS Detroit.

As of January 1974, the Navy operated 40 Naval Air Stations and Facilities within CONUS, as well as a number outside the U.S. Three bases were scheduled for closure in 1974 (Glynco, Quonset Point, and Albany), which brought to an end the Vietnam era winnowing of fields, which had included Sanford, Florida (1968), and reserve bases at Grosse Ile, Michigan (1969), Olathe, Kansas, Seattle, Washington, New York, NY, and Twin Cities, Minnesota (all in 1970), as well as Los Alamitos, California, in 1971. NAS Ellyson Field, the Navy's helicopter training base located in northeast Pensacola, was closed in December 1973 when its activities were moved up to Whiting Field.

The following listings include the field's ICAO three-letter identifier, where known. Navy/Marine air stations normally start with the letter "N." The actual airfield portions of some bases are named as

Located near the southern end of U.S. Highway 1, NAS Key West provides excellent clear weather training opportunities. Here a VF-171 det F-4N and A-4E are south of Boca Chica Key and the field on 10 Mar '81. (Bob Lawson)

well, usually in honor of naval heroes. Because detailed unit listings would consume more space than available, the author has chosen to show "slice in time" base loadings as of mid-1977.

NAS ALAMEDA (NGZ) Nimitz Field
Location: At Alameda, CA, across the bay from San Francisco
Alameda was an historic, old facility whose air station included a depot (NARF), as well as multiple reserve squadrons. Although it had been home to air wings and regular Navy units for many years, the last deploying squadron here was VAQ-130, which moved to Whidbey Island in 1974. The base was closed on 30 Sep 1997, with a large part being turned over to the Port of Oakland for commercial use, as well as providing a berth for the USS *Hornet* (CVS-12) Museum. The expansive runway and hangar areas have subsequently been made available for movie and TV productions, including "Matrix II," the motorcycle chase sequences being filmed on a "freeway" built over the old runway area. 1977 Units: CV-43, CVN-65, NARF Alameda, CVWR-30, VA-303, 304, VAK-208, -308, HM-15, HS-85, VR-30, -55, MAG-42, VMA-133, and HMH-769.

NAS ALBANY (NAB)
Location: 2 miles NE Albany, GA
The former Turner AFB, a Strategic Air Command (SAC) bomber base transferred to Navy 1 July 1967. Albany was home for the RA-5C community until closed in June 1974, with the *Vigilantes* moving to Key West. The facility was subsequently developed for light industry, as well as a brewery for the Miller Company.

NAS ATLANTA (NCQ)
Location: Marietta, GA, 6 miles NW of Atlanta.
NAS Atlanta is a Naval Reserve base located on the southwest corner of Dobbins AFB. This station replaced a previous (and much smaller) NAS Atlanta in April 1959, which was located ten miles to the east, and is the current Peachtree-De Kalb airport. The field also houses Marine Reserve functions and the Lockheed-Marietta plant, home to the C-5, C-130, and F-22. 1977 Units: VA-205, VR-54 det, VMFA-351, HML-765, HMA-773, VMO-4. Dobbins AFB: 94th TAW (AFRES, C-7A), 116th FW (GA ANG, F-100D/F)

NS BREMERTON
Location: Downtown Bremerton, WA
The Navy's major shipyard on the West Coast, Bremerton is located on Washington's Olympic Peninsula, and is a pleasant hour's ferry boat ride from Seattle. The base's drydock and extensive shipbuilding facilities provided the primary location in the Pacific Fleet to refuel nuclear surface ships and submarines, although carriers were done only at Newport News. Bremerton has been used as a homeport for nuclear powered carriers, since the arrival of *Nimitz* in 1987. She was replaced by *Carl Vinson* in 1997. The base was also home to a sizeable ship storage ("mothball") facility, which included several carriers and battleships during the period covered. The movie "An Officer and a Gentleman" features a view of the location early in the film.

NAS BRUNSWICK (NHZ)
Location: 1 mile SE of Brunswick, ME
The major patrol base for northeast U.S., Brunswick has been a NAS since 15 Sept 1951. As far as carrier aviators were concerned, Brunswick's value was largely as a place to stop at to buy cheap lobster. 1977 Units: PatWing-5, VP-8, -10, -11, -23, -26, -44.

NAS CECIL FIELD (NZC)
Location: approx. 7 mi SW of Jacksonville, FL
Auxiliary Field:
OLF White House (NEN) (5 mi north of field)
Primary home for Atlantic Fleet light attack (VA), strike fighter (VFA), and anti-submarine (VS) squadrons and support activities. Cecil Field closed on 30 Sept 1999, with the VFA units moving to Oceana, VA, and MCAS Beaufort, while the VS squadrons transferred to Jacksonville, FL. 1977 Units: LATWING ONE; AIRASWING ONE; CVW-1,3; CVWR-20; VA-45, -46, -72, -81, -83, -86, -105, -174, -15, -87; VS-22, -24, -28, -30, -31, -32

NAS CHASE FIELD (NIR)
Location: 5 mi east of Beeville, TX
Auxiliary Field: **NALF Goliad** (NGT) 12 mi NNE of field, 3 mi North of Berclair, TX
One of the Navy's three major jet training bases through the '70s and '80s. Closed 1 Feb 1993, and turned into a prison. 1977 Units: TraWing-3, VT-24, -25, -26.

NAS CHINA LAKE (NID) Armitage Field
Location: 1 mile north of China Lake, CA.
China Lake is located in the middle of nowhere, near beautiful downtown Inyokern, and almost within sight of Death Valley. It is a perfect place to test weapons, and is birthplace for a whole line of important aviation weapons, including *Shrike*, *Walleye*, *Rockeye*, *Snakeye*, *Zuni*, and *Sidwinder*. Disestablished as a formal NAS and separate command on 1 Dec 1977, with the base now being named Naval Weapons Center (NWC) China Lake. On 22 Jan 1992 it was again renamed, to Naval Air Weapons Station (NAWS) China Lake, with no real change in mission. 1977 Unit: VX-5

NAS CORPUS CHRISTI (NGP)
Location: 10 mi SE Corpus Christi, TX
Auxiliary Fields:
NALF Waldron Field, 3mi SSW of NAS,
NALF Cabaniss (NGW), 8mi W of NAS.
Home of the Chief of Naval Air Training (CNATRA) and Navy primary and multi-engine training, as well as an Army helicopter depot and a Coast Guard Air Station onboard. 1977 Units: TraWing-4, VT-27,28,31. USCG aviation det

NAF DAHLGREN (NDY)
Location: Dahlgren, VA, approx. 23 mi east of Fredericksburg, VA.
Renamed Naval Surface Warfare Center Dahlgren in 1987. A relatively obscure base located on the west bank of the Potomac River,

about 40 miles south of Washington, DC, Dahlgren was a significant test and development base (particularly for surface warfare systems) with no fleet or reserve flying units assigned. Among its many historical functions was its use as a test location for naval artillery up to and including 16", with firing being done into the river. The base features a short runway that saw reduced activity as time went on.

NAS DALLAS (NBE) Hensley Field
Location: Grand Prairie, TX, approx 10mi SW of downtown Dallas
A major Naval Reserve base, co-located with USMCR, TX ANG, Army Reserve activities, as well as the Vought plant, where F-8s and A-7s were built. Closed 30 Sep 1998, four years after surviving flight units had moved to NAS JRB Ft. Worth. 1977 Units: VF-201, VF-202, MAG-41, VMFA-112, HMH-777, 136th AREFW (TX ANG KC-97L)

NAS DETROIT (NFB)
Location: On Selfridge ANGB, at Mt Clemens, MI.
Reserve base, opened in Nov 1969 to replace tiny NAS Grosse Ile. NAS Detroit was itself closed 1 Apr 1994, although the last unit (Patron-93) lasted until 30 Sept '94. 1977 Units: VP-93, VR-52 det, VMO-4, HMM-766. Selfridge AFB: 127th TFW (MI ANG, F-100D/F) 191st FIG (MI ANG, F-106A/B) 927th TAG (AFRES, C-130A)

NAS EL CENTRO (NJK)
Location: In California's Imperial Valley, 4mi WNW of El Centro, CA
Located at the south end of California's Imperial Valley, and near the Mexican border, NAS El Centro's listed elevation is 42 feet ***below*** sea level, as a line encircling the control tower indicates. Deployed training base for fleet and TRACOM units, as well as the winter training home for the Blue Angels. "El Sweat-O" was the site for a Medium Attack Weapons Detachment operated jointly between VA-42 and -128 for many years.

NS EVERETT
Location: downtown Everett, WA, about 30 miles north of Seattle.
One of the Navy's newest facilities, Everett was one of the "Strategic Homeports" opened during the John Lehman buildup years. The Navy took a section of largely abandoned or lightly utilized harbor front, and rebuilt it to support a single nuclear carrier and a squadron of destroyers and frigates. The site was initially proposed in 1983, ground was broken in 1987, and the base was opened in April 1994.

Abraham Lincoln arrived on 8 Jan 1997 as the first permanent carrier based at the location. What aviation support is required is provided by NAS Whidbey Island, about 30 miles to the northwest. By 2001 Everett was one of the few Lehman-era new facilities still open.

NAS FALLON (NFL) Van Voorhis Field
Location: 6mi SE of Fallon, NV
Major training base for fleet units, controlled a large number of airspace and bombing ranges. Site of annual "WEPTRAEX" Air Wing training. Fallon became home to Naval Strike Warfare Center (NSWC, or "Strike U") from 1984, and its NSAWC follow-on. The base grew extensively during the 1980s, as it became the "Center of Excellence" for all Navy strike training. 1977 Units: VA-122 detachment

NAS JRB Ft WORTH (NFW)
Location: 2 mi NW of Ft Worth, TX
Established 1 Oct 1994, to consolidate military aviation in the Dallas-Ft Worth "Metroplex." It occupies the site of the former Carswell AFB, which was turned over to the Navy during a period of base realignment. The USAF moved its B-52 wing out of town on 30 Sep 1993, and claimed substantial savings, while the Navy shifted most of its former NAS Dallas units, while also spending millions of dollars to refurbish their new facility. Actual savings to the taxpayer depends on who you talk to. The 301st Fighter Wing, an Air Force Reserve F-16C/D unit, remains, and still calls the location Carswell Field. Lockheed's (former General Dynamics nee Convair) F-16 plant is located across the field. Many references, including some official, refer to this location as "NAS Ft Worth JRB," which gives some indication as to the level of confusion this title brought with it.

NAS GLENVIEW (NBU)
Location: Glenview, IL, roughly 12mi north of downtown Chicago.
The Navy's major aviation facility in "Chicagoland" was a large Reserve base through most of the period.

Fallon's large ranges were the home of at least six O-2 *Super Skymasters*. The former USAF forward air controller aircraft were assigned to VA-122 and, later, VFA-125 to spot bombs and carry out other odd jobs, including occasionally chasing errant motorcycle riders off Navy targets. The six Cessnas left the inventory in 1990, replaced by T-34Cs. 21365 (NJ293) is the former Air Force 67-21365 at NFL on 5 Feb 1984. (author)

Glenview's proximity to busy O'Hare International Airport (about five miles SSW), age, and land value led to its being vulnerable to closure. It was decommissioned on 30 Sep 1995, and was subsequently redeveloped into a mixed-use community of housing, recreation, and commercial properties, to the extent that it's now largely unrecognizable. 1977 Units: VP-60, 90, VR-51 det, VMGR-234, HML-776.

NAS GLYNCO (NEA)
Location: 5mi North of Brunswick, GA
Glynco was a training command base, and the former NAS Brunswick, gaining its later name in Jan 1943 so as not to confuse it with the base of the same name in Maine. The site was noted for its WWII-era blimp hangars, and was home for advanced Naval Flight Officer training until June 1974, when VT-86 moved to Pensacola. Glynco was closed December 1974, and turned over to other governmental agencies, who built the Federal Law Enforcement Training Center (FLETC) on site.

NAS IMPERIAL BEACH (NRS) Ream Field
Location:8 mi South of Coronado, CA
Barely a mile north of the Mexican border, "IB" had served as AirPac's center for rotary wing aviation since 1951. The base was turned into an Auxiliary field for North Island on 31 Dec 1974, when its HS, HC, and HSL units moved to NORIS.

NAS JACKSONVILLE (NIP) Towers Field
Location: on the St. Johns River, 5 miles south of Jacksonville, FL.
The larger of the two east coast VP bases, Navy Jax also holds the Atlantic Fleet HS units, which arrived from Quonset Point around 1973. The Atlantic Fleet's VS community moved in over 1999 with the closure of Cecil Field. 1977 Units: NARF Jacksonville, PATWING-ELEVEN, CVWR-20, VP-5, -16, -24, -30, -45, -49, -56, -62, VR-58, VA-203, VMA-142, HS-1, -3, -5, -7, -9, -11, -15, HC-2.

NAS KEY WEST (NQX)
Location: On Boca Chica Key, 5mi East of Key West proper on U.S. Highway 1.
By 1974 the base controlled four separate facilities spread throughout the Key West area, including the field located on Boca Chica ("Broken Chicken") Key, as well as support activities at Trumbo Point (home to the Navy's small PHM hydrofoil force, as well as a former seaplane facility), Truman Annex (the former destroyer and sub base located downtown), and Sigsbee Point housing area. Key West remains an important fair weather training location for east coast units, and occasional alert base for fighters watching Fidel Castro's Cuba. It was the last home for the Navy's *Vigilante* community, with VAQ-33 and VA-45 moving in after the retirement of the RA-5C. 1977 Units: RECONATTACKWING-ONE, RVAH-1, -3, -5, -6, -7, -9, -12, VF-101 det KW

NAS KINGSVILLE (NQI)
Location: 2mi East of Kingsville, TX.
Auxiliary Field:
NALF Orange Grove, 10mi NNE of Alice, TX, 27mi NNW of NAS.
A major jet training base, Kingsville would be the first location for T-45 training in the Navy. 1977 Units: TraWing-2, VT-21, -22, -23.

NAS/NAEC LAKEHURST (NEL)
Location: 3 miles NW of Lakehurst, NJ.
Lakehurst, famed as the location where the German Zeppelin *Hindenburg* burned in 1937, was the Navy's primary Lighter-Than-

Mayport is the service's "other" east coast carrier base, and normally homeport for one or two oil fueled carriers. Located right on the Atlantic Ocean, the facility features a very short "sea and anchor" detail, as ships are basically at sea once they cleared the south side of the pier. Here *John C. Stennis* is maneuvered into a berth while visiting Mayport on 5 Apr 1996. *John F. Kennedy*, the base's normal resident, sits at the pier to the right while it carries out routine maintenance. (U.S. Navy, PHAN L. Kanak)

Air (LTA) location on the East Coast. By the mid-1970s it was almost entirely a test and developmental base (largely for catapult and arresting gear), with only four deploying helo units (HC-2, HS-15, HSL-30, and -32) present. The NAS was disestablished as a separate command in Mar 1977, with the field coming under the main tenant, Naval Air Engineering Center (NAEC) Lakehurst. On 1 Jan 1992 it was renamed to Naval Air Engineering Station (NAES) Lakehurst. It has subsequently been renamed again to Naval Air Warfare Center (NAWC) Lakehurst. 1977 units: HC-2, HS-75

NAS LEMOORE (NLC) Reeves Field
Location: 6mi West of Lemoore, CA, and roughly 11mi West of Hanford.
Easily the Navy's most remote Master Jet Base, Lemoore is located in the middle of California's fertile San Joaquin Valley, and has served as home to the West Coast Light Attack and Strike Fighter communities. Lemoore was opened in 1960 to move jet units out of the rapidly growing San Francisco Bay area (from Alameda and Moffett Field), and it has remained one of the primary AirPac jet bases ever since. 1977 Units: CLAWPAC, CVW-9, 19, VA-22, -25, -27, -94, -97, -113, -122, -125, -127, -146, -147, -153, -155, -192, -195, -215.

NAF/NAS MAYPORT (NRB)
Location: Mayport, FL, 10 miles ENE of Jacksonville, FL
A relatively small base located at the mouth of the St. Johns River. Home port to aircraft carriers and LAMPS squadrons. Redesignated a NAS from NAF on 9 Sep 1988. On 1 Jun 1992 the airbase was consumed by the Naval Station, with the entire complex being called NS Mayport. *John F Kennedy* (CV-67) was moved to Mayport in 1995 in order to keep at least one carrier homported here. 1977 Ships: CV-42, -60.

NAS MEMPHIS (NQA)
Location: Millington, TN, about 18mi NNE of Graceland.
Memphis was one of the largest enlisted aviation training facilities in the Navy, as well as home to several reserve units. The NAS was deactivated on 31 July '98, when the base was redesignated Naval Support Activity Memphis. The Naval Personnel Command (BUPERS) was subsequently moved in to occupy the location, from Alexandria, VA.
1977 Units: VP-67, VR-53, VA-204, VMA-124

NAS MERIDIAN (NMM) McCain Field
Location: 12mi NNW of Meridian, MS
Auxiliary Fields:
OLF Alpha: roughly 35 mi NNE of the NAS, 2 mi S of Shuqualak, MS. Turned over to the USAF in 1970 for use as an Auxiliary to Columbus AFB, formally transferred in 1990.
OLF Bravo: (NJW) roughly 23mi NW of the NAS, 5 mi SSW of Lynville, MS. Named Williams Field in 1987.
Meridian was opened in 1961 as a primary jet training base, and has subsequently become home to Training Wing ONE. Meridian survived the post-*Desert Storm* BRAC cuts and reorganization to remain one of the two jet pilot training locations in the service. 1977 Units: TraWing-1, VT-7, -9, -19

NAS MIRAMAR (NKX) Mitscher Field
Location: On Kearney Mesa, roughly 10mi north of downtown San Diego.
Auxiliary Field: **NALF San Clemente IS**, (NUC) located on the northern tip of San Clemente Island, 74mi WSW from the NAS.

Originally built for the Marines in WWII, Miramar would be transferred to the Navy after the war, become a Master Jet Base known as "Fightertown USA," and the legendary home to the West Coast fighter community and WOXOF. The facility was returned to the Marines on 1 Oct 1997, becoming MCAS Miramar, with the remaining F-14 units moving to Oceana, while the E-2s headed up the coast to Pt Mugu. The CVW staffs were transferred to Lemoore, and *Topgun* became a department at NSAWC in Fallon. 1977 Units: FITAEWWINGPAC, CVW-2, -11, -14, -15, - VF-1, -2, -21, -24, -51, -111, -114, -121, -124, -126, -154, - 191, -194, -211, - 213, -301, -302; VFP-63, NFWS (*Topgun*), RVÀW-110, VAW-88, - 111, -112, -113, -114, -116, -117; VC-7, -13

NAS MOFFETT FIELD (NUQ)
Location: Near Palo Alto, CA.
Auxiliary Field:
OLF Crows Landing (NRC), 2 miles NW of town of same name (11 WSW of Turlock, CA).
The major patrol base for the West Coast, Moffett was noted for its huge dirigible hangar no. 1, as well as two smaller blimp hangars. Located in the rapidly expanding "Silicon Valley," the Navy was outpriced by the hot local economy, and it closed the field on 1 July 1994, with ownership transferring to NASA. 1977 Units: PATWINGPAC, RESPATWINGPAC, VP-9, -19, -31, -40, -46, -47, -48, -50, -91.

NAS JRB NEW ORLEANS (NBG) Alvin Callender Field
Location: About 6mi SE of downtown New Orleans.
"NAS NOLA" was a joint reserve base long before the term was coined. It was formally renamed as a NAS JRB in 1994. It held Navy Reserve, AFRES, ANG, and Army Reserve activities. 1977 Units: NAVAIRRES, VP-94, VR-54, HMM-767, -768. 159th TFG (LA ANG, F-100D/F), 926th TAG (AFRES, C-130B)

NAS NORFOLK (NGU) Chambers Field
Location: Roughly 4mi N of downtown Norfolk, VA.
The NAS was adjacent to Naval Station Norfolk, the self-styled "largest Navy base in the world."
The NS was home to CV-59, -62, -66, -67, and CVN-68. As of 1974 Norfolk had only a 7000 foot runway, and was home to largely prop or helo activities, as well as two VAQ units. It was extended to just over 8300 feet in the 1980s, and continues as a major east coast air facility. The NAS itself was deactivated as a separate command on 24 Nov 1998, with operations and other functions transferring to the Naval Station. 1977 Units: NARF Norfolk, AIRLANT, CAEWW-12, HELSEACONWING-ONE, RESPATWINGLANT, RVAW-120, VAW-78, -121 to -126, VRF-31, VAQ-33, -209, VR-1, -56, VRC-40, VRF-31, HC-6, HAL-4, HM-12, HSL-30, -32, -34, -36, HMM-774.

NAS NORTH ISLAND (NZY) Halsey Field
Location: Coronado, CA, across the bay from San Diego.
Auxiliary Field: **OLF Imperial Beach** (NRS) 10mi SSE from the NAS, near the Mexican border. A former NAS that became an OLF on 1 Jan 1975.

"NORIS" was home to AIRPAC, as well as Pacific Fleet carrier based ASW and helo units. Originally known as NAS San Diego, it was given its current name in early 1955. Along with Alameda, one of the two primary carrier bases in the Pacific Fleet. Home to the Pacific Fleet's HS, HSL, and VS activities, as well as AIRPAC itself. West Coast VAW units were based here until moved to Miramar in 1974. 1977 Units: CV-61, CV-63, CV-64; NARF North Island, AIRPAC, HELWINGRES, VS-21, -29, -33, -37, -38, -41 VC-3, VR-30 det, -57, HC-1, -3, -9, -11 HS-2, -4, -6, -7, -10, -84 HSL-31, -33, -35.

NAS OCEANA (NTU) Soucek Field
Location: 2mi SW of Virginia Beach, VA
Auxiliary Field: **ALF Fentress**, (NFE) 8mi SW of the NAS.
Master Jet Base. The East Coast home to Fighter and Medium Attack units. From 1999 the base was also home to the East Coast VFA community, which was moved from the newly closed Cecil Field. Oceana, which originally opened in WWII as a somewhat isolated adjunct to Norfolk, has subsequently become surrounded by civil growth in one of America's leading beach vacation areas. Noise complaints and encroachment continue to grow at this facility (as well as at its Auxiliary field at Fentress), and may well lead to the end of this large facility in time. 1977 Units: FITWING ONE, MATWING ONE, CVW-1, -6, -7, -8, -17, VF-11, -14, -31, -32, -33, -41, -43, -74, -84, -101, -102, -103, -142, -143. VA-34, -35, -42, -65, -75, -85, -176. VC-2, -12.

NAS PATUXENT RIVER (NHK) Trapnell Field
Location: 1mi East of Lexington Park, MD
A large test and developmental facility located along the Chesapeake Bay in a relatively isolated part of southern Maryland. "Pax River" was opened in 1943 to place all aviation testing at one location, and became well known for its leading edge (and highly dangerous) flight activities after being featured in the Tom Wolff book "The Right Stuff." In 1992 the Test Center was renamed Naval Air Warfare Center-Aircraft Division (NAWC-AD) as part of the massive realignment of Naval Air Systems Command ("NAVAIR"). NAVAIR itself moved on base from Crystal City (Alexandria), VA, in 1996-97. No carrier based fleet squadrons are located at Pax. 1977 Units: Naval Air Test Center (NATC), Naval Test Pilot School (NTPS), VX-1, VXN-8, VQ-4, VP-68, HAL-5.

NAS PENSACOLA (NPA) Forrest Sherman Field
Location: 5mi SW of downtown Pensacola, FL
Auxiliary Fields: (see NAS Whiting Field)
This is where all future Naval Aviators and Naval Flight Officers start their journey. Aviation Officer Candidate School (AOCS) was located here, as was Aviation Indoctrination (AI), the preflight portion of flight training for ROTC and Academy graduates. The movie "Officer and a Gentleman" was originally supposed to have been filmed here "on location," but official concerns with some of the plot lines led to it being shot without Navy support at an old Army coast artillery fort at Port Townsend, WA (which became the fictional "NAS Puget Sound"). 1977 units: NARF Pensacola, TraWing-6: VT-4, -10, -86, HCT-16, Naval Aviation Museum (later re-titled the National Museum of Naval Aviation), Naval Flight Demonstration Squadron (the *Blue Angels*).

NAS POINT MUGU (NTD)
Location: 5mi SE of Ventura, CA.
Auxiliary Field: **OLF San Nicholas Island** (NSI), 56mi S of the NAS on the east end of San Nicholas Is.
West Coast test and developmental base with some reserve activities. Long time home to the Pacific Missile Test Center (PMTC), Pt Mugu was renamed a Naval Air Weapons Station (NAWS) on 21 Jan 1992, and back again to NAS on 2 Dec 1998. In 2000 it was subsumed again, this time as part of regional Naval Base Ventura County, even though locals still refer to it as NAS Pt Mugu. Between 1983 and 1992 Pt Mugu was the home for FEWSG's VAQ-34. The Pacific Fleet E-2 *Hawkeye* community arrived from Miramar starting in July 1998. In December 1998 the California Air National Guard moved the 146th Airlift Wing on base from Van Nuys, CA, with their C-130Hs, calling its section Channel Islands Air National Guard Base. In a peculiar piece of notoriety, Pt Mugu was used as "Emerald Point NAS" in the mercifully short lived 1983 TV show of the same name, where the men were handsome, women gorgeous, and plots downright absurd. 1977 Units: VX-4, VXE-6, VP-65, VA-305.

The Navy's "Master Jet Base" at Virginia Beach, VA, hosted the Atlantic Fleet's Fighter and Medium Attack communities. A VF-43 T-2C heads for 23R on 21 Nov '89, while a VA-65 A-6E waits its turn to the right. (author)

NAS QUONSET POINT (NCO)
Location: 1mi North of Wickford, RI, roughly 10mi South of Providence.
Auxiliary Field: **OLF Charlestown** ("Charley Town"), 20 mi SW of Quonset Point.
When opened in 1939, Quonset Point was intended to be the largest NAS on the East Coast. 15 different carriers, 12 VS, and 8 HS units all called Quonset home at one time or another. It featured a deep water port and aviation depot that historically worked on S-2 and A-1 type aircraft. The base was home to the east coast's carrier based ASW community until the decision was made to put the SH-3s and new S-3s in northeast Florida. Squadrons started leaving in 1973, and NAS Quonset Point was closed on 28 June 1974.

NAS SAUFLEY FIELD (NUN)
Location: 7mi north of NAS Pensacola.
Saufley was the home for Navy primary training for many years, with two T-34B squadrons (VT-1 and -5) being assigned. The field was formally closed on 1 Dec 1976, and it became a NAAS at that time and, later, an OLF. The field continued to be used for landing practice by units out of Whiting Field.

NAS SOUTH WEYMOUTH (NZW) Shea Field
Location: 2mi NW of Rockland, MA, about 13mi SSE of downtown Boston.
South Weymouth replaced the former NAS Squantum in 1954, and was home for Boston area reserve activities. South Weymouth was closed 30 Sep 1997. 1977 Units: VP-92, HS-74, VMA-322, HML-771

NAF (NADC, NAWC) WARMINSTER (NJP)
Location: About 14 mi North of Philadelphia
Units: Naval Air Development Center
Located about two miles east of Willow Grove, Warminster was a weapons and systems research testing location that closed 30 Sep 1996. Formerly named NADC Johnsville (until 1965), the base hosted an odd lot of aircraft, from A-4s and A-7s up to EC-121s and P-3s. For whatever reason, the service renamed the facility Naval Air Warfare Center (NAWC) Warminster in March 1996, just months before it was closed.

NAF WASHINGTON (NSF)
Location: Occupies the north side of Andrews AFB, MD (ADW)
Home for DC area Reserve activities, NAF Washington sits across the runway from the Air Force's Andrews AFB. The base was opened in 1961 to replace NAS Anacostia, which is located across the Potomac River from Washington National Airport. The "NSF" code has long unofficially stood for "Navy Side of the Field." 1977 Units: VFP-206, -306, VR-52 det. VMFA-321. Andrews AFB: 89th MAW (VC-137 and other VIP aircraft), 113th TFW (DC ANG, F-100D/F), 459th TAW (AFRES, C-130E)

NAS WHIDBEY ISLAND (NUW) Ault Field
Location: 3mi West of Oak Harbor, WA.
Outlying field: **OLF Coupeville** (NRA) 8mi south
Home to West Coast Medium Attack activities, as well as all regular Navy EA-6B squadrons. Ault Field occupies Clover Valley, and is the main part of the facility. The former seaplane base portion of the complex is located about three miles east (on the other side of the island, and adjacent to Oak Harbor), and is now home to housing and support activities. 1977 Units: COMMATVAQWINGPAC. VA-52, -95, -128, -145, -165, -196; VAQ-129 through -138, VP-69, VR-51 det, HMM-770.

Whidbey Island on 24 June 1992, looking to the northwest towards Washington's San Juan Islands. The ramp is full of MatVAQWingPac's *Intruders* and *Prowlers*, as well as P-3Bs from Naval Reserve unit VP-69. (author)

NAS WHITING FIELD (NSE/NDZ)
Location: 5mi North of Milton, FL. Roughly 16mi NE of downtown Pensacola.
Auxiliary Fields: TraWing-FIVE uses a number of Navy owned and civilian fields for basic training purposes: Not all were necessarily open or used at any one time.

OLF Barin: ("Bloody Barin") 3mi East of Foley, AL.
Brewton Muni: 3mi South of Brewton, AL.
OLF Bronson: 5mi WNW of NAS Pensacola.
OLF Choctaw: 4mi NNW of Holley, FL.
OLF Evergreen/Middleton Field: 4mi West of Evergreen, AL.
OLF Holley: 1mi South of Holley, FL.
OLF Magnolia: 3mi North of Magnolia Springs, AL
OLF Santa Rosa: 4mi ESE of Milton, FL (predominantly rotary wing)
OLF Silverhill: 3mi WNW of Silverhill, AL
OLF Spencer: 2mi NE of Pace, FL (rotary wing)
OLF Summerdale: 4mi ENE of Summerdale, AL
OLF Wolf: 2mi NNW of Perdido Beach, AL
One of the Navy's two primary training facilities, and also site for all Navy/Marine/Coast Guard helo flight training. Whiting Field is actually two separate sets of runways connected by a taxiway. North Field (NSE) is used for fixed wing training, South Field (NDZ) for rotary wing. 1977 Units: TraWing-5, VT-2, -3, -6, HT-8, -18

NAS JRB WILLOW GROVE (NXX)
Location: About 14mi North of downtown Philadelphia, PA.
Home for Philadelphia area Navy and Marine Reserve activities, also has ANG, AFRES, and Army Reserve activities co-located. Was formally renamed NAS Joint Reserve Base Willow Grove in 1994. 1977 Units: VP-64, -66, VR-52, MAG-49, VMA-131, HMH-772. 111th TASG (PA ANG, O-2A), 913th TAG (AFRES, C-130E).

Master Jet Bases

The Cold War that "broke out" after World War II, and the introduction of jet aircraft to the fleet in the late 1940s led to a massive boom in base construction. The new aircraft required much longer runways and improved maintenance facilities, so in 1949 the Navy established a board to recommend how best to handle the new requirements.

Before long the service coined the term "Master Jet Base" to indicate those fields that were configured to handle large numbers of the new aircraft. Specifications for this title generally included parallel runways of no less than 8,000 feet in length (and usually longer), and appropriate instrument flight aids (radar and GCA) to allow operations down to 200 and 1/2 weather conditions. In initial plans, each was supposed to be able to support four carrier air groups and possess two jet capable Auxiliary fields.

They would also, at least initially, be located further away from the population in order to reduce noise complaints. (Oceana and Miramar would in time both be surrounded by public development, of course.) As of 1953 nine fields had been identified for the program: Miramar, Brunswick, Oceana, Cherry Point, El Toro, Cecil Field, Miami, Moffett Field, and Whidbey Island. In the end, only four Navy and two Marine fields would ever really come close to the full "Master Jet Base" criteria: Miramar, Oceana, Cecil Field, Lemoore, Cherry Point, and El Toro.

Marine Bases

MCAS BEAUFORT (NBC)
Location: 3mi NW of Beaufort, SC
The east coast's primary Marine fighter base. Actual location of the book and movie "The Great Santini," Beaufort was a WWII Naval Air Station, and was turned over to the Marines as an Auxiliary air station (MCAAS) on 26 Jun 1956, and became a full fledged MCAS on 1 March 1960. It has become the home of MAG-31, and the 2nd MAW's fighter and fighter-attack squadrons through the years. 1977 Units: MAG-31, VMFA-115, -122, -312, -333, -451

MCAF CAMP PENDLETON (NFG)
Munn Field (named 12 Jan '87)
Location: 6mi North of Oceanside, CA
Located at Camp Pendleton, CA. Home to 3rd MAW's light helicopter and observation units. 1977 Units: MAG-39, VMO-2, HML-267, HMA-169, HMT-303

MCAS CHERRY POINT (NKT) Cunningham Field
Location: 2mi NE of Cherry Point, NC, 14 SW of New Bern.
Auxiliary Fields: **MCALF Bogue Field**: (NJM) 1mi SE of Bogue, NC, 16 SW of Cherry Pt.
The major East Coast Marine fixed wing base, and home to a wide variety of 2nd MAW aviation units, as well as a sizeable depot (NARF) 1977 Units: NARF Cherry Point, 2nd MAW, MAG-14, -27, -32. VMA(AW)-533, -224, -533, VMAT(AW)-202, VMAQ-2, VMGR-252, VMA-231, -542, -331. VMAT-203.

MCAS EL TORO (NZJ)
Location: 6mi ESE of Santa Ana, CA
The major West Coast Marine fixed wing base until 2 July 1999, when it was closed, the Marines having moved the majority of 3rd MAW over to the "new" MCAS Miramar. 1977 Units: 3rd MAW, MAG-11, -13, -37, -46 VMA-134, -214, -311, -223, VMA(AW)-242, VMFA-314, -323, -531, VMFP-3, VMGR-352, VMO-8

MCAS (H) NEW RIVER (NCA)
Location: 2mi South of Jacksonville, NC
The major East Coast Marine rotary wing base, supporting the 2nd Marine Division. 1977 Units: MAG-26, -29, HMM-162, -261, -263, -264, HMH-362, -461, -464; HMT-204, VMO-1, HML-167, -267, HMA-269.

MCAS QUANTICO (NYG) Turner Field
Location: At Quantico, VA.
Called the "Crossroads of the Marine Corps," Quantico is a Headquarters, training, and support base for the DC area. Was redesignated a MCAF in 1980.
1977 Units: HMX-1.

MCAS (H) SANTA ANA/TUSTIN (NTK)
Location: 3mi SE of Santa Ana, CA
The major 3rd MAW rotary wing facility, was called Santa Ana until 1 June 1978, when renamed Tustin. It was closed 2 July 1999 after the Marines had basically moved both the Tustin and El Toro Groups to the newly acquired MCAS Miramar. 1977 Units: MAG-16, HMM-161, -163, HMT-301, HMH-361, -363, VMO-2.

MCB TWENTYNINE PALMS (NXP)
Location: At Marine Corps Base Twentynine Palms, roughly 10mi NW of the town of the same name.
Isolated Marine expeditionary training base in the California desert. No assigned flying units.

MCAS YUMA (NYL)
Location: 3 South of Yuma, AZ. Co-located with Yuma International Airport.
The former Vincent AFB, Yuma is a critical training location for Marine forces. Their highly regarded Marine Aviation Weapons Training Squadron ONE (MAWTS-1) is home to the Weapons and Tactics Instructor (WTI) program, and provides the Corps with a graduate level warrior training program. 1977 Units: MAWTS-1, MCCTG-10, VMFAT-101, VMAT-102, VMA-211, VMA-513.

Selected Overseas Bases

NS/NAF Adak, AK: (ADK)
Found near the end of Alaska's Aleutian chain, Naval Station Adak was typically a forward location for P-3 and other surveillance aircraft. The base was renamed a NAF on 1 July 1994, and subsequently closed on 18 Feb 1998 with a 30 Jan '98 official date. The desolate island was noted for its whimsical "National Forest," which consisted of a tiny plot of stunted trees surrounded by a fence.

Agana, Guam (NGM)
Agana provided an excellent mid-Pacific base for Naval operations, and was home to several units as well. It was closed on 31 March 1995, with Navy operations moving to the Air Force's **Anderson AFB** (UAM), which is located on the island's north end. 1977 units: VQ-1, -3.

NAF Atsugi JA: (NJA)
Located on the island of Honshu, Atsugi is home to CVW-5, which is assigned to the forward deployed carrier. 1977 residents: VF-151, -161, VA-56, -93, -115, VAW-115, HC-1 det, VRC-50 det. **NS Yokosuka** (typically pronounced by sailors "Ya-koos'-ka") is located about 20 miles away on Tokyo Bay, and is homeport for the navy's forward deployed carrier, as well as her support ships. The base includes pierside berthing, as well as several drydocks. 1977 resident: CV-41.

NAS Bermuda: (XKF)
Bermuda was another mid-Atlantic location for VP deployments, and was rarely visited by carrier aircraft. It was a USAF base until taken over by the Navy as a NAS on 1 July '70, and subsequently closed on 1 Sep 1995.

NAS Barber's Point Hawaii (NAX) John Rogers Field
Barbers was the Navy's primary aviation base in Hawaii during the period covered. Found just southwest of Honolulu, it was home to a Patrol Wing and other support activities. Barbers was disestablished on 23 Aug 1999 (1 July reported ceremonial date), with the surviving VP units being sent to either Kaneohe Bay or Whidbey Island. 1977 units: PATWING-TWO, VP-1, -4, -6, -17, -22; VQ-3; VC-1; HSL-37. **ALF Ford Island** (NPS) was another Hawaiian base, and is located in the middle of Pearl Harbor. A former NAS (until March 1962) and seaplane base, Ford Island had only 4000 feet of runway, which limited its use primarily to rotary wing traffic.

NAS Cubi Point RP (NCP)
Fabled Cubi Point was located in the Philippines, west of Manila, on the bay of the same name. The legendary liberty town of Olongopo was only a short walk outside the base's main gate, and across a bridge that spanned a ditch known fleet wide as the "S**t" River. Cubi was the primary U.S. Navy support base in West Pac throughout Vietnam, and up to its closure on 30 Oct 1992. Many carriers would leave part of their wing at Cubi while deployed to WestPac in order to make more flight deck space. The base provided pierside berthing for carriers (a rare thing outside of CONUS), and remained a vital facility throughout its existence. The base was subsequently developed by Federal Express (FedEx) for use as its Asian hub. 1977 units: VC-5, VRC-50.

NSA Diego Garcia BIOT (NKW)
Located on an English protectorate, Diego Garcia (also called "Day-Gar," or "Dodge") was built up to support Indian Ocean operations from the early 1980s. The base features a 12,000 ft runway, as well as an archipelago that allows anchoring of large vessels. Day-Gar has proven to be an absolutely vital logistics facility, as well as a regional bomber base for the USAF. NAF Diego Garcia was established on 26 Feb 1981, and disestablished in a late 1980s administrative change, with the base becoming a Naval Support Activity.

NAS Guantanamo Bay, Cuba (NBW).
Guantanamo was leased by the U.S. government for Navy use after the Spainish-American War. "Gitmo" (or "GTMO") possesses one of the best natural harbors in the Caribbean, and has proven valuable for fleet training ever since. Naval Aviation arrived during 1912. The U.S. refused to turn over the base after the Communist takeover of Cuba in 1959, as much to be a thorn in Fidel Castro's side as anything else. There are two airfields at Guantanamo: McCalla ("Windward") and Leeward. The Leeward field, located on the west side of the bay, re-

Roosevelt Roads, Puerto Rico, was a critical training location for the Atlantic Fleet until it was closed in 2004. A pair of VA-46 *Corsair IIs* take JP-5 in the fuel pits on 13 Oct 1981. (author)

mained the fixed-wing base, with an 8,000 ft runway. Approach was almost always to runway 10, which entailed a perpendicular approach and a hard 90 degree turn over the perimeter minefields into the break. A deep pattern would occasionally draw gunfire from the Cubans on the other side of the fence. The NAS designation was dropped 16 Feb 1993, with the entire facility coming under the larger Naval Station. 1977 unit: VC-10.

MCAS Iwakuni, Japan (NEU)
Located on the southern end of Honshu, Iwakuni is the home for the 1st Marine Air Wing, as well as the deployed location for fixed wing units rotated from CONUS under the Unit Deployment Program (UDP), where they came under the control of MAG-12. From 1974 to 2001 it was normal for single F-4 (VMFA), A-4 (VMA), and A-6 (VMA-AW) squadrons to be deployed here from the 2nd and 3rd MAWs. **MCAF Futenma** (NFO)**,** located on Okinawa, was home for WestPac deployed Marine helicopter units.

NAS Keflavik, Iceland (IKF)
"Kef" dates from May 1940, when the British "occupied" the location in order to establish a mid-Atlantic ASW base. It was opened as a NAF in July 1960, and became a NAS 1 Nov '85. Kef is best known for its Patrol deployments, and only rarely deals with carrier aircraft. The Air Force has long supported the base with interceptor units, with the 57th FIS, flying F-4Cs, being in residence as of 1977.

MCAS/MCAF Kaneohe Bay, Hawaii (NGF)
"K-BAY," located on Oahu's northeast side, was home to a single Marine Aircraft Group and its associated squadrons. By 1999 the Marines had shipped its VMFA units back to CONUS, and the Navy had moved in a Patrol Wing (with four VP units) from Barber's Point, along with single VR and HSL squadrons. The field was subsequently renamed a MCAF on 15 Apr '94, and placed under Marine Base Hawaii. 1977 Units: MAG-24, VMFA-212, -235, HMM-262, -463, VMO-6 det, HMA-369 det, HML-367 det.

NAF Lajes, Portugal (PLA)
Found in the Azores Group off the European Continent, Lajes was a VP deployment location, and only rarely visited by carrier aircraft. It was closed on 30 Sep 1993.

NAS/NAF Midway Island (MDY)
Famous location found at the end of the Hawaiian chain, and about 3200 miles west of San Francisco. Was the epicenter of the pivotal air and sea battle of June 1942. Midway was used by patrol squadrons, as well as a convenient stopping place for trans-pacific flights. The lonely little spit of sand was noted for its primary inhabitants, the flocks of Albatrosses that seemed quite ambivalent to the Navy's own flight activities. Was redesignated a NAF in Oct 1978, and disestablished 30 Sep 1993.

NAF Naha, Okinawa (NHC)
The Navy's primary air base on Okinawa during Vietnam, as well as a location for USAF fighters and interceptors, Naha was returned to the Japanese on 7 May 1975, with all remaining Navy activities moving to Kadena AFB by May 1976.

NS Roosevelt Roads, Puerto Rico (NRR). Ofstie Field
"Rosey Roads" was located on Puerto Rico's southeast coast, and entailed a harbor and airfield. It was a critical location due to the numerous live fire areas nearby, including the bomb range on Vieques Island, which is situated just across the channel. Political and environmental concerns led to the closure of Vieques, and Roosevelt Roads subsequently disestablished in 2004. 1977 unit: VC-8

NAS Cubi Point, located on Subic Bay in the Philippines, was the primary support facility in WestPac for the U.S. Navy through its closure in 1992. Carriers usually pulled into the pier adjacent to the ramp and airfield, although in this case *Kitty Hawk* sits across the bay at the balckshoe side of the base. Aircraft on the ramp in this July 1975 shot include a VA-215 A-7B and RVAW-110 E-1B from CVW-19 and *Oriskany*, as well as a VA-52 KA-6D and a pair of VF-114 F-4Js off the *Hawk*. (Doug Siegfried)

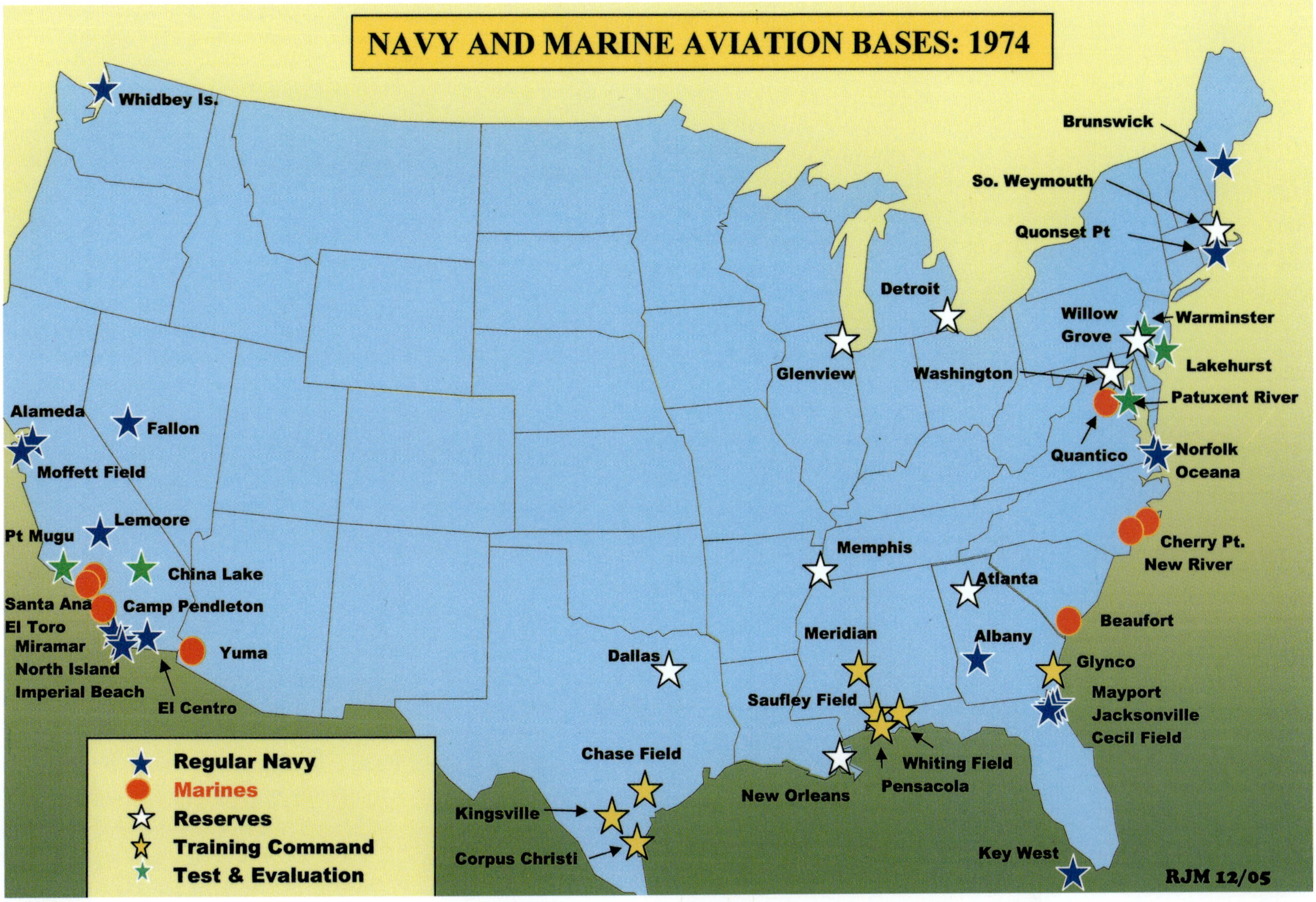

NS Rota, Spain (LERT)

Rota was the primary U.S. Navy support base for the Western Mediterranean and Eastern Atlantic. Although largely occupied by U.S. Navy activities, the base was actually owned and maintained by the Spanish. The small harbor was homeport for the Spanish carriers *Dedalo* and *Principe de Austurias*, as well as that service's Naval Air Force *Matador* and helicopter units. 1977 units: VQ-2, VR-24 det

NAS Sigonella, Italy (LICZ)

Located on the east coast of Sicily, and almost in the shadow of volcanic Mt. Etna, Sigonella was the fleet's primary divert airfield in the central Med. As with Cubi, many air wings dropped aircraft here while on cruise to increase flight deck space. The base was designated a NAF until 1 July 1981, when it became a NAS. 1977 unit: VR-24.

14

Plumage

"My plane isn't ugly—it's painted that way."
- Standard Naval Aviation comment about heavily weathered Tactical Paint Scheme (TPS)

Naval Aviation has a long history of colorful aircraft markings interspersed with periods of relative monotony. Through the 1930s the Navy used brilliant markings of silver fuselages and chrome yellow wings with multicolor tails and noses. This was followed by subdued markings during WWII in a series of shades of blues and grays. By the end of the war the standard paint scheme for carrier based aircraft was a single overall coat of Federal Specification (FS) 15042 Glossy Sea Blue. This lasted until 1956, when a new matt light gull gray (FS 36440) over gloss insignia white (17875) was adopted. In the fleet, the light gull gray paint could actually appear as either gloss (16440) or semi-gloss (26440), as well as the dull shade. This basic motif, which covered the entire period of the Vietnam War, was the one in effect as of 1974.

As opposed to the Air Force, which had gone through the war de-emphasizing its aircraft markings, and applying a new standard four-tone camouflage to its tactical airplanes, the Navy seemed to encourage its squadrons to apply vivid and colorful images that screamed for attention.

This practice started changing in the late 1970s, as a new direction was taken to reduce both the visibility and maintenance requirements of its paint jobs.

In 1977 the fighter and attack communities were authorized to use an interim single-shade overall gray (usually either 36440 or its gloss 16440 counterpart), and many squadrons started simplifying their elaborate squadron paint jobs, both to make visual detection harder, while also reducing the work load on their corrosion shops.

This trend was accelerated in 1981, when the Chief of Naval Operations (CNO) directed ComNavAirLant to develop a low visibility paint scheme for its aircraft. After several years of trials, AIRLANT and NavAirSysCom came up with an officially sanctioned Tactical Paint Scheme (TPS), which was authorized and formally described in MIL-STD-2161(AS), issued on 18 Apr 1985. The new standard directed that most carrier aircraft would be painted in three basic shades of dull (lusterless) gray, with F.S. numbers of 35237, 36320, and 36375. Each aircraft had its own distinct "scientifically designed counter-shaded" pattern applied using either two or all three of the specified dull gray colors. (36495, a very light gray shade, was also initially tested for the undersides of F/A-18, EA-6B, and A-7E types, but it was replaced by 1983 with the darker light compass ghost gray, 36375.)

While initial applications of the new paint could look sharp, they did not tend to last that way long, as TPS soon showed a tendency to decay when exposed to the sun and salt air environment. Whatever benefits it initially had from its "scientific design" were quickly lost in the real world, as it wasn't long before the entire aircraft started fading into one overall shade of dull gray that seemed to absorb dirt, as well. When squadrons carried out the prescribed corrosion control procedures, which officially allowed only "spot" touch-up repainting,

The *Golden Dragon* line at Fallon demonstrates how whole squadrons were painted in high visibility markings through the mid- to late '70s. These markings were basically the same the unit had carried since converting to *Corsair IIs* in 1970. NH307 taxis off the line on 18 July '76. (Mark Morgan)

By the late 1970s, the colorful Vietnam era paint schemes had started fading away, being replaced in many cases by more subtle and easier to apply renditions of existing markings. Two VA-25 *Corsairs* demonstrate the change at Chase Field on 30 Dec '79. (author)

their aircraft could become a disorganized mass of different shades of gray, or even light blue. To many observers, the Navy's aircraft looked perfectly awful—some described the resulting effect as either complex camouflage or even leprosy. It would actually take several years of experimentation and development of better paints and application procedures before this trend was reversed.

Unit markings were initially discouraged in many quarters (indeed, some aviators advocated the complete removal of ALL distinctive markings for what were described as both security and survivability reasons—the P-3 community actually went this route for several years), but the urge to decorate aircraft eventually returned and, by the mid-'90s, most wings allowed units to apply unit markings in dull gray, with one bird generally authorized per squadron to be painted up into an "easter egg" as a mark of unit pride. CAG markings, including the traditional "CAG rainbow," returned through the same period, with some wings (CVW-14 in particular) being more enthusiastic than others in its use.

Special experimental camouflage schemes were still allowed on a temporary basis, and were typically seen at places like Fallon or *Red Flag*. During the *Desert Storm* period at least three aircraft (two CVW-8 *Intruders* and a single CVW-3 *Corsair*) received desert camo, although most observers agreed that standard TPS was a better overall effect while operating at higher altitudes, which were the norm during the war. Adversary aircraft followed no specific rules, and seem to have been limited only by the imagination of the paint shop doing the work. Although some units (like VF-43) developed standard designs for their adversary aircraft, in other squadrons (such as VFA-127) every bird seems to have been different.

The Modex and Callsigns

The odd and obscure term "Modex" has been used for years to describe the distinctive side numbers the Navy applies to its airframes for individual aircraft identification. A modex, when attached to an air wing's tailcode, is frequently used as an aircraft's radio callsign (NG201 would be "November Golf 201"), or it may use its assigned tactical callsign with the modex on the radio—each squadron having its own unique tactical callsign assigned by the higher authority. ("Silver Kite 201" would be the same aircraft as NG201 when VF-92 was assigned to CVW-9.) Prior to the 1990s introduction of theater-wide Air Tasking Order (ATO) assigned callsigns, individual Navy flights normally used either their squadron callsign or, at times, the callsign of the flight leader himself.

Contrary to what some publications have stated, the U.S. Navy does not use a color/number based flight callsign like "Blue Flight" (with aircraft being numbered "Blue One," "Blue Two," etc.), or even European-style "Black 201," that would be based on the hue of the side number itself. In fact, your average Naval Aviator would have no idea what you were talking about if you referred to his aircraft as "Black 201"—they use the tailcode/modex, or just the side number when referring to an aircraft, say, November Hotel 201, or just 201.

Starting in the mid-'70s, the fighter and attack communities were de-emphasizing their markings, completely removing the insignia white belly paint, the better to reduce the "flash" caused under certain conditions. VF-32 F-14A AB201 (159009) shows the interim fighter scheme at Chase Field on 5 Apr '79. Note that while the previous wide swaths of yellow *Swordsmen* tail paint are gone, the nose still carries a full compliment of markings, including the conspicuous national insignia. TPS would soon remove or alter them as well. (author)

Fresh TPS presented a sharp and professional appearance under the right light. This VF-103 F-4S displays a distinct demarcation between the three shades of dull gray, as well as subdued squadron markings. The *Sluggers* joined CVW-17 in 1981, and only carried the 100 series for a short time before swapping with stablemate VF-74 for the 200 series. AA100, marked for MiG killer CAG Gene Tucker, is shown at Key West on 1 June 1981. (author)

While TPS was a superior camouflage under most conditions, it also tended to weather quickly into an unattractive image, as the multi-tone scheme blended into one overall color, and airframes took on a mottled appearance as a squadron's corrosion shop carried out an aggressive and "by the book" maintenance effort. VA-147 A-7E NG404 (157528) is shown at Fallon with a buddy store in December 1984. (Michael Grove).

By 1991 joint operations led to the routine use of daily changing callsigns, which were assigned by the local joint component commander through the daily ATO. Joint operations has generally led to an end to the confusion.

Modexes (side numbers) are assigned in accordance with an appendix in the general NATOPS instruction **OPNAV 3710.7**. Each squadron in the air wing is given a specific number series, with the five traditional primary mission (VF and VA) units being assigned to the 100, 200, 300, 400, and 500 series. Special mission units or detachments utilize a number of number sequences that can only loosely be described or predicted prior to about 1985.

The use of octal (base eight) IFF systems has led to normal use of only the digits 0 through 7 for side numbers, since most IFF systems do not use the numbers eight or nine. Not surprisingly, there are exceptions to this rule.

Colors have also been officially assigned to each number series by OPNAV 3710, but these standards are only mildly enforced, as many squadrons use their traditional colors instead of those prescribed. Some air wings take the color assignments more seriously than others, such as CVW-21 directing 200-series VF-24 to change the tail markings of their F-8s from red to the "proper" color, yellow, in 1969. They went right back to the squadron preferred shade of red once that CAG, or responsible member of his staff, moved on.

OPNAV 3710 assignments: (variations are not uncommon):

100 series: Insignia Red; Typically the first fighter (VF) squadron.

200 series: Orange-Yellow; Usually the second fighter squadron. Used by third VFA unit from 1990s.

300 series: Light Blue; first light attack (A-4, A-7) or strike fighter (VFA) unit

400 series: International Orange; second light attack or strike fighter unit.

500 series: Medium Green; Medium attack (A-6) unit. Used by VAQ squadrons, with maroon, from 1998.

The listed colors (red, yellow, blue, orange, and green) actually define the "correct" order of a "CAG rainbow," found on the tails of many air wing aircraft ending with the digits "00." As stated in chapter 3, CAG's name is traditionally placed on aircraft numbered "00" ("double nuts," as in 100, 200, 300, etc.), Commanding Officers in airframes ending "01" (101, 201, etc.), and Executive Officers "02." Most squadrons place aircrew names on other aircraft in the order of seniority, but this varies widely. Some squadrons find the time required to paint names is not worth the trouble, and may dispense with the tradition completely. It also needs to be repeated that, while a pilot or NFO may have his name on an aircraft, he will actually fly whatever bird is available, depending on the mission, where it is spotted on the flight deck, and many other factors. This seems to be lost to some photo caption writers, who frequently assume that the name on the canopy rail is the person at the controls.

"Support" squadrons (VAW, VAQ, VS, HS, HC) have occupied a wide array of side numbers over the years, including, but not limited to, the 00, 000, 010, 600, 610, 620, and 700 series. They have also been known to be placed in odd number areas that otherwise defy simple explanation (such as VFP-63 dets being numbered 115 to 117 for their last two deployments—which placed them in the number series set by AirPac for F-14 TARPS aircraft). Assignments were generally standardized by the mid-1980s to:

600 to 603: Dark Blue; VAW other series could be used when five aircraft assigned.

604 to 607: Maroon; VAQ changed to 620-624 when five EA-6Bs assigned, to 500 series from 1998.
610 to 617: Magenta; HS
700 to 711: Dark Green; VS does not usually include 708 or 709.

Once again, exceptions and variations to these "rules" are legion, and cannot be adequately covered here. Examples include VMFA-312's use of the 330/340 numbers with CVW-8 from 1993 to 1995, even after the 500 series was vacant. Similarly, CVW-3's second A-6 unit occupied the 540/550 series between 1983 and 1989, electing to stay within the traditional medium attack 500 numbers, even though both the 300 and 400 series were open.

Unit Awards

The Navy loves to give out awards, and Naval Aviation is certainly no slouch in that area. Needless to say, unit awards are meant to recognize the better squadrons in its organization. Some of these are familiar, some are obscure, and many end up being painted on the sides of aircraft by the proud winners. Each award has its own set of requirements, and most depend on some sort of objective evaluation being made by the awarding authority. Not surprisingly, there is frequently a subjective element involved in awards as well—politics, personalities, and other issues arise on occasion, particularly when one squadron that seems to have the normal elements required (things like flight time, time at sea, traps, participation in combat, enlisted retention, and no aircraft losses all are typically important categories) loses to another outfit that, say, hasn't gone to sea, or has lost an aircraft during the same period. To put it bluntly, sometimes awards just do not make sense. That being said, they are still hotly contested by most squadrons, and are usually a sign of a superior organization.

"Ribbon" awards: There are several such awards, listed below in the order of seniority. The unit commendations (PUC, NUC, MUC) are made at the Type Command level, or higher, following recommendations by the lower chain of command. All squadron members during the approved time frame are allowed to wear the respective ribbon on their uniforms, and they frequently show up on aircraft as well.[15] Once again, why some units get NUCs or MUCs is certainly open to discussion. Their award is frequently subjective in nature, and "award creep" was certainly present over the period, as the level that seemed to qualify a combat-blooded unit during Vietnam was not the case during the 1980s, when there were squadrons who received MUCs for little more than being established, and making their first peacetime deployment without embarrassing themselves.

PUC: Presidential Unit Commendation. PUCs are, almost without exception, given for exceptional unit performance in combat. None were awarded to carrier units between 1974 and 2000.

NUC: Navy Unit Commendation. The "middle" unit award, the NUC is less common than the MUC, although all Navy units that participated in *Desert Storm* received the award on a blanket basis.

MUC: Meritorious Unit Commendation. The lowest in precedence of the three unit awards. See the picture of RVAW-120 TE-2C on pg 161 for an example of an aircraft wearing a MUC.

Battle Efficiency Award: ("Battle E"): A periodic, and hotly contested, award given by Type Commanders for the top squadron in

VAW-115 pretty much swept the table for AEW awards in 1978, as this aircraft indicates. This E-2B shot on *Midway's* flight deck in Oct '79 displays three major awards behind the cockpit: a Battle "E," a Safety "S" (with second consecutive award bar), and the AEW Excellence award (the "I"). The *Liberty Bells* were the last fleet squadron to operate the "Bravo Hummer," finally getting "Cs" in 1985. (Rick Burgess).

each community. Once again, it comes with a uniform ribbon, which is frequently applied to aircraft as well—see the VFA-83 aircraft on p 90. The "E" goes well back in Navy history, and is believed to date from ship gunnery competitions (ships still qualify for "Es," as well as other letter awards in a variety of categories). Type Wing gives an "E" out on an annual basis, so that each community will normally have two "E" winners—one on each coast. Whidbey's VAQWING actually awards three "Es" annually: one each for AirLant and AirPac, and an additional one to the top Expeditionary EA-6B squadron. AirPac's "E" cycle was actually 18 months until 1988, when it matched AirLant's 12 month calendar schedule.

The criteria used to determine Battle "E" winners has varied considerably through the years, particularly during the relatively peaceful late 1970s and 1980s, when a variety of categories that had little or nothing to do with "Battle" could be used, including admin-related inspection results, and things as arcane as "dental readiness" (the author is not making this up), as wings sought to find ways to better differentiate highly competitive units. Surprisingly (but then again, maybe not), actual performance in battle has never seemed to be a particularly important contribution to this award, as proven by the reward of a 1991 community "E" to a squadron that was the only one of its type to have an aircraft actually shot down during *Desert Storm*, this over several sister squadrons who flew combat without loss.

"Name" awards: In typical American fashion, the Navy spends a lot of effort to determine who the top squadron of each type is. Usually called "Trophies," because each has some sort of hardware associated with it, these community excellence awards are named after notable Navy heroes, and are probably the closest thing available to determine who "the best" squadron in a respective warfare area is over a year—in other words, when a fighter squadron wins the Clifton Trophy, it can truly claim to be the "Number One." FitRon in the Navy for that year. Over the last 20 years each coast has nominated one squadron for each category (usually their Battle "E" winner), and the office of Chief of Naval Operations decides the winner. There is no standard way to apply these awards to aircraft, and they can take almost any form, including a name, a miniature trophy, or whatever else the squadron can think of.

Rear Admiral Joseph C. Clifton: The top fighter (VF) squadron in the Navy.
Rear Admiral Clarence Wade McClusky: The top Attack (VA) squadron in the Navy; subsequent to 1997 this award has gone to a fighter (VF) or strike-fighter (VFA) unit for "meritorious achievement in the air to ground mission area."
Captain Michael J. Estocin: The top Strike-Fighter (VFA) squadron in the Navy. (see VFA-83 *Hornet*, pg 90)
Admiral Arthur W. Radford: The top VAQ squadron in the Navy.
Rear Admiral Frank Akers: The top VAW squadron in the Navy.
Admiral John S. "Jimmy" Thach: The top HS squadron in the Navy.
Captain Arnold Jay Isbell: While a "major" award, the Isbell is given to eight ASW squadrons, with VP, HS, VP, and HSL (SH-2 and SH-60) units on each coast being awarded annually. This is occasionally applied to aircraft in the form of an ASW "A" (this award is in addition to the Thach trophy).
Note: With the end of the A-6 community, the McClusky is now given to the top squadron in the "Attack" role, which makes both VFA and VF "Bombcat" units eligible. VF-41, for instance, won the McClusky in 1999.

Other major awards:
Safety "S": Along with the "E," the Safety "S" is the most commonly seen letter award painted on squadron aircraft. It is given by community, with one squadron of each type on each coast being awarded a Safety "S" in the name of CNO. Needless to say, things like extensive operations with zero mishaps and limited personal injuries (on and off duty) are usually what it takes to win.
Golden Wrench: Usually given by CVWs and FuncWings to squadrons that have the best aircraft maintenance numbers for a specific period of time. There is no set presentation for these awards, and aircraft markings can include everything from a double-ended crescent wrench to a letter "M," among other things. See the picture of VS-21 S-3A on pg 192 for an example.
Golden Anchor: Normally awarded by a FuncWing, and given to the unit with the highest enlisted re-enlistment rate over a year. Not surprisingly, it is frequently displayed as a small gold anchor on aircraft. Ships that win this award will frequently paint their bow anchor gold as well.

Most communities and/or wings have additional awards that are given out for a variety or reasons. Some of these will show up on aircraft. One example is the "Mutha" award, which was given by the Miramar (and later, Oceana) fighter wing to the winner of an annual battle competition. Its name came from the fact that it was awarded by the Fighter RAG, or the "Mother" ("Mutha") squadron (see the picture of the VF-103 F-14B, pg 15). Another similar award is Whidbey's Battle Readiness Competition (BRC), which is a similar competition in the EA-6B community. The application of large "BRC" letters on *Prowlers* can be a head scratcher for the unknowing, or those used to single-letter awards, like the "E" and "S."

Paint and Marking Oddities

There are exceptions to every rule, and oddities in every system. The following pictures and captions depict only a small portion of the deviations possible in "normal" naval aviation paint schemes and markings.

This somewhat anonymous F-4N (AF111, 150442) belongs to Dallas based VF-201, and is painted in temporary baby blue over wash for the annual Reserve fighter derby held at Miramar in Feb 1978. How well the camouflage hides the *Phantom's* notorious smoke trail is open to conjecture. (Bob Lawson)

Some squadrons would use their Fallon det to test experimental camouflage paint schemes, and variations were numerous. There's a VA-146 *Blue Diamond* A-7E (NG305) hiding under this coat of desert camo, shown at Fallon in April 1988. Although it worked at lower altitudes, the standard Tactical Paint Scheme was considered to be more effective at most altitudes. This A-7E carries a practice AGM-88 HARM under its right wing. (Michael Grove)

Temporary camo could come in almost any form—the VF-2 *Bounty Hunters* applied an irregular two-tone-gray wash to NE203 (162600) for their 1988 Fallon det, although they did keep the rudder uncovered. (Michael Grove)

VF-171's Key West ACM detachment had a stable of A-4 *Skyhawks* assigned for use as adversaries. In 1981 their sole TA-4J was sent to the depot for work, and another was provided for the duration. When the det found out the "loaner" was painted white, and equipped with a less powerful motor (a J-52-P-6, instead of a P-8), they chose to put no distinctive markings on it other than the logo of a Key West gay bar. AD273 (153496) is shown at Boca Chica on 19 May 1981. (author)

Up to 1956 a single "N" tailcode would have indicated Carrier Air Group-NINE, but in Dec 1979, when this picture was taken at Chase Field, it means this F-14A (159827) is between air wings. Indeed, this aircraft has had CVW-14's NK slightly modified, and is ready to take CVW-2's NE. The name on the canopy rail is Rear Admiral "Punchy" Gillchrist, who was Commodore of FitAEWWingPac at that time. (author)

Fighter squadrons normally wear the 100-series modex, so this VA-87 *Corsair II* sporting an AE110 side number can be considered a wee bit out of the ordinary. Since Air Wing Six is deployed to the Med at the time of this shot (with the *Golden Warriors* being assigned the AE400 series), its presence with a VA-174 sister might indicate that this aircraft (159643) was left behind at Cecil for use by the RAG, and renumbered to avoid confusion with its own 400-series birds. Both are shown on the transient line at Scott AFB, IL, on 12 Nov '77. (author)

As of late 1989 CVW-13 had completed three deployments in *Coral Sea*, and was looking for another deck to move to after the retirement of CV-43. Aircraft from the wing would carry the names *Kitty Hawk* and *Lincoln* over the next year—CVW-13 did conduct at least one CQ period on the *Lincoln* in 1990, but never deployed on her. Elegantly marked VFA-132 F/A-18A AK203 (162871) displays the title "Honest Abe" for *Lincoln*, and is shown here at Nellis AFB, NV, on 19 Apr '90. The *Privateers* would move to CVW-6, make one more deployment, and then exit into history themselves. (Brian Rogers)

The Navy is not adverse to supporting motion pictures that help the service's image. While some movies used aircraft "as is," others required special paint for their screen work. In "Top Gun," Miramar F-14As and F-5s received temporary markings for fictional units. "The Flight of the Intruder" featured VA-165 A-6s modified with white noses and rudders, as well as markings to better reflect VA-196 aircraft during 1972. This *Boomer* A-6E ("NK520") was used as an A-6B in the movie—the Buno displayed in this case is bogus, and actually belongs to an A-4E *Skyhawk*. (author)

Appendix A: Kills and Losses 1974-2000

Air to Air Kills

1) 19 Aug 1981	**VF-41**	**CVW-8**	***Nimitz***	**AIM-9L**
Libyan SU-22	F-14A	160403	AJ-102	Cdr. Hank Kleeman/Lt. Dave Venlet
Libyan SU-22	F-14A	150390	AJ-107	Lt Larry Muczynski/Lt Jim Anderson
2) 4 Jan 1989	**VF-32**	**CVW-3**	***John F Kennedy***	**AIM-9/AIM-7**
Libyan MiG-23	F-14A	159610	AC-207	Lt. Herman Cook/LtCdr Steve Collins
Libyan MiG-23	F-14A	159437	AC-202	Cdr Joe Connelly/Cdr "Leo the Rio" Enwright
3) 17 Jan 1991	**VFA-81**	**CVW-17**	***Saratoga***	**AIM-9M**
Iraqi MiG-21	F/A-18C	163502	AA-410	Lt Nick Mongillo
Iraqi MiG-21	F/A-18C	163508	AA-401	LtCdr Mark Fox
4) 6 Feb 1991	**VF-1**	**CVW-1**	***Ranger***	**AIM-9M**
Iraqi MI-8	F-14A	162603	NF-103	Lt Stu Broce/Cdr Ron McElraft

Combat Losses

1) 4 Dec 1983 **VA-15** **CVW-6** ***Independence*** **Lebanon** **IR SAM**
A-7E 157468 AE-305 Cdr Ed "Hunyak" Andrews (CAG-6, recovered)
Note: A-7E AE-314, 157458 was hit during the same strike and recovered on *Independence*.

2) 4 Dec 1983 **VA-85** **CVW-3** ***John F Kennedy*** **Lebanon** **IR SAM**
A-6E 152915 AC-556 Lt Mark Lange (K)/ Lt Bobby Goodman (POW)

3) 17 Jan 1991 **VFA-81** **CVW-17** ***Saratoga*** ***Desert Storm*** **MiG-25**
F/A-18C 163484 AA403 LtCdr Scott Speicher
Note: Commander Speicher was initially declared KIA, which was later changed to MIA. He has subsequently been promoted to the rank of Captain while his status remains unknown.

4) 18 Jan 1991 **VA-35** **CVW-17** ***Saratoga*** ***Desert Storm*** **RF SAM**
A-6E 161688 AA-510 Lt Bob Wetzel/Lt Jeff Zaun (both POW)
Note: A-6E AA-502 (158539) was hit on same strike and recovered in Saudi Arabia, dismantled and returned to the U.S. for repairs and further service.

5) 18 Jan 1991 **VA-155** **CVW-2** ***Ranger*** ***Desert Storm*** **Prob. AAA**
A-6E 152928 NE-404 Lt. William Costen/Lt. Charles Turner (both KIA)

6) 21 Jan 1991 **VF-103** **CVW-17** ***Saratoga*** ***Desert Storm*** **Poss. RF SAM**
F-14A+ 161430 AA-212 Lt Devon Jones (recovered)/Lt Larry Slade (POW)

7) 2 Feb 1991 **VA-36** **CVW-8** ***Theodore Roosevelt*** ***Desert Storm*** ***UNK.***
A-6E 155632 AJ-531 Lt.Cdr. Barry Cooke/Lt Pat Conner (both KIA)

Operational Losses during Desert Storm

1) 25 Jan 1991	F/A-18A	163121	AJ-304	VFA-15	CVW-8	*Theodore Roosevelt*	pilot recovered
2) 26 Jan 1991	A-7E	158830	AC-403	VA-72	CVW-3	*John F Kennedy*	pilot recovered
3) 5 Feb 1991	F/A-18A	163096	AJ-401	VFA-87	CVW-8	*Theodore Roosevelt*	Lt B.J. Dwyer, CVW-8 staff, lost
4) 15 Feb 1991	A-6E	155602	AB-512	VA-85	CVW-1	*America*	crew recovered

Notable Fratricide Incidents

1) 22 July 1974 **SH-3D** **148034** **HC-1 det, CVW-2 *Ranger*** **six killed**
Shot down inadvertently by *Sidewinder* missile launched by VF-21 F-4J during firepower demo while deployed to the Western Pacific.

2) 17 Aug 1978 **F-4J** **155824** **VF-74** **CVW-17 *Forrestal*** **crew recovered**
Shot down inadvertently by *Sidewinder* missile launched by wingman during ACM while deployed to the Mediterranean.

3) 22 Sep 1987 **RF-4C** **69-0381** **26th TRW USAF** **crew recovered**
Shot down by *Sidewinder* missile from VF-74 F-14A (162707) during exercise while deployed to the Mediterranean.

4) 5 October 1992 ***Muavenet* (DM-357)** **five killed**
Turkish destroyer hit by two *Sea Sparrow* missiles shot in error by *Saratoga* during "Display Determination" exercise in the Mediterranean. Ship was the former USS *Gwin* (DD-772). Casualties included the ship's Commanding Officer.

5) 3 Jun 1996 **A-6E 155704** **VA-155** **CVW-5** ***Midway*** **crew recovered**
Was towing a gunnery banner when shot down by Phalanx CIWS on Japanese destroyer *Yuugiri* during RIMPAC exercises.

Sources:

Official squadron records; Naval Aviation History Office, Washington DC
"List of US Navy Aircraft Shootdowns Since 1950: Naval Historical Center
Gulf War Air Power Survey, Vol. V (Statistical Compendium & Chronology; public release)
US Military Aircraft Mishaps 1950-2004. Jan van Waarde, Dutch Aviation Society, 2005
"Naval Aviation News"
"Navy Times"

Appendix B: Carrier Aviation Tailcodes 1974-2000

This list contains carrier-based units as well as support and developmental organizations that flew carrier-type aircraft. This is not intended to be a comprehensive Navy tailcode list. The author recommends Patrick Martin's "Hook Code" to anyone interested in this subject.

AA:	CVW-17
AB:	CVW-1
AC:	CVW-3
AD:	AirLant Carrier-based FRSs
AE:	CVW-6
AF:	CVWR-20
AG:	CVW-7
AH:	HS-15
AJ:	CVW-8
AK:	CVW-13
AR:	AirLant Carrier-based ASW FRSs
AW:	CVSGR-70
BF:	HC-16
(CD):	VRC-40
GD:	VAQ-33, 34, 35, FEWSG
GE:	RVAW-120,VAW-122
GF:	VC-8
GH:	RVAH-1
GJ:	RVAH-3
GK:	RVAH-5
GL:	RVAH-7
GM:	RVAH-9
GN:	RVAH-11
GP:	RVAH-12
GR:	RVAH-13
GQ:	RVAH-14
HU:	HC-2
JA:	VX-1
JE:	VC-2
JH:	VC-10
JM:	VR-24
JQ:	VQ-2
NE:	CVW-2
ND:	CVWR-30
NF:	CVW-5
NG:	CVW-9
NH:	CVW-11
NJ:	AirPac Carrier FRSs
NK:	CVW-14
NL:	CVW-15 (1974-95) ComVAQWingPac (1995-c)
NM:	CVW-19 (1974-77) ComLatWingPac (c.1980-85) CVW-10 (1986-88)
NP:	CVW-21
NW:	CVSGR-80, ComHelWingRes
PP:	VFP-63
PR:	VQ-1
RA:	AirPac Carrier ASW FRSs
RG:	VRC-50
RW:	VR/VRC-30
SH:	VMFAT-101
TR:	VAQ-129
TT:	RVAW-110
UA:	VC-1
UE:	VC-5
UH:	VC-7
UP:	HC-1
XE:	VX-5
XF:	VX-4
6G:	NARU Alameda
7T:	Naval Air Systems Command

Appendix C: Glossary

ACM: Air Combat Maneuvering
AEW: (USAF)
Air Expeditionary Wing
AIS: Aircraft Instrumentation System
ALF: Auxiliary Landing Field
ARW: (USAF) Aerial Refueling Wing
ASW: Anti-Submarine Warfare
AVT: Auxiliary Training Carrier
Bird Farm: Irreverent term for an aircraft carrier
Blackshoe: Term used to differentiate officers in the surface ("ship driving") forces from their counterparts that fly aircraft, who are called "Brownshoes" due to traditional difference in footwear.
BRAC: Base Realignment And Closure
Bug: Slang name for McDonnell-Douglas (Boeing) F/A-18 *Hornet*
CAG: Commander, Air Group
CARIB: Caribbean
CONUS: Continental United States (the lower 48 states)
CVW: Carrier Air Wing
CVG: Carrier Air Group
CVWR: Reserve Carrier Air Wing
CVSG: Carrier Anti-Submarine Group
CVSGR: Reserve Carrier Anti-Submarine Group
CVA: Attack Aircraft Carrier
CVAN: Nuclear Powered Attack Aircraft Carrier
CVS: Anti-Submarine Aircraft Carrier
CV: Aircraft Carrier
CVN: Nuclear Powered Aircraft Carrier
DACM: Dissimilar Air Combat Maneuvering
DACT: Dissimilar Air Combat Training
DDG: Guided Missile Destroyer
Det: detachment
Disestab; Disestablished
ECS: (USAF) Electronic Combat Squadron
Electrolux: Slang name for Lockheed ES-3A *Shadow*.
EMI: Electro-Magnetic Interference
Estab: Established
FEWSG: Fleet Electronic Warfare Support Group
FID: Slang for USS Forrestal, from its motto "First in Defense"
FitFudd: Slang for Miramar's, Fighter AEW Wing PAC, "Fudd" coming from the unofficial name for the E-1B *Tracer*, the "Willy Fudd".
FLIR: Forward Looking Infra-Red
FRS: Fleet Readiness Squadron (frequently called Fleet Replacement Squadron)
FS: (USAF) Fighter Squadron
FW: (USAF) Fighter Wing
GQ: General Quarters
GWAPS: Gulf War Air Power Survey
HC: Helicopter Combat Support Squadron
HMH: Marine Heavy Helicopter Squadron
HMM: Marine Medium Helicopter Squadron
Hoover: Slang name for Lockheed S-3 *Viking*.
HS: Helicopter Anti-Submarine Squadron
HT: Helicopter Training Squadron
HUD: Heads Up Display
IADS: Integrated Air Defense System
IO: Indian Ocean
IR: Infra-Red
LSO: Landing Signal Officer
MAG: Marine Aircraft Group
MAW: Marine Aircraft Wing
MCAS: Marine Corps Air Station
MED: Mediterranean
MUC: Meritorious Unit Commendation
NAF: Naval Air Facility
NARF: Naval Air Rework Facility
NAS: Naval Air Station
NFO: Naval Flight Officer
NFWS: Navy Fighter Weapons School (*Topgun*)
NORLANT: North Atlantic
NS: Naval Station
NUC:Navy Unit Commendation
OLF: Outlying Landing Field
OPTAR: Operational Target: Budget allocated by higher authority to pay for a squadron's flight time
RAG: Readiness Air Group (frequently called Replacement Air Group)
RCH: Red Cat Hair
RefTra: Refresher Training
RS: Red Sea
RVAH: Reconnaissance Heavy Attack Squadron
RVAW: Readiness Early Warning Squadron (a replacement squadron)
SLUF: Slang name for LTV (Vought) A-7 *Corsair II*.
SOLANT: South Atlantic
TACTS: Tactical Air Combat Training System
TFW: (USAF) Tactical Fighter Wing
TPS: Tactical Paint Scheme
Turkey: Slang name for Grumman F-14 *Tomcat*.
TW: Training Wing

UDP: Unit Deployment Plan: Marine rotational assignment of squadrons to Iwakuni Japan
VA: Attack Squadron (Atkron).
VA(L): Unofficial term for Light Attack (A-4 and A-7) squadrons
VA(M): Unofficial term for Medium Attack (A-6) squadrons
VAH: Heavy Attack Squadron (Hatron)
VAW: Airborne Early Warning Squadron
VAQ: Tactical Electronic Warfare Squadron (to 1998), Electronic Attack Squadron (in 1998)
VC: Composite Squadron
VF: Fighter Squadron (Fitron)
VFA: Fighter-Attack Squadron (until 5/83), Strike-Fighter Squadron (from 5/83)
VFP: Light Photographic Reconnaissance Squadrons
VMA: Marine Attack Squadron
VMAQ: Marine Tactical Electronic Warfare Squadron
VMCJ: Marine Composite Squadron
VMFA: Marine Fighter- Attack Squadron
VMFP: Marine Photo-Reconnaissance Squadron
VQ: Fleet Air Reconnaissance Squadron
VT: Training Squadron
W-291: "Whiskey-291"- the large ocean training area off San Diego
Weptraex: Weapons Training Exercise: the annual air wing evolution at Fallon
Willy Fudd: Slang nickname for the Grumman E-1B (WF-2) "Tracer".
WP: Western Pacific. Also called "West Pac".

Notes

[1] Think in terms of all of the things you have to change other than just aircraft markings—parking spots, coffee mugs, patches, stationary—it soon adds up to real money!

[2] Although the "original" VF-17 apparently held a formal "decommissioning" (sic) ceremony when they returned to the U.S., the VF-17 designation was not actually ended, but held on paper without men and equipment until it was re-equipped later in 1944. The Naval Aviation History Office, which is the final authority in these matters, recognizes it as the true successor for lineage reasons.

[3] According to sources familiar with the change, the squadron was basically directed to take the "Jolly Roger" persona by leadership in the Oceana Fighter Wing.

[4] There was also the issue of service equivilancy; It had been noticed by some that while the Navy used men with the rank of Commander (Lieutenant Colonel equivalent) to run their CVWs the Air Force had Brigadier Generals (O-7s) in charge of many of their Fighter Wings.

[5] WOXOF being a term in aviation meteorological shorthand roughly meaning "weather reported as ceiling and visibility zero feet obscured in fog," which would suspend flying and might, in earlier days, encourage aircrew to do other things, like go to the bar.

[6] The *Phoenix* itself was known in the fleet by a number of nicknames, including "Pheeny Bomb," "Buffalo," and the "Great White Hope."

[7] The F-110 powered *Tomcat* was originally given the Navy developed and non-DOD approved designation F-14A+ ("F-14A plus"), which was changed to the officially sanctioned F-14B on 1 May 1991. Squadron listings show the title as it was when the unit deployed.

[8] In a somewhat macabre tradition, VF-84's ready room contained a glass case with the skull and crossed femurs said to be of Ens Jack Ernie, a *Hellcat* pilot killed in action during WWII. The *Jolly Roger* traditionally paint Ens. Ernie's name on the canopy rail of one of their aircraft, as well.

[9] During Vietnam there was a land based Heavy Attack unit (VAH-21, with AP-2Hs) and a formally recognized light attack squadron (VAL-4, with OV-10As). The discussion here will be limited to carrier based units.

[10] This arrangement would later change, and the school would come under Commander, Fleet Forces Command.

[11] Within the Navy, the term "RAG" is pronounced as a word, while FRS is always spelled out. The word "Replacement," while not quite right, is also frequently used in lieu of the officially sanctioned "Readiness."

[12] RVAW-110 and -120 were called "Carrier Airborne Early Warning Training Squadrons" in Navy documents, yet in everyday use the R was assumed to stand for Replacement. The VAW community was the only one in the Navy to use an "R" designation prefix for its FRSs, this as opposed to the *Vigilante* RVAH squadrons, where it was "R for reconnaissance." This odd quirk was corrected in 1983, when both of the *Hawkeye* FRSs dropped the "R" and became "straight" VAW units.

[13] Marine EA-6As also deployed on carriers on a limited basis through 1977. See chapter 11 for more details.

[14] The other two VQ units during this period (VQ-3 and 4) were equipped with EC-130s for the strategic communications ("TACAMO") role. They are well beyond the scope of this book.

[15] Dates are important, as one West Coast FRS wrote itself up for, and had approved, a MUC for "superior performance" in its duties over a one year period that fit neatly between two fatal mishaps.

Bibliography

Burgess, Richard; *The Naval Aviation Guide*; fifth edition; Annapolis, US Naval Institute, 1996.

Cohen, Elliot A. Dr. (Director); *Gulf War Air Power Survey, Vol V; Statistical Compendium and Chronology;* US Government Publishing Office, Washington DC, 1993.

Elliott, John M; *The Official Monogram US Navy & Marine Corps Aircraft Color Guide*. Monogram Aviation Press, Sturbridge MA.

Vol 2: 1940-1949; (published 1989)
Vol 3: 1950-1959 (1991)
Vol 4: 1960-1993 (1993)

Francillon, Rene; *Tonkin Gulf Yacht Club, U.S. Carrier Operations off Vietnam*; Naval Institute Press, Annapolis, MD, 1988

Friedman, Norman: *U.S. Aircraft Carriers, An Illustrated Design History*, Naval Institute Press, Annapolis MD, 1983.

Grossnick, Roy A: *Dictionary of American Naval Squadrons, Vol 1: VA, VAH, VAK, VAL, VAP, VFA,* Naval Historical Office, Washington DC, 1995

Grossnick, Roy A**:** *Dictionary of American Naval Squadrons, Vol II: VP*, Naval Historical Office, Annapolis MD, 1997

Kasulka, Duane: *USN Aircraft Carrier Air Units*; Carrollton TX, Squadron Publications.
Vol 2 1957-1963 (published 1985)
Vol 3 1964-1973 (published 1988)

Marloda, Edward J and Schneller, Robert J; *Shield and Sword, The United States Navy and the Persian Gulf War*; Washington DC; US Government Publishing Office; 1998

Martin, Patrick; *Hook Code*; United States Navy and Marine Corps Aviation Tail Code Markings; Self-Published, Vancouver BC; 1995

Michel, Marshall; *Clashes; Air Combat Over North Vietnam 1965-1972;*; Naval Institute Press, Annapolis, MD 1997.

Morgan, Mark L and Morgan, Rick: *Intruder, the Operational History of Grumman's A-6*. Schiffer Military Publishing, Atglen PA, 2004

Peacock, Lindsay; *US Naval Aviation Today*, West London Aviation Publishing, London UK 1977

Roberts, Michael; *United States Naval Aviation Patches*, Schiffer Military Publishing, Atglen PA.
Aircraft Attack Squadrons, Helicopter Squadrons, (1995)
Aircraft Fighter Squadrons, Strike-Fighter Squadrons, Reconaissance Squadrons (1995)

Shettle, Mel: *United States Naval Air Stations of World War II,* Vol I and Vol II, (Self-Published), 1995

Stanik, Joseph T: *Swift and Effective Retribution; The U.S. Sixth Fleet and the Confrontation with Qaddafi*, Naval History Office, Washington DC 1996

Bibliography

Tillman, Barrett: *U.S. Navy Fighter Squadrons in World War II*; Specialty Press, North Branch MN, 1997.

Wetterhahn, Ralph, *The Last Battle; The Mayaguez Incident and the End of the Vietnam War*, Carroll & Graf Publishers, NY NY, 2001.

Significant Articles:
"Welcome to El Dorado Canyon", LCDR Joseph T. Stanik, USN (Ret), Naval Institute Proceedings, April 1996.

"Operation Praying Mantis", Capt J.B. Perkins III and Capt "Bud" Langston, Naval Institute Proceedings, Naval Review 1989.

Magazines:
"Naval Aviation News", 1948 through 2005.

"The Hook", 1977 through 2005.

Official Web Pages:
Current instructions covering Naval squadron insignia:
http://www.history.navy.mil/branches/org4-29.htm

Officially recognized squadron insignia:
http://www.history.navy.mil/branches/org4-16.htm

Officially recognized squadron lineages:
http://www.history.navy.mil./branches/org4-9.htm

Photo Index

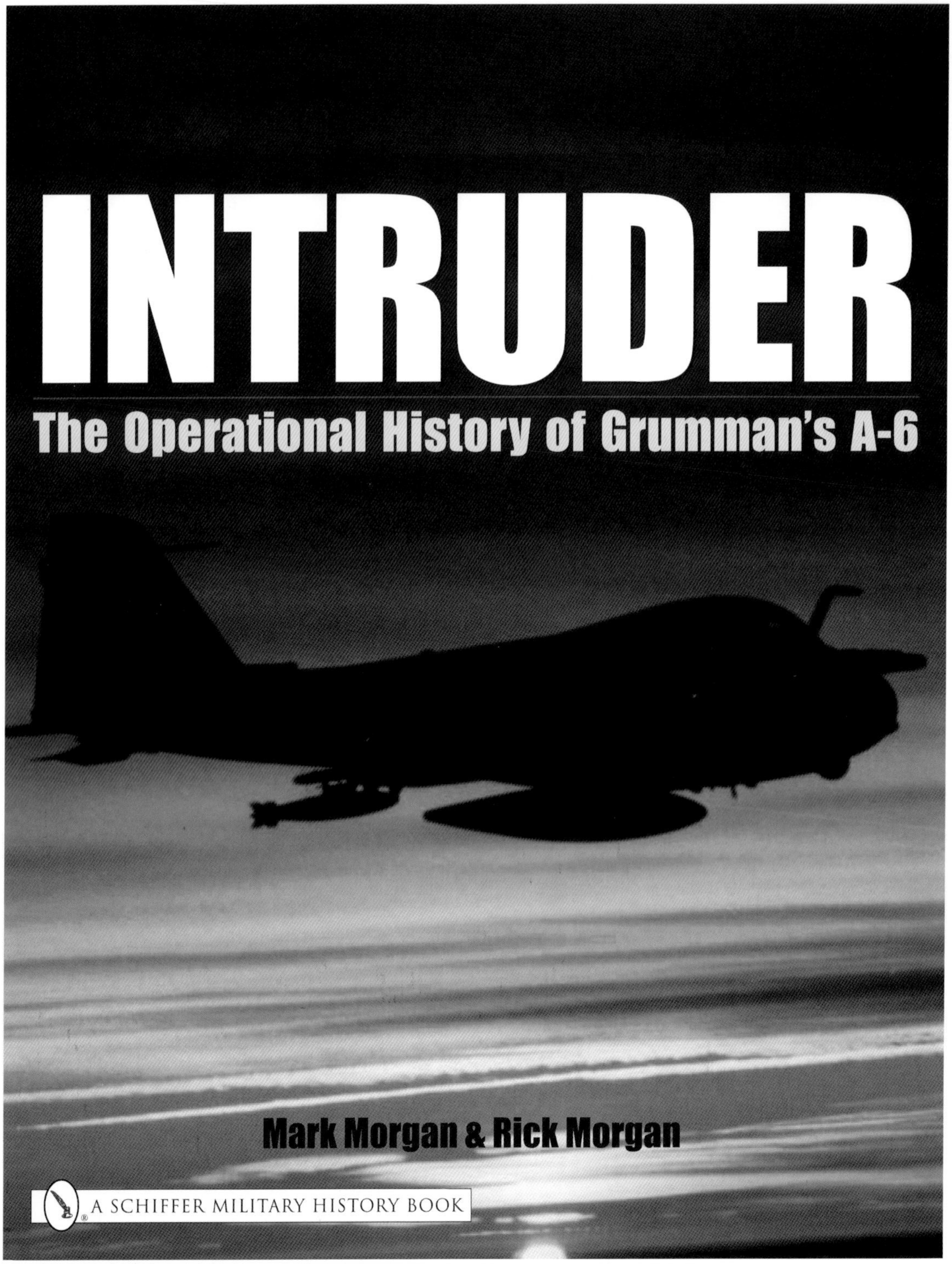

Intruder - The Operational History of Grumman's A-6

Mark Morgan & Rick Morgan

Covering both Navy and Marine Corps service, this is the operational history of the *Intruder* and the Naval service's "medium attack" community. Twelve chapters include detailed descriptions of the *Intruder's* combat record from its first deployment to Vietnam through the design's retirement in 1997. Every fleet version of the aircraft, and each squadron that flew the mighty A-6 are covered in detail. The authors, both carrier-experienced flyers, bring the exploits of the Intruder to life in the words of aircraft's aircrew. The most comprehensive operational history produced on this classic of Naval Aviation.

Size: 81/2"x11" ■ 250+ b/w & color photos ■ 296 pp

ISBN: 0-7643-2100-5 ■ hard cover ■ $59.95